CORINTH

———

VOLUME VII   PART III

CORINTHIAN HELLENISTIC POTTERY

CORINTH

RESULTS OF EXCAVATIONS

CONDUCTED BY

THE AMERICAN SCHOOL OF CLASSICAL STUDIES AT ATHENS

VOLUME VII   PART III

CORINTHIAN HELLENISTIC POTTERY

BY

G. ROGER EDWARDS

THE AMERICAN SCHOOL OF CLASSICAL STUDIES AT ATHENS

PRINCETON, NEW JERSEY

1975

Library of Congress Cataloging in Publication Data

Edwards, G   Roger, 1914–
  Corinthian Hellenistic pottery.

  (Corinth; results of excavations conducted by the
American School of Classical Studies at Athens, v. 7,
pt. 3)
  Bibliography: p.
  1. Pottery, Hellenistic — Corinth, Greece.
2. Pottery — Corinth, Greece. I. Title. II. Series: American School of Classical Studies at Athens. Corinth, v.
7, pt. 3.
DF261.C65A6 vol. 7 pt. 3 [NK3840] 738.3′0938′7
ISBN 0-87661-073-4   74-10623

PRINTED IN GERMANY AT J. J. AUGUSTIN, GLÜCKSTADT

PREFACE

This preface, written as the last element of this study, gives me the opportunity to recall in full and with pleasure and gratitude the assistance and cooperation which I have received from many in the course of its preparation. I acknowledge all cordially and think now with especial esteem of criticisms which have caused me to think harder and with greater pain than I might have done without them.

My acquaintance with Hellenistic pottery began in 1947 when Professor Oscar Broneer invited me to study the contents of the wells of the South Stoa at Corinth. It was for long envisaged that this study would include all the material from these wells, but it was ultimately seen that this would not be feasible in a single publication. Hence the decision was made that I should change my study to that of Corinthian pottery of Hellenistic times alone. The South Stoa wells have been intensively studied and employed in this volume, however, and they form a large block of the deposits important for the chronology of the pottery. For a time while studying the wells I had the collaboration of Dr. Judith Perlzweig (Frau Binder) and the stimulus of her ideas concerning categories of objects other than pottery from the wells and the larger implications of the archaeology of the area in which the South Stoa is located.

The study of Corinthian pottery and other material has not been pursued continuously over the years. During this time I have also been working on the Hellenistic pottery from the excavations of the Athenian Agora. This received primary attention during the decade of the 1950's. Many of the thoughts which I have had about Hellenistic pottery have been stimulated by the study of this cognate body of material and by the collaboration and criticism of my colleagues on the staff of the Agora excavations. Enlargement of my views is not the least benefit I owe to them.

It was not until 1962 that I returned to Corinthian studies. The present volume has resulted from opportunities to work in Corinth, since then largely during summer vacations. I wish to acknowledge with great pleasure the assistance provided by the Director of the American School of Classical Studies in Athens during those years, Professor Henry S. Robinson. One of the many invaluable aids which he provided was abundant space for spreading out the material for study. Such perspective and overall control of the pottery as I have achieved I owe to this enlightened and all too rare provision. It was, however, but one of many helpful varieties of assistance provided by him for a study which attempts to explore a new area of archaeology in which the guidelines have had all to be formed and established. I think also with warm pleasure of Mr. Charles K. Williams, Director of the Corinth excavations, whose enthusiasm and thought have given joy to my pursuits, and of many archaeological colleagues whose friendship I have had at Corinth.

Of general objectives in this study I wish to emphasize three. First, I have wished to express my ideas about Corinthian Hellenistic pottery so that excavators at Corinth and elsewhere who find this variety of pottery may as readily as possible be able to use it for dating in excavation. The written word cannot substitute for the pottery itself, a knowledge of it and repeated reference to it at first hand, but perhaps these pages can serve as some guide to those who work with the pottery in the field or in the storeroom. Second, I have wanted to present the material in such a way that future students of Corinthian pottery of the period here studied may be able to continue the work, adding to our knowledge of the pottery as additional evidence and information become available. For, as the reader will readily see, much remains to be known. This study should be thought of as only a beginning, with much that requires improvement and amplification. Third, I think of present and future scholars of Hellenistic pottery produced at other centers of manufacture, of which there were undoubtedly a great many. The chronology of Corinthian pottery of Hellenistic times, which has been the primary preoccupation in this book, will not be applicable to the dating of cognate pottery of other centers except in general ways; the establishment of the chronology of pottery produced at other centers must be developed independently. It is my thought, however, that the definition of the criteria for dating the Corinthian pottery set forth here may serve as a springboard or as a foil for those who undertake the study of the pottery of other centers.

It has been a matter of great interest and value to study the pottery of a very long tradition of craftsmanship, even in its last and least fortunate stages. I wish to acknowledge with warm appreciation the work of a number of students of Corinthian pottery of earlier times for in this study much reference has had to be made to the pottery produced at Corinth before the Hellenistic period. An invaluable framework for the chronology of earlier Corinthian pottery, subsequent to the work of Humfry Payne, has been provided by the devoted work of the late Agnes Newhall Stillwell, of Eva Brann, Mary Thorne Campbell (Mrs. Carl Roebuck), and Mary Zelia Pease (Mrs. John Philippides), as well as by the work of many others who have provided information in shorter studies and in field notes.

For the profile drawings published in this volume, I acknowledge my indebtedness to Nina Travlou (Einhorn), Helen Bezi and Ann Rafferty. The photographs were taken at various times by Lucretia Farr, James Heyle, Photo Emil, Ioannidou and Bartzioti, and Marcia Langer.

With these thoughts in mind I despatch my book, hoping that it may encounter as helpful and valuable critics and friends for its improvement as I have encountered in its preparation. One could not wish more for it.

University Museum, Philadelphia   G. Roger Edwards
March, 1970

As the manuscript of this book goes to the printer the Editor, Marian H. McAllister, has brought to my attention two developments at Corinth which may in some degree affect the chronology of the pottery published here. The first of these concerns the date of the construction of the South Stoa. Since the time this book was completed excavation has taken place in the area to the north of the Stoa which is relevant to its date and that of subsequent terracing in front of the building. A pertinent reference here is to Charles Williams' report of the excavation of Building II, part of which underlies the outer colonnade of the Stoa, the remainder extending to the north under the terracing. This appears in *Hesperia*, XLI, 1972, p. 171; for the position of Building II see p. 166, fig. 5. A further discussion of the Stoa, I am told, will appear in a forthcoming article by Mr. Williams in *Hesperia*. I understand that a date *ca.* 25 years later (i.e. toward the end of the 4th century B.C.) than that proposed here for the *completion* of the Stoa is being suggested. One must view these excavations with great respect and appreciation: the high standards and exemplary character of Mr. Williams' excavation cannot easily be matched in Greek lands. The second development concerns recleaning and re-examination of coins from some of the deposits used herein. I do not know the details nor how extensive the changes which reattribution by a present day numismatist may be.

It is of course not possible at this stage of publication to attempt to assess the effect of these new developments on the chronology of the pottery published here. Nor is it possible to try to evaluate them in relation to evidence already available. In how far the new evidence is obligatory remains to be considered. A general lowering of the dates of the pottery by 25 years is of course not to be thought of, but rather, if adjustment is actually indicated, perhaps a telescoping of upper stages of certain shape series or other entities—by no means all.

With the exception of references to O. Broneer, *Isthmia*, II, and the consequent redating of the filling of the Large Circular Pit, the manuscript stands as it was in 1970. The manuscript, however, was essentially completed in 1966; material discovered or published since then has only occasionally been included.

This addendum provides the welcome opportunity to express warmly my gratitude to the former editor, Lucy T. Shoe Meritt, who devotedly worked on the manuscript, as time permitted, from March, 1970, when the manuscript was submitted, until her retirement in June, 1972. Mrs. Meritt's work was taken over by the present editor at an advanced stage of the preparation of the manuscript for the printer. The benefit to the book of having the attention of two excellent editors will be readily apparent.

March, 1973   G. R. E.

TABLE OF CONTENTS

TABLE OF CONTENTS   xiii

Plates

LIST OF ILLUSTRATIONS

ABBREVIATIONS

A.J.A. = *American Journal of Archaeology.*

Arch. Anz. = *Archäologischer Anzeiger, Beiblatt zum Jahrbuch des deutschen archäologischen Instituts.*

*A.R.V.*² = Sir John Davidson Beazley, *Attic Red-figure Vase-painters*, 2nd edition, Oxford, 1963.

Asklepieion = Carl Roebuck, *Corinth*, XIV, *The Asklepieion and Lerna*, Princeton, 1951.

Ath. Mitt. = *Mitteilungen des deutschen archäologischen Instituts, Athenische Abteilung.*

B.C.H. = *Bulletin de correspondance hellénique.*

Boulter = Cedric Boulter, "Pottery of the Mid-fifth Century from a Well in the Athenian Agora," *Hesperia*, XXII, 1953, pp. 59–115.

Brann = Eva Brann, "A Well of the 'Corinthian' Period Found in Corinth," *Hesperia*, XXV, 1956, pp. 350–374.

Brann, *Late Geometric and Protoattic Pottery* = Eva T. H. Brann, *Athenian Agora*, VIII, *Late Geometric and Protoattic Pottery*, Princeton, 1962.

Broneer, *Isthmia*, II = Oscar Broneer, *Isthmia*, II, *Topography and Architecture*, Princeton, 1973.

Broneer, *S. Stoa* = Oscar Broneer, *Corinth*, I, iv, *The South Stoa and Its Roman Successors*, Princeton, 1954.

Broneer, *Terracotta Lamps* = Oscar Broneer, *Corinth*, IV, ii, *Terracotta Lamps*, Cambridge, Massachusetts, 1930.

Campbell = Mary Thorne Campbell, "A Well of the Black-figured Period at Corinth," *Hesperia*, VII, 1938, pp. 557–611.

Corbett = Peter E. Corbett, "Attic Pottery of the Later Fifth Century from the Athenian Agora," *Hesperia*, XVIII, 1949, pp. 298–351.

Courby = Fernand Courby, *Les vases grecs à reliefs*, Paris, 1922.

C.V.A. = *Corpus Vasorum Antiquorum.*

Davidson, *Minor Objects* = Gladys R. Davidson, *Corinth*, XII, *The Minor Objects*, Princeton, 1952.

Hesperia = *Hesperia, Journal of the American School of Classical Studies at Athens.*

Hill, *The Springs* = Bert Hodge Hill, *Corinth*, I, vi, *The Springs, Peirene, Sacred Spring, Glauke*, Princeton, 1964.

Howland, *Greek Lamps* = Richard Hubbard Howland, *The Athenian Agora*, IV, *Greek Lamps and Their Survivals*, Princeton, 1958.

Jahrb. = *Jahrbuch des deutschen archäologischen Instituts.*

J.H.S. = *Journal of Hellenic Studies.*

Kent, *The Inscriptions* = John Harvey Kent, *Corinth*, VIII, iii, *The Inscriptions, 1926–1950*, Princeton, 1966.

N. Cemetery = Carl W. Blegen, Hazel Palmer, Rodney S. Young, *Corinth*, XIII, *The North Cemetery*, Princeton, 1964.

Olynthus, V = David M. Robinson, *Excavations at Olynthus*, V, *Mosaics, Vases, and Lamps of Olynthus*, Baltimore, 1933.

Olynthus, XIII = David M. Robinson, *Excavations at Olynthus*, XIII, *Vases Found in 1934 and 1938*, Baltimore, 1950.

Payne, *NC* = Humfry Payne, *Necrocorinthia. A Study of Corinthian Art in the Archaic Period*, Oxford, 1931.

Pease = M. Z. Pease, "A Well of the Late Fifth Century at Corinth," *Hesperia*, VI, 1937, pp. 257–316.

Pfuhl, *M.u.Z.* = Ernst Pfuhl, *Malerei und Zeichnung der Griechen*, I–III, Munich, 1923.

Pnyx = G. Roger Edwards, "Hellenistic Pottery," *Hesperia*, Supplement X, *Small Objects from the Pnyx: II*, Princeton, 1956, pp. 79–112.

Pots and Pans = Brian A. Sparkes and Lucy Talcott, *Pots and Pans of Classical Athens*, Princeton, 1958.

PQ I = Agnes N. Stillwell, *Corinth*, XV, i, *The Potters' Quarter*, Princeton, 1948.

PQ II = Agnes N. Stillwell, *Corinth*, XV, ii, *The Potters' Quarter*, Princeton, 1952.

R.E. = *Paulys Real-Encyclopädie der classischen Altertumswissenschaft, Neue Bearbeitung*, Stuttgart, 1894–.

Rev. Ét. Gr. = *Revue des études grecques.*

Richter and Milne, *Shapes and Names* = Gisela Marie Augusta Richter and Marjorie J. Milne, *Shapes and Names of Athenian Vases*, New York, 1935.

Robinson = Henry S. Robinson, *Athenian Agora*, V, *Pottery of the Roman Period*, Princeton, 1959.

Schwabacher = W. Schwabacher, "Hellenistische Reliefkeramik im Kerameikos," *A.J.A.*, XLV, 1941, pp. 182–228.

Scranton, *The Lower Agora* = Robert L. Scranton, *Corinth*, I, iii, *Monuments in the Lower Agora and North of the Archaic Temple*, Princeton, 1951.

Talcott = Lucy Talcott, "Attic Black-glazed Stamped Ware and Other Pottery from a Fifth Century Well," *Hesperia*, IV, 1935, pp. 476–523.

Talcott (1936) = Lucy Talcott, "Vases and Kalos-names from an Agora Well," *Hesperia*, V, 1936, pp. 333–354.

Thompson = Homer A. Thompson, "Two Centuries of Hellenistic Pottery," *Hesperia*, III, 1934, pp. 311–480.

Vanderpool = Eugene Vanderpool, "The Rectangular Rock-Cut Shaft," *Hesperia*, XV, 1946, pp. 265–336.

Weinberg, *The Southeast Building* = Saul S. Weinberg, *Corinth*, I, v, *The Southeast Building, The Twin Basilicas, The Mosaic House*, Princeton, 1960.

Young = Rodney S. Young, "Sepulturae Intra Urbem," *Hesperia*, XX, 1951, pp. 67–134.

GENERAL INTRODUCTION

"The object of this study is to clarify and amplify that chapter in the ceramic history of Athens which covers the time between the end of the fourth and the end of the second century B.C." These words were written some time ago, introducing "Two Centuries of Hellenistic Pottery" by Homer A. Thompson, a study to which the archaeological world is deeply indebted, whose ideas and observations remain permanently fresh and evocative, and which needs no bibliographical footnote for reference in Hellenistic studies. The purposes of the present study are much the same: presentation, classification, chronology, in this case of the ceramic history of Corinth in its truncated Hellenistic years.

There can be no thought that this study presents a ceramic history of great intrinsic interest or of high artistic achievement, although in studying the pottery there has been great affection, and qualities have been seen in it to admire and enjoy. It is the pottery of a long and experienced tradition which had had its moments of high attainment. Even in its concluding phases it was still, to the end, the product of a craft, with much still of the requirements and discipline which the word craft implies, and with even an occasional flicker of the instinct for excellence.

Tangible indications of this instinct will, much too occasionally, be evident in the pottery illustrated. These pages, however, have other objectives in mind. Dating has necessarily been the major one and has, in the present early stages of our knowledge of this period in Corinthian pottery, occupied much space and primary attention. One can claim no more than a beginning here, using the evidence we have now and what it suggests as criteria for dating. One reflects that dating itself, after all, is only a beginning: ultimately one hopes that the Corinthian pottery of the times, through its dating, can tell us more[1] about the buildings and structures with which it is associated, when they were made, perhaps suggest by whom, and conceivably even give a clue as to why. Perhaps it may have something to say about the scantily documented history of Hellenistic Corinth in its many vicissitudes, about the peoples with whom Corinth came in contact, about the fluctuating material wealth of Corinth and her trade, her artistic taste in the period, something about Corinth's own contributions to the artistic world of these years, or about her derivations from pottery of other centers and her degree of suggestibility.

At the same time, there has been an immediate allied objective in mind: to express what this pottery has to tell us in such a way that those who excavate can use its information effectively, by clarifying one of the various means of dating available to archaeologists in the times concerned. As has been well said, one does not date by any one thing alone: the various categories of material providing chronological information, the contexts, the sources, the topographical implications involved, and much else all supplement and control each the others in the ultimate conclusions reached.

The pottery studied in this volume is Corinthian only, or what is believed to be Corinthian[2]: shape series or other entities believed to have been in production at Corinth during the Hellenistic period, or rather a part of it, from the time of Alexander the Great to the time of the destruction of Corinth

---

[1] In the section on Deposits and Chronology, below, pp. 188-198, some present indications of architectural, historical, and other connections are discussed.

[2] Much of the pottery discussed here is as recognizably Corinthian in characteristics of clay and glaze as any of the pottery products of Corinth of the preceding periods. There are, of course, some individual borderline cases in which there is doubt. Whether or not the cooking ware in general is of Corinthian manufacture has been a special problem for which a solution is sought rather than achieved.

by Mummius in 146 B.C. With a few minor exceptions[3] all the Corinthian pottery of this time found at Corinth has been studied: fine ware, coarse ware, cooking ware, blister ware, and moulded relief ware. These categories include vessels made entirely on the wheel, and vessels made partly on the wheel, partly by hand, either strictly so (e.g. blister ware) or with other mechanical assistance such as the beater and anvil (cooking ware) or moulds (moulded relief ware). There are no plastic vessels, that is vessels produced from piece-moulds.

The period covered in the study of this pottery actually extends much further back than the beginning of the Hellenistic period proper, for of the more than 100 shape series or other entities in production at Corinth in Hellenistic times 40% or more are shapes originally introduced into Corinthian pottery at much earlier periods, some in the 6th century, others in the course of the 5th and 4th centuries. To develop a chronology it was necessary to study the full histories of these earlier shapes whose periods of production extend in some instances part way into the Hellenistic period, in others all the way down to 146 B.C. It might be argued that one should separate the wheat from the chaff, as it were, and present in a Hellenistic study only what is strictly Hellenistic, but for chronological purposes this is not a practical suggestion. Hence full histories of all shapes, old and new, produced in Hellenistic times at Corinth, are included insofar as they can be traced at present.[4]

Although the present repertoire of vessels is extensive, it seems likely that in various ways it is not complete.[5] There are gaps in many series with respect to their periods of production and size series. There are evident or probable gaps in representation by function, some probably in the fine ware and some very certainly in coarse ware, whose representation here is comparatively slight. In sources there are also evident or probable gaps. Grave groups of the Hellenistic period proper are few in number and consequently varieties of vessels employed as grave offerings are probably not fully represented. There is extensive representation of material from private houses, from wells and cisterns. We form the impression, however, that few of these were the houses of the well-to-do, and we suspect that the pleasure of seeing Corinthian Hellenistic pottery of high quality awaits us in the future to a large extent. If any public antiquities were produced in pottery, they also await us. The absence of votive pottery will be evident. This, however, is a different kind of gap. Material from sanctuaries is present, but miniature[6] votive pottery, it would seem, was not a feature of Hellenistic Corinth, except possibly in the very early years. The practice of offering miniature vessels in sanctuaries, so prominent in earlier

---

[3] A few scantily represented shapes have not been discussed here. Their study will require fuller representation and documentation:

    Deep bowl, flat rim, West Slope decoration: C-40-16, Deposit 37.
    Double cruet: C-33-1466 and C-33-1466A; C-63-481 a–c.
    Small closed shape, fragment, West Slope decoration: C-28-70.

The following, found in the excavations during the spring, 1966, represent additional shapes not hitherto known in Corinthian Hellenistic pottery:

    Two different small closed shapes, both fragments, both with West Slope decoration: C-66-143; C-66-155.
    Small, shallow dish, flat rim: C-66-104; C-66-153.
    Bowl kantharos, kylix handles: C-66-159.

[4] During the present study and for long before, the question of the value of studying Greek pottery of post-Mycenaean times by the long-conventional and perhaps outmoded period units has persistently raised itself. Particularly in the cases of the plainer, undecorated, or simply decorated fine ware, the coarse ware, and the cooking ware it has seemed that much benefit in comprehension and utility could be derived from studies continuous from Protogeometric times through Hellenistic. The general picture seems one of successive shape series, overlapping one another in the course of the centuries, each of which could benefit much by an understanding of those which preceded and followed. Some shape series, in fact, have periods of production extending through several of the conventional time zones. Study of particular decorated shape series through the millenium should similarly be very rewarding, particularly of those most sensitive for dating, as, for instance, drinking cups.

[5] A summary listing of the pottery studied here, pp. 12-17, provides a means of appraising representation and lacunae in several respects.

[6] Some very small vessels are in fact included here, the ointment-pots, but these are not miniatures. Though tiny, they are not small versions of larger vessels, but rather are of the size required for their purpose.

times, seems to have ceased at Corinth in probably the late years of the 4th century or in the early 3rd. Representation by area in the city of Corinth is fairly widespread, as the locations of the deposits, most being indicated on the maps on Plates 85, 86, show; proportionately, however, a very large percentage comes from the area occupied in later times by the Roman Forum where excavation in Corinth has been most extensively undertaken.

CRITERIA FOR DATING

In the study of the pottery numerous criteria for dating have been indicated by the deposit evidence. That is to say, trends became evident when all the vessels of one kind were laid out in the chronological order indicated by the deposits from which they derive. In the cases of vessels for which the evidence is slight, potential criteria or trends of possible significance have been suggested here on the basis of the analogies of related, better established series; they can be tested when pertinent evidence is available in the future. It has seemed better to suggest lines of approach to criteria for dating, indicating them clearly as suggestions only, rather than to suppress opinion because objective evidence for demonstration was not possible.

Some of the criteria summarized here will be recognized as ones attested in pottery of other periods and other centers of manufacture. It should be emphasized that none of these was assumed for Corinthian pottery of Hellenistic times in advance of study. The position adopted has been that criteria applicable to pottery of earlier times had to be re-established and demonstrated for pottery of so late a period. Such criteria, not many, have been tested rather than taken for granted. Numerous others have suggested themselves, and there have been many surprises which could not have been anticipated. Much of the detail of the chronological evidence, from which the criteria for dating were derived, its gradual development and present state of establishment, is discussed below, pp. 188-192.

SHAPE

Shape is the primary and dominant consideration in the dating of three of the major categories of pottery here: the fine ware, the coarse ware, and the cooking ware. These categories are presented, then, in shape series, a shape series in this study meaning a series of vessels all having the same component elements of form, retained from the initial stage continuously throughout the period of production and modified only within the pattern originally set. In the discussions of shape series each one has been considered separately and in each discussion what seem to be chronologically significant criteria (as well as, often, what seem not to be) have been outlined in full. Though much can be said in a general way about trends in shape change for shapes of the same general character, e.g. broad shapes or deep shapes, study of particular shape series of either kind brings to light some unforeseen differences. Individual study of each shape without regard to others, however closely related, cannot be over-emphasized. The order of presentation adopted here for the various shape series whereby vessels of the same function, thus often related in the component elements of their forms, are grouped together will, it is thought, be of assistance in making this clear. In the fine ware, for instance, the bowls illustrate the individual development of the various shape series within a general form. Gradual constriction of the diameter of an originally broad ring foot appears to be a reliable criterion in the echinus bowl, the bowl with outturned rim, and probably also in the small dish with bevelled rim. This is not the case at all in the semi-glazed bowl in whose initial stage the foot was already constricted in relation to the rest of the form; the criteria for dating examples of its series derive from other elements. In the semi-glazed bowl and the bowl with outturned rim there is observable a chronologically significant trend toward the straightening out of an originally rounded wall profile, and toward the development of a distinctly concave upper wall profile, in later stages clearly set off from the lower wall by articulation.

The echinus bowl, on the other hand, originally also of rounded wall profile, retains this curvature throughout its Corinthian period of production from the first quarter of the 4th century to 146 B.C., the profile changing only by becoming a more shallow curve as its originally broad foot becomes more constricted, the incurving of its rim changing in no clearly definable way through all this time. One could go through the groups of interrelated wheelmade shapes and cite other general trends and exceptions in each. If one were to hazard a sweeping generality it would be only to the effect that in all shapes a gradual change can be observed from the shape initially adopted, usually within the limits of the form originally prescribed. But again "except": except when considerations of function prohibit, e.g., the already initially constricted foot of the semi-glazed bowl which could not become more constricted without rendering the shape too unstable for use.

Other trends also are not trends across the board, that is gradual trends equally affecting all pottery during the course of the period. There are trends from original carefulness in the execution of a form and its component elements toward careless formation, from clear articulation to blurred, from memory of the forms of the original elements to Lethe. There are trends toward loss of purely decorative niceties, toward vestigiality even of some functionally necessary components. There is a trend toward ease and speed of production. There is a trend from careful glazing to careless, from careful wheel glazing (or careful double dipping) to partial glazing by dipping.[7] But these are trends observable within particular shape series, not general trends of the period. A shape as it grows older in its period of production normally shows advancement along these lines. But a new shape introduced at whatever point in the Hellenistic period will invariably, in Corinthian pottery, exhibit in its initial stage all the care of execution one might desire for the purpose for which it was intended. A "set" of Corinthian pottery of all shapes of one moment in the period would show a gradation in quality of execution from high to low, the degree of quality depending on how long the given shape had been in production at the time. Grave groups composed of shapes varying in "age" provide partial illustration of this. Some vessels, it seems, had just come into production shortly before the destruction by Mummius in 146 B.C. Though they may not bear comparison with products of earlier periods at Corinth, they are still, in their chronological milieu, fresh, sharp, well done. It is humanly understandable: the increasing monotony of producing a shape of long tradition and well established on the market contrasts with the challenge and pleasure of craftsmanship in forming a new and interesting shape for different, new requirements, a shape which one hopes to introduce and induce sales for in the market.

Some shape series are more sensitive for dating than others, that is, more elements of their forms show trends of chronological significance. All show some chronologically useful trends, but the more sensitive ones are especially to be prized, particularly in excavation. In introductions to the general categories and to particular groups of shapes these have usually been noted. More particular attention in this regard should be paid to drinking cups. It seems highly probable that these, in the long run, will prove to be the most delicate chronometers of Hellenistic times. Conceivably they are also for earlier times, the special aspect of this kind of vessel being evidently an enduring interest in them on the part of fashion resulting in great variety and, in relatively short periods of production, comparatively rapid evolutions in their forms. If one were to grade the various shapes by their chronological utility those of even shorter periods of production might come next, shapes which appeared briefly on the market and for which demand was not sustained. Probably in this category, for instance, is the Corinthian unguentarium which one suspects made only the briefest of appearances on the market when the imported unguentarium was first introduced in Greece, in the course of the third quarter of the 4th century, and which probably did not continue in production because of the great technical superiority with which normal Corinthian clay could not compete, and the initially extremely attractive appearance of the imported products. Probably also within this category are the shapes thought to have been newly

---

[7] Partial glazing by dipping is not a phenomenon exclusive to the Hellenistic period in Corinth. It is known earlier, even in the 6th century; see, for instance, the trefoil olpe.

introduced shortly before Mummius' destruction of Corinth, which should be of great value for dating near the middle of the 2nd century at Corinth.

In the various discussions of shape series in this book the rare reader who reads the book through (most will naturally consult only particular entries) will find an insistent repetition of the words "size for size." It has become abundantly clear that for close dating of a given example in a given shape series comparison must be made between examples of the same size, or closely adjacent sizes.[8] Many shape series were produced in wide ranges of size from very large to very small. Comparison between large and small may yield something in the way of general placement but all too often the results are likely to be misleading. What the Corinthian potters thought to be standard sizes one can only estimate. In broad vessels, e.g. bowls, plates, and the like, it seems clear that sizes were based on diameters, in deep shapes normally on height. Here a somewhat arbitrary distinction of sizes has generally been adopted, and though at first it may seem finicky nicety, nonetheless it has been observed that a single centimeter's difference in size, whether by diameter or height, makes an appreciable difference in the appearance and proportions of a vessel, and hence, usually, a distinction is here made in sizes centimeter by centimeter. In some very small series, e.g. the smaller versions of the echinus bowl, an even slighter difference has an effect on the general appearance. In estimating dates for examples of particular series considerable use has been made of tables compiled from vessels of the same size, giving close measurements of those elements of the form affected by the trends of shape change which are chronologically significant and observable. Again this may be thought unrealistic nicety, as one can hardly expect mathematical precision to have been observed rigidly in the trends of shape series, in the course of the transmission of the shape from generation to generation in a master and apprentice sequence, yet one finds that the eye is all too fallible in judging placement according to shape trends. Close measurement is a necessary, objective control which the eye can and should often modify and interpret through consideration of trends other than those affecting proportions, particularly in advanced and late stages when the trends of shape and other kinds of change normally become less dependable. The desirability of using close measurement as one means of control is perhaps most clearly illustrated by comparison of examples of the Corinthian fish plate of Attic type of *ca.* 300 and 146 B.C., **132** and **131**. Differences in measurement between the two are slight, five millimeters in the height, four in the diameter of the foot, yet the difference in general appearance between the two is enormous. Another aspect of size perhaps is self-evident but seems to require some emphasis nonetheless: examples of a shape series of larger sizes seem likely to be more dependable for dating on the basis of shape trends and other considerations than examples of small size. This is humanly understandable again, for the potter of a given stage of production can produce a pattern of inherited shape and proportions more easily in a large shape than in a small one: he can see it better on the wheel and better control what he is forming.

With all these considerations of size in mind therefore, the arrangement of catalogues of shape series here is usually chronological by sizes, graduated from large to small, an annoying system perhaps until one gets used to it, but intended to facilitate as close dating as may be. Quite often in the placement of examples of particular shape series it has been necessary to assume a regular rate of shape change, which may well be unrealistic. Future evidence will, presumably, inform us better about these rates, and whether development occurred in spurts or at times remained on more or less static plateaus, or otherwise.

There are a number of more general considerations for dating the pottery which are more for future consideration than for the present study since the necessary information is largely not available at this time. One is relative dating of successive series of vessels of one function on the principle of functional

---

[8] Unfortunately it has not always been possible to illustrate in this book consecutive examples of shapes of the same size since the series now available for study are very frequently incomplete in respect to size. It is not, of course, feasible to illustrate the full range of sizes in all the various shape series, but extensive representation of sizes is provided in the cases of the echinus bowl (Pl. 2) and the Attic type of skyphos (Pls. 13 and 14).

replacements, especially in shapes for which there was an enduring need. The application of this principle will be clear in some instances, more difficult to apply in others. A clear instance is the functional replacement of the superannuated Classical krater shapes by new Hellenistic ones, e.g. the bolster and hemispherical kraters. The late stages of the bell krater in Corinthian are known; probably the calyx krater also continued late in production in Corinthian. The new kraters must have been introduced during one of the very late stages of the old, when it was seen that the old krater shapes were then functionally impractical. No lacuna in the production of krater shapes between Classical and Hellenistic seems likely. Old and new must have overlapped for a bit in time of production until the more satisfactory new shapes drove out the old. Estimates of the date of the last stage of the old and the initial stage of the new thus have to be considered together and an allowance made for overlap. Similar considerations have influenced the estimated dating of the undoubtedly overlapping periods of production of early Hellenistic drinking cups, the various kantharoi, and the later Hellenistic drinking-cup forms, including the moulded relief or Megarian bowl. It seems at present that moulded relief bowls came into production at Corinth somewhat later than at Athens, whose products the Corinthian potters imitated to a large extent. It seems then that the older wheelmade drinking-cup shapes necessarily continued in production longer at Corinth than perhaps they did at Athens, and their late stages are adjusted somewhat in time to overlap a bit the evidently advanced date of the introduction of moulded ware in Corinthian.

Consideration may also be given to shared elements of shape design which may serve to link different shape series together chronologically. This kind of chronological blocking out can perhaps be seen most clearly in a number of series of Hellenistic kantharoi: the use of similar forms of foot and handles in several different shapes suggests, in addition to deposit evidence, contemporaneity in periods of production. Somewhat more nebulous in application are the apparently dominant preferences in fashion for deep drinking-cup shapes in earlier Hellenistic times at Corinth and for broader, open shapes in the later; there is at least conceivable a chronological relationship between the introduction of the moulded-ware bowls and the later broad shapes, the introduction of the moulded bowls perhaps creating the fashion for the broad shapes. Another potential chronological linking concerns the effect of drinking-vessel forms on the oinochoai which were used to fill them. In the discussion of Decanter III below, at any rate, it is suggested that the introduction and preference for deep drinking cups in reaction to Classical broad shapes in the second quarter of the 4th century may have caused modification in the decanter form, requiring the makers of decanters to provide a more constricted neck and lip for pouring.

In connection with dating by shape two considerations which may seem attractive and potentially valuable chronologically have not been pursued. No attempt has been made to distinguish the products of different workshops; it has not seemed to the present writer that the material lends itself well to workshop identifications or groupings. Even if it were feasible to undertake such a study, one wonders if it would contribute sufficiently to be worthwhile except to the ceramic specialist. It is hoped that the expression and determination of the chronology of the pottery of this time may remain sufficiently simple and uncomplicated in its outlines to prove a usable tool for those relatively uninitiated in pottery. The second consideration not employed here has been deliberately avoided: dating of examples of Corinthian shapes on the basis of the dating of comparable shapes produced at other centers of pottery manufacture. There probably could be no greater pitfall in dating pottery of the Hellenistic era (or earlier?) than to assume that comparable shapes proceeded through the stages of their evolution in different fabrics *pari passu*. One may take the case of the perhaps twenty Attic shapes produced in Corinthian,[9] some of which were also produced at numerous other Hellenistic centers of manufacture throughout the Mediterranean. There is no reason to suppose that all these different imitations of Attic prototypes were adopted in the various centers at the moment when they first appeared in Attic, nor that they followed Attic shape changes step by step, nor that they ceased to be produced at all these

[9] For the list see below, p. 19, note 3.

centers at the time the corresponding Attic shape was abandoned. The more likely view, adopted here, is that such shapes were probably first imitated in the different centers at various stages of development, whenever a center came in contact with the Attic, perhaps generally in relatively early stages while the Attic was still attractive and excited imitation; that the Attic shape, once adopted at a center, went through a separate course of development at that center, perhaps faster, perhaps slower than the Attic; that production of the shape at the various centers may not have continued as long as in Attic or, on the other hand, may have continued much longer. These points cannot be proved on present information. Some indication that this is near the true picture is provided, however, by examples of similar shapes in several different fabrics, all probably in use at the time of the destruction by Mummius: if indeed all are of that moment, a variation in speed of shape development is thereby attested in a number of different fabrics in connection with the same shapes. It is possible indeed that some Corinthian shapes, originally imitated from the Attic, show a more rapid shape development than their contemporary Attic cousins. The picture of local individuality and enterprise which these suggestions envisage is not humanly an unlikely one. There was a certain superficial *koine*, one supposes, in Hellenistic pottery produced in various parts of the Greek world. There had been one to a greater or lesser extent in preceding periods, in Classical, Archaic, and earlier. The *koine* in Hellenistic times was probably no more closely knit than it had been previously (e.g. Classical Boiotian and Classical Attic?) and in time as more becomes known about the pottery products of the various local centers of Hellenistic times one may expect the degree of their differences one from another will become more evident. However, in default of other evidence, the fixed date provided by the Olynthos destruction for Attic skyphoi has been used here to give an approximate date for the Attic-type skyphoi found at Corinth.

One reads with great interest the acute observations of Eva T. H. Brann on Protoattic shapes and the "morphology of artifacts".[10] Shape developments of various kinds observed in Protoattic differ considerably from those observed here in Corinthian Hellenistic, no doubt because the Protoattic was a formative and experimental period in pottery and the Hellenistic comes at the end of long centuries of tradition and experience, and the evolvement of shapes is not, in the present Hellenistic wheelmade vessels at any rate, complicated in any evident way by the demands of major decoration. It seems clear that the morphology of artifacts will present different patterns in different periods. It will be interesting to learn of its character in different contemporary centers.

It is instructive and profitable in relation to these thoughts on the character of the Hellenistic *koine* to compare the situation in the Protogeometric period,[11] particularly with regard to differing periods of production of a style in different centers, adoption of it at advanced stages in some and production of it in some beyond the time when it had been abandoned elsewhere.

FABRIC

Criteria for dating Corinthian Hellenistic pottery are not limited to those of shapes and their elements alone, but also are concerned with fabric. In the case of coarse ware a chronological criterion is quite probably to be seen in the composition of the clay: heavy clay with many deliberate inclusions in the Classical period and earlier for the most part, in the later 4th century and following, a growing preference for purified clay, entirely similar to that used for fine ware, only thicker. In blister ware there is a distinct difference between its appearance in Classical times and that in Hellenistic: comparatively heavy and solid earlier, deliberately egg-shell thin in early Hellenistic, and still thin later. In it also a chronological distinction is to be seen in the method of manufacture: the shapes are primarily handmade in the earlier, evidently wheelmade in the Hellenistic. Even in intended color there is some clue for chronology: a dark color in Classical blister ware, and in Hellenistic evidently a pleasing, light, blond shade.

[10] *Late Geometric and Protoattic Pottery*, pp. 2–4.
[11] Vincent R. d'A. Desborough, *Protogeometric Pottery*, Oxford, 1952, pp. 294–295.

DECORATION

A more important body of criteria, however, is concerned with the decoration of various kinds appearing here in several of the major categories of pottery. Painted decoration appears on some wheelmade fine-ware series in the familiar West Slope technique (for detailed discussion see pp. 20-25) during the entire Hellenistic period in Corinthian. Though its course of development is chronologically informative, its requirements evidently do not affect the normal course of shape changes and trends, as they no doubt do in the case of the far more illustrious decoration of vessels of earlier times. The evolution of Corinthian painted decoration through the period is a somewhat curious one (it may, of course, be very different in other fabrics). During a long period, the first 75 years or so of the Hellenistic period, it is used in very minor ways, with no great distinction in execution. There follows a sudden bloom, on present dating in the third and last quarters of the 3rd century, resulting in decoration of excellent quality and considerable interest, as on the drinking-cup shapes on which it so often appears in Corinthian. It then gradually dwindles off to mediocrity and worse by the time of the city's destruction. The sudden and very pleasing flowering of West Slope decoration may owe something in composition and choice of designs to the introduction of moulded relief ware. Aside from these differences between the decoration of earlier Corinthian Hellenistic vessels and later, there is a special criterion for closer dating in West Slope decoration in the later phase: what has been called, and aptly in this case, the principle of the degeneration of the motif (a principle not confined to the Hellenistic period). The principle is actually no different from the trends of change in vessel forms, progressing gradually from early careful to later careless in execution. In Corinthian West Slope decoration no chronological information is to be derived from the use of incision or applied color since both are employed throughout the period.

The detection of individual artists in the earlier phase of Corinthian West Slope decoration seems not at all feasible because of the frequent loss of the fugitive glaze carrying with it the painted elements of the decoration. Their detection in the later phase when the decoration is better preserved and of more distinctive character may eventually be possible, but the body of material for this period is as yet slight. Chronological groupings of artists should in any case give way to more pressing aspects of dating. Art history is, perhaps fortunately, not seriously involved.

Other criteria in decoration for dating of fine ware are discussed in the general introduction to that class and in discussions of individual shape series in fine ware. To them other kinds of embellishment may perhaps be added as potentially of some interest for dating, e.g., the vertical grooving or ribbing on vessels such as some of the kantharos shapes, attested in Corinthian on present dating between *ca.* 330 and the third quarter of the 3rd century B.C.; also the horizontal, spiral grooving beneath the glaze employed on the conical bowls and the mastos to greater or lesser degree in the years of the third quarter of the 3rd century and following, perhaps a phenomenon exclusive to later Hellenistic days in Corinth.

Decorative criteria for dating are also present in the less likely categories of blister ware and cooking ware. The blister ware aryballoi of Classical times, being handmade, provide no criteria for dating by shape, but on them during their course of production from perhaps the second quarter of the 5th century into the later years of the 4th appears a simple kind of ribbed decoration which, as the deposit evidence indicates, goes through the pattern evolution of degeneration of the motif. Other handmade blister-ware shapes are also known in Classical times, decorated in other ways. Conceivably their decoration will, when studied, yield comparably useful indications for chronology. It may be somewhat surprising to find cooking ware included in a discussion of decoration, but in the cooking ware classed here as Corinthian there exists a kind of embellishment which has proved useful for dating. Its origins may be traced very far back in the history of cooking ware to the better known thin Archaic and Classical fabric.[12] In early days it appears as vertical stroke burnishing on the upper parts of vessels.

---

[12] Brann, *Late Geometric and Protoattic Pottery*, p. 3, dates the first appearance of the thin fabric in Attic in the 8th century. If indeed this is produced by the beater-and-anvil technique one wonders if it may not owe its introduction to imitation of the metal-work practice of hammering.

Subsequently this kind of treatment, which may conceivably have served some technical purpose, gives way to vertical lines seemingly in dull black glaze; these ultimately disappear from use around the middle of the 4th century.

Decoration, the present study suggests, is actually the dominant criterion for dating in one of the major categories of vessels considered here, the moulded relief ware. Though one cannot certify this on the basis of present evidence, it seems quite likely that its decoration was a major factor in its design and that shapes were changed and modified the better to enhance and exploit the particular style of decoration employed. A modification of form to suit decoration is perhaps to be seen, for example, in the bowl shape on which concentric semicircle decoration was employed (below, pp. 182-184). The presentation of the relief ware is therefore by different units, not of shapes but of what are regarded here as stylistic groups, which rest to some extent in a chronological limbo at present for lack of precise evidence. There is a small, presumably initial, class of Foliage Bowls, subdivided into stylistic groups, each group really a major motif: leaf-and-tendril bowls, pine-cone bowls, imbricate-leaf bowls, and other kinds of decoration derived from natural foliage and flora. In a second class, Figured Bowls, probably introduced a while after the beginning of the first, figured scenes play a major role in the decoration, and a final third class, the Linear Bowls, evidently just emerging shortly before the destruction of the city, has sub-groups of different motifs exploiting the possibilities of line decoration: long-petal bowls, net-pattern bowls and others. In the first and last classes some degree of chronological information can perhaps in future be derived from consideration of sequences in mould design. There is probably present to some degree a trend in mould designs from those comparatively difficult to produce toward those whose production is easier, a phenomenon not new in pottery. In the Figured Bowls the establishment of criteria for dating is more difficult. It seems likely that their dating will proceed through definition of the periods of use of particular scenes, and ultimately through these dating of subsidiary motifs may be possible.

GRAFFITO INSCRIPTIONS

There is a final possible criterion for dating related neither to shape nor to decoration, a special class of inscriptions which appear, in Corinthian, only on fine-ware kantharoi: graffito inscriptions (*grammatika ekpomata;* see pp. 64-65) incised on the vessels through the glaze before firing, most frequently the names of divinities or abstractions in the genitive. They appear on the Corinthian vessel forms only between *ca.* 330 and the third quarter of the 3rd century, on present dating, a period limited in time like that of the *kalos* names of Classical Attic pottery whose vogue was also fairly brief. For the talented student of calligraphy the identification of the handwriting of the individuals who inscribed them may provide closer relative dating and interconnections between the different drinking-cup series on which they appear. Perhaps these graffiti may be of papyrological or other interest since they are contemporary with the pots on which they appear.

CHARACTERISTICS OF CORINTHIAN HELLENISTIC POTTERY

In the present study it has been thought that it would be desirable in many ways to present the entire body of pottery of one Hellenistic center alone, without the distraction of the imported products of other centers[13] so that the individual characteristics of that center, in this case Corinthian, might be seen as clearly as possible in relation to those of other centers. Though the study of the distribution of

[13] Much imported pottery is actually noted here, however, and often dated, in introductions to various sections and in discussions of particular shape series or stylistic groups. In one of the stages of preparation of this volume most of it was given preliminary study. It is hoped that a volume combining the imported Hellenistic pottery of both Corinth and the Athenian Agora can be prepared in the future.

Corinthian in the Hellenistic period can provide considerable comment on Corinthian history and commercial enterprise, it has not been possible to undertake such a study here and hence it must remain a subject for future investigation.

FABRIC

In the fine ware, in much of the coarse ware, and in the moulded relief ware the clay in this period frequently has the characteristics familiar from Corinthian pottery of much earlier times: a light color, white, blond, sometimes light green, and normally rather soft, easily incised with a fingernail. In these characteristics it may differ markedly from the clay of distant centers, though it is possible that the clay employed in nearby centers, e.g. Sikyon, is not greatly dissimilar in appearance. Included in the study are some pieces varying from the norm in hardness and color. Coarse-ware mortars normally, and exceptionally among other Hellenistic coarse-ware shapes, have an inclusion of particles in the tradition of Classical and earlier Corinthian coarse ware. Blister-ware clay in Classical times, with relatively heavy walls, was fired to a very high temperature, often near vitrification, and apparently a dark color was intentionally induced, though reddish or orange shades appear, no doubt through accidental oxidization. Hellenistic blister ware, with thin walls, was also fired to a high temperature, but is normally blond in color. Cooking-ware clay is usually red, though shades of gray are included here. In appearance it probably does not differ greatly from that of cooking ware found at many other sites, though imported cooking ware of distinctively different appearance is known at Corinth.

GLAZE

The glaze is seldom lustrous and is very frequently fugitive, as often in earlier times in Corinthian. Sometimes it has completely flaked off. Possibly a peculiarity of Corinthian Hellenistic, inherited from earlier Corinthian, is the use of solid areas of glaze only on the interiors of some vessels (semi-glazed bowl, semi-glazed mastos, coarse-ware column krater, and one of the handle-ridge jugs) and also completely unglazed fine-ware vessels (some of the kyathoi, the trefoil oinochoe with shoulder stop, the juglet, the small water pitcher, the calyx cup, the lekanis, and the pyxis). Vessels whose exteriors are left unglazed, often with polished surfaces, and those with glaze only in wheel-run bands or lines are evidently not exclusive to Corinthian. This pleasing treatment is well attested in Classical Corinthian, e.g. the decanters, and is continued in Hellenistic Corinthian in the semi-glazed bowls.

SHAPES

It is not fully possible to assess what is peculiarly Corinthian in point of view of shapes. Candidates for native Corinthian shapes are the semi-glazed bowl, the saucer, the trefoil olpe, the small trefoil oinochoe with shoulder stop, the juglet (?), the decanters, the semi-glazed mastos (?), and the lekanis. Many other Corinthian shapes were certainly produced elsewhere as well and a good proportion of them probably were produced at Corinth in forms derived from those of other centers. Some 20 fine-ware shapes are evidently derivative from Attic (list, p. 19, footnote 3), and the moulded bowl forms to a large extent seem so, also. A few other fine-ware shapes are clearly derivative from other foreign shapes. For the remainder we are not now in a position to judge whether or not they are strictly Corinthian. The considerable interest in drinking-vessel shapes evident in Corinthian suggests that some of them are, however, native, if not in general design, perhaps in special characteristics of treatment. The blister-ware shapes may well be peculiar to Corinth, though other vessels in a similar fabric were probably produced elsewhere. Little can be said at the moment about individually distinctive shapes in coarse and cooking wares. The column krater is a very early local invention but certainly not confined to Corinth even in the Hellenistic semi-glazed version. The coarse-ware water pitcher and probably the handle-ridge jug are to be considered of foreign derivation. Many other coarse- and cooking-ware shapes are clearly, or probably, shared with other centers. A possible peculiarity in Corinthian vessels of these categories is the use of cooking-ware fabric instead of coarse clay for certain vessels because of the inadequacy of Corinthian clay for the purpose. In this connection the cooking-ware krater, bowls, plates, and pitchers may be cited.

The absence of certain shapes in the present repertoire may be an indication of Corinthian preferences or usage differing from those of other centers. The repertoire is evidently not as full, for instance, as Attic. A striking particular difference between Attic and Corinthian is in the West Slope amphora, a standard requirement in Athens throughout Hellenistic times, but a shape represented in Corinth only by a late diminutive example and by a very small number of imported amphorae. The absence of plastic vessels is also striking, and not least to be noted is the general lack of variants in the wheel-made ware.

DECORATION

Corinthian shares various kinds of decoration with many other centers. Special characteristics appear to be individual, notably the Corinthian use of a distinctive applied pink color in fine ware (below, p. 20). In the use and development of the West Slope type of decoration (restriction to certain shapes and unobtrusive employment in the earlier phases) Corinthian differs from the products of other centers. A certain degree of interest in figured representations in Corinthian West Slope is not widespread elsewhere, nor are the interesting Corinthian attempts at three-dimensionality in figured representations. A little Corinthian individuality and inventiveness is observable in certain representations on moulded bowls, though for the most part the moulded representations in Corinthian are widely shared. The use of stamping and rouletting are almost non-existent in the Corinthian vessels studied here. The characteristic Attic usage in moulded bowls of lines wheel incised through the glaze exposing color beneath is not present in Corinthian moulded ware.

It cannot be said that the Corinthian pottery of this time is outstanding in general quality in relation to the contemporary products of other cities, but in general most of its wares, cooking ware being excepted, stand out as recognizable: it is relatively easy to separate it out from imported pottery in Corinth. Conversely, although it is clear that a good number of different centers are represented in the imported Hellenistic pottery found in Corinth, it is often difficult, even impossible, to see clear distinctions among the imported pieces. Perhaps in this respect Corinthian can regain, through present day archaeological use, some of the luster it has lost, or obtain some never possessed, as a fabric for the most part recognizable without great difficulty, with much to tell us chronologically of the times when it was made, times in which archaeology stands still much in need of the kind of information which Corinthian can provide.

CONSPECTUS OF THE POTTERY

The following summary of all the categories of pottery in this book, and the shape series or other entities within them, has been provided for general comprehension of the pottery which at present exists in Corinth for study, and of the extent of present representation by function, by shape, by stage of production, by date, and by quantity.

Vessels in moulded ware have been presented in stylistic classes and groups. Vessels in fine ware, coarse ware, cooking ware, and blister ware have been presented by shape series (for definition see above, p. 3, and vessels of shape series of the same function have been grouped together. In each functional group of vessels an idea can thus be obtained not only of what we now have, but also of what is clearly missing at present, and what we may need in order to provide a complete picture of Corinthian vessels of that particular function, as well as for general chronological purposes.

It is emphasized that "attested periods of production" means very literally "attested" and no more. Most entries here provide specific dates attested for each shape series at present. These are not necessarily indications of the full period of production a given shape is thought to have had, but often is only that part of its period of production which we seem now to have represented by specific pots. Modifying explanations accompanying the dates will make this clear. "Initial to final stages" means that the beginning and end of production and perhaps some of the intermediate stages also are actually represented. Other terms indicate varying degrees of partial representation, e.g., early, advanced, intermediate, late, very late. With regard to lacunae it is safe to say that there is no series here that does not require further supplement in one or more aspects.

	ATTESTED PERIOD OF PRODUCTION	CATALOGUE NUMBERS
Wheelmade Fine Ware		
Vessels for Food		
Bowls		
Semi-glazed bowl	Early to final stages, 4th century, second quarter, to 146 B.C.	**1–14**
Echinus bowl	Advanced to final stages, 4th century, first quarter, to 146 B.C.	**15–71**
Bowl, outturned rim	Advanced to final stages, 4th century, second quarter, to 146 B.C.	**72–94**
Small dish, bevelled rim	Intermediate stages, 350 to 300 B.C.	**95–100**
Plates		
Rolled-rim plate	Very late and final stages, 200 to 146 B.C.	**101–106**
Flat-rim plate	Final stage only, 146 B.C.	**107–126**
Plate, offset rim	Initial and intermediate stages, 3rd century, third and fourth quarters.	**127–130**
Fish plate, Attic type	Intermediate and final stages, 300 to 146 B.C.	**131–133**

	ATTESTED PERIOD OF PRODUCTION	CATALOGUE NUMBERS
Fish plate, bevelled rim	Early to final stages, 275 to 146 B.C.	**134–137**
Saucer	Initial to final stages, 4th century, second quarter, to 146 B.C.	**138–186**
Vessels for Drink		
Containers		
Small West Slope amphora	Probably final stage, *ca.* 150 B.C.	**187**
Serving vessels		
Bolster krater	Early and advanced stages, early 3rd century to 3rd century, third quarter.	**188, 189**
Hemispherical krater	Early stage, 3rd century, first quarter.	**190**
Dippers		
Kyathos, loop handle, articulated wall	Early and advanced stages, late 4th century to early 3rd century.	**191–193**
Kyathos, pinch handle		
Articulated wall	Advanced stage, 2nd century, first half.	**194**
Articulated wall, inturned rim	Final stage, 146 B.C.	**195, 196**
Convex wall	Final stage, 146 B.C.	**197**
Pouring vessels		
Trefoil olpe	Initial to final stages, 550 to 146 B.C.	**198–244**
Small trefoil oinochoe	Intermediate stages, 475 to 300 B.C.	**245–270**
Small trefoil oinochoe, shoulder stop	Advanced to late stages, 5th century, last quarter, to 3rd century, first quarter.	**271–278**
Variant	Late stage, 3rd century, first quarter.	**279**
Juglet	Advanced stage, between 330 and 146 B.C.	**280**
Small water pitcher	Late stage, 2nd century, first half.	**281**
Decanter		
Decanter I	Initial stage and very late stages, 5th century, third quarter, and 2nd century, first half.	**282–286**
Decanter II	Initial to late stages, 5th century, third quarter, to 4th century, first quarter.	**287–300**
Decanter III	Intermediate stages, 4th century, third quarter, to 3rd century, first quarter.	**301–306**
Drinking vessels		
Deep shapes		
Skyphos, Attic type	Advanced to final stages, 425 to 275 B.C.	**307–371**
Calyx cup	Late stage, 3rd century, first quarter.	**372**

	ATTESTED PERIOD OF PRODUCTION	CATALOGUE NUMBERS
Calyx kantharos, kylix handles		
Pedestal foot	Late stage, 3rd century, first half.	**373–374**
Pedestal foot, moulded rim	Late stage, 3rd century, first half.	**375**
Metallic foot, moulded rim	Late stage, 3rd century, first half.	**376–377**
One-piece kantharos	Intermediate stages, 325 to 250 B.C.	**378–388**
Cyma kantharos	Early to final stages, 330 to 225 B.C.	**389–450**
Acrocorinth kantharos	Initial and intermediate stages, 330 B.C. to 3rd century, first quarter.	**451–457**
Articulated kantharos	Initial to late stages, 325 B.C. to 3rd century, third quarter.	**458–514**
Hexamilia kantharos	Intermediate stages, 3rd century, second quarter, to 3rd century, early last quarter.	**515–520**
Hexamilia mug	Advanced stage, 3rd century, third quarter.	**521–523**
Thorn kantharos	Final stage, *ca.* 150 B.C.	**524**
Broad shapes		
Hemispherical bowl, appliqué supports	Late stage, 2nd century, first half.	**525–526**
Wheelmade Megarian bowl	Initial to final stages, 3rd century, third quarter, to 146 B.C.	**527–531, 944**
Conical bowl	Initial to final stages, 3rd century, third quarter, to 146 B.C.	**532–549, 943**
Mastos	Early stage, 3rd century, last quarter.	**550**
Semi-glazed mastos	Advanced stage, 3rd century, second half.	**551**
Spouted, covered drinking bowl, recurved handles	Intermediate stages, 275 to 225 B.C.	**552–553**
Drinking bowl, recurved handles	Final stage, *ca.* 175 B.C.	**554**
Vessels for other purposes		
Covered vessels		
Lekanis	Initial, late, and final stages, 5th century, second quarter, to 146 B.C.	**555–558**
Pyxis, domed slipover lid	Intermediate stages, 350 B.C. to 3rd century, third quarter.	**559–583**
Vessels for perfume and ointments		
Unguentarium	Initial stage, 325 B.C.	**584–586**
Ointment-pot: amphoriskos	Advanced stage (?), *ca.* 225 B.C.	**587–588**
Ointment-pot: bulbous jar	Initial (?) and intermediate stages, 3rd century, first quarter, to 3rd century, last quarter.	**589–596**
Ointment-pot: piriform jar	Initial (?) to late stages, 350 B.C. to 3rd century, last quarter.	**597–603**

	ATTESTED PERIOD OF PRODUCTION	CATALOGUE NUMBERS
Vessels for writing		
Inkwell	Final stage (?), *ca.* 150 B.C. (?).	**604**
Vessels for other purposes		
Basketball askos	Initial stage, 330–300 B.C.	**605–607**
Coarse Ware		
Vessels for Food		
Stamnos lid I	Final (?) stage, 146 B.C.	**608**
Stamnos lid II	Early stage, *ca.* 300 B.C.	**609**
Stamnos lid III	Early stages, 350–300 B.C.	**610–611**
Stamnos lid IV	Early stage, *ca.* 300 B.C.	**612**
Column krater	Advanced stage, *ca.* 300 B.C.	**613–615**
Krater	Advanced stage, *ca.* 300 B.C.	**616**
Mortar I	Initial to final stages, 5th century, second quarter, to 275 B.C.	**617–625**
Mortar II	Late and final stages, 175 and 146 B.C.	**626–627**
Vessels for Drink		
Based amphora I	Advanced stage, 3rd century.	**628**
Based amphora II	Final (?) stage, 150 B.C.	**629**
Based amphora III	Advanced stage, Hellenistic prior to 146 B.C. (?).	**630**
Water pitcher	Intermediate stage, *ca.* 250 B.C.	**631–632**
Handle-ridge jug	Initial to final stages, 4th century, third quarter, to 146 B.C.	**633–642**
Funnel	Intermediate (?) stage, Hellenistic prior to 146 B.C.	**643**
Vessels for other purposes		
Ring stand I	Final stage, 146 B.C.	**644**
Ring stand II	Final stage, 146 B.C.	**645**
Cooking Ware		
Stoves		
Brazier	Very early stage, 2nd century, second quarter.	**646–647**
Vessels used over fire or in oven		
Chytra I	Early (?) and late stage, 550 (?) and 300 B.C.	**648–649**
Chytra II	Final stage, 146 B.C.	**650–655**
Stew pot	Final stage, 146 B.C.	**656**
Stew pot, one vertical, one tilted horizontal handle	Early and final stages, 300 and 146 B.C.	**657–658**
Casserole I	Early to late stages, 5th century, third quarter, to 146 B.C.	**659–670**
Casserole II	Early to final stages, *ca.* 450 to 146 B.C.	**671–682**
Casserole without handles	Early stage, *ca.* 146 B.C.	**683–685**
Large one-handled saucepan	Advanced stage, 146 B.C.	**686**
Small one-handled saucepan	Advanced stage, 3rd century.	**687**

	ATTESTED PERIOD OF PRODUCTION	CATALOGUE NUMBERS
Lid I	Early to final (?) stages, 6th century to 146 B.C. (?).	**688–692**
Lid II	Early to final stages, 6th century, second half, to 146 B.C.	**693–695**
Lid III	Early to final stages, 350 to 146 B.C.	**696–699**
Frying pan	Early stage, *ca.* 300 B.C.	**700**
Flanged plate	Early stage, 146 B.C.	**701**
Baking pan	Early stage, 146 B.C.	**702–703**
Small baking dish	Early stage (?), *ca.* 146 B.C. (?).	**704**
Vessels probably not intended for use with heat		
Vessels for Food		
Krater	Final stage, *ca.* 150 B.C.	**705**
Bowl	Final stage, *ca.* 150 B.C.	**706–708**
Bowl, vertical rim	Intermediate stage, *ca.* 200 B.C.	**709**
Plate	Early and final stages, *ca.* 300 and 146 B.C.	**710–718**
Rolled-rim plate	Final stage, 146 B.C.	**719**
Plate, low vertical rim	Intermediate stage, 146 B.C.	**720–721**
Vessels for Drink		
Round-mouth pitcher I	Early to final stages, 450 to 146 B.C.	**722–745**
Trefoil pitcher I	Intermediate stage, *ca.* 300 B.C.	**746**
Trefoil pitcher II	Intermediate stage, *ca.* 200 B.C.	**747–748**
Decanter	Final stage, 146 B.C.	**749**
Blister Ware		
Vessels for oil or perfume		
Squat aryballos	Initial to late stages, 450 to 300 B.C.	**750–775**
Duck askos	Early stage, 4th century, last quarter.	**776–777**
Vessels for other purposes		
Filter vase	Final stage, 146 B.C.	**778**
Cup	Initial stage, *ca.* 300 B.C.	**779**
Moulded Relief Ware		
Foliage Bowls		
Leaf-and-tendril bowl	Advanced stages, 225 and 200 B.C.	**780–782, 939**
Imbricate bowl		
Pine-cone bowl	Advanced stage, *ca.* 200 B.C.	**783–785**
Bowl decorated with small, veined, pointed leaves	– – – –	– – –
Bowl decorated with rounded petal tips	Final stage, 146 B.C.	**786–787, 940**
Bowl decorated with pointed petal tips	Final stage, 146 B.C.	**788–792, 941**
Bowl with encircling composition		
Ivy bowl	Advanced stage, *ca.* 175 B.C.	**793–794**
Unclassified Foliage Bowls	Early stage, 3rd century, last quarter.	**795**

	ATTESTED PERIOD OF PRODUCTION	CATALOGUE NUMBERS
Figured Bowls		
Figured Bowl	Early to final stages, 3rd century, last quarter to 146 B.C.	**796–872, 942**
Large bowl with appliqué relief supports	Advanced and final stages, 175–146 B.C.	
Comic mask supports		**873–883**
Tragic mask supports		**884–892**
Head of Athena		**893–894**
Unclassified		**895–896**
Handle (?)		**897**
Linear Bowls		
Long-petal bowl	Early stage, 150 to 146 B.C.	**898–907**
Net-pattern bowl	Early stages, 160 to 146 B.C.	**908–920**
Concentric-semicircle bowl	Early stage, 150 to 146 B.C.	**921–932**
Linear-leaf bowl	Early stage, 150 to 146 B.C.	**933–937**
Unclassified linear bowl	Early stage, *ca.* 150 B.C.	**938**

THE POTTERY

Dimensions are given in meters throughout the catalogues. Size ranges for categories within a centimeter are indicated by +, e.g., 0.09+ indicates the range from 0.090 to 0.099 m. Av. = average; D. = diameter; dim. = dimension; est. = estimated; H. = height; L. = length; max. = maximum; P. = preserved; rest. = restored; Th. = thickness; W. = width. Deposit numbers refer to those listed below under Deposits and Chronology.

WHEELMADE FINE WARE

1–607

INTRODUCTION

The term fine ware as used here includes wheelmade[1] vessels intended for relatively light use in the household: for serving food and drink, for the boudoir, and for various other minor purposes. Forty-two series of shapes in wheelmade fine ware of these functions are at present attested to have been produced in Corinthian pottery in Hellenistic times. This class of vessels is of relatively light fabric in general, and usually glazed in some fashion. It is on various members of this class, on examples of twelve of the shape series, that the painted decorative schemes of the period, in West Slope technique, were employed. As a class it is not ingratiating in appearance. The term fine ware as used here has to be understood in a very relative sense, especially by those accustomed to the fine ware of earlier periods. The imagination may restore to the present vessels some degree of the attractiveness they do not now possess, however, if it is realized that in the glazed series there has been considerable loss of the glaze due to its fugitive character, and consequently also loss of the decoration in colors applied over the glaze. A degree of the potential accomplishments of Corinthian decorators of pots can be recaptured from such vessels as the conical drinking bowl **532**, Plates 17, 55, which, though it cannot perhaps compete in quality with vessels of earlier periods, is yet a pleasing and tasteful achievement.

Contemplation of the 43 shapes now known and the general functions they served evokes some food for thought and speculation, not only in regard to what we do see represented among them, but also in what we do not find present. Shapes represented are: a moderate variety of bowls and plates for dining; for drink, a single, diminutive example of the serving amphora, a very slight representation of two kinds of kraters, a few dippers, a selection of wine pitchers, and in contrast an extremely full repertoire of drinking cups; for other household purposes, a slight representation for the boudoir (lekanis, pyxis, unguentarium), some ointment-pots, an inkwell, and a vessel possibly for specialized use (the basketball askos).

Spotty and scanty representation is evident within many of the series we now know. Future excavation will, presumably, fill in the present gaps and help to balance the uneven distribution which we now see in examples of pots for various functions. Students of Athenian Classical pottery will doubtless

---

[1] Moulded fine-ware vessels, below pp. 151-185, are treated separately since criteria for their dating are different due to their different method of manufacture.

note conspicuous absences of examples of fine-ware vessels serving other functions. Notable particularly is the almost total lack of shapes serving the purposes of the Attic Classical amphora, pelike, hydria, and stamnos, of vessels of ceremonial use such as the loutrophoros, lebes gamikos, the phiale, the rhyton, the plemochoe, and miniature vessels, not to mention those of special use such as the psykter and epinetron, and of plastic vases in general. These lacks may never be filled in Corinthian Hellenistic. Changes of fashion or belief may have eliminated them from the repertoire of shapes in the very early years of the period. Some may never have been part of Corinthian tradition and usage.

To return to the shapes we do have, it is of some interest to analyze them from the point of view of their times of origin. Of the 43 shape series some 17, possibly 18, were inherited from the Classical period, that is to say they were first introduced in Classical times and continued to be produced in Hellenistic, either for parts of the period or all the way through.[2] Twenty-four, possibly 25, are inventions of Hellenistic times. With one minor exception, a calyx kantharos, the "Classical" shapes are essentially undecorated. Decoration is otherwise restricted to the new shapes of Hellenistic times, though it does not occur in all the new shape series.

The degree of inventiveness in shape design of the Corinthian potters of Hellenistic times cannot yet be fully assessed. Survey of the various shape series in fine ware here, both "Classical" and Hellenistic, does show that the Corinthian industry was strongly influenced by the Attic. About half of the 43 shapes are known in Attic[3]; they were probably copied by the Corinthian potters at various stages of Attic production, and were subsequently developed independently by the Corinthian potters. About a few shapes, perhaps six or seven, we can feel some conviction that they are strictly in the Corinthian tradition.[4] Of the others a few are almost certainly derived from shapes originally produced in other centers of pottery manufacture.[5] About the remainder we are not yet in a position to say whether or not they were local Corinthian contributions to shape design or were taken over by the local potters from the traditions of other centers.[6]

Criteria for dating related to the elements of the forms have been fully discussed in the separate sections on the shapes below. At present the various drinking-cup shapes are, at least potentially, the most sensitive for chronology. In the sections below something has also been said about the decoration on specific shapes. However, a more general survey of the decoration is given here, its character, its general development through the Hellenistic period, and phases now discernible, which can provide general chronological guidelines.

DECORATION

Stamping and rouletting beneath the glaze, which is extensively employed in Attic decoration, plays almost no part in that of the Corinthian fine-ware vessels. Only two examples of its use are known, both on echinus bowls, one of the second quarter of the 4th century, **41**, one of *ca.* 300 B.C., **23**. In

---

[2] Semi-glazed bowl, echinus bowl, bowl with outturned rim, dish with bevelled rim, rolled-rim plate, fish plate of Attic type, saucer, trefoil olpe, trefoil oinochoe, trefoil oinochoe with shoulder stop, the decanters, the skyphos of Attic type, calyx cup, calyx kantharoi, lekanis, and pyxis with domed lid.

[3] Echinus bowl, bowl with outturned rim, dish with bevelled rim, rolled-rim plate, flat-rim plate, plate with offset rim, fish plate of Attic type, West Slope amphora, bolster krater, hemispherical krater, kyathos with loop handle, trefoil oinochoe (?), skyphos of Attic type, calyx cup, calyx kantharoi, thorn kantharos (?), hemispherical bowl with appliqué supports, wheelmade Megarian bowl, conical bowl, mastos, and pyxis with domed lid.

[4] The semi-glazed bowl, saucer, trefoil olpe, small trefoil oinochoai with shoulder stop, the juglet (?), the decanters, the semi-glazed mastos (?), and the lekanis.

[5] Small water pitcher, unguentarium, and the ointment-pots.

[6] The fish plate with bevelled rim, the kyathoi with pinch handles, the one-piece, cyma, Acrocorinth, and articulated kantharoi, the Hexamilia kantharos and mug, the drinking bowls with recurved handles, the inkwell, and the basketball askos.

certain Corinthian drinking-cup series, however, minor decoration of the foot, stem, and the bottom of the wall appears to an appreciable extent. The kind of decoration on these vessels probably owes to Attic practice its original introduction into Corinthian. Reservation of the underside of the foot with glazed wheel-run bands and lines and often a central dot of glaze on the reserved surface, is well attested on many Attic vessels in the 5th and 4th centuries. This practice is also attested among the Corinthian vessels studied here, either in close approximations of the Attic practice or in variations and reminiscences, from *ca.* 425 B.C. down into the third quarter of the 3rd century. Because of the pale color of the Corinthian clay, reserved areas are usually painted with a distinctive pink wash. The resting surface of the foot (never wheel grooved as it very commonly is in Attic) may also be reserved and painted pink, and similarly sometimes the top part of the foot, the stem, and a band around the bottom of the wall. Occasionally a reversed procedure is seen: wheel-painted pink circles or bands over the glaze. Such embellishment is best attested in the skyphoi of Attic type from *ca.* 425 B.C. into the second quarter of the 4th century: either the bottom is reserved, painted pink, and decorated with glaze bands and lines, or pink bands appear on the underside over the glaze, as well as, very occasionally, around the lower wall. Occasional use of such decoration appears on the underside of the echinus bowl and the bowl with outturned rim in the first and second quarters of the 4th century. Sporadic use of some form of this kind of embellishment is seen in three kantharos series, the one-piece, the cyma, and the Acrocorinth varieties, during their periods of production from the latter 4th down into the third quarter of the 3rd century.

The major and most distinctive type of decoration on the vessels presented here is, however, that in the West Slope technique, in incision or applied colors, often the two in combination. This appears on one variety of plate, that with offset rim, and on examples of eleven other series, all of which were devoted to the purpose of serving and drinking wine. Decoration of this kind is attested in Corinthian throughout the Hellenistic period, from about 330 B.C., on present dating, down to the time of the destruction of the city in 146. For purposes of analysis and discussion the designs employed are tabulated below, in the order of their first attested appearance. It will be noted that the designs are divided into those of an Earlier Phase and those of a Later Phase. With four exceptions the designs are exclusive to one phase or the other. Designs appearing in both phases are designated with an asterisk in the list below. In all cases designs appearing in both phases are rendered in one way in the Earlier Phase, in a different way in the Later Phase. It will be noted that in Corinthian West Slope decoration both incision and applied colors were used throughout the Hellenistic period; there is no indication that one was preferred over the other at any time. Some designs, e.g. the diminishing rectangles, were always rendered in incision only, while others, e.g. the figured representations, were always depicted through color alone.

EARLIER PHASE

Ca. 330 B.C. into the third quarter of the 3rd century.

*Running Ivy. Pls. 15, 39, 47, 52, 53.
　　　ca. 330 B.C. into third quarter of 3rd century.
　　　37 examples. One, **458**, in paint only, the rest in incision and paint.
　　　　On the two bolster kraters, **188** and **189**.
　　　　On 3 one-piece kantharoi, **386–388**.
　　　　On 21 cyma kantharoi, **390, 395, 403, 404, 406, 410, 412, 413, 415, 421, 422, 425, 437, 439–445, 449**.
　　　　On 6 Acrocorinth kantharoi, **451, 453–457**.
　　　　On 5 articulated kantharoi, **458, 460, 467, 489, 513**.

*Necklace. Pls. 39, 47, 51, 52.

    ca. 330 B.C. into third quarter of 3rd century.

    50 examples. Examples in incision and color frequent throughout the period. Examples in paint only also throughout the period, but less frequent.

    On hemispherical krater **190**.

    On calyx kantharos **373**.

    On one-piece kantharos **378**.

    On 23 cyma kantharoi, **391–393, 398, 401, 402, 405, 409-411, 414, 416, 419, 423, 426, 429, 431–436, 438**.

    On 25 articulated kantharoi, **459, 461–466, 468, 470, 472, 474–478, 481–483, 485–488, 490, 494, 496**.

*Bead-and-reel. Pls. 39, 47.

    Early 3rd century B.C.

    1 example, rendered entirely in paint.

    On bolster krater **188**.

Egg pattern. Pl. 39.

    3rd century B.C., second quarter.

    1 example, entirely in incision.

    On cyma kantharos **418**.

Lattice pattern. Pls. 39, 52.

    3rd century B.C., second quarter.

    1 example, rendered in incision and paint.

    On cyma kantharos **408**.

*Egg-and-dart. Pl. 39.

    ca. 250 B.C.

    1 example, in incision only.

    On cyma kantharos **428**.

Zigzag line and ivy leaf. Pl. 39.

    ca. 250 B.C.

    1 example, entirely in incision.

    On articulated kantharos **480**.

"Doric frieze." Pl. 39.

    3rd century B.C., third quarter.

    2 examples, entirely in incision.

    On 2 cyma kantharoi, **396** and **397**.

Quotation marks. Pl. 39.

    3rd century B.C., third quarter.

    1 example, in incision only.

    On cyma kantharos **441**.

LATER PHASE

From 3rd century, third quarter, to 146 B.C.

*Running Ivy. Pls. 40, 54, 84.

    3rd century B.C., third and last quarters.

    4 examples, in incision and paint.

    On plate, offset rim, **130**.

    On 2 wheelmade Megarian bowls, **527** and **944**.

    On conical bowl **536**.

*Necklace. Pls. 40, 55.

 3rd century B.C., third and last quarters.

 3 examples, in incision and paint.

  On 3 conical bowls, **532, 533,** and **537.**

*Egg-and-dart. Pl. 55.

 3rd century B.C., third quarter.

 1 example, in incision and paint.

  On conical bowl **535.**

Checkerboard. Pls. 40, 45, 55.

 3rd century, third quarter, to 146 B.C.

 9 examples, some in incision only, some in incision and paint.

  On 2 plates, offset rim, **129** and **130.**

  On 7 conical bowls, **532, 536, 537, 540, 544–546.**

Diminishing rectangles. Pls. 40, 45, 55.

 3rd century, third quarter, to 146 B.C.

 12 examples, in incision only.

  On 3 plates, offset rim, **127, 129** and **130.**

  On 9 conical bowls, **532, 536, 537, 539, 540, 544–546, 943.**

Hourglass pattern. Pls. 40, 55.

 3rd century B.C., third quarter.

 1 example, in incision and paint.

  On conical bowl **532.**

Butterfly pattern. Pls. 40, 55.

 3rd century B.C., third quarter.

 1 example, in incision and paint.

  On conical bowl **532.**

Suspended string of beading. Pl. 55.

 3rd century B.C., third quarter.

 1 example, in paint only.

  On conical bowl **535.**

Scale pattern. Pls. 40, 54, 55, 84.

 3rd century, third quarter, to 146 B.C.

 5 examples, in incision and paint.

  On 3 wheelmade Megarian bowls, **528, 529,** and **944.**

  On 2 conical bowls, **537** and **546.**

Imbricate pointed leaves. Pls. 40, 55.

 3rd century B.C., third quarter.

 1 example, in incision and paint.

  On conical bowl **532.**

Multipetalled flower. Pls. 40, 45, 54-56, 84.

 3rd century, third quarter, to 146 B.C.

 14 examples. Those of 3rd century, third quarter, in incision and paint, those later in paint only.

  On 3 plates, offset rim, **127–129.**

  On 3 wheelmade Megarian bowls, **528, 529** and **944.**

  On 7 conical bowls, **532–534, 536, 537, 541, 546.**

  On mastos **550.**

Encircling wheat. Pl. 55.

    3rd century B.C., third quarter.

    1 example, in incision and paint.

        On conical bowl **534.**

Dolphin. Pls. 40, 55.

    3rd century, third quarter, to 146 B.C.

    3 examples, rendered in paint only.

        On plate, offset rim, **127.**

        On 2 conical bowls, **539** and **541.**

Swan. Pl. 55.

    3rd century B.C., third and last quarters.

    2 examples, in paint only.

        On 2 conical bowls, **535** and **538.**

Winged hippocamp. Pl. 45.

    3rd century B.C., third quarter.

    1 example, in paint only.

        On plate, offset rim, **128.**

Pegasus. Pl. 84.

    3rd century B.C., last quarter.

    1 example, in paint only.

        On conical bowl **943.**

Filleted boukranion. Pl. 45.

    3rd century B.C., last quarter.

    1 example, in paint only.

        On plate, offset rim, **129.**

*Bead-and-reel. Pls. 54, 55.

    3rd century B.C., last quarter.

    3 examples, entirely in paint.

        On 2 wheelmade Megarian bowls, **529** and **944.**

        On conical bowl **538.**

Suspended festoons. Pls. 40, 55.

    3rd century B.C., last quarter.

    1 example, in paint only.

        On conical bowl **540.**

Suspended string. Pl. 55.

    3rd century B.C., last quarter.

    1 example, in paint only.

        On conical bowl **538.**

Suspended schematic garland. Pls. 40, 55.

    2nd century B.C., first half.

    1 example, in paint only.

        On conical bowl **541.**

Undulating line and dots. Pls. 40, 55.

    2nd century B.C., first half.

    1 example, in paint only.

        On conical bowl **541.**

Pentagonal net pattern. Pl. 54.

    160 to 146 B.C.

2 examples, in incision only.
> On 2 wheelmade Megarian bowls, **530** and **531**.
Undulating line. Pl. 47.
> *ca.* 150 B.C.
> 1 example, in paint only.
> On West Slope small amphora **187**.

The general picture of the Corinthian West Slope style which emerges from this chronological classification is in some ways a surprising one, viewed in the light of the development of preceding decorative styles on pottery and indeed in the light of the general development of the Attic West Slope style as it may be seen in part in Thompson's successive Hellenistic groups. The sequence in Corinthian, broadly outlined, shows a long period from *ca.* 330 B.C. into the third quarter of the 3rd century, the Earlier Phase, in which the style is employed rather unobtrusively and normally with little care or interest, making use of only a very limited repertoire of motifs, and then a sudden bloom of excellent work in the third quarter of the 3rd century, the beginning of the Later Phase, in which a wide variety of motifs is employed covering large areas, a bloom followed by gradually dwindling interest in rendition in the succeeding years down to the time of the destruction of the city in 146 B.C. The two phases presumably overlap to some extent during the third quarter of the 3rd century.

Some idea of the difference between the Earlier and the Later Phases can be obtained from statistics. In the Earlier Phase, 9 motifs are employed, in the Later, 24, including four also present in some form in the Earlier Phase. The difference is pointed up further by the fact that of the 9 motifs of the Earlier Phase only two appear on the overwhelming majority of the vessels of this time, the running ivy and the necklace. The seven other designs of the Earlier Phase are of extremely rare occurrence, there being only one or two instances of each: bead-and-reel, egg pattern, lattice pattern, the egg-and-dart, the zigzag line with ivy leaf, the "Doric frieze", and the quotation marks.

In the Earlier Phase the motifs are but rarely rendered in a competent fashion; more frequently they are indifferently executed. Comparatively little can be said of the stylistic development of the two major motifs, both of which were employed throughout the Earlier Phase, because of the high mortality rate of the elements of their rendition in applied colors. The necklace design seems never to have inspired much interest on the part of the decorators in this phase. Its rendition seems mostly perfunctory and stereotyped throughout. The necklace is usually shown as if hung outstretched on a wall, seemingly attached to two pins or pegs and for the most part loosely suspended between them, though sometimes taut, and in either case with dependent ends of the string or ribbon, on which the tear-shaped pendants were strung. The whole design may be rendered in paint throughout this phase. More often, also throughout the phase, the string is incised and the pendants are in paint. The running ivy, on the other hand, seems to have been found more interesting. The motif most frequently appears with incised, undulating tendrils and with the leaves, usually small, in color. No buds are indicated. In a few very early examples the undulations of the tendrils are closely spaced; in subsequent representations they are in broad, swelling curves. An attractive variation on the theme occurs on a few early vessels, notably on **489**, Plate 39, on which the fairly tight undulation of the ivy is accentuated by white quirks, between each pair of which is a single white dot above and below. Both the necklace and the ivy patterns appear again in the Later Phase, but the later renditions of these motifs are appreciably different. The designs of the Earlier Phase are restricted in use to the kraters and the kantharoi. Normally a single design is employed on both sides of the vessel, below the lip in many cases or, occasionally, in a somewhat lower zone.

The designs of the Later Phase appear on shapes not attested in the Earlier Phase, shapes probably for the most part newly introduced in Corinthian pottery, on present dating in the third quarter of the 3rd century, primarily the conical bowl (interior), but also the wheelmade Megarian bowl (exterior and interior), the mastos (interior), and the plate with offset rim (floor and rim). These all present broad surfaces to be decorated and the designs appear primarily in circular areas, e.g. as medallions, or in encircling zones in combinations of three or four. In the case of the plate with offset rim the complete floor and the top of the rim are so decorated. In the conical bowl the complete interior is covered, the scheme being a medallion and two or three encircling zones. In the case of the wheelmade Megarian bowl the complete exterior is decorated, again with a medallion and zones, and a painted medallion appears also on the interior. In the mastos (a fragment only is preserved) apparently only the interior was painted. In the West Slope small amphora decoration occurs only in the shoulder zone. The general approach to decoration has been completely revolutionized. Similarly striking is the high standard of composition and execution in the early part of the Later Phase. Both are excellent and their quality is only the more pleasing because in the preceding Earlier Phase of the use of the West Slope style there had been little which would have led us to expect it, and because it so very soon lost its freshness and proceeded quickly in the direction of schematization and thence to careless rendering.

There is considerable uniformity in the placement of the numerous designs of the Later Phase and nothing to suggest a period of experimentation in this respect. The multipetalled flower is exclusively employed in the medallion area and nowhere else. The necklace, the bead-and-reel, and the egg-and-dart (all in new and pleasing versions) are employed in the zones immediately encircling medallions and nowhere else. Twelve designs appear only in the main zones: the scale pattern, the imbricate pointed leaves, the encircling wheat, the winged hippocamp, Pegasus, the filleted boukranion, the dolphin, the swan, the suspended beading, festoons, strings, and schematic garland. The swan and dolphin appear in the main zone sometimes in combination with the suspended beading, strings, and garlands. Designs restricted to the outermost zone are the checkerboard and the diminishing rectangles, normally in alternation and also in combination with the hourglass and butterfly patterns in the only instance of their occurrence. The undulating-line-and-dots design, in its only attested occurrence, is placed in the outer zone. The simple undulating line appears, again in a single occurrence, on the shoulder of the small West Slope amphora. The only design to appear in more than one place is the running ivy, once in a main zone, twice in a rim zone on bowls, once as a tendril on the floor of a plate fragment. On all three bowls it is rendered as tightly undulating, once with white dots at regular intervals, above and below, and once with buds represented by three white dots.

In certain of the more frequently employed designs of the Later Phase a trend from an early careful toward a later very careless rendition (degeneration of the motif) may be observed which evidently is of chronological import since it accompanies comparable changes in the rendition of the pottery forms on which the motifs appear. The multipetalled flower shows gradation (Pl. 40) from an early naturalistic phase toward increased stylization and thence to a final stage in which the flowers are mere blobs of paint. A trend toward similar hastiness of execution is seen (Pl. 40) in the successive renditions of the dolphins, in those of the scale pattern, and also in those of the diminishing rectangles and checkerboard. The schematic garland (Pl. 40, **541**), may be a late rendering of a more realistic earlier motif, and conceivably also the careless undulating line and dots (also **541**), and the simple undulating line (Pl. 47, **187**), may be late renderings of the running ivy.

It is to be noted that in certain designs of the early part of the Later Phase there is visible a very remarkable interest in depicting them in a three-dimensional way. There are distinct suggestions of light and shadow and attempts to suggest roundness and other curving surfaces. Especially notable are early renderings of the multipetalled flower, the swan, dolphins, boukrania, hippocamps, and Pegasus, and in elements of the necklace and the bead-and-reel designs. This is an extremely interesting phenomenon of which more will be said below. It is notable chronologically now as a brief phase probably confined to the third and last quarters of the 3rd century B.C. Needless to say, in the late years of the Later Phase the rendering of these motifs reverts to two-dimensionality.

In sum, a number of main points of difference have been seen to exist between the Earlier and Later Phases of Corinthian West Slope decoration: the totally unexpected bloom in quality in the earlier years of the Later Phase; the remarkable increase in the number of designs employed in the Later Phase; the use of these designs on new, open shapes and in multiple areas and encircling zones covering broad surfaces; the sudden emergence of a set pattern for placement of the designs in particular positions on the vessels; and the appearance of a full-blown interest in three-dimensional rendering. What lay behind all this is of some interest. It seems quite reasonable to suggest that we need look no further for the inspiration for these sudden changes than the introduction of moulded relief bowls into the repertoire of Hellenistic pottery, which, according to present chronological estimates, probably took place in the years shortly before the beginning of the Later Phase, presumably not later than the middle of the 3rd century. Their introduction brought into the picture new open drinking-vessel shapes, conceivably inspiring the introduction of the new open wheelmade shapes which appear in the Later Phase of Corinthian West Slope. The decoration of the moulded bowls in their earlier phases, which are much more fully represented at present in Attic than in Corinthian, was of the highest quality. An almost infinite repertoire of new designs was employed in their decoration, some of them certainly represented in the new painted designs of the Later Phase (e.g., floral medallions, scale pattern, imbricate leaves, sea, land, and mythological creatures, etc.). Their walls were completely decorated with designs in circular areas and zones: a medallion; a medallion zone, or a corolla; a main wall design; a rim zone. Certain designs shown on them are also restricted to particular areas or zones. The sudden interest in three-dimensional rendering seen in some of the Corinthian West Slope motifs of the Later Phase seems in this light readily understandable. The decorators, insofar as they could, were evidently trying to reproduce in paint the actual three-dimensionality of the relief designs, floral, figured, and ornamental, on the moulded bowls. It seems corollary to this interpretation of the inspiration for the Later Phase of West Slope decoration in Corinthian that in the later conical bowls relief medallions are actually employed as appliqués in the center of their interiors, thus supplying, as it were, an explicit clue to the relief-ware origin of the decoration of the Later Phase in general. That painted medallions and encircling zones appear on the interiors of some of the vessels of the Later Phase, rather than on the exterior as in the moulded bowls, could conceivably be due to the decorators' contact with and observation of the moulds from which moulded bowls were made. In them the impressions to be produced on the outer walls of the bowls are on the interior surfaces. The inner surfaces of bowl moulds are quite often much more attractive than the bowls they produced, and they were certainly novel enough to inspire direct imitation.

Assessment of the general character and quality of Corinthian West Slope decoration, its degree of individuality and original contribution, must for the most part await the definition of the local variations in other centers where the style was employed, and with which it may be compared and contrasted. In the meantime, however, a reasonable degree of credit can be awarded the Corinthian artists who worked with it. They could, as has been seen, produce excellent results in quality of depiction, in composition, and in the effective combination of different motifs. They show, all too briefly, a perhaps original interest in three-dimensional representation in paint which is indeed to be commended. Even in the long and rather monotonous ranges of the Earlier Phase they displayed a quality of restraint and quiet good taste in using the style which should not be ignored. The style, as we know from its use elsewhere in centers as yet not identified, was capable of a floridity, not to say a flamboyance, which is not always pleasing to our eyes. That Corinthian West Slope decorators seem to have consciously avoided this kind of exploitation of the style throughout their use of it is surely a characteristic for which they (and their customers) deserve credit.

SHAPE HISTORIES

VESSELS FOR FOOD
BOWLS 1–100

INTRODUCTION

The shapes grouped under this heading conform in general to the modern meaning of the word bowl as a serving dish of broad proportions and of varying degrees of depth, although the word here includes shapes to which other terms might be applied in present day households, e.g., the saucer group of the echinus bowl and the dish with bevelled rim. The diameters now attested among the bowls range from 0.28+m. down to 0.06 m. Of the four forms under this heading the present examples of the echinus bowl show the widest range in diameter and the greatest number of gradations in size, from large (0.28+m.) to small (0.09 m.). It may be expected that future finds will show that the bowl with outturned rim had a nearly equal range and gradation of sizes. The more restricted present limits in range of size of the semi-glazed bowl, from moderate (0.19+m.) to small (0.10 m.) and miniature (0.06 m.) may be the full ancient range in this form. Its light fabric would seem to preclude the production of bowls of much larger capacity. The dish with bevelled rim may have been strictly a small receptacle in antiquity.

The semi-glazed bowl presents features worthy of special attention. In fabric it is very light, especially in the early stages, in contrast to the other forms. The scheme of glazing also sets it apart: full glaze, often red, on the interior, occasional single, thin glaze bands at intervals being the only embellishment of the exterior, accentuating the natural, pleasing color of the Corinthian clay, which, in early examples of this shape, is well polished. Semi-glazed (or glaze-banded) vessels of various forms were produced in Corinth from the late 6th century (if not before) onwards.[7] The present bowls attest the extension of production of this special class of Corinthian vessels down to the last days of the Greek city, and also the persistence of a strictly Corinthian tradition down through times in which imitation of vessels of other centers was largely the rule. The study of this special class would be a pleasing and rewarding undertaking. To this class of semi-glazed ware belong also, in the present volume, the decanters and the semi-glazed mastos.

The other bowls are in general of more substantial clay, serviceable, neither light nor heavy. They are either fully or partly glazed. Two of the echinus bowls have impressed decoration on the floor. One bowl with outturned rim is enlivened by reservation and the use of pink paint on the underside. Otherwise these forms are undecorated.

The echinus bowl is now attested to have been produced in Corinth from the first quarter of the 4th century to 146 B.C. The bowl with outturned rim and the semi-glazed bowl are attested for almost as long, from the second quarter of the 4th century down to the end. The echinus bowl is the most heavily represented in these years but it is likely that in actuality popularity was about equally divided among the three. The relative fragility of the fabric of the semi-glazed bowls presumably has worked against the preservation of complete bowls in contexts and toward the scattering of their fragments. On the other hand it seems likely that the fourth form, the dish with bevelled rim, probably a variant of the small echinus bowl, did not have a great popularity; probably its vogue was not of great duration, perhaps not much longer than at present attested, from ca. 350 B.C. to the end of the century.

Of the four shapes, the semi-glazed bowl and the bowl with outturned rim are, for chronological purposes, the most sensitive in form, quality of fabric, formation and glaze. The dish with bevelled rim will, of course, have value in chronology if, as it seems, it had a restricted period of production.

Imported examples of the echinus bowl, the bowl with outturned rim and the dish with bevelled rim are noted below in the pertinent sections. These imports include Attic and various other wares, the imported echinus bowls being by far the most numerous. The very restricted range of bowl forms

---

[7] E.g., Campbell 141, 142–152; Pease, p. 258 and nos. 144–173.

produced at Corinth in this period is supplemented by a number of examples of different shape imported from various centers, for the most part datable to the last years of the Greek city. These include bowls whose simple wall outline is a convex curve,[8] one with a horizontal rim,[9] a broad bowl whose wall is slightly canted inward above,[10] several whose wall profile is a gentle double curve, the lip outturned slightly above,[11] and a variety whose prominent upper wall has a flaring, concave outline.[12]

SEMI-GLAZED BOWL[13] **1–14**, Pls. 1, 43.
Early to final stages, 4th century, second quarter to 146 B.C.
Deposits: 39, 41, 42, 60, 90, 94, 96, 99, 102, 103, 110.

These bowls are characterized by a constricted ring foot, and a wall rising fairly steeply and broadly and incurving above to an outturned lip. The sizes now attested are eight: by diameter of shoulder, 0.19+, 0.18+, 0.17+, 0.13+, 0.12+, 0.11+, 0.10+, 0.06+m. The fabric is relatively light and in the best examples the walls are quite thin. The interior of all is fully glazed. The exterior is entirely unglazed except for one or more narrow wheel-glazed bands which may be placed on the edge or resting surface of the foot, on the wall at or just below the point of its greatest diameter, or around the outer edge of the lip.

The period of production of this series is attested by contexts from about the middle of the 4th century, or shortly after, to the end of Greek Corinth in 146 B.C. The actual beginning of production of this shape series may be still earlier. Five bowls seem typologically the earliest, probably very close to the initial stage of the shape. These, **1, 8, 11–13**, have accordingly been tentatively placed within the second quarter of the 4th century. Present indications suggest the estimate of *ca.* 375 for the beginning of production.

Bowls dated by context indicate that changes in the profile from foot to lip and a gradual decrease in quality of manufacture are criteria for relative placement and dating. In the profile the early outline is uninterrupted from the foot to the top of the lip. It rises in a rounding curve, turning in above and then sharply outward to form the lip. The progression is toward a profile in which the outline rises in almost a straight line to a sharply articulated shoulder at the point of greatest circumference of the wall, above which it changes abruptly to a strongly concave curve. The quality of manufacture progresses from a carefully executed form of relatively delicate and fine clay toward a more carelessly rendered form of rather less fine and thicker clay.

The series arranged according to these tendencies suggests several other criteria for dating. These concern the form of the foot, the relative depth of the bowl, the relationship of the diameter of the lip to that of the shoulder, and the employment of glaze bands on the exterior. The ring foot of those placed earliest is relatively low, and shallow on the underside, which is carefully tooled to form a central low cone. The feet of later bowls are more substantial, less carefully formed, and the central cone on the underside is either not present or slight by comparison. The early bowls are relatively deep, the later more open and shallower. In the earliest the lip is appreciably greater in diameter than the shoulder.

---

[8] E.g., C-48-104bis, Deposit 110, of the first half of the 2nd century; C-47-484, Deposit 113, of 146 B.C.; C-48-23, Deposit 112, probably of 146 B.C.; C-48-20, Deposit 112, Hellenistic prior to 146 B.C. These are from several different centers.

[9] C-48-32, Deposit 112, probably of 146 B.C.

[10] C-47-810, Deposit 46, of 146 B.C.

[11] C-33-1462, Deposit 98, of 146 B.C.; C-47-817, Deposit 46, of 146 B.C.; C-48-21, Deposit 112, Hellenistic prior to 146 B.C. These are probably of two different centers.

[12] C-33-1471, Deposit 98, of 146 B.C.

[13] An imported fully glazed bowl of substantial fabric, C-48-22, Deposit 112, is related to the present series in general form.

In subsequent instances the reverse is normal. Glaze banding after the initial examples is confined to a single band at or just below the shoulder. The foot is proportionately very constricted in all. When more examples and evidence are available it may be possible to determine whether or not there is an increase in the diameter of the foot, size for size, as the shape becomes more shallow and open. At present the representation in size series is too scanty to ascertain this point. Yet to be determined is the question of whether or not there is a progression toward decrease in height, size for size. This seems possible.

The placement of **4** at *ca.* 300, and **2** at *ca.* 250 B.C. is estimated within the long ranges of their contexts. Future evidence may suggest readjustment of these dates.

D. at shoulder 0.19+
  4th century B.C., second quarter
    1 (C-31-152), Deposit 41. Foot and lower wall missing. D. shoulder est. 0.193; D. lip est. 0.18; P.H. 0.082.
  ca. 250 B.C.
    2 (C-31-8), Deposit 39. D. shoulder 0.195; D. lip 0.198; H. 0.095; D. foot 0.063. Pls. 1, 43.
D. at shoulder 0.18+
  4th century B.C., third quarter, early
    3 (C-37-2667), Deposit 90. Lip and upper wall only. D. shoulder est. 0.18; D. lip est. 0.185; P.H. 0.06.
D. at shoulder 0.17+
  ca. 300 B.C.
    4 (C-47-126), Deposit 96. D. shoulder 0.171; D. lip 0.173; H. 0.107; D. foot 0.052.
  146 B.C.
    5 (C-34-21), Deposit 94. D. shoulder 0.175; D. lip 0.185; H. 0.076; D. foot 0.057.
    6 (C-47-235), Deposits 102 and 103. D. shoulder 0.174; D. lip 0.18; H. 0.078; D. foot 0.06. Pls. 1, 43.
D. at shoulder 0.13+
  ca. 200 B.C.
    7 (C-47-226), Deposit 99. D. shoulder 0.137; D. lip 0.137; H. 0.07; D. foot 0.048.

D. at shoulder 0.12+
  4th century B.C., second quarter
    8 (C-31-202bis), Deposit 42. D. shoulder 0.123; D. lip 0.116; H. 0.082; D. foot est. 0.05.
  4th century B.C., third quarter, early
    9 (C-37-2666), Deposit 90. Lip and upper wall only. D. shoulder est. 0.125; D. lip est. 0.13; P.H. 0.056.
  ca. 200 B.C.
    10 (C-48-94), Deposit 110. D. shoulder 0.126; D. lip 0.135; H. 0.07; D. foot 0.051.
D. at shoulder 0.11+
  4th century B.C., second quarter
    11 (C-31-201), Deposit 112. D. shoulder 0.118; D. lip 0.11; H. 0.068; D. foot 0.048. Pls. 1, 43.
D. at shoulder 0.10+
  4th century B.C., second quarter
    12 (C-31-202), Deposit 112. D. shoulder 0.103; D. lip 0.10; H. 0.058; D. foot 0.04.
D. at shoulder 0.06+
  4th century B.C., second quarter
    13 (C-31-203), Deposit 112. D. shoulder 0.067; D. lip 0.066; H. 0.043; D. foot 0.03.
  350–325 B.C.
    14 (T 2720), Deposit 60. D. shoulder 0.061; D. lip 0.063; H. 0.037; D. foot 0.03. *N. Cemetery*, 496-14.

ECHINUS BOWL[14] **15–71**, Pls. 2, 43, 44.
Advanced to final stages, 4th century, first quarter to 146 B.C.
Deposits: 20, 27, 36, 38–43, 46, 79–81, 90, 94, 102, 107, 110–113, 115.

The echinus bowl is so named since its wall profile resembles the outline of the echinus of the Doric capital at various stages. The Corinthian examples of the shape have (with one exception: **70**) a ring foot. The wall rises from it in varying degrees of convexity and steepness to a rim which is formed by a strong inward curve of the wall. Among the large bowls there are ten distinct sizes now represented: maximum diameter 0.28+, 0.21+, 0.20+, 0.17+, 0.15, 0.14, 0.13+, 0.12+, 0.11+, and 0.10+ m. A

[14] Numerous examples of the shape in foreign wares are also known in Corinth. There are 35 Attic bowls ranging in size from large to very small. 460–420 B.C.: C-34-1046, Deposit 10, Pease 48, and also, with disk base, C-34-1095, Deposit 10, Pease 132. *Ca.* 425–400 B.C.: C-37-493, Deposit 79. 4th century, second to third quarter: C-27-24; C-31-199, Deposit 42; C-31-405, Deposit 20; C-32-48, Deposit 23; C-34-278, Deposit 33; C-37-2532 through C-37-2535, C-37-2543, C-37-2545,

group of shallow bowls, which are here for convenience called the saucer group, shows ten gradations in size between 0.093 and 0.07 m. A third group of very small bowls, here called the salt-cellar group, of relatively greater depth than the preceding, also exhibits ten gradations in size, between 0.074 and 0.062 m. The bowls are usually made of clay of normal thickness though there are variations on either side, both fairly thin and rather thicker (though never massive). Some are fully glazed, but many are glazed fully on the interior and only partway down the exterior, by dipping. The glaze is very often fugitive. The quality of glaze and manufacture varies from quite good to quite bad. In only one, an early salt cellar, **48**, is the bottom decorated: a circular area, reserved and painted pink. The resting surface is in no case reserved or wheel grooved, and the point of juncture between foot and wall is in no instance reserved. Only two examples have impressed decoration on the floor: **23** and **41**.

The earliest stages of this series in Corinthian are evidently not represented among those reported here. The shape seems to have originated with one in Attic which was the prototype for the Corinthian series, in the early 5th century B.C.[15] The earliest Corinthian examples reported are of the third quarter of the 5th century.[16] Possibly Corinthian examples earlier than these will be found in the future. In Attic the shape, to judge from the published examples, was not made in any great quantity until about the second quarter of the 4th century when production became and long continued to be enormous. Also it would seem that in Attic only comparatively small examples of the shape (diam. 0.125 to 0.067 m.) were produced down to the second quarter of the 4th century when a much greater range of sizes was initiated. The rarity of Corinthian 5th century examples is thus readily understood as well as the fact that no Corinthian example of the large group is datable prior to the second quarter of the 4th century. The large group continued in production at Corinth until the time of the destruction of the city in 146 B.C. For the saucer group there is at present no evidence for production in Corinthian before or after the first half of the 4th century. The salt-cellar group is attested at present from the first quarter of the 4th century until (on estimate) about 200 B.C.

Deposit evidence indicates that for the examples reported here the main criterion for relative dating is a trend from a relatively broad ring foot toward a constricted one, size for size. This, of course, produced corresponding changes in the outline of the wall not unlike the development of the Doric echinus form in reverse, i.e., from the Classical broadly based back to the Archaic widely spreading outline. In the series arranged on this basis there are accompanying changes which support the sequence: loss of definition, particularly of the original form of the foot, and deterioration in the quality of form and glaze. There is no definable change in the form of the rim. If there is any increase in height, size for

C-37-2547, C-37-2604 through C-37-2609, all of Deposit 90; C-46-130, Deposit 87; C-53-66; C-53-246, Deposit 43; C-63-509, Deposit 84. 325–225 B.C.: C-31-195 through C-31-197, C-31-220, C-31-221, C-31-226, C-31-260, all of Deposit 42; C-53-247, Deposit 43; C-60-251, Deposit 22.

There are three gray-ware bowls, all dated 146 B.C. by context: C-34-1623, Deposit 102; C-35-718, Deposit 104; C-46-71, Deposit 107.

There are four of a single unidentified ware: C-31-194 and C-31-198, Deposit 42; C-34-17, Deposit 94; and C-47-417, Deposit 111.

There are four of a second unidentified ware. Two are dated 146 B.C. by context: C-34-1640, Deposit 102, and C-48-19, Deposit 112. Two are undated: C-31-259, Deposit 42, and C-47-227, Deposit 99.

Fifteen are of various other unidentified wares. Of these one is dated *ca.* 250–225 B.C. by context: T 2313, Deposit 70, *N. Cemetery,* 498-7, and another, C-34-1605, Deposit 102, is dated 146 B.C. The remainder are undated: C-31-9, Deposit 39; C-31-34 and C-31-36, Deposit 40; C-31-261, Deposit 42; C-36-2377; C-46-45 and C-46-62, Deposit 107; C-47-135, Deposit 115; C-47-330, Deposit 109; C-47-416, Deposit 111; C-48-104, Deposit 110; C-60-263, Deposit 34; C-62-247, Deposit 48.

There is one example of the shape in faïence, probably much earlier than its context: MF 9246, Deposit 46.

[15] The Attic series can be traced in various published examples. 5th century B.C., first and second quarters: Vanderpool 288; Corbett 154; Talcott (1936), P 5147, p. 341, fig. 9. 460–440 B.C.: Boulter 67, 69, 70, 74. 425–400 B.C.: Corbett 63–67. 4th century B.C., second quarter: *Olynthus,* XIII, 758, 759, 765, 768, 774, 785, 786, 789, 790; Corbett 155. Hellenistic: Thompson A 14–21; B 15; and probably D 8, 9.

[16] Not seen; from the Potters Quarter in Corinth. Cited, without number, in Pease under no. 48, which is an Attic example of that time.

size, over the years it cannot now be demonstrated. Such an increase is conceivable for the very large bowls (though evidently not for the smaller) and should be considered when more examples and evidence are available.

The main criterion, the decrease in the diameter of the foot, size for size, seems likely to be most dependable in the large bowls. The representation of sizes is very spotty. Since the deposit evidence for them for the stages between early and final for the most part covers an appreciable range in time, the placement of the intermediate large bowls is largely estimated and subject to future adjustment. The criterion seems also generally dependable in the saucer group. In the bowls of the salt-cellar group, however, it seems likely that, because of their small size and general quality of manufacture, it is only loosely applicable. These have, accordingly, been arranged in a sequence of larger periods.

A minor criterion for dating by form is provided by the underside of the foot of the saucer group. In the examples of the first quarter of the 4th century B.C. and in a few of the second quarter, a concave moulding appears between the inner edge of the foot and the underside (e.g. **42**). This embellishment is evidently borrowed from Attic in which it has been noted in the third and last quarters of the 5th century (Corbett, p. 329, under no. 67; p. 301 and note 12; cf. Boulter under no. 27).

It is to be noted that Attic bowls of the second quarter of the 4th century and for long thereafter are distinctively massive in fabric. No Corinthian large bowl of any time approaches the Attic in this characteristic. There is some slight reflection of it, however, in the saucer and salt-cellar groups. In contrast, two salt cellars, **48** and **64**, of the first quarter of the 4th century, are distinguished by great delicacy of fabric: conceivably this was a preference of that restricted period in this group.

Large bowls

Max. D. 0.28+
ca. 250 B.C.
  15 (C-63-736). Max. D. 0.287; D. foot 0.098; H. 0.082. Pls. 2, 43.
Max. D. 0.21+
146 B.C.
  16 (C-38-676), Deposit 115. Max. D. 0.212; D. foot 0.063; H. 0.089. Pls. 2, 43.
Max. D. 0.20+
146 B.C.
  17 (C-48-33), Deposit 112. Max. D. 0.20; D. foot 0.067; H. 0.088.
  18 (C-48-99), Deposit 110. Max. D. 0.201; D. foot 0.068; H. 0.093.
Max. D. 0.17+
4th century B.C., second quarter
  19 (C-33-390). Max. D. 0.176; D. foot 0.089; H. 0.056.
4th century B.C., early third quarter
  20 (C-37-2590), Deposit 90. Max. D. 0.171; D. foot 0.082; H. 0.056. Pls. 2, 43.
ca. 250 B.C.
  21 (C-60-63), Deposit 38. Max. D. 0.178; D. foot 0.065; H. 0.06. Pls. 2, 43.
Max. D. 0.15
ca. 250 B.C.
  22 (C-31-37), Deposit 40. Max. D. 0.15; D. foot 0.061; H. 0.061.

Max. D. 0.14
ca. 300 B.C.
  23 (C-60-64), Deposit 38. Max. D. 0.14; D. foot 0.068; H. 0.047. In center of floor, beneath glaze, four stamped palmettes and a circle of rouletting. Pls. 2, 43.
Max. D. 0.13+
ca. 250 B.C.
  24 (C-31-35), Deposit 40. Max. D. 0.134; D. foot 0.056; H. 0.05.
ca. 200 B.C.
  25 (C-47-483), Deposit 113. Max. D. 0.136; D. foot 0.051; H. 0.052. Pl. 2.
Max. D. 0.12+
ca. 300 B.C.
  26 (C-31-14), Deposit 39. Max. D. 0.126; D. foot 0.062; H. 0.054. Pls. 2, 44.
ca. 250 B.C.
  27 (C-53-264), Deposit 43. Max. D. 0.123; D. foot 0.055; H. 0.057. Pls. 2, 44.
  28 (C-31-13), Deposit 39. Max. D. 0.125; D. foot 0.055; H. 0.05.
ca. 200 B.C.
  29 (C-48-40), Deposit 112. Max. D. est. 0.126; D. foot 0.05; H. 0.06.
ca. 175 B.C.
  30 (C-34-22), Deposit 94. Max. D. 0.124; D. foot 0.047; av. H. 0.058. Pls. 2, 44.
146 B.C.
  31 (C-47-821), Deposit 46. Max. D. 0.123; D. foot 0.045; H. 0.055. Pls. 2, 44.

Max. D. 0.11+
ca. 250 B.C.
    32 (C-53-261), Deposit 43. Max. D. 0.11; D. foot 0.052; H. 0.057. Pls. 2, 44.
146 B.C.
    33 (C-34-1616), Deposit 102. Max. D. 0.114; D. foot 0.049; H. 0.052.
Max. D. 0.10+
ca. 300 B.C.
    34 (C-53-260), Deposit 43. Max. D. 0.103; D. foot 0.056; H. 0.044. Pls. 2, 44.

Saucer group

Max. D. 0.093–0.092
4th century B.C., early third quarter
    35 (C-30-116). Max. D. 0.093; D. foot 0.057; H. 0.028.
    36 (C-37-2544), Deposit 90. Max. D. 0.092; D. foot 0.055; H. 0.029.
Max. D. 0.087
4th century B.C., early third quarter
    37 (C-37-2611), Deposit 90. Max. D. 0.087; D. foot 0.051; H. 0.029.
    38 (C-46-15), Deposit 107. Max. D. 0.087; D. foot 0.052; H. 0.026.
Max. D. 0.086–0.082
4th century B.C., second quarter
    39 (C-40-57), Deposit 27. Max. D. 0.086; D. foot 0.054; H. 0.024. Pls. 2, 44.
    40 (C–35-645). Max. D. 0.085; D. foot 0.053; av. H. 0.027.
    41 (C-37-219), Deposit 80. Max. D. 0.082; D. foot 0.049; H. 0.023. In center of floor, beneath glaze, four stamped palmettes.
Max. D. 0.081–0.08
4th century B.C., first quarter
    42 (C-47-866), Deposit 81. Max. D. 0.081; D. foot 0.06; H. 0.024. Pls. 2, 44.
    43 (C-37-424), Deposit 79. Max. D. 0.08; D. foot 0.059; H. 0.022.
Max. D. 0.073–0.07
4th century B.C., first quarter
    44 (C-37-180), Deposit 80. Max. D. 0.073; D. foot 0.053; H. 0.022.
    45 (C-37-1083), Deposit 80. Max. D. 0.07; D. foot 0.046; H. 0.018.

Salt-cellar group

Max. D. 0.074–0.071
4th century B.C., second to third quarter
    46 (C-37-2538), Deposit 90. Max. D. 0.074; D. foot 0.045; H. 0.034.
    47 (C-53-8). Max. D. 0.071; D. foot 0.046; H. 0.037.
Max. D. 0.07
4th century B.C., first quarter
    48 (C-32-56). Max. D. 0.07; D. foot 0.049; H. 0.034. Fully glazed except circular area on

underside, D. 0.022, reserved and painted pink. Pls. 2, 44.
Max. D. 0.069
4th century B.C., second to third quarter
    49 (C-37-2536), Deposit 90. Max. D. 0.069; D. foot 0.043; H. 0.037.
4th century B.C., last quarter
    50 (C-33-395). Max. D. 0.069; D. foot 0.042; H. 0.035.
    51 (C-53-263), Deposit 43. Max. D. 0.069; D. foot 0.038; H. 0.036.
ca. 250 B.C.
    52 (C-60-65), Deposit 38. Max. D. 0.069; D. foot 0.034; H. 0.033. Pls. 2, 44.
Max. D. 0.068
4th century B.C., last quarter
    53 (C-47-264). Max. D. 0.068; D. foot 0.04; H. 0.037.
    54 (C-31-111). Max. D. 0.068; D. foot 0.039; H. 0.039.
    55 (C-31-262), Deposit 42. Max. D. 0.068; D. foot 0.038; H. 0.032. Pls. 2, 44.
Max. D. 0.067
4th century B.C., second to third quarters
    56 (C-47-386), Deposit 111. Max. D. 0.067; D. foot 0.042; H. 0.034.
Max. D. 0.066
4th century B.C., second to third quarters
    57 (C-37-2537), Deposit 90. Max. D. 0.066; D. foot 0.041; H. 0.029. Pls. 2, 44.
    58 (C-37-2540), Deposit 90. Max. D. 0.066; D. foot 0.044; H. 0.035.
4th century B.C., last quarter
    59 (C-31-263), Deposit 42. Max. D. 0.066; D. foot 0.039; H. 0.033.
Max. D. 0.065
4th century B.C., second to third quarters
    60 (C-40-399), Deposit 36. Max. D. 0.065; D. foot 0.044; H. 0.03.
    61 (C-37-2539), Deposit 90. Max. D. 0.065; D. foot 0.043; av. H. 0.034.
4th century B.C., last quarter
    62 (C-53-245), Deposit 43. Max. D. 0.065; D. foot 0.039; H. 0.031.
    63 (C-31-232), Deposit 42. Max. D. 0.065; D. foot less than 0.04; P.H. 0.024.
Max. D. 0.064
4th century B.C., first quarter
    64 (C-37-425), Deposit 79. Max. D. 0.064; D. foot 0.044; H. 0.036.
4th century B.C., second to third quarters
    65 (C-37-2610), Deposit 90. Max. D. 0.064; D. foot 0.04; H. 0.034.
    66 (C-31-409), Deposit 20. Max. D. 0.064; D. foot 0.044; H. 0.033.
ca. 200 B.C.
    67 (C-47-443), Deposit 113. Max. D. 0.064; D. foot 0.027; H. 0.032. Pls. 2, 44.

Max. D. 0.062
4th century B.C., second to third quarters
68 (C-31-147), Deposit 41. Max. D. 0.062; D. foot
0.038; H. 0.033.
69 (C-40-56), Deposit 27. Max. D. 0.062; D. foot
0.042; H. 0.032.

70 (C-40-437), Deposit 36. Max. D. 0.062; D. foot
0.04; H. 0.035. Solid foot conical in profile
beneath.
71 (C-33-106). Max. D. 0.062; D. foot 0.038; H.
0.031.

BOWL WITH OUTTURNED RIM[17] 72–94, Pls. 3, 44.
Advanced to final stages, 4th century, second quarter to 146 B.C.
Deposits: 43, 44, 46, 70, 90, 94, 95, 102, 107, 108, 110, 111, 113, 115.

These bowls have a ring foot, a broad, gently rising lower wall, a steep upper wall, and an outturned rim. The sizes at present represented in Corinthian are five: diameter of lip 0.25+, 0.14+, 0.12+, 0.11+, and 0.10+ m. (as well as a miniature, footnote 17). They are made of clay of normal thickness, strong but not heavy. The quality of manufacture and glazing varies from good to very poor. With two exceptions the bowls are carelessly glazed, by dipping, fully on the interior and partway down the wall on the exterior. The two exceptions are the earliest, 72 and 73, of the second quarter of the 4th century. 72 was fully glazed except for the resting surface and the underside within the foot, which were reserved and decorated. 73 is fully glazed. There is no example at present showing stamping or rouletting on the floor, nor does any show a reserved band at the join of foot and wall.

The earliest examples are probably near to the initial stage of production of the shape in Corinthian, though still earlier are to be expected. The shape was clearly derived from Attic in which production seems to have begun at least as early as the last quarter of the 5th century.[18] Production in Corinthian is attested by deposit evidence to have continued down to the destruction of the city in 146 B.C.

Deposit evidence makes clear enough the general trends which can be used for relative placement of examples of the series. Over the 200 or so years of production the foot becomes more constricted in diameter, size for size. The lower wall profile becomes more nearly straight. At the point of change from lower to upper wall a distinct line of articulation develops and above this the upper wall profile changes from convex to pronouncedly concave. It is also clear that there is, along with these changes, a loss of definition of the form of the foot, and that the good quality of the earliest examples and the early practice either of full glazing, or decoration of resting surface and underside, are in time abandoned in favor of careless manufacture and dipping. But we are not in a position to date with any precision the time when these changes took place, nor any particular intermediate stages of the form between the early and final periods. The intermediate examples are all of too small a size and of too poor a quality to afford dependable indications of relative placement. Larger examples of intermediate and final stages are needed.

Two of the intermediate small examples, 74 and 77, are considered fairly early since they seem to exhibit some memory of the original definition of the foot. They have been arbitrarily placed at ca. 250 B.C. Almost equally arbitrary (but supported by a little deposit evidence) are the thought that the

[17] A miniature Corinthian example, unglazed, is also known: C-61-39, Deposit 71, of the third quarter of the 3rd century B.C. The shape is also represented in Corinth in foreign wares. There are two Attic: C-37-216, Deposit 80, of ca. 425–400 B.C. and C-37-214, Deposit 80, of the first quarter of the 4th century. There are four gray-ware bowls. Three are of 146 B.C. by context: C-33-1119, Deposit 98; C-34-1618 and C-34-1623, both of Deposit 102. One is undated: C-47-415, Deposit 111.

There are eight of various other unidentified wares. Four are of 146 B.C. by context: C-33-1471, Deposit 98; C-34-474, Deposit 102; C-47-818, Deposit 46; C-48-103, Deposit 110. The others are undated: C-28-82; C-34-393, Deposit 94; C-34-2361; C-47-150, Deposit 98.

[18] Possibly a bit earlier? See Corbett 60–62, especially remarks under 62. The Attic series can be traced further in various publications. 4th century prior to 348 B.C.: *Olynthus*, XIII, nos. 754–756 (from graves); 770 and 773 (from rooms in houses). Hellenistic: Thompson A 7, A 9, A 71, C 3, D 5, E 33–44. Augustan: *Hesperia*, XXVIII, 1959, pl. 2, d.

sharp articulation between the lower wall and the upper wall (or lip) began at this time, and the placement of a number of examples which show this characteristic between the years 250 and 146 B.C. Those here dated in the final stage, in 146, are so placed entirely by context. This last group makes it quite clear that in the advanced examples of the small sizes little reliance can be placed on the degree of constriction of the foot as a criterion of date, though the sharp articulation and flaring rim present a fairly consistent impression.

D. of lip 0.25+
4th century B.C., second quarter
72 (C-36-251). D. lip est. 0.256; D. foot 0.11; H. 0.08. Fully glazed. Resting surface reserved and painted pink. Underside within foot reserved and decorated with two wheel-glazed circles and a central dot, between which are bands of pink. Traces of intentional(?) red glaze on upper wall. Pl. 3.

D. of lip 0.14+
4th century B.C., second quarter
73 (C-37-2589), Deposit 90. D. lip 0.147; D. foot 0.074; av. H. 0.048. Fully glazed. Pls. 3, 44.

D. of lip 0.12+
ca. 250 B.C.
74 (C-47-440), Deposit 113. D. lip 0.12; D. foot 0.051; max. D. lower wall 0.089; H. 0.042. Pls. 3, 44.
ca. 250–146 B.C.
75 (C-35-31), Deposit 44. D. lip 0.12; D. foot 0.049; max. D. lower wall 0.098; H. 0.039.
146 B.C.
76 (C-47-820), Deposit 46. D. lip 0.121; D. foot 0.041; max. D. lower wall 0.091; H. 0.041. Pls. 3, 44.

D. of lip 0.11+
ca. 250 B.C.
77 (C-37-2346). D. lip 0.116; D. foot 0.044; max. D. lower wall est. 0.086; H. 0.039.
ca. 250–146 B.C.
78 (C-47-362), Deposit 111. D. est. 0.119; D. foot 0.045; max. D. lower wall 0.084; H. 0.043.
79 (C-47-116), Deposit 95. D. lip 0.117; D. foot 0.044; max. D. lower wall 0.084; H. 0.041.
80 (C-47-313), Deposit 108. D. lip 0.11; D. foot 0.044; max. D. lower wall 0.088; H. 0.044.

81 (C-53-255), Deposit 43. D. lip 0.111; D. foot 0.039; max. D. lower wall 0.092; H. 0.042.
82 (C-34-24), Deposit 94. D. lip 0.113; D. foot 0.044; max. D. lower wall 0.086; H. 0.04.
83 (C-46-42), Deposit 107. D. lip 0.114; D. foot 0.044; max. D. 0.081; H. 0.046.
84 (T 2316), Deposit 70. D. lip 0.111; D. foot 0.046; max. D. lower wall 0.088; H. 0.038.
146 B.C.
85 (C-34-82), Deposit 102. D. lip 0.117; D. foot 0.046; max. D. lower wall 0.091; H. 0.044.
86 (C-48-97), Deposit 110. Av. D. lip 0.115; D. foot 0.046; max. D. lower wall, av. 0.086; av. H. 0.043.
87 (C-34-1620), Deposit 102. D. lip 0.112; D. foot 0.042; max. D. lower wall 0.086; H. 0.038.
88 (C-48-83), Deposit 110. D. lip 0.112; D. foot 0.041; max. D. lower wall 0.081; H. 0.039.
89 (C-47-819), Deposit 46. D. lip 0.113; D. foot 0.047; max. D. lower wall 0.085; D. foot 0.038.
90 (C-48-98), Deposit 110. D. lip 0.11; D. foot 0.044; max. D. lower wall 0.083; H. 0.04.

D. of lip 0.10+
250–146 B.C.
91 (C-46-46), Deposit 107. D. lip 0.108; D. foot 0.046; max. D. lower wall 0.082; H. 0.041.
92 (C-47-37), Deposit 107. Foot and lower wall missing. D. lip 0.10; max. D. lower wall, av. 0.077.
93 (C-47-35), Deposit 107. Upper part missing. D. lip. more than 0.088; D. foot 0.045; max. D. lower wall 0.084; P.H. 0.032.
146 B.C.
94 (C-47-55), Deposit 115. D. lip 0.107; D. foot 0.045; max. D. lower wall 0.094; H. 0.043.

SMALL DISH, BEVELLED RIM[19] 95–100, Pls. 4, 44.
Intermediate stages, ca. 350 to 300(?) B.C.
Deposits: 36, 42, 87, 90.

The small dishes of this series have a simple ring foot, a gently rising wall nearly straight in profile, with sharp articulation between the wall and the lip, which has a bevelled or only slightly convex profile,

[19] Two imported examples are also known in Corinth. Attic: C-31-406, Deposit 20, Asklepieion, pl. 48, no. 22, of perhaps 325 B.C. Other foreign: C-31-264, Deposit 42, of perhaps 300 or the first quarter of the 3rd century B.C. Both dates are on the basis of the present dating for Corinthian.

the slope from the top of the wall being upward and inward. Although there is less than a centimeter's difference in diameter between the largest and the smallest, it seems desirable to consider that various sizes exist since a difference of only a few millimeters makes a considerable change in appearance in this very small shape. The sizes, then, are four at present: greatest diameter 0.093, 0.088, 0.086, and 0.084 m. The clay of which they are made is quite thick. The quality of clay and manufacture in all is fairly good. All were fully glazed, the glaze in all now fugitive. None has stamped or incised decoration on the floor.

It is estimated that the beginning of production of this shape may lie within the second quarter of the 4th century B.C. The earliest examples here may not represent the very initial stage but would seem to be close to it. The examples placed latest here, at *ca.* 300, **95** and **100**, may not represent the final stage. Examples of more advanced stages may be expected in the future. The date assigned these two is on estimate and in need of future evidence for confirmation or revision. According to the context of **95**, the stage they represent would not seem to be later than *ca.* 275 B.C. at latest.

Criteria for placement of the examples are not well established by context dates since only **96**, **97**, and **99**, all of the same stage, are from a context of limited range. It is suggested on the basis of progressions in other shape series that in this one the criteria for placement are based on the foot and the wall profile, the foot progressing from a relatively broad diameter, size for size, toward a more constricted one, and the wall from a very gently and slightly rising profile toward a steeper one. The examples have accordingly been arranged below on this assumption. The series as so arranged shows supporting changes, a slight decrease in the heaviness of the fabric and some decrease in care of manufacture.

Max. D. 0.093
ca. 300 B.C.
> **95** (C-40-434), Deposit 36. Max. D. 0.093; D. foot 0.049; H. 0.031. Pls. 3, 44.

Max. D. 0.089–0.088
ca. 350 B.C.
> **96** (C-37-2541), Deposit 90. Max. D. 0.088; D. foot 0.052; H. 0.025.
> **97** (C-37-2542), Deposit 90. Max. D. 0.088; D. foot 0.054; H. 0.026. Pls. 3, 44.

ca. 325 B.C.
> **98** (C-46-122), Deposit 87. Max. D. 0.089; D. foot est. 0.053; P.H. 0.029.

Max. D. 0.086
ca. 350 B.C.
> **99** (C-37-2546), Deposit 90. Max. D. 0.086; D. foot 0.051; av. H. 0.019–0.02.

Max. D. 0.084
ca. 300 B.C.
> **100** (C-31–265), Deposit 42. Max. D. 0.084; D. foot 0.04; H. 0.03.

PLATES 101–186

INTRODUCTION

The term plate is used for convenience to classify this group of shapes. The examples have in common a ring foot and a wall rising from it in varying degrees of elevation from a gentle to fairly steep rise and with a slight gradation in curvature of profile from moderately convex to practically straight. They are not plates in the modern sense. Probably their function was as broad, open serving dishes. In the six series of plates now attested to have been produced in Corinthian pottery in Hellenistic times fourteen different sizes are represented, ranging in diameter from 0.27+ to 0.11 m. Though representation by sizes in the group is for the most part spotty and incomplete it seems likely that the first five series below were produced in Corinth primarily in the upper ranges of size, from moderately capacious to large. The sixth series, the saucer, the most fully represented, probably was always a small serving dish, in size the approximate equivalent of the modern saucer or bread-and-butter plate. In the saucer series we may have the full representation of sizes, between diameters 0.16+ and 0.11 m. All the plates were glazed, fully or in part. All are of serviceable thickness, relatively light. None are of the massively heavy fabric of certain early stages of cognate Attic plates and none are delicate. Only one series, the plate with offset rim, bears decoration. In the few examples of this series now known the floor and the upper surface of the rim display West Slope decoration in incision and applied colors. No use of stamping or rouletting is attested by any of the examples of Corinthian plates now known.

The full period of production is attested by examples only in the saucer series, in this case from some time in the second quarter of the 4th century to 146 B.C. In the other series we have in one case (the flat-rim plate) abundant representation of a single stage, the final one, and in the rest scanty representation of two, or at the most three, stages. Probably future evidence will show that the rolled-rim plate and the fish plate, Attic type, had as long a period of production in Corinthian as the saucer, or nearly so, the first two both being imitations of extremely popular Athenian shapes of wide distribution. It can be anticipated that future supplementation of the present evidence may show that the periods of production of the flat-rim plate and the fish plate with bevelled rim extend from the early years of the Hellenistic period to their now attested final stage of 146 B.C. The period of production of the plate with offset rim in Corinthian may have been more restricted, possibly only within the second half of the 3rd century.

The potential value of the criteria for dating provided by the plates as a whole is fairly good and attention on the part of future excavators at Corinth to filling the gaps in the various series by size and by stage of development is worthwhile. Distinction in date of 50 year intervals can be expected in all the series, and very likely even 25 year intervals or less will be possible to determine with some conviction, at least in early stages of the shape series. Although at present, due to scanty representation of stages and sizes in series and context evidence often of wide range in date, criteria for dating in some of the series is not well established, it seems likely that overall trends in shape development in the plates are from a broad ring foot to a constricted one, size for size, from a gently rising wall profile to a steeper one, and from a gentle concave curve in profile to a straighter one. Other trends, well attested in the saucer series and likely for others, include ones from full glazing to dipped, and from careful formation and clear definition of the component elements of the shape to less careful formation and blurring of the elements of the form. Other criteria for dating have been suggested in the discussions of the particular shapes, including one involving the decoration in the case of the plates with offset rim. At present, because of its extensive representation by stage and by size, the saucer series is the most valuable one to the excavator for close dating.

The spotty representation of plates in Corinthian Hellenistic pottery, with the notable exception of the saucer series, is to some extent supplemented by imported examples, Attic, gray ware and various other fabrics. An appreciable number of imported plates have been noted below in connection with the six Corinthian series. At least two other different shapes were known to the Corinthians in foreign examples, one with an upturned rim,[20] the other with an overhanging rim.[21]

ROLLED-RIM PLATE **101–106**, Pls. 4, 45.
Very late and final stages, *ca.* 200 to 146 B.C.
Deposits: 46, 107, 111.

This form, in the present examples, is characterized by a relatively quite constricted ring foot, and a fairly steeply rising wall profile more or less straight in outline. The rim is merely the upper termination

[20] In gray ware: C-33-998; of another imported fabric: C-47-804 and C-47-807, both of Deposit 46, and both in use in 146 B.C., *Hesperia*, XVIII, 1949, pl. 13, 3.
[21] In gray ware: C-47-812, Deposit 46, in use in 146 B.C.

of the wall. Close to the outer edge of the floor there appears either a slight tooled ridge or a wheel-run groove, both beneath the glaze, giving the rim a vestigially rolled appearance. Three sizes are now known: diameter of lip 0.27+, 0.21+, and 0.20+ m. The plates are substantially made, though not heavy, and are of merely adequate quality. The glaze, poor in all, was applied by dipping to the entire interior and to parts of the upper exterior. No stamping or rouletting appears on the floor of the present examples, but two wheel-run lines beneath the glaze encircle the center of the floor on **102**.

Five plates, by context, represent the last stage of the shape in Corinthian, of the time of the destruction of the city in 146 B.C. One, **104**, is evidently of a late stage not far removed in time from the end. It may be anticipated that examples of stages much earlier than those now known in the Corinthian series will be found in the future, and it seems likely the initial stage in Corinthian will prove to have been produced in imitation of some stage of the long series of Attic rolled-rim plates, first manufactured in Athens in the years just before 350 B.C. and widely exported.[22]

Criteria for dating in the Corinthian series are not as yet established since all with close context dates now known are of one time and stage. It may reasonably be assumed, however, on the analogy of other plate series, that the significant trends and criteria when ascertained will include ones toward constriction of the diameter of the foot, size for size, and toward increased elevation of the wall profile. On this assumption **104**, with a relatively broad foot and low wall profile, has been placed earlier than **105** of the same size series.

D. of lip 0.27+
  146 B.C.
    101 (C-47-354), Deposit 111. Rim and wall fragment. D. lip est. 0.27–0.28; P.H. 0.038.
    102 (C-46-43), Deposit 107. D. lip 0.275; D. foot 0.078; av. H. 0.064. Two wheel-run circles beneath glaze at center of floor, outer D. 0.04.
    103 (C-47-353), Deposit 111. Rim and wall fragment. D. lip est. 0.27, P.H. 0.05.

D. of lip 0.21+
  ca. 200 B.C.
    104 (C-34-29). D. lip 0.218; D. foot 0.069; H. 0.053. Pls. 4, 45.
  146 B.C.
    105 (C-46-66), Deposit 107. D. lip 0.125; D. foot 0.06; H. 0.058. Pls. 4, 45.
D. of lip 0.20+
  146 B.C.
    106 (C-47-816), Deposit 46. D. lip 0.208; D. foot 0.063; H. 0.07.

FLAT-RIM PLATE[23] **107–126**, Pls. 4, 45.
Final stage only, *ca.* 146 B.C.
Deposits: 46, 94, 95, 102, 104, 105, 107, 112, 115, 116.

The flat-rim plate, in the present examples, is characterized by a ring foot and a wall which rises fairly steeply. The wall profile is usually more or less straight but in some it is slightly everted and lightly tooled just below the lip. A narrow rim, normally flat and horizontal in plane, occasionally

[22] For the initial stage of the Attic rolled-rim plate see Corbett 153, and the examples cited there (under no. 41) from Olynthos. Also, *Olynthus*, XIII, nos. 847, 858, 861, 865, 866, all from houses. Examples of later stages of the Attic plate are Thompson A 70, C 1, E 1–15. Attic examples found in Corinth are the following. Of *ca.* 350 B.C.: C-31-236, Deposit 42; C-36-257; C-46-114, Deposit 87. 4th century B.C., third quarter: C-40-34, Deposit 28; C-40-468, Deposit 37; C-65-289, Deposit 31. 3rd century B.C.: C-30-100.
  Imported plates of this form from various other centers are also known in Corinth. Of *ca.* 200 B.C.: C-48-95 and C-48-96, both from Deposit 110. Of *ca.* 146 B.C.: C-34-1602 and C-34-1607, both from Deposit 102; C-35-831 and C-35-832, both from Deposit 104; C-47-49, Deposit 115. A gray-ware fragment, C-34-1856, is not from a datable context; presumably it is prior to 146 B.C.
[23] The shape is also represented by imported examples in Corinth. Gray ware: C-35-675, Deposit 108, of *ca.* 146 B.C. Unidentified ware: C-47-403, Deposit 111.

slightly bevelled, the slope upward and inward, is ordinarily formed by a wheel-run groove beneath the glaze around the outer edge of the interior. In one example, **126**, there is merely a tooled ridge between the floor and the rim. Five sizes are now known: diameter of rim 0.24+, 0.23, 0.22+, 0.21+, and 0.20+ m. All are of indifferent quality, though adequate to their purpose, and of medium thickness. The glaze is bad, usually fugitive, applied over all the interior and part way down the wall on the exterior by careless dipping. No stamping, rouletting or other decoration appears on them.

Extensive context evidence and considerations of form and quality of manufacture indicate that a single stage of this shape series in Corinthian is represented by the present examples: the final stage, of the time of the destruction of Corinth in 146 B.C. It may be anticipated that examples of earlier stages in Corinthian will be found in the future.[24] It is possible that the shape series had originally an Attic prototype. Conceivably such a prototype is to be seen in Thompson B 5, of a much earlier time: the distinct jog in its upper wall profile may be represented vestigially in the slightly everted profile below the lip seen in some of the Corinthian plates, as noted above.

Criteria for dating examples of this series can only be established with conviction when earlier examples from good contexts become available for study. It may tentatively be anticipated, however, that the criteria eventually ascertained will include trends toward constriction of the foot, size for size, and toward elevation of the wall profile. The present plates do show some variation in these respects, but not much. Though there may be, and should be, a slight gradation in date among them, the variations are probably due to their poor quality of manufacture rather than to any very appreciable difference in time of production.

D. of rim 0.24+
  146 B.C.
    107 (C-34-1603), Deposit 102. D. rim 0.246; D. foot 0.071; H. 0.062.
D. of rim 0.23
  146 B.C.
    108 (C-48-24), Deposit 112. D. rim 0.23; D. foot 0.07; H. 0.051.
    109 (C-34-1615), Deposit 102. D. rim 0.23; D. foot 0.065; H. 0.063. Pls. 4, 45.
    110 (C-35-649), Deposit 104. D. rim 0.23; D. foot 0.072; H. 0.055.
    111 (C-33-1451), Deposit 116. Rim and wall fragment. D. rim 0.23; P.H. 0.045.
D. of rim 0.22+
  146 B.C.
    112 (C-46-60), Deposit 107. D. rim 0.22; D. foot 0.062; av. H. 0.053.
    113 (C-33-306), Deposit 105. D. rim 0.22; D. foot 0.067; H. 0.05.
    114 (C-48-16), Deposit 112. D. rim 0.223; D. foot 0.069; av. H. 0.052.
    115 (C-47-57), Deposit 115. Rim and wall fragment. D. rim 0.22; P.H. 0.048.

D. of rim 0.21+
  146 B.C.
    116 (C-34-19), Deposit 94. D. rim 0.21; D. foot 0.064; H. 0.056.
    117 (C-48-18), Deposit 112. D. rim 0.215; D. foot 0.064; H. 0.055.
    118 (C-35-650), Deposit 104. Rim and wall fragment. D. rim 0.213; P.H. 0.033.
    119 (C-33-1450), Deposit 116. Rim and wall fragment. D. rim 0.21; P.H. 0.042.
    120 (C-48-17), Deposit 112. D. rim 0.218; D. foot 0.07; H. 0.054.
    121 (C-46-65), Deposit 107. D. rim 0.211; D. foot 0.06; H. 0.058.
    122 (C-47-117), Deposit 95. D. rim 0.212; D. foot 0.063; H. 0.055.
    123 (CP-515). D. rim 0.215; D. foot 0.065; H. 0.05.
D. of rim 0.20+
  146 B.C.
    124 (C-47-811), Deposit 46. D. rim 0.20; D. foot 0.06; H. 0.052.
    125 (C-48-25), Deposit 112. D. rim 0.208; D. foot 0.071; H. 0.055.
    126 (C-47-36), Deposit 107. D. rim 0.206; D. foot 0.071; H. 0.055.

---

[24] Since this was written an example of an appreciably earlier stage of the form and of a smaller size (D. 0.19 m.) has been found: C-66-158.

PLATE, OFFSET RIM[25] **127–130**, Pls. 4, 45.

Initial and intermediate stages, 3rd century B.C., third and fourth quarters.

Deposits: 94, 101.

This form of plate has a ring foot slightly spreading in profile, a gently rising wall, and an offset rim which is concave in profile below, convex above. Two sizes are now attested, diameter 0.20 and 0.168 m. The examples are strong but not heavy, the clay and quality of manufacture high. All are fully glazed, except for **127** on whose interior appear reserved zones painted white. Decoration in West Slope technique on the interior appears on all, on the two most fully preserved in three zones: medallion, outer floor, and rim.

The four examples probably belong to two adjacent stages of the shape series. Conceivably **127** and **128** represent the initial stage. **129** and **130** seem to represent the immediately subsequent stage. Further stages beyond them may be expected to be found in the future.

The full definition of the period of production of this plate series must await future evidence. The West Slope decoration on them associates them, of course, with the Hellenistic period. The context evidence of two, **128** and **129**, provides, however, only a very wide range, between *ca.* 330 and 146 B.C. The closer dating suggested here, the third quarter of the 3rd century for the examples of the first stage and the last quarter for the second, is based largely and perhaps not unreasonably on the close relationship between the flower medallion on these plates and those on the more extensive series of conical bowls below (p. 91). In the bowls there is a reasonably well-established relative progression in the rendition of this motif from naturalistic of high quality to schematic to careless. The rendition of the motif on the plates parallels the first two stages on the bowls, and the plates have been dated accordingly. It should be made clear, however, that the absolute dating of the bowls is only slightly stronger than that for the plates and that much more evidence is needed for them also. The flower medallion motif may well be of assistance in the future to establish more firmly the dating of these two series. It should be pertinent also to the dating of two other at present scanty series discussed below on which it appears, the mastos (**550**) and the wheelmade Megarian bowls (**527–531, 944**).

The plates arranged relatively on the basis of this progression in motif show two changes in shape which support the placement and which may, when the series is more extensively attested, prove to be criteria for dating: from a very slightly rising wall profile in the earlier to one rather steeper in the later; from a lip gently rounded on top to one which is rather flatter in profile. The differences in form between the two stages are clear but not so marked as to suggest that they are more than 50 years apart in date at most.

3rd century B.C., third quarter

127 (C-28-54). H. 0.023; D. est. 0.20; D. foot est. 0.07. Profile preserved except center of floor. Exterior fully glazed. On the interior only the rim, a broad band on the outer floor, and the medallion glazed. A groove wheel-run through the glaze is placed at the outer and inner edges of the rim and around the medallion. These probably were once colored, presumably pink. Two bands, one at the outer, one at the inner edge of the floor, were reserved and painted white. The decoration of the medallion is a multipetalled flower, petals in yellow, tendrils incised, and dot buds once in white. On the glazed band of the floor dolphins in yellow. On the section of the rim preserved only the incision of a block of diminishing rectangles remains. Pls. 4, 45.

128 (C-34-2499), Deposit 94. Part of foot and wall. Max. dim. 0.062; D. foot est. 0.07. Fully glazed except for a line, once painted, wheel-grooved through the glaze around the medallion. Medallion: multipetalled flower, petals in light gray with highlights in white, tendrils

---

[25] This shape, comparably decorated, is also represented in Corinth by imported examples. Attic: C-39-390. Two other foreign fabrics: C-53-267, Deposit 43; and C-63-86. Two other imported plates, black glaze and undecorated, of *ca.* 150 B.C., C-34-470, Deposit 102, and C-36-450, are of essentially the same form, the foot, however, relatively more constricted and the wall much steeper. In them the form has been transformed into a fish plate by the addition of a central depression. Also related in form and of late date are plates imported into Athens, Thompson D 1, E 22–26.

incised, dot buds in white. Floor: winged hippocamps in light gray, feathers and shading of form in white. Pl. 45.

3rd century B.C., fourth quarter

129 (C-48-53), Deposit 101. A section of the rim restored. H. 0.022; D. rim 0.168; D. foot 0.062. Fully glazed except for wheel-grooving through the glaze encircling the medallion and the inner and outer edges of the rim. Medallion: multipetalled flower with schematic outlines, petals in yellow with vertical and horizontal shading in yellow, white, and dilute black. On the outer floor four filleted boukrania rendered and shaded in the same colors. On the rim an alternation of three units of incised diminishing rectangles, each with a superimposed incised X from corner to corner, and a unit of incised checkerboard. No trace of color in these designs. *Hesperia*, XVIII, 1949, pl. 16, 14. Pls. 4, 45.

130 (C-37-2092). Fragment of rim and outer wall. Max. dim. 0.053; D. est. 0.20. Fully glazed except for a line wheel-grooved through the glaze at the inner edge of the rim. Floor: ivy tendril in yellow, white and incision. Rim: incised diminishing rectangles and checkerboard, the latter with three squares in white.

FISH PLATE, ATTIC TYPE[26] **131-133**, Pls. 5, 46.
Intermediate and final stages, *ca.* 300 to 146 B.C.
Deposits: 41, 47.

The examples of the Corinthian fish plate of Attic type now known closely resemble the Attic from which they derive, in form and in details of treatment. The Corinthian plate has a ring foot, a relatively gently rising wall profile, an overhanging rim, and a circular depression in the center of the floor. All the examples were evidently fully glazed (though **131** is uncertain since the glaze is almost entirely fugitive). There is no wheel-grooving of the resting surface and no employment of glazed circles on the underside of the foot. A groove wheel-run through the glaze, however, encircles the outer edge of the floor, and a second, except on **131**, is placed around the central depression. The grooves are painted pink on **132**. Three sizes are now known: diameter at highest point 0.19+, 0.17+, and 0.15 m. The quality of manufacture is good both in form and glaze (insofar as this is preserved).

Three stages of the shape series in Corinthian are represented. One, exemplified by **132**, is evidently early though probably not initial. The second, closely subsequent, is to be seen in **133**. The final stage in Corinthian, of the time of the destruction of the city in 146 B.C., is represented by **131**. It is to be expected that examples of stages earlier than **132** will be found in the future, perhaps extending the period of production in Corinthian back close to the time of its beginning in Attic, in which the earliest phase is to be placed at or shortly before 350 B.C.

Context evidence provides the relative placement of the earliest and the latest stages here. In the case of the earliest a date somewhat earlier than the lower limit of its context is suggested here on the basis of comparison with the Attic series (though, of course, the Corinthian series need not follow the Attic *pari passu*).

The placement of the two stages indicates that the criteria for relative dating of examples of the Corinthian series are based on the diameter of the foot, the wall and the rim profiles. Although the series is scanty the dependability of these criteria is supported by parallel developments attested in the Attic series. In the foot the trend is from one relatively broad to one more constricted. In the wall it is from one relatively low toward one rather steeper. In the rim it is from one of vertical

---

[26] The shape is also known in foreign examples in Corinth. There are seven Attic plates. Of *ca.* 350 B.C.: C-60-73, Deposit 38; C-60-269, Deposit 34; and CP-971. Of *ca.* 146 B.C., by context or attribution: C-47-400, Deposit 111; C-33-1463, Deposit 98; C-47-809, Deposit 46; C-47-118, Deposit 95. There are four gray-ware examples. Of *ca.* 146 B.C.: C-38-678, Deposit 115, and C-63-738, Deposit 47. Undated: C-35-962 and C-53-79. Two others are of a single, unidentified fabric, one of *ca.* 146 B.C. by context, the other by attribution: C-34-470, Deposit 102, and C-36-450. Another is of a still different unidentified ware, also of 146 B.C. by context: C-34-1604, Deposit 102.

profile toward one set at a pronounced outward angle. On this basis **133** is placed intermediate between the two stages and close to the earliest. The three so arranged suggest, for future observation, that there may also be a trend in the central depression from a very deep one toward one shallower. There is a suggestion also for future consideration that the Corinthian shape may have developed at a slightly faster rate than the Athenian.

The difference in appearance between the earliest and the latest examples is very marked. It is instructive to note, however, that this difference in form is accompanied by extremely slight differences in measurement, five millimeters in height, four in the diameter of the foot.

D. at highest point[27] 0.19+
   ca. 146 B.C.
      131 (C-63-737), Deposit 47. D. at highest point 0.195; max. D. 0.21; D. foot 0.08; av. H. 0.042; D. depression 0.04. Pls. 5, 46.
D. at highest point 0.17+
   ca. 300 B.C.
      132 (C-31-151), Deposit 41. D. at highest point 0.178; max. D. 0.181; D. foot 0.084; H. 0.037; D. depression 0.047. Pls. 5, 46.

D. at highest point 0.15
   ca. 275 B.C.
      133 (C-53-89). Profile preserved except most of rim. D. at highest point est. 0.15; max. D. est. 0.16; D. foot 0.08; H. 0.032; D. depression 0.04.

FISH PLATE, BEVELLED RIM[28] **134–137**, Pls. 5, 46.
Early to final stages, *ca.* 275 to 146 B.C.
Deposits: 36, 37, 94, 109.

This variety of fish plate has a ring foot and a wall rising broadly in a nearly straight profile, slightly everted at the top. The rim is narrow, set off from the floor by a distinct tooled ridge. It is bevelled in three examples, the slope downward and outward from the top of the floor. In the fourth, **135**, considered the latest, it is, however, flat and on a horizontal plane. A shallow depression encircled by a wheel-run groove beneath the glaze is set in the center of the floor. Two sizes are at present attested: diameter at outer edge of rim 0.23+ and 0.19+ m. They are relatively light plates with a variation from fairly thin to medium. In quality of manufacture they range from reasonably good to indifferent. Dipped glaze, carelessly applied, covers the interior and the upper part of the exterior of all.

Probably three stages of the shape series are at present represented. It may be anticipated that examples of the initial stage and of the intermediate stages now missing will be found in the future.

Criteria for dating examples of this series are not firmly indicated by context evidence as yet. **136** and **137** come from related contexts of considerable range, the lower limit being around 275 B.C. The contexts of the other two permit only general dating between *ca.* 330 and 146 B.C.

The four plates have been arranged below, then, in a sequence suggested by the criteria observed in comparable shape series, trends toward constriction of the diameter of the foot, size for size, and toward increased elevation of the wall profile. Accordingly, **136** and **137** are regarded as exemplifying the earliest (but probably not initial) stage, and they have, for the present, been placed at the lower limit of their contexts, *ca.* 275 B.C. The very considerable differences between them and **134** and **135** indicate that the latter are very much later and prompt the suggestion that they are of the penultimate and last stages of the shape series. The sequence so arranged shows supporting changes normal in a shape series. The earlier are much better formed than the later. The wall and rim are of thin clay in the earlier,

---

[27] This diameter is selected as the unit for distinguishing sizes since the rim varies in angle of placement in the course of the series.
[28] Other fish-plate shapes are noted above, footnote 26, in connection with the Fish Plate, Attic type.

heavier in the later. The foot is very low in the earlier and nicely tooled, higher and heavier in the later and cursorily formed. The quality of the glaze is fairly good in the earlier, poor in the later. The more precisely tooled ridge forming the rim and the more clear articulation of the groove around the central depression of **134** suggest that it is somewhat earlier than **135** in which both features are blurred. The placement of **135** at the end of the series in the time of the destruction is supported by the fact that its proportions and dimensions are within the range of plates of the same size in the cognate flat-rim plate series, dated by context to that time (**108–111**).

D. at outer edge of rim 0.23+
ca. 200 B.C.
    134 (C-34-23), Deposit 94. D. rim 0.235; D. foot 0.072; H. 0.058; D. depression 0.049.
ca. 146 B.C.
    135 (C-47-325), Deposit 109. Profile preserved but warped in firing. D. rim est. 0.23; D. foot 0.065; av. H. 0.058; D. depression 0.045. Pls. 5, 46.

D. at outer edge of rim 0.19
ca. 275 B.C.
    136 (C-40-467), Deposit 37. D. rim 0.19; D. foot 0.07; H. 0.035; D. depression 0.04. Pls. 5, 46.
    137 (C-40-433), Deposit 36. D. rim 0.194; D. foot 0.067; H. 0.035; D. depression 0.045.

SAUCER[29] **138–186**, Pls. 5, 46.
Initial to final stages, 4th century, second quarter to 146 B.C.
Deposits: 18, 19, 28, 36, 41–43, 45, 46, 48, 90, 97, 102, 107–111, 115.

A plain ring foot and a broadly rising wall profile uninterrupted in outline, whose upper termination is the rim, are the characteristics of this very simple form. It is generally very like the modern saucer, lacking only the central depression to receive a cup. Six sizes are attested at present: diameter of rim 0.16+, 0.15+, 0.14+, 0.13+, 0.12+, and 0.11+ m. The clay of which they are made is of normal thickness, neither fragile nor sturdy. All examples were glazed, either fully or in part.

For the period of production, examples of a somewhat advanced stage are from a deposit whose lower date is probably no later than the early third quarter of the 4th century. The earliest stage is thus placed within the second quarter. For the final stage the time of Mummius' destruction of Corinth in 146 B.C. is attested by deposit evidence. Representation of the series within this period is abundant, some 50 examples, and fairly uniform by stages. The representation in size series is less evenly distributed: a few of size 0.16+ m., good representation for sizes 0.15+, 0.14+, and 0.13+ m., two saucers each for 0.12+ and 0.11+ m.

The deposit evidence indicates three trends in shape development which are chronologically significant and which can be used as criteria for placement in sequence and dating. One is a trend from an originally broad ring foot toward one ultimately extremely constricted. The second is from an originally low wall outline toward one relatively extremely elevated. The third accompanies the second, a trend from a gently convex wall profile toward one essentially straight. Of these the first is probably the most dependable. The other two are generally true, but more subject to variation and inconsistency since the potters evidently could not as easily control the degree of elevation and curvature in these relatively small shapes of moderate thickness. The series arranged according to these trends exhibits other secondary trends which can also be used as criteria for dating. One is toward loss and modification of the original clear outline of the foot. The original form is retained for a while. It is still moderately recognizable down to the last years of the 4th century B.C. Thereafter it is much lower and of more irregular and inconsistent outline. The other secondary trend is toward loss of quality in the formation of the outer

---

[29] This shape has been discussed in greater detail by G. R. Edwards and M. Thompson in "A Hoard of Gold Coins of Philip and Alexander from Corinth," *A.J.A.*, LXXIV, 1970, pp. 343–350. Examples at Corinth attest that the shape was also produced in two other centers of manufacture: C-47-323, Deposit 109, and C-53-258, Deposit 43.

wall. Both inner and outer surfaces are initially well finished and this is usual to the end of the 4th century B.C. Thereafter, though the inner surface remains well finished throughout, examples with carelessly finished outer walls become more frequent.

D. of rim 0.16+

4th century B.C., early third quarter
138 (C-40-22), Deposit 28. D. rim 0.164; D. foot 0.068; H. 0.04.

4th century B.C., late third quarter
139 (C-40-432), Deposit 36. D. rim 0.16; D. foot 0.066; H. 0.035.

ca. 250 B.C.
140 (C-47-148), Deposit 97. D. rim 0.16; D. foot 0.056; H. 0.043.
141 (C-46-73), Deposit 107. D. rim 0.16; D. foot 0.047; H. 0.042.

D. of rim 0.15+

4th century B.C., second quarter
142 (C-37-2587), Deposit 90. D. rim 0.154; D. foot 0.071; H. 0.034.
143 (C-37-2619), Deposit 90. D. rim 0.154; D. foot 0.07; H. 0.037.
144 (C-37-2615), Deposit 90. D. rim 0.152; D. foot 0.069; H. 0.032.
145 (C-37-2614), Deposit 90. D. rim 0.155; D. foot est. 0.069; H. 0.037.
146 (C-61-381), Deposit 45. D. rim 0.15; D. foot 0.068; H. 0.035.

4th century B.C., early third quarter
147 (C-37-2582), Deposit 90. D. rim 0.152; D. foot 0.066; av. H. 0.036.
148 (C-37-2584), Deposit 90. D. rim 0.15; D. foot 0.066; H. 0.036.

3rd century B.C., third quarter
149 (CP-398). D. rim 0.158; D. foot 0.054; H. 0.047.
150 (C-62-249), Deposit 48. D. rim 0.155; D. foot 0.054; av. H. 0.05.

2nd century B.C., early second quarter
151 (CP-399). D. rim 0.154; D. foot 0.047; H. 0.049.

ca. 146 B.C.
152 (C-47-360), Deposit 111. D. rim est. 0.15; D. foot est. greater than 0.04; H. 0.047.
153 (C-34-1617), Deposit 102. D. lip 0.151; P.H. 0.031.
154 (C-48-102), Deposit 110. D. rim 0.158; D. foot 0.044; H. 0.05.
155 (C-47-814), Deposit 46. D. rim 0.156; D. foot 0.044; H. 0.046.

D. of rim 0.14+

4th century B.C., second quarter
156 (C-37-2585), Deposit 90. D. rim 0.146; D. foot 0.07; H. 0.038.
157 (C-37-2617), Deposit 90. D. rim 0.144; D. foot 0.07; H. 0.031.

158 (C-37-2586), Deposit 90. D. rim 0.145; D. foot 0.069; H. 0.037. Pls. 5, 46.

4th century B.C., early third quarter
159 (C-37-2588), Deposit 90. D. rim 0.142; D. foot 0.065; H. 0.035.
160 (C-33-391). D. rim 0.144; D. foot 0.065; av. H. 0.032.

ca. 300 B.C.
161 (C-31-246), Deposit 42. D. rim 0.146; D. foot 0.063; H. 0.043.

3rd century B.C., late second quarter
162 (C-31-148), Deposit 41. D. rim 0.148; D. foot 0.058; H. 0.033.
163 (C-31-223), Deposit 42. D. rim 0.145; D. foot 0.058; H. 0.039.

3rd century B.C., third quarter
164 (C-47-136), Deposit 115. D. rim 0.143; D. foot 0.055; H. 0.03. Pls. 5, 46.

2nd century B.C., early first quarter
165 (C-47-326), Deposit 109. D. rim 0.148; D. foot 0.05; H. 0.037.

2nd century B.C., second quarter
166 (C-47-312), Deposit 108. D. rim 0.146; D. foot 0.048; H. 0.038.
167 (CP-400). D. rim est. 0.14; D. foot 0.047; H. 0.034.

ca. 146 B.C.
168 (C-48-101), Deposit 110. D. rim 0.145; D. foot 0.046; H. 0.047. Pls. 5, 46.
169 (C-47-813), Deposit 46. D. rim 0.146; D. foot 0.045; H. 0.041.

D. of rim 0.13+

4th century B.C., second quarter
170 (C-37-2318). D. rim est. 0.132; D. foot est. 0.066; H. 0.029.

4th century B.C., early third quarter
171 (C-37-2583), Deposit 90. D. rim 0.132; D. foot 0.063; H. 0.03.

4th century B.C., late last quarter
172 (C-53-257), Deposit 43. D. rim 0.138; D. foot 0.059; H. 0.03.
173 (C-31-224), Deposit 42. D. rim 0.13; D. foot 0.058; H. 0.036.

3rd century B.C., early second quarter
174 (C-31-200), Deposit 42. D. rim 0.13; D. foot 0.055; H. 0.038.

ca. 250 B.C.
175 (C-47-265). D. rim 0.13; D. foot 0.053; H. 0.037.

3rd century B.C., early third quarter
176 (C-53-256), Deposit 43. D. rim 0.132; D. foot 0.052; H. 0.033.

177 (C-31-248), Deposit 42. D. rim 0.13; D. foot
0.051; H. 0.032.
3rd century B.C., last quarter
178 (C-31-247), Deposit 42. D. rim 0.13; D. foot
0.05; H. 0.041.
179 (C-61-382), Deposit 45. D. rim 0.132; D. foot
0.049; H. 0.042.
180 (C-53-259), Deposit 43. D. rim 0.134; D. foot
0.048; H. 0.035.
181 (C-61-424), Deposit 45. D. rim 0.13; D. foot
0.048; H. 0.034.
ca. 146 B.C.
182 (C-47-815), Deposit 46. D. rim 0.135; D. foot
0.046; H. 0.042.

D. of rim 0.12+
ca. 325–315 B.C.
183 (C-30-150), Deposit 19. D. rim 0.128; D. foot
0.061; H. 0.032.
3rd century B.C., early third quarter
184 (C-61-425), Deposit 45. D. rim 0.124; D. foot
0.052; H. 0.03.
D. of rim 0.11+
4th century B.C., last quarter
185 (KP 218), Deposit 18. D. rim 0.117; D. foot
0.058; H. 0.028.
2nd century B.C., early first quarter
186 (C-61-383), Deposit 45. D. rim 0.115; D. foot
0.044; H. 0.034.

VESSELS FOR DRINK

CONTAINERS

SMALL WEST SLOPE AMPHORA **187**, Pls. 6, 47.
Final(?) stage, *ca.* 150 B.C.(?).
Deposits: none.

The West Slope amphora takes its name from the first amphora of its kind to be found, discovered in the excavations of the West Slope of the Areopagus in Athens (Athens, National Museum, *Ath. Mitt.*, XXVI, 1901, p. 68, no. 1, pl. III). The shape would seem to have been a basic element of the equipment of an Athenian household all through the Hellenistic period. Thompson B 3, D 25, D 26, E 59–E 61 are among the many examples of usable size in Attic pottery.

At Corinth the representation of this shape is, in contrast, curiously slight. Four imported examples are known. Two are Attic, both fragmentary: C-47-803, Deposit 46, of the middle of the 2nd century B.C., and C-37-2226. The third, C-37-2422, is in gray ware. The fourth, C-34-38, Deposit 94, is of an unidentified fabric. In Corinthian Hellenistic pottery itself only the tiny **187** is at present known, and no functional substitute for the Attic shape in normal size is as yet known in Corinthian.

Diminutive West Slope amphorae such as the present one are rare. One Attic example close in size to it is known: Thompson D 27.

187 does not come from a datable context. The Corinthian potter who produced it may well have had the Attic shape in mind, but in imitating the Attic model he modified the form of the body so that a dependable date cannot be obtained by comparison with the Attic series. The date suggested is, therefore, necessarily an only slightly informed guess. Further examples and evidence for dating will be needed.

ca. 150 B.C.(?)
187 (C-33-424). D. rim 0.05; D. foot 0.036; D. body 0.078; H. 0.07. Ring foot. Sharp articulation between lower wall and shoulder. Neck concave in profile. Points of attachment of two vertical handles at outer edge of shoulder and just below lip. Fully glazed. A groove wheel-run through the glaze at the outer edge of the shoulder and at the base of the neck. In the zone so formed, A & B, a wavy line in applied yellow. A light wheel groove beneath the glaze around the profile of the lip. Pls. 6, 47.

SERVING VESSELS **188–190**

INTRODUCTION

The name krater chosen for the two shapes below is based only on the inference that these shapes served the same purpose as the familiar krater shapes of Classical times, as vessels in which wine was mixed and from which wine was served. Their capacities and forms are suitable for this purpose, though there is nothing to preclude their use as serving bowls for other contents. The modern spectator may find some conviction that the bolster krater, at any rate, served for wine because of its general resemblance in shape to some modern forms of the punch bowl. Both shapes were decorated with designs in the West Slope technique and would in this respect be suitable for festive occasions. All the examples now known are relatively well made, fully glazed, and decorated with a respectable degree of care. If sizes in the two series are reckoned by diameters, two are attested: 0.31 and 0.25+ m.

Both the bolster krater and the hemispherical krater were Hellenistic inventions, introduced in Corinthian pottery evidently fairly early in that period, both probably in imitation of Attic forms. Evidence for the period of production of each is scanty at present. It seems very unlikely that they were still in production at the time of the destruction of Corinth in 146 B.C. The present evidence for dating and the scarcity of examples tend to suggest that in fact they may have gone out of production much earlier than that time, perhaps even well within the 3rd century.

Future studies toward defining the limits of the periods of production of these shapes should keep in mind, in addition to the context dates of future examples, consideration of the functional predecessors and successors of these shapes, if they indeed served as kraters. In the former case, the lower limits of production of Corinthian bell and calyx kraters,[30] which the present kraters presumably replaced functionally, is of interest since the present krater forms were no doubt introduced contemporaneously with the late stages of the bell and calyx kraters. In the latter case, attention may be focused on the upper limits of production of large moulded bowls, such as those with appliqué relief supports discussed below, fragments of which are sufficiently numerous at Corinth to suggest that these may represent one of the forms which carried on the function of the krater after the bolster and hemispherical kraters went out of production.

The present representation of Hellenistic krater shapes in Corinthian may suggest a strong decline in this period in the use of kraters. The paucity of potential examples is only slightly supplemented by the existence of the coarse-ware column kraters below, unpretentious in appearance though pleasing, which could also have functioned as wine kraters in simpler households. An Attic bolster krater is noted below, probably of the fairly early 3rd century, and two other kraters, both of 146 B.C., imported from some other center, are also known, both interesting in that they are extremely late manifestations of the bell krater form in pottery.[31] The total number of Hellenistic kraters, even including the moulded bowl forms mentioned above, is not, however, great. Should we perhaps think that in Hellenistic times in Corinth (perhaps also in Athens) metal krater forms were preferred, at least in well-to-do houses?

It has already been suggested that the present krater forms may have been produced over only limited periods. In this respect they may prove to be valuable for purposes of chronology. The bolster krater may prove to be the more valuable of the two for close dating within its period of production.

---

[30] Corinthian black-glazed bell kraters known at present include three complete examples: C-38-563, Deposit 35; C-40-393, Deposit 36, *Hesperia*, XVII, 1948, p. 231, E 2, and pl. 85; C-40-62, Deposit 27; and three fragmentary: C-37-2345; C-38-560, Deposit 35; C-31-10, Deposit 39. The contexts involved are of wide range. The examples evidently represent several 4th century stages of the development of the form.

A fragment of an evidently very late Corinthian red-figure calyx krater has been found in the excavations of Halieis at Porto Cheli.

[31] C-33-304, Deposit 105; C-48-29, Deposit 112.

BOLSTER KRATER **188**, **189**, Pls. 7, 39, 47.
Early and advanced stages, *ca.* early 3rd century to 3rd century B.C., third quarter.
Deposits: 106, 113.

The bolster krater,[32] an invention of Hellenistic times, is named from the form of its handles, on the analogy of the names of the column and volute kraters of earlier days.

The foot is conical beneath, with a stepped profile on the exterior. The broad and deep bowl profile terminates above in a flat rim. The two handles are set on the upper wall, just below the rim. Both kraters are of much the same size. Both are fully glazed and decorated with West Slope designs in incision and applied color in a zone or zones just below the lip.

The contexts from which the two examples come provide only a general dating between *ca.* 330 and 146 B.C. Though further examples and deposit evidence will be needed for closer placement, something may be suggested at present on the basis of general considerations. The bolster krater is evidently a functional replacement for Classical krater shapes, particularly the bell and calyx krater forms. Little is known of the lower limits of production of these shapes in Corinthian, but they would seem probably to have persisted to the late 4th century, at any rate, as in Attic. Presumably the bolster krater will have been introduced contemporaneously with the very late stages of those shapes. On the basis of shape development principles **188** appears to be earlier by some years than **189**. It gives the impression, however, of being not of an initial stage but perhaps still early. It may thus be provisionally suggested that it is of the early 3rd century. An estimate of *ca.* 50 years difference in time seems required for **189** since its base and stem are appreciably more constricted, its handles are relatively vestigial in form and the incised patterns beneath its handles are similarly vestigial in treatment.

Early 3rd century B.C.

188 (C-47-451), Deposit 113. H. 0.156; D. lip 0.31; D. base 0.103. Substantial fabric. Handles 0.085 m. wide, each pierced vertically by a single hole for suspension. Below lip, A & B, two zones of decoration with bordering wheel-run lines incised through the glaze. Above, bead-and-reel in yellow. Below, ivy tendril in yellow and incision. Below each handle an incised pattern. *Hesperia*, XVIII, 1949, pl. 15, 11. Pls. 7, 39, 47.

3rd century B.C., third quarter

189 (C-47-269), Deposit 106. H. 0.173; D. lip 0.31; D. base 0.09. Somewhat lighter fabric than **188**. Handles 0.055 wide, only one pierced vertically for suspension. Below lip, A & B, between a pair of grooves wheel-run through the glaze, an ivy tendril design in incision and yellow. Beneath each handle an incised design similar to those on **188** but smaller. *Hesperia*, XVI, 1947, pl. 58, 11. Pls. 7, 39, 47.

HEMISPHERICAL KRATER **190**, Pls. 6, 39, 47.
Early stage, *ca.* 275 B.C.
Deposit: 38.

The simple hemispherical outline of the wall profile of this shape provides the name. It has a relatively constricted, very low ring foot for stability. There are no traces of any handles. The lip has a gentle bevel inward. The krater is made of moderately substantial clay and is fully glazed. Below the lip are two closely spaced wheel-run grooves incised through the glaze. From the lower groove three necklaces are represented suspended, the strings incised and the tear-shaped pendants in fugitive applied yellow.

The shape is evidently an invention of early Hellenistic times, perhaps first introduced in Attic and here copied in Corinthian, as a functional substitute, like the bolster krater, for the bell and calyx kraters. The context from which this single example comes would permit a dating within the period

---

[32] The form of a moulded relief krater from Delos, Courby, p. 330, fig. 62, XIII, is evidently in the general shape tradition of the bolster krater. Fragments of an Attic bolster krater in Corinth: C-66-165 a, b.

ca. 325 to *ca.* 250 B.C. The present placement within this range, at *ca.* 275 B.C., is entirely provisional since much more evidence is needed for dating examples of the shape. Though this example seems to be relatively early in shape development it would not seem to be of the initial stage.

ca. 275 B.C.

190 (C-60-58), Deposit 38. H. 0.155; D. 0.255; D. foot 0.073. Constricted ring foot. Lip bevelled, inward slope. Fully glazed. Below the lip, two grooves wheel-run, incised through the glaze. From the lower groove three necklaces are suspended, strings incised, tearshaped pendants in applied yellow. *Hesperia*, XXXI, 1962, p. 117, pl. 45, b, center. Pls. 6, 39, 47.

Dippers 191–197

INTRODUCTION

From at least the early Hellenistic period to the late Roman period a need was evidently felt for a very small (H. 0.03–0.05 m.), rather deep cup with a handle of a type which would permit dipping into liquid. Such cups were produced during this period in several forms, differing but related. They could have served many purposes connected with dipping, and presumably also sipping. In a wine-producing country they would have been very suitable in size and character for sampling before purchase varieties of wine sold in bulk.[33]

The several Hellenistic varieties which are recorded below are all interrelated in size and in having a flattened bottom. All have a wall profile broad below, constricted in varying degrees above, a characteristic devised perhaps so that the liquid could be swirled without spilling. Three varieties share a generally similar wall profile, more or less articulated below, and three share a similar form of handle. It is suggested, though on present evidence it cannot now be fully demonstrated, that the variety with a high loop handle, **191–193** below, may be the earliest, of the early Hellenistic period, and that the substitution of a solid, pinch handle for the loop handle, characteristic of all the others to the latest, may have been a practical innovation, less subject to breakage, of somewhat advanced Hellenistic times. The pinch handle in all cases, Hellenistic and Roman, is horizontally pierced for a string, perhaps merely for suspension, perhaps also to tie the vessels permanently near the place where they were to be used. The loop-handled variety could similarly be suspended or tied in place. Only the loop-handled variety was glazed.

Roman examples found in Athens are published by Robinson, G 215, 1st to early 2nd century after Christ; J 38, 2nd to early 3rd century; K 75, *ca.* A.D. 250 ; L 56, later 4th century. Robinson reports that they are "very common in the deposits of the 1st to 3rd century" in Athens. Another example, from Corinth (C-34-227), may also be of the Roman period.

KYATHOS, LOOP HANDLE, ARTICULATED WALL **191–193**, Pls. 8, 48.
Early and advanced stages, late 4th and early 3rd century B.C.(?).
Deposits: 99, 112.

The three examples of this variety are of one size (H. without handles 0.04 m.). **192** has a low disk base, **193** and **191** have a flat bottom with string marks. The point of greatest circumference is on the lower wall, this point sharply articulated only in **191**. Just below the lip there is a pair of wheel-run grooves beneath the glaze. The strap handle arches above the lip, the ends pinched together and attached to the edge of the lip and upper wall. All are of sturdy fabric and were fully glazed.

---

[33] Robinson, p. 44, G 215, has suggested that Roman examples may have been used as liqueur cups.

The shape is apparently a Hellenistic invention. Context evidence provided by **192** and **193** indicates only that these examples were produced sometime within the Hellenistic period prior to 146 B.C. Placement of the three in the early Hellenistic period is entirely provisional pending closer deposit evidence for dating. A slight indication of early date is provided by the fact that other types of kyathos are attested to have been in use in the later Hellenistic period. The relatively careful formation of **191** and the presence of sharp articulation around the lower wall in contrast to the other two suggests that it may be of an early stage and the other two of a somewhat more advanced stage.

Late 4th century B.C.(?)
191 (CP-198). Handle missing except for attachments. H. 0.04; D. 0.054; D. bottom 0.037. Pl. 8.

Early 3rd century B.C.(?)
192 (C-47-223), Deposit 99. H. without handle 0.04; D. 0.06; D. base 0.036. Pls. 8, 48.
193 (C-48-15), Deposit 112. H. without handle 0.04; D. 0.056; D. bottom 0.03. Pl. 48.

KYATHOS, PINCH HANDLE: ARTICULATED WALL **194**, Pls. 8, 48.
Advanced stage, 2nd century B.C., first half(?).
Deposit: 97.

The one example of this variety of kyathos has a flat bottom with string marks, a convex wall profile broadest near the bottom, constricted at the lip, and a handle formed by a solid pinch of clay pierced horizontally.

Its context indicates only that it is of Hellenistic date prior to 146 B.C. It seems possible, on the principle of loss of articulation in shape series, that its profile is a blurred late development of that of the kyathoi with loop handles, **191–193**. Hence an advanced date in the Hellenistic period is suggested for it.

2nd century B.C., first half
194 (C-47-149), Deposit 97. H. 0.037; D. 0.052; D. bottom 0.035; D. lip 0.04. Unglazed. Pls. 8, 48.

KYATHOS, PINCH HANDLE: ARTICULATED WALL, INTURNED RIM **195, 196**, Pls. 8, 48.
Final stage, 146 B.C.
Deposits: 113, 114.

This variety of kyathos has a flat bottom with string marks, a wall profile broadest below, straight but tapering inward toward the top. The top of the wall is folded inward forming a bevelled lip which slopes inward and is slightly overhanging within. It has a pinch handle, horizontally pierced, set on the upper wall. The two examples are unglazed.

The date of **195, 196** is established by context. It is understood that examples from Isthmia (IP 426, IP 427, IP 618), which are very similar to those catalogued here, were found in a 3rd century context. Hence the period of production of this variant may extend from some time in the 3rd century to 146 B.C.

ca. 146 B.C.
195 (C-47-430), Deposits 113 and 114. H. 0.03; D. 0.05; D. bottom 0.035; D. top 0.047. Pls. 8, 48.

196 (C-47-480), Deposit 113. H. 0.035; D. 0.052; D. bottom 0.035; D. top 0.042.

KYATHOS, PINCH HANDLE: CONVEX WALL **197**, Pls. 8, 48.

Final stage, 146 B.C.

Deposit: 46.

The single example of this variety of kyathos has a small flat bottom, a double convex wall profile, a constricted raised rim, and a pinch handle which was horizontally pierced.

ca. 146 B.C.
> **197** (C-47-851), Deposit 46. H. 0.03; D. 0.052; D. bottom 0.025; D. rim 0.033. Tip of handle missing. Pls. 8, 48.

POURING VESSELS **198–306**

INTRODUCTION

Vessels included under this heading are only those which could reasonably be considered serviceable for pouring wine or liquids of similar consistency, the main criteria for inclusion here being a neck and mouth of suitable size and form to provide a ready flow. Of the various series of such vessels here the decanters are the most capacious, their sizes, evidently to be reckoned by diameter of body, ranging between 0.21+ and 0.15 m. The examples of the other shapes now known have much more limited capacities, their sizes, reckoned by height, between 0.18 and 0.04 m., some of course being miniature versions of shapes represented also in usable sizes. Some of the very early examples are of rather fragile fabric but in the main they are made of clay of serviceable thickness. A number of the vessels are completely unglazed. The decanters have only glaze bands on the exterior, while nearly all the trefoil olpai and all the small trefoil oinochoai are glazed fully or in part. None of the vessels bears ornamentation of any kind.

Of all the shapes here the trefoil olpe has the longest period of production, believed to have extended from *ca.* 550 continuously down to the end of Greek Corinth in 146 B.C., although at present there is only slight representation of the shape in the years following 350. Other shapes were also inventions of Classical times with periods of production extending to some degree into the Hellenistic period: the varieties of small trefoil oinochoai, Decanter II with its modified descendant, III, and possibly also Decanter I. The limits of the period of production of the small juglet have yet to be ascertained. The only purely Hellenistic shape now known to have been produced in Corinthian, the small water pitcher, is represented by a single example of the first half of the 2nd century B.C. It may be anticipated, however, that its period of production in Corinthian will be shown by future examples to cover the entire Hellenistic period.

At present the most useful for chronology of the various series of vessels is the trefoil olpe, particularly in the period between 550 and 350 B.C. It may, however, be doubted that examples of the later 4th century and the Hellenistic period, the late stages of the shape, when they become more fully available will be as closely informative as their predecessors. One may anticipate rather that the series of small water pitchers will eventually provide some degree of precision in Hellenistic dating.

The Corinthian jugs now known to be actually made in the Hellenistic period are disturbing in two aspects, quite aside from their relatively slight representation at present. One would expect there to be decorated wine jugs to be used in connection with the very generous supply of decorated drinking cups, as there are in Attic Hellenistic. The present examples are, however, all plain. It may be, of course, that future excavation of wealthier Corinthian households of Hellenistic times will supply the present lack in this respect. The second strange aspect is the comparatively inadequately small size of most of the present Hellenistic fine-ware pouring vessels. It is possible, of course, that in simpler households the need for larger wine pitchers may have been supplied by examples in coarse ware, for instance the handle-ridge jug, or by such shapes in cooking ware as the round-mouth and trefoil pitchers. The thought remains, however, that our knowledge of Corinthian wine pitchers of the Hellenistic period is, like the present representation, very incomplete.

The picture of Corinthian Hellenistic vessels of this kind is somewhat amplified by imports. Two examples of imported olpai are noted below, and one probably Attic example of the small water pitcher. Other shapes evidently not produced in Corinthian are also represented by imported examples, the lagynos,[34] a small pitcher shape,[35] and four juglet forms.[36] An oinochoe shape in moulded ware is also attested in Corinth.[37]

TREFOIL OLPE[38] **198–244**, Pls. 9, 48.
Initial to final stages, *ca.* 550 to 146 B.C.
Deposits: 1–4, 6, 8–11, 13, 15, 18, 25, 42, 49, 79, 81, 90, 96, 102, 106, 109.

This form has a flat or concave bottom. The body, varying from moderately rotund to slender according to the period, rises in a swelling outline which, again depending on the period, may be either continuous in profile from foot to lip or articulated at the shoulder or the base of the neck, or both. The lip is trefoil. The handle rises from the shoulder area, arching above and down to the top of the lip. The sizes attested among the present examples[39] are eight: H. 0.18, 0.15+, 0.13+, 0.12+, 0.11+, 0.10+, 0.09+ and 0.08+ m. The clay of which they are made is fairly thin in early examples, of normally serviceable thickness later. Some early examples are unglazed, but the bulk are glazed in some degree.

It seems highly probable that both initial and final stages of the form are represented. There is quite full representation, though not of all sizes, in stages intermediate between 550, believed to be the approximate time of the introduction of the shape in Corinthian, and 350 B.C. With one exception, stages between 350 and 146 B.C. are at present completely lacking, but it is nonetheless believed that the latest are in a continuous tradition with the earlier.

Deposit evidence indicates that criteria for relative placement of examples of this shape include almost every aspect of the form, making it potentially an extremely useful one for dating in excavation even in fragments. The form begins, e.g. **199**, with a very thin disk foot, slightly lipped on the outer profile. The body is comparatively broad, rising in a gently rotund curve continuous in profile from the foot to

---

[34] Three lagynoi of probably three different imported fabrics, all black glazed: C-47-233, Deposit 102, and C-48-41, Deposit 112, both Hellenistic prior to 146 B.C.; CP 471, a miniature. The well-known white-ground lagynos is represented at Corinth only by one complete example, C-34-44, *A.J.A.*, XXXIX, 1935, p. 71, fig. 16, and Broneer, *S. Stoa*, p. 29, fig. 7 and pl. 7, 3, and by fragments of two others, C-36-2347 and C-36-2349. The extreme scarcity of examples of white-ground lagynoi from the excavations at Corinth tend to suggest that they were first beginning to be imported here only shortly before the destruction of the city. The excellence of the present pieces in point of care of formation, quality of the white ground, and of the decoration may also suggest that they are very early examples of their series and that production began only shortly before 146 B.C.

[35] C-47-282, Deposit 106, Hellenistic prior to 146 B.C.

[36] C-60-72, Deposit 38, *ca.* last quarter of the 4th century or first quarter of the 3rd century B.C.; C-34-16, Deposit 94, Hellenistic prior to 146 B.C.; C-33-123, and C-36-722. Four different fabrics seem to be represented.

[37] Gray ware: C-47-852, Deposit 46, of 146 B.C., *Hesperia*, XVIII, 1949, pl. 13, 1.

[38] The list of olpai included here is not fully exhaustive. They are those known at the time this was first written. 11 additional olpai are discussed in *N. Cemetery*, p. 133 ("Tall Trefoil Oinochoai"), and a few others from other parts of the Corinth excavations have since been noticed. Two others are known from Isthmia, IP 2303 and IP 2352, from the Large Circular Pit, Deposit 5, filled in after the middle of the 5th century B.C.: Broneer, *Hesperia*, XXXI, 1962, pp. 1–2; 23, nos. 6 and 7, and pl. 11, c; *Isthmia*, II, pp. 135–136. An apparently handmade example of the shape, C-47-752, Deposit 2, of the third quarter of the 6th century B.C., is also known. Two imported olpai, in addition: C-47-97, Deposit 96, and C-47-152, Deposit 98.

[39] An additional size, H. 0.07 m., is represented among those in *N. Cemetery*: X-197.

the base of the neck. The greatest diameter is near the middle. The shoulder is not articulated but the curve of the profile changes abruptly here from steep to incurving and low. There is a very slight ridge at the base of the neck. The neck is comparatively high and of trim profile. The handle rises from the outer edge of the shoulder in a flat curve, arches above the lip and down steeply to the top of the lip. The clay of which the earliest is made is quite thin and of high quality. The form is very competently made and its elements clearly defined. The changes in the form which ensued over the centuries result in a markedly different shape, e.g. **207**, in the final years of the city. The foot is no longer an element of the shape. The bottom is more deeply concave. The body is very slender, an attenuated, slightly swollen cylinder in outline from the bottom to the base of the lip. The greatest diameter is near the middle. The form is shoulderless and neckless, the trefoil lip set like a frill around the top of the wall. The ends of the handle are set close together and the handle outline is distinctly ear-shaped. The clay of which the final examples are made is comparatively thicker. The shape is carelessly formed and only the handle shows any indication of craftsmanlike shaping.

Between these two extremes certain changes of limited duration occur which are of chronological usefulness. The original foot is present only from about 550 to 500 B.C. The fairly rotund early body profile is of the same period. It remains fairly broad from 500 down to *ca.* 350 B.C. but examples of this time are more nearly cylindrical, the outline rising in a flatter curve, and often the greatest diameter is at the shoulder. The latest examples are much more slender than those of 350. The shoulder remains unarticulated until about 500 B.C. A quite sharp definition of the outer shoulder, however, begins then and is usual, in some degree, throughout the 5th century. In the 4th century this becomes somewhat blurred on the way toward its entire deletion and full blending of its identity with the other elements of the shape in the latest olpai. The slight ridge at the base of the neck is seen only in the olpai of 550 to 500 B.C. The neck has only semi-articulation thereafter, through 350 B.C., and there is, of course, no definition here in the latest. The originally trim profile of the neck persists only into the early years of the 5th century when it develops a curiously bulging outline, rather resembling a double chin, between its base and the lip. This is retained throughout the 5th century, becoming blurred by 350 B.C. The handle was originally formed of two coils of clay. This form had been replaced by a strap handle by 500 B.C., if not before, and the new form is canonical throughout the rest of the series. The handle profile remains more or less in the original outline, though perhaps more roundly arching after 500, until about 350 B.C. when blurring of the shoulder outline permits the lower attachment to be placed higher and the final ear-shaped profile begins to develop.

The quality of execution is high in the 6th century, mediocre in the 5th and 4th centuries, poor in the latest examples. The glaze, at no time of high quality, is at its best in the 5th century. Intentionally unglazed examples are known only in the 6th century. Olpai glazed on the exterior occur contemporaneously with them and throughout the rest of the series. A few of these, of the 6th and 5th centuries, are glazed on the underside of the bottom. Most examples of these years are not, nor are any of the 4th century and later. Fully glazed exteriors occur in some 6th and 5th century examples, but none later are known. Exteriors glazed down to a low point on the wall occur in the 6th, 5th and 4th centuries. The latest examples are glazed only down to a point high on the wall. It seems likely that dipping was employed as early as the last quarter of the 6th century in this series: e.g. **202**.

H.[40] 0.18

350 B.C.

> **198** (C-37-2520), Deposit 90. H. 0.18; D. foot 0.07; max. D. 0.09; D. shoulder 0.082. Pls. 9, 48.

H. 0.15+

550 B.C.

> **199** (C-47-750), Deposit 2. H. 0.15; D. foot 0.06; max. D. 0.088; D. shoulder 0.08. Unglazed. Pls. 9, 48.

[40] H. in this catalogue means without handle.

6th century B.C., third quarter

200 (C-39-253), Deposit 8. H. 0.158; D. foot 0.057; max. D. 0.09; D. shoulder 0.075. Unglazed.

201 (C-47-751), Deposit 2. H. 0.15; D. foot 0.053; max. D. 0.085; D. shoulder 0.078. Unglazed.

6th century B.C., fourth quarter

202 (C-37-949), Deposit 3. H. 0.158; D. foot 0.061; max. D. 0.086; D. shoulder 0.082. Campbell 63.

203 (C-37-1081), Deposit 3. P.H. 0.09; D. foot 0.062. Unglazed. Campbell 68.

204 (C-37-1051), Deposit 3. P.H. 0.065; D. foot 0.06. Unglazed. Campbell 67.

350 B.C.

205 (C-31-192), Deposit 42. H. 0.158; D. foot 0.057; max. D. 0.085; D. shoulder 0.078.

146 B.C.

206 (C-47-299), Deposit 106. P.H. 0.155; D. foot 0.045; max. D. 0.061.

207 (C-47-300), Deposit 106. P.H. 0.153; D. foot 0.038; max. D. 0.063. Pls. 9, 48.

H. 0.13+

5th century B.C., second quarter

208 (C-39-99), Deposit 8. H. 0.132; D. foot 0.048; max. D. at shoulder 0.07.

209 (C-39-102), Deposit 8. H. 0.133; D. foot 0.047; max. D. 0.071; D. shoulder 0.064.

4th century B.C., first to second quarter

210 (C-37-484), Deposit 79. P.H. 0.105; max. D. 0.069; D. shoulder 0.063.

211 (C-36-976), Deposit 15. P.H. 0.131; D. foot 0.05; max. D. 0.072; D. shoulder 0.06.

212 (C-47-872), Deposit 81. H. 0.13; D. foot 0.048; max. D. 0.07; D. shoulder 0.062.

146 B.C.

213 (C-34-1619), Deposit 102. P.H. 0.105; D. foot 0.044.

H. 0.12+

6th century B.C., third quarter

214 (C-47-748), Deposit 2. P.H. 0.092; D. foot 0.055. Unglazed.

215 (C-37-973), Deposit 3. P.H. 0.09; D. foot 0.049. Campbell 65.

6th century B.C., fourth quarter

216 (C-37-972), Deposit 3. P.H. 0.088; D. foot 0.05. Unglazed. Campbell 64.

Early 5th century B.C.

217 (C-31-171), Deposit 4. H. 0.127; D. foot 0.048; max. D. 0.073; D. shoulder 0.069.

218 (C-31-172), Deposit 4. H. 0.122; D. foot 0.049; max. D. 0.075; D. shoulder 0.07.

5th century B.C., second quarter

219 (KP 361), Deposit 6. H. 0.12; av. D. foot 0.046; max. D. at shoulder 0.072.

220 (C-34-347), Deposit 10. H. 0.123; D. foot 0.05; max. D. at shoulder 0.064.

450 B.C.

221 (C-34-1020), Deposit 10. H. 0.125; D. foot 0.048; max. D. 0.068; D. shoulder 0.061. Pease 124. Pls. 9, 48.

222 (C-39-101), Deposit 8. H. 0.12; D. foot 0.042; max. D. 0.066; D. shoulder 0.062.

5th century B.C., third to fourth quarter

223 (KP 930), Deposit 13. H. 0.12; D. foot 0.05; max. D. 0.073.

146 B.C.

224 (C-47-128), Deposit 96. H. 0.122; av. D. foot 0.032; max. D. 0.054.

H. 0.11+

500 B.C.

225 (C-40-39), Deposit 25. P.H. 0.107; D. foot 0.051; max. D. 0.071; D. shoulder 0.061.

226 (C-40-40), Deposit 25. P.H. 0.109; D. foot 0.047; max. D. 0.068; D. shoulder 0.06.

5th century B.C., second quarter

227 (C-39-100), Deposit 8. H. 0.115; D. foot 0.049; max. D. at shoulder 0.064.

228 (C-39-7), Deposit 8. H. 0.111; D. foot 0.05; max. D. 0.073; D. shoulder 0.068. Pls. 9, 48.

5th century B.C., third to fourth quarter

229 (KP 715), Deposit 13. H. 0.117; D. foot 0.045; max. D. 0.067; D. shoulder 0.062.

230 (C-36-1074), Deposit 11. P.H. 0.102; D. foot 0.042; max. D. at shoulder 0.066.

4th century B.C., first to second quarter

231 (C-37-485), Deposit 79. P.H. 0.116; D. foot 0.049.

232 (C-36-977), Deposit 15. H. 0.115; D. foot 0.044; max. D. 0.063; D. shoulder 0.054.

3rd century B.C.

233 (C-47-322), Deposit 109. H. 0.117; D. foot 0.042; max. D. 0.061. Pls. 9, 48.

H. 0.10+

350 B.C.

234 (KP 121), Deposit 18. H. 0.104; D. foot 0.037; max. D. 0.053; D. shoulder 0.047.

H. 0.09+

550 B.C.

235 (C-53-153), Deposit 1. P.H. 0.082; D. foot 0.05. Unglazed. Brann 58.

6th century B.C., third quarter

236 (C-47-749), Deposit 2. P.H. 0.078; D. foot 0.045.

237 (KP 367), Deposit 9. H. 0.099; D. foot 0.04; max. D. 0.056; D. shoulder 0.052.

5th century B.C., third to fourth quarter

238 (KP 719), Deposit 13. H. 0.098; D. foot 0.042; max. D. 0.06; D. shoulder 0.055.

H. 0.08+

550 B.C.

239 (C-53-93), Deposit 1. H. 0.088; D. foot 0.037; max. D. 0.058; D. shoulder 0.054. Unglazed. Brann 56.

240 (C-47-755), Deposit 2. H. 0.088; D. foot 0.044; max. D. 0.061.

5th century B.C., third to fourth quarters

241 (KP 964), Deposit 13. H. 0.089; D. foot 0.038; max. D. 0.054; D. foot 0.052.

242 (CP-829), Deposit 49. H. 0.088; D. foot 0.033; max. D. 0.053; D. shoulder 0.05.

243 (C-37-510), Deposit 79. P.H. 0.074; D. foot 0.038; max. D. 0.056.

350 B.C.

244 (KP 834), Deposit 18. P.H. 0.077; D. foot 0.035; max. D. 0.051; D. shoulder 0.049.

SMALL TREFOIL OINOCHOE[41] **245–270**, Pls. 10, 48.

Intermediate stages, 475 to 300 B.C.

Deposits: 7, 8, 13, 15, 18, 41, 42, 50–52, 63, 93, 98, 107, 113.

Oinochoai of this series have a disk foot and a bulging wall profile which is continuous in curve from the base to the trefoil lip. The handle rises from just above the middle of the wall and arches above and down to the top of the lip. The quality of manufacture is only adequate throughout the series. The walls are fairly thin. Normally, from the earliest to the latest here, dipped glaze covers the interior of the lip and the outer wall down to about the point of greatest circumference or slightly below. Six sizes are known, representing each centimeter of height between 0.09 and 0.04 m. The size series height 0.07+ m. has the most extensive representation. The larger sizes are usable. The smaller sizes are miniatures. Some examples of height 0.07+ m. and smaller were found in graves.

Possibly production of this series of small pitchers may have begun as early as the first quarter of the 6th century. A seemingly related Middle Corinthian figured example of that time is attested (T 1550: *N. Cemetery*, 168-5, pl. 27). A gap of about 100 years exists at present, however, between it and the earliest below. It is also possible that the series may have continued in production later than the latest here, of the end of the 4th century B.C. This consideration prompts the inclusion of the series in this publication.

Examples from deposits indicate that several criteria exist for placement of oinochoai of this series in a relative chronological order. These criteria will be more valid, of course, for the larger oinochoai than for the miniature size series. One criterion is a trend toward constriction of the diameter of the base. A second is a trend toward a gradual rise of the point of greatest circumference of the wall, the outline changing with the rise from an initial dumpy to a later rotund and thence to a subsequent pear shape. The series arranged on the basis of these trends exhibits others to be expected in the advancing age of a shape series. The initial thin disk foot, nicely finished beneath and sometimes slightly concave here, becomes thicker as it becomes more constricted in diameter and the bottom is left unworked, with string marks. Bases carefully finished beneath occur until the end of the 5th century in the present examples. Ones unfinished beneath, however, may occur as early as the third quarter of the 5th century. All 4th century examples are unfinished here. The general outline of the handle may be an additional criterion, though comparatively few are preserved. Initial and early examples, through the third quarter of the 5th century, have a handle which rises nearly straight up from the body and straight down to the lip. Beginning with those of the last quarter of the 5th century and continuing to the end of the 4th century the handle curves out both ascending and descending, giving the outline an ear-shaped profile.

H. 0.09

4th century B.C., last quarter

245 (C-47-151), Deposit 98. H. 0.09; D. base 0.038; max. D. 0.07; H. to max. D. 0.035.

H. 0.08+

430–420 B.C.

246 (KP 963), Deposit 13. H. 0.08; D. base 0.045; max. D. 0.069; H. to max. D. 0.027.

---

[41] It has not been possible to examine all the "Small Trefoil Oinochoai" listed in *N. Cemetery*, pp. 132–133. Some of them for this reason not included in the present catalogue may actually belong to the present series. Others listed under this heading in the North Cemetery volume clearly belong to quite different shape series.

4th century B.C., last quarter
  247 (C-47-467), Deposit 113. H. 0.085; D. base 0.033; max. D. 0.069; H. to max. D. 0.037.
  248 (C-47-468), Deposit 113. H. 0.085; D. base 0.035; max. D. 0.069; H. to max. D. 0.036.
  249 (C-46-58), Deposit 107. Fragment. P.H. 0.075.

H. 0.07+
  5th century B.C., second quarter
  250 (C-36-973), Deposit 15. H. 0.074; D. base 0.049; max. D. 0.068; H. to max. D. 0.023.
  251 (CP-371). H. 0.078; D. base 0.048; max. D. 0.07; H. to max. D. 0.025. Pls. 10, 48.
  252 (CP-370). H. 0.072; D. base 0.048; max. D. 0.064; H. to max. D. 0.023.
  5th century B.C., third quarter
  253 (C-39-86), Deposit 8. H. 0.079; D. base 0.043; max. D. 0.07; H. to max. D. 0.03.
  254 (C-31-131), Deposit 41. H. 0.079; D. base 0.043; max. D. 0.07; H. to max. D. 0.03.
  5th century B.C., last quarter
  255 (CP-608), Deposit 50. H. 0.076; D. base 0.041; max. D. 0.07; H. to max. D. 0.033. Pls. 10, 48.
  4th century B.C., first quarter
  256 (KP 2525), Deposit 18. H. 0.076; D. base 0.038; max. D. 0.068; H. to max. D. 0.028.
  4th century B.C., third quarter
  257 (T 2413). H. 0.075; D. base 0.035; max. D. 0.06; H. to max. D. 0.032. *N. Cemetery*, X-176.
  4th century B.C., last quarter
  258 (T 2617), Deposit 52. H. 0.076; D. base 0.031; max. D. 0.062; H. to max. D. 0.031. *N. Cemetery*, 463-2, pl. 26. Pls. 10, 48.

H. 0.06+
  5th century B.C., second quarter
  259 (KP 1312), Deposit 7. H. 0.065; D. base 0.045; max. D. 0.056; H. to max. D. 0.023.

5th century B.C., last quarter
  260 (KP 688), Deposit 18. H. 0.063; D. base 0.035; max. D. 0.06; H. to max. D. 0.023.
350 B.C.
  261 (C-31-274), Deposit 42. H. 0.064; D. base 0.031; max. D. 0.055; H. to max. D. 0.025.
  262 (T 2533), Deposit 51. H. 0.064; D. base 0.032; max. D. 0.054; H. to max. D. 0.026. *N. Cemetery*, 442-5.
325 B.C.
  263 (T 1164), Deposit 63. H. 0.067; D. base 0.035; max. D. 0.058; H. to max. D. 0.025. *N. Cemetery*, 491-6, pl. 76.

H. 0.05+
  5th century B.C., third quarter
  264 (KP 835), Deposit 18. H. 0.053; D. base 0.035; max. D. 0.053; H. to max. D. 0.018.
  265 (KP 684), Deposit 18. H. 0.054; D. base 0.034; max. D. 0.054; H. to max. D. 0.018.
  4th century B.C., first quarter
  266 (C-28-85). H. 0.059; D. base 0.035; max. D. 0.052; H. to max. D. 0.021.
  267 (C-33-116), Deposit 93. H. 0.054; D. base 0.034; max. D. 0.051; H. to max. D. 0.021.
  268 (T 2666). H. 0.057; D. base 0.032; max. D. 0.052; H. to max. D. 0.023. *N. Cemetery*, X-181.
  4th century B.C., last quarter
  269 (T 2582). H. 0.05; D. base 0.027; max. D. 0.042; H. to max. D. 0.02. *N. Cemetery*, X-179.

H. 0.04+
  4th century B.C., third quarter
  270 (MP 143). H. 0.049; D. base 0.029; max. D. 0.042; H. to max. D. 0.02.

SMALL TREFOIL OINOCHOE, SHOULDER STOP **271-278**, Pls. 10, 48.
Advanced to late stages, 5th century, fourth quarter to 3rd century B.C., first quarter.
Deposits: 18, 53, 54.

The pieces catalogued below appear on present information to be members of a basic shape series which has a number of collateral relatives.[42] The series is small and incompletely documented. The demonstration of its own validity as a single shape series and the relationship of the allied oinochoai will require reconsideration when additional examples and evidence for dating are available.

The examples here are characterized by a very thin, inconspicuous flat base or foot, a steep, gently rounded wall profile, a more or less strongly concave neck profile beginning at the shoulder, and an

---

[42] The related oinochoai are as follows: IP 557, from Isthmia, and **279** (profile continuous from lip to base); KP 711 (thickened neck); T 1060, *N. Cemetery*, X-197 (no base, bottom concave, straight wall, articulation at shoulder and base of neck); T 2560, *N. Cemetery*, D 23-d (round mouth). The following do not appear to be related to the series: T 1440 (*N. Cemetery*, 301-3, pl. 41); T 602 (*ibid.*, X-195); and T 603 (*ibid.*, X-196). The fragmentary T 1067 (*ibid.*, X-198) may belong.

outturned lip which is only slightly pinched in to make it a trefoil. A broad strap handle rises from the shoulder and arches above and down to the top of the lip. The mouth was intended to receive a "cocked hat" lid: two examples from graves have their original lids. The walls of the earlier oinochoai are fairly thin, their quality of manufacture pleasing. The walls of the latest are heavier and the quality of execution less satisfactory. All are unglazed. Four sizes are represented: heights 0.09+, 0.08+, 0.07+, and 0.06+ m.

It seems possible that the initial stage of production of the shape is not represented by the earliest examples below since the definition of the shoulder stop (the point at which the concave profile of the neck and the convex profile of the wall meet) is not as sharp as might be expected in an entirely new shape. The date of the earliest examples here is also only vaguely defined. For the single late example there is no evidence for date by context. Its stage in the series may well be close to the final one for the shape.

The evidence available indicates that the trends of shape change in the series are toward constriction of the diameters of the various elements of the shape, base, greatest diameters of wall, shoulder, and neck. Arrangement of the series on this basis indicates that a corresponding trend toward carelessness of execution may be expected to accompany these changes, when more late examples are known. All the examples through those of *ca.* 350 B.C. have a flat or slightly concave bottom set off from the wall by a shallow groove. In all of these the bottom is carefully finished except one of 350 B.C., which is left unfinished with string marks. In the latest example the groove is retained, but the underside is pared so as to form an irregular, low ring foot. The formation of the wall of the latest is correspondingly casual as compared with those of earlier examples.

H. 0.09+
  5th century B.C., fourth quarter
    271 (KP 230), Deposit 18. H. 0.097; D. base 0.08; max. D. 0.095; D. shoulder 0.075; D. neck 0.052.
  350 B.C.
    272 (KP 231), Deposit 18. H. 0.096; D. base 0.065; max. D. 0.084; D. shoulder 0.0705; D. neck 0.05.
H. 0.08+
  4th century B.C., first quarter
    273 (KP 876), Deposit 18. H. 0.08; D. base 0.06; max. D. 0.079; D. shoulder 0.06; D. neck 0.045. Pls. 10, 48.
  350 B.C.
    274 (T 2651), Deposit 54. H. 0.087; D. base 0.057; max. D. 0.076; D. shoulder 0.06; D. neck 0.041. *N. Cemetery*, D 28-b. Pls. 10, 48.

3rd century B.C., first quarter
    275 (C-65-169). H. 0.089; D. base 0.045; max. D. 0.073; D. shoulder 0.052; D. neck 0.033. Pls. 10, 48.
H. 0.07+
  350 B.C.
    276 (T 2370), Deposit 53. H. 0.072; D. base 0.046; max. D. 0.072; D. shoulder 0.056; D. neck 0.039. *N. Cemetery*, D 36-c, pl. 73.
H. 0.06+
  5th century B.C., fourth quarter
    277 (KP 702), Deposit 18. H. 0.066; D. base 0.047; max. D. 0.066; D. shoulder 0.056; D. neck 0.037.
  350 B.C.
    278 (KP 682), Deposit 18. H. 0.065; D. base 0.04; max. D. 0.063; D. shoulder 0.053; D. neck 0.038.

SMALL TREFOIL OINOCHOE, SHOULDER STOP, VARIANT **279**, Pls. 10, 48.
Late stage, 3rd century B.C., first quarter.
Deposit: 113.

The single example of this shape is perhaps in some way related to the small trefoil oinochoe with shoulder stop (**271–278**). It has a crudely formed false ring foot. Its body, plumply pear-shaped in outline, has walls on which the wheel marks have not been finished off, and whose profile is continuous from base to lip. The broad lip is very slightly pinched in at two points, no doubt a vestigial trefoil form. The strap handle rises from the upper wall and arches above and down to the top of the lip. It is made of thin clay. There is no trace of glaze. It would seem to be a late example of the series to which it belongs.

Its context provides only a general dating between *ca.* 330 and 146 B.C. The more precise date offered is merely an estimate based on its presumed relationship to the oinochoe with shoulder stop.

3rd century B.C., first quarter
279 (C-47-444), Deposit 113. H. 0.086; D. base
0.049; max. D. wall 0.084; D. neck 0.047.
Pls. 10, 48.

JUGLET **280**, Pls. 10, 49.
Advanced stage, Hellenistic prior to 146 B.C.
Deposit: 111.

This form, of which only a single example is known at present, has a flat bottom of small diameter (0.026 m.). The greatest diameter of the body is somewhat low, just below the level of the lower handle attachment. Above this the profile constricts gradually in a steep outline, turning outward without articulation to form a simple lip round in plan. The plain, vertical strap handle, set somewhat askew, rises only slightly above the level of the top of the lip. The vessel is made of fairly thin but strong clay. There is no trace of glaze.

No Classical antecedent for the form seems to be known at present. The context of this example provides only a general dating between *ca.* 330 and 146 B.C. The treatment of the elements of the form suggests that this example is not early in its shape series.

Hellenistic, prior to 146 B.C.
280 (C-47-410), Deposit 111. H. 0.06; D. 0.062;
D. bottom 0.026. Flat bottom. Profile of body
continuous from bottom to top of lip. Vertical
strap handle. Pls. 10, 49.

SMALL WATER PITCHER **281**, Pls. 10, 49.
Late stage, 2nd century B.C., first half.
Deposit: 110.

The shape is a small version, in the fabric of glazed ware, of the coarse-ware water pitcher (**631, 632**, *q.v.*). It has a ring foot, constricted in diameter relative to the greatest diameter of the body which is at the shoulder. The slope of the shoulder is very gentle. There is distinct articulation between the shoulder and the neck. The neck has a tapered profile, broader above. The overhanging lip has a rounded profile. The attachments of the strap handle are at the outer shoulder and on the upper neck. Two wheel-run grooved lines encircle the neck about a third of the way down. There is no indication of glazing.

The single example is dated by context. In form it has been discussed below in connection with the Corinthian coarse-ware pitchers of the same shape and their foreign counterparts. Although this pitcher is perfectly usable for carrying and pouring a small quantity of liquid and the reason for producing this small version of an ordinarily sizable shape may be no more than pure utility, it is perhaps notable that in Athens small pitchers[43] of the same shape (differing in profile because they are early Hellenistic

---

[43] Athenian Agora: P 18580, P 18471, *Hesperia*, XX, 1951, pl. 52, a, 13, and pl. 54, a, 11. An Attic small water pitcher (H. 0.125 m.), C-65-391, probably of the 3rd century B.C., has been found in Corinth.

versions of the form) and of much the same size (H. 0.104 and 0.125 m.) were found in pyre groups, perhaps of a sacrificial nature.

2nd century B.C., first half
   281 (C-48-127), Deposit 110. H. 0.123; D. foot 0.04; max. D. 0.08; H. to max. D. 0.06; D.

lower neck 0.048; D. upper neck est. 0.058; H. of neck and lip 0.055; D. lip est. 0.067. Pls. 10, 49.

DECANTER **282–306**.

Introduction

The name decanter is here used to mean a two-handled jug, adopting the interpretation of the function of such vessels offered by Corbett (p. 334, under no. 92).

The idea of a decanter seems to have been introduced into Corinthian pottery in the later Archaic period. Although the present representation of decanters in succeeding centuries is sporadic it would seem that a need was felt for these specialized vessels throughout the remaining Greek period of Corinth down to the time of the destruction by Mummius in 146 B.C.

At present a total of six versions of the idea are known in Corinthian pottery. Three seem to have been short-lived experiments which did not create enough demand for their repetition.[44] Two versions, however, were evolved in the third quarter of the 5th century which met with approval. These are the forms designated below as Decanters I and II. Both, it would seem, derive from a long tradition of shape design, going back to the Early Corinthian period, in which there was lively experiment in and adaptation of an oinochoe shape to which Patricia Lawrence and D. A. Amyx propose to give the name of the Corinth Oinochoe.[45] Decanter I is possibly directly antecedent to the latest, Hellenistic, decanter. Decanter II seems almost certainly antecedent to the sixth version, Decanter III. III was evidently introduced to meet new requirements in the second quarter of the 4th century. Its survival into the 3rd century B.C. is attested.

Decanter I **282–286**, Pls. 11, 49.

Initial and very late stages, 5th century, third quarter to 2nd century B.C., first half.
Deposits: 10, 109.

The single Hellenistic example of this form, **286**, has a very thin, constricted disk foot. The flaring lip, the short neck, the broad, steeply rounded shoulder and the lower body are in a continuous curve of profile except for a suggestion of articulation, perhaps not accidental, just above the greatest diameter. Two plain strap handles are attached, at an angle of about 60° to one another, on the upper shoulder and at the lip. Three fingers and a thumb on one handle provide the most convenient grip for using the

[44] Each of the three is known in only a single catalogued example. The probably earliest is from a context of 550–480 B.C., C-37-2056, Deposit 3 (Campbell 150). The second variety in time, probably of the first half of the 5th century B.C., is C-39-22, Deposit 8. The third, of the third quarter of the 5th century, is C-36-1116, Deposit 11. This is one of the "two vases with two handles on the same side of the vase" to which reference is made in Pease, p. 294, under nos. 151–153. Evidently the second vase was not catalogued, and it is thus permissible to infer that it was of the same form as the first. C-36-1116 has a strong resemblance in form to an Athenian version of the decanter which Amyx has suggested (*Hesperia*, XXVII, 1958, pp. 208–211) may in ancient times have been called *myke*. It may be a Corinthian adaptation of the Athenian form. The Athenian myke seems to have been produced in Athens only over a short period, from the third quarter of the 5th century to the middle of the 4th century B.C. (Corbett, p. 334, under no. 92).

[45] The variations on the theme are considerable and the connection between the decanters and the Corinth Oinochoe is the loose but nonetheless real one of shape design. No specific oinochoe design within the term Corinth Oinochoe is closely antecedent in actual shape to the forms of Decanters I and II, though clearly the potters working in the Corinth Oinochoe tradition invented them.

vessel. The fabric would ordinarily be taken for coarse but it is of a more efficient and durable consistency than is usual in Corinthian coarse ware. The surfaces are covered with a fine slip. There is no decoration of any kind.

The context from which it comes provides only a wide dating between *ca.* 330 and 146 B.C. That this decanter is late in this long period is indicated by its general resemblance in form to a cooking-ware decanter, **749**, Deposit 46, of the time of Mummius' destruction of Corinth in 146 B.C.

The suggestion is here made that this decanter represents one of the latest stages in a direct shape development of a form introduced in Corinthian pottery in the third quarter of the 5th century, represented by **282–285** in the catalogue below. The difference in time between it and these is indeed considerable, probably approaching three centuries, and certainly the connection in a single shape series of vessels so widely separated in time, without intermediate examples, will require more assured demonstration. At present the connection seems a fair possibility since strong likenesses in form exist between the early group and the late decanter, the differences are ones to be expected in a long shape development, and the elements present in the earlier, lacking in the later, are ones which could readily be expected to disappear in the course of production.

In the 5th century examples the disk base is broad. A wheel groove is set well within the perimeter on the underside. As in the late example, the profile is continuous from the outturned lip to the base save for semi-articulation just above the greatest diameter. The strap handles are also set at mid-shoulder and at the edge of the lip, though rather more widely, at an angle of about 90⁰ to one another. The handles have each a central vertical rib (an embellishment which is seen to have disappeared in the late examples of Decanter III), and since they are short only two fingers and a thumb can be used for gripping. The forms of the 5th century decanters are decorated with glaze bands, one around the outer profile of the base, one below and one above the greatest diameter, one on the top of the lip; an additional line appears just within the neck of two of the four. Aside from the solid base and fairly substantial handles, the form is made of thin but strong clay which is fairly highly polished on the exterior surface.

D. 0.17+ – 0.16+
  460–420 B.C.
    282 (C-34-947), Deposit 10. Max. D. est. 0.17; av. H. 0.162; H. to max. D. 0.07; D. base 0.117; D. lip 0.095. Pease 152.
    283 (C-34-946), Deposit 10. Max. D. 0.163; av. H. 0.158; H. to max. D. 0.065; D. base 0.103; D. lip 0.089. Pease 151. Pls. 11, 49.
    284 (C-34-948), Deposit 10. Base and part of lower wall missing. Max. D. 0.17; P.H. 0.147; est. D. lip 0.085. Pease 153.

285 (C-34-1194), Deposit 10. Base and much of lower wall missing. Max. D. *ca.* 0.173; P.H. 0.095; D. lip 0.088.
2nd century B.C., first half
  286 (C-47-314), Deposit 109. Max. D. 0.167; av. H. 0.208; H. to max. D. 0.09; D. base 0.067; D. lip 0.09. Pls. 11, 49.

Decanter II[46] **287–300**, Pls. 12, 49.

Initial to late stages, 5th century, third quarter to 4th century B.C., early first quarter.
Deposits: 10, 20, 79, 80.

This variety has throughout what is essentially a broad, slightly spreading disk base, with modifications in later examples which give it the superficial appearance of a shallow ring foot. The profile of the

---

[46] Athens, Agora, P 10941 (Corbett 165) evidently is also an example of Decanter II, of the large size (H. 0.154; D. 0.181). Corbett, p. 335, under no. 92, suggested that it was possibly of Corinthian manufacture. From a deposit of the last quarter of the 5th century, it seems to correspond to the contemporary Corinthian examples of Decanter II in every way except in having a base unfinished on the underside.
For the relationship of Decanter II to the Athenian Oinochoe shape 9 see footnote 48.

broadly pulvinated body is continuous in curve with that of the neck. The lip is overhanging and its outer profile is bevelled in varying degrees of steepness nearly to perpendicular. The two strap handles are attached a few centimeters apart, at an angle of about 45° to one another, on the middle of the shoulder and on the lower edge of the lip. Two fingers, not more, and a thumb can be used to grip the handle. No doubt ordinarily a single handle was used in this fashion for gripping and pouring, since any other method of grasping this kind of decanter is rather awkward and unsatisfactory for the purpose. Apart from the solid base and fairly thick handles the form is made of relatively thin clay which is polished, sometimes (early) to a high degree of luster, on all the exterior. Glaze bands are wheel painted around the profile of the base, below and above the greatest diameter, and around the outer edge of the lip. One or two further bands appear also on the inside of the lip or neck, where these are preserved, and a few have in addition still another on the lower wall just above the base. The underside of the base has no glaze decoration. It would seem that a distinction in sizes in the series is to be made on the basis of the greatest diameter measurements of the body. They are two: *ca.* 0.18 m. and *ca.* 0.15–0.16 m. Conceivably this unusual circumstance may have something to do with the liquid capacity of the vessels.[47] All are of much the same height, between 0.154 and 0.166 m.

Context evidence and other considerations indicate that Decanter II was introduced well within the third quarter of the 5th century, the fragmentary examples **298** and **299** being the earliest. The placement of these fully within the third quarter, of others at 425 B.C., and those of a subsequent stage in the early first quarter of the 4th century is prompted in part by contexts and in part by estimates backward from the earliest examples of Decanter III below, whose body form (with modifications of other elements to meet new requirements) is believed to be in a direct line of shape development with that of Decanter II. The body form of the earliest examples of Decanter III, by context evidence not later than the early third quarter of the 4th century, is very advanced. Between it and that of the latest examples of Decanter II a very considerable time allowance must be made, placing the latest examples of II probably no later than the early first quarter, *ca.* 50 years earlier. As a result the earlier two stages of II must be placed back as far as their context evidence permits.[48] For the end of production of Decanter II reasons have been developed below (p. 61) for thinking that it may have continued into the second quarter of the 4th century, although we have no examples of so late a date at present.[49]

In the series some differences in form exist. One, in the form of the handle, between those of 425 B.C. and those of the early 4th century, is probably due only to manufacture in two different workshops and may represent only individual idiosyncracies. The former, **287**, **288**, and **300**, have a strap handle with a central vertical rib. The latter, all from one deposit and probably from one workshop, have the reverse one with a central vertical groove. The other differences are more likely to be chronological. Those in the form of the bottom of the base provide a natural shape progression. In the earlier, of the third quarter of the 5th century and 425 B.C., it is a true disk base, slightly concave beneath, with a shallow wheel-run groove set well within the periphery giving just the slightest suggestion of a broad ring foot. In those of the early first quarter of the 4th century the base looks much more like a ring foot. The groove is deep and set closer to the outer edge, and the surface within it has been turned so as to form a rounded surface between the groove and the shallow central conical depression. Four of the earlier are

[47] Cf. Amyx' comments on the capacities of the Attic decanter (myke), *Hesperia*, XXVII, 1958, p. 210.

[48] The dating of those assigned to 425 B.C. is somewhat strengthened by the context of Athens, Agora, P 10941, for which see footnote 46.

The dating of those assigned to the third quarter of the 5th century is strongly supported by their close resemblance in form (aside from the single arching handle) to an Athenian Oinochoe shape 9 by the Shuvalov Painter (*A.R.V.²*, p. 1208, no. 41; Pfuhl, *M.u.z.*, fig. 787).

[49] Since the above was written an example from Isthmia, IP 2843, has been noted. In form it may be of the second quarter of the 4th century. H. 0.116; D. base 0.095; max. D. 0.154; H. to max. D. 0.07; D. lip 0.079. The handles are of the plain strap variety without ribbing or grooving.

of high quality, the surfaces highly polished. The latest are uniformly of somewhat less high quality, the surfaces, though polished in some degree, dull.

D. 0.18+
425 B.C.

287 (C-37-451), Deposit 79. Max. D. 0.184; H. 0.154; H. to max. D. 0.06; D. base est. 0.124; D. lip 0.092. Pls. 12, 49.

288 (C-37-454), Deposit 79. Base and much of wall missing. Max. D. est. 0.184; P.H. 0.088; D. lip 0.103.

4th century B.C., early first quarter

289 (C-37-245), Deposit 80.[50] Max D. 0.186; H. 0.164; H. to max. D. 0.065; D. base 0.125; D. lip 0.10.

290 (C-37-242), Deposit 80. Max. D. 0.187; H. 0.159; H. to max. D. 0.06; D. base 0.124; D. lip 0.10.

291 (C-37-243), Deposit 80. Max. D. 0.187; H. 0.165; H. to max. D. 0.068; D. base 0.123; D. lip 0.102. Pls. 12, 49.

292 (C-37-241), Deposit 80. Max. D. 0.19; av. H. 0.169; H. to max. D. 0.07; D. base 0.12; D. lip 0.097.

293 (C-37-240), Deposit 80. Max. D. 0.186; H. 0.166; H. to max. D. 0.065; D. base 0.123; D. lip 0.10.

294 (C-37-244), Deposit 80. Max. D. 0.181; H. 0.158; H. to max. D. 0.058; D. base 0.128; D. lip 0.099.

295 (C-37-247), Deposit 80. Neck, lip and handles missing. Max. D. 0.182; P.H. 0.104; H. to max. D. 0.07; D. base 0.125.

296 (C-37-246), Deposit 80. Neck, lip and handles missing. Max. D. 0.19; P.H. 0.105; H. to max. D. 0.07; D. base 0.123.

297 (C-37-248), Deposit 80. Neck, lip and handles missing. Max. D. 0.183; P.H. 0.113; H. to max. D. 0.065; D. base 0.124.

D. 0.16+ – 0.15+
5th century B.C., third quarter

298 (C-34-1195), Deposit 10. Neck, lip and handles missing. Max. D. 0.168; P.H. 0.107; H. to max. D. 0.06; D. base 0.13.

299 (C-34-1196), Deposit 10. Neck, lip and handles missing. Max. D. 0.155; P.H. ca. 0.09; H. to max. D. 0.05; D. base 0.113.

425 B.C.

300 (C-31-66), Deposit 20. Max. D. 0.168; H. 0.155; H. to max. D. 0.055; D. base 0.098; D. lip 0.098. *Asklepieion*, p. 135, no. 60, and pl. 50 (for C-3217 read: C-31-66).

Decanter III[51] 301–306, Pls. 12, 49.

Intermediate stages, 4th century, early third quarter to 3rd century B.C., first quarter.
Deposits: 36, 42, 88, 90.

Decanter III has a solid disk foot, finished plain and slightly concave beneath. The profile of the body, pulvinated in outline, and that of the neck form a continuous curve. It has a prominent collar lip, broader above. The strap handles are set at an angle of about 45° to one another in the smaller examples, at one of about 60° in the large example, 301. The neck of Decanter III is taller and the handles longer than those of Decanter II. Consequently examples of Decanter III can be grasped more strongly, using more fingers, than was possible with examples of Decanter II. Aside from the solid base the form in the earlier examples is made of relatively thin clay and the quality of manufacture is good. In the later, the clay is somewhat more substantial and the quality rather less good. Glaze bands, wheel painted, appear on the body and on the inner and outer lip. Possibly, as among the examples of Decanter II, a distinction in sizes is to be made on the basis of the greatest diameter of the body. If so, there are three: *ca.* 0.21 (not represented in Decanter II), *ca.* 0.18 (corresponding to 287–297, Decanter II), and *ca.* 0.16–0.15 m. (corresponding to 298, 299, and 300, Decanter II).

[50] Those from Deposit 80 are presumably the ones to which reference is made in Pease, p. 294, under 151–153: "several vases from under the Agora floor: more bulbous in shape."

[51] Thompson B 33 is evidently a foreign version of Decanter III. Corbett, p. 335, under no. 92, has already noted that it may be an import to Athens. It would also seem not to be Corinthian. The fabric as described is not like that of any Corinthian decanter. It differs from any known Corinthian example also in having a very steep shoulder, short neck and rolled rim. Although 301 has, exceptionally in the series, five glazed bands on the body their position is different from that of the bands on B 33. No Corinthian example has *four* bands inside the lip. It is notable also that the size of B 33 (D. 0.195 m.) is not represented among the Corinthian decanters.

The time of the introduction and the beginning of production of Decanter III can perhaps be suggested by inference with some precision as within the second quarter of the 4th century. It has already been suggested (above, p. 59) that Decanter III is a modified continuation of Decanter II. The reason for modification may plausibly be thought to be a need for a more concentrated and more precisely directed flow of the wine which the vessels presumably contained. Decanter II, with its broad neck splaying widely above to a lip bevelled outward, provided a rather broad flow of liquid and could be used economically and acceptably only with a broad receptacle. Decanter III, with its nearly cylindrical neck and closely fitting collar lip, provided a narrow flow which could be more accurately directed, and hence would have been efficient even with receptacles of quite constricted diameters. It has been suggested above that a period of about 50 years must be allowed between the latest known examples of Decanter II and the earliest of III, between the early first quarter of the 4th century and the early third quarter. It seems not coincidental that during this time old broad forms of the drinking cup, the kylix in its many varieties, began to go out of use and that within the second quarter of the 4th century new series of drinking cups, the various calyx kantharoi and other forms with constricted mouths, were introduced and quickly became enormously and very widely popular. The preference for relatively narrow and deep drinking cups,[52] once introduced, prevailed for many years, and it is not until well along in the 3rd century that there is any strong reversion to broader drinking vessels. It may be supposed, then, with some reason, that as long as broad drinking cups were popular, perhaps into the second quarter of the 4th century, Decanter II, suitable for them, continued to be produced and that, as soon as the new drinking cups began to supplant the old, Decanter III was introduced in replacement of II to meet their requirements. The two varieties may have overlapped in production for a short while. The earliest examples of Decanter III in the catalogue below are presumably, then, of an early stage of the new shape, not long after its first appearance.

The end of production of Decanter III is not yet as clearly indicated. On context evidence the earliest examples of Decanter III here are not later than the early third quarter of the 4th century. The contexts, both of wide range, of the two later examples would permit a date as late as the second quarter of the 3rd century for one, the last quarter for the other. The degree of difference in shape development between the earlier and the later is not great, however; hence an allowance of 50 years difference in time between them seems sufficient, with placement in the first quarter of the 3rd century (probably early in it) for the later. To what further stage the shape may have been produced remains to be seen.

Notable differences exist between the earlier and later which may be significant for relative chronology. Those in clay and quality of manufacture have already been noted. Others concern the forms of the lip and handle, the treatment of the shoulder, and the placement of the glaze banding. The broad collar lip of the earlier, approaching perpendicular in profile, is transformed to a narrower one in the later which is much greater in diameter above. The central vertical rib of the strap handle of the earlier has flattened out and disappeared in the later. The rather abrupt transition in profile between neck and body in the earlier has become a more gradual curve in the later. The earlier examples have glaze banding in the tradition of Decanter II: one below, one above the greatest diameter of the body, one around the exterior of the lip and one inside. In the later the syntax has relaxed as far as the body is concerned. One, 306, has three bands, one each below, at, and above the greatest diameter. The other, 301, has five, from the greatest diameter up to the handle roots.

---

[52] In this connection one of the old standard drinking cups, the skyphos of Attic type (307–371), popular in Corinth as well as in Athens through the 4th century B.C., is notable. In the 5th century and in the early years of the 4th century it was a broad, generously open vessel. By the middle years of the 4th century it had become very much more constricted.

D. 0.21+

3rd century B.C., first quarter

  301 (C-40-413), Deposit 36. Max. D. 0.217; av. H. 0.214; H. to max. D. 0.08; D. base 0.108; D. lip 0.09. Pls. 12, 49.

D. 0.18+

4th century B.C., early third quarter

  302 (C-37-2521), Deposit 90. Max. D. 0.187; av. H. 0.188; H. to max. D. 0.075; D. base 0.103; D. lip 0.078. Pls. 12, 49.

  303 (C-37-2662 a, b), Deposit 90. Much of wall missing. Max. D. est. 0.182; P.H. 0.131; D. base 0.105; D. lip 0.075.

304 (C-53-60), Deposit 88. Neck, lip and handles missing. Max. D. 0.185; P.H. 0.115; H. to max. D. 0.075; D. base 0.105.

D. 0.16+ − 0.15+

4th century B.C., early third quarter

  305 (C-31-238), Deposit 42. Base and most of wall missing. Max. D. more than 0.15; P.H. 0.097; D. lip 0.069.

3rd century B.C., first quarter

  306 (C-31-280), Deposit 42. Max. D. 0.166; H. 0.184; H. to max. D. 0.07; D. base 0.092; D. lip 0.078.

DRINKING VESSELS 307–554

INTRODUCTION

The fine-ware, wheelmade drinking cups produced in Corinth during the Hellenistic period which are grouped here have been classified below under two main headings, deep shapes and broad shapes. The deep shapes will be fairly easily recognizable to the modern, non-professional eye as drinking cups, even though they differ in form from our modern ideas of what a drinking vessel, especially one for wine, should be, one major difference being, normally, the provision of two handles, the exception being the Hexamilia mug which has one. About the broad shapes the modern spectator may feel much less conviction. These include handleless shapes of hemispherical, conical, or breast-shape outline with no separate foot or at most appliqué supports for stability. They have no modern connotations as drinking vessels, but the idea of vessels of such broad, open forms as drinking cups was the predominant one in the advanced and late years of the Hellenistic period in Corinth, best exemplified in the more familiar moulded drinking bowls discussed separately below. The two varieties of broad drinking cups with recurved handles are also strange to us, but their use as drinking vessels becomes plausible in the light of the broad kylix forms with two handles which had been popular in Classical times in Greece.

The sizes and capacities of the drinking vessels here, viewed in the light of their probable use as wine cups, will also cause some consternation to the present day spectator. A gradation of sizes is represented in most of the series of drinking vessels here, in the deep shapes a range between heights 0.22 and 0.06 m., in the broad shapes between lip diameters 0.18 and 0.11 m. Of the examples now known the fairly capacious sizes are the most numerous. As a rough index, in the deep shapes ca. 67% occur in sizes between heights 0.13 and 0.09 m. with estimated capacities between ca. 1000 and ca. 200 cc.,[53] ca. 22% occur in the larger sizes, heights 0.22 to 0.14 m., and ca. 11% in the smaller, 0.08 m. and below. The most numerous size is, by height, 0.09–0.10 m., with a capacity of ca. 300 cc. It is normally assumed that wine was ordinarily served diluted in these times and the representation of sizes in the present cups attests the probability of this assumption.

A number of the shapes were produced in serviceable fabric: the skyphos, the calyx cup and kantharoi, the Hexamilia kantharos and mug, and the drinking bowls with recurved handles. The others have either lighter or really delicate walls. Only one vessel, the calyx cup, seems never to have been glazed. A second vessel, a calyx kantharos, now unglazed, 376, may have been gilded. A third, the semi-glazed

---

[53] Eight intact drinking vessels have been measured with water. Acrocorinth kantharos, 451, H. 0.12–0.13 m., ca. 1000 cc. One-piece kantharos, 385, H. 0.09 m., ca. 200 cc. Hexamilia kantharos, 520, H. 0.09–0.10 m., ca. 300 cc. Attic type of skyphoi, 341, 343, and 344, H. 0.09 m., ca. 250, 200, and 200 cc. respectively; 353 and 355, H. 0.08 m., each ca. 200 cc.

mastos, has glaze only on the interior. Examples of a few series were glazed by dipping, fully on the interior and part way down on the exterior: all the Hexamilia kantharoi and mugs, all the drinking bowls with recurved handles, and one very late example of the skyphos. The other cups, the great majority, were all given full treatment, either full glazing or glazing with minor areas reserved and painted. This is true throughout their series, early to late, and is exceptional in Corinthian fine ware of the time since most shapes originally fully glazed are found in their later stages to be partially glazed by dipping. No doubt the full treatment throughout in these is due in part to considerations of avoiding loss by seepage of wine through the walls, perhaps also to the use of these vessels on more or less formal occasions.

Generally speaking, cups of the serviceable fabric were not decorated, one example of the calyx kantharos being the only exception; those of lighter fabric were decorated. This thought can be carried further: the cups of the most delicate fabric were the most lavishly and attractively decorated of all. The decoration, that is to say decoration with ornamental patterns, where it occurs is in the West Slope technique of incision through the glaze, sometimes seen to expose pink color beneath, and applied colors usually on the glaze.

Context evidence for the limits of the periods of production of the various cup series and the dating of the various stages of their shape development is not abundant and much in need of future supplement. The general picture is, however, reasonably assured and to some extent the present evidence provides indications for absolute chronology. The picture shows, in broad outlines, an overlapping succession of three major groups of shape series. The first group was introduced in Corinthian in the Classical period and continued in production down to some time in the first half of the 3rd century, probably appreciably within that half century. It includes the skyphos of Attic type, for which a possibly extreme lower date of 275 B.C. has been suggested, and the varieties of calyx cup and kantharos, whose lower date in Corinthian can only be suggested very loosely at present.[54] The second major group may be considered purely Hellenistic since it seems likely at present that all were first introduced in Corinthian within Alexander's short reign. These are four, all kantharoi: one-piece, cyma, Acrocorinth, and articulated. The evidence provided by pottery and coins in some pertinent contexts suggests that the periods of production of all had come to an end by the third quarter or early last quarter of the 3rd century B.C., if not indeed before that. Interrelationships in details of form (or shape design) and decoration among these four series help to unite this group as contemporary in production. Two other shapes, the Hexamilia kantharos and the allied Hexamilia mug, were probably in production during the same time, though evidently with a rather later introductory date than the kantharoi. The time of the introduction of the third group is at present estimated backward from the destruction of the city in 146 B.C., with which are connected deposits containing advanced stages of many of the shapes. The estimate includes considerations of functional replacement of the earlier forms: it is, of course, evident that the earlier shapes were not abandoned until after successors in function had appeared in the market. Whatever may be true of vessels of other functions it is clear that there was no lacuna in the production of drinking cups in Corinth. Initial dates around the middle of the 3rd century or shortly thereafter thus seem indicated for a number of the new shapes. This may, of course, be a conservative dating. These new shapes include the wheelmade Megarian bowls and the conical bowl. Others, the hemispherical bowl with appliqué supports, the mastos, the semi-glazed mastos, and the thorn kantharos, are at present known only in examples of advanced stages beyond this time. Future evidence may well show that their introduction was more or less contemporary with the preceding broad forms. The idea of the drinking bowl with recurved handles, seen below in two versions, seems likely to have been introduced a bit earlier and to have disappeared from the scene by the time of the destruction of the city.

---

[54] Other Classical cup shapes, not studied here, also probably continued to be produced in Corinthian during the early years of the Hellenistic period. These include the bolsal, the one-handler, and the Corinthian type of skyphos.

In the general succession of shapes produced in Corinth in the Hellenistic period we may see two main overlapping phases in popular preference in drinking-cup forms: a major preference for deep forms in the earlier half of the Hellenistic period in Corinth, comprising the first two successive groups, a major preference for broad, open forms in the later half, the third group, still prevalent at the time of the destruction of the city. The picture of the later major preference is, of course, extensively supplemented by the extremely popular moulded bowl forms of that time.

All the cup forms will eventually, it is hoped, be of considerable value in archaeological dating. In this aspect it is to be emphasized that all seem to have had relatively short periods of production, which by itself is a fact peculiar to drinking-cup forms, very desirable in archaeological dating, and not true of vessels of other functions except for sporadic series. The desirability of future supplementation of the present evidence for dating of any Corinthian Hellenistic drinking-cup series is thus considerable. All the cup forms will eventually provide some degree of utility for closer dating within their periods of production, some in a few aspects, others in many. At present the two potentially most useful and most sensitive shapes chronologically, in that fragments of almost all elements of their forms provide clues for dating, are the skyphos of Attic type, covering the period from the late 5th century well down into the earlier Hellenistic period, and the cyma kantharos, from very early Hellenistic years down into the later part of the 3rd century. To the further supplementation of the evidence for dating these two forms excavators at Corinth and elsewhere will be well advised to pay particular attention.

The criteria for dating provided by the cups are mainly ones of shape changes during their periods of production. It might be hoped that the extensive elements of decoration present on a number of the cup series might also contribute to chronology in a manner comparable to the decoration of vessels of earlier periods. The value of the decoration for this purpose is severely restricted in Corinthian cups of these times, however, due to the fugitive nature of the glaze employed which all too frequently has caused the disappearance of the painted ornament. This is particularly true in the case of the various kantharos series. Preservation, however, is appreciably better in the series of wheelmade Megarian bowls, in the conical bowls and the mastos. In these it seems quite likely that the principle of degeneration of the motif may be operative for relative chronological placement, accompanying the advancing stages of shape development. There is, incidentally, at present no strong reason for supposing that the decoration of Corinthian wheelmade wine cups ever influenced the trends of the shape development.

Another aspect of the wine cups is of some interest, the presence on examples of several series of graffito inscriptions (Pls. 41, 42), the names of divinities or abstract ideas, normally in the genitive, a few in the nominative. A total of 43 are now known. For cups so inscribed the term *grammatika ekpomata* has been adopted here from Athenaeus.[55] These names are for the most part inscribed through the glaze on examples of the cyma, Acrocorinth, and articulated kantharoi, in a zone below the lip on one side only. A fragment, possibly of a one-piece kantharos, or conceivably of a hemispherical bowl, C-66-96, is also known, while a dipinto inscription appears on a lip fragment of a Corinthian calyx kantharos, C-31-451 (*Asklepieion*, p. 135, no. 69, and pl. 51). A large number of the inscriptions on cups from the South Stoa, all of which are included here, have already been discussed by Broneer.[56] The list below takes advantage of his comments and restorations of incomplete graffiti, supplementing his list with examples found subsequently or of other proveniences.

Ἀλυ[πίας]	: **510.**
Ἀντέρωτος	: **438.**
Ἀσφαλείας	: **475, 501, 502.** One complete, two restored.

---

[55] 11, 466 d; cf. also 15, 692 e. For Attic *grammatika ekpomata* and references to studies concerning them, Thompson B 23. Broneer, *S. Stoa*, p. 63, footnote 27, cites also, in connection with Corinthian examples: Martin P. Nilsson, *Geschichte der griechischen Religion*, II, Munich, 1950, p. 177; and *Eranos* (Acta philologica suecana, Upsala, 1890–1906, Goteburg, 1907–), L, 1952, p. 39.

[56] *S. Stoa*, pp. 62–64.

Διονύσου	: **409, 464**. Both complete.
Διὸς Σωτῆρος	: **424, 447, 458, 474, 498, 499, 503, 514**. Two complete, six restored.
Εἰ]ράνας	: **437**.
Ἔρωτος	: **480**.
Ἐυ]νοίας	: **500**.
Ἡδ[ο]νῆς	: **476, 493**. Both in part restored.
Ἡ]δυλ[	: C-66-96. Below, footnote 75.
Ἡδύοινος	: **454, 512**. One complete, one restored.
Ο]ἰνῶπ[ος]	: **407**.
Ολ[—] or ομ[—]	: C-65-379. Below, footnote 79.
Παυσικρηπά[λου	: **416**.
Πι[——]	: **511**.
Πιωνε[——]υς	: **492**.
[Ποδα]λ[ίρι]ος(?)	: **389**. Complete dipinto: C-31-451, *Asklepieion*, p. 135, no. 69, and pl. 51.
Σώζων	: **491**.
Ὑ]γεῖας	: **448**.
Ὑγιείας	: **400, 505**. One restored.
Φιλίας	: **483**.
Ὤ παρ'ἐλπίδας φανεῖς	: **489**.
]α[	: **506**.
]ας	: **507**.
]ας	: **452**.
]ιας	: **509**.
]ιας	: **467**.
]νερεις[?]	: **508**.
]υη[	: **504**.

The majority of the inscriptions call for no special comment. Attention, however, may be called to the enigmatic broken graffiti, πιωνε [——] υς, and]νερεις, which still seek satisfactory restorations. The name Σώζων is unusual. It can either[57] refer to an Anatolian divinity apparently first attested in Hellenistic times, or be an epithet of Zeus or Apollo. The significance, religious, convivial, or both, of these inscriptions does not concern the present study. The proveniences, however, it may be noted, show an extremely large majority to be from within the area of the South Stoa, many from contexts associated with the use of the building in the Greek period. One, C-66-96, is from the Peribolos of Apollo. A second, **454**, is from Deposit 43, at the northwest corner of the peribolos of Temple E, and a third, C-65-379, is from a well still further to the west of the Agora area. It seems worthy of comment, for future appraisal, that in Corinthian pottery this kind of inscription on drinking vessels seems to have had a limited period of vogue, from around 330 down into the third quarter of the 3rd century B.C. Conceivably the presence of such inscriptions on Corinthian drinking cups can be used as a criterion for dating.

There is a certain amount of variation in letter forms observable in the inscriptions, enough perhaps to prompt question as to whether or not they were inscribed at the time the cups were made or subsequently. It is the present writer's opinion that the inscriptions, with one or two possible exceptions, were inscribed before firing and that they are thus of the same date as the pots on which they appear.

---

[57] *R. E.*, *s.v.* Sozon. Roscher, Wilhelm Heinrich, *Ausführliches Lexikon der griechischen und römischen Mythologie*, Leipzig, 1909–1915, *s.v.* Sozon.

Their appearance, with usually carefully and delicately incised letters, differs markedly from graffiti inscribed on other vessels after firing, comparing very favorably in quality with and sometimes to the disadvantage of the incised elements of the decoration. This is especially clear in many of the cursive letters which are inscribed easily and with fluid lines. Professor Broneer, though believing that they were inscribed after firing, has pointed out previously that the decorators of the cups were aware in decorating them that they were to receive inscriptions since they omitted the decoration in the zone on the side on which the inscriptions are placed.

Imported wheelmade drinking cups are not numerous in Corinth in these times. Those of forms related to the Corinthian (a few are Attic) are noted below in the pertinent sections. Only a single imported shape of a form not represented in Corinthian is at present attested, a broad drinking bowl with a constricted ring foot, a lower wall rising broadly, a prominent nearly vertical upper wall, and horizontal loop handles.[58] The two examples of this shape are of the years close to and somewhat prior to the destruction of the city.

DEEP SHAPES

Skyphos, Attic type[59] **307–371**, Pls. 13, 14, 50, 51.
Advanced to final stages, 425[60] to 275 B.C.
Deposits: 15, 17, 20, 22, 23, 27, 28, 34, 36, 42, 43, 59, 61, 63, 66–69, 79–82, 87, 88, 90.

In basic form the Corinthian skyphoi of this series correspond closely to the Attic skyphoi which they, at least initially, copy.[61] The ring foot has an outer profile recognizable as of more or less torus outline throughout the series except for two very blurred late examples. The wall swells upward in varying degrees of curvature in an outline continuous from the foot to the top of the lip. The two horizontal loop handles are set below the lip. Aside from three fragmentary skyphoi of very great size (H. est. 0.22 m.: **307–309**) all of the first quarter of the 4th century, seven sizes are now attested: heights 0.13+, 0.12+, 0.11+, 0.10+, 0.09+, 0.08+, and 0.07+ m. Sizes 0.09+ m. and 0.08+ m. are at present much the most common. The clay of which they are made, except for one clumsy example, **362**, is uniformly of serviceable thickness. Full glazing seems to have been the rule, the one exception being the very late **366** which was dipped, leaving the lower wall and foot unglazed. Dipping may have been used more extensively in the series than is evident from their present appearance. **319**, of the third quarter of the 4th century B.C., was fully glazed but clearly was dipped, in two overlapping operations, top and bottom. In early stages certain areas (lower wall and top of foot, resting surface, underside within foot) of many examples received special treatment (reservation or paint over glaze) which will be noted in detail below. Although the series extends through the period when many drinking cups bore special inscriptions (*grammatika ekpomata*), for example the articulated and cyma kantharoi, none of the skyphoi is so inscribed.

[58] Gray ware: C-47-352, Deposit 111, of 146 B.C. Other: C-48-100, Deposit 110, of the first half of the 2nd century.

[59] Skyphoi of late stages of this shape have been discussed in *N. Cemetery*, p. 128. Of the 13 examples listed there one (491–5) is included here: **361** (T 1158).

[60] Two examples of the shape of a date prior to 425 B.C. are known to me: C-34-1092, Deposit 10, Pease 222, is of 460–420 B.C.; C-39-168, Deposit 8, is probably of the early 5th century. H. 0.085; D. foot 0.078; max. D. (at lip) av. 0.112. Fully glazed. A pair of purple lines wheel painted below the handles. They may be representative of occasional sporadic imitation of the Attic form rather than of the beginning of full production and the establishment of the Corinthian tradition in this shape. C-34-1093, Deposit 10, Pease 223, does not seem to be Corinthian.

[61] *A.R.V.*[2] Type A: Richter and Milne, *Shapes and Names*, fig. 174. Advanced examples of the series are on the order of Richter and Milne, fig. 177.

In Attic the production of the shape seems to have begun in the early years of the 5th century B.C.[62] Although a Corinthian example of about this time is known (above, footnote 61) it seems at present likely that large-scale production of the shape in Corinthian did not begin until some time in the last quarter of the 5th century. Production of the shape in Corinthian is well and continuously attested from that time onward. The latest skyphoi, whose regrettable forms lend high conviction to the thought that they are of the very final stage in Corinthian, show the shape carried to an even greater extreme than any now known in Attic.

For absolute dating in the series the latest examples from Olynthos, presumably close to 348 B.C., have been used. These are probably Attic, and thus not strictly relevant to the dating of Corinthian, but perhaps the degree of difference in form between the Attic of that time and the Corinthian was not too great. The date of the end of production in Corinthian is still largely a matter of estimate. Coins from deposits of limited range pertinent to the later stages of the form are not, at least in the present state of information, helpful in suggesting a close final date.[63] It is here estimated that the series came to an end about 275 B.C. This 75 year extension of the series beyond the stage of that reached at Olynthos is in part prompted by the extreme stage of the form ultimately reached in Corinthian. Five grave groups, in which skyphoi and unguentaria[64] are associated, provide some evidence supporting this considerable extension. Unguentaria, not present at Olynthos, probably first began to be imported into mainland Greece during the third quarter of the 4th century B.C. An indication of the date of the initial stage of the unguentarium in this quarter century is provided by Deposit 58, a grave in which a very early unguentarium and a coin of Corinth of 338 B.C. were associated. In two grave groups, Deposits 59 and 63, skyphoi somewhat more advanced than the Olynthian stage were found with unguentaria of the very early stage. In three other graves, Deposits 68, 67, 66, still more advanced skyphoi and advanced unguentaria were found associated. The final stage of the skyphos represented by **365** and **366** must be placed appreciably beyond these. Any precision in dating reached through future evidence in either the unguentarium or the skyphos series will be pertinent to both.

Deposit evidence indicates that the main criteria for relative dating of examples of this series concern all elements of the shape, making the skyphos one of the most useful forms in dating, even in fragments. In general the trends are from a generously capacious form very broad above and moderately constricted below, with a gently upswelling wall profile whose termination above is the lip, toward one of very restricted capacity, moderately broad above, much broader near the middle, constricted to the utmost extent possible at the foot, with a wall profile strongly flaring in outline from foot to mid-point where it recurves inward up to a strongly outcurved lip. The series arranged according to these trends exhibits other supporting changes: toward modifications in the form of the handle, toward carelessness in the application of decoration to the lower wall and foot resulting in the eventual abandonment of decoration entirely, and toward a decrease in the quality of manufacture and glazing.

The earliest examples in the Corinthian series have their greatest circumference above, either at the lip or slightly below. The profile of the upper wall of these skyphoi is visibly convex. The lower wall constricts very gradually, its curve slightly convex in profile, to the base, where its diameter is much constricted in relation to the upper part, yet very broad in relation to that of later skyphoi. The ring foot, a torus slightly flattened in profile, is a little greater in diameter than the bottom of the wall.

---

[62] 5th century B.C., prior to 480: Vanderpool 247; Talcott (1936), fig. 8, P 2732; Campbell 42–45. The subsequent stages of the Attic shape can be followed in various publications. 480–460 B.C.: Talcott (1936), fig. 8, P 5145. 460–440 B.C.: Boulter 29–30. 460–420 B.C.: Pease 23–28. 440–425 B.C.: Talcott 21 and Talcott (1936), fig. 8, P 2297. 425–400 and 400–374 B.C.: Corbett 24–25, 138, 139. *Ca.* 350 B.C.: *Olynthus*, XIII, nos. 581, 583, 585, 587 (from houses). Early Hellenistic: Thompson A 26; Young pyres 6 and 12.

[63] Two grave groups, Deposit 68 and 66, each contained a silver coin of Corinth, the one dated 400–338, the other (tentatively dated by Henry S. Robinson), 350–315 B.C.

[64] I.e., those of the best known ware, described by Thompson, pp. 472–474.

The attenuation of the form which gradually ensued in the succeeding years was brought about by a constriction of the diameter of the base and lower wall, of the maximum diameter of the upper wall, and that of the lip. In the stages between 400 and 350 B.C. the lip usually has the largest of these three diameters, the maximum diameter of the body being somewhat less, those of the lower wall and foot markedly smaller. The lip and upper wall in this period are occasionally of equal diameters. In the few instances in which the wall diameter is broader than the lip it is not so by much. In the first quarter of the 4th century the lower wall becomes slightly concave in profile, and in the second quarter strongly so. The profile of the upper wall becomes flatter and there is a slight outcurve to form the lip. In the second quarter this change produces a sharply outturned lip as a distinct element of the shape which is characteristic of all of this quarter and of all the rest of the entire series. In the stages after 350 B.C. the upper wall has usually the broadest of the three diameters, the lip one slightly less, and the base and lower wall are progressively more strongly constricted in relation to them. The lower wall, as the base constricts, becomes more deeply concave in profile. In the latest examples the base and lower wall are so tiny that the form is functionally impractical. It is evident that the series ends here. The household requirement for drinking cups in Corinth was supplied henceforth by other shapes, most immediately by the various forms of kantharos (e.g. articulated and cyma kantharoi) which were in production contemporaneously with advanced stages of the skyphos and which seem to have continued in production for many years after its demise.

Several other criteria are useful for dating examples belonging to the Corinthian series. The first is the handle form, its placement and its outlines in section and plan. Those of the period from 425 to 375 B.C. are set high on the wall, just below the lip, with only a slight upward tilt. The relatively heavy coil of clay (Pl. 51, **311**) from which they were formed is nearly circular in section, and the ends of the coil are set on the wall with a very wide interval between them. The handle in plan flares out slightly from the roots. In examples of the second quarter of the 4th century and later the handles are placed lower on the wall (because of the development of the distinct lip) and have a more pronounced upward tilt. The relatively thinner coils of clay (Pl. 51, **317**) from which they are formed usually have a flatter outline in section on the vertical surfaces. The interval between the roots of the handle is less and the degree of flare outward in plan is greater. Extreme examples (Pl. 51, **347**) of these changes are seen in some skyphoi of *ca.* 300 and 275 B.C., with the roots close together, the coil strongly tilted, and in several the outer part of the loop recurving.

A second criterion for dating concerns the decoration (or lack thereof) on the underside. In all examples of 425–375 B.C. (Pl. 51, **336**) the resting surface and the bottom within the foot are reserved. Both are painted pink and the latter is decorated with glaze over the pink, sometimes with a central dot and always with either a single circle or concentric circles, line or band, wheel painted.[65] A few examples of 375–350 B.C. are similarly decorated, either in the same technique or in an allied one (Pl. 51, **316**), more easily applied, in which the skyphoi are fully glazed but have pink, white, or buff paint applied over the glaze to simulate the reserved areas: **310**, **315**, **316**, **324**, **325**, **328**. On two of these, **310** and **324**, a band of pink is also applied around the lower wall immediately above the foot. A single example, of *ca.* 375 B.C., **368**, seems to be transitional for on it the two techniques are combined, a white band over glaze on the lower wall, the resting surface and the underside reserved, painted pink, and decorated with a glazed dot and circles. No fully glazed, undecorated skyphos of the series is known prior to the stage of the second quarter of the 4th century. Most of those of this quarter century are fully glazed and all of those of 350–275 B.C. with the lone exception of one of the two latest, **366**, which was glazed by dipping, as already remarked, the lower wall and foot left unglazed for handling.

---

[65] This type of decoration is attested on Attic skyphoi from the early 5th century at least into the first quarter of the 4th century B.C.: examples cited above, footnote 62, in Vanderpool, Campbell, Boulter, Pease, Talcott, and Corbett. The examples cited from Olynthos were apparently not so decorated nor were those in Thompson and in Young, of the late years of the 4th century.

The fabric and glaze of those of 425–375 B.C. are of very high quality. Examples of 375–325 B.C. vary from good quality to poor (two, **359** and **362**, are outright bad). Those of 325–275 B.C. would be acceptable only to the least demanding.

A minor criterion for dating concerns the foot. Two very late skyphoi, **364** of *ca.* 300 B.C., and **366** of *ca.* 275 B.C., depart from the standard torus foot. In both, the profile of the foot spreads outward in a more or less bevelled outline.

H. est. 0.22
  4th century B.C., first quarter
    307 (C-47-858b), Deposit 81. H. est. 0.22; D. foot 0.134. Bottom of wall, top of foot, resting surface, and underside reserved and painted pink. Underside: glazed dot, two glazed bands and two glazed lines.
    308 (C-47-859), Deposit 81. H. est. 0.22; D. foot 0.129; max. D. wall est. 0.209. Bottom of wall, top of foot, resting surface, and underside reserved and painted pink. Underside: glazed dot and two glazed lines.
    309 (C-47-858a), Deposit 81. H. est. 0.22; max. D. wall est. 0.22; D. lip est. 0.23.

H. 0.13+
  350 B.C.
    310 (C-37-2526), Deposit 90. H. 0.132; D. foot 0.07; max. D. wall 0.13; D. lip 0.132. Fully glazed. Pink bands over glaze on bottom of wall, resting surface, and underside. Pls. 13, 50.

H. 0.12+
  5th century B.C., fourth quarter
    311 (C-40-407), Deposit 36. H. 0.125; D. foot 0.089; max. D. wall 0.148; D. lip 0.147. Line wheel incised through glaze at bottom of wall. Resting surface and underside reserved and painted pink. Underside: glazed dot and two glazed lines. *Hesperia*, XVII, 1948, p. 231 and pl. LXXXV, E 3. Pls. 13, 50.
  4th century B.C., second quarter
    312 (C-37-2492), Deposit 90. H. 0.126; D. foot 0.071; max. D. wall 0.132; D. lip 0.132. Fully glazed.
  300 B.C.
    313 (C-31-230), Deposit 42. H. 0.123; D. foot 0.05; max. D. wall 0.10; D. lip 0.092. Fully glazed. Pls. 13, 50.

H. 0.11+
  4th century B.C., second quarter
    314 (C-53-58), Deposit 88. H. 0.117; D. foot 0.062; max. D. wall 0.116; D. lip 0.111. Fully glazed.
    315 (C-37-2494), Deposit 90. H. 0.11; D. foot 0.057; max. D. wall 0.102; D. lip 0.108. Fully glazed. Pink bands over glaze on resting surface and underside.
    316 (C-37-2528), Deposit 90. H. 0.11; D. foot 0.062; max. D. wall 0.101; D. lip 0.105.

Fully glazed. White bands over glaze on resting surface and underside. Graffito on outer wall under lip: Δ I. Pl. 51.
  350 B.C.
    317 (C-53-59), Deposit 88. H. 0.112; D. foot 0.055; max. D. wall 0.111; D. lip 0.105. Glaze entirely fugitive. Pls. 13, 50.
  4th century B.C., third quarter
    318 (C-40-61), Deposit 27. H. 0.118; D. foot 0.051; max. D. wall 0.11; D. lip 0.109. Fully glazed.
    319 (C-40-60), Deposit 27. H. 0.114; D. foot 0.051; max. D. wall 0.103; D. lip 0.105. Fully glazed: top and bottom halves dipped separately.
  300 B.C.
    320 (C-60-280), Deposit 34. H. 0.111; D. foot 0.045; max. D. wall 0.092; D. lip 0.088. Fully glazed. Pls. 13, 50.

H. 0.10+
  400 B.C.
    321 (C-37-435), Deposit 79. H. 0.101; D. foot 0.078; max. D. wall 0.126; D. lip 0.125. Resting surface and underside reserved and painted pink. Underside: glazed dot and glazed line. Pls. 13, 50.
  4th century B.C., first quarter
    322 (C-47-857), Deposit 81. H. 0.10; D. foot 0.065; max. D. wall 0.111; D. lip est. 0.121. Resting surface and underside reserved. Underside: glazed dot and two glazed lines.
  375 B.C.
    323 (C-47-856), Deposit 81. H. 0.102; D. foot 0.067; max. D. wall 0.105; D. lip 0.102. Resting surface and underside reserved. Underside: two glazed lines. Pls. 13, 50.
  4th century B.C., second quarter
    324 (C-37-2491), Deposit 90. H. 0.108; D. foot 0.056; max. D. wall 0.103; D. lip 0.107. Fully glazed. Pink bands over glaze at bottom of wall, on resting surface and on underside.
    325 (C-52-1), Deposit 82. H. 0.105; D. foot 0.058; max. D. wall 0.103; D. lip 0.103. Fully glazed. Pink bands over glaze on resting surface and on underside. Broneer, *S. Stoa*, pl. 24, 3, upper right.
    326 (C-37-2523), Deposit 90. H. 0.104; D. foot 0.054; max. D. wall 0.107; D. lip 0.104. Fully glazed.

327 (C-31-391), Deposit 20. H. 0.10; D. foot 0.065; max. D. wall 0.103; D. lip 0.107. Resting surface and underside reserved. Underside: two glazed bands. *Asklepieion*, p. 132 and pl. 48, no. 7.

328 (C-37-2493), Deposit 90. H. 0.10; D. foot 0.054; max. D. wall 0.098; D. lip 0.101. Fully glazed. Pink bands over glaze on resting surface and underside.

350 B.C.

329 (C-37-2525), Deposit 90. H. 0.108; D. foot 0.055; max. D. wall 0.11; D. lip 0.104. Fully glazed. Pls. 13, 50.

325 B.C.

330 (C-32-214). H. 0.105; D. foot 0.048; max. D. wall 0.098; D. lip 0.096. Glaze entirely fugitive. Pls. 13, 50.

300 B.C.

331 (C-31-229), Deposit 42. H. 0.102; D. foot 0.039; max. D. wall 0.084; D. lip 0.08. Fully glazed. Pls. 13, 50.

H. 0.09+

5th century B.C., fourth quarter

332 (C-37-434), Deposit 79. H. 0.099; D. foot 0.079; max. D. wall 0.133; D. lip 0.133. Resting surface and underside reserved and painted pink. Underside: glazed dot and glazed line. Pls. 13, 50.

333 (C-37-428), Deposit 79. P.H. 0.031; D. foot est. 0.08. Resting surface and underside reserved and painted pink. Underside: glazed line.

4th century B.C., first quarter

334 (C-37-171), Deposit 80. H. 0.097; D. foot 0.067; max. D. wall 0.106; D. lip 0.109. Resting surface and underside reserved and painted pink. Underside: glazed dot and two glazed bands.

335 (C-37-170), Deposit 80. H. 0.09; D. foot 0.065; max. D. 0.104; D. lip 0.109. Resting surface and underside reserved and painted pink. Underside: glazed dot and glazed line.

336 (C-36-969), Deposit 15. P.H. 0.06; D. foot 0.06. Resting surface and underside reserved and painted pink. Underside: two glazed lines and a glazed band. Pl. 51.

337 (C-31-455), Deposit 20. P.H. 0.045; D. foot 0.062. Resting surface and underside reserved and painted pink. Underside: glazed dot and glazed line. Graffito: Σ. *Asklepieion*, pl. 47, no. 73.

4th century B.C., second quarter

338 (C-31-390), Deposit 20. H. 0.099; D. foot 0.061; max. D. wall 0.099; D. lip 0.103. Resting surface and underside reserved and painted pink. Underside: glazed dot and band. *Asklepieion*, pl. 48, no. 6.

339 (C-31-453), Deposit 20. P.H. 0.06; D. foot 0.055. Resting surface and underside reserved and painted pink. Underside: two glazed lines. Graffito: THΛ. *Asklepieion*, pl. 47, no. 71.

340 (C-31-454), Deposit 20. P.H. 0.055; D. foot 0.05. Resting surface and underside reserved and painted pink. Underside: glazed line. Graffito: TE. *Asklepieion*, pl. 47, no. 72.

350 B.C.

341 (C-31-249), Deposit 42. H. 0.092; D. foot 0.043; max. D. wall 0.082; D. lip 0.081. Fully glazed. Pls. 13, 50.

4th century B.C., third quarter

342 (C-40-59), Deposit 27. H. 0.094; D. foot 0.045; max. D. wall 0.08; D. lip 0.08. Fully glazed.

343 (C-60-250), Deposit 22. H. 0.09; D. foot 0.038; max. D. wall 0.08; D. lip 0.076. Fully glazed.

325 B.C.

344 (C-31-250), Deposit 42. H. 0.093; D. foot 0.039; max. D. wall 0.08; D. lip 0.075. Traces of glaze. Pls. 13, 50.

345 (C-28-90). P.H. 0.066; max. D. wall 0.081; D. lip 0.075. Fugitive glaze.

4th century B.C., fourth quarter

346 (C-32-50), Deposit 23. H. 0.093; D. foot 0.039; max. D. wall 0.078; D. lip 0.073. Fully glazed.

300 B.C.

347 (C-60-221), Deposit 67. H. 0.095; D. foot 0.037; max. D. wall 0.073; D. lip 0.067. Fully glazed, fugitive. Pls. 13, 50.

348 (C-60-229), Deposit 68. H. 0.093; D. foot 0.038; max. D. wall 0.078; D. lip 0.07. Fully glazed.

H. 0.08+

4th century B.C., second quarter

349 (C-53-238), Deposit 43. H. 0.087; D. foot 0.044; max. D. wall 0.082; D. lip 0.084. Fully glazed.

350 (C-35-114). H. 0.087; D. foot 0.047; max. D. wall 0.08; D. lip 0.084. Fully glazed.

351 (C-46-113), Deposit 87. H. 0.085; D. foot 0.045; max. D. wall 0.081; D. lip 0.084. Fully glazed.

352 (C-50-29), Deposit 87. H. 0.086; D. foot 0.046; max. D. wall 0.084; D. lip 0.084. Fully glazed. Broneer, *S. Stoa*, pl. 24, 1, left.

353 (C-53-237), Deposit 43. H. 0.082; D. foot 0.046; max. D. wall 0.084; D. lip 0.085. Fully glazed.

354 (C-37-2522), Deposit 90. H. 0.082; D. foot 0.047; max. D. wall 0.087; D. lip 0.084. Fully glazed.

355 (C-31-251), Deposit 42. H. 0.08; D. foot 0.042; max. D. wall 0.073; D. lip 0.075. Fully glazed.

350 B.C.

356 (C-37-2524), Deposit 90. H. 0.086; D. foot 0.044; max. D. wall 0.084; D. lip 0.084. Fully glazed.

357 (C-40-439), Deposit 36. H. 0.085; D. foot 0.041; max. D. wall 0.078; D. lip 0.078. Fully glazed. *Hesperia*, XVII, 1948, p. 231 and pl. LXXXV, E 4. Pls. 14, 50.

4th century B.C., third quarter

358 (C-31-231), Deposit 42. H. 0.086; D. foot 0.041; max. D. wall 0.082; D. lip 0.076. Fully glazed.

359 (C-61-31). H. 0.084; D. foot 0.041; max. D. wall 0.074; D. lip 0.074. Fully glazed.

360 (C-30-1), Deposit 59. H. 0.083; D. foot 0.039; max. D. wall 0.076; D. lip 0.073. Fully glazed.

361 (T 1158), Deposit 63. H. 0.08; D. foot 0.04; max. D. wall 0.078; D. lip 0.074. Fully glazed. *N. Cemetery*, no. 491-5, pl. 76.

362 (C-60-232), Deposit 61. H. 0.086; D. foot 0.046; max. D. wall 0.082; D. lip 0.074. Fully glazed.

325 B.C.

363 (C-40-465), Deposit 17. H. 0.086; D. foot 0.039; max. D. wall 0.08; D. lip 0.077. Fully glazed. Pls. 14, 50.

300 B.C.

364 (C-63-658), Deposit 66. H. 0.089; D. foot 0.038; max. D. wall 0.075; D. lip 0.07. Traces of glaze. Pls. 14, 50.

275 B.C.

365 (C-61-14), Deposit 69. H. 0.085; D. foot 0.031; max. D. wall 0.08; D. lip 0.075. Fully glazed. Pls. 14, 50.

366 (C-61-18). H. 0.083; D. foot 0.037; max. D. wall 0.083; D. lip 0.083. Dipped, lower wall and foot unglazed.

H. 0.07+

400 B.C.

367 (C-37-172), Deposit 80. H. 0.076; D. foot 0.055; max. D. wall 0.08; D. lip 0.082. Resting surface and underside reserved and painted pink. Underside: glazed dot and glazed line. Pls. 14, 50.

375 B.C.

368 (C-37-173), Deposit 80. H. 0.074; D. foot 0.05; max. D. wall 0.081; D. lip 0.083. Bottom of wall painted white over glaze. Resting surface and underside reserved and painted pink. Underside: glazed dot and two glazed lines. Pls. 14, 50.

4th century B.C., second quarter

369 (C-37-2527), Deposit 90. H. 0.073; D. foot 0.041; max. D. wall 0.075; D. lip 0.077. Fully glazed.

4th century B.C., third quarter

370 (C-36-2420). H. 0.078; D. foot 0.042; max. D. wall 0.074; D. lip 0.07. Fully glazed.

325 B.C.

371 (C-40-21), Deposit 28. H. 0.076; D. foot 0.037; max. D. wall 0.067; D. lip 0.068. Fugitive glaze. Pls. 14, 50.

Calyx cup and calyx kantharoi[66] 372–377, Pls. 14, 51

Introduction

3rd century, first half.

Deposits: 28, 113, 115, 118.

The four distinct but related shapes here all have a lower wall convex in outline and an upper wall concave in outline and flaring outward above. These elements are, on a small scale, those which are seen in the calyx krater, hence the name given to them. It is desirable to class these drinking cups all under the same name since it serves to indicate their close relationship, which is apparently a chronological one as well as one of form. The basic form is seen most clearly in the calyx cup, **372**. In the three forms of calyx kantharos here handles and a foot are added to this basic form. The handles are all of one variety, which is ultimately derived from that employed in Attic kylikes of Classical times. In two of the kantharos forms the foot is the same. It may be called a pedestal foot: a spreading profile, stepped in outline, beneath a constricted stem. The foot of the third kantharos form, missing but restorable, was more elaborate. It is comparable to that employed on some metal kantharoi, hence it is referred

---

[66] A lip fragment of another Corinthian calyx kantharos: C-31-451, Deposit 20, *Asklepieion*, p. 135, no. 69, and pl. 51, is inscribed in dipinto: Ποδαλίριος.

to as a metallic foot. In two of the varieties of kantharos a moulded rim was added to the lip. In each of the three varieties there is an example of embellishment of the lower wall with impressed or incised reeding. The calyx cup may never have been glazed. The examples of two of the varieties of kantharos are fully black glazed. Of the two representatives of the third form one is now completely unglazed. It also may never have been glazed but there is a possibility that it may have been gilded.

All four shapes now known in Corinthian are imitations, or derived from Corinthian imitations, of Attic in which were produced still other varieties of calyx kantharos.[67] The representation of the calyx cup and calyx kantharos shapes in Corinthian is very slight, but in Attic it is enormous. Attic examples were very widely exported and evidently imitated in a great many local centers around the Mediterranean.

For the period of production of this group of shapes in Attic, it is evident that all but one variety was introduced during the course of the second quarter of the 4th century B.C. Examples of initial and of slightly advanced stages were found in the houses of Olynthos, evidently in use at the time of its destruction in 348 B.C. The lower limit of production in Attic is not yet fully established. It would seem that the lowest date within the realm of probability is *ca.* 250 B.C. It may be a bit earlier. These two limits have immediate bearing on Attic only. The shapes may have been and probably were adopted from Attic in other fabrics at various of the Attic stages. In foreign fabrics the shapes may have been produced longer than in Attic[68] and in those fabrics the shape development may be different, more accelerated, or slower. The examples of the Corinthian calyx cup and kantharoi now known are all of a very advanced stage, seemingly all to be dated within a short span of time, probably within one quarter century some time in the first half of the 3rd century B.C. From the point of view of numerical representation at present it is probably safe to say that the quantity of production of the shapes in Corinthian was minuscule compared to that in Attic. Future evidence may well, however, indicate that the shape was introduced in Corinthian at a stage earlier than at present attested.[69] The present deposit evidence is not sufficiently precise to indicate closely what the date of the examples here is, and consequently we are not in a position to say what the lower limit of production in Corinthian may be. The date suggested here may well be emended when more evidence is available.

Calyx cup **372**, Pls. 14, 51.
Late stage, 3rd century B.C., first quarter.

There is no foot. The potter ensured stability by tooling a circular area 0.014 m. in diameter on the bottom. The lower wall is convex in outline, approaching hemispherical. The upper wall, concave in outline and flaring outward above, is set off, but only in a blurred way, from the lower. The outer surfaces were well polished, but not the inner, on which there are wheel marks visible. The clay of which it is made is of normal thickness and of good quality. There is no trace of glaze and it may never have been glazed.

The initial stage of the form in Attic is datable around 350 B.C. or in the second quarter of the 4th century. An example of this stage[70] from Olynthos was evidently in use at the time of the destruction of the city in 348 B.C. An example more or less contemporary with the Olynthian one is known in Corinth, C-33-394, and also an Attic example of a more advanced stage, MP 124. The final stage in Attic is probably represented by Athens, Agora, P 902. In relation to the Attic series the Corinthian cup is seen to be of a stage very near the final one. The deposit from which the Corinthian cup comes

---

[67] Notably, spur-handled varieties, with or without a moulded lip. Plain lip: *Olynthus*, XIII, 510A (= 513A); Thompson A 27–29; *Hesperia*, XXXI, 1962, pl. 20, nos. 15, 35–38. Moulded lip: *Olynthus*, XIII, nos. 512–516, 522B.

[68] The Corinthian skyphos of Attic type (**307–471**) seems to be a case in point. At least its most extreme, final stage in Corinthian is more advanced than the most extreme Attic example of the shape known at present.

[69] Attic examples of earlier stages were well known in Corinth. Some 25 have been noted among catalogued examples.

[70] *Olynthus*, XIII, 521A.

covers a span from *ca.* 350 at least to *ca.* 300 B.C. The cup is regarded as the latest piece in it and in view of the nature of the deposit we are perhaps not justified in placing it later than the first quarter of the 3rd century.

3rd century B.C., first quarter
372 (C-40-32), Deposit 28. H. 0.081; D. lower
wall 0.067; D. lip 0.083. Pls. 14, 51.

Calyx kantharos, kylix handles: pedestal foot **373–374**, Pls. 14, 51.
Late stage, 3rd century B.C., first half.

The shape has a stemmed, pedestal foot, a variety which for visual purposes may be roughly compared to the base and lower part of an Ionic column. The lower part resembles the torus moulding, but spreading with a small astragal above, and the stem may be compared to the apophyge. The kylix handles are attached at the top of the lower wall. They rise steeply and recurve at the top so as nearly to touch the lip. The lower wall is plain in one example, vertically reeded in the other. The lip is plain, as on the calyx cup. The clay of which both are made is of normal thickness. Both are fully glazed on all surfaces. **373** had West Slope decoration in incision and applied paint on each side of the upper wall. Neither was otherwise embellished.

The initial stage of the form in Attic is datable in the second quarter of the 4th century B.C. An example of the early phase is *Olynthus*, no. XIII, 497. Two examples of later, more advanced stages come from Thompson's Group B, a cistern of which sections were abandoned and filled in a sequence. A fairly advanced example, B 46, comes from a section abandoned first. A very advanced example, B 17, comparable in stage to that of the two Corinthian examples, comes from a section abandoned last.

The two Corinthian examples come from one filling, a context providing only a general dating between *ca.* 330 and 146 B.C. On estimate they are probably not earlier than *ca.* 300, and are for the present placed only generally, within the first half of the 3rd century.

3rd century B.C., first half
373 (C-47-452), Deposit 113. H. 0.15; D. foot
0.056; H. foot and stem 0.026; D. lower
wall 0.097; D. lip 0.096. On upper wall,
A & B, necklace design, strings incised, traces
of pendants once in applied color. Pls. 14, 51.

374 (C-47-453), Deposit 113. Handles missing. H.
0.145; D. foot 0.049; H. foot and stem 0.024;
D. body 0.103; D. lip est. 0.099. Lower wall
ribbed. Pl. 51.

Calyx kantharos, kylix handles: pedestal foot, moulded rim **375**, Pls. 14, 51.
Late stage, third century B.C., first half.

This variety is essentially identical with the preceding, differing only in that the lip is given the appearance of having an appliqué rim composed of two mouldings.[71] The clay of which it is made is of normal thickness, and it is fully glazed on all surfaces. The lower wall is reeded beneath the glaze. There is no other decoration.

The initial stage in Attic is datable to the second quarter of the 4th century, since examples of this stage and a slightly advanced one were found in houses at Olynthos and were thus probably in use there at the time of the destruction of the city in 348 B.C.[72]

The probable context of **375** provides only a general dating between *ca.* 330 and 146 B.C. On estimate it is probably not earlier than *ca.* 300 and is for the present only generally dated, within the first half of the 3rd century.

---

[71] In Attic examples the entire moulded rim is often actually separately applied. In this Corinthian example only the lower part of the rim is appliqué.

[72] Initial: *Olynthus*, XIII, no. 503. Slightly advanced: *Olynthus*, XIII, nos. 504, 505; cf. also, handles complete, no. 506, from a grave.

3rd century B.C., first half
375 (C-33-42), Deposit 118. Handles missing except for attachments. H. 0.145; D. foot 0.054; H. foot and stem 0.026; D. lower wall 0.095; D. lip 0.102. The lower wall is reeded beneath the glaze. Pls. 14, 51.

Calyx kantharos, kylix handles: metallic foot, moulded rim 376–377, Pls 14, 51.
Late stage, 3rd century B.C., first half.

The shape is essentially identical to the preceding except that it had a foot and stem of special form, restorable as having been in imitation of that employed for some metal kantharoi. This is best seen in a silver kantharos from Tarentum.[73] The two pieces below are respectively a kantharos complete from the top of the stem upward, and a foot. The stem between would have been tall and slender and with a projecting moulding or mouldings between foot and body. The foot, 377, is from a black-glazed kantharos. The clay is of normal quality and thickness. The kantharos, 376, is made of clay of normal thickness, but rather soft, not unlike Corinthian terracotta clay. There is no trace of glaze preserved. It may never have been glazed; it is possible that it was, however, gilded. A fragment of a similar, probably Corinthian kantharos of this form from Sikyon, excavated in 1966, is of similar clay, and on its lower wall traces of gilding over white sizing are preserved.

This special form of kantharos may not have been introduced in Attic contemporaneously with the other varieties of calyx kantharos. The earliest known at present is of perhaps 325 B.C.[74] A very advanced example, lacking stem and foot, relatively about contemporary with 376, comes from one of the sections last abandoned of Thompson's Group B cistern: B 20.

There is no deposit evidence for dating 377. The deposit from which 376 comes provides only a general dating between *ca.* 330 and 146 B.C. On estimate it is not earlier than *ca.* 300 B.C. and is for the present placed only generally, within the first half of the 3rd century.

3rd century B.C., first half
376 (C-47-77), Deposit 115. Foot missing and stem, except for a bit of the top. In the illustrations the lowest "moulding" should be disregarded: it is plaster from an incorrect restoration which cannot be removed. P.H. 0.144; D. lower wall 0.098; D. lower moulding of rim 0.098; D. lip 0.092. Above stem, at bottom of wall, a small convex moulding.

Lower wall irregularly reeded, A & B. Beneath each handle a few random strokes of reeding. Pls. 14, 51.
377 (C-40-469). Foot, and attachment of stem. P.H. 0.02; D. foot 0.072; D. base of stem 0.021. Fully glazed except for a narrow band around the outer edge of the top of the foot reserved and painted pink. Pls. 14, 51.

One-piece kantharos 378–388, Pls. 15, 52.
Intermediate stages, 325 to 250 B.C.
Deposits: 39, 40, 42, 43, 115.

The kantharoi of this series have been called one-piece kantharoi since the convex profile of the wall is uninterrupted from bottom to top. The form has a ring foot with a stem initially slight, later prominent. The lip is not a separate element, but is merely the upper termination of the wall. Two types of handle occur throughout the series. One is a strap handle with strap thumb-rest (that of 378 is exceptional in that it terminates above in a small bolster). The other is a double loop with a Herakles knot as thumb-rest. A handle zone is delimited on most by means of a fine wheel groove (or double, closely

[73] P. Wuilleumier, *Le Trésor de Tarente*, Paris, 1930, pp. 41–47, pls. V and VI. For pottery kantharoi of this kind see: Brussels, Musée du Cinquantenaire, inv. nos. A 1710, A 1709, and A 1708, *C.V.A.*, Brussels 3 (3), III L and III N, pl. 3 (138), nos. 7, 11, and 22.
[74] *Hesperia*, XII, 1943, p. 294, fig. 15, d; now Athens, Agora Museum, PN P 510.

spaced) beneath the glaze at a level between the handle attachments. Decoration in this zone occurs in only a few, however. Two designs[75] are attested. A necklace design with incised strings and pendants in added color is seen on one, **378**. Running ivy, with incised tendrils and white leaves, occurs on three, **386–388**. Only **378** is fully glazed. On all others the body inside and out is fully glazed but the stem and the resting surface of the foot are reserved and often painted pink. On these the outer and inner vertical profiles of the foot were glazed. Exceptional treatment of the area within the foot on some of these is noted below. The quality of manufacture (clay, glazing) is relatively good in the earlier and fair in the later. Four sizes are now attested: heights 0.12+, 0.11+, 0.09, and 0.08+ m.[76]

Evidence for the absolute dating of the period of production of this series is very slight at present. The shape does not occur at Olynthos. In Attic pottery a possibly cognate shape, Thompson A 39, suggests that the form may have come into production not too many years later than the time of Olynthos' destruction. The treatment of the underside of the foot of the earliest examples, **380, 382**, and **384**, with wheel-painted bands and lines is evidently in imitation of 4th century Attic, and some indication that we must look toward the years close to the time of Olynthos' destruction for the beginning of the series is found in the abandonment of this type of decoration on Corinthian skyphoi of Attic type about the middle of the century (cf. **307–371**). **378**, of a somewhat advanced stage, is from a context subsequent to *ca.* 330 B.C. 75 or 100 years is probably very ample allowance for the shape development observable in this series. A probably extreme *terminus ante quem* for the lower limit of production of the shape is provided by the occurrence of examples in deposits of considerable range whose terminal date, according to both the indications of the pottery and coins, is in the third quarter or early last quarter of the 3rd century.

The significant changes in shape development in the series would seem to be, size for size, toward constriction of the diameter of the foot, the development of a prominent stem (with a corresponding decrease in the depth of the body), and toward a decrease in the diameter of the lower wall and lip which result in a change of the initial full, deep, convex profile of the body to a more ovoid one. There is a corresponding change in the profile of the foot. Early examples have a spreading ring foot, its outer profile encircled by a wheel-run groove, the area within it broad and flat. As the foot becomes more constricted the wheel grooving broadens into a concave moulding, and the area within becomes conical. The special treatment of the underside of the foot referred to above seems to be entirely an early feature, occurring only on the three examples here dated *ca.* 325 B.C., **380, 382**, and **384**. In these the underside is reserved. Two are painted pink under wheel-painted glaze dot and circle. The other has, conversely, a wheel-painted pink band and line. A reminiscence of this is seen in **383** in which this now constricted area is reserved and painted pink. On all the others the area was probably or certainly painted fully black. There would seem to be no significant change in the greatest diameter of the body in the course of the shape development.

It seems possible that the series is incomplete. We may not yet have the initial stage of the series. Possibly also the shape was carried further than the most extreme examples now known. In the following catalogue fragments are listed separately since they do not preserve enough information for relative placement in the series.

---

[75] A rim fragment excavated since this was written, C-66-96, if it is actually from a one-piece kantharos, attests a third design, a horizontal ivy garland interrupted by a six-petal rosette. The ivy tendril and the outlines of the rosette are incised, the leaves and petals are in added white. They are set in a zone formed by two lines wheel incised through the glaze. Beneath the lower is part of a graffito, incised before firing: H]ΔΥΛ[ΟΓΙΑC (?). No other one-piece kantharos known at present is a *grammatikon ekpoma*, nor does any other have a zone of two lines. It is conceivable that this fragment may actually be from another form, perhaps a hemispherical bowl such as *Hesperia*, XII, 1943, p. 359, fig. 60, a.

[76] A still smaller size, H. 0.066 m., has been found at Isthmia, IP 688. It is of the same stage of development as **379**.

H. 0.12+
  300 B.C.
    378 (C-47-75), Deposit 115. av. H. 0.12; D. foot
      0.053; max. D. 0.112; D. lip 0.099; H. to top
      of stem 0.008. A, necklace. B, missing.
      Pls. 15, 52.
  250 B.C.
    379 (C-31-39), Deposit 40. H. 0.126; D. foot 0.05;
      max. D. 0.112; D. lip 0.095; H. to top of
      stem 0.023. Pls. 15, 52.
H. 0.11+
  325 B.C.
    380 (C-31-206), Deposit 42. H. 0.112; D. foot
      0.067; max. D. 0.118; D. lip 0.105; H. to
      top of stem 0.014. Pls. 15, 52.
  275 B.C.
    381 (C-53-230), Deposit 43. H. 0.111; D. foot
      0.046; max. D. est. 0.106; D. lip 0.096; H.
      to top of stem 0.018.
H. 0.09
  325 B.C.
    382 (C-31-207), Deposit 42. H. 0.09; D. foot
      0.057; max. D. 0.094; D. lip 0.089; H. to top
      of stem 0.10.

275 B.C.
  383 (C-53-236), Deposit 43. H. 0.09; D. foot
    0.037; max. D. 0.086; D. lip 0.076; H. to top
    of stem 0.014.
H. 0.08+
  325 B.C.
    384 (KP 213). H. 0.08; D. foot 0.046; max. D.
      0.081; D. lip 0.073; H. to top of stem 0.01.
  250 B.C.
    385 (MP 76). H. 0.084; D. foot 0.035; max. D.
      0.08; D. lip 0.069; H. to top of stem 0.015.
Fragments
  ca. 300–250 B.C.
    386 (C-31-25), Deposit 39. Part of a double loop
      handle with Herakles knot attached to section
      of rim and wall. Handle zone: running ivy.
    387 (C-31-26), Deposit 39. A double loop handle
      with Herakles knot attached to section of rim
      and wall. Handle zone: running ivy.
    388 (C-31-29), Deposit 39. Wall fragment. Handle
      zone: running ivy.

Cyma kantharos 389–450, Pls. 15, 39, 41, 52, 53.
Early to final stages, 330 to 225 B.C.
Deposits: 36, 38, 39, 40, 43, 75, 94, 95, 96, 106, 108, 110, 111, 113, 114, 115, 118.

The name cyma kantharos has been given this shape since, in advanced stages, the profile of its wall resembles a cyma reversa. It has a spreading ring foot whose outer, vertical profile is wheel-grooved beneath the glaze. In later examples it is conical in profile within. The resting surface is flat, never grooved. A stem appears throughout the series, slight at first, more prominent later. Its wall profile is convex below, curving inward above to an outturned lip. It normally has a strap handle with strap thumb-rest. One early exception has a grooved strap handle. A few others have a double loop handle with a Herakles knot thumb-rest. Ten sizes are known, one perhaps height 0.20 m., the others representing each centimeter of height between 0.16 and 0.08 m. The clay of the walls is fairly thin throughout the series. Full glazing also occurs throughout. There is no certain example of dipping. A number, otherwise fully glazed, have a reserved stem and resting surface (some also a circular area inside the foot) which are painted pink. In most the body is plain; some examples, however, have a reeded body. Decoration in incision, color or both occurs only at the level of the handles: in a single zone (the handle zone), A & B, delimited by wheel grooving, in early kantharoi; in two zones (lip zone and shoulder zone) in the later. Decoration in the zones is usual, although a few examples were not decorated. Incised designs sometimes show traces of pink color.

Possibly the shape was introduced into Corinthian pottery in imitation of a form of a foreign fabric. A fragment of the upper wall of a possible foreign prototype, conceivably but not certainly Attic, C-50-26 (Pl. 53), would appear to be fully as early as the earliest of the Corinthian series, if not a bit earlier. The vine-pattern decoration in its handle zone is rendered with considerable elegance in applied clay.

The period of production of this series is delimited generally by the occurrence of examples of all stages (except possibly the very earliest)[77] in use fillings of the South Stoa wells. The period of their

---

[77] Since the above was written a fragment probably representing the earliest stage has been brought to my attention by Professor Cedric G. Boulter. It is KP 2702, found in the courtyard of the Terracotta Factory of the Potters' Quarter.

manufacture and use thus falls between *ca.* 330 and 146 B.C. With regard to the end of production the shape seems almost certainly not to have been current at the time of Mummius' destruction of Corinth in 146 B.C. Only two fragmentary pieces, probably strays, occur in the fillings attributed to this event, though examples of other varieties of drinking cups are present. We can also believe that production had ceased before 200 B.C., for none occur in the second use filling of Deposit 110 of *ca.* 200–146 B.C. Examples of penultimate and final stages do occur, however, in deposits with terminal dates at present placed in the third quarter of the 3rd century and into the fourth quarter, according to the indications of both pottery and coins. We seem to be justified in looking for the end of production in the years around 225 B.C. At the upper end there seems to be good reason for assuming that the shape came into production very close to the time of the beginning of use of the South Stoa. Examples of one stage occur in Deposits 36 and 38 whose lower limits are in the vicinity of 275 B.C. The stage is so far advanced that it seems necessary to place the earliest stage as far back as our evidence permits.

The deposits support in small part the reasonable assumption that the shape development in this series is in the direction of attenuation and constriction. The series has been arranged in a chronological sequence[78] on this principle, primarily on the line of a gradual decrease in the greatest diameter of the wall, size for size. Kantharoi of incomplete size series have been placed both with respect to one another and to adjacent size series.

The sequence so arranged suggests that certain other criteria can be used for relative dating. These are fairly numerous and the series seems potentially of more than normal value to field archaeologists since fragments of various elements of the form can be used to indicate a relative date.

In the present sequence, on present dating and size for size, the following criteria seem to be the most useful, in addition to the degree of constriction of the wall. The degree of constriction of the diameter of the bottom of the foot can be used, in part. A broad low ring foot with a shallow groove around the outer vertical profile and a very low stem is characteristic of those prior to 300 B.C. The lower wall is correspondingly broad. The foot in subsequent examples is markedly constricted, the profile within in these is conical, and the groove is more pronounced, producing a strongly stepped profile of two mouldings, lower and upper. The stem is similarly constricted and appreciably taller and the lower wall is correspondingly constricted in its diameter. Beyond 300 there is no particular decrease in the diameter of the bottom of the foot, nor is there any marked, further increase in the combined height of foot and stem. There is generally, however, a further development toward constriction of the diameter of the upper moulding of the foot and of the diameter of the stem, though an occasional example departs from the norm, as might be expected.

The profile of the upper wall and lip and the placement of zones of decoration also seem to provide useful criteria. The earliest examples have walls of entirely convex profile, the lip formed by a sharp outturning above. They have only a single zone of decoration delimited by a pair of wheel grooves within the limits of the levels of the handle attachments. In examples of 300 to 275 B.C. the upper wall is nearly straight in profile and the lip is less pronounced as a separate element of the form. These also have a single zone of decoration. In examples of 275 and following, the upper wall profile is distinctly concave and the lip is merely an outward curve of the upper profile. In these, two zones for decoration are provided by a slight ridge at about mid-point between the levels of the two handle attachments. Decoration appears in either the upper or the lower zone. On only one are both zones decorated. The

---

It is part of the lip and wall of a kantharos of about the size of **400**. Criteria which place it earliest are the relatively high quality of the fabric, the quite gentle outcurve of the lip, and the careful reeding of the body. Exceptionally, in the lip zone appears a row of impressed egg pattern, upside down.

[78] A question to be reconsidered when more evidence is available concerns the kantharoi here assigned to the years 330 and the early fourth quarter of the 4th century B.C. Although they are clearly related to the rest of the present series they are not fully satisfactory as the earliest stage. A second group, the Acrocorinth kantharoi, again related, has also been considered as providing possible prototypes. These also do not seem to mesh in a convincing fashion with the rest of the present series and accordingly have been treated as a collateral rather than a lineal development.

three inscribed kantharoi of this time have the graffito in the upper zone, decoration in the lower. Only one example has a single element of decoration occupying both zones.

Some decorative aspects may be useful as criteria also. These include special features of the grooving beneath the glaze, which appear on the bodies of 19 examples. This grooving is primarily seen as vertical parallel lines, rather crude reeding, fairly closely spaced, from about the level of the lower handle attachment nearly to the stem, on both sides. It is omitted in the area just below the handles. Here in examples from 330 into the second quarter of the 3rd century B.C. a crude grooved X often appears. On one example of around 325 a large vertical branch pattern occupies this position. A single example of *ca.* 300 has here a vertical line with a long squiggle on either side. On one example of 275, to the left of each handle two panels interrupt the reeding and in each appears a single vertical squiggle. On one of 250 B.C. a panel with one squiggle and a group of 4 lines of reeding alternate around the entire wall.

One might expect that the designs, incised or painted (or both), in the zones would also be helpful in relative chronology. This, however, is only in part true since the painted elements have all too seldom survived because of the fugitive character of the glaze on which they were placed. The running-ivy design, which appears on 20 of the kantharoi, can provide a distinction between early and later. The earliest (Pl. 39, **442**), of about 330, has short tendrils and the garland they form is narrow, the leaves close together. In ivy of *ca.* 300 B.C. and later (Pl. 39, **412**) the tendrils sprawl widely, and the leaves are few and far apart. Designs of rare occurrence may, in this series, represent experiments of brief duration (either ivy or the necklace design are standard in these kantharoi). Such are the incised egg pattern of the second quarter of the 3rd century B.C. (Pl. 39, **418**); the incised egg-and-dart of *ca.* 250 (Pl. 39, **428**); the incised lattice pattern with white dots of *ca.* 250 (Pl. 39, **408**); the incised "quotation marks" design of the third quarter of the 3rd century B.C. (Pl. 39, **441**); and the incised "Doric frieze" of the same time (Pl. 39, **396**).

It would appear, conversely, that although many aspects of the kantharoi suggest means of relative dating others do not. Such include the form of the handle. No definable difference is seen in any of the handles of strap form with strap thumb-rest, a form employed throughout the series. The rare occurrence of the double loop handle with Herakles knot thumb-rest probably has no chronological significance, though conceivably the use of the grooved strap handle is only an abortive experiment of the early years. Similarly uninformative is the occasional practice from 300 B.C. onward of reserving and painting pink the stem and resting surface and sometimes a circular area on the underside of the foot. This is probably only a survival of 4th century practice. Among the designs in the zones the necklace, entirely painted or with painted pendants and incised string, is not useful, although it occurs throughout the series and even more frequently than the ivy. The rendering is cursive and the painted pendants have seldom survived. There seems finally to be no chronological information to be derived from the use of incision versus painting in the designs. Both occur in combination throughout the series. Designs rendered in paint only also occur throughout. They are infrequent early in the series, but increase somewhat toward the end.

Of the series ten are *grammatika ekpomata*. The names which occur are: Ἀντέρωτος; Διὸς Σωτῆρος (twice); Διονύσου; Εἰ]ράνας; Ο]ἰνῶπ[ος; Παυσικρηπά[λου; [Ποδα]λ[ίρι]ος; Ὑ]γ[ι]εῖας (twice). Seven occur on kantharoi dated between 330 and 300 B.C. The others are of the second and third quarters of the 3rd century B.C.

H. est. 0.20
330 B.C.

389 (C-47-288), Deposit 106. Fragment of lip and wall. D. lip est. 0.21. A, [ΠΟΔΑ]Λ[ΙΡΙ]ΟΣ. Cf. a fragment of the rim of a calyx kantharos (probably Corinthian, not Attic) on which the name of Podalirios is painted: C-31-451, Deposit 20, *Asklepieion*, p. 135, no. 69, and pl. 51. Note also that the name Hygieia appears on two kantharoi of the present series, **400** and **448**, both contemporary with **389**. Reeded body. Pls. 13, 41.

H. 0.16+

3rd century B.C., second quarter

390 (C-47-461), Deposit 113. H. 0.164; D. foot 0.057; max. D. wall 0.125; D. lip 0.106; H. foot and stem 0.024; D. upper moulding 0.049; D. stem 0.036. A–B, shoulder zone, running ivy. Fully glazed.

3rd century B.C., third quarter

391 (C-47-463), Deposit 113. H. 0.166; D. foot 0.055; max. D. wall 0.118; D. lip 0.12; H. foot and stem 0.028; D. upper moulding 0.043; D. stem 0.035. A–B, shoulder zone, suspended necklace, painted. Fully glazed.

392 (C-47-74), Deposit 115. H. 0.16; D. foot 0.053; max. D. wall 0.113; D. lip est. 0.109; H. foot and stem 0.027; D. upper moulding 0.038; D. stem 0.032. A–B, shoulder zone, suspended necklace, painted. Fully glazed.

393 (C-47-92), Deposit 96. H. 0.16; D. foot 0.054; max. D. wall 0.113; D. lip 0.12; H. foot and stem 0.024; D. upper moulding 0.04; D. stem 0.031. A–B, shoulder zone, suspended necklace, painted. Fully glazed.

394 (C-47-292), Deposit 106. P.H. 0.113; D. foot 0.052; max. D. 0.112; H. foot and stem 0.024; D. upper moulding 0.038; D. stem 0.031. A–B, missing. Fully glazed.

395 (C-47-271), Deposit 106. H. 0.163; D. foot 0.053; max. D. wall 0.11; D. lip 0.108; H. foot and stem 0.023; D. upper moulding 0.04; D. stem 0.031. A–B, running ivy, incised and painted. Fully glazed.

396 (C-47-356), Deposit 111. P.H. 0.14. B, "Doric frieze," shoulder zone, incised. Pl. 39.

397 (C-47-357), Deposit 111. Fragment of lip and wall. B, "Doric frieze," shoulder zone, incised.

225 B.C.

398 (C-47-93), Deposit 96. H. 0.168; D. foot 0.055; max. D. wall 0.107; D. lip 0.111; H. foot and stem 0.027; D. upper moulding 0.041; D. stem 0.031. A–B, shoulder zone, suspended necklace, painted. Fully glazed.

399 (C-47-122), Deposit 96. H. 0.16; D. foot 0.054; max. D. wall 0.105; D. lip 0.112; H. foot and stem 0.026; D. upper moulding 0.038; D. stem 0.031. Undecorated. Fully glazed. Pls. 15, 53.

H. 0.15+

4th century B.C., early fourth quarter

400 (C-47-119), Deposit 95. P.H. 0.14; max. D. wall 0.14; D. lip 0.12. Foot and stem restored, perhaps incorrectly. A, ΥΓΙΕΙΑC. B, part of curving white vertical line preserved. Grooved strap handle. Reeded body; grooved branch beneath handles. *Hesperia*, XVI, 1947, pl. LIX, 15, right; Broneer, *S. Stoa*, pl. 14, 5, right. Pls. 15, 41, 52.

300 B.C.

401 (C-47-66), Deposit 115. H. 0.15; D. foot 0.064; max. D. wall 0.132; D. lip 0.128; H. foot and stem 0.028; D. upper moulding 0.054; D. stem 0.045. A, missing. B, suspended necklace, string incised. Reeded body. Fully glazed. Pls. 15, 52.

402 (C-47-63), Deposit 115. P.H. 0.128; max. D. wall 0.13; D. lip 0.116. A–B, suspended necklace, string incised. Reeded body. Foot missing.

403 (C-31-24), Deposit 39. Rim and wall fragment. B, running ivy, tendrils incised, leaves painted. Reeded body.

275 B.C.

404 (C-60-70), Deposit 38. H. 0.155; D. foot 0.057; max. D. wall 0.123; D. lip 0.124; H. foot and stem 0.025; D. upper moulding 0.04; D. stem 0.033. A–B, lip zone, running ivy, incised tendrils. Reeded body. Fully glazed except for reserved stem and resting surface painted pink. Pls. 15, 52.

405 (C-47-462), Deposit 113. H. 0.158; D. foot 0.055; max. D. wall 0.123; D. lip 0.117; H. foot and stem 0.022; D. upper moulding 0.043; D. stem 0.035. A–B, suspended necklace, incised string, shoulder zone. Fully glazed.

3rd century B.C., second quarter

406 (C-31-23), Deposit 39. Fragment of lip and wall. B, running ivy, incised tendrils, lip zone. Fully glazed.

407 (C-50-1). Fragment of lip. A, O]ΙΝΩΠ[OC lip zone. Pls. 13, 41.

250 B.C.

408 (C-47-61), Deposit 115. H. 0.155; D. foot 0.058; max. D. wall 0.118; D. lip 0.127; H. foot and stem 0.026; D. upper moulding 0.04; D. stem 0.03. A–B, lip zone, incised lattice pattern, white dots. Fully glazed. *Hesperia*, XVI, 1947, pl. LIX, 14, left. Pls. 15, 39, 52.

3rd century B.C., third quarter

409 (C-47-86), Deposit 96. H. 0.155; D. foot 0.057; max. D. wall 0.108; D. lip 0.112; H. foot and stem 0.025; D. upper moulding 0.042; D. stem 0.032. A, lip zone, ΔΙΟΝΥCOY; shoulder zone, suspended necklace. B, shoulder zone, suspended necklace. Necklace design painted. Fully glazed. Pls. 13, 41.

H. 0.14+

3rd century B.C., first quarter

410 (C-47-65), Deposit 115. H. 0.149; D. foot 0.057; max. D. 0.125; D. lip 0.113; H. foot and stem 0.021; D. upper moulding 0.043; D. stem 0.032. A, necklace. B, running ivy; incised tendrils. Fully glazed except for stem and resting surface reserved and painted pink.

275 B.C.

411 (C-47-62), Deposit 115. H. 0.149; D. foot
0.062; max. D. wall 0.118; D. lip 0.118; H.
foot and stem 0.02; D. upper moulding 0.05;
D. stem 0.041. A–B, shoulder zone, suspended
necklace, incised string. Fully glazed.

3rd century B.C., second quarter

412 (C-36-713). H. 0.143; D. foot 0.055; max. D.
wall 0.116; av. D. lip 0.113; H. foot and
stem 0.025; D. upper moulding 0.045; D.
stem 0.03. A–B, shoulder zone, running ivy,
incised tendrils. Fully glazed except for stem,
resting surface, and circular area on underside of foot reserved and painted pink. Pl. 39.

250 B.C.

413 (C-47-272), Deposit 108. H. 0.148; D. foot
0.05; max. D. wall 0.113; D. lip 0.114;
H. foot and stem 0.025; D. upper moulding
0.038; D. stem 0.03. A–B, shoulder zone,
running ivy, incised tendrils. Reeded body.
Fully glazed except for stem and resting
surface reserved and probably painted pink.

414 (C-47-67), Deposit 115. H. 0.146; D. foot
0.058; max. D. wall 0.113; D. lip 0.113; H.
foot and stem 0.022; D. upper moulding
0.048; D. stem 0.038. A–B, shoulder zone,
suspended necklace, painted. Fully glazed.

415 (C-48-107), Deposit 110. P.H. 0.137; D. foot
0.05; H. foot and stem 0.024; D. upper
moulding 0.038; D. stem 0.031. A, missing.
B, shoulder zone, running ivy, tendrils incised.
Reeded body. Fully glazed except for stem
and resting surface reserved and painted pink.

3rd century B.C., third quarter

416 (C-47-87), Deposit 96. H. 0.148; D. foot 0.06;
max. D. wall 0.103; D. lip 0.104; H. stem
and foot 0.023; D. upper moulding 0.047;
D. stem 0.038. A, lip zone, ΠΑΥϹΙΚΡΗΠΑ̣
[ΛΟΥ]; shoulder zone, suspended necklace, incised string. B, missing. Fully glazed. Pls. 13, 41.

H. 0.13+

3rd century B.C., second quarter

417 (C-47-123), Deposit 96. H. 0.13; D. foot
0.048; max. D. wall 0.111; D. lip 0.116; H.
foot and stem 0.022; D. upper moulding
0.035; D. stem 0.028. No trace of decoration.
Fully glazed.

418 (C-47-64), Deposit 115. H. 0.137; D. foot
0.05; max. D. wall 0.10; D. lip 0.102; H.
foot and stem 0.023; D. upper moulding
0.036; D. stem 0.027. A–B, lip zone, egg
pattern, incised. Fully glazed. Pl. 39.

250 B.C.

419 (C-47-70), Deposit 115. av. H. 0.135; D. foot
0.048; max. D. wall 0.098; D. lip 0.098; H.
foot and stem 0.024; D. upper moulding
0.033; D. stem 0.026. A, shoulder zone,

suspended necklace, painted. B, undecorated.
Fully glazed.

3rd century B.C., third quarter

420 (C-47-290), Deposit 106. av. H. 0.132; D.
foot 0.05; max. D. wall 0.095; D. lip 0.093;
H. foot and stem 0.025; D. upper moulding
0.035; D. stem 0.025. Undecorated. Fully
glazed.

421 (C-31-38), Deposit 40. P.H. 0.092; max. D.
wall 0.094; D. lip 0.09. Foot and stem missing. A–B, lip zone, running ivy, incised tendrils. Double loop handle with Herakles knot
thumb-rest.

422 (C-31-22), Deposit 39. Fragment, lip, wall
and handle. B, lip zone, running ivy, incised.

H. 0.12+

300 B.C.

423 (C-47-71), Deposit 115. H. 0.128; D. foot
0.048; max. D. wall 0.108; D. lip 0.103; H.
foot and stem 0.018; D. upper moulding
0.041; D. stem 0.032. A–B, suspended necklace,
incised string. Reeded body. Fully glazed.

424 (C-34-392 a, f), Deposit 94. Fragment of
wall. A, [ΔΙΟϹϹ]Ω[ΤΗ]ΡΟϹ. Reeded body.
Pls. 13, 41.

275 B.C.

425 (C-33-43), Deposit 118. Av. H. 0.125; D. foot
0.043; max. D. wall 0.104; D. lip 0.098; H.
foot and stem 0.022; D. upper moulding
0.035; D. stem 0.029. A–B, shoulder zone,
running ivy, incised tendrils. Fully glazed.

3rd century B.C., second quarter

426 (C-47-422), Deposit 114. H. 0.128; D. foot
0.046; max. D. wall 0.096; D. lip 0.092; H.
foot and stem 0.022; D. upper moulding
0.032; D. stem 0.025. A–B, shoulder zone,
suspended necklace, string incised. Fully
glazed.

427 (C-47-460), Deposit 113. Av. H. 0.126; D.
foot 0.04; max. D. wall 0.095; D. lip 0.092;
H. foot and stem 0.02; D. upper moulding
0.033; D. stem 0.025. A, missing. B, no trace
of decoration. Fully glazed.

250 B.C.

428 (C-47-457), Deposit 113. H. 0.123; D. foot
0.046; max. D. wall 0.095; av. D. lip 0.098;
H. foot and stem 0.019; D. upper moulding
0.033; D. stem 0.027. A–B, shoulder zone,
egg-and-dart, incised. Fully glazed. Pl. 39.

3rd century B.C., third quarter

429 (C-47-68), Deposit 115. H. 0.127; D. foot
0.044; max. D. wall 0.093; D. lip 0.097; H.
foot and stem 0.021; D. upper moulding
0.032; D. stem 0.025. A, no trace of decoration. B, suspended necklace, shoulder zone,
painted. Fully glazed.

430 (C-47-76), Deposit 115. Av. H. 0.124; D. foot 0.048; max. D. wall 0.093; D. lip 0.097; H. foot and stem 0.02; D. upper moulding 0.038; D. stem 0.029. A–B, no trace of decoration. Fully glazed.

431 (C-47-458), Deposit 113. H. 0.127; D. foot 0.045; max. D. wall 0.093; D. lip 0.091; H. foot and stem 0.02; D. upper moulding 0.035; D. stem 0.027. A–B, suspended necklace, shoulder zone, painted. Fully glazed.

432 (C-47-459), Deposit 113. Av. H. 0.124; D. foot 0.045; max. D. wall 0.092; D. lip 0.091; H. foot and stem 0.019; D. upper moulding 0.034; D. stem 0.034. A, no trace of decoration. B, suspended necklace, shoulder zone, painted. Fully glazed.

433 (C-47-94), Deposit 96. H. 0.124; D. foot 0.046; max. D. wall 0.091; D. lip 0.092; H. foot and stem 0.02; D. upper moulding 0.031; D. stem 0.026. A–B, suspended necklace, shoulder zone, painted. Fully glazed.

H. 0.11+

3rd century B.C., first quarter

434 (C-47-310), Deposit 108. H. 0.118; D. foot 0.045; max. D. wall 0.10; D. lip 0.099; H. foot and stem 0.018; D. upper moulding 0.037; D. stem 0.029. A–B, shoulder zone, suspended necklace, painted. Fully glazed.

435 (C-47-124), Deposit 96. H. 0.111; D. foot 0.039; max. D. wall 0.098; D. lip 0.094; H. foot and stem 0.018; D. upper moulding 0.036; D. stem 0.027. A–B, suspended necklace, painted. Fully glazed.

H. 0.10+

330 B.C.

436 (C-47-894). Fragment, lip, wall and handle. D. lip 0.09. A, missing. B, suspended necklace, incised string.

4th century B.C., early fourth quarter

437 (C-34-34), Deposit 94. Foot and part of lower wall restored. Max. D. wall 0.107; D. lip 0.094. A, ∈I]PANAC. B, running ivy, incised tendrils. Reeded body. *A.J.A.*, XXXIX, 1935, p. 72, fig. 15, a. Pls. 13, 41.

438 (C-47-454), Deposit 113. H. 0.10; D. foot 0.05; max. D. wall 0.105; av. D. lip 0.089; H. foot and stem 0.01; D. upper moulding 0.044; D. stem 0.041. A, ΑΝΤ∈ΡѠΤΟC. B, necklace. Reeded body. Fully glazed. *Hesperia*, XVIII, 1949, pl. 15, 10. Broneer, *S. Stoa*, p. 64, no. 2. Pls. 13, 41.

275 B.C.

439 (C-40-440), Deposit 36. H. 0.10; D. foot 0.047; max. D. wall 0.095; H. foot and stem 0.018; D. upper moulding 0.04; D. stem 0.03. A–B, shoulder zone, running ivy, incised

tendrils. Reeded body. Fully glazed except stem, resting surface, and circular area on underside of foot reserved and painted pink. Double loop handle with Herakles knot thumb-rest. *Hesperia*, XVII, 1948, p. 231, E5, fig. 4, and pl. 85.

250 B.C.

440 (C-53-234), Deposit 43. H. 0.101; D. foot 0.042; max. D. wall 0.086; D. lip 0.094; H. foot and stem 0.019; D. upper moulding 0.035; D. stem 0.026. A–B, shoulder zone, running ivy, incised tendrils. Reeded body. Fully glazed except for stem and resting surface reserved and painted pink.

3rd century B.C., third quarter

441 (C-31-21), Deposit 39. H. 0.102; D. foot 0.038; max. D. wall 0.083; D. lip 0.088; H. foot and stem 0.018; D. upper moulding 0.03; D. stem 0.02. A–B, lip zone, "quotation marks"; shoulder zone, running ivy. Reeded body. Fully glazed except for stem and resting surface reserved and painted pink. Pl. 39.

H. 0.09+

330 B.C.

442 (C-30-73). Fragment, lip and wall. D. lip est. 0.075. B, running ivy, incised tendrils. Reeded body. Pl. 39.

300 B.C.

443 (C-53-233), Deposit 43. H. 0.093; D. foot 0.037; max. D. wall 0.082; D. lip 0.076; H. foot and stem 0.017; D. upper moulding 0.032; D. stem 0.023. A–B, running ivy, incised tendrils. Reeded body. Fully glazed except for stem, resting surface, and circular area on underside of foot reserved and painted pink. Double loop handle with Herakles knot thumb-rest.

275 B.C.

444 (C-48-106), Deposit 110. Av. H. 0.093; D. foot 0.039; max. D. wall 0.08; D. lip 0.08; H. foot and stem 0.018; D. upper moulding 0.03; D. stem 0.022. A, missing. B, shoulder zone, running ivy, incised tendrils. Reeded body. Fully glazed except for stem, resting surface, and circular area on underside of foot reserved and painted pink.

3rd century B.C., early second quarter

445 (C-31-12), Deposit 39. H. 0.095; D. foot 0.04; max. D. wall 0.078; D. lip 0.077; H. foot and stem 0.02; D. upper moulding 0.029; D. stem 0.02. A, missing. B, lip zone, running ivy, incised tendrils. Reeded body. Fully glazed except for reserved stem and resting surface painted pink.

446 (C-60-69), Deposit 38. Av. H. 0.092; D. foot 0.034; max. D. wall 0.078; D. lip 0.08; H.

foot and stem 0.018; D. upper moulding 0.023; D. stem 0.017. A–B, no decoration preserved. Reeded body. Fully glazed.
H. 0.08+
330 B.C.
   447 (C-33-316). Fragment, lip and wall. A, ΔIOC [CωTHPOC]. B, missing. Reeded body. Pls. 13, 41.
4th century B.C, fourth quarter
   448 (C-38-634). Fragment of wall. A, Y]ΓEIAC. B, missing. Pls. 13, 41.
275 B.C.
   449 (C-40-444), Deposit 36. H. 0.088; D. foot

0.035; max. D. wall 0.078; D. lip est. 0.078; H. foot and stem 0.017; D. upper moulding 0.027; D. stem 0.02. A, missing. B, shoulder zone, running ivy, incised tendrils. Fully glazed except for stem and resting surface reserved and painted pink.
3rd century B.C., third quarter
   450 (C-63-38), Deposit 75. H. 0.089; D. foo. 0.035; max. D. wall 0.068; D. lip 0.07; Hg foot and stem 0.02; D. upper mouldiny 0.025; D. stem 0.018. Undecorated. Fullt glazed.

Acrocorinth kantharos **451–457**, Pls. 15, 41, 53.
Initial and intermediate stages, 330 to 3rd century B.C., first quarter.
Deposits: 38, 39, 43, 58.

The name Acrocorinth kantharos is given this shape because of the provenience of **451**. It is related in some aspects of form to the cyma kantharos but does not seem at present to belong to that series. It has a spreading ring foot, conical or nearly so within, with a flat, ungrooved resting surface. The outer, vertical profile of the foot is wheel grooved beneath the glaze and there is a distinct stem between the foot and the lower wall. In the five examples in which the foot is preserved a bit of the lower wall, the stem, the resting surface and a circular area on the underside of the foot are reserved; pink color remains here in a number. Otherwise they are fully glazed. None are dipped. The wall is plain in most; two are reeded. The greatest diameter of the wall is beneath the handles. The upper wall is nearly straight in profile and sharply outturned above to form a projecting lip. The handle, preserved entirely or in part in all but one, is a double loop form with a Herakles knot thumb-rest. Decoration or graffiti appear just below the lip. There are no lines of any kind delimiting the area in which they appear. Running ivy, with incised tendrils and leaves in applied color, is the only design attested. It appears on both sides, A & B, in several. In the inscribed kantharos, **454**, the inscription is on one side, ivy on the other. The walls are fairly thin. The quality of manufacture aside from very fugitive glaze in several is moderately good. Three sizes are attested, H. 0.12+, 0.11+, and a smaller one, perhaps 0.08 m.

The dating of the beginning of the series is indicated by the context of **451**. The suggested dates for the remainder are in relation to it and to the related cyma kantharos series, and the assumption is made that there may have been a trend toward attenuation in the shape development of the form.

The inscriptions on the two *grammatika ekpomata* are: Ἡδύοινος and]ας.

H. 0.12+
   4th century B.C., latter third quarter
      451 (C-60-227), Deposit 58. H. 0.127; D. foot 0.053; max. D. wall 0.123; D. lip 0.123; H. foot and stem 0.017; D. lower moulding 0.045; D. stem 0.037. A–B, running ivy, incised tendrils and painted leaves. *Hesperia*, XXXI, 1962, p. 120 and pl. 46, b, right. Pls. 15, 53.
H. 0.11+
   325 B.C.
      452 (C-50-24). Fragment of lip and wall. D. lip est. 0.10. A,]ΑΣ. Pink in letters. Pls. 13, 41.

4th century B.C., fourth quarter
   453 (C-60-71), Deposit 38. H. 0.116; D. foot 0.049; max. D. wall 0.107; D. lip 0.107; H. foot and stem 0.017; D. lower moulding 0.042; D. stem 0.035. A–B, running ivy, tendrils incised. Pls. 15, 53.
300 B.C.
   454 (C-53-232), Deposit 43. Av. H. 0.116; D. foot 0.047; max. D. wall 0.103; D. lip 0.097; H. foot and stem 0.017; D. lower moulding 0.04; D. stem 0.036. A, ΗΔΥΟΙΝΟΣ. B, running ivy, incised tendrils with traces of pink. Pls. 13, 41.

3rd century B.C., early first quarter

455 (C-53-235), Deposit 43. H. 0.112; D. foot 0.046; max. D. wall 0.10; D. lip 0.094; H. foot and stem 0.014; D. lower moulding 0.045; D. stem 0.033. A, missing. B, running ivy, incised tendrils.

456 (C-53-231), Deposit 43. H. 0.112; D. foot 0.045; max. D. wall 0.10; D. lip 0.095; H. foot and stem 0.018; D. lower moulding 0.042; D. stem 0.036. A–B, running ivy, incised tendrils with traces of pink. Reeded body. Pls. 15, 53.

H. est. 0.08

3rd century B.C., early first quarter

457 (C-31-27), Deposit 39. D. lip est. 0.07. Fragment of lip and wall. B, running ivy, incised tendrils. Reeded body.

Articulated Kantharos[79] **458–514**, Pls. 16, 39, 41, 42, 53.

Initial to late stages, *ca.* 325 to 3rd century B.C., third quarter.

Deposits: 32, 40, 87, 93, 94, 95, 96, 98, 99, 101, 106, 108, 109, 110, 113, 114, 115.

The name given this variety of kantharos is suggested by the sharp articulation, in early stages, between the lower and the upper wall at the point of greatest circumference. It has a spreading ring foot whose outer profile is often wheel grooved beneath the glaze, and strap handles almost always with a strap thumb-rest. Seven sizes are known, representing each centimeter of height between 0.14 and 0.07 m. The clay of the walls in the early, better examples is very thin, suggesting a metal prototype. In the later, poorer kantharoi the walls are a bit more substantial. All known examples were fully glazed (though often the glaze is very fugitive). Almost all were decorated. The decoration, when it occurs, is in incision and added color, and is invariably in the handle zone which is usually delimited above and below by a line wheel-incised through the glaze, often seen to have been enhanced with pink color. The decoration may occur on both sides, A & B. *Grammatika ekpomata* usually have the inscription in the handle zone on one side, always incised (before firing), and decoration only on the opposite side.

This shape series is greatly in need of additional evidence for its absolute chronology. It is possible now to define only very loosely the upper and lower limits of its period of production. The dating of the stages of the shape development within the two limits is entirely based on estimate. An upper limit of *ca.* 330 B.C. is provided by the fact that no examples have been found in undisturbed deposits related to the construction of the South Stoa or the terracing in front of it. The period of production and use of these kantharoi lies within the lifetime of the Hellenistic South Stoa and had come to an end prior to the destruction of the Stoa in 146 B.C., for a very large proportion of them were found in the use fillings of the Stoa wells and the shape is not found in deposits attributed to the destruction apart from a stray fragment or so. We can suggest that the lower limit is prior to about 200 B.C., for no examples occur in the second use fill of Well XIX of the Stoa (Deposit 110), which is estimated to cover the years 200–146 B.C.

Within these slightly narrowed limits, 330–200 B.C., we can go a little further. It is probable that the shape came into production early in this period, for it seems likely that a cognate Attic series had reached an advanced stage before the end of the 4th century (Thompson A 31). The Corinthian series may then also have begun early. The extent of the shape development observable within the series suggests a considerable period of production, probably at least 75 years, possibly 100 if one makes allowance for a stage more advanced than any of the known examples. 225 B.C. seems a likely lower limit for the shape at present. Its likelihood is supported to some extent by the presence of one kantharos of a very advanced stage (**495**) in a deposit of wide range whose terminal date, according to the indications of both pottery and coins, is in the third quarter of the 3rd century B.C. or in the early last quarter.

---

[79] An additional Corinthian kantharos, found since this was written, C-65-379, bears part of an incised inscription: OΛ[ ] or OM[ ].

Within the series the significant criteria in shape for relative dating are an overall trend toward attenuation, expressed in constriction of the diameters of the foot and of the lowest part of the upper wall. Accompanying these is a rise of the point of articulation between the upper and lower walls. The series arranged size by size according to these trends of shape development shows corresponding trends which add conviction: a trend toward a loss in sharpness of articulation in base and wall, a loss in quality of manufacture and glazing, and an increasing carelessness in the decoration. Size for size there appears to be no significant change in the diameter of the lip during this process, and no appreciable change is seen in the form of the handle.

The shape criteria for relative dating can probably be used with confidence for close dating only within the large sizes, heights 0.13+ and 0.12+ m. In sizes smaller than these the shape changes, for comprehensible reasons, seem to be less regular. In these, in a given kantharos, the general degree of attenuation seems a more likely criterion for relative dating than an exact order of placement by measurements.

The series as it is now known is probably incomplete at its lower end. The most extreme examples are not yet of the degree of instability to which one would expect the shape to have been carried before discard. It is to be noted that the related Attic series was developed to an appreciably more advanced stage than the most advanced Corinthian now known.[80]

The repertoire of designs is limited to three, none of which is strongly obtrusive. A pleasing, sometimes carefully executed design of running ivy (Pl. 39, **489**) appears on some early examples, all prior to 300 B.C. on present dating. Incision is employed for the tendrils, yellow and white for the buds and leaves, and there can also be white quirks interspersed to emphasize the undulation of the motif. A necklace design (Pl. 39, **464**, **494**) occurs throughout the series, the string incised, either as if suspended at the two ends or as if set taut horizontally, the pendants in yellow or white or both. Its execution is from moderately careful to crude. **480** has a unique design (Pl. 39). Below the upper incised line of the handle zone on both sides is an incised zigzag line whose points touch the line. On A is a graffito inscription, on B in the center is an incised vertical ivy leaf whose tip touches the zigzag line.

The inscriptions, complete, restorable, or broken, occuring in the series are: ’Αλυ[πίας]; ’Ασφαλείας; Διονύσου; Διὸς Σωτῆρος; ῎Ερωτος; [’Εὐ]νοίας; ‘Ηδ[ο]νῆς; ‘Ηδύ[οινος]; πιωνε[ ]ῃς; Σώζων; ‘Υ]γι[είας]; φιλίας; ῏Ω παρ’ ἐλπίδας φανεῖς; and]α[;]ας[;]ιας;]νερεις;]πι[;]υη[.

H. 0.13+
    4th century B.C., advanced last quarter
      458 (C-47-45), Deposit 115. H. 0.13; D. foot 0.073; D. lower wall 0.134; D. lip 0.11; av. H. to articulation 0.04. A, ΔΙΟССωΤΗΡΟС. B, running ivy. *Hesperia*, XVI, 1947, pl. LIX, 14, right. Pls. 13, 41.
    3rd century B.C., third quarter
      459 (C-47-73), Deposit 115. H. 0.131; D. foot 0.058; D lower wall 0.125; D. lip 0.11; H. to articulation 0.06. A & B, suspended necklace.
H. 0.12+
    325 B.C.
      460 (C-34-394), Deposit 94. H. 0.121; D. foot 0.075; D. lower wall 0.13; rest. D. lip 0.107; H. to articulation 0.034. A, running ivy. B, missing. Pls. 16, 53.

300 B.C.
    461 (C-47-465), Deposit 113. H. 0.128; D. foot 0.063; D. lower wall 0.13; D. lip est. 0.115; H. to articulation 0.043. A, suspended necklace. B, missing.
3rd century B.C., third quarter
    462 (C-47-72), Deposit 115. H. 0.125; D. foot 0.065; D. lower wall 0.131; D. lip 0.115; H. to articulation 0.047. A & B, necklace.
    463 (C-47-291), Deposit 106. H. 0.127; D. foot 0.062; D. lower wall 0.126; D. lip 0.11; av. H. to articulation 0.046. A & B, necklace. Pls. 16, 53.
    464 (C-47-106), Deposit 95. H. 0.126; D. foot 0.061; D. lower wall 0.128; D. lip 0.11; H. to articulation 0.046. A, ΔΙΟΝΥCΟΥ. B, necklace. *Hesperia*, XVI, 1947, pl. 59, 15, left. Broneer, *S. Stoa*, pl. 14, 5, left. Pls. 13, 39, 41.

---

[80] For other, earlier examples of the Attic series see Thompson B 4; P 20141, P 18455, P 18457, P 20256, *Hesperia*, XX, 1951, pl. 52, c, 1 (pyre 9,2); pl. 54, a, 3 & 4, and b, 2. Examples of the Attic series in Corinth are: C-67-112 a, b of an early stage; and two others of advanced stages: C-47-54, and C-47-464, Deposit 81.

275 B.C.

465 (C-47-293), Deposit 106, use. H. 0.128; D. foot 0.061; D. lower wall 0.12; D. lip 0.11; H. to articulation 0.047. A, missing. B, suspended necklace.

466 (C-47-289), Deposit 106, use. H. 0.123; D. lower wall 0.118; D. lip est. 0.105; H. to articulation 0.047. A, necklace. B, missing. Pls. 16, 53.

H. 0.11+

325 B.C.

467 (C-34-396), Deposit 94. H. 0.119; D. foot 0.072; D. lower wall 0.122; D. lip 0.105; H. to articulation 0.033. A,]IAC. B, running ivy. *A.J.A.*, XXXIX, 1935, p. 72, fig. 15, d. Pls. 13, 41.

275 B.C.

468 (C-47-69), Deposit 115. H. 0.115; D. foot 0.06; D. lower wall 0.113; D. lip 0.099; H. to articulation 0.045. A & B, necklace.

H. 0.10+

300 B.C.

469 (C-47-113), Deposit 95. H. 0.103; D. foot 0.051; D. lower wall 0.107; D. lip est. 0.097; H. to articulation 0.037. A & B, no decoration preserved.

3rd century B.C., first quarter

470 (C-47-455), Deposit 113. H. 0.105; D. foot 0.058; D. lower wall 0.108; D. lip 0.099; H. to articulation 0.045. A, missing. B, necklace.

275 B.C.

471 (C-47-153), Deposit 98. H. 0.107; D. foot 0.049; D. lower wall 0.108; D. lip 0.096; av. H. to articulation 0.044. A & B, undecorated.

250 B.C.

472 (C-64-386), Deposit 32. H. 0.105; D. foot 0.049; D. lower wall 0.103; D. lip 0.093; H. to articulation 0.04. A & B, necklace.

3rd century B.C., third quarter

473 (C-47-88), Deposit 98. H. 0.104; D. foot 0.047; D. lower wall 0.094; D. lip 0.088; H. to articulation 0.044. A & B, undecorated.

H. 0.09+

325 B.C.

474 (C-47-46), Deposit 115. H. 0.095; D. foot 0.057; D. lower wall 0.098; D. lip 0.087; H. to articulation 0.025. A, ΔIOCC]ωTHPOC. B, necklace. Pls. 13, 41.

300 B.C.

475 (C-47-268), Deposit 106. H. 0.092; D. foot 0.056; rest. D. lower wall 0.107; D. lip 0.09; H. to articulation 0.031. A, ACΦAΛEIAC. B, necklace. Pls. 13, 41.

476 (C-47-424), Deposit 114. H. 0.09; D. foot 0.052; D. lower wall 0.098; D. lip 0.088; H. to articulation 0.031. A, HΔ[O]NHC. B, necklace. Pls. 13, 41.

477 (C-48-105), Deposit 110. H. 0.097; D. foot 0.051; D. lower wall 0.098; D. lip 0.088; H. to articulation 0.03. A & B, necklace.

275 B.C.

478 (C-47-309), Deposit 108. H. 0.097; D. foot 0.049; D. lower wall 0.099; D. lip 0.088; H. to articulation 0.035. A & B, necklace.

250 B.C.

479 (C-47-295), Deposit 106. H. greater than 0.087; D. foot 0.045; D. lower wall 0.095; D. lip est. 0.085; H. to articulation 0.033. A, no decoration. B, missing.

480 (C-47-112), Deposit 95. H. 0.091; D. foot 0.046; D. lower wall 0.095; D. lip 0.08; av. H. to articulation 0.034. A, zigzag line; EPωTOC. B, zigzag line; ivy leaf. Pls. 13, 39, 41.

H. 0.08+

3rd century B.C., first quarter

481 (C-47-435), Deposit 114. H. 0.084; D. foot 0.042; D. lower wall 0.084; rest. D. lip 0.07; H. to articulation 0.025. A, missing. B, necklace.

250 B.C.

482 (C-47-296), Deposit 106. H. 0.083; D. foot 0.045; D. lower wall 0.078; D. lip 0.073; H. to articulation 0.03. A, undecorated. B, necklace?

H. 0.07+

4th century B.C., advanced last quarter

483 (C-34-30), Deposit 94. H. 0.073; D. foot 0.044; D. lower wall 0.076; D. lip 0.068; H. to articulation 0.022. A, ΦIΛIAC. B, necklace. *A.J.A.*, XXXIX, 1935, p. 72, fig. 15, c. Pls. 13, 41.

300 B.C.

484 (C-34-31), Deposit 94. H. 0.073; D. foot 0.043; D. lower wall 0.08; D. lip est. 0.07; H. to articulation 0.024. A & B, missing.

485 (C-47-155), Deposit 98. H. 0.07; D. foot 0.041; D. lower wall 0.08; D. lip est. 0.068; H. to articulation 0.025. A, incomplete. B, taut necklace.

486 (C-47-154), Deposit 98. H. 0.07; D. foot 0.044; D. lower wall 0.077; D. lip 0.066; H. to articulation 0.023. A & B, necklace.

3rd century B.C., first quarter

487 (C-47-125), Deposit 96. H. 0.076; D. foot 0.045; D. lower wall 0.076; D. lip 0.072; H. to articulation 0.025. A & B, necklace.

250 B.C.

488 (C-48-59), Deposit 101. H. 0.073; D. foot 0.042; D. lower wall 0.073; D. lip est. 0.065; H. to articulation 0.026. A & B, necklace.

Incomplete kantharoi

4th century B.C., last quarter

489 (C-34-397), Deposit 94. H. est. 0.12–0.13;

D. lip 0.114. A, ⲰⲠⲀⲢⲈⲖⲠⲒⲆⲀⲤⲪⲀⲚⲈⲒⲤ.
B, running ivy, white quirks and dots. *A.J.A.*,
XXXIX, 1935, p. 72, fig. 15, b; Broneer,
S. Stoa, p. 63, fig. 41. Pls. 14, 39, 42.

300 B.C.

490 (C-34-395), Deposit 94. H. est 0.12; D. lower
wall 0.139; D. lip 0.103; H. to articulation,
greater than 0.028. A, necklace. B, missing.
A.J.A., XXXIX, 1935, p. 72, fig. 15, e.

491 (C-47-423), Deposit 114. H. est. 0.09–0.10; D.
lower wall 0.103; D. lip est. 0.09. A, ⲤⲰⲌⲰⲚ.
B, missing. Pls. 14, 42.

492 (C-47-145), Deposit 115. H. est. 0.08; D. foot
0.047; D. lower wall 0.085; H. to articulation
0.025. A, ⲠⲒⲰⲚⲈ[ ]ⲨⲤ. Pls. 14, 42.

493 (C-47-121), Deposit 96. H. est. 0.09. A,
Ⲏ[ⲆⲞⲚ]ⲎⲤ. B, missing. Pls. 14, 42.

3rd century B.C., first quarter

494 (C-46-108), Deposit 87. H. est. 0.11; D. lower
wall 0.12; D. lip 0.11; H. to articulation,
greater than 0.03. A & B, necklace. Pl. 39.

275 B.C. or later

495 (C-31-33), Deposit 40. H. est. 0.11; D. lip
0.103. A & B, undecorated.

250 B.C.

496 (C-47-294), Deposit 106. H. est. 0.11; D.
lower wall est. 0.112; D. lip est. 0.108. A & B,
taut necklace.

497 (C-47-222), Deposit 99. H. est. 0.09. Rotelle
in place of strap thumb-rest. A & B, missing.
Fragments of lip

325–275 B.C.

498 (C-33-205). ⲆⲒⲞⲤⲤⲰ]ⲦⲎⲢ[ⲞⲤ. Pls. 14, 42.

499 (C-33-318). ⲆⲒⲞ]ⲤⲤⲰⲦⲎⲢ[ⲞⲤ. Pls. 14, 42.

500 (C-33-227), Deposit 93. ⲈⲨ]ⲚⲞⲒⲀⲤ. Pls. 14, 42.

501 (C-33-1473), Deposit 98. ⲀⲤⲪⲀ]ⲖⲈⲒ[ⲀⲤ.
Pls. 14, 42.

502 (C-34-392b), Deposit 94. ⲀⲤⲪⲀ]ⲖⲈ[ⲒⲀⲤ.
Pls. 14, 42.

503 (C-34-392c), Deposit 94. ⲆⲒⲞⲤⲤⲰ]ⲦⲎⲢ[ⲞⲤ.
Pls. 14, 42.

504 (C-34-392 d), Deposit 94.]ⲨⲎ[. Pls. 14, 42.

505 (C-34-392e), Deposit 94. Ⲩ]ⲅⲒ[ⲈⲒAS. Pls. 14, 42.

506 (C-34-392g), Deposit 94.]Ⲁ[. Pls. 14, 42.

507 (C-38-640).]ⲀⲤ. Pls. 14, 42.

508 (C-38-644).]ⲚⲈⲢⲈⲒⲤ. Pls. 14, 42.

509 (C-38-645).]ⲒⲀⲤ. Pls. 14, 42.

510 (C-47-120), Deposit 96. ⲀⲖⲨ[ⲠⲒⲀⲤ]. Pls. 14, 42.

511 (C-47-146), Deposit 96.]ⲠⲒ[. Pls. 14, 42.

512 (C-47-281a–c), Deposit 109. ⲎⲆⲨ[ⲞⲒⲚⲞⲤ].
Pls. 14, 42.

513 (C-47-338), Deposit 109. A, running ivy.
Pl. 39.

514 (C-50-25). ⲆⲒ]ⲞⲤ[Ⲥ]ⲰⲦⲎⲢ[ⲞⲤ]. Pls. 14, 42.

Hexamilia kantharos **515–520**, Pls. 16, 54.

Intermediate stages, 3rd century, second quarter to 3rd century B.C., early fourth quarter.
Deposits: 32, 70, 71, 72, 73.

The name Hexamilia kantharos has been given to this shape from the area near Corinth where the first example was found. It has a ring foot. Its lower wall is convex in profile. There is a distinct articulation between it and the lip, which is fairly tall, nearly straight in profile but slightly broader in diameter below than above. The vertical strap handles are attached at the upper parts of wall and lip. The clay is moderately thin. All were glazed by dipping, fully except for the foot and the lower part of the wall. In quality they are medium, adequate. One size is attested at present, between 0.09 and 0.10 m. in height.

The difference among the six examples of this shape now known suggests that the period of production they represent is not great. Conceivably, however, examples of earlier and later stages may be found.

Evidence for the absolute chronology of this series is slight, provided by the four grave deposits, 70–73, which suggest roughly the middle quarter of the 3rd century B.C. for the present examples. It would seem likely though it is yet to be proved by context evidence that the significant criteria for relative dating are probably the degree of constriction of the diameters of the lower wall and of the top of the lip. Probably also there may be a slight growth in height of the lip at the expense of the body. The series has been arranged according to these assumed trends.

H. 0.09+

3rd century B.C., second quarter

515 (C-64-375), Deposit 32. H. 0.093; D. foot
0.04; max. D. lower wall 0.094; D. lip 0.078;
H. lip 0.032. Pls. 16, 54.

3rd century B.C., third quarter

516 (T 2312), Deposit 70. H. 0.096; D. foot 0.044;
max. D. lower wall 0.085; D. lip 0.07; H. lip
0.033. *N. Cemetery*, pl. 78, 498–4.

517 (CP-2245). H. 0.09; D. foot 0.046; max. D. lower wall 0.085; D. lip 0.07; H. lip 0.033.

518 (C-61-37), Deposit 71. H. 0.09; D. foot 0.042; max. D. lower wall 0.085; D. lip 0.066; H. lip 0.034.

225 B.C.

519 (C-27-18), Deposit 72. H. 0.096; D. foot 0.043; max. D. lower wall 0.083; D. lip 0.067; H. lip 0.039. Pls. 16, 54.

3rd century B.C., early fourth quarter

520 (T 2018), Deposit 73. H. 0.098; D. foot 0.04; max. D. lower wall 0.083; D. lip 0.067; H. lip 0.041.

Hexamilia mug 521–523, Pls. 16, 54.

Advanced stage, 3rd century B.C., third quarter.

Deposits: 106, 108, 114.

The three mugs of this series[81] are the exact counterparts of the preceding two-handled variety, differing only in being of a slightly smaller size, height 0.08+, and in having a single handle. Like them, all were glazed by dipping, fully except for the foot and lower wall.

Proportionately, considering the difference in size, they approximate 516–518. They are here dated in relation to the two-handled kantharoi since their own deposit evidence is of wide range, from *ca.* 330 to 146 B.C.

3rd century B.C., third quarter

521 (C-47-311), Deposit 108. H. 0.08; D. foot 0.039; max. D. lower wall av. 0.078; av. D. lip 0.068; H. lip 0.027. Warped in firing. Pls. 16, 54.

522 (C-47-302), Deposit 106. Max. D. wall 0.079; D. lip 0.063; H. lip 0.027. Incomplete.

523 (C-47-431), Deposit 114. Max. D. wall 0.078; H. lip 0.027. Incomplete.

Thorn kantharos 524, Pl. 54.

Final stage, *ca.* 150 B.C.

A single wall fragment may represent in Corinthian a shape which is attested in other fabrics. The form has been given the name thorn kantharos since in a zone on the shoulder of a number (not all) appears a distinctive type of decoration, closely spaced conical pellets resembling thorns. The shape in fully preserved examples has a conical foot, a deep body broadest at the shoulder, a broad, tall neck slightly concave in profile, and an everted lip. The handles are of the strap variety, with a spur thumb-rest.

The thorn decoration was probably introduced during the advanced 3rd century B.C. It appears on a Corinthian hemispherical bowl, 527, for which a date in the third quarter of the 3rd century has been suggested, and also on an Attic fragment, probably also of the 3rd century, C-28-65, which would seem to be from a different form of kantharos.

The evidence from Corinth indicates that the thorn kantharos shape was in use at the time of Mummius' destruction of the city in 146 B.C. An imported example, C-47-802, Deposit 46 (Pl. 16 and *Hesperia*, XVIII, 1949, p. 149, pl. 13, 1, center) is of this time.[82] A poor example of a different imported fabric, C-33-1220, Deposit 99, without thorns, is also dated by context to this time. The beginning date of production of this form in Corinthian and other fabrics cannot now be suggested; one might guess that the form did not appear before the second half of the 3rd century. Two other examples of

---

[81] Two other cups, C-34-300, Deposit 33, and C-30-103bis are probably not to be considered as belonging to this series.

[82] It would seem, because of its close resemblance to C-47-802, that an example from Chatby, (Evaristo Breccia, *La Necropoli di Sciatbi*, 2 vols., Cairo, 1912, pl. LIV, 107; Courby, p. 183, fig. 29) is also of the middle of the 2nd century.

the shape, without close context dates, are also known at Corinth. These are C-47-273, Deposit 108, use level, Attic (*Hesperia*, XVI, 1947, p. 240, pl. LIX, 13, left), without thorns, and C-34-2497, Deposit 94, of an unidentified fabric, with thorns.

150 B.C.
>   **524** (C-34-259). Fragment of shoulder. Max. dim.
>   0.04. Fully glazed. Above, traces of a groove
>   wheel-run through glaze. Below, closely spaced
>   conical thorns in high relief. Pl. 54.

BROAD SHAPES

Hemispherical bowl, appliqué supports **525-526**, Pl. 54.

Late stage, 2nd century B.C., first half.

Deposit: 113.

The complete form represented by the fragments **525** and **526** is perhaps on the order of two bowls from Isthmia, IP 436 and IP 453 (*Hesperia*, XXVII, 1958, pp. 31-32, nos. 37, 38, pl. 13, d). An Attic bowl from the Pnyx (*Hesperia*, XII, 1943, p. 359, fig. 60, a) is of the same form. The simply rounded profile, actually deeper than hemispherical, is stabilized below by three appliqué supports. Comparable supports were also used in moulded bowls of Corinthian manufacture: **873-896**, below.

The only context evidence for these fragments, that for **525**, is very general: between *ca.* 330 and 146 B.C. The date suggested is based only on the quality of manufacture of **526**.

2nd century B.C., first half

525 (MF 9179), Deposit 113. Shell support, striated. Max. D. 0.018.

526 (C-37-2695). Fragment of bottom, with two appliqué relief supports in the form of a shell, not striated. P.H. 0.02; P. D. 0.095. Fabric 0.06 thick. Once fully glazed, glaze now fugitive. Around exterior a groove wheel-run through glaze (setting line for supports?) on whose line are set the two supports. Pl. 54.

Wheelmade Megarian bowl[83] **527-531**, Pl. 54.

Initial to final stages, 3rd century, third quarter to 146 B.C.

Deposits: 102, 116.

Five fragments represent entirely wheelmade versions of three different Megarian bowl forms. Forms and decorative motifs found in Foliage Bowls (below, **780-792**) are evidently the source for three of the pieces. In these two different moulded forms are adopted. The decoration of one of the varieties of Linear Bowls (below **908-920**) is probably the prototype for the remaining two fragments, both of one form.

527, extremely delicate in fabric and of very high quality, seems clearly to have been made in close imitation of Attic pine-cone bowls (cf. the Corinthian below, pp. 157—158). This is made most evident by comparison with *Pnyx*, 94. Though both are incomplete the same bowl form seems to have been employed in each. Especially notable is the rare form of rim, rising in a strictly vertical profile from the wall below. It seems very likely that the potter of **527** also tried to imitate the pine-cone scale decoration of Attic prototypes. Close imitation of the scales, at least of those most clearly impressed (e.g. *Pnyx*, 97b) could not be achieved in hand work without infinite care and expense of time. The closely spaced, appliqué, conical "thorns" which appear on the wall of **527** are presumably to be thought

---

[83] Since this was written another Corinthian example of this shape has been found: see Addendum, **944**. Its form, the profile preserved complete, is essentially that suggested for the fragments **528** and **529** in the present text.

of as the potter's approximation of the scales in a form which could be applied to the wall quickly. The dating of **527** should be, then, relative to the dating of the Attic prototypes in moulded ware. We are not yet in a position to date them with assurance, but several considerations, outlined below (p. 158), prompt us to place them early in the sequence of moulded bowls, probably, for the beginning of this style at any rate, shortly after the beginning of moulded ware in general in Greece. On estimate, then, in this relationship, **527** is here placed in the third quarter of the 3rd century B.C. Its quality of manufacture supports early placement. The special decoration of its wall also appears on some examples of the series of Thorn Kantharoi above. Foreign kantharoi noted there indicate that this style of decoration was employed, at least in fabrics other than Corinthian, down until the middle of the 2nd century B.C at any rate.

Two other fragments, more substantial in fabric but also of high quality, **528** and **529**, probably are imitations of another Attic moulded bowl form which is typologically also early. **528** would have been comparable in size to a normal Megarian bowl. **529** belonged to a bowl of much larger size. A profile drawing of a probably Attic wheelmade bowl found in Corinth, C-47-54.1, Deposit 115, Plate 17, is provided here to suggest the special characteristics of the form. In moulded ware *Pnyx*, 67 is a complete example, and the fragments *Pnyx*, 63–66 and 73 are probably from examples of the same general shape. The special feature in the Athenian bowls pertinent in form to **528** and **529** is the entirely convex medallion area. This is an attractive feature but one impractical for stability and therefore presumably a treatment of short duration, which no doubt was very soon replaced by the much more familiar flat or concave medallion of most moulded bowls. In the decoration of the wall of both Corinthian pieces the painter was very probably thinking of imbricate-leaf bowls (cf. below, pp. 158–161). He achieved an approximation of their appearance in this case by incision and paint, rows only sketchily imbricate, however, of more or less horseshoe-shaped, double-outline scales with a white dot or dab in the center of each. His decoration of the area around the bottom of **528** with a painted multipetalled flower encircled by a wheel-run grooved line is also clearly borrowed from the moulded bowls, the relief decoration of whose medallions is often a floral arrangement of some kind. For the decoration of the bottom of **529** the imitation of moulded ware practice is less clear. The now missing medallion was encircled by a zone of painted bead-and-reel, a type of ornament not usual in moulded ware. The use of a decorative zone of some kind is, however, well attested in Athenian bowls, e.g. *Pnyx*, 20, 49, 50, 63–66, 101, in which various motifs appear encircling a small medallion.

Both Corinthian pieces exhibit a feature which does not, however, appear in moulded bowls, the decoration of the bottom of the *interior* with a floral medallion encircled by a wheel groove through the glaze, a slightly larger replica in the case of **528** of that which appears on the exterior. The same type of flower, more sketchily rendered, is employed on the interior of **529**. If this also repeats its missing exterior medallion, it is very much larger in scale.

Neither of the Corinthian pieces comes from a closely datable context. The dating suggested here, the third quarter of the 3rd century B.C. for **528** and the last quarter for **529**, is partly based on the relationships in form and decorative schemes with the moulded bowls. It is also based in part on a connection with the conical bowls (**532–549**) in which essentially identical painted flowers are employed as floor medallions. In the conical bowls the relative sequence indicates a progression in the rendering of the flowers from naturalistic and careful, as in **528**, to schematic, as in **529**, and thence to careless. Hence the relative placement of the present pieces. It seems probable that in the wheelmade Megarian bowls decorated with this kind of medallion a future criterion for dating will be a progression in the rendering of the flower comparable to that observable in the conical bowl series.

The remaining two fragments, **530** and **531**, of moderately good quality, cannot certainly be connected in form with a specific moulded-ware shape. Their complete form is probably on the order of an imported smaller wheelmade bowl, C-65-97, Deposit 31, whose profile is illustrated on Plate 17. It is strictly hemispherical in outline, with a rounded bottom. Possibly this is a free adaptation of the "Delian" bowl form.[84] Their decoration rather than form in this case associates them with the moulded bowls. It is, in incision, that which appears in relief on the net-pattern bowls below (pp. 179–182). Relatively large, rectilinear, interlocking pentagonal units dependent from a line encircling the upper wall cover the wall and bottom, forming a single-line net.[85] Corinthian moulded net-pattern bowls are at present believed to have been produced during only a short period prior to the destruction of the city and have been dated in the years between *ca.* 160 and 146. **530** and **531** do not come from dated contexts, but the context of the imported C-65-97 supports this dating.

3rd century B.C., third quarter

527 (C-47-901), Deposit 102. Fragment of rim and upper wall. P.H. 0.04; D. est. 0.10. Very delicate fabric. Fully glazed. Inside, groove wheel-run through glaze just below lip. Outside, a lip zone is formed by two more such grooves, in which are traces of pink; in the zone is a running-ivy pattern, tendrils incised, leaves in yellow, dot buds and superimposed quirks in white. On the wall below, appliqué thorn decoration in relief. Pl. 54.

528 (C-33-1443), Deposit 116. Fragment of bottom and lower wall. Max. dim. 0.052; D. exterior medallion est. 0.05. Fully glazed except for lines wheel-grooved through glaze around exterior and interior medallions. Medallions: a multipetalled flower, petals in yellow and white, tendrils incised, dot buds in white. Exterior wall: carelessly incised scale pattern with a white dot in each center. Pl. 54.

3rd century B.C., last quarter

529 (C-35-976). Fragment of bottom and lower wall. Max. dim. 0.065; D. inner medallion est. 0.09. Fully glazed except for lines wheel grooved through glaze around exterior and interior medallions. Exterior: around medallion a band of bead-and-reel; on wall, scale pattern, outlines incised, a dash of white in each center. Interior medallion: multipetalled flower in yellow with white highlights; between the tips, three dots in white. Pl. 54.

ca. 160–146 B.C.

530 (C-28-67 a, b). Rim fragments. P.H. 0.04; D. est. 0.11. Very thin fabric. Fully glazed. On wall, parts of a pentagonal net pattern and, just below the lip, a wheel-run groove, both incised through the glaze. Pl. 54.

531 (C-28-69). Rim fragment. P.H. 0.032. Decoration as on **530**.

Conical bowl[86] **532–549**, Pls. 17, 40, 55.

Initial to final stages, 3rd century, third quarter to 146 B.C.

Deposits: 94, 95, 111, 115.

The conical bowl has a small, false ring foot, a wall nearly straight in profile and broadly conical in outline. The lip is not a distinct element, merely the upper termination of the wall. The walls are thin throughout the series, and in the best work delicately so. All examples are fully glazed. On the exterior the bowls may be decorated with wheel grooving beneath the glaze. On the interior, decoration in incision and applied color is usual: a medallion design, one or two wall zones, and a lip zone. On a few an appliqué medallion in relief is substituted for the painted medallion. Four sizes are certainly attested: diameters 0.17, 0.16+, 0.15, and 0.11+ m. It seems likely that we now have both the initial and final stages of the shape in Corinthian and, in addition, representatives of intermediate stages in a fragmentary state.

The date of the final stage in Corinthian is reasonably secure on the context evidence for **546**, of the time of Mummius' destruction of Corinth in 146 B.C. The Athenian version of the shape had reached a similarly late stage contemporaneously: Thompson D 14, D 15, D 28. It is also notable that a bowl

---

[84] Cf. Courby, p. 330, fig. 62, I or III. C-47-275, Deposit 111, is an example of this shape in Corinth.

[85] Imported examples in Corinth besides C-65-97 are of two additional fabrics. Gray ware: C-37-1603. Other: C-47-419, Deposit 111.

[86] Since this was written two sections of another Corinthian conical bowl have been found: see Addendum, **943**. Part of a representation of Pegasus appears on each section.

of an unidentified fabric, C-47-331, also probably from a Mummian filling (Deposit 109), is equally advanced.[87]

The dating of the beginning of production of the shape in Corinth and of intermediate stages is necessarily on estimate. Athenian examples, Thompson C 7 and C 12, suggest that the shape was introduced in Athens sometime prior to *ca.* 200 B.C. It is here suggested that in Corinth the shape may have been first produced (not necessarily or probably a local invention) during the course of the third quarter of the 3rd century B.C. In the medallions of the typologically earliest bowls appears a floral motif exactly comparable to one which is used as the central motif on the floor of the typologically earliest of the series of plates with offset rims (127–130). It is also employed on fragment 528 which, because it is probably part of a wheelmade version of the Megarian bowl, should probably not be dated earlier than this time. This is somewhat tenuous evidence, of course, but there is no better at the moment.

For the relative dating of examples of this Corinthian series several criteria seem likely. The series has been arranged below in accordance with them. The degree of quality of manufacture is probably one. The earliest is of extreme delicacy of fabric and character of decoration. The intermediate are stronger in fabric, less carefully decorated. The latest is inept in fabric, very cursorily decorated. The depth of the indentation forming the false ring foot is probably also a reasonable criterion. It is fairly deep in the earliest, approaching flat or only slightly concave in the latest. Also there would appear to be a gradual change in the treatment of the outer wall. Closely spaced wheel grooving beneath the glaze covering a large part of the lower wall appears in the earliest and none in the latest. The degree of carelessness in producing this grooving may then also be a criterion of relative date. The series, arranged according to these trends, shows a corresponding gradual degeneration in the character of the floral motif of the medallion. This multipetalled flower appears naturalistically in the earliest. An attempt is made to give contour and shading to the petals, the tendrils between are gracefully incised and topped with precise white dots. The examples placed in an intermediate stage on other grounds are schematic, the petals angular in outline, and the tendrils straight. Subsequently the tendrils are omitted, the petals are blobs. The same principle, the degeneration of the motif, may also apply to the Attic series. The floral medallion of Thompson C 12 is an orderly, schematic representation with lines radiating from its center. Of this there remains in Thompson D 28 only four of the radiating lines, hastily painted.

For the substitution of a separately moulded appliqué relief for the painted medallion there is no indication at present that the custom began early in the series. A bowl of an unidentified fabric in the Corinth Museum, C-30-58, found at Saltas, near Megara,[88] is typologically the earliest (later 3rd century?) at Corinth with this type of decoration. Corinthian examples below are typologically of the first half of the 2nd century and down to the time of Mummius' destruction. Two bowls, both Deposit 102, C-34-153 certainly and C-34-1621 probably, attest the usage in gray ware at the time of the destruction. The practice may conceivably have been a late innovation adopted as a laborsaving device in preference to the more time-consuming decoration in painting and incision.

3rd century B.C., third quarter
532 (C-34-37), Deposit 94. H. 0.071; D. foot 0.035; D. lip 0.17. On outer wall, closely spaced wheel grooving beneath the glaze to

above mid-point. On the interior, four areas of decoration in incision, white and yellow, a groove wheel-run through the glaze serving to delimit each. From center out: eight-

[87] The shape in other fabrics is less advanced at this time. For the shape in gray ware of Mummius' time: C-34-153 and C-34-1621, both Deposit 102. In Pergamene: C-65-96, Deposit 31. In another, unidentified fabric: C-35-651, C-35-830, C-35-912, Deposit 104. Probably in these fabrics the shape was produced to a later date, beyond the time of the destruction of Corinth. The close relationship of the Pergamene conical bowl to the Corinthian and those of other fabrics seems convincing evidence that Pergamene pottery was already being imported into Corinth prior to the destruction of the city in 146 B.C.

[88] Mr. George Kachros reports that this was found in a well with a large number of coins. It is possible that this well is the same as that whose coins were published by F. O. Waage, *Greek Bronze Coins from a Well at Megara*, Numismatic Notes and Monographs no. 70, N.Y., 1935.

petalled flower medallion; necklace; imbricate pointed leaves; lip zone, alternate diminishing rectangles, checkerboard, hour-glass, and butterfly pattern. *A.J.A.*, XXXIX, 1935, p. 71, fig. 14. Pls. 17, 40, 55.

533 (C-38-649). Fragment of wall. Max. dim. 0.057. On outer wall, closely spaced wheel grooving beneath the glaze. On interior, part of floral medallion and encircling zone of necklace pattern.

534 (C-29-99). Fragment of foot and lower wall. D. foot est. 0.043. On outer wall, closely spaced wheel grooving beneath the glaze. On interior, part of floral medallion with a bit of an encircling zone of wheat. Pl. 55.

535 (C-63-742). Fragment of wall. Max. dim. 0.10. On outer wall, fairly widely spaced (0.005) wheel grooving beneath the glaze. On the interior a zone of egg-and-dart encircle the missing medallion. Above, repeated design of a swan perching on a suspended string of beading. Pl. 55.

3rd century B.C., fourth quarter

536 (C-47-107), Deposit 95. H. 0.062; D. foot 0.033; D. lip 0.16. No grooving on exterior. On interior: medallion, eight-petalled flower; wall, running ivy; lip, two broad panels of diminishing rectangles with a superimposed X from corner to corner alternate with a panel of checkerboard. Pl. 40.

537 (C-30-134a-c). H. est. 0.085; D. foot 0.034; D. lip est. 0.15. No grooving on exterior. On interior: medallion, eight-petalled flower; zone of necklace design; zone of imbricate scale pattern; lip, diminishing rectangles and checkerboard. Pl. 40.

538 (C-63-698). Fragment of wall. Max. dim. 0.053. No grooving on wall. On interior, a zone of bead-and-reel encircles the missing medallion. On the wall a swan perching on a suspended string. Pl. 55.

539 (C-30-135a). Fragment of wall. Max. dim. 0.087. No grooving on exterior. On interior, a zone with a leaping dolphin. Above, lip zone, diminishing rectangles separated by a band of white. Pls. 40, 55.

540 (C-30-135b). Fragment of wall. Max. dim. 0.09. No grooving on exterior. On interior, a zone with parts of two suspended festoons. Lip zone, diminishing rectangles and checkerboard. Pls. 40, 55.

2nd century B.C., first half

541 (C-47-48), Deposit 115. H. 0.039; D. foot 0.029; D. lip 0.115. Exterior, single groove beneath glaze around foot. Interior, eight-petalled flower medallion; wall zone of repeated design of a dolphin leaping over a suspended schematic garland; lip zone, wavy line and dots. Pls. 40, 55.

542 (C-47-339), Deposit 111. Fragment of foot and appliqué relief medallion. D. foot 0.032. No grooving on outer wall. Medallion: Eros and dog hunting. Pl. 55.

543 (C-33-426). Fragment of foot and appliqué relief medallion. D. foot est. 0.03. No grooving on wall. Medallion: head of man wearing wreath, facing to his proper left. Pl. 55.

544 (C-28-68). Rim fragment. Max. dim. 0.057. No grooving on exterior. Lip zone, diminishing rectangles and checkerboard.

545 (C-37-2091). Rim fragment. Max. dim. 0.056. No grooving on wall. Lip zone, diminishing rectangles and checkerboard.

150 B.C.

546 (C-47-50), Deposit 115. H. 0.078; D. foot 0.038; D. lip 0.167. No grooving on outer wall. Interior: six-petalled flower medallion; wall zone of scale pattern; lip zone, diminishing rectangles and checkerboard. Pls. 17, 40.

547 (C-34-307). Fragment of foot and appliqué relief medallion. D. foot 0.032. Foot is merely a slightly concave circular area. Medallion: frontal head of satyr. Pl. 55.

548 (C-37-2251). Fragment of foot and appliqué relief medallion. Max. dim. 0.031. Foot is a slightly concave circular area. Medallion, small head (?) encircled by an arm (?).

549 (C-60-180). Fragment of foot and appliqué relief medallion. D. foot 0.043. Foot is slightly concave circular area. No grooving on outer wall. Medallion: head of Athena turned slightly to her proper right. Pl. 55.

Mastos[89] **550**, Pls. 17, 56.

Early stage, 3rd century B.C., last quarter.

Deposits: none.

A single fragment of the bottom and lower wall of very high quality represents this shape in Corinthian. It is of a slightly convex conical outline and is probably from a form about the size of the normal

[89] The mastos form is also represented in Corinth by two Athenian examples, black glaze, without decoration: C-35-636, Deposit 108 and C-46-104, both of *ca.* 150 B.C.

Megarian bowl. It is fully glazed. Closely spaced, spiral, wheel grooving beneath the glaze decorates the exterior. On the interior, within a groove wheel-run through the glaze, is an incomplete eight-petalled flower, the petals in yellow with white highlights, groups of dots in white between the tips.

There is no context evidence for the dating of the form in Corinthian at present. A date for the piece may be suggested, however, by its relationships to the conical bowls (532–549). The treatment of the outer wall and the employment of the floral motif is also seen in them. The careful grooving is a characteristic of the earlier conical bowls, though in them there is the minor difference that the wheel grooves are not spiral but parallel and independent. The somewhat schematized rendition of the flower appears in an early but not initial phase of the bowls. Comparable rendition of the flower in the bowls has been placed at present in the last quarter of the 3rd century B.C. and that is accordingly the date suggested for this piece. The same flower motif appears also on the plates with offset rim (127–130), and the wheel-made Megarian bowls (527–531).

3rd century B.C., last quarter
  550 (C-37-2668). Fragment, bottom and lower wall. P.H. 0.02; P. D. 0.072. Moderately thin wall. Fully glazed. Exterior: closely spaced, wheel-run spiral grooving beneath the glaze.

Interior: in a medallion framed by a groove wheel-run through the glaze, an eight-petalled flower, petals in yellow with white highlights, white dots between the tips. Pls. 17, 56.

Semi-glazed mastos **551**, Pls. 17, 56.

Advanced stage, 3rd century B.C., second half.

Deposit: 115.

The bottom is slightly flattened and the profile of the wall curves inward slightly above, its upper termination forming the lip. The wall is thin. The piece was not finished with any particular care since wheel lines and ridges are visible on both surfaces. The interior was fully glazed, the exterior left entirely unglazed.

The bowl was found in a context which permits only a wide dating between *ca.* 330 and 146 B.C. The closer dating suggested for it is intended only as a rough approximation since the other considerations which are brought to bear on its date are not very strong. Its light fabric and interior glaze associate it with the series of semi-glazed bowls (1–14). In fabric and quality of manufacture it relates best to examples of that series of advanced 3rd century date. Conceivably also the form of the bowl may have been suggested by such fully glazed shapes as the hemispherical bowl (525, 526). Its quality of manufacture would again suggest an advanced date in relation to that series.

3rd century B.C., second half
  551 (C-47-60), Deposit 115, use. H. 0.095; max. D. 0.146; D. lip 0.14. Pls. 17, 56.

Spouted, covered drinking bowl, recurved handles **552, 553**, Pls. 17, 56.

Intermediate stages, 275 to 225 B.C.

Deposits: 34, 42.

This form has a low ring foot, a broad body moderately deep, a lip distinctly set off from the body and flanged within for a cover. Each handle is formed of a coil of clay, the ends attached at the points of greatest circumference, the coil recurved in the middle upward to meet the lip. Halfway between the handles and at the same level a short spout projects horizontally. The fabric of the two examples is of indifferent quality, substantial in thickness. Both are glazed by dipping, fully within but on the exterior only to just below the level of the handles and spout.

The two are of nearly the same size (diameters of lip 0.133 and 0.143 m.). Three appreciable differences in form exist between them, differences which may prove to be criteria for relative dating of the series when more are known. In **553** the foot is more constricted than in **552**. In it also the sharp articulation at the top of the wall and the distinct concave profile of the lip of **552** are blurred over. It is also slightly taller. These differences suggest that **553** may be as much as 50 years later than **552**. The contexts and quality of the two suggest in part their placement in time. The advanced stage of a bowl entirely cognate except for the lack of the spout and flange, **554** below, and its context have also been considered in the dating of these two.

275 B.C.

552 (C-60-283), Deposit 34. H. 0.061; D. foot 0.071; D. top of wall 0.13; D. lip 0.135. Pls. 17, 56.

225 B.C.

553 (C-31-225), Deposit 42. H. 0.064; D. foot 0.065; max. D. wall 0.141; D. lip 0.143. Pls. 17, 56.

Drinking bowl, recurved handles **554**, Pls. 17, 56.

Final stage, *ca.* 175 B.C.

Deposit: 110.

The one example of this shape now known has a constricted ring foot and a steeply rising wall which recurves above to a low lip with a rounded upper profile. Each handle is formed of a coil of clay, the ends attached at the point of greatest circumference, the coil recurved in the middle to touch the lower part of the lip. The fabric is of indifferent quality and moderate thickness. It was glazed by dipping, fully within but on the exterior only to just below handle level.

In basic form it is essentially of the same series as **552, 553** above, though of a much more advanced stage of shape development than they. It may be anticipated that bowls of this kind parallel in time of production to **552, 553** will be found.

For the dating of **554**, although its context would permit a date as late as the time of Mummius' destruction of Corinth in 146 B.C. it seems likely not to be so late since no others have been found in the various destruction fillings of that time. The shape would not seem to have been current then. The degree of instability of **554** suggests that it is at the end of its series.

175 B.C.

554 (C-48-93), Deposit 110. H. 0.094; D. foot 0.056; max. D. wall 0.189; D. lip 0.185. Pls. 17, 56.

VESSELS FOR OTHER PURPOSES 555–607

COVERED VESSELS

LEKANIS **555–558**, Pls. 18, 57.

Initial, late and final stages, 5th century, second quarter to 146 B.C.

Deposits: 8, 22, 46, 113.[90]

Nearly 100 unglazed lekanides from the excavations at Corinth are now known. Seventy-one come from grave groups and other deposits in the North Cemetery.[91] An additional 25 come from deposits of various kinds, including grave groups, in other parts of Corinth. It seems clear that in this total

[90] Additional examples are known from other deposits studied in connection with this publication: Deposits 10, 11, 41, 43, 81, 90.   [91] *N. Cemetery*, pp. 146–148.

probably several distinct shape series, and no doubt a number of variants, are represented. And in the total some 64 deposits, of which only 11 have been studied in this publication, are also represented. These 64 include many grave groups for whose close relative and absolute placement numerous other shape series need to be considered as well. Wisdom, time, and human frailty alike suggest that sorting of the various series of lekanides, definition of their chronologies, and accounts of their shape histories demand a special effort far beyond the scope of the present publication. It seems likely, however, that a special study of them would be very rewarding chronologically. Not only were these lekanides produced over a very long period but also the numerous grave groups involved suggest the possibility of very close placement and the definition of very sensitive criteria for dating. In view of what is involved in a full study, however, the present account must be restricted to a very limited scope. It is intended merely to supplement information previously published, providing examples of later date than those hitherto known and suggesting criteria to be tested in an extended study.

Four lekanides are reported here. Three seem to exemplify three different stages, including the final one, of one shape series all within the Hellenistic period. The fourth may represent a very early stage of the same series.

The four have a ring foot. The wall rises from it in a broad curve to the lip, which is flanged above to receive a cover. A horizontal strap handle, the ends recurving, is set at the top of the wall just below the lip. The cover is preserved in only one of these, **556**. The profile of its top is a continuous curve, steep around the edge, in a low, upward slope above. The knob has a constricted stem, and the profile of its top has a slightly flaring outline. The four are of different sizes: diameter, without handles, 0.23, 0.17+, 0.15+, and 0.08+ m. All are made of clay of normally serviceable thickness.

The earliest, **555**, is from a deposit of very great range, from the early 6th century perhaps into the third quarter of the 5th century B.C. The evidence from the North Cemetery seems to indicate that unglazed lekanides were introduced during the second quarter of the 5th century, hence presumably **555** is to be placed very late in the range of its deposit, and to be regarded as near to if not of the initial stage. **558** is by context of the time of the destruction of the city in 146 B.C., and is thus of the final stage in Corinthian. The deposits from which the two others come are of appreciable range between these two dates. The context of **556** covers the period from the second quarter of the 4th century through the last quarter. **556** has been placed somewhat arbitrarily at the lower limit, in the last quarter. The filling in which **557** was found covers the period from *ca.* 330 to 146 B.C. It has been placed in the 3rd century.

The present placement of the latter two within the ranges of their contexts is based on criteria which it is thought may prove, when the series is fully studied, to have validity. They are suggested here primarily for testing when the evidence is fully assessed. The criteria indicated for other shape series provide these suggestions in part, and also the fact that we do have the end result of the progression. These are trends toward a constriction of the original broad foot, a possible one toward elevation of the wall profile, one toward loss of definition of the shape of the handle, and one toward a decrease in the quality of manufacture. Though four different sizes of receptacle are represented, it is evident that in the three later the foot is proportionately much smaller than in the earliest, and that the elevation of the wall profile of the latest is proportionately greater than that of the earliest. In the handle form the vestigial character of the later as compared with the earliest is also evident: the clearly defined loop of the earliest is reduced to a sharp pinching in the later, and the strongly projecting ends of the earliest are mere protrusions in the later. In quality the earliest is perfectly formed and finished with great care, the exterior surface highly polished. The two successive examples are reasonably well done, the feet defined with some precision. The latest is still adequate, but with an uneven, unpolished surface and the foot, comparatively, is crudely formed. A minor criterion of late date may concern the upper wall. It is notable that in contrast with the first two, which have a wall continuous in curve from foot to lip, the later two have a definite outcurve in profile just below the lip.

In the lid two potential criteria for dating are worthy of future attention. Many early lids (cf. those from the North Cemetery) show a stepped profile, the steps carefully tooled. It is possible that there is a trend toward loss of definition of this nicety and eventual abandonment. In this respect three grooves around the outer wall of **556b** may represent a late, vestigial stage of this kind of embellishment. The other may concern the form of the knob, a trend toward the gradual abandonment of the vertical cavity which appears in the tops of the knobs of early lids. None appears in the knob of **556a**. The top is, however, ornamented with wheel grooving.

5th century B.C., second quarter
555 (C-39-211), Deposit 88. Receptacle only. H. 0.078; D. foot 0.12; D. outer edge of lip 0.23. Pls. 18, 57.

4th century B.C., last quarter
556 a–b (C-60-254 a–b), Deposit 22. Receptacle and lid. Combined H. 0.065. Receptacle: H. 0.034; D. foot 0.035; D. outer edge of lip 0.083. Lid: H. 0.04; D. 0.08; D. top of knob 0.025. Three wheel grooves around outer edge of top, two around top of knob. Pls. 18, 57.

3rd century B.C.
557 (C-47-470), Deposit 113. Receptacle only. H. 0.058; D. foot 0.05; D. outer edge of lip 0.153. Pls. 18, 57.

146 B.C.
558 (C-47-822), Deposit 46. Receptacle only. H. 0.064; D. foot 0.064; D. outer edge of lip 0.172. Pls. 18, 57.

PYXIS, DOMED SLIPOVER LID[92] **559–583**, Pls. 19, 57.
Intermediate stages, 350 to 3rd century B.C., third quarter.
Deposits: 18, 28, 42, 43, 53, 55, 62, 63, 113.

The receptacle of this kind of pyxis normally has a flattened circular area on the bottom serving as the base, the one exception being **563** which has a low ring foot. The bottom rises in a bevel around the edge to a pronounced keel on which the lid rests. A high flange rises from the inner edge of the keel, decreasing in diameter from bottom to top. The lid has a lower wall about equal in height to the flange of the receptacle, straight or slightly concave in profile. The outer edge of the domed top projects outward beyond the line of the wall to a diameter close to that of the keel. The fabric is light and of fair quality. All examples are unglazed except **572** whose receptacle and lid are both fully glazed. The lid is normally ornamented with wheel grooving around the center and the outer edge of the dome. In one there is also grooving at mid-point on the dome, and in another there is also grooving around the middle of the wall.

Ten sizes are now attested, representing all but two centimeters of diameter between 0.16 and 0.04 m. Representation in these size series is very spotty. The initial stage of the shape may not be represented in the examples catalogued here. A decorated pyxis in Oxford (1879.183; Payne, *NC*, p. 333, no. 1513, fig. 178), dated by Payne in the late 6th or early 5th century, seems essentially the same in form. Conceivably then the date of the beginning of production of the shape in Corinthian is to be placed around the year 500 B.C. There seem to be at present, however, no known examples of the shape datable in the long period intermediate between the Oxford pyxis and the earliest below. For the end of production of the shape we may or may not have examples of the final stage. The shape was produced in

[92] Examples of the shape, all of which are included here, have previously been discussed by Miss H. Palmer in *N. Cemetery*, p. 144. The present shape is to be distinguished from the powder pyxis (e.g., *N. Cemetery*, p. 144, "Powder pyxides with pattern decoration"), which would seem to have had an independent development. The powder pyxis has features similar to the present shape (receptacle with a high flange, and a lid whose wall overlaps the flange) but differs in having a flat top and bottom. A few 4th century B.C. examples in Corinth with slightly domed lid, C-31-421, Deposit 20 (*Asklepieion*, p. 134, no. 37, pl. 49); C-37-202, Deposit 80; C-37-2597, Deposit 90; and C-60-239, Deposit 56, appear to be intermediate between the two series.

Athenian pottery contemporaneously with the stages represented below in Corinthian, but in Athens the shape continued in production far beyond the latest date proposed for the Corinthian examples here, well into the 1st century B.C. Corinthian potters need not necessarily, of course, have continued to produce it *pari passu* with the Athenian, though they may have done so down to the time of the destruction of the city.

Deposit evidence provides some indication that the main trend in shape development in this series is toward an increase in height in both the receptacle and the lid. In the catalogue below the two components have been arranged separately in a relative chronological order on this basis, the various size series placed in relation to one another insofar as is possible with so few representatives of each size. The series so arranged gives a slight indication that three other criteria may be valid for relative chronology. For the receptacles there may be a trend toward constriction of the flattened area forming the base, and there may be a rise in the angle of the bevel of the outer part of the bottom also. For the lid there seems to be an increase in the degree of convexity of the dome.

In the catalogue separate treatment of receptacles and lids has been dictated by the examples themselves and by the requirements of field archaeologists. Only five, possibly six, complete pyxides are known in Corinth. The five certain examples are **561, 562, 578, 579,** and **582**. Three of these are illustrated in complete form in *N. Cemetery*, pls. 73, 76, 78. **560**, a receptacle, and **573**, a lid, found together in a well filling, may also belong to one vessel.

Receptacles
D. 0.16
350 B.C.
559 (T 2369), Deposit 53. D. keel 0.16; H. 0.062; D. base 0.085. D. top of flange 0.126; H. to keel 0.025. *N. Cemetery*, D 36-f, pl. 73. Pls. 19, 57.

D. 0.15+
3rd century B.C., second quarter
560 (C-47-471), Deposit 113. Lower wall and base missing. D. keel 0.158; P.H. 0.057; D. base less than 0.09; D. top of flange 0.135; P.H. to keel 0.03. The lid, **573**, may belong. The combined preserved height of the two is 0.099. Pls. 19, 57.

D. 0.13+
4th century B.C., third quarter
561 (CP-2253 b). D. keel 0.132; H. 0.059; D. base 0.065; D. top of flange 0.111; H. to keel 0.018. The lid, **575**, belongs. The combined height of the two is 0.082.

D. 0.12+
350 B.C.
562 (T 2371 b), Deposit 53. D. keel 0.127; H. 0.05; D. base 0.08; D. top of flange 0.11; H. to keel 0.018. The lid, **577**, belongs. Their combined height is 0.07. *N. Cemetery*, D 36-e, pl. 73. Pl. 57.

D. 0.11+
4th century B.C., fourth quarter
563 (T 1097 b), Deposit 55. D. keel 0.113; H. 0.051; D. foot 0.06; D. to top of flange 0.089; H. to keel 0.024. The lid, **578**, belongs. The combined height of the two is 0.08. Low ring foot. *N. Cemetery*, 494-2, pl. 76.

3rd century B.C., first quarter
564 (MP 208 b). D. keel 0.113; H. 0.053; D. base 0.048; D. top of flange 0.094; H. to keel 0.028. The lid, **579**, belongs. The combined height of the two is 0.084. Pl. 57.

D. 0.10+
350 B.C.
565 (KP 701), Deposit 18. D. keel 0.103; H. 0.39; D. base 0.056; D. top of flange 0.086; H. to keel 0.018.

D. 0.08+
4th century B.C., third quarter
566 (C-31-237), Deposit 42. D. keel 0.084; H. 0.04; D. base 0.044; D. top of flange 0.063; H. to keel 0.013.

D. 0.07+
4th century B.C., third quarter
567 (KP 837), Deposit 18. D. keel 0.075; H. 0.036; D. base 0.035; D. top of flange 0.055; H. to keel 0.013.

4th century B.C., fourth quarter
568 (CP-350). D. keel 0.078; H. 0.039; D. base 0.042; D. top of flange 0.061; H. to keel 0.013.

D. 0.06+
350 B.C.
569 (KP 677), Deposit 18. D. keel 0.067; H. 0.025; D. base 0.044; D. top of flange 0.05; H. to keel 0.008.

4th century B.C., fourth quarter
570 (C-33-416). D. keel 0.063; H. 0.031; D. base 0.035; D. top of flange 0.042; H. to keel 0.01.

D. 0.05+

4th century B.C., third quarter

571 (T 1159), Deposit 63. D. keel 0.057; H. 0.026; D. base 0.031; D. top of flange 0.038; H. to keel 0.012.

572 (T 2703 b), Deposit 62. D. keel 0.052; H. 0.028; D. base 0.037; D. top of flange 0.036; H. to keel 0.01. Fully glazed. The lid, **582**, belongs. The combined height of the two is 0.039. *N. Cemetery*, 495–5, pl. 78.

Lids

D. 0.15+

3rd century B.C., second quarter

573 (C-47-469), Deposit 113. D. dome 0.155; H. 0.063; H. wall 0.033; H. dome 0.03. Wheel grooving on dome: two broad grooves around center; three lines around edge.

D. 0.13+

350 B.C.

574 (C-40-24), Deposit 28. Fragment. D. dome 0.13; P.H. 0.037; P.H. wall 0.014; H. dome 0.022. Wheel grooving on dome: one line around edge.

4th century B.C., third quarter

575 (CP-2253 a). D. dome 0.13; H. 0.062; H. wall 0.037; H. dome 0.025. Wheel grooving on dome: in center, a shallow depression, D. 0.025, and a broad groove; around edge, three lines. Lid of **561**.

3rd century B.C., third quarter

576 (C-53-250), Deposit 43. D. dome 0.138; H. 0.065; H. wall 0.034; H. dome 0.031. Wheel grooving on dome: in center, a broad groove and a line; around edge, two grooved lines. Pls. 19, 57.

D. 0.12+

350 B.C.

577 (T 2371 a), Deposit 53. D. dome 0.128; H. 0.052; H. wall 0.032; H. dome 0.02. Wheel grooving on dome: in center, a shallow depression, D. 0.025, and a broad groove; midpoint, two broad grooves; around edge, one line. Lid of **562**. *N. Cemetery*, D 36-e, pl. 73. Pl. 19.

D. 0.11

4th century B.C., fourth quarter

578 (T 1097 a), Deposit 55. D. dome 0.11; H. 0.053; H. wall 0.03; H. dome 0.023 Wheel grooving on dome: in center, shallow depression, D. 0.03, and line; around edge, two lines. Lid of **563**. *N. Cemetery*, 494–2, pl. 76.

D. 0.10+

3rd century B.C., first quarter

579 (MP 208 a). D. dome 0.108; H. 0.057; H. wall 0.031; H. dome 0.026. Wheel grooving on dome: in center, low cone, D. 0.016, and two lines; around edge, two lines. Pl. 57.

D. 0.08+

350 B.C.

580 (C-36-467). D. dome 0.082; H. 0.033; H. wall 0.021; H. dome 0.012. Wheel grooving on dome: in center, shallow depression 0.007; around edge, two lines. On side of wall, two wheel-grooved lines.

D. 0.07+

4th century B.C., third quarter

581 (KP 685), Deposit 18. D. dome 0.077; H. 0.035; H. wall 0.019; H. dome 0.016. Wheel grooving on dome: in center, shallow depression rising in cone, D. 0.018, and broad groove; around edge, one broad groove.

D. 0.05+

4th century B.C., third quarter

582 (T 2703 a), Deposit 62. D. dome 0.051; H. 0.026; H. wall 0.016; H. dome 0.01. Fully glazed. Wheel grooving on dome, beneath glaze: in center, two lines; around edge, one line. Lid of **572**. *N. Cemetery*, 495–5, pl. 78.

D. 0.04+

3rd century B.C., first quarter

583 (C-31-269), Deposit 42. D. dome 0.048; H. 0.029; H. wall 0.018; H. dome 0.011. Wheel grooving on dome: in center, shallow depression, D. 0.003, and one line; around edge, two lines.

VESSELS FOR PERFUME AND OINTMENTS

UNGUENTARIUM **584–586**, Pls. 20, 58.

Initial stage, probably very restricted period of production, *ca.* 325 B.C.

Deposits: 65B, 110.

The unguentarium form was evidently produced in many different centers of manufacture. The prototype series employed by all, for imitation and adaptation, was presumably the abundant one which has been described by Thompson, pp. 472–474. The very distinctive fabric of the prototype series may, for the sake of definition, be called the Unguentarium Fabric. The three here are easily distinguishable from those of Unguentarium Fabric since they are made of normal Corinthian clay. They are covered with fugitive black glaze.

The dating proposed here for them is based primarily on a study of unguentaria of Unguentarium Fabric found in Corinth which will be published elsewhere. All three seem to reflect in varying degrees a stage of the original form reached soon after the beginning of importation into mainland Greece, which, on present evidence, is thought to have been in the latter third quarter of the 4th century B.C. **584** is closest to the original in form, differing only in having a greater degree of constriction of the lower wall. **585** and **586** are much freer adaptations of the original.

It seems likely that unguentaria were imitated in Corinthian only for a brief time when they first became known to the potters. Importation of unguentaria of the original fabric is well attested throughout the Hellenistic period in Corinth. It seems probable that the great technical superiority of the imported examples and their evident ready availability would have tended to limit and discourage production of the form in Corinthian.

ca. 325 B.C.

584 (C-48-119), Deposit 110. Intact. Fully glazed on exterior and on inner lip. H. 0.082; D. 0.038; D. base 0.021; D. lip 0.022; H. neck 0.022; D. lower neck 0.113; D. upper neck 0.018. Disk foot, slightly concave beneath. Jog in profile at base of neck. Neck greater in diameter above than below. Lip projecting, bevelled above. Possibly traces of wheel-painted lines in white on body. Pls. 20, 58.

585 (C-63-662), Deposit 65B. Intact. Fully glazed (dipped) on exterior and on inner lip. H. 0.076; D. 0.041; D. base 0.022; D. lip 0.028; D. lower neck 0.015. Disk foot, flat beneath. Lip bevelled in profile above. Traces of wheel-painted lines in white on neck and body. Pl. 58.

586 (C-63-654). Intact. Fully glazed (fugitive) on exterior and on inner lip. H. 0.085; D. 0.047; D. lip 0.03; D. mid-neck 0.014; D. foot 0.026. Pl. 58.

OINTMENT-POTS **587–603**

Introduction

Diminutive ointment-pots of clay and lead have been extensively discussed by Sjöqvist in *A.J.A.*, LXIV, 1960, pp. 79–83, in connection with numerous pottery examples found at Morgantina. Many bear the stamped (or, in the case of lead, moulded) word ΛΥΚΙΟΝ, referring to the type of ointment they contained. Some also bear the stamped or moulded name of a druggist.

Although no inscribed pottery examples, and no examples of lead, have been found as yet in Corinth it would seem that the original characteristic containers of lykion must have been known at Corinth, for an appreciable number of pottery imitations of them were produced there.[93]

Three of the various forms found at Morgantina were also produced in Corinthian pottery, the Corinthian shapes showing minor differences, as would be expected in a different fabric. To Sjöqvist's very full and careful study the Corinthian examples can add only a few comments. Sjöqvist reports that of the examples from Morgantina "there is no evidence for any one specimen being older than the third century B.C." In Corinthian, however, one variety,[94] perhaps best equated with an example of Sjöqvist's type 4 (*ibid.*, p. 80, and pl. 20, fig. 11:7) seems to have come into production in the middle years of the 4th century.[95] For the lower limit of production at Morgantina (or, perhaps better, use,

---

[93] Two Corinthian examples have not been included in the present catalogue since it was not possible to see them. These are: T 2346 and T 655 (*N. Cemetery*, 487–6, pl. 78, and X-205, respectively). Several foreign examples of the shape have also been found at Corinth: C-29-149, perhaps of *ca.* 300 B.C.; C-46-93, perhaps of the middle of the 3rd century B.C.; C-53-239, Deposit 43, perhaps of the last quarter of the 3rd century B.C.

[94] **602** and **603**.

[95] Another example from Corinth, T 2346 (*N. Cemetery*, 487–6, pl. 78), evidently of the same type, was found in a grave of the third quarter of the 4th century B.C.

since Sjöqvist does not indicate that any from Morgantina are of local manufacture) Sjöqvist reports that his types 1, 2, and 4 survived into the 2nd century B.C. Context evidence for the dating of the Corinthian series is at present weak. Such as it is, there are no Corinthian (nor imported) examples at present datable by context or other considerations beyond the end of the 3rd century.

Sjöqvist is able to suggest that two of his types were employed for secular purposes only, that one appears at Morgantina in both secular and religious contexts, and that a fourth type, his type 3, seems to have been used only for religious purposes, appearing in shrines of Demeter and Kore. Some examples of this type also have an entirely appropriate association with Asklepios, since a stamped likeness of him appears on them. It seems surprising that none of any variety have been found in the Asklepieion at Corinth.[96] The current excavations of the sanctuary of Demeter and Kore at Corinth also seem not to have produced examples. The excavation of the site and the study of the enormous amount of material from it, however, is still in progress. Of the known Corinthian examples none is from a context certainly identified as religious in character. However, one of the puzzling deposits (90) from which two examples, **602, 603**, come may possibly be a favissa group. Two others, **595** and **596**, come from wells of the South Stoa. Considerable evidence points to the possibility that this structure was intended for religious use.[97] Possibly, then, these two may derive from a religious context also. To the secular and religious uses of these vessels for which the excavations at Morgantina have provided evidence the Corinthian examples add employment as grave offerings. Pots of all three Corinthian varieties have been found in graves, in several instances, like other tiny vessels used as grave offerings in the later 4th century and in the Hellenistic period at Corinth, in pairs.

Amphoriskos 587, 588, Pls. 20, 58.

Advanced stage, *ca.* 225 B.C.
Deposit: 72.

The form corresponds best, though not exactly, to Sjöqvist's type 2 A (*ibid.*, p. 80, and pl. 20, fig. 11:3). It has a flat bottom, unfinished, with string marks, and a heavy stem. To the rounded body are attached a pair of horizontal handles formed by a string of clay pinched into place. The lip flares slightly. The two examples, unglazed, from the same grave, are essentially identical.

225 B.C.
587 (C-27-22), Deposit 72. H. 0.034; max. D.
0.032; D. base 0.024; D. lip 0.025. Pls. 20, 58.
588 (C-27-19), Deposit 72.

Bulbous jar 589–596, Pls. 20, 58.

Initial (?) and intermediate stages, 3rd century, first quarter to 3rd century B.C., fourth quarter.
Deposits: 70, 71, 73, 110, 113, 114.

The form of this variety approximates Sjöqvist's type 3, having some relationship to both 3 A and 3 B (*ibid.*, p. 80, and pl. 20, figs. 11:5 and 11:6). The vase has a flat bottom, unfinished, with string marks. The body is well rounded, constricting above in varying degrees to a fairly wide mouth. Some of the examples have a mouth with no distinct lip; others have a slightly everted lip. Of the examples two only are glazed. The fabric is substantial. The eight examples are each of a different height, ranging between 0.043 and 0.026 m.

---

[96] There is no published example and none has been noted among the unpublished material from this sanctuary.

[97] This suggestion has been made by Miss Judith Perlzweig, who has studied the considerable body of material of religious import from the area of the South Stoa and from the adjacent area of the Greek "Agora."

The dated examples provide some slight indication that there may be trends of shape change in the series, even though the jars are tiny and of rather indifferent quality. It would seem that there may be a tendency toward constriction of the diameter of the base and also of the greatest diameter of the body and of the mouth. These changes would appear to be accompanied by an increase in the thickness and prominence of the base and by a rise in the point of greatest circumference. It is notable that, in the series so arranged below, the one placed earliest on this basis corresponds most closely in form to inscribed lead containers of lykion (from the Athenian Agora: *Hesperia*, XVII, 1948, pl. LXIX, 4), examples of which may well have served as the prototypes for the Corinthian series. The date for the beginning of production of this series in Corinth is entirely on estimate.

H. 0.043 to 0.040
  3rd century B.C., third quarter
    589 (T 2314), Deposit 70. H. 0.041; D. base 0.0305; H. to max. D. 0.018; max. D. 0.047; D. lip 0.031. *N. Cemetery*, 498-9, pl. 78.
    590 (T 2317), Deposit 70. H. 0.040; D. base 0.033; H. to max. D. 0.018; max. D. 0.043; D. lip 0.029. *N. Cemetery*, 498-10, pl. 78.
    591 (C-61-36), Deposit 71. H. 0.043; D. base 0.025; H. to max. D. 0.02; max. D. 0.045; D. lip 0.031. Pls. 20, 58.
H. 0.038-0.036
  3rd century B.C., second quarter
    592 (CP-2250). H. 0.037; D. base 0.03; H. to max. D. 0.016; max. D. 0.044; D. lip 0.032.
  3rd century B.C., third quarter
    593 (CP-2251). H. 0.038; D. base 0.027; H. to max. D. 0.016; max. D. 0.042; D. lip 0.027.

3rd century B.C., early fourth quarter
    594 (T 2023), Deposit 73. H. 0.036; D. base 0.026; H. to max. D. 0.018; max. D. 0.041; D. lip 0.027.
H. 0.033
  3rd century B.C., second quarter
    595 (C-48-118), Deposit 110. H. 0.033; D. base 0.026; H. to max. D. 0.016; max. D. 0.038; D. lip 0.032. Fully glazed.
H. 0.026
  3rd century B.C., first quarter
    596 (C-47-425), Deposit 114. H. 0.026; D. base 0.022; H. to max. D. 0.01; max. D. 0.03; D. lip 0.021. Fully glazed. Pls. 20, 58.

Piriform jar[98] **597-603**, Pls. 20, 58.
Initial (?) to late stages, 350 to 3rd century B.C., fourth quarter.
Deposits: 74, 90.

This form corresponds fairly closely to one example of Sjöqvist's type 4 (*ibid.*, pp. 80-81, pl. 20, fig. 11:7). The bottom of the base is flat, unfinished, with string marks. The greatest circumference of the wall is low. The upper wall may be straight or flare out slightly. The fabric is substantial. Only three of the examples were glazed. The seven examples are each of a different height between 0.036 and 0.021 m.

Only two examples are from a dated context, both from the same deposit. In these circumstances the series has been arranged hypothetically on the assumption that there may be a trend in shape change toward constriction of the various elements of the form, an increase in the prominence of the base, and a rise in the point of greatest diameter, on the analogy of the bulbous jar.

H. 0.036
  ca. 300 B.C.
    597 (C-60-149). H. 0.036; D. base 0.029; H. to max. D. 0.012; max. D. 0.036; D. lip 0.025.

H. 0.034-0.032
  3rd century B.C., third quarter
    598 (C-61-29), Deposit 74. H. 0.033; D. base 0.024; H. to max. D. 0.013; max. D. 0.028; D. lip 0.018.

---

[98] T 2346 (*N. Cemetery*, 487-6, pl. 78), not seen, from a grave group of the third quarter of the 4th century B.C., is probably also of this form.

599 (C-61-28), Deposit 74. H. 0.032; D. base 0.023; H. to max. D. 0.012; max. D. 0.03; D. lip 0.02.

3rd century B.C., fourth quarter

600 (C-28-89). H. 0.034; D. base 0.019; H. to max. D. 0.015; max. D. 0.029; D. lip 0.023. Fully glazed. Pls. 20, 58.

H. 0.03

3rd century B.C., third quarter

601 (C-28-86). H. 0.03; D. base 0.02; H. to max. D. 0.012; max. D. 0.027; D. lip 0.021. Fully glazed.

H. 0.023–0.021

ca. 350 B.C.

602 (C-37-2641), Deposit 90. H. 0.021; D. base 0.018; H. to max. D. 0.007; max. D. 0.022; D. lip 0.017. Pls. 20, 58.

603 (C-37-2645), Deposit 90. H. 0.023; D. base 0.016; H. to max. D. 0.007; max. D. 0.022; D. lip 0.016.

Vessels for Writing

INKWELL **604**, Pls. 20, 58.

Final stage (?) *ca.* 150 B.C. (?)

Deposit: 101.

In form the missing bottom (only the point of attachment is preserved) of the single Corinthian[99] example of an inkwell was evidently flat or slightly concave, set flush with the bottom of the wall. The wall is concave in profile. The top is domed, appreciably greater in diameter than the wall. Its profile slopes down in the center to a dipping hole. This is encircled by two lines of wheel grooving, and around the outer edge of the dome is a single wheel groove. Traces of black on the exterior are presumably of glaze. More extensive and better preserved matt-black on the interior may be ink stain.

The inkwell comes from a context which indicates that it was in use in 146 B.C. It is, however, easily possible that it may be of earlier date, a stray in its context. Some indication of an earlier date for it is provided by its general resemblance to the form of the lid of the pyxis with domed, slipover lid (**559–583**). The resemblance may not be fortuitous since in addition to a similar form of top with overhanging edge it has wheel grooving applied in much the same manner as do some of the pyxis lids.

ca. 150 B.C. (?)

604 (C-48-245), Deposit 101. H. 0.028; D. lower wall est. 0.067; D. top 0.071; D. dipping hole 0.019. Pls. 20, 58.

Vessels for other Purposes

BASKETBALL ASKOS **605–607**, Pls. 19, 58.

Initial stage, short period of production (?): *ca.* 330 to 300 B.C. (?).

Deposit: 96.

Three identical askoi, of excellent fabric, have a body in the form of a sphere, the bottom flattened. The neck, with trefoil lip, preserved in **605** only, is set at mid-point on one side and rises vertically. Enough of the handle is preserved in **605** and **607** to show that it was in the form of a broad flat ring set at somewhat less than a right angle to the neck and tilted a bit forward toward it. The body was

---

[99] Two further Hellenistic examples of the shape at Corinth appear to be of foreign manufacture, from two different sources. C-47-98, Deposit 96, is in form like a small bowl with a constricted foot and a domed top. Its context provides only a very general date, between *ca.* 330 and 146 B.C. C-48-108, Deposit 110, is also bowl shaped, but with a flat top. It is of *ca.* 146 B.C. by context. For inkwells in general see Sjöqvist, *A.J.A.*, LXIII, 1959, pp. 275–277.

fully glazed (fugitive) and decorated with a net pattern of interlocking pentagons incised through the glaze and filled with pink color. The pentagons are laid out with careful attention to the form, one framing the neck and lip, a second the top, a third the handle. Those around the lower body all have the edge of the bottom as their fifth side. The treatment gives the body the appearance of a modern basketball. Comparison with a terracotta representation of an ancient ball from Samothrace (*Archaeology*, XII, p. 168, 8) is also pertinent.

The three askoi were found together in a single filling. This context, however, provides only a general dating between *ca.* 330 and 146 B.C. Excellence of fabric and execution would seem to suggest that they are to be dated early in this period. On the other hand, the use of incised pentagons or net pattern may suggest that they are actually late, in the vicinity of 150 B.C., since this kind of decoration is well attested at that time (e.g. moulded relief ware, net-pattern bowls, below, pp. 179–182). Further evidence is needed for the placement of these vessels. The present placement, though plausible, is tentative.

Mr. and Mrs. Robert M. Cook and Mlle. Anne Bovon have provided information on three more askoi of this shape elsewhere. One of these in Mykonos (no. 109) has a handle formed by the coils of a plastic snake whose forward part and head rise up to peer into the lip. An appliqué plastic head is set on the top. The second, in the British Museum (93.11–1.1), stated by the dealer from whom it was purchased to have been found in Galaxidi near Delphi, has a triple ring handle and an appliqué comic mask on top. The third was seen in Alexandria. I have not examined these and do not know whether or not they are Corinthian.

ca. 330–300 B.C.
605 (C-47-89), Deposit 96. H. 0.098; D. 0.10; D. bottom 0.04. Pls. 19, 58.
606 (C-47-90), Deposit 96. Pl. 19.
607 (C-47-91), Deposit 96. Pl. 19.

COARSE WARE

608-645

INTRODUCTION

The fabric of the Corinthian coarse ware of Classical times has been well described in Pease, under nos. 174–175: "As almost always when Corinthian clay is used in any degree of thickness (i.e., in architectural terracottas and sculpture...) the original clay has been mixed with sand or even tiny pebbles to strengthen it." This applies to many different forms of strictly utilitarian household vessels of the Classical and earlier periods in Corinth. The clay employed in them is apt to be very thick and their surfaces often present a very uneven appearance due to the protrusion of the admixture.

This very characteristic fabric, however, is not typical of Corinthian Hellenistic coarse ware, as it is now known. Ordinarily the clay employed for coarse ware of this time is without admixture, and the fabric is, by comparison with the earlier, thinner. Essentially it is the same as that employed for finer ware, merely thicker. It ideally is warm buff, on the soft side in texture. Often the vessels are carefully made and of pleasing appearance.

At present only a very limited amount of Corinthian Hellenistic coarse ware is known and only such vessels of Classical times as are pertinent to the Hellenistic have been considered.[1] In addition the dating of Corinthian Hellenistic coarse ware can for various reasons seldom be precise or even reasonably close. Conclusions, then, about the change-over from the earlier to the later type of coarse fabric in vessels are thus of very restricted value at this time. The present information, such as it is, suggests that the earlier type began to go out of use for some forms as early as *ca.* 350,[2] and that it was gradually restricted to fewer and fewer of the forms until by the time of Mummius' destruction in 146 B.C. it is found to be employed only for the mortars in the series catalogued below.[3]

The interior of some of the pieces, the column kraters and one of the jugs, **633**, was glazed a dull, thin red so that they might better retain their liquid contents. The color is presumably intentional (or expected) since the plain ware in general would be fired under oxidizing conditions. Such blackening as is seen would be only accidental.

The present paucity of examples of Corinthian coarse ware of the Hellenistic period is to some extent supplemented by imported vessels. Many of these are noted in the pertinent sections below. It is also supplemented by shapes produced in cooking ware, e.g. below, the krater, bowls, and pitchers. It seems likely that Corinthian housewives preferred to have these shapes made in cooking ware because of its greater strength and durability.

---

[1] It is, as might be expected, not always easy to decide whether or not an example of Hellenistic coarse ware is Corinthian or imported. It is quite possible that some of the pieces here accepted as Corinthian may not be, and that among those not accepted some Corinthian may be present. The repertoire of forms known in Corinthian Hellenistic coarse ware would not, in any case, be greatly expanded by the inclusion in Corinthian of vessels which are at present considered imports.

[2] Among the various stamnos lids below some of 350 B.C. employ the old fabric, some of the same date do not. Of those of later date only **611** still employs the old fabric.

[3] It continued in use in Hellenistic times for architectural terracottas, of course. It undoubtedly continued for pithoi, but no Corinthian example of the Hellenistic period is at present known to me. It may have continued for some time in the Hellenistic period for wine amphorae, but this shape perhaps did not survive to very advanced Hellenistic times.

SHAPE HISTORIES

VESSELS FOR FOOD

STAMNOS LID 608-612

INTRODUCTION

Below, four types of Corinthian coarse lids, I–IV, have been distinguished. They have been called stamnos lids since there seems to be no other form for which they are suitable. As it happens, no certain example of a Corinthian Hellenistic stamnos is at present known.[4]

The lids in general are all of one form. Each has a flange beneath to keep the lid from sliding off. The top slopes upward from the edge to a substantial knob. All are of rather heavy fabric. In the classification below a distinction has been made largely on the degree of slope of the top and on the shape of the knob. These probably reflect differences in the character of vessels to which the lids belonged since it can presumably be assumed that potters even of coarse vessels took some thought to providing lids suitable in design to a particular shape. The height or degree of constriction of the flange seems not significant and probably had no close relationship to the size of the mouth of the vessels concerned.[5]

Two peculiarities of the knobs are notable. III and IV have strongly tapered knobs with the greater diameter above. This is a very convenient form for lifting and it would also have been handy for tying on the lid to the handles. In connection with these varieties two lids have been noted which are vertically pierced from the top of the knob to the underside of the lid. Seemingly this device (seen also in some coarse amphora lids) was intended as a safety valve for some particular type of contents stored in the vessels. It is also conceivable that the stamnoi they covered were intended as cinerary urns. This suggestion is provided by the presence of holes, made before firing and thus intentional (for libation?) in the lids, C-62-111b and T 2250, which belong to two very late Hellenistic (ca. late 1st century B.C.) cinerary urns which seem to have been designed for this purpose alone. Two bowls, C-62-105, C-62-113, used as substitute lids, one for a similar cinerary urn and one for a stamnos used as an urn, are also pierced, one before firing, one after.[6]

To judge from the rims of the contemporary foreign and the later stamnoi (footnote 4) the lids may have been set in position in several ways. They may have been set on their outer edge just within the rim on a bevel. They may have been set on their outer edge in a groove just within the lip. They may have been set so that the outer edge rested on top of the lip. Or with rims whose outer profile is rounded they may have rested on their under surface between the edge and the flange, overlapping the rim.

STAMNOS LID I **608**, Pls. 19, 59.
Final (?) stage, 146 B.C.
Deposit: 111.

The single example of this variety has a very low flange, constricted in relation to the edge of the top, and with the greater diameter above. The top is low, very broadly conical. The solid knob is cylindrical in profile, roughly finished flat on top. The lid is made of thick clay.

[4] There are, however, imported stamnoi of the Hellenistic period at Corinth. One example is of ca. 250–200 B.C.: C-62-26, Deposit 76. C-62-107 and C-62-109 are evidently Roman examples of this shape. The following are examples of various other forms in use in 146 B.C. Deposit 110: C-48-67, C-48-75, and C-48-72 (*Hesperia*, XVIII, 1949, pl. 16, 16 left; pl. 16, 17; and pl. 17, 19, respectively). Deposit 109: C-47-900. Deposit 110: C-48-69 through C-48-71; C-48-72 bis through C-48-74; C-48-76; C-48-77; C-48-82. Of uncertain date: C-46-84.

Still another shape, which was probably in production in the Hellenistic period, is represented at Corinth evidently only in examples of late stages, certainly or probably of the early Roman period: C-27-7; C-62-8; C-62-24; C-62-106; C-62-108; C-62-112. These were used as cinerary urns. The context in some cases and the evidently early Roman bowl form used as a cover (in substitution for the original cover) for three indicate their dating.

[5] A lack of close correspondence in diameter between flange and mouth has been noted in connection with Corinthian pyxides, even of high quality, of earlier times.

[6] Other bowls of similar form used as substitute lids for stamnoi employed as urns, C-62-9, C-62-25, C-62-27, and C-62-110, are not, however, pierced.

It may belong to either of two fillings in a well. The one provides only a wide dating between *ca.* 330 and 146 B.C., the other is of the time of Mummius' destruction in 146 B.C. It cannot certainly be assigned to either. Its rather cursory quality of manufacture as compared with other lids provides the only basis for suggesting that it may belong to the latter.

146 B.C.

608 (C-47-391), Deposit 111. H. 0.052; D. est. 0.17; H. flange 0.013; max. D. flange 0.092; Projection of flange below level of edge of top 0.003; H. knob 0.014; max. D. knob 0.036. Pls. 19, 59.

STAMNOS LID II **609**, Pls. 19, 59.
Early stage, *ca.* 300 B.C.
Deposit: 110.

609, the only example, has a very broad flange in relation to the edge of the top, with the greater diameter above. The top is very low, only slightly and very broadly conical. The knob is somewhat tapered in profile with the greater diameter above. A deep, half-ovoid depression is wheel formed in the top, of a depth nearly equal to the height of the knob. The lid is made, with care, of heavy clay, and covered on both surfaces with slip.

It was found in a context which permits a fairly wide dating between *ca.* 330 and *ca.* 200 B.C. Its quality of manufacture is the only basis for suggesting an early date in this period.

ca. 300 B.C.

609 (C-48-110), Deposit 110. H. 0.05; D. 0.162; P.H. flange 0.007; D. flange 0.117; Projection of flange below level of edge of top more than 0.006; H. knob 0.017; max. D. knob 0.042; Depth of depression 0.015; D. depression 0.026. Pls. 19, 59.

STAMNOS LID III **610, 611**, Pls. 19, 59.
Early stages, 350 to 300 B.C.
Deposits: 90, 111.

The two examples of Stamnos Lid III have a flange constricted in diameter in relation to the edge of the top, with the greater diameter above. The top is more steeply conical in outline than in Lids I and II. The knob is tapered in profile, with the greater diameter above. In the center of the top of the knob is a pronounced but shallow, wheel-formed, conical depression. The clay of which the lids are formed is substantial.

The later lid, **611**, may belong to either of two fillings in a well. The one provides a wide dating between *ca.* 330 and 146 B.C., the other is of the time of Mummius' destruction of Corinth in 146 B.C. It cannot certainly be assigned to either filling. Its fairly close resemblance to the earlier lid, **610**, is the basis for suggesting that it may be early in the Hellenistic period. How long this kind of lid may have remained in production cannot now be determined.

Two lids of about 350 B.C. are related to these in having a tapered knob and a top similar in its conical profile. One, C-63-504, Deposit 90, with a flange of diameter comparable to them, may belong to a vessel of a design similar to that for which these two were intended. It differs in having a knob slightly concave on top, with a very small central hole, and in having a step in the profile of the top about equal in diameter to the flange. A second example of the same time, C-53-54, Deposit 88, was intended for a vessel perhaps differing in design and evidently differing in purpose (described above, p. 105). In this the flange is very broad and the knob is pierced all the way from the top to the underside by a steeply conical, wheel-formed hole.

The series is too small to permit suggestions of criteria for relative dating.

4th century B.C., early third quarter
610 (C-63-503), Deposit 90. H. av. 0.075; D. 0.176; H. flange 0.028; max. D. flange 0.102; Projection of flange below level of edge of top *ca.* 0.13; H. knob 0.023; max. D. knob 0.041; Depth of depression 0.01; D. depression 0.022. Pls. 19, 59.

300 B.C.
611 (C-47-390), Deposit 111. H. 0.073; D. more than 0.154; H. flange 0.02; max. D. flange 0.098; Projection of flange below level of edge of top less than 0.015; H. knob 0.024; max. D. knob 0.04; Depth of depression 0.01; D. depression 0.019.

STAMNOS LID IV **612**, Pls. 19, 59.
Early stage, *ca.* 300 B.C.
Deposit: 110.

The single example of this variety probably had a very low flange evidently rather broad in relation to the edge of the top, and with its greater diameter above. The top is fairly strongly conical in about the same degree as that of Lid III. The solid knob is tapered, with its greater diameter above, and its top is flat, with a broad bevel around the edge. The clay of which it is made is substantial and the surface is covered with slip. The quality is very good.

The context from which it comes permits only a wide dating between *ca.* 330 and 200 B.C. The resemblance of the lid to three others of about the middle of the 4th century B.C. is the basis for suggesting that it is early in this long period.

The three are related in having a similar knob and tops of similarly conical form. One, C-37-584, Deposit 92, may perhaps come from a vessel of a design similar to that for which **612** was intended. It differs in being somewhat larger, and in having a smaller knob. The second, C-53-14, Deposit 88, and the third, C-53-53, Deposit 88, were perhaps intended for vessels of other designs for both differ in having taller flanges and knobs of other sizes. The knob of C-53-53 is pierced vertically through to the underside by a wheel-formed cylindrical hole.

ca. 300 B.C.
612 (C-48-112), Deposit 110. P.H. 0.05; D. more than 0.13; P.H. flange 0.01; max. D. flange 0.091; Projection of flange below level of edge of lip not determinable; H. knob 0.018; max. D. knob 0.039. Pls. 19, 59.

COLUMN KRATER **613–615**, Pls. 21, 59.
Advanced stage, *ca.* 300 B.C.
Deposits: 111, 114, 115.

The column krater, which first appeared in Corinthian pottery in the late years of the 7th century,[7] in the early Corinthian period (Payne, *NC*, pp. 300–301), continued in production at Corinth in the Classical period and in the Hellenistic, changing its function in the course of its production from that of a decorated krater for hospitable occasions to one of less pretentious and more utilitarian service. Examples of the shape of 550–480 B.C. (C-37-942, 984, 985, 1066: all of Deposit 3, Campbell, p. 583, nos. 59–62) are plain black glazed. Two examples of 460–440, produced at or near Corinth (Athenian Agora, P 21928, P 21927: Boulter 98–99), are also plain black glazed except for certain reserved areas. Another Corinthian example of 460–420 B.C. (C-34-979, Deposit 10: Pease 146) is partly glazed by dipping.

[7] Miss Patricia Lawrence suggests that the form considered here may be lineally descended from a form of column krater without a handle plate, introduced at the same time as the more familiar krater with a handle plate. In the form lacking the plate the handles rise to the level of the rim and are attached to the rim by a narrow bridge of clay.

A much more cheerful appearance was restored to the form by its translation into coarse ware, cleanly unglazed outside and with a pleasant red glaze or wash on the interior. The date when this occurred and the duration of the production of the column krater in this fabric in Corinth is not at present determinable. The three examples in the catalogue below, closely alike and thus contemporary, were produced, on estimate, about 300 B.C. The shape in this fabric may have been first produced much earlier and may have continued in production to a much later date. The contexts of the three provide only a wide dating between *ca.* 330 and 146 B.C. The difference between their form and that of the example of 460–420 B.C., primarily in the handle, in these constricted and no longer touching the lip, and in a somewhat less rotund wall profile, suggests that probably they are no more than 125 years, if that much, later.

For later manifestations of the column krater, in cooking fabric, the kindest comment which can be made about them is that they pay tribute to the original inventor of the form. Corinthian housewives of perhaps sixteen generations, down to the end of the Greek period in Corinth, and others of the Roman colony, found it useful. C-47-827, Deposit 46, was in use in 146 B.C. Another example, in form scarcely recognizable, C-60-89, from a well deposit of the 1st to 3rd centuries after Christ, may represent a reintroduction of the shape from another center in Roman times.

H. est. 0.21
   ca. 300 B.C.
      613 (C-47-129), Deposit 115. Lower wall and foot restored. P.H. 0.197; D. foot less than 0.13; max. D. 0.225; D. neck 0.21; D. lip 0.25. Pls. 21, 59.

614 (C-47-401), Deposit 111. Section from rim to lower wall. P.H. 0.143; max. D. est. 0.22; D. neck est. 0.19; D. lip est. 0.25.
615 (C-47-433 a, b), Deposit 114. Sections from rim to lower wall. P.H. 0.132; max. D. 0.21; D. neck est. 0.20; D. lip est. 0.24.

KRATER 616, Pls. 21, 59.

Advanced stage, *ca.* 300 B.C.
Deposit: 113.

The single example of the form has a relatively small ring foot and an overhanging lip. Two horizontal handles, each formed of a thick coil of clay, are attached to the wall just below the lip. These curve upward in the middle to touch the underside of the lip. The fabric is thick and the quality of manufacture is good.

Since the evidence of the context from which this krater comes provides only a very general date between *ca.* 330 and 146 B.C. a close date for it must be based on other considerations. The best indication at present is its evident relationship in elements of form to two Athenian kraters of the last quarter of the 5th century B.C. (Athenian Agora: P 11009, P 11010: Corbett 85 and 86, pl. 96). The relationship is sufficiently close to suggest that the krater should be placed early within the long period indicated by its context.[8]

      ca. 300 B.C.
      616 (C-47-477), Deposit 113. H. 0.215; D. foot 0.142; D. lip 0.42. Pls. 21, 59.

---

[8] There seem to be at present no Corinthian antecedents for the shape. The same function at Corinth earlier was probably served by lug-handled kraters such as, of 550–480 B.C., C-37-2048, Deposit 3, Campbell, p. 600, no. 172; and, 460–420 B.C., C-34-955, C-34-956, Deposit 10, Pease, p. 291, nos. 144–145. For another Athenian series of kraters see Talcott, p. 511, nos. 69–71, and p. 512, fig. 25. Of the Athenian basin fragments in Thompson, fig. 122, only B 40 would seem to be at all comparable to **616**.

MORTAR I[9] **617–625**, Pls. 22, 59.

Initial to final stages, 5th century, second quarter to 275 B.C.

Deposits: 10, 13, 35, 38 (?), 43, 80.

Examples of this series of mortars have either a disk foot or a flattened bottom. The wall is low, broadening out as it rises. The heavy, projecting rim has a steeply rounded profile and at its level is set a horizontal spout, open above. A bolster hand-grip is provided on each side, attached on the outer edge of the rim, often a little forward of center, toward the spout. The clay is mixed with abundant coarse grits. Probably all are wheel made.[10] The surfaces are covered with a fine slip. On a large circular area of the interior, reaching partway up the wall, it would appear that on the surface immediately beneath the slip a concentrated quantity of grits was applied giving this part of the surface a texture which in some resembles sandpaper and in others is coarser, the grits being sharp fragments of appreciable size. The forms are massively heavy in the earlier examples, lighter in the latest two (**624, 625**). Six sizes are attested. In addition to those in the catalogue below, which range between diameters 0.35+ and 0.23+m., a diminutive size, 0.14 m., and one 0.28–0.29 m. are represented among examples from the Asklepieion. (Cf. footnote 9.)

It seems probable that the present examples include both the initial and final stages of the shape series. Since representation in the various size series is very spotty what seem to be probable trends of shape development cannot be clearly demonstrated. They are offered as suggestions to be checked when additional examples and evidence are available. These include one toward a constriction of the diameter of the base or bottom and one toward an eventual increase in height, size for size. Changes in the bottom and wall may also be useful for chronology. The 5th century examples have a thick disk foot and a gently convex wall with distinct articulation between the two. In the early 4th century the two elements are blended into one, with a resultant concave profile. In the 3rd century example this profile has become straight. The profile of the rim is a simple quarter-round in the 5th and 4th century mortars. A distinct lip is introduced in the 3rd century pieces. The 5th century spout is like a tube cut in half lengthwise. In the early 4th century the tube is splayed in plan. In the example of 325 B.C. the splaying has changed to fluking. A seemingly very consistent change occurs in the form of the bolster hand-grip, which may have a single reel or several beads between the ends. It is initially large and well

---

[9] Six others of this series, found in the Asklepieion, are not included in the present catalogue since it was not possible to examine them in detail or in conjunction with the rest. These include C-31-443, C-31-448, both of Deposit 20 (*Asklepieion*, p. 135 and pl. 50, nos. 61 and 66). Four others are uncatalogued. All appear, insofar as it has been possible to examine them, to correspond to the present 4th century B.C. examples. Two mortars from Isthmia of *ca.* 350 B.C. are also of this series, IP 2232 and IP 2240, Deposit 16 (*Isthmia*, II, p. 41, note 37; pl. 19, d [IP 2240]). The beads of their bolsters are still fairly well defined, but cursorily treated and small. There are no signs of wear from pounding or grinding on the surface of their floors.

The following are other Corinthian mortars which are not related in form to the present series: 625–600 B.C.: Weinberg, *Hesperia*, XVII, 1948, p. 228, D 78–79. 600–540 B.C.: Brann, p. 366, no. 64. 550–480 B.C.: Campbell, p. 601–602, nos. 176–183. 460–440 B.C.: Boulter, p. 98, no. 127. 460–420 B.C.: Pease, pp. 299–301, nos. 193–194. For discussion of mortars, especially those of Roman times, see R. Cagnat and V. Chapot, *Manuel d'Archéologie Romaine*, Paris, 1920, vol. II, pp. 434–435; H. B. Walters, *History of Ancient Pottery*, London, 1905, vol. II, pp. 550–551; Charles Victor Darenberg, ed., *Dictionnaire des antiquités grecques et romaines*, 5 vols. in 10, Paris, 1877–1919, *s.v.* Mortarium.

[10] The question of the method of manufacture of the mortars is of some interest, both technically and in connection with their usefulness for archaeological dating. Miss Marie Farnsworth has stated that Corinthian mortars were mould-made: *A.J.A.*, LXVIII, 1964, p. 224: "Moldmade wares are common, especially for the mortars and wash-basins produced by the Corinthian tile factories and regularly imported to Athens." This seems to the present writer open to question, at least in part. The changes in shape observable in mortars discussed here over the centuries do not seem to be ones likely in a series of moulded vessels, and, on the other hand, they do seem reasonable for a wheelmade series. It is true that in the examples studied here wheel marks are not generally in evidence, but it is also clear that a slip has been added to the surfaces, evidently by immersion, which effectively conceals any working of the surface beneath. Fairly convincing wheel marks do exist, moreover, on two examples, **624** here and **627**, an example of Mortar II, below. Spouts and handle grips were necessarily added separately. It seems likely that they were hand formed. Both go through changes in the course of time which suggest the approach of successive generations of potters accustomed to wheel work, primarily changes toward vestigiality of form and gradual forgetfulness of the niceties of the original forms.

defined. Those of the early 4th century are less sharply defined. In that of 325 the bolster is small, the beads vestigial. In the one of 275 B.C. only shallow random incisions in a very slight strip of clay represent the beads.

For the use to which these vessels were put a note by deWaele (*A.J.A.*, XXXVII, 1933, p. 447, footnote 3) seems valuable. "Their use, however, cannot have been limited to that of grinding corn, but probably they were also a kind of milk basin, if not cheese-vat. In modern times similar milk basins are in frequent use in Switzerland. The basins, made of clean-washed clay, have a rough inner surface which is intended for accelerating the coagulation of the milk stored in the receptacle. After the process of coagulation is over, the milk water is poured out through the spout." The condition and character of the present examples would tend to cast doubt on their ever having been used for a grinding, or pounding, process, and to favor their use as milk basins or cheese vats. It has been noted that the granular surface of the interior of the examples seems deliberately produced,[11] and not to be the result of abrasion. It is also notable that the pebble fragments project above the surface and are sharp, not worn down or polished as from grinding or pounding. And, though the vessels are durably constructed, admirably fit for long years of use, none shows any perceptible wearing down of the surface or a decrease in thickness in the center such as continual and prolonged pounding or grinding would produce. The off-center position of the handles provides a good fulcrum for the kind of tipping involved in the cheese process he suggests. The introduction of the lip in the early Hellenistic example, a feature more prominent in the examples of Mortar II, was no doubt prompted by the desire to prevent spilling over the rim when the contents were poured out, a precaution seemingly more pertinent to use with liquid than with dry contents.[12]

D. 0.35+
460–420 B.C.
617 (C-34-926), Deposit 10. D. rim 0.351; H. 0.066; D. base 0.248. Disk base, finished beneath. Plain bolster. Pease 190.
618 (C-34-2513), Deposit 10. Rim fragment. Bolster with one reel. Pease 191. [For "1584" read: 2513.]
619 (C-34-2514), Deposit 10. Rim fragment. Bolster with one reel. Pease 192. [For "1585" read: 2514.]

D. 0.31+ – 0.30+
4th century B.C., first quarter
620 (C-38-571), Deposit 35. D. rim 0.312; H. 0.082; D. base 0.208. Flat bottom, finished beneath. Bolster with three beads.
621 (C-37-312), Deposit 80. D. rim 0.305; H. 0.071; D. base 0.185. Flat bottom, finished beneath. Bolster with three beads.

D. 0.26+ – 0.25+
430–420 B.C.
622 (KP 2503), Deposit 13. D. rim 0.264; H. 0.062; D. base 0.18. Thick disk base, finished beneath. Bolster with three beads. Pls. 22, 59.
4th century B.C., first quarter
623 (C-37-313), Deposit 80. D. rim 0.256; H. 0.066; D. base 0.168. Flat bottom, finished beneath. Bolster with three beads.

D. 0.23+
325 B.C.
624 (C-53-269), Deposit 43. D. rim 0.232; H. 0.057; D. base 0.123. Flat bottom, finished beneath. Bolster with six vestigial beads.
275 B.C.
625 (C-60-67), Deposit: possibly from 38. D. rim 0.232; H. 0.075; D. bottom est. 0.115. Bottom finished, slightly concave. Bolster with very vestigial beads. Pls. 22, 59.

---

[11] A fragment of a mortar, C-61-453, from an early Roman context prior to A.D. 10 (possibly itself of much earlier date?) supports the view that the granular surface was deliberately produced. It has large pieces (the size of a little fingernail) of volcanic stone embedded in the floor. They project above the surface of the floor slightly. In R. Cagnat and V. Chapot, *op. cit.*, II, p. 435, it is remarked in connection with Roman mortars: "la paroi interne était souvent recouverte de poussière de tuileaux . . ." Evidently the vessels are regarded as mortars since the explanation of the purpose of this surfacing of the interiors offered is: ". . . pour amortir les effets du choc." Stone mortars of similar shape are, of course, well known. One found in the debris of a house in Athens destroyed in A.D. 267 was evidently used for light pounding since a small stone finger pestle was found, evidently *in situ*, inside it: *Hesperia*, XVIII, 1949, pl. 41, 1 and 2.

[12] The vessels have commonly been identified as mortars in archaeological literature, and Amyx, *Hesperia*, XXVII, 1958, has on the basis of this identification of their purpose suggested that the ancient name for this kind of vessel was *holmos* (ὅλμος). Perhaps, in view of the indications provided by the Corinthian examples, the question of the ancient name for them should be reconsidered.

MORTAR II[13] **626, 627**, Pls. 22, 59.

Late and final stages, 175–146 B.C.

Deposits: 102, 111.

Mortar II has a relatively constricted disk foot, slightly concave beneath. The wall is nearly straight in profile. The overhanging rim is undercut and its rising upper profile is almost flat. At its inner edge is set a prominent lip. This rises to the level of the top of the spout which, in the one example in which it is preserved, is set at a descending angle and splays outward in plan. On the rim at each side, forward of center, a row of four pie-crust impressions are placed to serve as a hand-grip. Both examples are of substantial fabric though they are relatively lighter and thinner than those of the Classical period of Mortar I. The clay (mixed with sizable grits) of **626** is like that of Mortar I and is similarly covered with a fine slip. Over most of the interior a liberal application of sharp pebble fragments, pressed into the surface, protrudes through the slip. The clay of **627** and the slip covering its interior are, however, free of grits. There is no indication of abrasion on the interior of either example. The two sizes, D. *ca*. 0.30 and 0.34 m., are each represented by a single example.

The two by context were probably in contemporary use. It would be expected, however, that constriction of the diameter of the base would be a trend of shape development in this form, size for size, as it seems to be in the Mortar I series. On this basis **626** is placed earlier, for though it is the smaller its base diameter is the same as that of the larger example.

For the use of the shape see under Mortar I.

D. 0.34 – 0.29+
175 B.C.
   626 (C-47-242), Deposit 102. D. rim 0.298; av. H. 0.075; D. base 0.14. Spout missing except attachment. Pls. 22, 59.

146 B.C.
   627 (C-47-399), Deposit 111. D. rim 0.34; av. H. 0.102; D. base 0.142. Pls. 22, 59.

VESSELS FOR DRINK

BASED AMPHORA I **628**, Pls. 23, 60.

Advanced stage, 3rd century B.C.

Deposit: 97.

This variety has a thin disk base, finished and slightly concave beneath. The greatest diameter of the wall is just above the middle. Articulation is lacking between the shoulder and the nearly cylindrical neck. A line at this point probably merely indicates that the neck was made separately and joined here. Just beneath the simply rolled lip are two closely spaced, wheel-grooved lines. The thickened strap handles are attached at the middle of the shoulder and on the upper neck. The fabric is fairly thick and the quality of manufacture is very good.

The context of the amphora provides only a wide dating, with *ca*. 330 B.C. as the upper date and possibly the end of the 3rd century as the lower. It is not later than 146 B.C., presumably, in any case.

3rd century B.C.
   628 (C-47-147), Deposit 97. H. 0.37; D. base 0.108; H. to max. D. 0.18; max. D. 0.26; D. lower neck 0.099; D. lip 0.096. Pls. 23, 60.

---

[13] An example of this shape in a foreign fabric: C-47-355, Deposit 111. Also of this shape: Thompson E 124.

BASED AMPHORA II 629, Pls. 23, 60.

Final stage (?): 150 B.C. (?).

Deposit: 30.

The single example of this shape has a constricted, low, ring foot. The greatest diameter is just above the middle of the wall. The broad, short, cylindrical neck is set at a sharp angle to the line of the shoulder, though there is no strong line of articulation. The exterior profile of the projecting lip forms a double bevel. The short handles, of the strap variety with light, vertical, triple grooving, are attached at the middle of the shoulder and just below the lip. The fabric is thick and the quality of manufacture good.

The context from which it comes, a filling deposited not earlier than the early 1st century B.C., perhaps not until the early years of the Roman colony of Corinth, after 44 B.C., is not helpful for deciding whether this amphora was produced in the Hellenistic period prior to 146 or in the late 1st century B.C. The filling included fragmentary Hellenistic material which is in favor of the present date, as is, of course, its fabric, which is close to that of other Corinthian Hellenistic coarse ware. The degree of completeness of the amphora, however, would favor the later date.

150 B.C. (?)
629 (C-63-718), Deposit 30. H. 0.414; D. foot est. 0.115; H. to max. D. 0.225; max. D. 0.32; D. lower neck 0.115; D. lip 0.13. Pls. 23, 60.

BASED AMPHORA III 630, Pls. 23, 60.

Advanced (?) stage, Hellenistic prior to 146 B.C. (?).

Deposit: none.

Based Amphora III, a single example, has a spreading ring foot, its vertical profile nearly straight. The greatest diameter of the body is well above mid-point. The profile of the fairly tall, cylindrical neck is continuous with that of the body. The profile of the projecting lip is a double bevel, that above being the broader. The thickened strap handles rise from the middle of the shoulder and are attached just below the lip. The fabric is relatively thin, the quality of manufacture good.

No objects were found associated with the amphora in excavation. Its attribution to the Hellenistic period thus rests only on its very general resemblance to the other based amphorae preceding.

Hellenistic period prior to 146 B.C.
630 (C-63-661). H. 0.366; D. foot 0.122; H. to max. D. 0.17; max. D. 0.256; D. lower neck 0.095; D. lip 0.103. Pls. 23, 60.

WATER PITCHER 631, 632, Pls. 24, 60.

Intermediate stage, ca. 250 B.C.

Deposit: 115.

The shape has a ring foot (preserved in one example). The greatest diameter of the deep body is at the shoulder. There is distinct articulation between the shoulder and the neck, which is cylindrical. A strap handle rises from the outer shoulder. At the point of its upper attachment to the neck a broad wheel-formed groove provides the transition between the neck and the outturned lip, which is of a simply rounded profile. The quality of manufacture is satisfactory. The walls are of moderate thickness. Two sizes are at present attested in Corinthian: Hts. 0.29+ and 0.20 m. (est.). A small example of the shape, perhaps to be considered a miniature, 281, in the Corinthian fine-ware fabric, is also to be noted in connection with the present series.

The context of the two examples provides only a very wide dating between *ca.* 330 and 146 B.C. The date suggested within the period for the present examples derives from several other considerations.

A date early in the Hellenistic period for the beginning of production of the shape in Corinthian is likely, for the shape was known in Corinth then from imported examples.[14] The likelihood of an early introduction of the shape in Corinthian is perhaps strengthened by the fact that the shape came into use in Athens in early Hellenistic times (Thompson A 53–55; B 39). That the shape was produced in Corinth into the first half of the 2nd century is indicated by the miniature, **281**, and the likelihood that it was in production here down to the time of the destruction of the city is conceivable again because of the continued popularity of the shape in Athens down to this time and well beyond (Thompson E 127). The minimal representation[15] of the shape in Corinthian at present is probably an entirely incorrect index of the true popularity of the shape in Corinth. The short supply of examples of this shape at present available for study in Corinth may be due to the fact that comparatively few household wells of the Hellenistic period have as yet been excavated here. Quantities of examples of the shape have been found in such well deposits in the Athenian Agora (Thompson, p. 465), and it may be supposed that one of the primary uses for the shape was the drawing of water. On the other hand, it may be that the Corinthians preferred the cooking-ware fabric for this purpose. Numbers of cooking-ware pitchers (below, pp. 137–143) have been found in use fillings of wells at Corinth and there would seem to be no doubt that they were indeed used for drawing water, although their handles, particularly those of large pitchers, seem fragile for the purpose.

For the closer dating suggested below for the two examples, the early 1st century pitcher from Athens, Thompson E 127, and the 2nd century miniature, **281**, provide a working indication. In the example from Athens we may note a foot much more constricted than in early examples there, and also a body form which is more bulbous, with a much flatter slope in the shoulder. The neck has a tapered profile, broader above, in contrast to the almost perfectly cylindrical necks of the early Hellenistic examples cited. Generally speaking the same differences may be observed between the Corinthian miniature and the two large Corinthian pitchers. These tend to suggest that the latter are appreciably earlier than the former, although in shape development in general a very small example provides only a very shaded index for dating those of larger size.

H. 0.29+
    ca. 250 B.C.
        631 (C-47-130), Deposit 115. H. 0.297; D. foot 0.11; H. to max. D. 0.13; max. D. 0.208; D. lower neck 0.10; H. neck and lip 0.105; D. lip 0.113. Pls. 24, 60.

H. est. 0.20
    ca. 250 B.C.
        632 (C-47-131), Deposit 115. Lower wall and foot missing. Max. D. 0.16; D. lower neck 0.076; H. neck and lip 0.073; D. lip 0.092.

HANDLE-RIDGE JUG **633–642**, Pls. 24, 60.

Initial to final stages, 4th century, third quarter, to 146 B.C.

Deposits: 27, 60, 61, 102, 103, 113, 115.

Examples of this shape have either a disk base, finished and broadly conical beneath, or a ring foot, both types constricted in diameter in relation to the greatest diameter (at the shoulder) of the rounded body. The neck is slender and of moderate height. Its profile is continuous with that of the body. The

---

[14] Similar to the Corinthian in form: C-60-62, Deposit 38. Differing in form in the substitution of a sharp, projecting ridge for the groove on the upper neck: C-40-64, Deposit 27; C-60-285, Deposit 34. These may be from three separate foreign centers of manufacture. The fabric of none corresponds to the description provided in Thompson, p. 465, for the examples found in the Athenian Agora.

[15] It is pertinent that nine examples of this shape have been found in the excavations of Isthmia. Four are of Corinthian manufacture, the rest seem to be foreign.

lip is undercut and overhanging. The strap handle rises from just above the shoulder, turning in sharply at a level distinctly below the lip; at the upper point of attachment a sharp ridge encircles the neck, providing the name for the shape used here. The quality of manufacture is competent, the walls usually comparatively thin. Only on **633** does glaze appear, in this example as a full coating of the interior. Seven sizes are attested, some by incomplete pieces: Hts. *ca.* 0.35, 0.26+, 0.22+, *ca.* 0.20, *ca.* 0.18, 0.16+, and 0.12+ m.

It is likely that the two earliest examples below, **639** and **641**, of the third quarter of the 4th century, represent the initial stage of production of the shape in Corinthian pottery. It is here assumed that **633** represents the end of production of the shape in Corinth, although this is open to question.[16]

The relative placement of the examples on the evidence of deposits indicates that two trends of shape change may be useful chronologically. These are constriction of the diameter of the base or foot, and a change in the profile of the lip. The earliest examples have a lip with a profile which can best be described as a convex bevel. In later examples the lip has a straight or slightly rounded perpendicular profile. Insofar as can be determined with present examples there would appear to be no appreciable change in the greatest diameter of the body, size for size, through the series, nor is there any suggestion of a rise in the point of greatest circumference as there is in other shape series.

This kind of vessel could, of course, be used for containing and pouring any kind of liquid. It seems likely, however, that the shape was primarily intended to be used as a sealed container for wine. It is readily seen that the narrow mouth is very suitable for a stopper of some kind. The ridge around the neck might well be advantageous for tying on a stopper. That it was a useful rather than an ornamental element of the shape is indicated by its continued presence throughout the series. Purely ornamental embellishments of so slight a character as this are apt to disappear in the course of a shape series. A fairly decisive indication of this purpose for the form is the fact that in five examples (**635, 636, 638, 640, 642**) the interior is abundantly coated with resin.[17] That this is a deliberate coating rather than one due to long settling of a resinated wine is indicated by the fact that it covers the entire upper surface of the lip in the four examples in which this element is preserved.[18] To these considerations may be added the unusual circumstances of a respectably high standard of manufacture maintained throughout the series, for ordinarily in a shape series good quality is not be to expected beyond relatively early stages. It was evidently important in this series to keep up an attractive appearance. If these indications provide a correct interpretation for the main purpose of this shape it would then antedate the lagynos, in functional respects a kindred form, as a special container for wine.[19] The capacities of the various sizes of this type of jug cannot, unfortunately, be measured since none is intact.

H. est. 0.35
146 B.C.
   633 (C-47-234), Deposits 102 and 103. P.H. 0.231; D. foot 0.095; H. to max. D. 0.15; max. D.

0.238. Ring foot. Adherent red glaze wash on interior. Pl. 60.

[16] The question in this regard is as to whether or not **633** actually is a member of this shape series since it is incomplete, lacking neck, lip, and handle. Several factors are in favor of its identification with the series. The form, so far as preserved, is plausible as a late manifestation of the shape. The preserved point of attachment suggests that the handle was of the strap variety. It is determinable that the neck was slender. No other shape is known at Corinth with which it can be better identified. Elements which create doubt are its size, very much greater than the others, and the treatment of the interior with a red glaze wash, which does not occur otherwise in the series. The chronological placement of certain of the advanced examples of the series is in part dependent on the identity of **633** since they can be dated otherwise only very generally by context between *ca.* 330 and 146 B.C. The series should be reconsidered when examples from more closely dated deposits become available.

[17] A sample from one melted when burnt.

[18] Conceivably the red glaze wash (cf. footnote 16, above) on the interior of **633** was an innovation of the series in substitution for the coating of resin.

[19] For the lagynos as a special container for the shipment of small quantities of wine see Virginia Grace, *Hesperia*, Suppl. VIII, p. 180.

H. 0.26+

4th century B.C., fourth quarter

634 (C-40-63), Deposit 27. H. 0.264; D. foot 0.108; H. to max. D. 0.11; max. D. 0.22; D. lip 0.082. Pls. 24, 60.

ca. 330–146 B.C.

635 (C-47-134), Deposit 115. Fragment, lip, neck and handle. P.H. 0.113; D. lip 0.086.

H. 0.22+

2nd century B.C., second quarter

636 (C-47-79), Deposit 115. H. 0.225; D. base 0.084; H. to max. D. 0.09; max. D. 0.166; D. lip 0.072. Ring foot. Pls. 24, 60.

H. est. 0.20

2nd century B.C., second quarter

637 (C-47-139), Deposit 115. Section, foot to shoulder. P.H. 0.101; D. base 0.071; H. to max. D. 0.082; max. D. 0.138.

H. est. 0.18

ca. 330–146 B.C.

638 (C-47-58), Deposit 115. Fragment, neck, lip and handle. P.H. 0.072; D. lip est. 0.052.

H. 0.16+

4th century B.C., third quarter

639 (C-60-236), Deposit 61. H. 0.164; D. base 0.07; H. to max. D. 0.075; max. D. 0.118; D. lip 0.047.

2nd century B.C., second quarter

640 (C-47-133), Deposit 115. Lip missing. P.H. 0.156; D. base 0.052; H. to max. D. 0.075; max. D. 0.113.

H. 0.12+

4th century B.C., third quarter

641 (T 2722), Deposit 60. H. 0.126; D. base 0.052; H. to max. D. 0.055; max. D. 0.092; D. lip 0.041. *N. Cemetery*, 496–12, pl. 77.

2nd century B.C., second quarter

642 (C-47-466), Deposit 113. H. 0.121; D. base 0.04; H. to max. D. 0.058; max. D. 0.09; D. lip 0.038.

FUNNEL **643**, Pls. 25, 60.

Intermediate (?) stage, Hellenistic prior to 146 B.C.

Deposit: 106.

The profile of the single example is missing in the lower part. Of the spout nothing is preserved except a slight change in profile at the lower break, providing a limit for its diameter. The rim was formed by turning in horizontally the upper termination of the wall. No trace of a handle appears on the preserved section of the wall. The general form is analogous to that of a Corinthian funnel, C-34-923, Deposit 10 (Pease 204)[20] except that the rim of the latter is rounded inward.

The context in which the funnel was found permits only a wide dating between *ca.* 330 and 146 B.C.

Hellenistic prior to 146 B.C.

643 (C-47-298), Deposit 106. P.H. 0.085; D. spout est. 0.05–0.06; max. D. 0.215; rim 0.015 wide. Section of spout restored in plaster. Pls. 25, 60.

VESSELS FOR OTHER PURPOSES

RING STAND I **644**, Pls. 25, 60.

Final stage, 146 B.C.

Deposit: 112.

The wall has a gently concave profile spreading at the bottom. The profile of the heavy, projecting lip is rounded. The fabric is thick (0.006–0.01 m.) and strong. The lip and the lower wall were dipped separately in glaze.

---

[20] For funnels found in Athens see: Vanderpool, *Hesperia*, VII, 1938, p. 401, no. 40; *Pots and Pans*, fig. 48; Amyx, *Hesperia*, XXVII, 1958, pp. 255–259, pl. 49, f; Thompson E 136; Robinson F 63, F 64, M 9, M 119.

146 B.C.
> **644** (C-48-2), Deposit 112. H. 0.045; D. bottom
> 0.094; D. lip 0.095. Pls. 25, 60.

RING STAND II **645**, Pls. 25, 60.

Final stage, 146 B.C.

Deposit: 112.

Although the wall is very thick (0.012 m.) and strong it is further strengthened below by the addition of a heavy, rounded moulding. The stand is unglazed. Irregular black smudges may be due to its use in connection with fire.

146 B.C.
> **645** (C-48-39), Deposit 112. H. 0.023; D. bottom
> 0.075; D. top 0.072. Pls. 25, 60.

COOKING WARE

646–749

INTRODUCTION

Household vessels in cooking ware are at present attested to have been in use in Corinth in Greek antiquity from about 625 to the time of the city's destruction in 146 B.C. The cooking-ware shapes discussed here are those known in the Hellenistic period; in connection with certain shapes, their antecedents in form as far back as the 5th and 6th centuries have been included. Shapes known only in the periods prior to the Hellenistic have not been included though some which have some relevance in distinguishing Classical from Hellenistic have been mentioned. Some shapes of the Roman period have been considered and mentioned as well, also for the purpose of making clear the character of the Hellenistic.

Much cooking ware is here classified as Corinthian. It is necessary to point out that this identification of these pieces is primarily a suggestion for future consideration and examination, not a statement. Other Corinthian ware can usually be quite readily distinguished from foreign imports. For the cooking ware objective criteria for this distinction have yet to be established.

The identification of pieces as Corinthian here is not based on microscopic examination.[1] It seems unlikely, actually, that such examination of all the pieces could practically be undertaken. In the selection of pieces to be classified here as Corinthian the criterion has largely been on the basis of shapes, particularly those with very long traditions of use in Corinth. A long series of pitchers, Round-mouth Pitcher I below, in which there is full representation from *ca.* 450 to 146 B.C., and a consistent shape development over the years, was used as a nucleus. Such a series is likely to be (though foreign manufacture and a long tradition of import, of course, is not excluded) of local manufacture. This series has provided the criteria by which some shapes have been added to the Corinthian repertoire and others excluded as foreign. These criteria include the color of the clay and the range of its variations. The pitcher series shows a wide variety of warm colors up to brick red. There are also examples of slate gray. This may represent a different composition of the clay, perhaps one containing a high percentage of manganese.[2] The criteria also include details of the form by which other varieties of pitcher have been associated. They include in addition a special decoration with glaze lines which appears on some examples of the 5th and 4th centuries, a late survival of the earlier stroke burnishing (below, pp. 138–139). There are a few other shapes of long tradition in Corinth which have contributed support to the criteria (e.g. casseroles, lids). For an occasional form, indication of imitation of Corinthian black-glaze or other

---

[1] See Marie Farnsworth, *A.J.A.*, LXVIII, 1964, pp. 221–228. P. 224: "Corinthian clay was unsuitable for the manufacture of high-grade cooking pots . . ." This may imply, however, that conceivably cooking pots of a lower grade could be made with Corinthian clay. It has, in fact, been noted among the pots studied here that in general the quality of Corinthian cooking ware, whether Classical or Hellenistic, is not high, and the contrast in quality between cooking pots considered Corinthian of the Classical period and those of the Hellenistic period is not as marked as, for instance, the contrast between Athenian Classical and Hellenistic cooking-ware vessels. In favor of a local Corinthian manufacture and a tradition of production it is to be noted that cooking-ware vessels of *ca.* 615 B.C. occur in the filling of a well at Corinth whose source was a Corinthian potters' factory. Two of these are noted below (p. 120, footnote 7).

[2] Cf. Farnsworth, *A.J.A.*, LXVII, 1963, pp. 393–396.

shapes has provided a suggestion of Corinthian origin. And for others, the apparent cessation of the form at the time of Mummius' destruction of Corinth has also given an indication that they may be of Corinthian manufacture. All of these criteria are vulnerable and, though there is consistency traceable in a graded way in series and some also across series contemporaneously, one will not feel the same assurance that the entire group is Corinthian as one might with pieces of finer Corinthian ware of the same span in time. The classification of these vessels as Corinthian may not prove satisfactory on these grounds. It has, however, seemed better to make the attempt to distinguish what is Corinthian than not to do so.

Descriptions of cooking fabric of the 6th and 5th centuries have been provided by Campbell, under nos. 159–161, and by Pease, under nos. 205–209. Broneer, *Terracotta Lamps*, p. 58 provides the following in reference to lamps of similar fabric of the Roman period:

> An objection to the conclusion that type XVI was producd in Corinth may seem to arise from the quality of the clay. The Corinthian clay is well known from the early classical pottery and has often been referred to in connection with the preceding types. The clay of type XVI, however, is quite unlike the soft yellow clay of the Corinthian pottery, but the difference is only apparent. Nearly all the coarse pottery [i.e. of cooking ware fabric] from Corinth of all periods is made of that same coarse red clay, yet it is incredible that all that ware was imported. The same may be said of bricks and tiles from Hellenistic and Roman times. This makes it sufficiently clear that the red color of the coarse ware is due, not to the clay itself, but to the admixture of sand and loam which it contains and to a difference in temperature at the baking.

The methods of manufacture of cooking ware have been described by M. Farnsworth (*A.J.A.*, LXVIII, 1964, p. 225). The thin walls and finely burnished surfaces of some of the pieces of the 6th to 4th centuries may be due to the beater-and-anvil process. One may question that it was employed in the later examples here, particularly in those of relatively thick fabric.

Many of the pieces derive from fillings attributed to the Mummian destruction of 146 B.C., which did not usually reach their final place of deposit until, presumably, the early Roman period in Corinth. In cooking ware the problem of distinguishing what is really Mummian in date from what is of early Roman manufacture is a much more vexing one than in Corinthian pottery of other wares. It has been possible to do so fairly readily with shapes of long traditions in Corinth prior to Mummius. Fortunately the Roman preference in forms often seems to have differed appreciably in shapes of the same functions. Shapes occuring only in the Mummian debris have presented a more difficult problem. It may be expected that some of these will be shown by future evidence to be of other dates than here proposed.

Shape development in cooking-ware vessels is rather more slow moving than in vessels of other wares. Nonetheless it has been possible often to suggest useful criteria for dating, some of which can be used in connection with other evidence for fairly refined chronology. Several shapes would seem to have been introduced only shortly before Mummius' destruction. Their presence in a filling may thus provide really close dating for the middle of the 2nd century in Corinth.

It will be noted that a number of the shapes produced in cooking ware seem ill suited for use over the fire or in the oven, e.g. the pitchers with indented bottom or disk foot, the decanter, the krater, the bowls and plates. One naturally wonders why it was thought desirable to produce these shapes in this special fabric. A possibility, not tested, is that the cooking fabric in addition to being heat resistant might also retain heat well and that food could be kept warm longer in vessels of this fabric. A second possibility is that the low porosity of the fabric was a factor. Both may well have contributed in part to their production. A third consideration is perhaps the most likely, however: that the cooking fabric was tougher and more durable than the ordinary Corinthian coarse ware and that for that reason vessels which in foreign parts would normally be produced only in coarse ware were in Corinth produced in the cooking fabric. Comparison between the cooking-ware krater, **705**, and its parallel shape in

Corinthian coarse ware, **616**, brings home this point. The former is light and extremely strong, the surface tough. The latter is heavy, readily breakable, and the surface is vulnerable even to light abrasion in use. There is no question as to which of these a sensible Corinthian housewife would choose in the market.

SHAPE HISTORIES

STOVES

BRAZIER **646**, **647**, Pls. 26, 61.

Very early stage, 2nd century B.C., late second quarter.

Deposits: 46, 110.

646 and **647** are Corinthian imitations of a foreign brazier form[3] which achieved great popularity in the latter half of the Hellenistic period. Of the two, **646** is nearer to the original series. The outer edge of the broad base is lipped upward. The broadly conical bottom is vertically pierced in the center by a hole for draught, diameter estimated 0.02 m. The wall, concave in profile, has a rectangular opening below the level of the fire bowl both for draught and the removal of ashes. A thick coil of clay forms each handle, the two ends attached below, the loop recurved above to touch the upper wall. The floor of the fire bowl, in which the charcoal was placed, is pierced by five holes for draught. Three lugs project both above and inward from the rim to support cooking vessels. In this brazier the lugs are plain. The canonical imported brazier often has lugs in the form of a bearded head. Two from imported braziers, C-48-247, Deposit 112, and C-48-132, are typical examples. **647** exhibits three abnormal features, the omission of the lipping of the base, a leaf-shaped opening instead of the rectangular draught hole in the wall, and directly opposite, a second, smaller opening covered by an appliqué comic mask with whose open mouth it communicates. It would have been appreciably taller than **646**. Its wall, missing above, rises to a greater height than that of **646**, but there is still no trace of the attachment of the fire bowl even at its highest preserved point.

Both braziers are made of thick clay with many prominent grits. That of **647** was fired to a warm buff, the texture of the fabric comparatively soft, its appearance relating it with conviction to that of Corinthian architectural terracottas and Corinthian coarse pottery of Classical and earlier times.[4] The clay of **646** has fired hard and red, quite comparable in appearance to cooking fabric. One might suppose that **646** is of foreign manufacture, but, instructively enough, one section of one handle, perhaps broken off prior to intensive use of the brazier in cooking, has retained the normal appearance of Corinthian coarse ware. The composition of the clay of the two braziers, however different their general appearance, would seem to be the same.

Evidence from the Athenian Agora (P 7039) indicates that this type of brazier was in production prior to the construction of the Stoa of Attalos (159–138 B.C.); Thompson, p. 468, implies a date of

---

[3] The original place of manufacture of these braziers is not known. Moulds for lugs for such braziers have been found in Alexandria: now Athens, Agora P 26396, P 26397 (one "from Egypt," one from "Canopus"). This provenance need not imply, however, that Alexandria was the original producer. The form may have been copied there, as at Corinth, the Alexandrian moulds being imported or secondary.

For the braziers see Conze, *Jahrb.*, V, 1890, pp. 118 ff.; Mayence, *B.C.H.*, XXIX, 1905, pp. 373–404; Thompson, pp. 466–468. For earlier braziers of other forms see Boulter 123; Talcott 106; Pease 213; *Pots and Pans*, fig. 44; Amyx, *Hesperia*, XXVII, 1958, pp. 229–231 and pl. 49, b, c.

[4] This fabric is rare in Corinthian Hellenistic coarse pottery (see above, p. 104).

around 200 for the introduction of the form. The contexts of **646** and **647**, combined[5] with the extreme paucity of examples (four, including the two imports mentioned above) known at Corinth, would suggest, however, a lower initial date and imply that they were beginning to be made and had begun to achieve popularity in the export market only shortly before Mummius' destruction of Corinth in 146 B.C. (If indeed this is true, the form will be of value for close dating in Corinth.) The few examples from Corinth may also suggest that the popularity and period of production of this type of brazier was over by the time of the establishment of the Roman colony in 44 B.C. Confirmation of this suggestion is supplied by Henry S. Robinson, who tells me that deposits of early Roman times in Athens indicate that this type of brazier was no longer in use at that time there.

2nd century B.C., late second quarter

646 (C-47-836), Deposit 46. H. to top of lugs 0.285; D. lip 0.255. Pls. 26, 61.

647 (C-48-126), Deposit 110. Upper part, including fire bowl, missing. P.H. 0.255; D. bottom 0.23. Draught hole in floor plausibly restored on the analogy of **646**. Outline of leaf-shaped hole in wall partly restored. The eyes of the mask are preserved. A similar mask: Athens, Agora, *Hesperia*, XVIII, 1949, pl. 17, 23. Pls. 26, 61.

VESSELS USED OVER FIRE OR IN OVEN
CHYTRA 648–655

INTRODUCTION

The name chytra is here used to refer to vessels of cooking ware of several related shapes. These all have a rounded bottom and body form, both in a continuous curve of profile up to the neck, which is set off from the body by articulation in some degree. They may be covered vessels with some provision within the lip, such as a flange, for a lid, or they may be open vessels, i.e. with no specific provision for a lid. They have either one or two vertical handles. The name is known to have been applied to one of these varieties in Hellenistic times.[6] It is convenient to use it for the others also since the use of the same name for them all implies their actual close relationship in form.

Cooking-ware vessels of shapes which are included under this name are[7] attested in Corinth as early as the last quarter of the 7th century and examples of one variety (Chytra II) are attested to have been

---

[5] A fifth brazier, Corinthian, C-65-394, has been excavated since this was written. Incomplete above, though the floor of the fire bowl is present, it is of roughly the same scale as the two examples published here: P.H. 0.205; D. bottom 0.25 m. It differs from the others in several minor ways: a flat bottom with no draught hole, a profile more widely spreading below and stepped around the lower wall, the large draught opening in the side of M-shaped outline, handle only slightly recurved, and a prominent simple moulding around the wall at a point only just above the level of the handle. There are four draught holes 0.02 m. in diameter in the floor of the fire bowl.

[6] C-48-65, Deposit 110, an imported vessel in use in 146 B.C., bears a dipinto inscription which in referring to the amount of the vessel's contents identifies the shape (two handles, covered) as a chytra. It should be emphasized that the inscription was probably not put on the pot in Corinth but more likely, considering its character, at the unknown foreign source from which the pot and its contents were exported. Publications: *Hesperia*, XVIII, 1949, p. 152 and pl. 16, 15–16. Marie Farnsworth, "Ancient Pigments," *Journal of Chemical Education*, XXVIII, 1951, pp. 28–29 and fig. 2. Amyx, *Hesperia*, XXVII, 1958, p. 212 and notes 89–90. Sparkes, *J.H.S.*, LXXXII, 1962, p. 130, note 77. In the latter two articles the name chytra has been discussed with reference to vessels known in Athens.

[7] *One-handled, open chytrai*

625 B.C.: C-62-640. 610–600 B.C.: C-62-239. These are from a well filled with great quantities of rejects from a Corinthian potters' factory. It is thus entirely likely that they are of local Corinthian manufacture. They have been dated by Miss Patricia Lawrence who, with D. A. Amyx, is preparing a publication of the material from this well (*Corinth*, VII, ii, forthcoming).

550–480 B.C.: C-37-2058 through C-37-2060, Deposit 3. Campbell 159–161, not seen; however, probably also of this variety.

Ca. 350 B.C.: four contemporary examples from Isthmia, Deposit 16: IP 2234–IP 2236, IP 2241 (*Isthmia*, II, pl. 19, d, center).

4th century B.C., third quarter: T 2698 b, Deposit 62, *N. Cemetery*, 495–6, pl. 78, is a miniature example.

in production at the time of Mummius' destruction of Corinth in 146 B.C. In connection with Chytra II below a few cognate examples of the Roman period have also been noted.

In the two series, Chytra I and II below, there is perhaps some indication of local manufacture to be seen in the possibly long tradition in shape of Chytra I (though this is tentatively questioned) and in the coherence in form of the graduated sizes of Chytra II. Their clay varies between red and slate gray in color.

CHYTRA I **648**, **649**, Pls. 27, 61.
Early (?) and late stages, *ca.* 550 (?) to *ca.* 300 B.C.
Deposits: 1, 38.

The two chytrai classed together here have a widely pulvinated body profile constricting above to a moderately broad lip which has a nearly vertical, straight profile. A flange of fairly slight projection is provided for a lid at the base of the lip within. The vertical handle, preserved in small part in one only, was of the strap variety, attached just above the greatest diameter and at the lip. Both are made of very fine, red clay and the quality of manufacture is excellent. There are probable traces of wheel marks on the interior of **648**, but no others are evident in either.

For the period of production of the form the date suggested for **648** would indicate that it is of the initial stage of the shape series or very near it. It could reasonably be expected, however, that the shape continued in production much later than the time of **649**. The examples of Chytra II are the much later successors in function of this shape. It seems unlikely, however, that they are of the same shape series.

In connection with the date of **649** it should be noted that 300 is merely an arbitrary date within the range of its context, *ca.* 325 to the early second quarter of the 3rd century B.C. Future evidence may provide a basis for adjustment.

Criteria for dating examples of this form cannot be suggested with any conviction with only two examples. In fact, despite the very considerable difference in time indicated between them the two examples show no real difference in general form except possibly a trifle less projection of the flange in the later. This is extremely puzzling since even in the comparatively slow-moving shape development of cooking-ware forms much more difference would be expected.[8]

Traces of blackening from cooking fires appear on both examples.

ca. 550 B.C. (?)
    648 (C-53-134), Deposit 1. P.H. 0.15; H. to max. D. more than 0.07; max. D. 0.215; D. lip 0.13. Brann 69.

ca. 300 B.C.
    649 (C-60-60), Deposit 38. H. 0.12; H. to max. D. 0.05; max. D. 0.158; D. lip 0.094. Pls. 27, 61.

Two-handled, open chytrai
    4th century B.C., presumably: C-61-432.
    Context date between *ca.* 330 and 146 B.C.: C-47-78, Deposit 115 and C-47-301, Deposit 106, miniature examples in Corinthian unglazed fine ware. Compare Thompson D 71, of a usable size, in cooking ware.
One-handled, covered chytrai
    See Chytra I and II below. In addition to these there are three which are thought to be foreign:
    Context date between *ca.* 425 and 375 B.C.: C-37-535, Deposit 79.
    Context date between 325 and the early second quarter of the 3rd century B.C.: C-60-61, Deposit 38.
    Context date between *ca.* 330 and 146 B.C.: C-48-123, Deposit 110.
    The list of examples of the one-handled, covered chytrai at present known in Corinth is believed to be complete. For the other varieties the lists are not intended to be exhaustive. I have not noted any examples in Corinth other than C-48-65 of the two-handled, covered chytra of either Classical or Hellenistic times. Thompson D 70 may be compared in this connection.

[8] When more examples and information about the shape series are available it would seem worthwhile to consider whether or not **648** may not be a much later addition (i.e., though still prior to *ca.* 330 B.C.) to the well filling from which it is reported. One might suspect that it came from the top of the well, though there is no way of determining the depth at which it was found in the records of the excavation.

CHYTRA II **650–655**, Pls. 27, 61.

Final stage, 146 B.C.

Deposits: 103, 107, 110, 112.

These chytrai have a broadly piriform body constricting above to a moderately broad lip which is separated from it by semi-articulation. The lip broadens outward from its base in a nearly straight profile, its top is ordinarily bevelled, the slope inward, and at its base within there is a vestigial flange for the lid. A thickened strap handle is attached just above the greatest diameter and at the lip. The clay of which they are made varies from moderately fine to coarse. It is fairly thin, though by no means as thin as in Chytra I. The quality of manufacture is adequate, but no special care has been devoted to the form. Sizes are graduated between heights of 0.14 and *ca.* 0.09 m., each centimeter between being represented.

Only one stage of the shape is at present represented, evidently a very advanced one, and, if the examples are actually Corinthian, the last one. It may be anticipated that examples of earlier stages will be forthcoming. The form of the body of Chytra I is so different that it seems unlikely, however, that the examples of Chytra II stem from it.

Cognate forms of the late 1st century B.C. and the 1st century after Christ are also known in Corinth. One of the last quarter of the 1st century B.C., C-60-220, has a very close resemblance to these. It differs, however, size for size, in a greater breadth of the lip and in having a slightly less pronounced flange within. The others, C-46-79 and C-46-28, both Deposit 107, and C-60-196, differ more markedly. All are articulated between bottom and wall, the general profiles of bottom and wall are different, two have a different lip profile, without a flange, and one has a ring handle.

All the examples below show indication of use over cooking fires.

146 B.C.

650 (C-48-124), Deposit 110. H. 0.14; H. to max. D. 0.05; max. D. 0.154; D. lip 0.13.

651 (C-48-37), Deposit 112. H. 0.134; H. to max. D. 0.055; max. D. 0.147; D. lip 0.092. Pls. 27, 61.

652 (C-48-120), Deposit 110. H. 0.127; H. to max. D. 0.05; max. D. 0.14; D. lip 0.096.

653 (C-46-38), Deposit 107. H. 0.12; H. to max. D. 0.045; max. D. 0.142; D. lip 0.098.

654 (C-47-246), Deposit 103. H. 0.115; H. to max. D. 0.05; max. D. 0.13; D. lip 0.095.

655 (C-47-247), Deposit 103. P.H. 0.073; D. lip 0.089.

STEW POT[9] **656**, Pls. 27, 61.

Final stage, 146 B.C.

Deposit: 46.

The single example of this shape has a broad, rounded bottom above which, without articulation, the convex wall profile very gradually constricts upward to a broad lip. This flares outward in a straight profile on the exterior. Its top is bevelled, with the slope inward, and at the bottom of the lip within

---

[9] It seems quite likely that future evidence will show that this form had a long period of production in Corinthian prior to the time of the present example.

It is conceivable that the incomplete **658** below is also of this form. It has, however, been restored as and is placed with the Stew Pot, one vertical, one tilted horizontal handle.

C-47-303, Deposit 106, generally related in form, is here considered an import. By context it is dated within the period *ca.* 330 to 146 B.C. It is likely to be of a very advanced date within this range, however, possibly *ca.* 200 B.C. It shares several features with Thompson C 70, of that time: indented bottom, position of handles, and two wheel grooves at handle level. It is, however, deeper than the latter and of more constricted body form.

A stew pot of *ca.* 350 B.C. from Isthmia, IP 2243, Deposit 16, *Hesperia*, XXXI, 1962, p. 24, no. 15 and pl. 12, b, is almost certainly the direct antecedent of **656** in form. On its shoulder appear vertical stripes of dull glaze, irregularly spaced. On the significance of this decoration for dating see p. 138.

there is a slight flange for the cover. Two handles, circular in section, rise from the wall just below the lip to a point slightly above the level of the top of the lip, nearly touching it. At the level of the handle attachments a wheel groove encircles the wall. The pot is wheelmade of dark gray, rather coarse clay. The quality of manufacture is adequate.

It seems quite likely that future evidence will show that this form had a long period of production in Corinthian prior to the time of the present example.

The form is known also in the 1st century B.C.: Athenian Agora, P 11906, Robinson F 81. In general appearance this example is very similar. Its lip profile is, however, quite different in detail and there is no flange comparable to that of **656**. It is also notable that the handles of F 81 actually touch the lip. These differences may, of course, be either chronological or due to manufacture in a different center of production.

146 B.C.
>   **656** (C-47-826), Deposit 46. Av. H. without han-
>   dles 0.152; H. to max. D. 0.06; max. D. 0.188;
>   D. lip 0.14. Pls. 27, 61.

STEW POT, ONE VERTICAL, ONE TILTED HORIZONTAL HANDLE[10] **657, 658**, Pls. 28, 61.
Early and final stages, 300 to 146 B.C.
Deposits: 28, 102.

The body of the one certain example of this form, **657** of *ca.* 300 B.C., is globular in outline up to the lip, which is set off from it by semi-articulation. The lip flares outward in a straight profile. The lip is flat on top and at its base within is set a very pronounced flange. On one side a strap handle is attached at the outer shoulder and at the lip. On the opposite side on the wall just below the lip a handle circular in section rises nearly vertically to a point just above the lip, which it almost touches. The pot is made of fine, red clay, quite thin, and is of excellent quality. There are no certain traces of the wheel on either the exterior or interior. The date suggested for **657** is merely an arbitrary one, within the range of the context from which it comes, between *ca.* 350 and the first quarter of the 3rd century B.C. Future evidence may suggest adjustment of this date.

The incomplete **658** has been tentatively associated with it and has been restored to resemble it. It may conceivably be, alternatively, of the form of the Stew Pot above, **656**. Of the time of Mummius' destruction in 146 B.C., it is suitable in form as a much later version of **657**. It is made of rather thicker, coarser clay, and has a more baggy outline. Other slight differences, also to be expected as the result of gradual progression over a long period, are the bevel of the top of the lip, sloping inward, and the vestigial character of the flange within.

The same general form, with differences, is known in the 1st centuries B.C. and after Christ: Robinson F 84, F 85, and G 116. In these the horizontal handle is set entirely free of the lip, and the lip profiles themselves are in detail slightly different, notable being the form of the top of the lip and the absence of a flange within.

Both of the examples below show traces of blackening, presumably from cooking.

---

[10] The incomplete C-46-41, Deposit 107, has been restored as of this form. The placement of its one preserved, horizontal handle well down the wall and fully independent of the lip, makes this association doubtful. It may, perhaps, have had two handles of the same kind instead, but there is no Hellenistic parallel for this at present. It is therefore omitted. It seems in form likely to be prior to the destruction of 146 B.C., or of that time, though its context permits a dating as late as the 1st century after Christ.

ca. 300 B.C.

657 (C-40-29), Deposit 28. H. 0.20; H. to max. D. 0.09; max. D. 0.233; D. lip 0.15. Pls. 28, 61.

146 B.C.

658 (C-34-1613), Deposit 102. H. 0.158; H. to max. D. 0.06; max. D. est. 0.182; D. lip est. 0.15. Pls. 28, 61.

CASSEROLE I[11] 659–670, Pls. 29, 62.

Early to late stages, 5th century, third quarter to 146 B.C.

Deposits: 10, 15, 79, 80, 87, 88, 90, 105, 113.

This form of casserole has a broad, gently convex bottom and a low wall, the two separated by semi-articulation. The low lip, set off from the wall sometimes also by semi-articulation, sometimes with sharper definition, is broader above. A flange for a lid is provided at the join between rim and wall within. Two handles, triangular in plan, circular in section, are normally attached on the outside of the rim and rise from it at about a 45° angle to a point well above the lip. The shape was probably wheelmade though there are seldom visible traces since all surfaces are usually fairly well finished. The clay employed is red. Six sizes are attested: diameters 0.22+, 0.18+, 0.17, 0.16+, 0.15+, and 0.12+ m.

For the beginning of production the earliest known at present, 669, is from a deposit of 460–420 B.C. Its quality does not necessarily suggest that it is among the earliest of the series. Possibly the shape was introduced still earlier. The series is well represented down to the early third quarter of the 4th century. Only two pieces are of later date, by form and by context. How much later they actually are is an open question for which future evidence may provide a more secure answer. That they provide indication that the shape continued to be produced down to the time of Mummius' destruction of Corinth in 146 B.C. is only tentatively suggested. 662 is from a Mummian context. It is, however, a fragment and can well be an earlier stray. 670, a complete, very small casserole, comes from a context of wide range, between *ca.* 330 and 146 B.C. Its form does differ appreciably from those of the third quarter of the 4th century. That it is almost two centuries later seems difficult to believe. It is, however, placed near the end of its long range in context since there is a foreign version of the form known from a Mummian context, C-47-248 (footnote 11). Similarity in the flange and in the placement of the handles seem to suggest that the two are more or less contemporary. The equally long period of production of Casserole II may tend to support the placement of the end of production of the present series at so late a date.

Some criteria for dating in the series may be suggested. The wall in the examples down through the first quarter of the 4th century is canted inward above. In subsequent examples it is canted outward a little and is nearly straight in profile. The rim through the first quarter of the 4th century is fairly strongly everted. In subsequent examples it is normally more nearly vertical (the very small 670 is an exception). The flange down to the early third quarter of the 4th century is comparatively wide and prominent. In the later two it is vestigial. There is no change in the handle form between the third quarter of the 5th century and the third quarter of the 4th, and evidently the form and placement of the handle of the later 662 was the same. In 670 the form is the same but the placement is different. They attach to the wall, not the rim, and rise glued to the outside of the rim. Their appearance above

---

[11] C-37-2506, Deposit 90, of *ca.* 350 B.C., is a variant (possibly foreign?). The handles, circular in section, are attached to the outer surface of the rim, rise vertically, and form a low arch above the lip. Two other casseroles are believed to be foreign versions of the shape. C-53-268, Deposit 43, is from a context of wide range, from the second quarter of the 4th century to the last quarter of the 3rd. Comparison with examples of the present series tends to suggest that it may be of the last quarter of the 4th century. Its handles are in the form of a cursive mu in plan. C-47-248, Deposit 103, is of 146 B.C. The lip starts at the edge of the bottom, is deeply concave in profile and flaring above. The handles, rounded loops, are attached just above the edge of the bottom. They are set at an angle and as they rise they nearly touch the outer surface of the lip.

is as the earlier. This different placement may have no chronological significance. It may be different because of the very small size of this casserole. **670** also differs in the interior. In those prior to the third quarter of the 4th century and in **662** the wall and floor below the flange are in a single curve of profile. In **670** there is strong articulation between wall and floor. The fabric of those dated between the third quarter of the 5th century and the third quarter of the 4th is good, the clay is thin, and the quality of manufacture is high. Those later are of coarser, rather thicker clay. They are less well formed. In no examples of this series is there indication of stroke burnishing or glaze-line decoration.

Blackening from cooking normally appears on the exterior only. On **659** the black is all within.

D. 0.22+
> 4th century B.C., second quarter
>> **659** (C-37-559), Deposit 80. D. lip 0.228; H. 0.072; D. bottom 0.208; max. D. wall 0.215.
>
> 350 B.C.
>> **660** (C-53-63), Deposit 88. D. lip 0.223; H. 0.063; D. bottom 0.208; max. D. wall 0.21.
>> **661** (C-53-62), Deposit 88. D. lip 0.225; H. 0.064; D. bottom 0.20; max. D. wall 0.207.
>
> 146 B.C.
>> **662** (C-34-2419), Deposit 105. D. lip est. 0.22; P.H. 0.045.

D. 0.18+
> 4th century B.C., second quarter
>> **663** (C-37-560), Deposit 80. D. lip 0.182; H. 0.055; D. bottom 0.172; max. D. wall 0.178.

D. 0.17
> 4th century B.C., second quarter
>> **664** (C-36-971), Deposit 15. D. lip 0.17; H. 0.05; D. bottom 0.158; max. D. wall 0.168.
>> **665** (C-46-133), Deposit 87. D. lip 0.17; H. 0.05; D. bottom 0.163; max. D. wall 0.168.

D. 0.16+
> 4th century B.C., first quarter
>> **666** (C-37-540), Deposit 79. D. lip est. 0.16–0.17; H. 0.054. Pl. 29.
>
> 350 B.C.
>> **667** (C-37-2509), Deposit 90. D. lip 0.163; H. 0.053; D. bottom 0.153; max. D. wall 0.16. Pls. 29, 62.

D. 0.15+
> 350 B.C.
>> **668** (C-46-128), Deposit 87. D. lip 0.153; H. 0.045; D. bottom 0.13; max. D. wall 0.132.

D. 0.12+
> 460–420 B.C.
>> **669** (C-34-943), Deposit 10. D. lip 0.126; H. 0.039; D. bottom 0.118; max. D. wall 0.116. Pease 207.
>
> 150 B.C.
>> **670** (C-47-478), Deposit 113. D. lip 0.123; H. 0.035; D. bottom 0.102; max. D. wall 0.112. Pls. 29, 62.

CASEROLE II[12] **671–682**, Pls. 29, 62.

Early to final stages, *ca.* 450 to 146 B.C.

Deposits: 10, 15, 80, 81, 87, 104, 105, 107, 118.

This form has a rounded bottom and a low wall, normally with articulation in some degree between the two. The rim is also low, always greater in diameter above. It is also normally set off from the wall. The handles, formed of a loop of clay circular in section, rise at an upward angle from the shoulder usually to a level just above the rim. One of the earliest casseroles, **676**, may have had a non-functional spout. (For attachment of a wooden handle? Cf. the frying-pan handles below.) The clay is usually seen to be or to have been red. There is no indication of stroke burnishing or of glaze lines as decoration in this series. The earliest do not show traces of the wheel since all surfaces are well finished. The later, in which the exterior is less well finished than the interior, do show traces of it. Five sizes are known: diameters 0.27+, 0.21+, 0.19+, 0.18+, and 0.12 m.

The earliest of this series known at present in Corinth are from a deposit of *ca.* 460–420 B.C. They are here dated, within this range, at 450 because of the degree of difference in form between them and

---

[12] Of this series also is a casserole from Isthmia, of *ca.* 350 B.C., IP 2239 A, Deposit 16, *Hesperia*, XXXI, 1962, p. 24, no. 17 and pl. 12, e. Its lid, IP 2239 B, was found with it. In form it is a member of the Lid II series, below, p. 130.

their closest successors. It seems possible that the form may have been introduced still earlier. The latest, of 146 B.C., although there is a considerable gap in the series, show indications that they are in one tradition with the earlier. Thus they are likely to be Corinthian and hence of the last stage of the form in Corinth.

No later casseroles known at present show real affinities with this series. Robinson F 76, of the early Augustan period, has been indirectly connected with the casserole without handles below, and C-65-323 is probably an example of the same type. Robinson F 77, also of the 1st century B.C., is entirely different from Casserole II. Others of subsequent date differ in other basic ways: C-65-15, of the early 1st century after Christ; Robinson G 190, of the late 1st to early 2nd century after Christ; C-62-58, of the first half of the 2nd century after Christ; and Robinson J 22, of the early 3rd century after Christ.

For Casserole II several criteria for dating can be suggested. In commenting on them here "early" is equated with the period 450 through the second quarter of the 4th century B.C.; "late" is equivalent to the time of Mummius' destruction of Corinth in 146 B.C. The bottom, in the early examples, is known to be or is thought to be, where it is not preserved, gently rounded. In the late it is deeper, with a straighter profile, generally conical in outline. Articulation between it and the wall is fairly well defined in those of 450 B.C., less clearly defined in those of the second quarter of the 4th century, sharp in the late. The wall is low throughout. The line of its profile, sometimes rounded, is inward in the early, slightly outward in the late, and straight. There is articulation in some degree between it and the lip throughout except that in the late **673** it is omitted, wall and lip merging in one straight line of profile. The rim is always low, and always broader above. It has a straight profile in those of 450 B.C. In those of the second quarter of the 4th century the lip is everted a bit. In the late examples it is nearly straight. The handles in the early examples are set well free of the rim and approach rectilinear in plan. In the late they are very generally of the same form, although abbreviated, and are glued to the profile of the wall and rim. The flange in the early examples is fairly broad and prominent. In the late it is vestigial. In the early the inner wall and floor are in one line of profile with only a suggestion of articulation between. In the late there is sharp articulation. The clay in the early is thin and of high quality, and the forms are carefully defined. In the late the clay is coarser, a bit thicker, and though the forms are adequately constructed no niceties of definition and modelling are present.

Quite thorough blackening from cooking on all surfaces is seen in a number of examples.

D. 0.27+
146 B.C.
 671 (C-46-91), Deposit 118. D. lip 0.27; H. 0.075; D. bottom 0.233; D. wall 0.244. Pls. 29, 62.
 672 (C-46-68), Deposit 107. D. lip 0.27; P.H. 0.08; D. bottom 0.238; D. wall 0.246.
 673 (C-47-261), Deposit 104. D. lip 0.273; H. 0.08; D. bottom 0.223.
 674 (C-33-1001), Deposit 105. D. lip est. 0.27; P.H. 0.045.

D. 0.21+
4th century B.C., first quarter
 675 (C-47-889), Deposit 81. D. lip 0.217; H. 0.07; D. wall 0.208.

D. 0.19+
460–420 B.C.
 676 (C-34-944), Deposit 10. D. lip 0.19; P.H. 0.046; D. wall 0.20. Pease 208 (not illustrated). Pl. 29.

 677 (C-34-1139a), Deposit 10. D. est. 0.19; P.H. 0.042.
 678 (C-34-1135a), Deposit 10. D. est. 0.19.
4th century B.C., second quarter
 679 (C-46-135), Deposit 87. D. lip 0.193; H. 0.07; D. bottom 0.184; D. wall 0.18. Pls. 29, 62.

D. 0.18+
4th century B.C., second quarter
 680 (C-37-564), Deposit 80. D. lip 0.183; H. 0.083; D. bottom 0.183; D. wall 0.17.
 681 (C-36-986), Deposit 15. D. lip est. 0.18; P.H. 0.05.

D. 0.12
146 B.C.
 682 (C-46-59), Deposit 107. D. lip 0.12; H. 0.043; D. bottom 0.098; D. wall 0.11. Trace of attachment of one handle.

Casserole without Handle 683-685, Pls. 30, 62.

Early stage, 146 B.C.

Deposits: 102, 104, 107.

The three examples have a broad, convex bottom, a low wall set off from the bottom by sharp articulation, and a wide lip straight in profile set off from the wall by semi-articulation. Within, a slight flange for a lid is provided at the join between the lip and wall. The red clay is of fairly good quality, and reasonably thin. The three are wheelmade. The quality of manufacture is rather careful. The finish is quite good on both surfaces, though better on the interior. Three sizes are represented: diameters 0.27, est. 0.25, and 0.21+ m.

All three are believed to be of the time of Mummius' destruction of Corinth in 146 B.C. Their close resemblance to Thompson E 141 does not necessarily imply that they must be later, since shape development is relatively slow-moving in cooking ware. It is also quite possible that E 141 is appreciably earlier than the time when it was deposited, for the filling from which it comes seems to cover a considerable range.[13] A rather stronger consideration taken together with their contexts, the general resemblance of the three examples in form to Thompson D 72, a casserole with two vertical handles, makes their placement in the years near to 150 B.C. not only plausible but probable.

For the period of production of this shape it seems likely that it may have been introduced only shortly before the time of Mummius' destruction. If so, the shape will be useful for close dating in Corinth. There is no Hellenistic precedent for just this form in Corinth. Comparison with the contemporary two-handled casseroles will make it readily apparent that it is not just a handleless version. It is a different kind of casserole. The degree of care given to the manufacture of all examples, with clear definition of the various elements, suggests that the shape is a new one for the potter. Comparison in quality with the contemporary two-handled casseroles, of long and by now rather tired tradition, points up this aspect.

The three examples form a coherent group and give the impression of contemporaneity, and the context evidence for them indicates this also. In one way, however, they are somewhat puzzling in this regard. They differ strongly in the form of the wall. The largest of the three has a wall profile rather less canted than the first and slightly convex. The smallest has a profile much more nearly approaching the vertical. Such divergences might be explained in various ways. The walls are of differing forms because the shape is a new one; the potters are still experimenting before settling down to a pattern of shape which is acceptable to customers and will sell well. Or the three are from three different centers of manufacture. This does not seem at all probable in this case. Or the differences are merely due to size, for in shape series of many sizes there is certainly a wide difference between the profiles of small examples and large. In this case, size does seem to have something to do with it, for it seems likely that the potter in making them this way was thinking about stacking them effectively and economically in the kiln. Examples of this shape, without handles, can readily be stacked, and if there is a series of graduated sizes more can be stacked together than would be possible with casseroles all of one size. The graduated differences in wall profile were, it would seem, a device which had the stacking of graduated sizes in mind. This difference would facilitate circulation of the kiln atmosphere among the pots in a stack. There would be considerable risk of spoilage if the walls of all sizes were made to correspond and fit together tightly. The housewife would have found a graduated set of casseroles convenient, just as now, but in this respect the difference in wall profiles would not be an especial advantage. The technical and economical reasons for making them this way would seem to have been the primary consideration.

---

[13] Miss Virginia Grace has expressed the opinion that the latest stamped amphora handles from Group E date "perhaps down to somewhere about 110 B.C." See V. R. Grace and M. Savvatianou-Pétropoulakou in Ph. Bruneau and others, *Exploration Archéologique de Délos*, XXVII, *L'Ilot de la Maison des Comédiens*, p. 322. A few other pottery shapes also suggest a fairly wide range for the deposit.

Casseroles without handles do not seem to be known at present in the Roman period. The present shape, via other centers presumably, may have contributed to the design of a two-handled casserole perhaps of early Augustan times, Robinson F 76, a deeper casserole with a rim perhaps a bit more compressed.

The three examples are all extensively blackened from cooking, primarily on the exterior, very little within the covered area.

D. 0.27
   146 B.C.
      683 (C-46-26), Deposit 107. D. lip 0.27; rest. H. 0.073; D. bottom 0.216; max. D. wall 0.245. Pls. 30, 62.

D. est. 0.25
   146 B.C.
      684 (C-35-723), Deposit 104. D. lip est. 0.25; P.H. 0.052; D. bottom est. 0.19; max. D. wall est. 0.21. Pls. 30, 62.

D. 0.21+
   146 B.C.
      685 (C-34-1611), Deposit 102. D. lip 0.211; H. 0.065; D. bottom 0.16; max. D. wall 0.17. Pls. 30, 62.

Large one-handled Saucepan 686, Pl. 30.

Advanced stage, 146 B.C.

Deposit: 102.

Two fragments of one vessel attest this shape in Corinth. The complete shape is known, however, from unpublished examples found elsewhere. The bottom part has a broad and shallowly rounded profile. Above this the curve changes to nearly vertical, without articulation, and slightly canted inward, its upper termination forming a plain lip. A single horizontal strap handle is set on the wall just below the lip. There is fairly sharp articulation at the outer edge of the floor within. The clay is of fairly substantial thickness and is red throughout. There are some traces of blackening from cooking on the exterior.

The context provides the date for this vessel. The rendition of the elements of the form suggest that it is fairly advanced in its series, though not particularly late. Presumably the form had been in production for some time prior to the manufacture of this piece.

   146 B.C.
      686 (C-34-2489 a, b), Deposit 102. Two fragments giving the profile except for much of the center and part of the handle. D. lip est. 0.22; P.H. 0.04. Pl. 30.

Small one-handled Saucepan 687, Pls. 30, 62.

Advanced stage, *ca.* 3rd century B.C.

Deposit: 97.

The center of the bottom of the single example of this shape is missing. It may have been either fully rounded or slightly indented. The wall rises in a broad, fairly steep curve which, without articulation, changes to a vertical curve above, slightly canted inward, its upper termination forming a plain lip. A single, horizontal, thickened, strap handle, triangular in plan, is set slightly askew just below the lip. The clay is of substantial thickness and the surface is gray, perhaps not its original color but merely acquired in cooking.

The context from which it comes provides only a general indication of date between *ca.* 330 and 146 B.C., with a slight possibility that it may be before *ca.* 200 B.C. The rendition of the elements of the form suggests that it is probably of an advanced stage of its series.

It seems possible that it is a late, one-handled version of a two-handled vessel shape of early origin. Possible two-handled antecedents in form are C-37-2062, Deposit 3, Campbell 163, of the later 6th or early 5th century, and C-47-870, Deposit 81, of the first or second quarter of the 4th century B.C. C-61-386, Deposit 45, *Hesperia*, XXXIV, 1965, pl. 3, c, is also cognate, but with two handles squared in plan.

ca. 3rd century B.C.
687 (C-34-25), Deposit 97. Center of bottom restored. D. lip 0.182; H. 0.06; max. D. 0.192. Pls. 30, 62.

LID I 688–692, Pls. 31, 62.

Early to final (?) stages, 6th century to 146 B.C. (?).
Deposits: 8, 10, 62, 108, 111.

Five lids found in Corinth and one lid found in the excavations at Isthmia, IP 2239 B[14], are classed together in this series.

They are characterized by a broad, relatively low top of various degrees of convexity from well rounded to nearly straight. Their knobs are small and solid, consisting of two elements, a thick stem and a cap of rising outline whose greatest diameter is somewhat greater than that of the stem. Five sizes are attested: diameters 0.17+, 0.16+, 0.14, 0.06+, and 0.04+ m. The clay employed originally in all seems to have been of several shades of red, though three are now extremely gray, no doubt from use. The outer surface in the larger lids is better finished than the inner.

The date of the beginning of production of this kind of lid cannot now be closely determined. The seemingly earliest lid, 688, comes from a deposit of great range, from the early 6th century to perhaps the third quarter of the 5th century B.C. The degree of difference in the form of the top and knob between it and 689, from a deposit of 460–420 B.C., prompts its placement well within the 6th century. The date of the end of production is not certainly established at present. 692, one of the late examples by context, could be assigned to either of two fillings in its well, one covering the period *ca.* 330 to 146 B.C., the other of 146 B.C. It is suggested, subject to review when more examples and evidence are available, that it is of *ca.* 146 B.C. on grounds of form and character of manufacture. The tiny lid, 691, cannot be placed more closely than within the range of its context, *ca.* 330–146 B.C.

It seems likely that several criteria for dating will prove useful in this series. These concern the form of the top, the shape of the knob, and the quality of manufacture. It would seem that there is a progression in the form of the top from a fairly generously convex profile toward one of much straighter outline. The earliest lid, 688, here assigned to the 6th century, is the most rounded. There is a reminiscence of this in the two succeeding, 689 of the 5th century, and IP 2239 B of *ca.* 350 B.C. The later lids are almost straight in profile. The initial shape of the knob, seen in 688, is a well-formed bud-like finial with a pointed top. In the 5th century 689 it still has this form, carefully made but squatter. In that of 350 B.C., IP 2239 B, the form is a rather crude reminiscence of the earlier.[15] In the later examples the top is only slightly rounded. The two earliest lids, of the 6th and 5th centuries, are carefully made. The 4th century lid is of adequate execution only. The three later are cursorily rendered. The practice of stroke burnishing or application of glaze lines in reminiscence of burnishing may prove useful for dating

[14] Deposit 16, *ca.* 350 B.C. H. 0.05; D. 0.18; D. knob 0.018. *Hesperia*, XXXI, 1962, p. 24, no. 18 and pl. 12, e.
[15] The form of the knob of a closely similar lid, Athenian Agora, P 14655 b, *Pots and Pans*, fig. 44 left (on casserole), is not unlike that of IP 2239 B, though it is more carefully finished.

with future examples of this series (for its utility with other shapes see below, p. 138). Among the present lids only the 5th century **689** is so embellished, with stroke burnishing on the top.

The larger lids may have been intended for casseroles. IP 2239 B was found together with a casserole, IP 2239 A, to which, though warped, it evidently belongs. The very tiny **690** was found in a grave on a small chytra, which it does not, however, fit very well.

Blackening from cooking is seen on two, **689** (more heavily on the underside), and **692** (about equally on both surfaces).

6th century B.C.
    688 (C-39-278), Deposit 8. D. 0.165; H. 0.06; D. knob 0.012. Pls. 31, 62.
460–420 B.C.
    689 (C-34-945), Deposit 10. D. 0.14; H. 0.036; D. knob 0.015. Pease 209. Pls. 31, 62.
350–325 B.C.
    690 (T 2698 a), Deposit 62. D. 0.046; H. 0.015; D. knob 0.012. *N. Cemetery*, 495–6, pl. 78.

330–146 B.C.
    691 (C-47-307), Deposit 108. D. 0.062; H. 0.02; D. knob 0.013.
146 B.C. (?)
    692 (C-47-402), Deposit 111. D. 0.178; H. 0.043; D. knob 0.016. Pls. 31, 62.

Lid II 693-695, Pls. 31, 62.

Early to final stages, 6th century, second half to 146 B.C.
Deposits: 3, 80, 98.

Of the three lids in this series **693** is known only from its published illustration.

The lids of this series have a broadly conical top. The small solid knob is in form like a button mushroom, the stem constricted, the cap overhanging and gently rounded above. Two sizes are attested: diameters 0.22 and 0.16 m. Both red and gray clay are employed. The outer surfaces of the two examples seen are better finished than the inner.

The earliest, **693**, to judge from its quality in illustration, may be near the time of the beginning of production of this kind of lid. Its context is, however, of considerable range, from *ca.* 550 to 480 B.C., hence it cannot be closely dated. The series, though sparsely represented, would seem to have continued in production to the end of Greek Corinth in 146 B.C. on the evidence of the context of **695**.

Criteria for dating of examples of this series would seem to include primarily quality of manufacture and a special embellishment of the top surface. The two earliest are clearly of high quality in execution and with well-finished surfaces. The latest is roughly formed of rather coarse clay. The two earliest both show lines on the surface of the top radiating from the knob, produced in both probably by stroke burnishing. This is not present in the latest example. The significance of this treatment for dating in other shape series is discussed below, pp. 138–139. The shape of the knob in the three examples is not markedly different.

6th century B.C., second half
    693 (C-37-2062a), Deposit 3. "H. of cover 0.045. D. of cover 0.22 m." Campbell 163.
ca. 375 B.C.
    694 (C-37-561), Deposit 80. D. 0.16; H. 0.042; D. knob 0.02. Pls. 31, 62.

146 B.C.
    695 (C–33-985), Deposit 98. D. est. 0.16; H. 0.045; D. knob 0.021. Pls. 31, 62.

Lid III 696-699, Pls. 31, 62.

Early to final stages, 350 to 146 B.C.
Deposits: 87, 90, 102, 113.

This form of lid has a very broad, shallow, conical profile. The knob is not unlike a doorknob, the center depressed, however, in varying degrees. The clay employed is of good quality and fairly thin.

Wheel marks are in evidence only in one. The outer surfaces are much better finished than the inner. Two sizes are known: diameters *ca.* 0.18 and *ca.* 0.14 m. In form they are sufficiently alike to have been used for the same form of pot.

The careful definition of the knob may suggest that the earliest, **697**, of *ca.* 350 B.C., is near to the beginning of production of the shape. If the lids are indeed Corinthian, **699** of 146 B.C. represents the last stage.

The series is obviously very slightly represented. A few suggestions, however, as to possible criteria for dating examples may be made for future testing. Character of the fabric and quality of manufacture are probable criteria. In the three placed earliest the clay is quite thin, the top and the knob are quite well defined. In the latest the clay is thicker and the form rather cursorily rendered. Decoration of the lid with dull glaze lines radiating from the knob is also a very probable criterion. This usage has been noted in connection with the cooking-ware pitchers (p. 138). In them decoration of this kind is not known after about 350 B.C. It may well apply to the lids also. It appears on the two here placed earliest, the date of one being by context. A possible and attractive criterion concerns the form of the knob. The earliest by context, **697**, has a well-formed, deep, conical depression in the center of the top. In the latest by context, **699**, the depression is so shallow that it would seem due to carelessness rather than intent if its predecessors were not known. This is the kind of change in form which is often seen in elements of a shape, particularly in embellishments and niceties such as this, which have no useful function. The degree of depth of the depression of the knobs in this series may then prove to be chronologically significant. These various criteria have been used in the placement of the two examples **696** and **698** whose contexts provide only wide ranges for dating.

Blackening from cooking does not appear in two, and is slight in the others, one on the underside, the other on both surfaces.

ca. 350 B.C.

  696 (C-46-129), Deposit 87. D. 0.148; H. 0.032; D. knob 0.028; Depth of depression 0.004. Pls. 31, 62.

  697 (C-37-2512), Deposit 90. D. 0.182; H. 0.058; D. knob 0.043; Depth of depression 0.01. Pls. 31, 62.

250 B.C.

  698 (C-47-479), Deposit 113. D. est. 0.178; H. 0.033; D. knob 0.022; Depth of depression 0.005. Pls. 31, 62.

146 B.C.

  699 (C-34-1612), Deposit 102. D. more than est. 0.13; P.H. 0.022; D. knob 0.03; Depth of depression 0.001. Pls. 31, 62.

FRYING PAN **700**, Pls. 32, 62.

Early stage, *ca.* 300 B.C.

Deposit: 94.

The pan of this single example is circular, moderately convex beneath, the edges rising in a continuous curve from the bottom. The top of the lip has a slight bevel, the slope inward. The cylindrical handle is attached in a horizontal position to the edge and ends in a knob which is a quarter-round in profile and which has a shallow central depression. A small hole in the bottom of the depression, which reveals that the handle is hollow for a length of 0.027 m. from its end, appears to have no value for function and is presumably accidental. All surfaces including the shaft of the handle are finished plain. The clay, relatively thick for cooking ware, is red, of excellent quality, and the utensil is very well made.

The context from which this pan comes provides only a wide date between *ca.* 330 and 146 B.C. The early date in this period suggested for it is based only on the quality and character of the clay and manufacture.

The period of production of this kind of pan cannot now be determined with any certainty. If **700** is actually of the early Hellenistic period, pans of its general form may perhaps be expected to have been available throughout the remaining years of Greek Corinth. By the 1st century B.C. an improved version of the form was on the market elsewhere. Robinson F 81, of that time, has a handle set in the same position as that of **700**. It is reported to be hollow, and one suspects that this change was introduced as a means for attaching a more heat-proof grip, perhaps of wood. It is differentiated from **700** also by the presence of spiral ridges around the shaft. Subsequent examples of the Roman period are more sharply differentiated. Robinson G 113–115 and M 11 of the 1st century after Christ are deeper pans with flat bottoms and straight walls set at an angle to the bottom and with grooved handles set at the same angle from the rim. A deep conical hole penetrating the handle from the end is provided, again presumably for an attachment for gripping.

The underside of the pan shows blackening from cooking.

ca. 300 B.C.
> **700** (C-34-35), Deposit 94. D. lip 0.237; H. without handle 0.025; L. handle 0.085; D. knob 0.03. Pls. 32, 62.

FLANGED PLATE **701**, Pls. 32, 62.

Initial stage, 146 B.C.

Deposit: 112.

This form presents rather puzzling aspects. It is large, well made on the wheel, of thin red clay of very good quality. The floor has only a slight rise in profile from the center to about two-thirds of the distance to the rim where it begins to rise more steeply. Beneath is a simple, very low cylinder of clay which is very thin and fragile and extremely constricted in relation to the very considerable diameter of the floor.

The form was evidently not made to be a lid. The potter clearly thought of it as a plate, for like the forms definitely classifiable as plates the inner surface is well finished, the outer surface is left rough. The reverse is true of the forms known to be lids. The only interpretation which seems feasible is that the cylinder is to be regarded as a kind of flange on the order of the flanges projecting downward on the underside of the Stamnos Lids (**608–612**), and that it had the same purpose as the flanges of those lids, to keep the plate from sliding off what it was set on. Perhaps it was used for cooking some kind of food which required rotating or constant shaking, for parching, for example. It would be possible to use it on a brazier, but with one of the only type now known for Corinth in the Hellenistic period (**646, 647**) the flange would be pointless. Hence it was probably used with some other form of cooking stove which we do not yet know for Corinth, one with a simple opening above such as the Athenian cooking stand, Athens, Agora P 17822 (*Pots and Pans*, fig. 44).

The high quality of the clay and manufacture of the plate suggest that it may be of an early stage of its shape series and that the form was introduced only shortly before the time of this example. If so, examples of this form will be valuable for close dating in Corinth.

The only blackening from cooking on the plate is a bit odd, if the interpretation of the form is correct. It appears only around the edge on the inner surface. Perhaps it was *used* as a lid, even though this was not its real purpose. Plate forms no doubt often did substitute as lids in ancient kitchens just as now.

146 B.C.
> **701** (C-48-42), Deposit 112. D. 0.311; H. 0.038; D. flange est. 0.07. Pls. 32, 62.

Baking Pan 702, 703, Pls. 32, 62.

Early stage, 146 B.C.
Deposits: 46, 118.

The two pans each have a flat bottom. The wall rises from it at a steep angle. The slightly overhanging lip is a quarter-round in profile with a light, thin, wheel groove, too slight to serve as a flange for a lid, around its inner edge. They are wheelmade of fairly good quality, rather thick clay, one of red, the other of pale gray, and the quality of manufacture is careful. The inner surface is better finished than the outer. They are of two sizes: diameters 0.32+ and 0.28+ m.

For the period of production of such pans only a little can be said at present. It seems possible that they may have come into production only shortly before the time of the present examples. If so, the shape will be of value for close dating in Corinth. The care with which these examples were made would suggest that the shape was a comparatively new one for the potters. They stand out in quality of form in relation to contemporary vessels with long previous traditions. Flat-bottomed pans with a variety of differing wall profiles and lip forms are well attested in later contexts: Thompson E 139, E 140, and Robinson F 78 for the 1st century B.C.; Robinson G 112, G 191, K 89, M 100, and Corinth C-60-92, C-60-99 for the 1st to 3rd centuries after Christ.[16]

Cooking-ware shapes with flat bottoms do not seem to be numerous prior to the Roman period. This is the only shape with a flat bottom known at present in Hellenistic cooking ware at Corinth. A flat-bottomed form presumably antecedent in function is attested in some quantity in the 5th century B.C. at Corinth: C-34-940, Deposit 10, Pease 214.[17]

It might be assumed from their form that these pans would be used for baking and they are indeed entirely similar to the modern pie plates. Blackening from cooking is concentrated primarily on the bottom, however, hence it would appear that they were actually used over an open fire. They would seem to be too large to be used over the ordinary Hellenistic brazier (see 646, 647).

D. 0.32+
146 B.C.
702 (C-47-835), Deposit 46. D. lip 0.327; H. 0.059; D. bottom 0.265.

D. 0.28+
146 B.C.
703 (C-46-92); Deposit 118. D. lip 0.286; H. 0.05; D. bottom 0.245. Pls. 32, 62.

Small Baking Dish 704, Pls. 32, 62.

Early stage (?), 146 B.C. (?)
Deposit: 102.

The single example has a gently convex bottom. The wall is set off from it by distinct articulation and rises from it at about a 60° angle. The lip is outturned and is flattened on top. Inside, at the point corresponding to the articulation on the exterior, a pair of light, shallow, wheel grooves encircle the wall. The clay is a bit coarse and fairly thick. The quality of manufacture is moderately good. It is a bit better finished on the interior.

There is no precedent at present known for this kind of dish in Hellenistic Corinth. There is a chance that it is actually of early Roman manufacture since the Mummian destruction debris filling from which it comes was not disposed of until that time. There seems, however, to be no Roman example like it

---

[16] C-46-80, Deposit 107, a pan with a convex bottom and a straight wall set off from it by articulation may perhaps also be of the Roman period, although there seems to be no close parallel for it in form at present.
[17] A very similar shape in Athens, *Pots and Pans*, fig. 40.

either. It is here attributed to the Hellenistic period in Corinth. Future evidence will no doubt decide its correct placement.

Blackening from cooking appears on both surfaces.

146 B.C. (?)
> **704** (C-34-1608), Deposit 102. D. lip 0.137; H.
> 0.035; D. bottom 0.102. Pls. 32, 62.

VESSELS NOT FOR USE WITH HEAT

Vessels for Food 705–721

KRATER **705**, Pls. 33, 63.
Final stage, *ca.* 150 B.C.
Deposit: 102.

The single example of this form has a very constricted, slightly spreading ring foot. The wall profile expands broadly from it and at its top are set the two horizontal, strongly reflex handles. Just above the level of the roots of the handles a reverse curve provides the transition from the body to the still more broadly flaring lip. The nearly vertical outer profile of the lip has a single wheel groove. Within, a broad and shallow, slanting wheel groove may have served as the flange for a lid. The clay is comparatively thick for cooking fabric, no doubt because of the considerable breadth above, and very strong. The execution of the form is adequate but cursory, with many wheel marks.

A date for this vessel close to the time of Mummius' destruction in 146 B.C. is here suggested. It may even have been in use at the time of the destruction. It was found at a level in a well which would permit its assignment to either of two fills, one of *ca.* 330 to 146 B.C., the other associated with the destruction of the city. The quality of its manufacture in part suggests the date proposed here, as well as its resemblance in form and proportions to the cooking-ware bowls below, **706–708**, which are assigned to the same date.

It seems possible that this form in cooking ware may have had a long period of production and that this is an example of the final stage, if it is actually of Corinthian manufacture. In basic form it is clearly related to krater forms which were presumably first introduced in Corinthian pottery in the early Hellenistic period, i.e. the Bolster Krater in fine ware, **188, 189**, and the coarse-ware krater, **616**. One might expect that examples of stages of the 3rd century would be forthcoming.

There are no certain traces of use over the fire on this example, and its form is certainly ill adapted for such use. Perhaps, with a cover, it was used for keeping food warm.

ca. 150 B.C.
> **705** (C-47-256), Deposit 102. D. lip 0.408; av. H.
> 0.185; D. foot 0.121; H. to max. D. 0.136;
> max. D. wall 0.37. Pls. 33, 63.

BOWL **706–708**, Pls. 33, 63.
Final stage, 150 B.C.
Deposits: 30, 46, 94.

In form the three bowls at present known of this series are in every way, except for the lack of handles, smaller counterparts of the cooking-ware krater, **705**. They have a constricted ring foot, a broadly expanding wall profile, a reverse curve above broadening out still further to the lip. The lip has a single wheel groove in its outer profile and there is also a possible flange for a lid (a shallow, slanting wheel groove) within. They are wheelmade, of fairly thin, strong red clay. They are better formed than the krater, with more distinct articulation separating the wall from the reverse curve above in two (blurred, however, in **707**). Three sizes are represented: lip diameters 0.29+, 0.27+, and 0.24+ m.

The contexts of two of the bowls are of considerable range, in the case of **706** between 330 and 146 B.C., in the case of **707** even greater, a mixed filling containing material from Geometric times down to the middle of the 2nd century B.C. and with some additions during the period of desolation after Corinth's destruction. The context of **708**, however, is attributable to the time of the destruction. This date seems indicated for all three, which appear to be sufficiently similar in forms and proportions to have been produced more or less contemporaneously.

As with the cooking-ware krater it is to be expected that this form had a considerable period of production prior to 146 B.C., and that examples even of 3rd century stages of the shape will probably be forthcoming.

None of the bowls shows traces of use over the cooking fire.

D. 0.29+
  ca. 150 B.C.
    706 (C-34-471), Deposit 94. D. lip 0.295; av. H. 0.12; D. foot est. 0.094; H. to max. D. wall 0.08; max. D. wall 0.25. Pls. 33, 63.

D. 0.27+
  ca. 150 B.C.
    707 (C-63-717), Deposit 30. D. lip 0.273; H.
0.101; D. foot 0.088; H. to max. D. 0.065; max. D. wall 0.245.

D. 0.24+
  ca. 150 B.C.
    708 (C-47-891), Deposit 46. D. lip 0.248; H. 0.102; D. foot 0.08; H. to max. D. wall 0.067; max. D. wall 0.207.

BOWL, VERTICAL RIM **709**, Pls. 33, 63.
Intermediate stage, 200 B.C.
Deposit: 110.

The single example has instead of a base or foot a constricted circular indentation on the bottom on the edge of which the bowl rests. The wall above it broadens widely in a very nearly straight profile. At the top of the wall the upward direction of the profile changes to vertical, with sharp articulation at the point of change. The horizontal lip above is overhanging and of a low, rounded profile on top. The red clay of which it is formed is fairly thin and of very good quality. The bowl was made by the potter with considerable care.

It comes from the use filling of a well which provides only a wide dating between *ca.* 330 and *ca.* 200 B.C. The extensive preservation of the bowl may suggest that it is one of the fairly late additions to this accumulative filling following one of the later cleanings of the well.

Only a few blackened spots on the exterior suggest that the bowl may have been used over the fire. The provision of an indented bottom (cf. the long tradition of such bottoms in cooking-ware pitchers, below, pp. 137–138), may suggest that the potter expected that this bowl would be carried on the head.

200 B.C.
    709 (C-48-121), Deposit 110. D. lip 0.323; av. H. 0.115; D. bottom 0.075; Depth of indenta-
tion 0.015; H. to max. D. wall 0.072; max. D. wall 0.294. Pls. 33, 63.

PLATE **710-718**, Pls. 32, 63.
Early to final stages, *ca.* 300 to 146 B.C.
Deposits: 36, 98, 102, 104.

This form of plate has a ring foot, a broadly conical wall profile whose termination forms the rim. Both red and gray clay are used. The inner surfaces of all are better finished than the outer. Two sizes are known, a small one, diameter 0.13+, and a larger, diameter 0.21 m.

The date of the beginning of production cannot be closely determined by context evidence, for the earliest, **710**, comes from a filling whose range of date is between the last quarter of the 5th century and the early second quarter of the 3rd century B.C. **710** is, however, very small, and it would seem that there may well be a relationship in form between it and the small black-glazed saucers (above **138–186**). Perhaps, as with the rolled-rim plate (**719**) in cooking fabric, the potter produced this cooking-ware shape in imitation of the more pretentious saucer series. If so, it may be suggested that **710** is to be dated around 300 B.C. or in the first quarter of the 3rd century as an adaptation of the stage of the black-glazed saucers of that period. The freshness and crispness of the form, with an extremely well defined foot, would suggest that it is of the initial stage of this cooking-ware series. The connection with the saucers would imply a Corinthian origin for the shape. If the latest examples, of 146 B.C., are also of Corinthian manufacture they would represent the final stage of the shape.

Several probable criteria for dating can be suggested for examples of this series. Character and quality of the clay and manufacture provide one. The earliest is made of very thin clay of high quality and, as noted above, it is excellent in manufacture. The latest are of rather coarse, thick clay, adequately but hastily made. The ring foot is sharply defined in the earliest and with a spreading profile. The foot of the later is defined only in the sense that it is recognizable as a ring foot. There is no attempt to model the outlines of the ring. For its size the earliest has a fairly broad foot. For theirs the latest have a fairly constricted one, as in other late stages of plate and bowl series. The wall profile of the earliest rises at a shallow angle from the foot, that of the latest rises much more steeply. The degree of constriction of the foot, then, size for size, and the degree of elevation of the wall profile can be expected, with probability, to be criteria for dating in this series when more examples are known.

Blackening from cooking occurs on most, on both surfaces. Two, entirely red, could conceivably have been recent purchases, unused as yet, at the time of Mummius' destruction.

In those below of 146 B.C. the diameters of the foot range between 0.06 and 0.07 m., heights between 0.042 and 0.06 m.

D. 0.13+
  ca. 300 B.C.
    710 (C-40-435), Deposit 36. D. rim 0.135; H. 0.025; D. foot 0.055. Pls. 32, 63.
D. 0.21
  146 B.C.
    711 (C-34-1609), Deposit 102. D. rim 0.21; H. 0.058; D. foot 0.064. Pls. 32, 63.

712 (C-33-986), Deposit 98.
713 (C-34-1610), Deposit 102.
714 (C-34-1614), Deposit 102.
715 (C-34-1738), Deposit 102.
716 (C-35-720), Deposit 104.
717 (C-35-721), Deposit 104.
718 (C-35-833), Deposit 104.

ROLLED-RIM PLATE **719**, Pls. 32, 63.
Final stage, 146 B.C.
Deposit: 110.

The single example has a low, constricted ring foot, a moderately steeply rising wall profile and a rim thickened above and given the effect of being rolled by tooling at its inner edge. The clay of which it is made is of fair quality, red, and quite thick. The quality of manufacture is fair. The surface of the interior is better finished than that of the exterior.

The plate is analogous in form to the Corinthian rolled-rim plates (above, **101–106**), though in its distinctly thickened rim it shows a greater resemblance to the earlier Attic plates of this shape, e.g. Thompson C 1.

The underside is much blackened from cooking.

146 B.C.
  719 (C-48-66), Deposit 110. D. rim 0.205; H. 0.048; D. foot 0.068. Pls. 32, 63.

PLATE, LOW VERTICAL RIM **720, 721**, Pls. 32, 63.

Intermediate stage, 146 B.C.

Deposits: 108, 115.

The two examples have a ring foot, a broadly conical wall profile, and a very low rim, sharply upturned but not defined by articulation. The clay is red and fairly thin. The quality of manufacture is good. The interior surface of both plates is well finished, the exterior surfaces left in a rather rough state. Two sizes are known: diameters est. 0.25+, and 0.17 m. By context both are of the time of the destruction of Corinth.

Blackening from cooking is seen only on one, in a small section near the rim on both the exterior and interior, the interior blackening being the more extensive.

D. 0.25+
   146 B.C.
     720 (C-35-674), Deposit 108. D. rim est. 0.257;
     H. 0.052; D. foot 0.069. Pls. 32, 63.

D. 0.17
   146 B.C.
     721 (C-38-679), Deposit 115. D. rim est. 0.17;
     H. 0.04; D. foot 0.056.

VESSELS FOR DRINK

PITCHERS **722-748**

Introduction

It may be suggested, on present information, that pitcher forms in cooking fabric came into use, if not production, about 450 B.C. in Corinth. Context evidence indicates that they had certainly come into use in the close vicinity of 400 B.C. Two without certain context may be as much as 50 years earlier, perhaps, on considerations of form.[18] In the period between this time and 146 B.C. six forms which are here taken to be Corinthian are attested. Two other forms are believed to be foreign imports.[19]

Probably one of the earliest of the six Corinthian forms is what may be called the Hydria Pitcher, so called since the form of its shoulder, neck, lip, and handle relate it to the Classical hydria. The single example, C-35-638, could on rather tenuous indications of context (Deposit 14) be perhaps as early as 450 B.C.

The most popular and longest-lived form of pitcher, the first of three varieties, Round-Mouth Pitcher I[20] (**722-745**), probably came into production at about the same time. Its continuous series extends to and evidently came to an end in 146 B.C. Two other varieties of Round-Mouth Pitcher are attested only in the years around 400. II is known in a single example, in a context of *ca.* 425-375 B.C.[21] III,[22] entirely similar to early examples of I except in having a disk foot, is attested in contexts ranging between *ca.* 425 and the early second quarter of the 4th century B.C. Two varieties, below, of pitchers with trefoil mouths, Trefoil Pitcher I and II, are attested only in the Hellenistic period.

Some observations applying to the pitchers in general will be useful for dating, particularly of fragments. Two forms of base are used in the pitchers. The first is a circular indentation of the bottom

---

[18] Deposit 14: **733** and C-35-638.

[19] There is a single example of each of these forms and the two are thought to be from two different, unidentified, foreign centers of manufacture. C-47-476, Deposit 113, is possibly to be dated *ca.* 200 B.C.: similar bolster thumb-grips appear on the handle fragments Athenian Agora P 4043-4044, Thompson C 71, C 72. C-48-195, Deposit 110, is of *ca.* 150 B.C.

[20] Three round-mouth pitchers are incomplete and hence cannot be certainly classified. C-37-537, Deposit 79, late 5th or early 4th century B.C. (possibly an early Round-Mouth Pitcher I). C-53-57, Deposit 88, *ca.* 350 B.C. (possibly foreign?). C-48-34, Deposit 112, Hellenistic prior to 146 B.C. (possibly Round-Mouth Pitcher I).

[21] C-60-247, Deposit 21. Indented bottom; hemispherical lower body; low, straight shoulder; neck with concave profile; arched handle; semi-articulation at outer shoulder and base of neck; dull glaze stripes imitating stroke burnishing.

[22] Deposit 80: C-37-557; C-37-569; C-37-576. Deposit 21: C-60-246. Deposit 14: C-35-641; C-35-642.

serving as a base.[23] It occurs on the Hydria Pitcher, Round-Mouth Pitchers I and II, and on Trefoil Pitcher II. In examples of these varieties dated between 450 and 350 B.C. the indentation is shallow. In those of *ca.* 325 to 275 B.C. it is moderately deep. In those of 225 to 146 B.C. it is very deep. The second variety, a thin but distinct disk base, is at present attested only in examples dating between *ca.* 425 and 300 B.C., in Round-Mouth Pitcher III and Trefoil Pitcher I. The body forms are in general well rounded. Semi-articulation at the shoulder is seen only between 450 and 400 B.C., in the Hydria Pitcher and in Round-Mouth Pitcher II. Sharp articulation here is seen only in a foreign pitcher of *ca.* 200 B.C. (C-47-476; p. 137, footnote 19). A very distinct shoulder stop is seen only in the earliest example of Round-Mouth Pitcher I of *ca.* 450 B.C. Subsequent examples of this form show sometimes a blurred reminiscence of the shoulder stop down as late as the end of the 4th century B.C. The neck in most forms is in a continuous curve of profile either with the shoulder or with the shoulder and body. In only two varieties, the Hydria Pitcher and Round-Mouth Pitcher II, in examples dating between 450 and 400 B.C., is it an element of the form distinct from the shoulder and body, with articulation at its base. In all varieties it is in greater or less degree concave in profile. The mouth is accentuated by wheel grooves (two) beneath it in only one example, of 450 B.C., the earliest Round-Mouth Pitcher I.

Round mouths of simple profile occur throughout the period from 450 to 146 B.C. There is no discernible difference between earlier and later except that the profile of the single example of Round-Mouth Pitcher II, of *ca.* 400 B.C., has a low bevel as opposed to the plain rounding of the others. A steep bevel without and a slanted groove within appear only on the Hydria Pitcher of 450 B.C. The form of the mouths of the two foreign pitchers stand apart from the Corinthian. In one, C-48-195, of 150 B.C., the mouth is simply rounded but around the edge appears a thin wheel-run groove, and within the profile has a slight recess to receive a lid. In the other, C-47-476, of 200 B.C., the profile within is concave, with also a flange for a lid. A plain strap handle is employed on all Corinthian varieties. The strap handle form which rises only to the level of the lip is employed throughout, from 450 to 146 B.C., and the only notable difference among them is that in examples of the 5th century and early 4th it is by comparison ovoid in section, while in later examples the outer and inner surface approach flat. The only example of a strap handle which rises above the lip is of *ca.* 400 B.C., in the one example of Round-Mouth Pitcher II. In the handle again the two foreign examples are distinctive. The thin strap handle of C-47-476, of 200 B.C., has above a rotelle thumb-grip. The handle of C-48-195, of 150 B.C., is of the twisted-rope variety.

The fabric might be expected to show a pronounced difference between Classical and Hellenistic, but in the Corinthian there is little change to be seen. The Classical pitchers are perhaps (though not always) a shade better in fineness and in smoothness of the surface and the forms may be a bit more carefully executed, but not much. In fabric and execution of form two Hellenistic pitchers, surprisingly enough, are much the best: the two foreign examples.

In a kind of decoration a stronger distinction can, however, be made between Corinthian cooking-ware pitchers of Classical times and those of Hellenistic. In many examples of 450 to 350 B.C. closely but irregularly spaced, long, vertical lines of dull glaze are painted on the exterior. These are not known on any example of later date. They may appear only on the neck or only on the shoulder, or they may appear as long continuous lines on both neck and shoulder or on neck, shoulder, and body down nearly to the base.[24] These evidently are a late, traditional reminiscence of a much older practice of stroke

---

[23] An indented bottom also appears on two other cooking-ware shapes, a bowl with vertical rim, **709**, and an imported deep stew pot, C-47-303, Deposit 106, both of *ca.* 200 B.C.

[24] Cooking-ware vessels from Isthmia, from an evidently contemporary deposit of *ca.* 350 B.C. (Deposit 16), also show decoration of this kind. On three one-handled, open chytrai, IP 2234, IP 2236, and IP 2241, vertical strokes extend from the lip to the shoulder. In IP 2234 they are dull black-glaze strokes, in IP 2236 the glaze is a dull yellow, in IP 2241 the strokes are more inconspicuous, much the color of the clay (just possibly real stroke burnishing). A stew pot, IP 2243, shows strokes of dull glaze in the same position. A cooking-ware pitcher, IP 2233, shows an unusual variation. There are

burnishing attested in Corinth as early as the last quarter of the 7th century on cooking pots.[25] A special treatment of the shoulder, with somewhat swirled incised lines, appears only once, on an example of Round-Mouth Pitcher I, **724**, of *ca.* 325 to 300 B.C. This kind of decoration may also be a vestigial survival of stroke burnishing.

The clay employed in all varieties attributed to Corinth is sufficiently consistent in texture to suggest that they are all of a single local center of manufacture (above, p. 117), i.e. that they are all of Corinthian manufacture, although no doubt produced in several different workshops. Perhaps the best indication for local manufacture is provided by the long, consistent tradition of form and shape development seen in the series of Round-Mouth Pitcher I and the probable end of production of this form coincident with Mummius' destruction of the city. The reminiscence of the earlier practice of stroke burnishing which appears on early examples also ties in this series with the Corinthian tradition. The other, more sparsely represented shapes can be associated with this series in various ways. The full range of clay colors in these is within the range of those of the Round-Mouth Pitcher I series. They are also to be related in aspects of form which would seem to indicate the same tradition, e.g. the indented bottom (Hydria Pitcher, Round-Mouth Pitchers I and II, Trefoil Pitcher II); similar body, neck and lip forms (Round-Mouth Pitcher III); similar handle form (all but Round-Mouth Pitcher II). The practice of decoration with glaze lines is shared by all varieties produced prior to 350 B.C. For Trefoil Pitcher II possible evidence for local manufacture is seen in **748** whose warped form may be a result of a kiln mishap, though there may be other circumstances to account for its present condition.

A possible indication of foreign manufacture may be seen in the pitchers of several varieties in which the clay is fired a slate gray. Most are of warmer colors, from tan to brown to brick red, often mottled. Presumably all would have been fired in an oxidizing atmosphere and the gray must represent a different composition of the clay, perhaps one with a high percentage of manganese. It does not seem necessary here, however, to assume that clays of different composition could not be used in a single center, and certainly the use of clay of only one type of composition is not characteristic of earlier Corinthian pottery.

All varieties appear to have been wheelmade. The potters, no doubt to decrease porosity, took care in all periods represented to provide a fairly smooth surface on the exterior, with the result that few traces of the wheel are visible here, but on the interior this precaution was evidently not thought necessary, and wheel marks are frequently seen within the neck and on the inner surface of the body. The clay of all varieties of the entire period from 450 to 146 B.C. is of a uniform degree of thinness. Sizes vary between heights 0.31+ and 0.15 m.

Round-Mouth Pitcher I[26] **722-745**, Pls. 34, 63.

Early to final stages, *ca.* 450 to 146 B.C.

Deposits: 14, 22, 24, 29, 34, 45, 46, 79, 90, 94, 98, 103, 110, 112, 113, 118.

Instead of a foot or base these pitchers have a circular indentation on the bottom the edge of which serves adequately to stabilize the vessel. The deep, broad and well-rounded body profile constricts

the normal vertical strokes on the neck, but also there are horizontal glaze stripes, irregularly spaced at intervals around the body. It is a flat-bottomed variant of Round-Mouth Pitcher I. This kind of decoration does not appear on IP 2235, a fourth chytra, presumably a symptom that the practice is at this time beginning to be abandoned.

[25] On two one-handled chytrai, C-62-639, C-62-640. Evidently "the vertical marks of the paring knife" on Campbell 159-161 (not seen) of 550 to 480 B.C. are also stroke burnishing.

[26] There are two other examples of this series which are not included in the catalogue since it was not possible to re-examine them in connection with the preparation of the present text. C-40-419, Deposit 36, without comparison with the others, can only be dated within the limits of its context, which ranges between the last quarter of the 5th century

gradually above, originally without interruption, to a relatively narrow neck which flares upward to an entirely simple, rolled lip. A plain strap handle rises vertically from the outer edge of the shoulder and curves in sharply above to its attachment to the lip. The clay of which the pitchers are formed is fairly thin throughout. The quality of manufacture is very satisfactory for the purpose and certainly is technically successful. In the execution of the form, however, none of any part of the period of production shows evidence of really careful attention. A fairly smooth outer surface was seemingly technically necessary since throughout the long period wheel marks were obliterated on the exterior though many show clear traces of the wheel on the interior surface. The surface color of the pitchers is of many shades between brick red and slate gray. For those of the latter color see above (p. 117). In the series seven sizes have been distinguished: heights 0.31+; 0.28+-0.27; 0.24+-0.23; 0.22+-0.21; 0.20+; 0.17-0.16; and 0.15 m. The representation in these size series is sporadic and though several cover wide ranges of the period of production the largest size is represented only by very late examples and the two smallest sizes only by three fairly early examples.

Production of this form in cooking fabric may have begun as early as *ca.* 450 B.C. Context evidence indicates that production had certainly begun by the years around 400 B.C. One example, however, without certain context, **733**, Deposit 14, appears to be antecedent in form to the rest of the series and an estimate backward of *ca.* 50 years seems indicated for it. The form is known to have continued in production to its probable end in 146 B.C.[27] In connection with dating proposed below for specific examples within the period of production it is to be noted that many examples from use fillings of the South Stoa wells have been placed relatively late in the wide period (*ca.* 330-146 B.C.) which their contexts offer. This is in part due to their greater resemblance to those of 146 B.C. than to those of the 4th century and early 3rd. In part also their extensive preservation suggests that they accumulated in the wells after one of the latest cleanings.

Several criteria for dating examples of the form can be suggested. Of these the degree of indentation of the bottom is one. It is quite shallow in those of 450 to 350 B.C., moderately deep by the time of those of *ca.* 325-275 B.C., very deep in the time of those placed late, *ca.* 225-146 B.C. A second criterion concerns the form of the body. In the earliest example, **733**, it is well rounded and with a distinct shoulder stop. This rotund form, with only an occasional blurred reminiscence of the shoulder stop, is prevalent through the 4th century. In those of 300 to 146 B.C. the desired form was evidently a double lentoid, with no apparently intended shoulder stop. In the neck a distinctly concave curve in profile is characteristic from 450 to 300 B.C. From 300 to 146 B.C. the curve is much shallower. For the handle, the shape within the period 450-350 B.C. is fully known only in the earliest. In it it is nearly ovoid in section. Those subsequent to 350 have a handle in which the outer and inner surfaces approach flat. There is no perceptible difference in any of these. The lip shows no definable change throughout the series, and for fabric little difference is evident between earlier and later save that in the two earliest, of the 5th century, it is a bit finer and has a somewhat smoother finish.

and the second quarter of the 3rd B.C. C-37-2390 was found in a filling which contained Augustan material beneath the foundations of the paving of the Roman Agora. A previous note suggests that it was comparable to those of the time of the destruction of 146 B.C. Conceivably the filling from which it comes was Mummian destruction debris to which material of the early colony had been added prior to the paving of the area. Other examples which might belong to this series but which are incomplete, lacking lip or bottom or both, and hence not classifiable, are noted above (p. 137, footnote 20). Examples of other series (above, pp. 137-138) may, in an incomplete state, be confused with the present series. Similar indented bottoms are seen on the Hydria Pitcher, Round-Mouth Pitcher II, and Trefoil Pitcher II. Round-Mouth Pitcher III is entirely similar to early examples of the present series except in having a disk foot.

[27] A point somewhat in favor of local production of the series is the seeming lack of examples certainly datable after the founding of the Roman colony in 44 B.C. and of a stage of shape development appropriate to that time (in this connection see footnote 26, with reference to C-37-2390). If the series were an imported one presumably late 1st century versions would have been available to the early Roman colonists.

One peculiarity in the treatment of the neck and upper shoulder will be of assistance, however, in distinguishing those quite early from those subsequent. This has been discussed above (p. 138) with regard to cooking-ware pitchers in general. In the three earliest, of 450 to 350 B.C., long vertical, irregularly placed brush strokes in dull black glaze appear here. They occur in no later examples known at present, though rough, incised strokes, perhaps a late survival, appear on the shoulder in one example of 325–300 B.C., **724**.

The purposes to which these pitchers could be put in household life are numerous. They are known to have been used for drawing water from wells, since use fillings are the contexts of a large number, even though, particularly in the large pitchers, the handles seem insufficiently strong for the purpose. It was evidently expected that they would be used for carrying water from the water source, whether well or fountain. The indentation of the bottom seems to have been specially devised for ease of carriage on the head. The nature of the fabric implies, perhaps, that they were expected to be used over the fire, presumably for warming or boiling, and some of those of lighter color, though not all, do show a type of blackening which looks more like the effect of household cooking than of an accidental reducing atmosphere in the kiln. The modern tea kettle comes to mind. Use of one-handled pitchers for cooking is attested as early as the late Geometric period in Athens (Rodney S. Young, *Hesperia*, Suppl. II, p. 199).

H. 0.31+

3rd century B.C., fourth quarter

722 (C-48-122), Deposit 110. H. 0.315; D. bottom 0.085; Depth of indentation 0.016; av. H. to max. D. 0.12; max. D. 0.273; D. neck 0.088; D. lip 0.127.

146 B.C.

723 (C-47-831), Deposit 46. Av. H. 0.312; D. bottom 0.08; Depth of indentation 0.012; H. to max. D. 0.123; max. D. 0.275; D. neck 0.098; D. lip 0.13.

H. 0.28+ and 0.27+

4th century B.C., fourth quarter

724 (C-60-288), Deposit 34. Av. H. 0.285; D. bottom 0.088; Depth of indentation 0.01; H. to max. D. 0.11; max. D. 0.257; D. neck 0.087; D. lip 0.13.

225–146 B.C.

725 (C-46-90), Deposit 118. Av. H. 0.288; D. bottom 0.085; Depth of indentation 0.015; H. to max. D. 0.10; max. D. 0.256; D. neck 0.093; D. lip 0.123.

726 (C-47-159), Deposit 98. Av. H. 0.282; D. bottom 0.078; Depth of indentation 0.013; H. to max. D. 0.105; max. D. 0.254; D. neck 0.092; D. lip 0.117.

727 (C-47-472), Deposit 113. H. 0.275; D. bottom 0.085; Depth of indentation 0.015; H. to max. D. 0.115; max. D. 0.251; D. neck 0.089; D. lip 0.12. Pls. 34, 63.

728 (C-47-473), Deposit 113. H. 0.27; D. bottom 0.075; Depth of indentation not determinable; H. to max. D. 0.095; max. D. 0.24; D. neck 0.09; D. lip 0.112.

H. 0.24+ and 0.23+

400 B.C.

729 (C-37-545), Deposit 79. H. 0.234; D. bottom 0.073; Depth of depression 0.003; H. to max. D. 0.098; max. D. 0.218; D. neck 0.093; D. lip est. 0.118.

4th century B.C., fourth quarter

730 (CP-2169), Deposit 24. H. 0.246; D. bottom 0.075; Depth of depression 0.008; H. to max. D. 0.09; max. D. 0.228; D. neck 0.078; D. lip 0.109.

225–146 B.C.

731 (C-34-33), Deposit 94. H. 0.234; D. bottom 0.068; Depth of depression 0.011; H. to max. D. 0.095; max. D. 0.192; D. neck 0.085; D. lip 0.108.

146 B.C.

732 (C-47-830), Deposit 46. H. 0.243; max. D. 0.20.

H. 0.22+ and 0.21+

450 B.C.

733 (C-35-640), Deposit 14. Av. H. 0.22; D. bottom 0.08; Depth of indentation 0.005; H. to max. D. 0.085; max. D. 0.203; D. neck 0.09; D. lip 0.114. Pls. 34, 63.

350 B.C.

734 (C-37-2510), Deposit 90. Av. H. 0.215; D. bottom 0.063; Depth of depression 0.005; H. to max. D. 0.09; max. D. 0.19; D. neck 0.082; D. lip 0.106.

4th century B.C., fourth quarter

735 (C-60-289), Deposit 34. Av. H. 0.22; D. bottom 0.06; Depth of depression 0.006; H. to max. D. 0.088; max. D. 0.195; D. neck est. 0.092; D. lip 0.12.

736 (C-61-385), Deposit 45. Av. H. 0.215; D. bottom 0.055; Depth of indentation not preserved; H. to max. D. 0.085; max. D. 0.193; D. neck 0.081; D. lip 0.113. *Hesperia*, XXXIV, 1965, pl. 3, b.

275 B.C.

737 (C-47-475), Deposit 113. Av. H. 0.22; D. bottom 0.063; Depth of depression 0.008; H. to max. D. 0.078; max. D. 0.198; D. neck 0.084; D. lip 0.113.

225-146 B.C.

738 (C-47-158), Deposit 98. H. 0.224; D. bottom 0.062; Depth of depression 0.012; H. to max. D. 0.09; max. D. 0.195; D. neck 0.088; D. lip 0.113.

739 (C-47-474), Deposit 113. Av. H. 0.022; D. bottom 0.06; Depth of depression 0.01; H. to max. D. 0.09; max. D. 0.186; D. neck 0.082; D. lip 0.113.

740 (C-48-36), Deposit 112. H. 0.218; D. bottom 0.067; Depth of depression 0.009; H. to max. D. 0.08; max. D. 0.196; D. neck 0.09.

H. 0.20+

4th century B.C., fourth quarter

741 (C-63-687), Deposit 29. H. 0.205; D. bottom 0.055; Depth of depression 0.006; H. to max. D. 0.075; max. D. 0.182; D. neck 0.084; D. lip 0.106.

225-146 B.C.

742 (C-47-245), Deposit 103. Av. H. 0.205; D. bottom 0.06; Depth of indentation 0.012; H. to max. D. 0.07; max. D. 0.183; D. neck 0.082; D. lip 0.104.

H. 0.17 and 0.16+

4th century B.C., fourth quarter

743 (C-60-290), Deposit 34. H. 0.17; D. bottom 0.05; Depth of indentation 0.003; H. to max. D. 0.07; max. D. 0.162; D. neck 0.074; D. lip 0.098.

744 (C-60-261), Deposit 22. Av. H. 0.162; D. bottom 0.05; Depth of indentation 0.005; H. to max. D. 0.06; max. D. 0.162; D. neck 0.078; D. lip 0.102.

H. 0.15

3rd century B.C., first quarter

745 (C-60-270), Deposit 34. H. 0.15; D. bottom 0.048; Depth of depression 0.004; H. to max. D. 0.06; max. D. 0.149; D. neck 0.072; D. lip 0.094.

Trefoil Pitcher I **746**, Pls. 34, 63.

Intermediate stage, 300 B.C.

Deposit: 34.

The single example has a thin, constricted disk foot, slightly concave beneath. The profile from the base to the lip is continuous in curve, the body being rotund and with a low point of greatest diameter. The aperture for pouring is broad (0.07 m.) as compared with that of (the later) Trefoil Pitcher II. The thickened strap handle rises vertically from the outer shoulder and rounds smartly above to its attachment to the lip. It is of slate-gray clay, thin, and of fairly good quality of manufacture.

The context, in the middle of which it has been placed, provides a date between *ca.* 330 and 275 B.C. The limits of the general period during which this form was produced cannot now be suggested.

300 B.C.

746 (C-60-287), Deposit 34. H. 0.225; D. base 0.087; H. to max. D. 0.07; max. D. 0.19; D. neck 0.073; D. lip 0.103. Pls. 34, 63.

Trefoil Pitcher II **747, 748**, Pls. 34, 63.

Intermediate stages, *ca.* 200 B.C.

Deposits: 44 (?), 112.

This variety has a fairly deep, indented bottom serving as the base. The profile is in a continuous curve from base to lip. The aperture for pouring is moderately narrow (0.05 m.). The thickened strap handle rises vertically from the outer shoulder and curves inward abruptly to its attachment to the lip. The quality of manufacture of **747**, fired a brick red, is good. **748** is badly warped and discolored, including a large area of blackening. It could be used, though awkward, and was in fact found in the use filling of a well. It may be a still salable kiln mishap, though it seems also possible that its present condition is due to having been involved in a subsequent intense fire, after which it was discarded down the well.

The contexts of both provide only general suggestions for dating. For **748**: between *ca.* 330 and 146 B.C. For **747**, if it is actually from Deposit 44: some time between 250 and 146 B.C. The depth of the indentation of the bottom corresponds to that of the Round-Mouth Pitchers of *ca.* 225 to 146 B.C. The dating at 200 B.C. is thus an averaging of these indications. The limits of the general period of production of this variety cannot now be suggested.

200 B.C.

747 (C-35-557), Deposit: perhaps 44. H. 0.21; D. bottom 0.07; Depth of indentation 0.015; H. to max. D. 0.08; max. D. est. 0.178; D. neck 0.08; D. lip 0.106. Pls. 34, 63.

748 (C-48-35), Deposit 112. H. *ca.* 0.218; D. bottom 0.06; Depth of indentation *ca.* 0.10; av. H. to max. D. 0.07; av. max. D. 0.175; av. D. neck. 0.08; D. lip *ca.* 0.10.

Decanter[28] **749**, Pls. 34, 63.

Final stage, 146 B.C.

Deposit: 46.

The single example of this form in cooking ware has a flat bottom with wheel marks. The uninterrupted profile from the bottom to the outturned, simply rounded lip is plumply piriform. The two plain strap handles are attached below, at an angle of about 45⁰ to one another, on the outer shoulder. One rises vertically to the level of the lip and arches downward to its attachment on the neck below the lip. The other, canted slightly away from the first, rises in a curve to a point slightly above the level of the lip before arching down to its point of attachment to the neck. Two fingers only and a thumb provide the most convenient grip with either handle. The decanter is wheelmade of good quality, fairly thin but substantial, red clay. The execution of the form is cursory, and no care was taken to remove traces of the wheel from the exterior.

The relationship of this vessel to Decanter I (above, **282–286**) has already been noted. It seems likely that this is an adaptation in cooking fabric of that form.

It is, of course, not possible with a single example of a form to suggest the period of production of the series to which it belongs. In view, however, of the much earlier tradition of decanter forms in fine ware (above, pp. 57–62) a considerable period of production may well be anticipated. None later are known at present, and if this decanter was indeed manufactured in Corinth, it would, by date, represent the end of the series. There is no indication on the vessel of use over the fire. It may have seen use only as an unpretentious wine pitcher.

146 B.C.

749 (C-47-829), Deposit 46. H. 0.184; D. bottom 0.078; H. to max. D. 0.07; max. D. 0.158; D. lip 0.093. Pls. 34, 63.

---

[28] For the name, see above, p. 57.

BLISTER WARE

750–779

INTRODUCTION

Blister ware was first isolated and named by Thompson in 1933 (Thompson A 68, C 78, and pp. 470–471). The pieces known at that time were all of the Hellenistic period, two vessel shapes and a lamp. The period of production of this special fabric was extended backward to the years 460–420 B.C. by Miss Pease (Pease, p. 259 and nos. 138–143), who published two additional shapes and suggested that the pieces she published were of Corinthian manufacture. Hellenistic lamps of the fabric were published by Howland in 1958,[1] and most recently, in 1964, vessels of *ca.* 450 B.C. and the third quarter of the 5th century found in graves of the North Cemetery at Corinth were added.[2]

Present knowledge indicates that blister ware was in continuous production from about 450, if not a bit earlier, to 146 B.C. There is reason to believe that Corinth was an important center for its production during this time. It seems quite possible, however, that the ware was also produced in other centers and that conceivably elsewhere this special fabric had been in production earlier than the initial date now attested for Corinth.[3] If this ware was indeed produced in other centers there is no reason why it should not have continued in them beyond 146 B.C. None beyond this date seem to be known at present, however.[4]

Some vessels and lamps made of blister ware are very attractive in appearance. In general, however, it is clear that the aesthetic possibilities of blister ware were not the main factor motivating the 300 or more years of demand for its production and supply. The primary reason obviously is that the fabric is to an extremely high degree non-porous, far better in this respect than vessels and lamps of normal fabric.[5] This characteristic was evidently obtained by firing the pieces to a much higher temperature than that used normally for firing clay, to such a high degree that the clay employed for them is extremely hard and brittle, approaching the stage of vitrification. The characteristic was found to be desirable to prevent loss of oil in lamps in Hellenistic times. This evident use in connection with oil, in addition to their shapes, suggests that the most numerous series of vessels, the squat aryballoi (below **750–775**) and kindred larger jugs, were intended to contain either oil for household use or perfumed oil, with either of which loss through seepage would be a factor worth considering and avoiding.

Of the shapes now known in blister ware the squat aryballos is the most numerous and probably the most extensive in point of length of period of production. Of long duration also are larger jugs

---

[1] Howland, *Greek Lamps*, pp. 91–94, Types 28 A and 28 B.

[2] *N. Cemetery*, pp. 137–138.

[3] Examples generally similar in fabric (though distinguishable from that of examples from Corinth) are known from Nemea, now in the Corinth Museum: Nem. P. 424, 428. All three are miniature hydriai of the kalpis variety, a shape not attested in this fabric in Corinth. They come from a votive deposit to be published by Miss Marion Rawson. If Attic analogy is pertinent the kalpis forms indicate that they are not earlier than the late 6th century B.C.

[4] Miss Judith Perlzweig tells me that lamps in blister ware were apparently no longer in production at the time of Mummius' destruction of Corinth in 146 B.C.

[5] Blister ware would seem to be very satisfactory as regards porosity. A lamp of the fabric was filled with olive oil in 1962 and allowed to stand for several weeks to test this aspect. It showed little or no seepage at the end of the period.

related in form.[6] Other vessel shapes are rare. The duck askos (below, **776, 777**) would have been very suitable also for oil or perfume, and conceivably the filter vase as well (below, **778**), though its function is not clear. In the case of two drinking vessels, a mug shape, evidently inspired by an Attic form,[7] and a cup, the decorative possibilities of the fabric may be the principal factor in their production, in the one case the relief ornament, in the other the delicacy of the clay. The reason for the production of the neck amphora[8] in blister ware is not as clear. Thompson A 68 is the only example of the unguentarium shape[9] known in this fabric. Three of these shapes were imitated in Corinthian in normal fabric: the squat aryballos (see below, footnote 14), the jug (e.g. Pease 128), some examples provided with a ring foot, and the mug (C-37-511, Deposit 79). Four neck amphorae in normal Corinthian clay[10] may have been produced under the influence of blister ware since their shoulders are decorated with rows of impressed "thumb prints," a type of decoration known in blister ware. The existence of these copies has been taken to support the view that Corinth was an important producer of blister ware. The existence of the two long shape series, consistent in tradition, also contributes.[11]

The criteria for dating vessels of this fabric includes considerations of fabric. The vessels now known of the 5th and 4th centuries are made of clay of normal, if not slightly substantial, thickness. Evidently the surface color desired in this period was dark, on the order of slate gray, though accidentally oxidized or partially oxidized examples are known. The vessels and lamps of the Hellenistic period, on the other hand, are much lighter in respect to thickness of the clay and it seems that the production of surfaces of warm tones through oxidizing firing was often, if not always, the intention. This seems true of one Hellenistic aryballos below, **775**, and the cup **779**. These are of very thin clay and fired completely a light buff. The Hellenistic lamps are of fairly thin clay. Many are completely fired in warm tones, though some are dark.

Considerations of fabric also appear to have bearing on the curious fact that the *floruit* for vessels in this fabric in Corinth is the 5th and 4th centuries B.C. They are numerous in these years, very rare thereafter. Quite likely the reason for the strong decline in the quality of production of vessels in this fabric in Hellenistic times is that in this time the need for non-porous containers for oil or perfume was being supplied from abroad by the technically and, at least in the early stages, aesthetically very superior unguentaria.[12] These, according to present evidence (see p. 99), first began to be imported into mainland Greece in the third quarter of the 4th century. Demand for them seems to have developed quickly and their desirability, as is well known, persisted without interruption throughout the Hellenistic period. They evidently severely restricted the market for blister-ware vessels.

Conceivably the generally thinner fabric of Hellenistic blister ware may have been introduced in emulation of the very thin unguentarium fabric. It may be that the extremely thin fabric seen in the aryballos, **775**, and the cup, **779**, represents early attempts along this line, a phase of brief duration which had to be abandoned for practical reasons because of great fragility, and that producers of blister ware subsequently in the Hellenistic period reverted to a rather more substantial, though still relatively thin, fabric. At least the filter vase, of 146 B.C., and the Hellenistic lamps which have been examined are appreciably more substantial in fabric than the aryballos and cup. It is odd that the possibilities

[6] Pease 139–141; *N. Cemetery*, 364–6, 382–2; *Hesperia*, XVII, 1948, pl. 85, E 10; and a good many other unpublished examples in Corinth.

[7] Two examples, Pease 142, 143. Cf. *A.R.V.*², Oinochoe Shape VIII.

[8] C-60-244, Deposit 21, probably of the last quarter of the 5th century B.C.

[9] The neck and lip are incorrectly restored in Thompson, fig. 9. A 68 was first identified as an amphoriskos. Some early unguentaria do, in fact, have vestigial handles such as appear on it.

[10] C-37-467, C-37-468, C-37-469, all of Deposit 79; and C-36-551.

[11] Professor Jack L. Benson tells me that a few examples of blister ware were found in the Potters' Quarter at Corinth but that there is no reason to suppose that blister-ware vessels were actually produced there. Presumably the blister-ware vessels found at Corinth could have been produced in a factory located elsewhere in the city.

[12] I.e., those of the best known ware, described by Thompson, pp. 472–474.

of blister ware for lamps seem not to have been realized until Hellenistic times. No Classical lamp of the fabric is at present known.

Among the other criteria for dating there is a technical aspect of the formation of the vessels. None of the examples of the 5th and 4th centuries examined provides indication that it was formed on the wheel. That is to say, none of the bodies at any rate. These appear all to have been handmade. It is conceivable that necks and lips may have been wheel thrown and attached separately. Production of handmade vessels is a curious phenomenon at so late a period, but the probability that it is so is strengthened by the evidence of the Hellenistic filter vase and lamps. On these traces of the wheel are clearly evident. It would appear that wheelmade blister-ware vessels are a phenomenon of the Hellenistic period only. The present evidence, however, does not provide indication of the time within the Hellenistic period when the wheel began to be employed for them.

In connection with the squat aryballoi below it has been indicated that the main criterion for dating them concerns the impressed and incised decoration appearing on their walls, and that, on this criterion, they can be dated as closely, within a quarter of a century probably, as examples of other shape series. The elements of the shape, however, perhaps due to their having been made by hand, offer no criteria for dating. The same may be true of other 5th and 4th century vessels of blister ware. Future study of the shape series not published here[13] will no doubt indicate whether it is or not. The decorative schemes which are used in the aryballoi, impressed vertical ribbing and incised vertical lines, also appear on a number of the jugs and may go through on them a similar evolution. Other kinds of decoration also appear on shapes other than the aryballos. Relief hobnails, closely spaced, are attested on the mugs. Rows of thumb-print impressions and ones of a lunate design, probably fingernail impressions, are attested on the jugs. The latter two are sometimes employed in connection with an impressed and incised encircling ivy garland. The duck askos has, exceptionally, five zones of incised motifs: herringbone, wave pattern, ivy garland, zigzag line, and closely spaced dots. These other decorative motifs may perhaps prove to be of brief duration or to show patterns of evolution which will help to make the series on which they appear chronologically useful. For the wheelmade vessels of Hellenistic times criteria for dating can be suggested only when sufficient examples and further evidence are available.

SHAPE HISTORIES

VESSELS FOR OIL OR PERFUME
SQUAT ARYBALLOS **750-775**, Pls. 35, 64.

Initial to late stages, *ca.* 450 to 300 B.C.
Deposits: 10, 11, 20, 22, 35, 36, 39, 43, 79, 81, 87, 102, 106.

These vessels have a flat or slightly concave, broad bottom. The body is low, greatest in diameter at the bottom, the wall profile constricting in diameter as it rises, giving the body the general outline of the top of a mushroom. The neck is slender, concave in outline. The thin lip is low and flares widely in profile. The narrow handle, when preserved (rather rarely), is of the strap variety. There is no real articulation employed to set off the elements of the form from one another. The entire outline is essentially a single continuous curve. All examples are small, ranging in height between 0.05 and 0.075 m., in greatest diameter between 0.07 and 0.093 m., and there seems to have been no intentional distinction of sizes.

---

[13] I.e., particularly the jug series and its imitations in normal Corinthian clay. The mug is perhaps, in blister ware, a shape of brief duration. Neither of these shapes is known to have been produced during the Hellenistic period.

The clay of which they are made is of normal thickness, fired to an extremely high temperature. One exception, the latest example, **775**, is extremely thin. Typical blisters which give the ware its name are comparatively little in evidence on the exteriors among the present examples except for the bottom, on which they appear frequently. They do appear on the exteriors of the two latest examples, however. Broken examples show them on the interior. The appearance of the aryballoi suggests that the bodies, at least, may have been handmade. Conceivably the neck and lip may have been made separately on the wheel. If the bodies were actually made on the wheel also, all traces have vanished in the high temperature of their firing, and certainly there is little to suggest the wheel in the body outlines. Presumably they were fully glazed on the exterior surfaces, though if so the glaze is fully adherent. It would seem that the intended effect was a black or slate-gray surface, though some are fired orange and others are various shades between the two, often mottled or in streaks, no doubt accidentally partly oxidized in firing. A single exception, the latest, **775**, may have been deliberately fired a warm tone. Most examples are decorated, either by impression or incision, the two latest examples being the only exceptions. Conceivably this kind of decoration served as a kind of safety valve, preventing blisters from forming on the visible surfaces. At any rate, it is notable that blisters have formed on the walls of only the two latest, undecorated, aryballoi.

The period of production of this shape in this fabric seems to cover about 150 years. The initial stage is to be placed in the vicinity of 450 B.C.,[14] possibly a bit on the upper side. The form seems certainly to have continued down beyond *ca.* 330. The two latest examples come from contexts only widely dated between 330 and 146 B.C. Their close resemblance in general form to those of *ca.* 350 and the rarity of the shape in Hellenistic deposits suggests that they are to be dated high in range of their contexts. The latest has, accordingly, been placed at *ca.* 300 B.C. It is, however, of quite high quality, and we may not, then, have the final stage of the form.[15]

Deposit evidence indicates that the main criterion for relative placement of examples of this series concerns the decoration. The general trend is toward degeneration of the original motif. The original motif in this case is evidently very pronounced, widely spaced, "pumpkin" ribbing, e.g. **750**, which goes through probably three successive stages of less strong, more shallowly impressed and more closely spaced ribbing, e.g., for the first, heavy ribbing: **751**; for the second, moderately ribbed: **752–754**; for the third, closely spaced ribbing: **755–761**. The most advanced of these is to be placed, by deposit evidence, in the first quarter of the 4th century B.C. In the final stage of this decoration the original ribbing is reduced to fine, lightly incised, closely spaced, vertical lines: linear aryballoi. This kind of decoration was evidently current in the second quarter of the 4th century.[16] It may well have continued for a little while beyond 350 B.C. It would seem, and this is a natural progression, that decoration was evidently abandoned entirely, as indicated by the two latest examples.

Two minor criteria for dating are also indicated, both for future testing when more examples and evidence are available. They concern the fabric and the handle form. It is conceivable that toward the end of the 4th century, the normal fabric of serviceable thickness, fired dark, was abandoned in favor of extremely thin clay of almost eggshell thinness and delicacy, fired buff, of which the single, last aryballos, **775**, is an example, and that these may in the future provide distinctions between Classical

[14] **751**, from Deposit 10, is of 460–420 B.C. Other aryballoi, which, to judge from illustrations, seem to be of a very early stage, come from graves in the North Cemetery dated *ca.* 450 B.C. and in the third quarter of the century: *N. Cemetery*, 354-3; 355-4; D 11-a. (Note that 364–6 and 382–2 belong to a different shape series of small jugs, the shape on the order of Pease 139–141; also, that D 14-b appears to be somewhat later than the third quarter of the 5th century.) **750** seems typologically to be earlier than any of the published aryballoi.

[15] The fragment, Thompson C 78, if it is indeed contemporary with its context, would seem to indicate that the shape continued to be produced until *ca.* 200 B.C.

[16] Two aryballoi so decorated, IP 2230 and IP 2231, from the Isthmia Pottery Pit, Deposit 16, are of *ca.* 350 B.C. by context: Broneer, *Hesperia*, XXXI, 1962, pl. 12, f; *Isthmia*, II, p. 41, note 37, pl. 19, d.

and Hellenistic aryballoi. The handle form of the same aryballos is also unprecedented and may be a criterion of late date: the effect of a double loop handle is given to what is essentially the earlier, canonical strap handle, by a strong, vertical line of incision. The aspects of thinness, light color, and forms of handle are paralleled in the blister-ware cup, **779**, also of late date with respect to the aryballos series.

The deposit evidence indicates that there is no essential change in the basic form over the long period of production. This is a very unusual phenomenon and it may well be a point in favor of the thought that these aryballoi were handmade, in addition to the exceptional lack of real articulation.

The form was closely imitated in normal Corinthian clay. Three of the imitations are decorated with very advanced ribbing and two are linear.[17] The interiors of two broken examples have traces which may indicate that they were wheelmade but none of the exteriors suggests this. All were covered with black glaze.

Pumpkin ribbing
  ca. 450 B.C.
    750 (C-36-1057), Deposit 11. P.H. 0.036; max. D. 0.074. Neck, lip, and handle missing. Pl. 64.
Heavy ribbing
  5th century B.C., third quarter
    751 (C-34-1028), Deposit 10. H. 0.06; max. D. 0.074. Handle and part of lip restored. Pease 138. Pl. 64.
Moderately ribbed
  5th century B.C., fourth quarter
    752 (C-32-38).
    753 (CP-464).
    754 (CP-465). H. 0.057; max. D. est. 0.078. Pl. 64.
Closely spaced ribbing
  4th century B.C., first quarter
    755 (C-47-878), Deposit 81.
    756 (C-31-418), Deposit 20. H. 0.058; max. D. 0.073. *Asklepieion*, pl. 49, no. 34. Pl. 64.
    757 (C-37-416), Deposit 79.
    758 (CP-463).
    759 (C-37-415), Deposit 79.
    760 (CP-20).
    761 (C-31-417), Deposit 20. H. 0.061; max. D. 0.088. *Asklepieion*, pl. 49, no. 33. Pl. 35.

Linear
  4th century B.C., second quarter
    762 (C-38-592), Deposit 35.
    763 (C-40-423), Deposit 36.
    764 (C-38-629).
    765 (C-31-15), Deposit 39.
    766 (C-40-424), Deposit 36. *Hesperia*, XVII, 1948, pl. 85, E 11.
    767 (C-53-227), Deposit 43.
    768 (C-38-628). H. 0.06; max. D. 0.083. Pl. 64.
    769 (CP-21).
    770 (C-53-229), Deposit 43.
    771 (C-46-119), Deposit 87.
    772 (C-47-873), Deposit 81.
    773 (C-60-255), Deposit 22.
Undecorated
  ca. 325 B.C.
    774 (C-47-297), Deposit 106. P.H. 0.068; max. D. 0.093. Handle and most of lip missing. Pl. 64.
Undecorated, thin fabric
  ca. 300 B.C.
    775 (C-47-228), Deposit 102. Bottom and much of wall missing. P.H. 0.055; max. D. est. 0.09. Pls. 35, 64.

DUCK ASKOS **776**, **777**, Pl. 64.

Early stage, short period of production (?), 4th century B.C., last quarter.
Deposits: 38, 102.

The nearly complete piece, **776**,[18] has the schematized form of a duck. The fragment, **777**, is very similar to it in decoration and evidently also came from a form modelled freehand. It may have come from

[17] Closely spaced ribbing, first quarter of the 4th century: C-47-874, Deposit 81; C-37-466, Deposit 79; and CP-466. Linear, second quarter of 4th century B.C.: C-53-228, Deposit 43, and C-47-266.

[18] Since this was written a large section of a very similar askos has been catalogued from context pottery, C-32-290. It supplies the form of the neck and lip missing in **776**. They are exactly the same as in the blister-ware squat aryballoi. The upper wall has zones of incised decoration, from bottom to top: herringbone; a swirling tendril design; ivy; and, at the top behind the neck, closely spaced dashes.

a similar vessel, though some other theriomorphic shape is not excluded. They are both made of clay of normal and substantial thickness, smoothly finished on the exterior surfaces. No blisters are in evidence. Both were evidently covered with a dilute glaze which has fired a mottled, slate gray and buff. Both are decorated with incised patterns, **776** beneath the glaze, **777** through the glaze.

Their close similarities indicate that they are nearly contemporary. The approximate date for them is indicated by the context of **776**, a range between *ca.* 325 and some time in the second quarter of the 3rd century B.C. **777** is regarded as much earlier than its context, a filling associated with the destruction of Corinth in 146 B.C. The substantial fabric provides a suggestion for a date for them high in the range of the context of **776** on the analogy of the squat aryballoi (**750–775**). For them it has been suggested that the characteristic 5th and 4th century substantial fabric was abandoned in favor of a much lighter fabric in the late years of the 4th century.

4th century B.C., last quarter

776 (C-60-68), Deposit 38. Neck and lip missing. Sections of upper body, lower body, and bottom restored. P.H. without handle 0.054; P.L. 0.122; max. W. 0.073; bottom W. est. 0.045; L. est. 0.07. Flat bottom, oval in plan. Lower wall nearly straight in profile. Slight articulation at join of lower and upper walls; at front at this level, just below the missing spout, an oval indentation 0.015 x 0.012 m., probably a thumb impression. The upper wall is decorated with a series of zones of incised decoration separated from one another by an incised line. These encircle the top longitudinally, interrupted below the neck and handle. Bottom to top: herringbone; wave pattern; ivy garland; zigzag line. The triangular area behind the handle has closely spaced dots. The handle, nearly circular in section, is decorated on top with closely spaced incised diagonal lines. Pl. 64.

777 (C-34-1645), Deposit 102. Fragment. Max. dim. 0.028. A line of sharp articulation near the lower break. From it outward, a longitudinal line of herringbone and ivy. No line separating the two. Pl. 64.

VESSELS FOR OTHER PURPOSES

FILTER VASE **778**, Pls. 36, 64.

Final stage, 146 B.C.

Deposit: 46.

The single example of this form, fragments only, had a flat bottom. The deep body has a convex profile greatest in diameter in the lower part. The funnel-shaped, high lip, straight in profile, much greater in diameter above than below, is distinctly set off from the body. The attachments of the vertical strap handle are preserved at the base of the neck and on the outer shoulder. Presumably there was a spout on the wall but of this no indication is preserved. Five vertical holes 0.005 m. in diameter pierce the bottom of the lip inside between it and the body cavity. The clay of which it is made is of normal thickness. There are distinct wheel marks on the interior of both body and lip. Blisters appear on both the exterior and the interior. The core is gray. The exterior was evidently covered with a slip which has fired various shades of buff with some gray mottling.

The context of this example provides its date and is the evidence for continuation of production of blister-ware vessels down to the time of the destruction of Corinth in 146 B.C.

146 B.C.

778 (C-47-853), Deposit 46. H. est. 0.14; D. body est. 0.10; D. lip est. 0.07. Pls. 36, 64.

CUP 779, Pls. 35, 64.

Initial stage, *ca.* 300 B.C.

Deposit: 98.

The single example of this shape has a flat bottom and a rotund body profile, greatest in diameter below the middle. The low lip, straight in profile, is sharply set off from the wall. The thickened strap handle is attached at the middle of the wall and at the edge of the lip, with a triangular projection at each side at the upper attachment. On its outer surface a strong groove runs the entire length, giving the effect of a double rolled handle. The clay is of eggshell thinness. Small blisters and craters are in evidence inside and out. There are some lines on the interior which suggest rotary manipulation of the shape but other irregularities in profile and plan suggest that they are due to hand formation rather than wheel. Evidently the cup was covered inside and out with a slip which has fired a warm buff.

The context from which it comes provides only a general dating between *ca.* 330 and 146 B.C. A date early in the period is here suggested for it since its special and rare characteristics of extremely thin fabric and light surface color and a resemblance in handle form are shared with a blister-ware aryballos, **775**, for which there is some indication of a date early in the Hellenistic period. The handle form is also closely similar to that employed on some lamps, e.g. Broneer, *Terracotta Lamps*, no. 175.

ca. 300 B.C.
> **779** (C-47-157), Deposit 98. Av. H. 0.06; D. bottom 0.045; max. D. 0.078; av. D. lip 0.066.
> Pls. 35, 64.

MOULDED RELIEF WARE

780-942

INTRODUCTION

Probably in archaeological studies and circles the term Megarian bowl will always be a current one, and desirably so, since it is a good name. What it describes is readily apparent to all archaeologists interested in Greek antiquity. The serviceability of the term, however, unfortunately becomes qualified when one wishes to discuss Megarian bowls of various different centers and it will become more so when more fabrics are localized. One can, of course, speak of the Megarian bowls of Athens, the Megarian bowls of Corinth, but Athenian Megarian, Corinthian Megarian, *et al.* are obviously not desirable. And there is difficulty too with forms based on the bowl mould which are not bowls at all, but quite other shapes (cf. Courby, p. 330, fig. 62). The name *hemitomos*, which may be the ancient one for Athenian bowls of this kind (*Pnyx*, pp. 83-84; and Pontus Hellstrom, *Labraunda*, II, i, *Pottery of Classical and Later Date, Terracottas, Lamps, and Glass*, Lund, 1965, p. 19), also involves complications when other moulded forms are being considered (e.g., Athenian hemitomic amphora?). For purposes of classification here, then, with regret, the more colorless term moulded relief ware is used. A more succinct and at the same time more sharply descriptive term would be welcome.

Courby (chapter XX, pp. 327-366) some forty years ago distinguished the general category of moulded ware to which Corinthian belongs. He gave it the name of the *bols à glaçure*, meaning bowls with a high, glossy glaze, differentiating it, rightly, from *bols à vernis mat*, bowls with matt glaze. The distinction is generally an apt one, for in addition to differing preferences in the appearance of the glaze there are basic differences between the two in traditions of shape and consequently in some aspects of decorative treatment. In the *bols à glaçure* he isolated four classes, I, the *bols à godrons;* II, *bols à bossettes et à imbrications;* III, *bols à décor végétal et floral;* and IV, *bols à décor varié et corolle végétale.* Thompson, subsequently studying the Hellenistic pottery of the Athenian Agora, made it clear that the major center producing the *bols à glaçure* was Athens. He retained Courby's classification, clarifying it by defining the general chronology of the four classes relative to one another. He expressed the thought, however, that a new form of classification would eventually be needed. This need has become very apparent in the present study dealing with the Corinthian moulded ware. It would seem that the time has come to take steps toward such a classification.

All students of moulded ware find and will find in Courby's work a never-failing source of ideas. However, a much more numerous and varied corpus of moulded bowls is available than was at hand for Courby. To treat the present material in a comprehensible way and to make provision for more which will become known in the future requires a more general and more elastic terminology. Courby's approach to a meaningful classification of the bowls, on the basis of the main emphases of decoration, was certainly the correct one. That proposed and used here is essentially on the same lines as his and the nucleus of his contribution will be found in all the present classes.

The present classification is threefold: (1) Foliage Bowls, in which are included Courby's II, *bols à bossettes et à imbrications*, and III, *bols à décor végétal et floral*, along with others; (2) Figured Bowls, in which are included his IV, *bols à décor varié et corolle végétale;* and (3) Linear Bowls, in which, with other related groups, appears his I, *bols à godrons.* Each of the three, on the basis of the material we have now which is very extensive, is thought to be a basic class, representing one of, seemingly, the only three major interests in the design of moulded ware in Athenian pottery and its probably very extensive circle of derivative local centers of manufacture, of which Corinthian is one. Imported pieces found in Corinth testify to the existence of a considerable number of other centers of moulded-ware production which also stemmed from Attic. A classification which will serve for Corinth applies equally well to Athenian and to other fabrics presumably, in what might be called, for lack of local designations, the Attic orbit. How well it may apply to the many centers of production of moulded ware which followed other traditions, the *bols à vernis mat*, has yet to be tested. It may apply in some degree. It will be noted in this connection, particularly in the Foliage and Linear Bowls, that reference has been made to a large number of imported bowls found in Corinth of the non-Attic traditions. In many cases it will be seen that there is a good deal in common in decorative aspects between the Athenian tradition and theirs. The application of the present classification to that category of bowls, however, can be judged only by those who know them more familiarly.

The details of the definitions of the terms Foliage, Figured, and Linear are given in the introduction to these classes below. In sum, they each refer to the major interest of the decoration on the walls of the bowls. The sequence, Foliage, Figured, Linear, is a deliberate one. This is almost certainly the order in which these classes were first introduced.

The exact date, or a close one, when moulded bowls first began to be produced in Greece has yet to be defined. In the present study, 250 B.C. has been adopted as the approximate date. It may conceivably be late by perhaps a quarter century or so. It does not, on the other hand, seem at all likely on present evidence that it is any later, at least in Athens. It may well prove that other centers did not take up the practice of mould production of drinking cups contemporaneously with Athens.[1] There may be a period during which old wheelmade drinking-cup forms continued to be produced and used and a consequent lag before the new kind of cup came into sufficient demand to be produced in local centers. This may be the case in Corinthian. There is certainly no strong indication at present that moulded bowls were used or made to any extent in Corinth before *ca.* 225 or the last quarter of the 3rd century B.C. And, on present evidence, some of the old Corinthian drinking-cup forms do seem to have continued to be produced down into the later years of the 3rd century (e.g., articulated kantharos, cyma kantharos, Hexamilia kantharos), and one at least not only to that time but through it and beyond (conical bowl).

Foliage Bowls were almost certainly the first to be produced in Athens, ushering in the new form of drinking cup and the new techniques of manufacture. The quality of bowls of this class considered early is certainly high enough to inspire a world of imitation both of the designs and the technique of manufacture. The leaf-and-tendril variety below, scantily represented in Corinth, was perhaps the earliest of this class. No doubt it was quickly followed by the imbricate bowls and the pine-cone bowls, and before too long, perhaps in the last quarter of the 3rd century, by the Foliage Bowls of encircling design. Some of these varieties continued to be produced for some time, others may prove to have been of short duration. It seems likely at present that Figured Bowls first came on the market in Athens and Corinth some time in the last quarter of the 3rd century. They were still in very active production at the time of the destruction of Corinth in 146 B.C., though probably for 10 or 15 years before that the third of the major groups had been emerging, the Linear Bowls, which were to dominate production in Athens during the second half of the 2nd century and perhaps into the earlier 1st century B.C.

The chronological framework of moulded ware is still in the very early stages of erection. The main outlines are blocked out very roughly. General sequences are observable but all too seldom provable by context evidence. In details of chronology the work has hardly begun. In devising the present major

---

[1] It also seems possible that some Greek centers of pottery manufacture did not take up the production of moulded bowls at all. Dr. James McCredie tells me, for instance, that only a very few fragments of moulded bowls have been found at Samothrace. I do not know if these are of local manufacture or are imported.

classification of moulded ware much thought has been given to devising one which will be workable in building up a relative chronology which in time can be resolved into one more nearly absolute. The establishment, or suggestions of, criteria by which bowls may eventually be dated has been very much in mind. In each major class some suggestions have been made as to approaches which may yield chronological information.

In bowls in which much of the mould design was produced by hand, this applying particularly to some examples of the Foliage Bowls and, I think, to all of the Linear Bowls here,[2] it would seem that a general approach through the establishment of stylistic groups would be the most rewarding. A stylistic group here is meant in the sense of a single basic theme of decoration, e.g. the long-petal bowls. A number of such groups have been outlined below in which the original theme and some of the subsequent stages of its development in successive moulds can be suggested. In such groups, as one result, it has been possible by inference to suggest that a sequence of mould designs will progress from an original idea fairly difficult for a designer to produce in the mould toward one which can be produced with greater ease and expedition, though an interest in the elaboration of the possibilities of the given theme is also present. This trend toward ease of production is not a new one exclusive to the Hellenistic period. It is a very old one and a natural one, almost inevitable especially in freehand work. It underlies the change from, for instance, Protocorinthian to Corinthian, from Attic black figure to red, and the gradual abandonment of relief line in red-figure work is also on the same lines. In moulded ware itself it underlies evidently the change from early hand work in the Foliage Bowls to the introduction of the individual stamps which are used so extensively and evidently with great ease in advanced Foliage Bowls and in the Figured Bowls. In the stylistic groups this trend has practical application for chronology in that it puts one in a position to distinguish mould designs which, because of relative difficulty for the designer to produce in the mould, are apt to have been discarded and to have had relatively limited periods of employment. One can, conversely, have a basis for opinion about those which would have been employed longest.

In the Figured Bowls, whose decoration was entirely produced by stamping, the approach must be different. Here it would seem that relative chronology can best be established on its general lines perhaps by means of the individual scenes represented. It seems likely that in the period of production of this class of bowls the scenes were introduced not all at once but from time to time. One may, perhaps, with good context evidence, succeed in defining the times of introduction of the various scenes. We may also be able to define limited periods in which they were employed. Theoretically a scene once introduced might be reproduced indefinitely; but is this necessarily so? Given a sequence based on the scenes it should be possible, as a result, to do more with the auxiliary designs of medallions, corollas and rim zones.

From bowl forms, also, some chronological information will eventually be obtainable. Some suggestions on this line are made here, though in general shape development cannot be expected to be operative in moulded ware as it is in wheelmade vessels. Moulded forms are less subject to modification of an established pattern and such changes of form as are distinguishable are subject to different, as yet hardly explored, influences from those which prevail in wheelmade pottery.

That Corinth was a center of production of moulded ware is abundantly clear from the bowls themselves which are normally in a fabric as distinctively recognizable as Corinthian as any of the products of earlier Corinth in its Orientalizing and black-figure styles, or for that matter, of the intervening centuries which followed the end of production of Corinthian figured ware. Very recently, in 1965 and 1966, the evidence for local manufacture has been further increased by the discovery of four fragments of moulds for bowls, the first to be found in Corinth. These are catalogued in the Addendum below,

---

[2] In this connection, however, a stamp for a long-petal bowl in Brussels (Musée du Cinquantenaire, inv. no. M 723) should be kept in mind. Production of linear designs in moulds by hand was not, perhaps, a universal practice.

p. 186, **939–942**. Three are for bowls of normal size, one for a large bowl. Three are for Foliage Bowls, one probably for a Figured Bowl. Conceivably the proveniences of these pieces provide clues for the location of a shop or shops which produced the bowls, whose place of manufacture at Corinth (and, for that matter, that of Corinthian Hellenistic pottery in general) has yet to be determined. One is from a well a distance to the west of the present village of Old Corinth, two are from the area occupied in Roman times by the North Market, and one from an area in the northern part of the village, some distance north of the North Market. Evidence of Corinthian manufacture is also provided by a badly overfired, though still usable, bowl, **813**. Its provenience, a well in the South Stoa, is clearly not pertinent to the location of the workshop which produced it.

Incomplete potters' (or more probably, mould designers') signatures are found on a few Corinthian bowls. The names include:

> **838.**]OΔI[. Retrograde?
> **904.** ?]ΠP[
> **909.** A/T[   ] or [ ]A/T[ ]
> **911.** /   /A/Tω/ 3 to 6 letters /O/Y
> **912.** A/T[   ] or [ ]A/ T[ ]
> **913.**]A[or A[ ]
> **914.** ?]P[?
> **915.**]A[or A[ ]

Bowl forms of various sizes, from very small to very large, primarily of the normal drinking-cup size, are the principal products of the Corinthian moulded-ware industry attested at present. One form, based on an Attic model, was evidently current from the beginning of production in Corinth to the end of the city. It has a fairly flat medallion area, a broad lower wall, and a rim with a fairly high wheel-made section, slightly outturned above. One complete example, **802**, Plates 36, 67, of the last quarter of the 3rd century, is known and a fairly large number of the time of Mummius,[3] represented by **843**. A very large proportion of the Corinthian bowls are of this form. Though Athenian in inspiration, none of these bowls nor any other Corinthian bowl form employs the characteristically Attic embellishment of incised lines exposing red miltos (cf. Thompson, p. 454). A possible distinction between early and late in this bowl form lies in the wheelmade rim, fairly vertical in the one early example, more flaring in those of Mummius' time. Three pieces, a bowl, **805**, Plate 37, and two fragments, **840** and **780**, illustrate a probably early variety of bowl which is clearly related in form to the first in its basic moulded section. The wheelmade section of its rim is, however, of minimal height, just enough to provide a lip. Bowls with such rims are perhaps an inheritance from early Athenian bowl design of the middle years of the 3rd century (e.g., *Pnyx*, 62, pl. 44). Of the time of Mummius two other bowl forms are in evidence also. Both, represented by **919** and **921**, Plate 36, are of a more conical form, the former with a high wheelmade rim, the latter with one of moderate height. How long previous to Mummius' time these forms may have been used in Corinth is not known. The latter conceivably had been improvised fairly recently to suit its particular style of decoration, a linear one with relationship to the Macedonian shield and coin type.

But few moulded shapes other than the drinking-bowl form were produced in Corinthian. Very large examples of the most popular bowl form were probably made to serve as kraters, e.g. the Figured Bowls with appliqué supports below, and a huge Linear Bowl, **901**, Plate 38. A kantharos (?) form of the time of Mummius, **850**, Plates 38, 75, is attested, with a second perhaps of the same time, **792**, Plates 35, 65. The form of another piece, **912**, signed and closely contemporary, is not yet determinable.

---

[3] **796, 797, 798, 807, 811, 821, 829, 843, 845, 933.**
Other complete or substantially complete bowls without context dates are: **810, 813, 816, 842, 908.**

The average quality of Corinthian moulded ware is not high. It seems less high than it is because of the characteristic fugitive Corinthian glaze and the wear of the often fairly soft clay. There are, however, a few surprisingly well designed pieces.[4] One would like to think that their moulds were Corinthian, not imported. There is possibly a little local inventiveness in figured stamps and some local imagination in their use. Present pieces may well fail to provide a fully representative sampling of the Corinthian industry. General considerations of the topography of Corinth from which they derive, the distribution of the examples over the period of production, the paucity of pieces likely to be early, suggest that perhaps we will be underestimating the quality of the industry if we judge it by what we know at present. Those from a single, evidently well-to-do household, Deposit 46,[5] are, for instance, in striking contrast in quality to most of the others. Perhaps those from this deposit will prove to be more symptomatic of the true potentialities of Corinthian production in moulded ware as we may come to know them in the future.

STYLISTIC CLASSES

FOLIAGE BOWLS
780–795
INTRODUCTION

Ca. 250 to 146 B.C.

The term Foliage Bowls as here used is intended to include all bowls in which the main focus of design and interest is in plant life of whatever kind, naturalistically rendered or rendered in a limited stylized way. It is intended to be a comprehensive term under which stylistic groups additional to those represented in Corinth may be included when they have been distinguished. The term would exclude stylized representations of foliage which fall more naturally under the class of bowls with linear decoration, below, in which, whatever the basic element of the design, the interest of the designer and our interest lies in the possibilities of patterns based on line. The term Foliage Bowls seems an apt one in that one of the main focuses of interest in moulded-bowl design is clearly in motifs taken from nature, i.e., flora, and the possibilities which they provided for composition of bowl decoration. The term thus includes two of Courby's groupings, *bols à bossettes et imbrications* (Courby, p. 334) being one. These are the pine-cone bowls and the imbricate-leaf bowls such as those below. The other, *bols à décor uniquement végétal et floral* (Courby, pp. 334–337), applies only to the leaf-and-tendril bowls, of which there are Corinthian examples also. Courby's two groupings are actually related, and fall readily under the present more comprehensive heading, in that both are either closely or in a derivative way naturalistic.

This class of bowls is potentially a large one and probably many stylistic groupings can be made within it. The Corinthian designers of Foliage Bowls are known at present to have interested themselves in only a limited repertoire of this kind. A number of varieties of Foliage Bowls are known elsewhere. Among these the difficult, probably initial style of Foliage Bowls, the leaf-and-tendril style, is scantily represented. The stamped imbricate patterns had evidently more appeal. In Corinthian, however, there appears a style of foliage decoration of encircling composition (below, pp. 161–162), which has not been isolated for attention previously. And a single Corinthian bowl, **795**, may be the nucleus for the formation of an additional style of normal (i.e. vertical) composition. This bowl is an astonishing accomplishment in mould design in the general picture of Corinthian mould making known at present.

---

[4] **780, 795.**
[5] *Hesperia*, XVIII, 1949, pls. 13–14.

One or two fragments of leaf-and-tendril bowls also suggest that there were Corinthian mould designers of considerable competence.

The Corinthian style of mould design in the Foliage Bowls, as in other classes, seems to be derived from the Athenian. In Athens the possibilities of foliage designs seem to have been much more richly exploited. The likelihood of additional stylistic groupings in Attic Foliage Bowls can be suggested by illustrations of fragments which do not have connection with the bowls below, e.g. Schwabacher, pl. VII B, 16; *Pnyx*, pl. 43, 57–59; pl. 46, 75–79, 81, 82. Still further stylistic groups are suggested by imported bowls in Corinth which are also in the Attic tradition. They include examples of Foliage Bowls without corollas (most of the Corinthian examples lack corollas also) and some in which a corolla is introduced, as in Figured Bowls, to set off the main focus of attention on the wall. In the use of a corolla such bowls have a link, presumably of chronological import, with the Figured Bowls, which are similarly decorated.

Decoration with foliage is thought to be the earliest kind of decoration on moulded bowls. The period during which foliage was of greatest interest in Athens probably lies within the second half of the 3rd century B.C. Elsewhere, in derivative or other fabrics, the time of greatest interest may not coincide. Outside Athens it seems perhaps to have had a recurring vogue and examples of it are known even in the late days of Greek moulded-bowl production (e.g. Thompson E 79).

LEAF-AND-TENDRIL BOWL[6] **780–782**, Pl. 65.

Advanced stages, 225 and 200 B.C.

The style of decoration which appears on the walls of these bowls was first distinguished by Courby (pp. 334–337). Its chronological position among Athenian bowls was established subsequently by Thompson (p. 455). Additional examples have since been provided by Schwabacher (pl. VIII B, 11–22), and in *Pnyx*, 67–69, 71–74.

Courby used the name *bols à décor uniquement végétal et floral*. In *Pnyx* this was translated as Leaf and Tendril Bowls and the name is retained here since, though it is not fully comprehensive, it conveys an idea of what seem to be the original, basic elements of the style. A constant element is the division of the wall into perhaps six, eight, or sometimes more vertical areas by the placement of a single, long, lotus petal or leaf at fairly wide intervals. The field between them is often filled with grapevine (e.g. Thompson A 74). For this a more involved, delicately intricate convolution of tendrils is frequently substituted (e.g. Thompson C 16, 17). On some, a tiny bird rests among the tendrils (Thompson C 17), or an even tinier Eros is seen hovering (Schwabacher, pl. VIII B, 20–21). Tall spikes (Thompson C 16) may be substituted for some of the petals or leaves. These have been identified as the fruit stems of the date palm. On one probably late imported bowl at Corinth, C-30-144, a date-palm tree appears in full as an additional alternative for the vine or the tendrils.

The style at its best is superlative. There is no difficulty in supposing it to be one of the earliest to appear on moulded ware. The degree of technical skill demanded for the design of vines and tendrils as they appear in the best of this style and the entirely splendid creative imagination which the best exhibit warrant their position as the earliest, providing the initial impetus and enthusiasm for the whole craft of moulded ware. Bowls of precious metal decorated in this style are attested[7] to have provided the suggestion for the style and it may be that jewellers or metalworkers were employed in early work with the moulds for the pottery style.

---

[6] Since this was written a fragment of a mould for a bowl probably pertinent to this group as a late manifestation of the style has been found, **939**. It is catalogued in the Addendum below, p. 186.

[7] Three bowls found in the Athenian Agora, P 5813, P 11436, and P 16621 were fully impressed in the mould from complete, probably gold, bowls.

It is not easy yet to place the moment of the introduction of this style in Athenian moulded ware. Thompson's suggestion, based evidently in part on the stratigraphical position of A 74, an early example of this style, that moulded ware was introduced in Athens near the end of the first quarter of the 3rd century B.C., seems a bit early in the light of information available since his writing. For the present a date around 250 B.C. for the introduction of moulded ware in Athens seems preferable and the introduction of the leaf-and-tendril style must be relatively contemporary with that introduction. The style evidently was current in Athens at least to the end of the 3rd century (Thompson C 16, 17, 38). It seems not to have been produced in any great quantity, probably primarily because of the infinitely intricate handwork involved in the delineation of vines and tendrils in the moulds for effective representation of them. Producers of moulds turned more readily, it would seem, to the design of moulds which could be produced, and with very attractive results also, with individual stamps.

Corinthian evidence indicates that the style was adopted by other centers of bowl production outside Athens and that in some of these it may well have persisted for some time into the 2nd century B.C. Context evidence for this probably late and derivative phase of the style is at present lacking, aside from the general chronological implications of its existence in Corinth. The character of mould design and manufacture, and the bowl forms represented in imported examples of the style, however, suggest this.[8]

In Corinthian the style may have been adopted from Athens[9] during a fairly advanced phase of the Athenian style. Only two very small fragments, **780** and **781**, may be considered to be of this time. A third, more hastily designed, is perhaps a bit later than they. None has context evidence for dating. This absence, combined with the paucity of examples, makes the suggestion that the style was used in Corinthian during the later years of the 3rd century only a working hypothesis.

225 B.C.

780 (C-34-2508). Upper wall and rim. Max. dim. 0.06. Rim: very low wheelmade section, outturned above. Rim zone, a line of small carets, above a line. Wall, outline leaf and rosette; cf. *Pnyx*, 67, for this combination. Pl. 65.

781 (C-28-53). Wall fragment. Max. dim. 0.04. Leaf and tendril. Pl. 65.

200 B.C.

782 (C-35-977). Edge of medallion and lower wall. Max. dim. 0.038. Leaf (?) and tendrils with dotted buds. Pl. 65.

IMBRICATE BOWL

PINE-CONE BOWL[10] **783–785**, Pl. 65.

Advanced stage, *ca.* 200 B.C.

The characteristic decoration by which these bowls may be recognized is unfortunately not clearly discernible in the three Corinthian fragments representing this style since all the impressions are blurred, either because the bowls were poorly impressed in the moulds or because the moulds themselves were secondary. For those in Greece the nearest pine tree will provide clear comprehension of what the imbricate scales of the decoration are supposed to look like. For others, a cone and bowl fragments are shown in *Pnyx*, pl. 48. The cone scales are often graduated in size on the bowls, small to larger from bottom to top as are those on the actual cones. The only other decorative element of the Corinthian bowls

---

[8] Imported pieces representing probably four different centers of manufacture in which the Attic bowl form was employed: C-30-144 (vine, date palm, and tendrils); C-35-971; C-37-1567; C-37-2717; C-47-335, Deposit 109.

[9] One Athenian example of the style, a fragment, is known at Corinth: C-29-202.

[10] There is one foreign example of these bowls, a fragment, C-35-936.

which can be reported is the use of a single rim zone, formed by two lines, between which appears an ivy-leaf guilloche, on **784**. For the form, the three fragments may all be from different ones. For **785** one might suggest something like *Pnyx*, 94. **783** is evidently from a very large bowl where form cannot be characterized. **784** is a large example of a familiar variety, probably one with a broad lower wall, the wheelmade section of whose rim is high (0.03 m.) and slightly outturned above. Aside from the dimness of the impressions the quality of mould design and manufacture is good enough.

For the period of production of these rather rare bowls Corinth at present provides no evidence by context, aside from the negative fact that such bowls do not occur in deposits related to the destruction of the city in 146 B.C. This fact, however, is in support of previous Athenian evidence and suggestions that the style is of earlier date (for Attic: Thompson, pp. 455–456, with reference to C 29 and C 53; *Pnyx*, pp. 90–91). We may perhaps add a further suggestion in support of their ascription to a fairly early period of production. It seems likely that we are justified in seeing in a type of decoration, to which Courby gave the name *bossettes* (Courby, pp. 334 and 386; fig. 80, 6), and which we might call pyramidal bosses, a late stylization of the pine-cone scale motif. Evidence that this type of decoration is late is provided by an imported fragment,[11] C-48-87, Deposit 110, whose context is ascribed to the Mummian destruction. Perhaps one may see a further, this time linear, stylization of the motif in designs such as those which Courby described and illustrated (Courby, p. 386 and fig. 80, 7) as *petits losanges juxtaposés*, juxtaposed lozenges. Even though these three, the pine-cone scales, the pyramidal bosses, and the lozenges, may prove to be phases of one style of decoration, it will be perhaps best to retain a difference in nomenclature for them, on the order of the names suggested here, since each is distinctive.

The evidence then, at present, can suggest for the pine-cone scale bowls a date on the earlier side of 200 B.C., probably between 250 and 200. The rarity of the examples of the style may suggest that its period was brief. The Corinthian pieces do not seem early in this style and are accordingly placed at the end of its supposed period of production. The phase of pyramidal bosses may be expected to fall within the first half of the 2nd century, being still known at the time of Mummius. The linear, juxtaposed lozenges can perhaps be appropriately associated with the general linear style of 160 B.C. and later.

ca. 200 B.C.

783 (C-30-148). Wall fragment of a large bowl. Max. dim. 0.062. Curvature of profile nearly flat. Interior glaze almost entirely fugitive. Pl. 65.

784 (CP-909). Fragment of upper wall and rim of large bowl. Max. dim. 0.06; D. lip est. 0.20. Rim zone: ivy-leaf guilloche between two lines.

785 (C-31-481). Wall fragment. Max. dim. 0.069. Small scales: evidently from lower wall.

BOWL DECORATED WITH SMALL, VEINED, POINTED LEAVES

Elsewhere, in Attic and in at least one other foreign fabric, there seems definitely to have existed a style of decoration in which closely spaced, small, diagonally veined, pointed leaves, imbricate, covered the entire wall of the bowls. An example of the kind of leaf employed is seen on **850**, Plates 38, 75. The decoration was produced by repeated impressions of a single stamp. In the finest work there is meticulous graduation of sizes from very tiny around the medallion (perhaps made with the tip of the stamp) to larger up the wall. Athenian bowls on which this style is certainly attested are: Thompson C 28, C 34, and Schwabacher, pl. VII B, 19A, 19B, 22, 23. On bowls from Delos it may also be employed: Courby, pl. XII, 8, 13. On a foreign bowl found in Corinth, C-47-274, Deposit 111, comparable leaf decoration appears also.

---

[11] Two additional imported fragments with pyramidal bosses, both without contexts, have been found in Corinth: C-34-2340, and probably also C-35-877.

The style is distinctive and deserving of attention. The present indications, provided by evidence in Athens, are that it may be a fairly early style produced within the second half of the 3rd century B.C., and perhaps, in view of the rarity of such bowls, a style of brief duration. It is seen in Thompson C 28 and C 34, of about 200 B.C. These examples do not appear to be early in the aspect of mould design, which is rather careless and hasty, an aspect which suggests that the early phase of the style lies on the upper side of 200 B.C. The possibilities of the style and suggestions as to its appearance in its early phase are perhaps best realized from some of the examples shown in *Pnyx*, pl. 47. These particular pieces *may* belong to the style but cannot be proved to be examples of it, for they are lower wall fragments, and the same leaf design is often used for corollas of Figured Bowls, sometimes extending far up the wall. The style, completely imbricate, is not seen in Thompson's Group D of the mid-2nd century, nor in Group E of the late 2nd and early 1st century B.C. Absence from these groups of examples of the style is appropriate if indeed its period of production is earlier than that of these groups.

The existence of the style in Corinthian[12] has yet to be demonstrated for no bowl complete as to wall, nor any fragment of upper wall, on which these leaves are employed is yet known.

There is no doubt that the use of these imbricate leaves *as corollas* was in practice in Athens at the time of Mummius' destruction of Corinth in 146 B.C. An Attic bowl of this time, C-35-115, Deposit 108, demonstrates this. Thompson D 36, of the same time, shows a similar scheme of decoration. For how long the leaves had been employed in this fashion has yet to be determined: perhaps from the point at which figured decoration was first introduced. One may suppose, in view of their date, that two Corinthian pieces of lower wall, **850**, Deposit 98, Plates 38, 75, and **851**, Deposit 117, may represent figured bowls with corollas of this kind rather than completely imbricate bowls. Two other Corinthian wall fragments and three foreign fragments,[13] all five without context, cannot be certainly classified as one or the other. The Corinthian pieces have been catalogued below, for purposes of report, as unclassified Figured Bowls.

BOWL DECORATED WITH ROUNDED PETAL TIPS[14] **786, 787,** Pl. 65.
Final stage, 146 B.C.
Deposit:[15] 112.

Elsewhere, in Attic and in other foreign fabrics, there existed a distinct style of decoration in which closely spaced, imbricate, outline petal tips with a central spine covered the entire wall of the bowls. The decoration was probably produced by repeated impressions of a single stamp. The size of the tips in good work graduates from fairly small around the medallion zone (probably the top of the stamp was used here) to larger and more elongated up the wall. The effect in the best examples, of a fairly taut and naturalistically dynamic sheathing of the wall, is extremely pleasing. It is sometimes inconspicuously enlivened by the addition of a few feathered leaves, either in the top row or in one close to the medallion.

There is no context evidence at present for the time of the introduction of the style. It seems likely that it may have originated in Athens, and one may suggest as a working hypothesis that it was introduced

---

[12] A foreign fragment, top of wall and rim, C-34-2511, without context, is, however, evidently an example of the production of the style elsewhere.

[13] Corinthian: **852** and **853**. Foreign: C-35-683, C-36-2051, and C-37-1564.

[14] Since this was written a fragment of a mould for a large bowl, with large stamped petal tips, has been found, **940**. This is catalogued below in the Addendum, p. 186.

A complete bowl of normal size decorated in much the same fashion has also been found, C-67-56. The graduated rows of petal tips are, however, not stamped. Their outlines were engraved individually in the mould and the petal surfaces are not plastically rendered as in **940**, but flat.

[15] The contexts of imported bowls similarly decorated is also pertinent: Deposits 46, 107, 111, 112.

there about 225 B.C. Examples found there, *Pnyx*, 60, 62–66, pls. 43–44,[16] are clearly of the earliest phase of the style on the grounds both of mould design and high quality of manufacture. They may also claim to be early in bowl form. This is seen in the medallions of *Pnyx*, 63–66 for one aspect of the form. It is also seen in *Pnyx*, 62 for the form of the rim in which only the barest minimum was added on the wheel. *Pnyx*, 60 is probably still early, though it shows a bowl form which is connected, evidently antecedent, to one prevalent in the 2nd century B.C. in Athens and elsewhere.

How long the style remained current in Athens is not yet known. The period of its production there may have been short if its absence from Thompson's Group C is significant. The evidence from Corinth may be taken to suggest that the style was, however, adopted in other fabrics, both in ones which adopted the Athenian bowl form (i.e. on the order of *Pnyx*, 60), including Corinthian, and ones in which other bowl forms were employed.[17] In both, Corinthian evidence attests that the style was still in production at the time of Mummius' destruction of the city in 146 B.C. In two of the foreign fabrics the bowls of this time decorated in this style are of quite high quality. At what point the style may have been introduced in these fabrics is at present unknown.

The two Corinthian pieces are wall fragments. It is, of course, possible that they are not from examples with walls fully covered with these leaves. It is not known, however, to what extent this petal design was used as a corolla. In a single Athenian example, *Pnyx*, 54, the employment of such a corolla seems a bit distracting for use in a bowl in which figures were expected to receive the focus of attention; perhaps its use in corollas was, therefore, infrequent. **787** is without context. Criteria for suggesting a difference in date between it and **786** cannot at present be ascertained. Certainly both are static in design as compared with the Pnyx bowls, a difference which may be of assistance in discerning what examples may be early, and what late.

146 B.C.

786 (C-48-51), Deposit 112. Wall fragment. Max. dim 0.054. The ragged outline of the surface near the edge and the lack of glaze on the petals indicates that this piece was the point of attachment of a support of some kind, a relief head, mask or shell. Pl. 65.

787 (C-36-2006). Wall fragment. Max. dim. 0.054. Pl. 65.

BOWL DECORATED WITH POINTED PETAL TIPS[18] **788–792**, Pls. 35, 65.

Final stage, 146 B.C.

Deposit: 102.

The typical decoration by which these bowls may be recognized consists of outline, pointed, imbricate leaves with a central spine. They are of moderate size and cover the wall up to the rim zone. In the examples of this style known at present in Corinth there is no indication of a graduation in size among the petal impressions. No medallion or medallion zone is preserved in present examples. The rim-zone treatment shows several interconnected variations. A single zone of guilloche between two pairs of lines occurs on one. The same arrangement is elaborated on a second by introducing a line of jewelling between the lines and adding a line of egg-and-dart dependent from the lower line. On the third variety three single lines form two zones, one of the same guilloche and the other of the same egg-and-dart. Four of the pieces are bowls. The same bowl form seems to have been employed in all, one with a fairly broad lower wall and a rim whose wheelmade section is fairly high (0.025 m.) and slightly outturned

---

[16] Schwabacher, pl. VIII A, 4–9, and *Pnyx*, pl. 46, are examples in which a broader leaf of the same kind is used.

[17] In probably two foreign fabrics employing the Attic bowl form: C-47-342, Deposit 111, and C-48-30, Deposit 112; C-46-69 a–c, Deposit 107. Delian (?) bowls: C-47-792 and C-47-794, both Deposit 46; and C-37-2719.

[18] Since this was written a fragment of a mould for a bowl of this group has been found, **941**. It is catalogued below in the Addendum, p. 186.

above. The size in these is evidently much the same, H. *ca.* 0.08 m. and D. lip 0.125 m. In the fifth piece, **792**, the same general form, but smaller, may have been employed. The addition of a rim of different form and a handle indicate that it was probably a kantharos. Four moulds were employed for the five pieces, **790** and **791** probably being from the same mould. The quality of mould design and manufacture is only fair.

For the date of the introduction of the style in Corinth there is no context evidence. A suggestion, however, by way of a working hypothesis, can perhaps be made. The style was, by the context evidence of **789**, still in production in Corinth at the time of the destruction of the city in 146 B.C. Probably all of the pieces are of much the same date. The rim designs, the bowl form, the character and quality of the mould design and manufacture suggest contemporaneity for the four fragments of bowls, and there is no discernible reason for supposing that the kantharos fragment is earlier. The character of the mould design and manufacture do not suggest that the style was entirely new to Corinth but perhaps an advanced phase. If so, perhaps an estimate of 25 or 30 years backward would be appropriate to cover the time of the introduction of the style and its earlier phases.

The same style is also employed on bowls of several different fabrics found in Corinth.[19] It seems quite possible that all the fabrics, including the Corinthian, derived the style from one which was originally produced in Athens, first introduced there perhaps about 225 B.C. Examples of the Athenian style, evidently of the earliest phase there, are *Pnyx*, 61a–c, and 63, pls. 44 and 51. These are closely related to and probably contemporary with Athenian examples from the Pnyx of the style with rounded petal tips (see pp. 159–160). The same early form of medallion is used in both. If the absence of this style from Thompson's Group C is significant it may suggest that the duration of the style in Athens was short. The difference in quality and character of the individual leaves between those on the Athenian pieces and those appearing on bowls of Corinthian and other fabrics at Corinth may suggest a fairly long period of transmission between the Athenian and the derivative styles.

146 B.C.

788 (C-37-2423). Fragment of upper wall and rim. Max. dim. 0.067. Rim zone, between two pairs of lines an ivy-leaf guilloche.

789 (C-34-1622), Deposit 102. Profile preserved from rim to upper wall. P.H. 0.065. Rim zone, two pairs of lines in the center of which is an ivy-leaf guilloche and between each pair of lines a line of jewelling. Dependent from the lowest line, egg-and-dart. Pl. 65.

790 (C-37-2704). Fragment of upper wall and rim. Max. dim. 0.075. Two rim zones formed by three lines. Above, ivy-leaf guilloche. Below, egg-and-dart.

791 (C-37-2259). Fragment of upper wall and part of rim. Max. dim. 0.085. Same decoration as **790** and probably from the same mould. Pl. 65.

792 (C-33-1468). Fragment of the upper wall and rim of a kantharos. Max. dim. 0.065. No rim zone. Upper and lower points of attachment of a vertical strap handle. Pls. 35, 65.

BOWL WITH ENCIRCLING COMPOSITION

IVY BOWLS **793**, **794**, Pl. 66.

Advanced stage, *ca.* 175 B.C.

Deposits: none.[20]

In other Foliage Bowls the composition of the designs of the walls may be considered vertical ones. That is to say, the mould designer in them has thought primarily of building up his decoration from

---

[19] Bowls of possibly four different fabrics in which the Athenian bowl form was employed: CP-526, C-35-972, C-37-2264, C-37-2424, C-37-2700. Bowls of perhaps two different fabrics employing a different bowl form: C-37-2693, C-37-2743.

[20] The contexts of foreign bowls decorated with encircling compositions are relevant: Deposits 102, 104, 109, 111.

the medallion zone to the rim zone. Two Corinthian bowls exhibit a different approach in that the main focus of attention on the wall is on a design whose line of direction encircles the bowl. The design chosen in both cases lends itself readily to this treatment: running ivy. In the one example, **793**, it is in a free field, above a corolla but without a rim zone. In the other it is confined within a pair of relief lines above a leaf corolla with interspersed clusters of grapes; again there is no rim zone.

This kind of foliage composition is attested in an Athenian ivy bowl found in Corinth, C-30-141, whose scheme is: corolla; running ivy confined in a zone; two rim zones. For the dating of this bowl there is no context evidence, but one may estimate that it is of the last quarter of the 3rd century B.C. It may be that this concept of composition originated in Athens; this bowl would suggest it. One may expect that it was introduced there contemporaneously with Figured Bowls, for the approach to the composition of their decoration is the same.

Encircling compositions, confined either by a rim zone or by a wall and a rim zone (rather than in a free field), and with or without a corolla are well attested in other foreign fabrics. In Corinth compositions of these varieties are employed in a number of imported pieces.[21] The designs employed include wheat, grapevine, a foliage scroll, and olive leaf.

The date of the introduction of foliage decoration of encircling composition in foreign fabrics cannot now be suggested. In at least two if not more of the foreign fabrics, Corinthian evidence indicates that it was still being employed at the time of Mummius' destruction of Corinth in 146 B.C. In the fabrics in which it is attested at this time there is no reason to suppose that it did not continue to be employed for some time thereafter.

There is no context evidence for the period of production in Corinthian aside from the general implications provided by the destruction of the city. In mould design the pieces do not seem to represent early phases. In character of manufacture they seem suitable for almost any time within the first half of the 2nd century. A mid-way point is therefore suggested for them.

175 B.C.

793 (C-33-1467). Profile preserved from lip to lower wall. P.H. 0.045; D. est. 0.075. Below, a large, veined leaf of the corolla. Above, running ivy. No rim zone. Pl. 66.

794 (C-63-697). Profile preserved from lip to lower wall. P.H. 0.078; D. est. 0.11. Below, part of the leaf corolla and in the field a grape cluster. Above, between two relief lines forming a zone, running ivy. No rim zone. Pl. 66.

UNCLASSIFIED FOLIAGE BOWL **795**, Pl. 66.

Early stage, 3rd century B.C., last quarter.

A single Corinthian bowl of considerable elegance may well belong to a distinctive stylistic group not otherwise attested. The medallion and its zone are not preserved. The decoration of the wall was probably based on the medallion zone and covers the entire wall. The design is an alternation around the wall of a long, outline leaf, probably pointed at its base and with a pointed tip, and a frond of equal height. The field between them is minutely filled with fine jewelling. The rim zone occupies nearly half of the moulded height of the bowl. Strictly speaking there is only one rim zone, though the effect of

---

[21] In two or three different fabrics employing the Athenian form of bowl large foliage compositions cover the wall between a corolla and the rim zone. Encircling wheat: C-31-117; C-37-2120 a. Encircling grapevine: certainly in CP-1926; CP-1928; and probably in the fragments C-28-72; C-30-137; and C-47-258, Deposit 104.

Among Delian (?) bowls found in Corinth a number have large encircling foliage designs covering the wall between the medallion and the rim zone. Foliage scroll: CP-1607; C-34-1624, Deposit 102; C-34-1740, Deposit 102; C-37-1570. In other Delian (?) bowls a small foliage design in a zone encircles the wall between a very large corolla and the rim zone. Foliage scroll: CP-522; C-47-344, Deposit 111; C-48-28, Deposit 112. Olive leaf: C-47-328, Deposit 109.

three is given. A delicate guilloche with jewelling in its intervals is set between two pairs of lines on each of which a line of jewelling is imposed. Below the lowest line there is a line of fine egg-and-dart. Above the topmost line is a line of fairly large coil spirals. The design is in craftsmanship a *tour de force* and technically in design and manufacture the bowl is the finest Corinthian piece.

There is no context evidence for its date. If one supposes that moulded-bowl design began with naturalistic foliage, we can perhaps see in this bowl a suggestion of a foreseeable advanced trend toward stylization of naturalistic motifs, and expect that such a trend, one of probably a number, might develop within perhaps the last quarter of the 3rd century B.C.

ca. 225–200 B.C.
795 (C-37-2212 a and b). Non-joining fragments.
Profile preserved from lip to lower wall. Pl. 66,

FIGURED BOWLS[22]
796-897
INTRODUCTION

3rd century, last quarter to 146 B.C.

The term Figured Bowls is intended to include all moulded pieces on which the main focus of design and interest is in figure representations of whatever kind: divine and mythological, literary, human, animal, inanimate. This class corresponds to Courby's *bols à décor varié et corolle végétale* (Courby, pp. 338–362), but would not include Foliage Bowls on which a corolla is employed.

The decoration of the Corinthian bowls of this kind now known was produced entirely with small stamps. The bowl form employed in the Corinthian Figured Bowls is generally consistent. It is the Attic type, with a fairly flat medallion area and a broad lower wall. In a very large percentage of the Figured Bowls known at present the rim has a fairly high wheelmade section and it is usually outturned slightly above. The normal scheme of decoration includes a fairly small medallion, a simple medallion zone (usually a pair of concentric circles), and a corolla of foliage of some kind, often a single row of large leaves, sometimes imbricate small leaves or petals. The principal stamped figures or groups are usually placed above the corolla in a single line encircling the bowl, although a few examples of double, figured zones are known. Normally there is one rim zone, though up to four are attested.

An analysis of the figured representations now known in Corinthian appears below (pp. 165–168). It will be seen that many of them are the same as ones already known in Attic, the identifications being based on the work of Courby and Schwabacher. References under each heading provide access to their work, often to clearer representations than are available in Corinthian, in which fugitive glaze and wear of the often fairly soft clay are frequently in evidence. A number of representations, however, seem not to have received particular attention before. Conceivably some of them are local Corinthian contributions to iconography. These are: a standing Artemis (?); Eros bound (?); a Hermes type; the agitated woman; the girl dancing; and a cavalryman. Various other figures in Corinthian are not specifically identifiable as yet.

As in most fabrics, few of the Corinthian bowls show scenes of connected theme. Usually a variety of scenes, to our mind totally unrelated, are placed in no particularly comprehensible order in the figured area. A few Corinthian bowls may be singled out as exhibiting some consciousness of a single theme. One hunting bowl, **843**, is entirely consistent in its decoration. A chariot race among Nikai is

---

[22] Since this was written a fragment of a mould (medallion and corolla), possibly for a Figured Bowl, has been found, **942**. It is catalogued below in the Addendum, p. 186.

evidently the designer's single thought on **821** and **822**. The designer of **829** clearly intended to depict a circular dance of girls. We may perhaps give even more credit to the mould maker of **805** for an awareness of content and imagination. Between repeated scenes of Cassandra taking refuge at the palladion he has interspersed agitated women admirably suited to Cassandra's plight, heightening its terror like a Greek tragic chorus such as many with which he may have been familiar.

For the dating of the beginning of the use of figured scenes in Corinthian bowls a little evidence by context seems to indicate that it is to be placed within the last quarter of the 3rd century B.C. This is essentially in agreement with the evidence for Athenian Figured Bowls from which the Corinthian clearly derived. The Figured Bowls of Thompson's Group C of *ca.* 200 B.C. are evidently products of a well-established practice. The Corinthian evidence makes it abundantly clear that bowls with figured scenes were still in very active production at the time of Mummius' destruction of Corinth in 146 B.C. Again there is correspondence with the evidence for Athenian bowls, provided by Thompson's Group D. In Athens, apparently, some Figured Bowls were still being produced (Group E) many years later. Their period of production in Athens seems probably, then, to cover a full hundred years.

Context evidence for dating is available for many Corinthian bowls of this class, though a very large number of pieces lack it. The evidence is, however, very one-sided. Most of the pertinent contexts are of the time of Mummius' destruction. Only two examples come from contexts prior to that time, one, **805**, from a filling of very great range, the other, **802**, also of great range but probably extending no later than the last quarter of the 3rd century. In this situation we are not in a strong position to make many worthwhile observations on criteria for refined dating within the period of production of the class. The two earlier bowls are here assigned to the last quarter of the 3rd century. This assumption provides a few suggestions for consideration with regard to dating. Two concern the form of the bowl. The moulded part would seem to be essentially the same throughout the period. There may, however, be an appreciable difference in the rim, which was added on the wheel. A minimal wheelmade section is probably to be regarded as early in the period. Such a rim appears on **805**, and in only one other example, **840**, which is without context. There is no example of this kind of rim among the many bowls of Mummian contexts, all of which have a quite high wheelmade rim. This is not to suggest that *only* a minimal rim was employed early, for **802** has a high, wheelmade one also. One notes, however, that the latter is relatively vertical in profile, lipped slightly at the top, whereas the Mummian rims have a more pronounced flare outward. Probably another useful distinction between early and late among these bowls is to be seen in the character of the medallion motif. It might be expected that medallions to whose design careful attention had been paid would be early and those more carelessly designed late. So far as present evidence goes this seems to be the case. The medallion of **805** is, though in sorry condition, a pleasing design, a tiny rosette superimposed on a bed of radiating leaves. It is comparable to *Pnyx*, 75 and 87, pls. 46, 47. That of **802**, though less interesting, was done with care: radiating, pointed, veined leaves, four larger ones at the cardinal points, smaller ones, as if in the range below them, on a slightly lower plane, radiating in the intervals between their tips. The rendition of medallion motifs in Mummian bowls is at best routine, with no great variety of choice available, it would seem, and often it is downright poor.

It is of interest that the early **805** is one of the few to exhibit attention to the content of the scenes portrayed. One might be tempted to think that early bowls may have been so characterized and that lack of interest in content and multiplicity of themes is a later phenomenon. This, on present evidence, would seem certainly not to be the case generally in the class, for **802**, though a competent early bowl, shows a mixture of five representations, repeated already with a factory-like monotony. Interest in content in Corinthian would seem to be, in a very understandably human way, a phenomenon only of an occasional more imaginative craftsman. Bowls exhibiting an interest in content, in this light, could be expected to appear only fairly rarely and sporadically over the period of production. It seems just possible, however, that there may have been somewhat *more* interest in content toward the end of the period of production of Figured Bowls in Corinth, the reverse of what we might be inclined to suspect. The hunting bowl, the chariot race (?) bowl, and the dance bowl are all of Mummian times. We may in this connection note still another bowl, **798**, of Mummian times, in which there is what is to us a virtue, that only one scene is used all the way around, Apollo Kitharoidos. We are to be reminded that these are all of the time of the epoch-making, narrative Telephos frieze. It is the time also of the Homeric bowls.[23] Interest in narration on bowls is not at all strong in Attic, and is equally slight in Corinthian. We may, however, perhaps occasionally see a reflection of the new major interest in narration, appearing in the second quarter of the 2nd century, among the bowls of these two fabrics and of those related.

The Corinthian evidence indicates at present that certain representations were known early in the period of production of Figured Bowls, and most of these, if not all, are to be expected throughout the period. Athena, the trophy, and the trophy girl appear on both early and late bowls. Cassandra and the agitated woman are attested by context only on early bowls. But this lack on certainly later bowls known in Corinth at present is probably not chronologically indicative. One supposes that a type once known probably continued for a long time, though we may come to modify this view. We do not yet know at what point other representations were introduced into the figured repertoire. Quite conceivably there was a stepped introduction of new representations from time to time throughout the entire period, in Corinthian, Attic, and other fabrics. One may perhaps think of this as a possible clue to be explored in the future, with closer evidence, toward providing further criteria for the relative and absolute dating of Figured Bowls.

It will be noted that one group of Figured Bowls has been separated out from the rest. This group shows considerable promise for close chronology. It consists of very large bowls, perhaps quite ornate in appearance, with appliqué supports in high relief (pp. 171–175). These were very much in evidence at the time of the destruction. They may represent a fashion, not only in Corinthian, of quite a short period prior to that event. They, like the representations on the other Figured Bowls, warrant the careful attention of those who will be in a position to provide evidence for closer dating in the future.

At the end of the catalogue are listed, for purposes of report, fragments consisting only of sections of medallions, corollas, and rim zones. Lacking indications of the figured scenes they emphasized they are not classifiable according to main categories. The character of present evidence for dating being as it is, these aspects of the bowls cannot yet provide useful clues for dating. Given, however, the means to set up a relative chronology of the Figured Bowls based on other elements they can be expected in time to be informative.

Amymone
Courby, p. 345, fig. 70, 18
Schwabacher A 2
796. with Poseidon. 146 B.C.
797. 146 B.C. Pl. 67.
801. with Poseidon. Pl. 67.
811. with Poseidon. 146 B.C.
824. with Poseidon. 146 B.C.
825. with Poseidon. Pl. 70.

Aphrodite (seated, with Eros)
Courby, p. 387, fig. 80, 10 (2nd from left). Part of Judgment of Paris.
810. Pls. 37, 69.
Apollo Kitharoidos, seated
Courby, p. 345, fig. 70, 14
Schwabacher A 3
798. 146 B.C.
799.
814. with Leto. Pl. 68.
815. with Leto.

---

[23] Ulrich Hausmann, *Hellenistische Reliefbecher aus attischen und boötischen Werkstätten*, Stuttgart, 1959, p. 50. A Homeric bowl found in Corinth, C-47-449, Deposit 113, *Hesperia*, XVIII, 1949, pl. 15, 8–9; Hausmann, *op. cit.*, pl. 40, 1–2, is probably of the time of Mummius.

Artemis
1. Seated, with bow
Courby, p. 345, fig. 15 b
800. Pl. 67.
2. With stag
Schwabacher A 8
801. Pl. 67.
3. Artemis (?): standing, short chiton
803. Pl. 67.
Athena
Courby, p. 387, fig. 80, 10 (third from left). Part of Judgment of Paris. *Hesperia*, XVIII, 1949, pl. 14, 4 (C-47-796, Deposit 46; imported)
796. 146 B.C. (?)
802. 3rd century B.C., last quarter? Pl. 67.
803. Pl. 68.
804.
Cassandra
Cf. Courby, p. 308, fig. 59 (not entirely similar)
802. 3rd century B.C., last quarter? Pl. 67.
805. 3rd century B.C., last quarter. Pls. 37, 67.
Demeter (?)
Courby, p. 345, fig. 70, 17
801. Pl. 67.
Dionysos group
Courby, p. 342, fig. 69, 3 (illustration number missing)
Schwabacher A 1
807. 146 B.C. Pls. 37, 68.
810. Pls. 37, 69.
Eros
1. With Aphrodite. See Aphrodite.
2. Standing, frontal pose, wings spread, arms (tied?) behind back
873. 146 B.C. Pls. 38, 76.
875. Pl. 76.
3. Striding to left
808. Pl. 68.
4. On mount
808. Pl. 68.
809.
873. On lion (?). 146 B.C. Pls. 38, 76.
Ganymede and the Eagle. Large eagle with wings outspread, the right one behind head of frontal Ganymede. See also Zeus.
827.
873. 146 B.C. On medallion, scene incomplete. Pls. 38, 76.

Hermes, facing right, wearing cloak and petasos, one foot forward on rock, his left elbow on knee. For a different pose see Courby, p. 387, fig. 80, 10 (left). In Judgment of Paris scene.
810. Pls. 37, 69.
811. 146 B.C.
812. Pl. 68.
Leto
Courby, p. 345, fig. 70, 16
Schwabacher A 3
812. Pl. 68.
813.
814. Pl. 68.
815.
Nike
1. Frontal
Courby, p. 345, fig. 70, 20
Schwabacher D 3, 1
797. 146 B.C. Pl. 67.
816.
817. Pl. 69.
818.
819.
820. 146 B.C.
831. Pl. 70.
832. 146 B.C.
2. Winged Nike driving biga of panthers toward right
821. 146 B.C. Pl. 70.
822. 146 B.C.
Poseidon
Courby, p. 345, fig. 70, 19
Schwabacher A 2
796. 146 B.C. (?) with Amymone.
801. with Amymone. Pl. 67.
811. with Amymone. 146 B.C.
813.
823. Pl. 71.
824. with Amymone. 146 B.C.
825. with Amymone. Pl. 70.
826.
833.
Zeus, with Ganymede and Eagle
Courby, p. 345, fig. 70, 26 b
Schwabacher A 6
See also: Ganymede
827. Pl. 70.
828.

Agitated woman
  802. 3rd century B.C., last quarter? Pl. 67.
  805. 3rd century B.C., last quarter. Pls. 37, 67.
  806.
Girl dancing. Two similar, one head left, one head right, arms outstretched, long chiton.
  829. 146 B.C. Pls. 37, 70.
Trophy
  Courby, p. 349, fig. 72, 30
  Schwabacher A 4
  796. 146 B.C. (?) with trophy girl.
  802. 3rd century B.C., last quarter? with trophy girl. Pl. 67.
  815. with trophy girl.
  826.
  830. with trophy girl.
  831. with trophy girl? Pl. 70.
Trophy girl (girl in act of placing crown or wreath)
  Courby, p. 349, fig. 72, 30
  Schwabacher A 4
  796. with trophy. 146 B.C. (?)
  802. with trophy. 3rd century B.C., last quarter. Pl. 67.
  806.
  807. 146 B.C. Pls. 37, 68.
  811. 146 B.C.
  815. with trophy.
  820. 146 B.C.
  826. with trophy.
  831. with trophy. Pl. 70.
  832. 146 B.C.
  833.
  834.
  835.
Unidentified human figures
  796. female. 146 B.C. (?)
  797. cloaked. 146 B.C. Pl. 67.
  810. woman in long chiton, in profile facing right, right arm extended toward second figure at right: perhaps a stag. Artemis? Pls. 37, 69.
  812. parts of three figures. Pl. 68.
  833. small nude figure (?) in profile toward right, holding out something large in right hand. At left, a small column?
  836. male. Pl. 71.

  837. cloaked figure. 146 B.C.
  838. satyr (?) running toward right. Pl. 70.
  839. 146 B.C.
Armed combat: cavalry
  841. Pl. 71.
Hunting scenes (hunters, dogs, boar, hare, lion, etc.)
  Schwabacher C I-II
  Animals: Courby, p. 347, fig. 71, 29
  Male hunter: cf. Courby, p. 347, fig. 71, 29 a (not closely similar).
  842. Pls. 72, 73.
  843. Pl. 73.
  844. Pl. 74.
Land animals (other than those in hunting scenes): goats
  Cf. Courby, p. 342, fig. 69, 9 a–b
  Schwabacher B 1
  Thompson C 23
  841. Pl. 71.
  845. antithetic, with krater, 146 B.C. Pl. 74.
  846. antithetic, with krater, 146 B.C. Pl. 75.
  847. antithetic, over frond.
  848. antithetic, over frond. Pl. 75.
  895. antithetic, over frond (?).
Birds
  800. Pl. 67.
  807. Pls. 37, 68.
  817. Pl. 69.
Marine creatures, including mythological
  Cf. Courby, p. 345, fig. 70, 23–25
  Cf. *Pnyx*, pl. 36
  849. Triton? Pl. 75.
Fruit: cluster of grapes
  842. Pls. 72, 73.
Objects
  1. Thymiaterion
    825. Pl. 70.
  2. Krater
    Cf. Courby, p. 342, fig. 69, 10 a–c
    Cf. Schwabacher, p. 201
    823.
    838. with satyr (?). Pl. 70.
    842.
    845. with goats. 146 B.C. Pl. 74.
    846. with goats. 146 B.C. Pl. 75.

3. Masks
  a. comic
    873. 146 B.C. Pl. 76.
    874. Pl. 76.

  b. satyr (?)
    840. 3rd century B.C., last quarter. Pl. 74.
4. Boukranion, dotted fillet
  842. Pls. 72, 73.

FIGURED BOWL

796 (C-65-98), Deposit 31. H. 0.086; D. est. 0.125. Much of wall and rim missing. Medallion: quadruple (?) linear rosette. Medallion zone: two concentric circles. Corolla: a single row of large acanthus leaves; between tips, a hare. Wall, l. to r.: unidentified female figure; Amymone; Poseidon; Athena; female figure; trophy girl; trophy. Rim zone: ivy-leaf guilloche between two lines. 146 B.C. (?)

797 (C-47-237), Deposits 102 and 103. Profile preserved from rim zone to medallion. Medallion: eight-petal rosette. Medallion zone: two concentric circles. Corolla: single row of large fronds. Wall, l. to r.: frontal Nike; unidentified cloaked figure striding toward left; Amymone. 146 B.C. Pl. 67.

798 (C-63-487), Deposit 47. Medallion, much of wall and rim missing. H. 0.078; D. est. 0.14. Medallion zone: two concentric circles. Corolla: a single line of large acanthus leaves. Wall, repeated at close intervals: seated Apollo Kitharoidos. Rim zone: between two lines, repeated double spiral. 146 B.C.

799 (C-37-2231). Fragment of wall. Max. dim. 0.068. Corolla: a line of large leaves. Between tips, seated Apollo Kitharoidos.

800 (C-28-51). Profile from lip to mid-wall. Max. dim. 0.082. Wall, l. to r.: seated Artemis with bow; bird carrying fillet. Two rim zones: below, guilloche; above, flying birds, dolphins (?), rosettes. Pl. 67.

801 (C-46-10). Section of rim and upper wall. Max. dim. 0.081. Wall, l. to r.: Amymone; Poseidon; Demeter; Artemis and stag. Two rim zones, between dotted lines: below, dogs. Pl. 67.

802 (C-64-335), Deposit 32. Part of wall and rim missing. H. 0.077; D. lip 0.13. Medallion: eight veined leaves, radiating from center. Medallion zone: two concentric circles. Corolla: a single line of large fronds, a rosette between the tips. Wall, group of four repeated probably four times: Athena; agitated woman; trophy girl; Cassandra. Rim zone: ivy-leaf guilloche between two lines. 3rd century B.C., last quarter? Pls. 36, 67.

803 (C-30-133). Wall fragment. Max. dim. 0.063. L. to r.: Athena; Artemis (?), standing, short chiton. Pl. 68.

804 (CP-953). Wall fragment. Max. dim. 0.042. Athena.

805 (C-47-450), Deposit 113. H. 0.07; D. 0.123. Medallion: small eight-petal rosette superimposed on radiating veined leaves. Medallion zone: two concentric circles. Corolla: a line of small fronds, a flying bird between the tips. Wall: Cassandra (repeated six times) alternating with one or more agitated women (repeated eight times). Two rim zones, between lines: below, rosettes; above, pointed leaves, points up. 3rd century B.C., last quarter. Pls. 36, 37, 67.

806 (C-34-2504). Wall and rim fragment. Max. dim. 0.055. Wall, l. to r.: rosette; agitated woman; rosette; trophy girl. No rim zone.

807 (C-38-683), Deposit 115. H. 0.084; D. lip 0.148. Medallion: multipetalled rosette (of leaves?) encircled by a single line. Corolla: a single row of large fronds. Wall: Dionysos group and three trophy girls repeated four times. Rim zone: guilloche between two lines. 146 B.C. Pls. 37, 68.

808 (C-30-37). Fragment of rim and upper wall. Max. dim. 0.065. Wall, l. to r.: Eros striding to left; Eros on mount. Two rim zones formed by three lines: below, leaves, points down; above, rosettes. Pl. 68.

809 (C-28-37). Fragment of rim and upper wall. Max. dim. 0.078. Wall: Eros on mount, riding to left. Rim zone: row of leaves, tips down.

810 (C-33-1008). Much of wall and rim missing. H. 0.078; D. lip 0.13. Medallion: eight-petal rosette. Medallion zone: two concentric circles. Corolla: two imbricate rows of pointed, outline leaves with central spine. Wall: Hermes; Dionysos group; Aphrodite and Eros; and unidentified figure, the four repeated probably three times in differing orders. Rim zone: between lines, guilloche. Pls. 37, 69.

811 (C-47-795), Deposit 46. Section from rim to middle of wall. P.H. 0.065; D. est. 0.125.

Wall, l. to r.: trophy girl; Amymone; Poseidon; Hermes. Rim zone, ivy-leaf guilloche. 146 B.C.

812 (C-30-39). Fragment of wall, or large bowl, perhaps the variety with appliqué supports (below, pp. 171–175). Two zones, separated by a relief line. Above, parts of three figures. Below, l. to r.: Leto; Hermes. Pl. 68.

813 (C-46-64), Deposit 107. H. 0.07; D. 0.113. Medallion: eight-petal rosette. Medallion zone: two concentric circles. Corolla: line of independent, ovoid, veined leaves. Wall: Leto, Poseidon, alternating. Bowl badly overfired but usable.

814 (C-30-38). Wall fragment. Max. dim. 0.065. Possibly two figured zones. Below, l. to r.: Apollo; Leto. Pl. 68.

815 (C-30-40). Wall fragment. Max. dim. 0.062. Corolla: large fronds. Wall, l. to r.: Apollo; Leto; trophy girl; trophy.

816 (C-47-893). Profile preserved corolla to rim. P.H. 0.093; D. 0.14. Corolla: large fronds. Wall: below, zone of bead-and-reel between two lines; above, in a zone of two lines, repeated frontal Nike. Rim zone: guilloche.

817 (CP-1929). Profile preserved medallion to rim zone. Max. dim. 0.10. Medallion: four radiating fronds. Medallion zone: two concentric circles. Corolla: a row of large fronds. Wall: frontal Nike alternating with a flying bird. Rim zone: between two lines, a guilloche. Pl. 69.

818 (C-37-2737). Section, medallion zone and corolla. Max. dim. 0.07. Medallion zone: two concentric circles. Corolla: a row of large fronds with a pointed petal between the bases. Between the tips, a frontal Nike.

819 (CP-1572). Section, medallion and wall. Max. dim. 0.07. Medallion: eight-petal rosette. Medallion zone: two concentric circles. Corolla: a row of large fronds. Between the tips, a frontal Nike.

820 (C-47-798), Deposit 46. Section of wall and rim. Max. dim. 0.085. Wall: alternate trophy girl and frontal Nike. 146 B.C.

821 (C-47-787), Deposit 46. H. 0.08; D. 0.138. Medallion: eight-petal rosette. Medallion zone: two concentric circles. Corolla: four rows of imbricate, outline, pointed petal tips with central spine. Wall: repeated Nike (?) in biga driving to right. Rim zone: guilloche between lines; line of pointed leaves, points down, dependent from lower zone. 146 B.C. Pl. 70.

822 (C-47-236), Deposits 102 and 103. Fragments of wall and rim. D. lip est. 0.18. Wall: parts of Nike (?) driving biga to right; above, a

line of birds flying to left. Rim zone: vertical spirals between lines. 146 B.C.

823 (C-28-59). Section, medallion to rim zone. Max. dim. 0.093. Medallion: swirling (?) leaf (?) design. Medallion zone: two concentric circles. Corolla: row of large fronds. Wall, l. to r.: dog; hare; krater; hare; Poseidon; hare; krater; hare. Rim zone: line of lozenges. Pl. 71.

824 (C-48-86), Deposit 110. Section of rim and wall. D. 0.155. Wall, l. to r.: Poseidon; Amymone; Poseidon. Rim zone: guilloche. 146 B.C.

825 (C-46-57), Deposit 107. Section rim to corolla. Max. dim. 0.075. Corolla: frond and krater (presumably between tips). Wall, l. to r.: Amymone; Poseidon; thymiaterion; animal (?); above, relief line. No rim zone. Pl. 70.

826 (C-31-478). Profile preserved medallion to just below rim. Max. dim. 0.075. Medallion: four radiating leaves. Medallion zone: two concentric circles. Corolla: three rows of imbricate, pointed petal tips. Wall: Poseidon; trophy girl; trophy. Rim zone: leaves, points down.

827 (C-31-480). Wall fragment. Max. dim. 0.07. Corolla: frond (?), rosette beside tip. Wall, l.: Zeus, Ganymede and Eagle; r.: Nike (?); above, rosette. Pl. 70.

828 (C-28-74a). Wall fragment. Max. dim. 0.04. Wall, l.: branch (?); r.: Zeus (?) and Ganymede (?).

829 (C-38-681), Deposit 115. H. 0.075; D. est. 0.14. Medallion: small rosette superimposed on circle of linear petal design. Medallion zone: two concentric circles. Corolla: two rows of imbricate, pointed, outline petal tips. Wall: ten girls dancing circular dance around bowl. Rim zone: row of vertical spirals between lines; dependent from lower line, a row of egg pattern. 146 B.C. Pls. 37, 70.

830 (C-47-351), Deposit 111. Wall fragment. Max. dim. 0.027. Wall, r.: upper part of trophy. 146 B.C.

831 (C-38-698). Wall fragment. Max. dim. 0.062. Wall, l. to r.: trophy girl (?); trophy; frontal Nike. Pl. 70.

832 (C-47-241), Deposits 102 and 103. Fragments of all elements. Medallion: four radiating fronds. Medallion zone: two concentric circles. Corolla: a line of leafy fronds. Wall: trophy girl; frontal Nike. 146 B.C.

833 (C-28-52 and C-28-57). Profile lacking medallion. P.H. 0.09; D. est. 0.13. Corolla: a row of large fronds. Wall, l. to r.: dog; unidentified human figure; trophy girl; Poseidon; trophy girl; dog; hare; Poseidon; trophy girl. Rim zone: between lines, a row of lozenges.

834 (C-28-46). Wall and rim zone fragment. Max. dim. 0.055. Wall: trophy girl. Rim zone: between lines, large egg-and-dart.

835 (CP-1931). Section rim to corolla. Max. dim. 0.11. Corolla: row of large fronds. Wall: alternate trophy girl and dog. Rim zone: between lines, a dim pattern.

836 (C-46-56), Deposit 107. Much of wall and rim missing. H. 0.055; D. est. 0.08. Medallion zone: two concentric circles. Corolla: large fronds. Wall: running, nude male figures. Pl.17.

837 (C-48-49), Deposit 112. Profile preserved. H. 0.068; D. est. 0.13. Medallion: radiating fronds. Corolla: large fronds. Wall: between tips of corollas, tiny blurred human figures. Rim zone: between two lines, an ivy-leaf guilloche. 146 B.C.

838 (C-32-281). Wall fragment. Max. dim. 0.045. Wall, r.: satyr (?) approaching a krater (?); part of signature at left, retrograde (?),]OΔI[. Pl. 70.

839 (C-47-797 a–b), Deposit 46. Section of rim and upper wall of large bowl. Max. dim. 0.08. Wall: blurred figures. Rim zone: guilloche between two lines; dependent from the lower line, a row of egg-and-dart. 146 B.C.

840 (C-38-705). Section of wall and rim. Max. dim. 0.06. Wall: satyr (?) mask. Rim: two relief lines; dependent from lower, egg pattern widely spaced; rising from upper line, pointed leaves. No wheelmade section of rim. 3rd century B.C., last quarter. Pl. 74.

841 (C-30-143 a–c). Section of upper wall and rim of very large bowl. Max. dim. 0.16. Wall: below, top of a frond; rampant goat; above, two armed cavalrymen advancing to right. Four rim zones, bottom to top: ornamental fillet; vertical spirals; ornamental fillet; line of vertical leaves and horizontal spirals. Rim once decorated with West Slope design of which only curved incisions remain. Pl. 71.

842 (CP-520). Medallion and parts of wall missing. P.H. 0.105; D. 0.16. Corolla: large, separate, veined leaves, a rosette between the tips. Wall: naked hunter with spear; boars; lions; dogs; boukrania; cluster of grapes. Rim zone: between lines, vertical spirals. Stamps deeply impressed. Pls. 72, 73.

843 (C-48-14), Deposit 112. H. 0.083; D. 0.15. Medallion: eight-petal rosette. Medallion zone: two concentric circles. Corolla: a line of large fronds. Wall: dogs and boar. Rim zone: between two lines, a guilloche. 146 B.C. Pls. 36, 73.

844 (C-30-36). Fragment of upper wall and rim zone. Max. dim. 0.09. Wall, l.: hunter with shield and spear; r.: dogs. Pl. 74.

845 (C-35-117 + C-35-719), Deposit 104. Much of wall and rim missing. H. 0.085; D. est. 0.16. Medallion: eight radiating leaves. Medallion zone: two concentric circles. Corolla: a line of tall fronds. Wall: repeated groups of antithetic goats and krater. Rim zone: between two lines, an ivy-leaf guilloche. 146 B.C. Pl. 74.

846 (C-47-340), Deposit 111. Fragments of corolla, wall and rim. Max. dim. 0.12. Corolla: large frond. Wall: groups of antithetic goats and krater; above, a relief line on each side of which is a line of egg-and-dart, the upper upside down. 146 B.C. Pl. 75.

847 (C-34-2059). Section of wall and rim. Max. dim. 0.07. Wall: antithetic goats over the tip of a large frond. Rim zone: a row of vertical spirals over two relief lines.

848 (C-48-92), Deposit 110. Lower wall fragment· Max. dim 0.06. Corolla: large fronds, on either side of which is an antithetic goat. 146 B.C. Pl. 75.

849 (C-32-280). Wall fragment. Max. dim. 0.045. Corolla: veined leaves. Wall: above a rosette, the forked tail of a Triton (?). Pl. 75.

Unclassified:

Fragments with corollas (?) of imbricate, pointed, veined leaves:

850 (C-33-1461), Deposit 98. Part of base, stem and lower wall of a kantharos (?). P.H. 0.055; max. D. 0.085. Spreading foot. Hollow stem. Medallion: rosette (?). Lower wall: corolla (?) of imbricate, small, pointed, veined leaves. 146 B.C. Pls. 38, 75.

851 (C-33-204), Deposit 117. Medallion and lower wall. Max. dim. 0.055. Medallion: four radiating leaves. Medallion zone: two concentric circles. Corolla (?) of small, imbricate, pointed, veined leaves. 146 B.C.

852 (C-37-2738).

853 (C-34-2060).

854 (C-34-2507).

855 (C-28-74).

Fragments with corollas of fronds:

856 (C-48-50), Deposit 112. 146 B.C.

857 (C-28-55).

858 (C-28-58).

859 (C-28-71).

860 (C-29-146).

861 (C-33-1377).

862 (C-35-978).

863 (C-37-2244).

864 (C-37-2716).

865 (C-37-2724).

866 (C-37-2731).

Fragments with corollas of various leaves:
867 (C-33-1378).
868 (C-36-2113).
869 (C-37-2705).

870 (C-37-2734).
Rim fragments:
871 (C-28-60).
872 (C-37-2250).

LARGE BOWL WITH APPLIQUÉ RELIEF SUPPORTS 873–897, Pls. 38, 76.

INTRODUCTION

Although the classification of Figured Bowls here is primarily according to the identity of the figures or figured scenes represented, it seems desirable to single out a fairly large group of pieces, all of which probably represent a particular, large bowl form, regardless of what figured decoration they may have had. One of the perhaps several special peculiarities of this bowl form is that it had appliqué supports, three evidently on each bowl, in the form of heads in high relief. Comic masks, tragic masks and a head of Athena are attested. Probably the three heads on each bowl were the same type. The bowl form attested in the most extensively preserved pieces (e.g. **873**, Pl. 76) has a fairly flat medallion area and a fairly broad lower wall. There may have been a special form of rim, and they may conceivably have had handles of special form (cf. p. 172, note 25). These bowls are, of course, unsuitable as drinking cups. No doubt they were used as small kraters.

The Corinthian examples are supplemented by numerous foreign fragments of this kind of bowl. All the contexts known for such pieces are attributable to the destruction of Corinth by Mummius in 146 B.C. It would appear that this kind of bowl was especially popular at that time. For how long these special bowls had been in production by 146 B.C. in Corinthian and other fabrics there is no context evidence. Wheelmade bowls with relief supports had been known for many years in the Hellenistic period (cf. the hemispherical bowls with appliqué supports above, **525, 526**). It seems possible, however, that this particular class may have been the special effort and interest of a limited period. A period of production of about a quarter century is here suggested as adequate. The general conception of these bowls is rather too rich, if not overripe, to have lasted long, it would seem. Very probably in the practice of adding appliqué reliefs to the moulded bowls there is to be seen a chronological link of some kind, probably of shorter duration, with that of adding relief heads as medallions to the wheelmade conical bowls above (p. 91).

Such wall decoration as exists at present is figured. There is nothing to exclude the possibility that many of these fragments may have belonged to bowls decorated in other ways. At the time attested by context for these bowls figured decoration seems the most likely. Figures seem more suitable with the head supports than foliage or linear decoration.

LARGE BOWL WITH APPLIQUÉ COMIC MASK SUPPORTS **873–883**, Pls. 38, 76.
Ca. 175 to 146 B.C.
Deposits:[24] 46, 109, 110.

Only one Corinthian bowl of this class, **873**, is extensively preserved. Four other pieces provide a section of the lower wall with mask attached. One other example provides other sections of wall. The rest are masks only. The masks are in high relief. Evidently only three, probably all the same, were used on a bowl, the resting surface in all (shown by wear) being on the forward part of the tops of the heads. The type of mask is the same in all, with broadly open mouth, a pug nose and strongly projecting

---

[24] The contexts of imported examples are also relevant: Deposits 46, 110.

brows. A rounded fillet encircles the head at forehead level. The bowl form, as far as attested, had a flat medallion area and a broad lower wall. On **873** part of a rim zone is preserved. Quite possibly it had three rim zones. A fragment, **874**, very likely from the same mould, has the same rim zone plus parts of two more above. The treatment of the level above the rim zones is not certainly attested in Corinthian.[25] The attested dimensions are preserved height, without masks, 0.09 m. and greatest preserved diameter 0.24 m.

The only medallion motif known is Ganymede and the Eagle. Its zone is composed of two relief lines with a low convex band between. The only corollas known consist of, evidently, a single line of fairly large leaves, fronds of two varieties. On **876** between each of the fronds is the top of a pointed, outline leaf with vertical linear divisions. For the wall on **873** the principal decoration is a row of fairly large, widely spaced, frontal Erotes, their hands (presumably tied) behind their backs. Similar Erotes were used on **875**. Above their heads, a procession of Erotes riding on lions (?), on a smaller scale, moves around the bowl toward the right. There is some indication on **875** that there could be two zones of decoration on a bowl. The rim zone has a repeated line of small comic masks.

Among the Corinthian pieces at least three bowl moulds are represented. Conceivably **877** and **878** are from the same mould. Among the masks, attached or separate, perhaps seven or eight moulds are attested. Probably **882** and **881** are from one mould; **873** and **876** are from another. One, **883**, may be from a secondary mould. The quality of mould design and manufacture is fair.

The Corinthian pieces give the impression of being fairly closely contemporary. Probably all were produced close to the time of Mummius' destruction of the city in 146 B.C. Two come from contexts attributed to this event. The period of production of this class prior to that time may, however, have been of some duration since the pieces do not give the impression of belonging to an earlier phase.

Corinthian evidence attests that bowls of this kind were also being produced in other foreign fabrics at this time.[26]

146 B.C.

873 (C-36-499 a–e + C-48-62), Deposits 109 and 110. One mask restored, bowl profile preserved to top of one rim zone. P.H. with masks 0.115; max. preserved D. 0.245. Medallion: Ganymede and the Eagle. Medallion zone: between two relief lines, a low, convex moulding. Corolla: a line of fronds. Wall, center: repeated frontal Eros, wings spread, hands (tied, presumably) behind back. Rim zone: repeated comic masks above a relief line. Pls. 38, 76.

874 (C-30-130). Fragment, rim zones. Max. dim. 0.043. Three zones: below, line of comic masks; middle, egg pattern; above, lower part only, bead-and-reel (?). Relief line be-

tween each zone. Possibly from same mould as **873**. Pl. 76.

875 (C-39-351 a, b). Wall fragments. Max. dim. 0.068. Wall: repeated frontal Eros, wings spread, hands (tied, presumably) behind back; above, part of relief line, possibly of a rim zone, and, perhaps more likely, indication that there was a second zone of decoration above. Cf. **812**, Pl. 68.

876 (C-39-352). Section of lower wall and one mask. Max. dim. 0.105. Corolla: a line of large fronds between each of which is the tip of an outline leaf with four vertical inner linear divisions.

877 (C-31-104). Section of rim zone, lower wall, and one mask. Max. dim. 0.085. Medallion

---

[25] Two pieces of gray-ware bowls of comparable size provide suggestions for the treatment above. On C-32-231 there are three rim zones. Above the topmost the rim begins to flare outward sharply. It also may have had some sort of vertical handle, at the base of which, superimposed on the rim zones, is an appliqué comic mask in relief. On a second gray-ware bowl fragment, C-37-1604, a bit more of a similarly outturned rim is preserved. **897**, Deposit 109, is conceivably a handle for such a bowl as this. It is a female torso in the round. From the back projects part of a strap handle. The lower part was evidently attached to something below, perhaps the rim. A less baroque possibility for the appearance of the rim may, however, be suggested by the very large bowl with linear decoration, **901**, below.

[26] In one foreign fabric: C-47-796, Deposit 46, *Hesperia*, XVIII, 1949, pl. 14, 4. In a second, C-48-117, Deposit 110. There are also examples without context of perhaps two other different fabrics: MF 1040, MF 1041, C-29-115, C-34-356, C-34-2179, C-37-2322, C-59-21.

sunk within a medallion zone consisting of a convex moulding within a wheel groove. Corolla: dim impressions of large fronds (?).

878 (C-33-1470). Section of lower wall and one mask. Max. dim. 0.075. Corolla: fronds. Possibly from same mould as **877**.

879 (C-47-854), Deposit 46. Mask only. Max. dim. 0.05. Pl. 76.

880 (C-28-125). Mask fragment.

881 (C-63-19).

and

882 (C-28-113). Masks, probably both from the same mould. Max. dim. 0.05.

883 (C-33-185). Mask with a bit of wall. Max. dim. 0.05. Perhaps from a secondary mould.

LARGE BOWL WITH APPLIQUÉ TRAGIC MASK SUPPORTS **884–892**, Pl. 77.

Ca. 175 to 146 B.C.

Deposits: 107.[27]

The evidence for the existence of bowls of this kind in Corinthian consists of a number of mask supports to some of which bits of the lower wall are still attached. The bowl form was presumably similar to that of those with comic mask supports above (p. 172). A foreign example, of which a large section of the wall is preserved, is noted below (footnote 28). A set of three masks, probably all the same, presumably served as the supports for a single bowl. The type of mask is generally similar in all the examples. The frontal head is probably female, the lips parted. A rounded fillet encircles the head just above the forehead level. A medallion zone is attested on one piece: two concentric relief circles with a broad wheel-run groove between them. A corolla of fronds similar to those on the bowls with comic masks is attested on **884**. An oak (?) leaf in corolla position appears on **885**, and in the same position, a small petal with a central spine (cf. **786**) on **886**, and part of a much larger one on **887**. Four bowl moulds are attested among the pieces and perhaps six mask moulds. Conceivably **887**, **888**, and **889** are from the same mask mould. The quality of mould design and manufacture is fair. The pieces appear to be, in these aspects, contemporary.

Bowls of this kind are attested to have been in production at the time of Mummius' destruction of Corinth in 146 B.C. Presumably, since they do not suggest that they are of an early phase, the period of production may have been of some duration prior to that time.

Corinthian evidence shows that bowls of this kind were also being produced in other foreign fabrics[28] contemporaneously with the Corinthian.

146 B.C.

884 (C-35-88). Mask, part of medallion, and of lower wall. Max. dim. 0.085. Medallion zone: two relief lines with broad wheel groove between. Corolla: fronds.

885 (C-29-116). Mask and part of lower wall. Max. dim. 0.06. Wall: oak (?) leaf.

886 (C-37-2681). Mask and part of lower wall. Max. dim. 0.06. Wall: outline petal tip with central spine; cf. **786**.

887 (C-35-116 A). Mask and part of lower wall. Max. dim. 0.055. Wall: lower part of large outline leaf.

888 (CP-908). Mask and bit of wall. Max. dim. 0.055.

889 (C-31-102). Mask and bit of wall. Max. dim. 0.047. Pl. 77.

890 (C-31-113). Mask and bit of wall. Max. dim. 0.053.

891 (C-36-1991). Part of mask and bit of wall. Max. dim. 0.045.

892 (C-47-43), Deposit 107. Part of mask. Max. dim. 0.04.

[27] The context of a foreign bowl of this kind is also pertinent: Deposit 104.

[28] In one foreign fabric: C-35-116, Deposit 104, with section of wall showing a boar hunt. Probably of the same fabric, without context, CP-889. In a second fabric, both without context: C-35-45; C-61-64. In a third, all without context, CP-991, CP-1923, C-37-2230, C-38-637, C-38-660, C-49-33, C-61-51.

LARGE BOWL WITH APPLIQUÉ SUPPORTS: HEAD OF ATHENA **893, 894**, Pl. 77.

Ca. 175 to 146 B.C.

Two heads with bits of the lower wall of their bowls attest the existence of moulded bowls with high-relief heads of Athena. The bowl form was presumably similar to that more fully attested with comic and tragic masks above. Both heads are of the same type. Athena's head is turned toward her proper left. There are some possible indications of a helmet. A bit of a medallion zone is preserved on one piece, a single large relief line, and blurred traces of moulded decoration are seen adjacent to the heads on both. The heads are probably from two different moulds.

The two pieces are without context. Presumably they were produced contemporaneously with the other relief-support bowls above.

> *ca.* 175–146 B.C.
> **893** (C-31-107). Head of Athena, part of medallion zone and bit of lower wall. Max. dim. 0.07. Pl. 77.
> **894** (C-34-166). Head of Athena and bit of lower wall. Max. dim. 0.06.

LARGE BOWL WITH APPLIQUÉ SUPPORTS: UNCLASSIFIED[29] **895, 896**.

Ca. 175 to 146 B.C.

Two fragments of the lower wall of large moulded bowls from which the relief supports have been separated may have belonged to one of the three groups of such bowls above. One, **895**, had a corolla of large fronds between which appear a goat's hind legs. On the wall of the other there was probably a design of small leaves. They are considered to be contemporary with the other bowls with appliqué supports above. The context of **786** (footnote 29) supports this dating.

> 175–146 B.C.
> **895** (C-30-145). Section of lower wall, traces of relief-support attachment. Corolla: fronds between two of which a goat's hind legs.
> **896** (C-35-975). Section of lower wall, traces of relief-support attachment. Small leaves.

LARGE BOWL WITH APPLIQUÉ SUPPORTS: HANDLE (?) **897**, Pls. 35, 77.

Ca. 175–146 B.C.

Deposit: 109.

The possibility that bowls of this kind may have had handles of a special form has been discussed above (p. 172, note 25). **897**, a fragment of a female torso with a bit of a strap handle projecting from her upper back, is conceivably a candidate for the handle form, if one was employed in these Corinthian bowls. It was found in a well from which part of the best preserved bowl of this kind also came, **873**. The back of the figure is only sketchily modelled in contrast to the other surfaces, indicating that this part of the figure was expected not to be visible. Both legs and both arms were evidently outstretched. In the break below is a segment of a circular depression which evidently represents the point of attach-

---

[29] For an additional unclassified fragment, also lacking the support, see **786**, Deposit 112. **812**, a figured wall fragment, may also have belonged to a bowl of this kind.

ment of the figure. This and the position of her arms and legs suggests that she may have been, for instance, on horseback, or shown as the rider of some other of the various possible mounts in Greek mythology.

ca. 146 B.C.
897 (C-47-329), Deposit 109. P.H. 0.05. Pls. 35, 77.

LINEAR BOWLS

898–938

INTRODUCTION

The term bowls with linear decoration or Linear Bowls has not been used previously with reference to moulded relief ware. The terms are intended to include all moulded bowls the major decoration of whose walls is based on linear patterns designed freehand in the mould.[30] In the sections below only such varieties of Linear Bowls as are known at present in Corinth are discussed, but the term is intended to be more comprehensive and to be applied also to other varieties in whose major decoration line is the predominant element. Other varieties are known elsewhere, particularly in Athens, and still others may well be identified in the future. The name is suggested as an apt one in recognition of the apparent fact that line decoration was a, if not the, predominant and most popular form of ornament for the moulded bowls in the period from about 160 B.C. to the end of the 2nd century and perhaps into the 1st century B.C. This seems to be true of Athens. It seems likely to be true of centers of moulded-bowl manufacture which followed the Athenian fashions. Conceivably it may be true of centers with differing traditions, though little is known of these at present.

The terms include the well-known long-petal bowls, a name introduced by Thompson (p. 456) as the English equivalent of Courby's *bols à godrons* (Courby, pp. 329–334). It includes other varieties also made known by Courby and Thompson: the net-pattern bowls and those decorated with concentric semicircles. A new, but perhaps minor variety, the linear-leaf bowl, is here introduced for the first time as an entity.

Several varieties known in Athens but not in Corinth would be suitable to include among the Linear Bowls. One is an additional phase of the long-petal bowls: Schwabacher, pl. VIII A, 7, 8[31] in which the independent petals have fine inner divisions, evidently an early phase of the long-petal style. Others are perhaps of advanced date in the Linear period. Those with interlocking linear flowers (Schwabacher, pl. IX A, 9–10) seem to form a distinctive style. And no doubt some stylistic identity or identities can be distinguished among a group of pieces associated with Ariston from the Kerameikos: Schwabacher, pl. IX A, 1–8, and B, 18; from Delos: Courby, pl. IX, e. In these, closely spaced, tiny leaves or jewelling form the background for large leaf designs and evidently also for concentric semicircles. Their relationship to groups defined at present is not fully evident. Still another Kerameikos fragment (Schwabacher, pl. IX A, 12) suggests the existence of a totally distinct class of linear decoration, possibly imbricate, linear leaves of graduated sizes.

How significant the absence of these classes or groups in Corinth may be chronologically has yet to be explored. It may, of course, mean for most that they were introduced into moulded-bowl design after Corinth's destruction in 146 B.C.

---

[30] Or, for that matter, produced by stamps. A stamp for a Linear Bowl is known, Brussels, Mus. du Cinq. no. M 723. Linear Bowls known at present, however, seem all to have been produced by freehand work.

[31] A more complete example has been found in the Athenian Agora: P 23095. Its context is prior to the construction or completion of the Middle Stoa.

It is believed that generally bowls with linear decoration at Corinth, Corinthian or foreign, are to be dated prior to the destruction of the city. As might be expected, a few foreign examples are attributable to the time of the Sikyonian occupation, between 146 and 44 B.C., probably well before its end. These, an appropriately small percentage, are noted below (footnote 32). There is no reason or evidence, known at present, for supposing that Linear Bowls were produced at Corinth or in the areas from which Corinth imported in the years after the founding of the Roman colony at Corinth in 44 B.C.

LONG-PETAL BOWL[32] 898–907, Pls. 38, 77.

150 to 146 B.C.

Deposits:[33] 47, 112.

The typical decoration by which this kind of bowl may be recognized consists of long, tapering, narrow, linear, relief petals completely covering the wall, based on the medallion zone and extending up to the rim zone. The petals may be contiguous, each vertical line serving both as the right outline of one petal and the left outline of the next, or they may be independent petals. Both varieties may be placed vertically on the wall, or their outlines may be undulating (swirling long petals). Between the independent petals a line of jewelling often appears. Eight varieties of this kind of decoration are known. They will be described specifically below. Only four variations are known in Corinth at present, but the others are attested in foreign examples found there (footnote 32). The Corinthian examples are few (10), and all are fragments. Accordingly little is known of the decoration of other areas of these bowls. The medallions known are small, and the only motif known to occur in them is a multipetalled linear rosette. The only medallion zone is a pair of concentric circles. Both single and double rim zones are attested, however. In the former the zone may be delimited by a line above and a line below, or the upper line may be omitted. In the latter there are two lines below, two in the middle, and one above. The motifs employed in the zones are: a line of jewelling; a line of multipetalled linear rosettes, separated; an ivy-leaf guilloche; and egg-and-dart. The sizes of the bowls on which this decoration appears seem to vary from fairly small to average to large to extremely large (D. 0.34 m.: **901**, the largest moulded bowl known). They were all probably of one form which had, apparently, a flat medallion area, and a fairly broad lower wall. The wheelmade section of the rim was relatively high and slightly outturned above. Each of the ten Corinthian pieces was made in a different mould. The quality of mould design and manufacture among these pieces is uniformly quite good.

The period of production of long-petal bowls in Corinth prior to the Mummian destruction in 146 B.C. was evidently very short. The number of Corinthian examples is extremely few by comparison with bowls with other kinds of decoration. The restricted number of variations of the design in Corinthian

---

[32] A total of 28 examples of imported bowls with this kind of decoration has also been found in Corinth. (This number does not include five imported examples which in character look as if they may be attributable to the period of the Sikyonian occupation of Corinth and datable perhaps in the earlier part of the 1st century B.C.: C-33-1375; C-36-2035; C-37-2095; C-37-2249 b and c; C-37-2732.) Among the imported included in the total there are many which are either Attic (2), or whose form would suggest that they were produced in centers in which the Attic form of bowl was adopted (20). Attic: swirling long petals, C-39-438; swirling long petals and jewelling, C-37-1652. Gray ware: independent long petals, relief centers, C-37-2229; contiguous long petals, raised centers, C-63-699; contiguous long petals, flat centers, C-46-63, Deposit 107. Other fabrics: contiguous long petals, raised centers: C-30-129; C-38-691; contiguous long petals, flat centers: CP-1932; C-33-1003; C-33-1383; C-33-1464 (signed]XOY); C-34-213; C-36-2041; C-37-2232; C-37-2249 a; C-37-2714; C-37-2718; C-37-2742; C-38-704; C-47-347, Deposit 111; long petals, raised centers and jewelling: C-37-2735; long petals, flat centers, and jewelling: C-38-692. The remainder are of other fabrics not employing the Attic bowl form. "Delian": long petals, raised centers and jewelling, C-37-1572. Other fabrics: long petals, flat centers and jewelling: C-35-552 (stamnos [?] fragment); contiguous long petals, flat centers: CP-521; C-37-2702; C-47-345 and C-47-346, both from Deposit 111.

[33] The contexts of foreign examples with this kind of decoration are also pertinent: Deposits 107, 111.

bowls and the uniform good quality of their mould design and manufacture are also indicative of the very short period suggested. The general evidence for the design at Corinth would tend to suggest that the idea of decorating bowls in this fashion was adopted, either directly or indirectly, from Athens, where it may well have been in use for a more extensive period. One might estimate that it had been introduced there about 155 B.C. In footnote 32 the imported long-petal bowls have been classified. The Attic imports are only two[34] but a total of 20 others were made in centers which seem to have adopted the Attic bowl form. The implications of this would seem to be that in Attic a sufficient period of time must be allowed for this decoration to be introduced and to have become sufficiently popular abroad to be imitated. 155 B.C. as the date of introduction in Athens is probably a fair and likely estimate. An earlier date does not seem probable since further extension backward in time for the introduction would provide an improbably long period of production for them in Athens, a period which was evidently very long in any case. Athenian bowls of this kind of excellent quality, therefore presumably still early, are known to have been in use in Athens around 150 B.C.[35] They continued in popularity there to the end of the 2nd century and perhaps even into the early first quarter of the 1st century B.C.,[36] according to the evidence of Thompson's Group E. If they did indeed continue to be produced until the time of Sulla's destruction of Athens in 86 B.C. the period of production would thus have been some 69 years. Despite the enormous popularity of bowls so decorated in Athens there would seem to be no justification for estimating a longer period of production for them. If anything, the estimate should probably be reduced. One may, conceivably, be justified in thinking that perhaps the long-petal bowls found in Group E are not so late by some years as the time of the final disposal of the material it includes.[37] Possibly a terminal date of around 100 B.C. would be realistic.

Eight[38] steps in mould design can be distinguished among the bowls of various fabrics found in Corinth including the Corinthian, only four steps being attested in Corinth itself. This may seem a large number for the short period allowed before the destruction of Mummius. In other types of decoration this might suggest that a longer estimate was in order. In this the interpretation indicated seems to be, all considerations being taken into account, that the decoration became quickly popular and its popularity stimulated variation and experiments on the part of the mould designers. It also seems likely, and perhaps more conducive to celerity in making changes, that demand forced the designers of moulds to invent variations which could be more quickly incised in the moulds than was possible with the original concept. This interpretation is indicated by the fact that the design which ultimately won out and persisted was in fact certainly the easiest of all to incise in the mould. This may seem somewhat in contrast to the suggested developments in the bowls with concentric semicircles and those with net pattern, since in them the mould designers seem to have begun with simple patterns and developed them into complicated ones. But in their changes the amount of effort and concentration on the part of the mould maker was not really increased. In fact some of their advanced designs, more complicated in appearance, could perhaps have been executed with less effort. It would, for instance, be easier to dot a net pattern than to incise it accurately.

The initial phase in the long-petal bowls is probably to be seen in bowls whose petals, closely spaced, have linear outlines independent of one another and centers in relief (a gray-ware example, C-37-2229). Two lines per petal, and rather fussy intaglio engraving of the relief center, all to be closely and accurately

[34] Attic imports in Corinth are generally rare in the Hellenistic period in any case.

[35] Contiguous long petals: Thompson D 39, D 42–D 44, D 48. Long petals and jewelling: Thompson D 40. Swirling petals and jewelling: Thompson D 41.

[36] Contiguous long petals: Thompson E 75, E 76. Long petals and jewelling: Thompson E 74, E 86. Swirling long petals and jewelling: Thompson E 85.

[37] It has been suggested, p. 127, that the material in Group E may cover an extended period of time prior to the Sullan sack.

[38] For a ninth phase, known in Athens but not in Corinth, see above, p. 175. This, which has long independent petals with fine, vertical linear divisions, is evidently a quite early phase, clearly among the most difficult to incise in the mould.

aligned, were involved in this design for the mould maker. The engraving of a presumably contemporary variation involved even more care in alignment, one in which to the first design was added a line of jewelling between each of the petals. (A "Delian" example, C-37-1572, and other foreign: C-37-2735.) Two efforts to reduce the amount of concentration in engraving would seem to be subsequent, perhaps simultaneous. In one the relief center was omitted. Examples of this have independent petals with high-relief outlines and lines of jewelling, **898-900**. In the other the number of petal outlines was reduced by about half by making the petals contiguous. Examples of this have contiguous petals with relief centers: **901-903**. As a result of these trials a further experiment seems to have been undertaken: contiguous petals with high-relief outlines (rather like ribs), and with flat centers, of which there are two Corinthian examples, **904** and **905**. The effect is not and apparently, to judge from the rarity of such bowls, was not pleasing. The final solution, a modification, was entirely satisfactory from all points of view it would seem: contiguous petals with outlines in low relief and flat centers, **906** and **907**. This was to prove elsewhere to be the standard variety, the one produced in the greatest numbers. Two other variations were evidently produced more or less contemporaneously with it, two with swirling petals, one with jewelling, one without (Attic: C-37-1652; C-39-438; cf. Thompson D 41 and Courby, pl. IX, c for the former; for the latter: Schwabacher, pl. VII A, 9). They must have been difficult for the mould maker to engrave and it is perhaps for this reason that they are relatively rare. Their very pleasing appearance must be the reason, however, why they continued long in production alongside the standard style. Bowls with swirling petals and jewelling seem to have been produced just as long as the standard style: Thompson E 85. Those with long straight petals and jewelling mentioned above seem to have continued also: Thompson E 74, E 86.

This outline is, of course, intended to suggest a relative sequence. Further observation of the frequency of the examples of the various phases will perhaps provide a measure of control for the validity of the sequence or provide other suggestions or modifications. But, however true the sequence may prove to be, it can be only of somewhat shaded value for suggesting the actual time of manufacture of bowls of the various phases. It is a sequence of mould design, only in part a sequence of the bowls produced from the moulds. A mould of a given phase, once made, could be used for a considerable period.[39] One would, however, perhaps be justified in supposing that a mould of a superseded, discarded phase would have a less long life than those of the general style to which it belongs. Perhaps a third of the period allotted to the general long-petal style will be sufficient as an estimate for the time of use of moulds of the earlier phases.

Only one of the Corinthian bowls is signed by the mould designer, **904**, with two letters of his name only, reversed in the bowl: ΠР. A signature on a foreign bowl of this kind has been noted (p. 176, note 32). A fair number of names of mould designers are known on Linear Bowls.[40] To us it may seem odd and perhaps unsuitable that long-petal bowls, oftentimes, particularly in the standard variety, failing to suggest the degree of creative imagination which a signature is apt to imply, should be signed. However, in the light of the fact that these bowls among all the hand-engraved linear styles were the most exacting to incise, signatures seem less surprising. One who had perhaps contributed a solution to the problem of their manufacture, as perhaps ΠР had, or thought he had, would well deserve notice, by signature, as an individual.

150-146 B.C.
Independent long petals and jewelling
   898 (C-37-2698). Wall fragment. Max. dim. 0.075.
     Pl. 77.

899 (C-37-2715). Part of medallion and lower wall. Max. dim. 0.051.
900 (C-37-2709). Wall fragment. Max. dim. 0.045.

---

[39] Depending, of course, on the durability of the fabric of which the mould is made. Athenian moulds could have been used indefinitely; and the Corinthian moulds now known (Addendum, p. 186) are equally durable in fabric.

[40] Courby lists six signed pieces representing at a minimum four individuals (Courby, p. 331). One of the four names also appears on a bowl in Yale University (Baur, *A.J.A.*, XLV, 1941, p. 236, no. 199).

Contiguous long petals, relief centers

901 (C-63-490 a–c), Deposit 47. Two sections, upper wall and rim. P. H. 0.153; D. est. 0.34. Two rim zones: two lines below, two in the middle, one above; below, ivy-leaf guilloche; above, egg-and-dart. Rim: two wheel-run lines beneath the glaze. Fully glazed. Pl. 38.

902 (C-36-2422). Section of upper wall and rim zone. Max. dim. 0.06. Rim zone: ivy-leaf guilloche. Pl. 77.

903 (C-48-244 a, b), Deposit 112. Two fragments of wall and rim. Max. dim. 0.033. Rim zone: rosettes, probably eight-petal, isolated.

Contiguous long petals, high-relief outlines, flat centers

904 (C-34-304). Section of medallion and lower wall. Max. dim. 0.09. Medallion, multi-petalled rosette; zone of two concentric circles. Between petals on wall:?]ΠΡ[? retrograde. Pl. 77.

905 (C-37-2739). Upper wall and rim zone. Max. dim. 0.045. Rim zone: two lines, no decoration.

Contiguous long petals, flat center

906 (C-33-1463bis). Rim and upper wall. Max. dim. 0.06. Rim zone: line of jewelling over single line. Pl. 77.

907 (C-35-973). Section of lower wall to upper rim. Max. dim. 0.068. Rim zone: between two lines, a line of dots.

NET-PATTERN BOWL **908–920**, Pls. 36, 38, 78–80.

160 to 146 B.C.

Deposits:[41] 46, 94, 98, 101, 104, 110.

The typical decoration by which these bowls may be recognized is a rectilinear net pattern, of pentagonal units, usually in two, one in three registers. It depends from the rim zone or its level and extends far down the lower wall, sometimes connecting with the zone around the medallion, sometimes terminating just above it. The net may be formed in several ways, by single lines and also by double lines, the latter with a line of dots between. It may also be formed by triple lines, or by a single dotted line. The pentagons of the net formed by all these methods are usually interlocking, but among those formed by a single line some examples have nets composed of independent units. Usually the field within the pentagons is plain, but on four a single decorative motif appears in each. A linear ivy leaf, point down, in the lower register, is known, and, in the upper register, a rosette, linear or dotted. In several of the pieces the mould maker has distributed the letters of his name around the bowl in one or other of the registers, a letter, or two, in each pentagon. The Corinthian examples provide little information about the medallion. The few that are preserved show only a quadruple palmette pattern, and possibly a rosette of some sort as the main motif. A blank medallion may have been used on **909**. Only one type of encircling zone for the medallion is known, a pair of concentric circles. One example of a double rim zone is known, on **916**, egg-and-dart and ivy-leaf guilloche, with line borders. A single rim zone is known in three examples. It is formed by two lines, the motifs in it being guilloche in two forms, and spirals. One has in the rim-zone position a continuous linear herringbone spray without borders. In others the rim zone is entirely omitted.

The bowls on which this decoration appears were of perhaps three main sizes: H. 0.07, D. lip 0.12 m.; H. 0.085, D. lip 0.135–0.15 m.; and one appreciably larger, **912**. The forms of bowl employed appear to be three. Two forms share a flat medallion area and the wheelmade section of the rim is high (0.02–0.025 m.). The one has a broad lower wall: **908, 911,** and **916** are certainly and **909** and **918** are probably of this form. The other has a conical outline: **919**. The third form, represented by **912**, is puzzling. It is here taken to be a bowl form, since both surfaces of this wall fragment are fully glazed. The profile is a single, continuous, convex outline. There is only a shallow moulded section below and the wheelmade part above broadens out widely from it. Each of the thirteen pieces here is from a different mould.

---

[41] The contexts of foreign and wheelmade vessels with net decoration are also pertinent: Deposits 31, 46, 96, 102, 103, 111.

The quality of mould design and manufacture varies from very competent and entirely pleasing to adequate but crude and thence to poor.

A number of considerations prompt the suggestion that bowls with this kind of decoration had been in production for perhaps fifteen years prior to the destruction of Corinth in 146 B.C. The number of examples attested is not great, though appreciably greater than the number of bowls with concentric-semicircle decoration to which a shorter span has been assigned. In addition to the thirteen Corinthian there are six foreign[42] bowls plus two more foreign[43] with related decoration. Also to be taken into consideration are eight wheelmade vessels, Corinthian and other, on which this decoration is incised.[44] The variety of motifs known to have been employed on these bowls is not great. There are, however, discernible among the bowls a number of phases of design, representing first acquaintance and subsequent experiments with the possibilities of the basic net pattern. The initial stage is presumably to be seen in the bowls with nets of single lines. To this simple line pattern are added in several only motifs which are predominantly linear: small spirals in the rim zone or a herringbone spray at that level, and in the pentagons only the linear letters of the mould maker's signature. On **910**, however, the most satisfactory in design of all, the very delicately simple line net is appropriately in contrast to a rich and involved guilloche rim zone. Another, **911**, substitutes a leaf (?) for the verticals of the lower register of the net. Four essays toward varying this scheme, three good, one definitely not, are presumably subsequent. Independent single-line pentagons with a floral motif in each is an attractive one. The double-line pentagons with inner dots are very satisfactory in a restrained way. The dotted-line net is very successful in a more elegant way, reminding one of the gold nets attached to medallions of the same metal (e.g., Amandry, Pierre, *Collection Hélène Stathaton, Les bijoux antiques*, Strasbourg, 1953, no. 235, pl. XL). The triple-line net is merely incompetent.[45] These steps are not far apart in time, it would seem, for examples of all but one are known to have been in use at the time of Mummius. The one, without context in Corinth, the double-line net, **917**, is presumably also of the same time because of its close resemblance to Thompson D 38. Several examples, all of the earliest variety, come from use fillings of wells whose contents accumulated up to the time of Mummius. They were perhaps among the latest pieces to be discarded before that event. The degrees of quality in design and manufacture among the bowls suggest that there had been time in production for the style to have lost its freshness for the mould maker. In respect to their range of quality they make a fairly strong contrast with the uniformly rather good quality of the concentric-semicircle bowls whose period of production is believed to have been quite short in Corinth. Although interest had perhaps fallen off a bit with some mould makers, others had made advances toward sophistication and some elegance, it would seem, if one compares such pieces as **908** with **910** and **919**. For the relative dating there is possibly a suggestion of contemporaneity, in part at least, between these bowls and those with concentric semicircles in that two of the bowl forms employed for each are much the same. The connection is perhaps strengthened by the use in both of the double circle as a zone for the medallions, which are of similar size. With these considerations in mind, some suggesting a distinct span of time of production, more than momentary, others indicating that the several varieties are closely interlocked in time, the present estimate for the date of the introduction of the design seems fully adequate and not subject to much, if any, extension earlier.

[42] "Delian": C-47-275, Deposit 111. Gray-ware oinochoe: C-47-852, Deposit 46, *Hesperia*, XVIII, 1949, pp. 148–149, pl. 13, 1, right. Other foreign: C-35-698; C-37-2703; C-30-149; CP-519.

[43] C-47-238, Deposits 102 and 103; C-36-2424.

[44] Corinthian basketball askoi: **605–607**, Deposit 96. Corinthian wheelmade Megarian bowls, **530** and **531**. Gray-ware wheelmade Megarian bowl: C-37-1603. Wheelmade Megarian bowl, other fabric: C-47-419, Deposit 111; C-65-97, Deposit 31. All these are decorated with a single-line, interlocking net.

[45] The foreign bowls noted above (footnotes 42, 43) from Corinth show types of net similar to those on the Corinthian bowls, adding only one variety not present in the Corinthian: a single-line net with short cross strokes at close intervals: C-30-149; CP-519. Thompson D 38; Schwabacher, pl. IX A, 11; and Courby, p. 387, fig. 80, 1, are double-line nets, the former two with a line of dots between the lines.

Athenian evidence (Thompson D 38[46] and D 51) has already provided the indication that this style was prevalent about 150 B.C. The evidence of contexts for bowls of this kind in Corinth strongly enforces this dating. How much later it survived is not yet clear. In Thompson's Group E bowls with other types of decoration were popular and none of this kind appear, although a wheelmade inkwell, E 58, is decorated with an incised net pattern. Schwabacher seems to imply, perhaps unintentionally,[47] a connection between the net-pattern bowls and the mould maker Ariston. If so, this may suggest a continuation of production of net-pattern bowls into the latter second century. At an estimate it seems reasonable to suppose that the style in moulded ware had its greatest popularity perhaps between 160 and 120 B.C., though this estimate may be too great. The style may not have had an enduring appeal for the market. Among the linear styles of the latter second century those with long petals probably soon won out over the others. Observation of the number of further experiments with the basic motif in the various fabrics in which it was employed will no doubt provide a fairly close index for the period of production of this kind of bowl.

It would be of interest chronologically to know how many mould makers were involved among the six signed pieces from Corinth. One may perhaps have made three of the pieces. His name so far as preserved was either:

$$ATω\,[3\ to\ 6\ letters]\,OY$$
or:
$$]ATω\,[3\ to\ 6\ letters]\,OY$$

This name appears most fully preserved on **911**, and the first two letters appear on **909** and **912**. The letter forms, where comparable, are the same in all (alpha with a diagonal bar is notable), and so is the position of the letters, all in the upper register of the net, and all upside down, with reference to the rim. The three other signed pieces may perhaps have also been those of one man, and though as far as the letters of the name are concerned he could be the same as the first, the letter forms and their position suggest that he is a different man. The letters preserved are two broken-bar alphas, one each on **913** and **915**, and a rho, on **914**. One of the two alphas, on **913**, is initial, the other two letters are of undeterminable position. All appear in the lower register of the net, and all are in right-side-up position with reference to the rim. The possibility of Ariston[48] as the maker of these three has been considered, but seems unlikely in view of present information that his period of activity was much later (Thompson, p. 464; Howland, *Greek Lamps*, p. 176).

160–146 B.C.
Single-line net
908 (C-35-128), Deposit 94. H. 0.085; D. lip est. 0.15. Medallion missing except the border, two concentric circles. Net does not connect with border. Rim zone: between two lines, a row of separate double spirals. See footnote 46, above. Pl. 78.
909 (C-37-2701). Fragment, part of medallion and wall. Max. dim. 0.068. Medallion blank(?). Net joins border of medallion. In upper register of net, upside down, part of signature: A/T[ ] or [ ]A/T[ ]. Pl. 78.

910 (C-28-66). Fragment, wall and rim zone. Max. dim. 0.099. Rim zone: between two lines, guilloche. Pl. 78.
911 (C-35-653), Deposit 104. Medallion missing except outer line of border. H. 0.075; D. lip 0.12. For verticals of lower register of net a large motif, possibly a leaf, is substituted. In upper register, upside down, letters of maker's signature: / /A/Tω/ (space of three pentagons; 3 to 6 letters possible) /O/Y. No rim zone. Pl. 38.
912 (C-37-2256). Section of wall convex in profile. Max. dim. 0.135. Clay thicker than in

---

[46] It is to be noted that the bowl from Corinth mentioned under D 38 is **908** and that its deposit, 94, extends down to the time of Mummius rather than to the end of the 3rd century B.C.

[47] In *A.J.A.*, LXV, 1941, pl. IX A, 11, a fragment of a net-pattern bowl is illustrated with others under the general caption: "Ariston-werkstatt, etc." This fragment does not seem to be mentioned in the text, and the illustration is too dim to see if it may have been signed.

[48] The forms of the alpha and rho are not unlike those in a number of Ariston's signatures. Cf. Howland, *Greek Lamps*, nos. 687, 688, 689, 850, 851.

other bowls: 0.006. Fully glazed on both surfaces, therefore from open vessel, possibly a bowl. In upper register of net, upside down, part of maker's signature: A/T[ ] or [ ]A/T[ ]. Above, continuous herringbone spray without border. A fragment of a wheelmade hemispherical bowl with appliqué supports, **526**, is comparable in character of fabric. Pl. 79.

Single-line net, independent pentagons

913 (C-36-2350). Lower wall fragment with border, two concentric circles, of medallion. Max. dim. 0.054. Lower register: a linear ivy leaf, point down, in each pentagon, and in one also a letter of the maker's signature: a broken-bar alpha, in initial position, since the pentagon to the left has no letter. Upper register: a seven-petal rosette in each pentagon. Pl. 79.

914 (C-33-433), Deposit 98. Lower wall fragment. Max. dim. 0.047. Lower register: a linear ivy leaf in each pentagon, point down diagonally; in one pentagon also a letter of the maker's signature, position in name undeterminable: rho. Pl. 79.

915 (C-48-61), Deposit 101. Wall fragment. Max. dim. 0.04. Considered probably to have been decorated with net pattern because of similarities to **913** and **914**. Left: a linear ivy leaf; right: part of the maker's signature, position

in name not determinable: a broken-bar alpha. Pl. 79.

916 (CP-1933). Profile complete to just below rim. P.H. 0.062; D. lip est. *ca.* 0.11. Medallion: rosette (?) between two concentric circles. Two rim zones: below, egg-and-dart; above, ivy-leaf guilloche.

Double-line net, dots between lines

917 (C-31-483). Wall fragment. Max. dim. 0.092. Thompson D 38 employs the same variety of net. Pl. 79.

Triple-line net

918 (C-48-90), Deposit 110. P.H. 0.068; D. lip est. 0.14. Lines of net fine and closely spaced. No rim zone. Pl. 79.

Dotted-line net

919 (C-47-790), Deposit 46. H. 0.085; D. lip 0.138. Medallion: quadruple palmette within two concentric circles. Net in three registers: base line of net is a line of dots around medallion zone; suspended from a line of dots under a straight line beneath rim zone; verticals of top register are a dotted line between two straight lines. Rim zone: between two lines, a guilloche. Pls. 36, 80.

920 (C-33-1053). Wall fragment. Max. dim. 0.048. Part of one pentagon in which is a dot rosette. Pl. 79.

CONCENTRIC-SEMICIRCLE BOWL **921–932**, Pls. 36, 80, 81.

150 to 146 B.C.

Deposits: 46, 102.

The typical decoration by which these bowls are distinguished consists of groups of large semicircles on the walls, depending from the rim zone and extending down to the lower wall. A single ornament (asterisk or triskeles) may appear within the inner semicircle of each group. The rest of the decoration is equally characteristic, for though there is variation it is limited. In the field between the groups of semicircles and extending down to the zone or zones encircling the medallion are bosses, large or small. The only medallion design attested is the triskeles, and the medallion where preserved is always within two concentric circles. It is, in a few, also encircled by a third circle, with a line of bosses between it and the inner two. There are either one or two narrow, decorated rim zones. A single line of bosses in a single zone, a double line of bosses in a single zone, two zones each with a single line of bosses all occur. As variations there are two zones, one a line of bosses, the other a row of thick vertical strokes, and two zones, each with a line of alternating tear-shaped drops and rosettes.

The bowls on which this decoration appears seem all to have been about one size: H. *ca.* 0.08–0.085 and D. lip *ca.* 0.145 m. The forms among these bowls are three, not strongly dissimilar. One, attested by **929** and **930**, has a fairly flat medallion area and a broad lower wall. The wheelmade section of the rim is high (0.02 m.) and slightly outturned above. The second, known from **923** and **924**, is similar except in having a concave medallion. The third, seen in **921**, whose medallion is missing, has a generally more conical outline and the wheelmade section of the rim is low (0.01 m.). Eleven different moulds were used with the twelve pieces, **921** and **922** being probably from the same mould. The clay employed in all is of about the same thickness (wall *ca.* 0.004 m.) and the glaze, where preserved (fugitive in some), is uniformly a matt black except in one fired red. The quality of mould design and manufacture is uniform, reasonably careful, and pleasing.

The present suggestion that the period of production of bowls with this kind of decoration in Corinth is short is based on several considerations. The paucity of examples, as compared with bowls of other types of decoration, is one. There are twelve Corinthian examples and four foreign,[49] plus two more foreign examples with related decoration.[50] Two other considerations suggest that this type of decoration was fairly new to the Corinthian designers of moulds and that the examples represent a formative stage of the style with them. Variety of motifs and complications of their possible combinations and permutations are presumably indications in moulded bowls of long tradition. In these the number of motifs employed, already noted, is few, and the basic approach to their use in these bowls is elemental. The process of experiment with these motifs had just begun. The wall designs are extant or preserved to a restorable extent in all but one piece. In their planning only two stages can be distinguished, a simple, presumably initial one and the beginnings of experiment with more complicated arrangements. Both are closely tied together and characterized by the use of groups of only three semicircles, plain wide arcs, perhaps compass drawn, and bosses. In the initial stage four large groups appear, with large, widely spaced bosses: **921–927**, and perhaps **928**. In the second, two experiments toward providing a more sophisticated and a livelier overall effect are made. In one the step has been taken toward this end by reducing the size of the semicircles and increasing the number of groups from four to perhaps five or six, retaining the original large bosses: **929, 930**. The other is a mirror experiment of the first. The four large groups of semicircles are retained and the effect is enlivened by reducing the size of the bosses and increasing their number so that they pepper the available surface in the field: **931, 932**. The early and experimental character of the decoration of these bowls in best seen by contrast with others which exhibit some of the complications and variations which could be achieved, and which perhaps unfortunately were achieved, with the basic motifs themselves and by the addition of others (for example, ones from Athens, Thompson E 78, by context later than the Corinthian, and Schwabacher, pl. IX B, 18; from Delos: Courby, fig. 80, 2; and from Pergamon: Courby, fig. 87, 13 and 24).

The stages of experiment in design in the Corinthian bowls do not suggest that any great amount of time is represented among them. An example of the first stage and an example of one of the two experiments of the second were in fact found in contexts of the Mummian destruction. On present evidence it seems justifiable to suggest that this kind of decoration was introduced in Corinth close to the year 150 B.C. and had hardly begun to be exploited when the end came. Should, of course, more complicated designs on this pattern be found in Corinth the date of the introduction would have to be increased accordingly.

If this short period of production proves to be the case, examples of these bowls will be of value for close dating in Corinth in the mid-second century. Elsewhere bowls so decorated were presumably produced for a much longer period, perhaps, for instance, into the early first century in Athens (Thompson E 78). Another indication that the semicircle bowls were still in production at this time is provided by the signature of Ariston on bowls of this type found in Delos (Courby, pp. 365, 386). His period of

---

[49] Two bowls evidently from one center: C-33-1472 and C-38-699. They seem close in form and decoration to Yale University, Gallery of Fine Arts, 1913, 202. For this bowl Baur (*A.J.A.*, XLV, 1941, pp. 240–241, no. 202) suggested a Macedonian origin because of the resemblance of its decoration to that appearing on Macedonian coins. The suggestion is attractive, and this source for the design seems plausible. Bowls with this design from Macedonia do not seem to be known as yet, however. Perhaps the source of the design is purely numismatic.

Two others from different centers: C-30-138, C-28-130.

[50] Gray ware: C-37-2720 (concentric decoration of uncertain type). Other: C-37-2098 (bosses and very small semicircles).

activity is understood to have occurred in the late 2nd and early 1st centuries B.C.[51] The period of 50 or 60 years thus indicated for the duration of the popularity of this kind of decoration in Greece would seem to be much more than adequate. If it really lasted into the early 1st century there is then still stronger reason for placing its introduction as close to the time of Mummius as possible.

150–146 B.C.

921 (C-47-791), Deposit 46. P.H. 0.08; D. lip 0.144. Missing medallion encircled by three concentric circles, a line of bosses between the outer two. Wall: four groups of three semi-circles, an asterisk within the inner semicircle of each; bosses in field. Two rim zones formed by three lines, a line of alternate tear-shaped drops and rosettes in each. Pls. 36, 80.

922 (C-37-2712). Wall fragment. From same mould as **921**.

923 (CP-1930). Section, rim to medallion. Triskeles within the inner semicircle.

924 (C-37-2399). Part of medallion and wall.

925 (C-37-2225). Fragment, wall and rim.

926 (C-30-131). Fragment, wall and rim. Asterisk within inner semicircle.

927 (C-37-2740). Fragment, wall and rim.

928 (C-37-1569). Fragment, medallion. Max. dim. 0.053. Triskeles within two concentric circles; at edge, traces of bosses. Pl. 81.

929 (C-34-1742), Deposit 102. Section, rim to outer medallion zone. P.H. 0.075; D. est. *ca.* 0.145. Outer medallion zone: line of bosses. Wall: parts of two groups of three semicircles, an asterisk within the inner semicircle of one; bosses in field. Single rim zone: a line of bosses. Pl. 81.

930 (C-33-102). Section, medallion to rim.

931 (C-31-479). Section, medallion to upper wall. Max. dim. 0.082. Medallion: triskeles within two concentric circles. Wall: parts of three groups probably each of three semicircles. Small bosses in field. Pl. 81.

932 (C-34-2503). Section, edge of medallion to rim zone.

LINEAR-LEAF BOWL[52] 933–937, Pls. 81, 82.

Ca. 150 to 146 B.C.

Deposits: 109, 112.

The characteristic decoration by which these bowls may be recognized consists of contiguous, long, outline leaves of two kinds, one lanceolate, the other broadly triangular in outline above. These cover the entire wall, alternating. They are based on the medallion zone and rise sheathing the wall to about its mid-point where they separate to form their characteristic tips, which touch the rim zone. No other decoration appears on the walls of the present examples except, on **937**, for a line of large jewelling at the level of the tips of the leaves. The medallion is not preserved except for its zone which (preserved in **935**) is a pair of concentric circles. The rim zone in the known examples is single or double. The rim-zone patterns used are: ivy-leaf guilloche, a repeated leaf (?) pattern of two varieties, upside down egg-and-dart, and a lattice pattern (X's between dotted lines). The form of bowl employed (medallion form unknown) had a fairly broad lower wall. The wheelmade section of the rim is high (0.025 m.) and slightly outturned above. Probably all the pieces belong to bowls of about the same size: H. *ca.* 0.085 and D. lip 0.15 m. Four certainly, perhaps five, moulds were employed for the five pieces (possibly but not probably **934** and **935** were produced in the same mould). The quality of mould design is not very good. The quality of manufacture is uniformly fair.

Assessment of the period of production of this class of bowls depends at present on the connection in which they are to be regarded, and too little is known about them for a good opinion. They may represent either the final feeble stylization of an earlier, more naturalistic motif or else they may be feeble local imitations of quite a fresh conception. On the one hand the leaf forms were certainly used

---

[51] See Broneer, *Terracotta Lamps*, pp. 64–65; Thompson, p. 464; Schwabacher, p. 222; Howland, *Greek Lamps*, p. 176.

[52] The same style of decoration is also employed on a "Delian" bowl found in Corinth, C-47-328, Deposit 109. In it, however, the decoration appears in a minor position (lower wall) as the corolla for the medallion, and the leaves are independent of one another. This link between it and the Corinthian may, even so, prove to be chronologically significant.

earlier in a plastic way, and certainly no pleasure in their design is evident, as would be expected to be visible in bowls representing first acquaintance with a new idea. On the other hand their designs seem plausibly to be associated with those of other Linear Bowls which began to be produced *ca.* 160 B.C., and the context of one example, **933**, is known to be of this period (the context of another, **936**, may possibly be of the same time). In addition they probably share the same design with an Attic fragment, C-36-2425, which can be more closely associated with the Linear Bowls. The Attic fragment does give the impression of a new scheme of design. It is crisp, sharp, and spacious in design and execution. It is connected with the long-petal bowls and with the bowls decorated with double-line net pattern of this time by the use of a pair of lines, with a line of jewelling between, as the spine of the leaves. The Attic fragment is a rarity. The present interpretation of the Corinthian bowls, then, is that they are inept imitations of a very short-lived linear style of decoration which had its period of popularity in the years around 150 B.C.[53]

Two different approaches to the design are seen among the pieces, one in which the outline leaves, of about equal breadth, have only a single line as spine, the other in which the triangular leaf is much broader than the other, and in which the lanceolate leaf has multiple vertical linear divisions (three or five interior lines). Possibly they are dim reflections of stronger and competent phases of design in the parent bowls.

ca. 150–146 B.C.
Leaves with single-line spine

933 (C-48-31), Deposit 112. Profile preserved from lip to lower wall. P.H. 0.085; D. est. 0.15. Outline leaves. Rim zone: between two lines, an ivy-leaf guilloche. Pl. 81.

934 (C-34-2007). Wall fragment. Max. dim. 0.045.

935 (C-37-2725). Fragment, medallion zone and lower wall. Max. dim. 0.05.

Broad triangular leaves, lanceolate leaves with multiple divisions

936 (C-47-337 a–e), Deposit 109. Fragments pre-serving profile from rim to lower wall. Max. dim. 0.095. Lanceolate leaves with three inner lines. Two rim zones: below, upside down egg-and-dart; above, lattice pattern (X's between dotted lines). Pl. 82.

937 (C-31-482). Fragment of rim and upper wall. Max. dim. 0.07. Lanceolate leaf with five inner lines. On wall at level of tip, a line of large jewelling. Two rim zones, each with a line of leaves (?), a different one in each zone.

UNCLASSIFIED LINEAR BOWL **938**, Pl. 82.

Ca. 150 B.C.

A single bowl represents a style of linear decoration differing from the preceding groups. It may well be a variant of the linear-leaf bowls. Its major decoration is independent, long, outline leaves with a single line as spine, extending from the medallion zone to the rim zone. The very small medallion has an eight-petal flower and its zone is formed by two concentric circles. The rim zone, formed by a pair of lines, seems to have a continuous line of dots. The form has a fairly flat medallion area and a broad lower wall. The wheelmade section of the rim is high (0.025 m.) and slightly outturned above. The quality of the mould design is adequate. That of manufacture was evidently good, though marred by misfiring.

Its context is unknown. Its linear decoration, the kind of medallion and rim zones, and its form have relationships among the Linear Bowls sufficient to suggest that it is to be dated in the time of their production at Corinth.

ca. 150 B.C.
938 (CP-518). H. 0.068; D. lip 0.132. Pl. 82.

---

[53] I.e., evidently short lived as far as Corinth is concerned. Conceivably further information and observation will show that the style was employed for a longer period elsewhere.

ADDENDUM: RECENT FINDS

939-944

MOULDS FOR CORINTHIAN RELIEF WARE

939-942

After the text on moulded relief ware had been prepared four fragments of moulds for bowls, the first to be found in Corinth, were discovered. They are, accordingly, catalogued here below. A word of comment on them has been inserted in the introduction to the bowls above, p. 153, and references to them have been inserted in footnotes in the pertinent sections.

The decorative schemes they were intended to produce are not exemplified by any of the bowls or fragments known at present. Two are readily recognizable as of Corinthian manufacture, **939** and **942**. They are made of clay similar to that employed for the bowls and for other Corinthian Hellenistic pottery. In these the clay has, however, been fired above the normal temperature so that they are extremely hard and of a pale green color. The two others, of buff clay of very fine texture, were also fired hard, but not overfired. Possibly they are imports, though they resemble to some degree the appearance of moulds for Corinthian terracotta figurines. One, **939**, was found in a Hellenistic context of the mid-2nd century B.C. The contexts of the others are of much later times.

Moulds for Foliage Bowls:

939 (C-65-372). From a well west of Old Corinth in a context of the middle of the 2nd century B.C. Fragment of lower wall and false ring foot of a mould for a bowl of normal size. P.H. 0.045; max. Th. 0.017. From the outer edge of the missing medallion spring long leaves with central spines alternating with vertical rows of (in the mould) horizontal dashes. Evidently a late manifestation of the leaf-and-tendril bowls. See pp. 156–157; Pl. 83.

940 (C-66-3). From the area occupied in Roman times by the North Market. Wall fragment of a mould for a very large bowl. Max. dim. 0.068; Th. 0.01. Stamp impressions of part of two rows of large, imbricate, rounded petal tips. See pp. 159–160; Pl. 83.

941 (C-66-225). From northern part of village of Old Corinth (grid: L-15/C 5). Wall fragment of a mould for a bowl of normal size. Max. dim. 0.04; Th. 0.005. Stamp impressions: below, parts of two rows of imbricate, small, pointed petal tips; above (rim zone), egg-and-dart. The impressions of the stamps are reflected in the surface of the outer wall. See pp. 160–161; Pl. 83.

942 (C-66-4). From the area occupied in Roman times by the North Market. Fragment of base and lower wall of mould for a bowl of normal size. P.H. 0.035; D. bottom 0.045. Underside of base left unfinished, with string marks. Medallion (in cast) 0.029 in diameter, decorated with five overlapping, pointed petal tips. Corolla: feathered leaves with a bunch of grapes between their tips. Possibly from a mould for a Figured Bowl. See pp. 163–175; Pl. 83.

CONICAL BOWL
(see pp. 90–92)

3rd century B.C., last quarter

943 (C-66-151). Two sections preserving the profile from the rim to the edge of the medallion. Max. dim. 0.105. No grooving on the exterior. Interior: edge of medallion (multipetalled flower?) encircled by a groove wheelrun through the glaze. Wall: parts of two Pegasi supplementing one another to provide a representation complete except for the forelegs and head. For the possible position of the front feet compare the hippocamp on **128**. Rendered entirely in paint of various shades of brown, yellow, and white. Rim zone set off by a wheel groove through the glaze below; repeated diminishing rectangles in incision with a vertical band of white between each. Pl. 84.

WHEELMADE MEGARIAN BOWL
(see pp. 88–90)

3rd century B.C., last quarter

944 (C-65-377). Large section, profile complete. H. 0.095; D. est. 0.145. Fully glazed except for lines wheel grooved through glaze, one around exterior and interior medallions, one on lower wall, two on upper wall as borders of rim zone. Medallions: multipetalled flower rendered entirely in paint. Medallion zone: bead-and-reel rendered in paint only, in white with yellow highlights. Wall: 3 rows of scale pattern, each scale of double outline, entirely in incision. Rim zone: running ivy, tendrils incised, leaves in yellow. Pls. 38, 84.

THE DEPOSITS AND CHRONOLOGY

INTRODUCTION

Below are summarized 118 deposits[1] of various kinds. These include all which have been employed for the chronology in this book. In addition are included others, a number only partially studied, which it is thought will be useful for future chronological investigations, whether of Corinthian or of imported pottery. They include as well a few questionable deposits about which comment seems required. In each summary an attempt has been made to provide all pertinent bibliography and an indication of the location[2] of the deposit. In the case of deposits in which fillings are concerned some indication or suggestion as to the nature of the fillings has been provided where this is possible. Occasionally it has also been possible to suggest potential sources for the material in a deposit, e.g. 90, from a sanctuary, or 2, from a pottery shop or factory. The deposit bibliographies provide means of access to objects from them already published. Following each deposit summary is a list of the pieces from them published or mentioned in this study.

In the summaries of all deposits an indication of the range in date has also been provided. An appreciable number of the deposits have had the benefit of attention by many other scholars in varying degrees, either full study, partial, preliminary notice in excavation reports, or opinions recorded in field notebooks. The present writer is deeply indebted to these various scholars in the present attempt to form the necessary framework for the chronology of the pottery. In all cases the dates they have suggested for deposits have necessarily been subject to testing in the course of outlining the histories of the many shape series and other entities in this volume. Often the present material has strongly supported their dating. Sometimes, however, in the case of dates proposed in preliminary notices and especially in cases where additional pertinent information from other deposits has been available, some modifications of their dating has seemed indicated. In such cases the bibliographies provide access to their opinions, and the dates expressed here for the deposits are those of the writer. On the other hand, many deposits (absence of bibliography will make them evident) have been studied up to the present, aside from examination for purposes of field recording, only by the present writer. Future comment on them by others will be both welcome and certainly chronologically extremely desirable.

It is candidly expected that the present dates proposed for the deposits, particularly those for which the writer is responsible, will also be subject to scrutiny and further modification. In the range of time covered by the deposits, the upper ranges of some extending into the 7th century B.C., the lower limits of others extending far into the Roman period, it cannot be expected that there will be present full control of all chronological evidence pertinent to the dating of the deposits. Further studies by others of pottery, in the deposits, of numerous varieties additional to those published here will undoubtedly

---

[1] The original records pertaining to these deposits are on file in the Corinth Museum. Copies of the deposit lists, transcripts of field records, and other notes compiled and used in the preparation of this study are to be placed on file there also.

[2] At the time of writing it was not possible to give references to Corinth grid designations for the deposits. Such designations will, however, eventually be assigned to all deposits. In the present study the designations which appear in excavation diaries and records are employed, supplemented by references to publications in which specific locations can be ascertained. The general location of the deposits can be determined also from the indications provided on plans of Corinth illustrated on Plates 85 and 86 in this book.

suggest modification and refinement of the present dating, particularly in the case of deposits of times prior to the Hellenistic period. Similarly, studies of other categories of objects in the deposits which may be susceptible of providing criteria for close archaeological dating will also occasion tests, furnish controls, and indicate the need for modification. This writer's conclusions as to dates have in their background, in addition to the criteria for dating provided by the pottery here as they have been developed through hand-in-hand study of shape series and deposits, the information provided by both coins and stamped amphora handles in periods where these are pertinent. For the coins, much of the information has been that provided by various scholars recorded in the Corinth coin files. No doubt future close studies of particular coin series represented among them will produce modification of the present conclusions as to deposit dates. The writer has had, however, the especial advantage of the recent opinion of Mr. Martin Price in connection with an important block of the coins. Mr. Price kindly made available a preliminary draft of his study of the coins from the South Stoa wells which has formed the basis for the comments on the coins of these deposits. He also very kindly provided his preliminary opinions on the date of a number of bronze coins (Deposits 35-37, 39, 40) of Corinth in the Pegasos/Trident series. It is a great satisfaction to record general agreement between his conclusions on the date of deposits via the coins and the writer's conclusions from the pottery, either fairly close pin-pointing in some cases, or dating within the range covered by the pottery.[3] Miss Margaret Thompson has studied an important group of Ptolemaic coins from Deposit 110. She has also undertaken a study of the gold hoard of Deposit 19, to be published in conjunction with a note by the writer on the black-glazed saucer which concealed it. For the dating of the amphora handles in the deposits the writer is deeply indebted to Miss Virginia Grace. Her dating of handles, of which there were a large number, in the initial study of the material from the South Stoa well deposits, which composed the original nucleus of the study here and which form an important block of the chronology, was of the greatest value. It is very gratefully recorded that, when the criteria for dating the pottery were ultimately developed, her dating and the dating provided by the pottery (as well as the coins) were found to be in entire agreement in the cases of deposits studied subsequently, the handles from which were referred to her only after study of the other material.

The exacting critic will no doubt wish to be informed to what extent the dating proposed here is actual and historical as opposed to "archaeological," i.e. estimated from criteria established or envisaged for relative dating, and in both cases how reliable or likely the dating may be.

For actual and historical dates it will quickly become evident that aside from deposits to whose dating coins contribute, there are only two historical connections involved:[4] the destruction of Olynthos in 348 B.C.,[5] and the destruction of Corinth by Mummius in 146 B.C.[6] For the latter, particular comment

---

[3] M. J. Price, "Coins from some Deposits in the South Stoa at Corinth," *Hesperia*, XXXVI, 1967, pp. 348–388.

It would, in the summaries, be most desirable to be able to give references to the specific coins in the deposits so that future changes in dating and attribution could readily be assimilated. Specific references, however, to the coins concerned in this study would, for the most part, be intolerably cumbersome. It is a pleasure, however, to note that as of recent date coins found at Corinth are being given catalogue numbers, which will make such necessary reference possible in the future.

[4] Their significance and utility in chronology should, however, not be minimized. In archaeological chronology two historical connections, both providing abundant material, are much to be prized and not given to all. The hidden fringe benefits are far reaching and, in the present case, the two are more than usually basic since they often provided, or assisted in providing, dates for both early (or initial) and final stages of many shape series.

[5] In the main, use has been made in this study only of material found in the houses at Olynthos since this in general has been assumed to have been in use at the time of the destruction. Since shape development is an important criterion for dating here, especial effort has been devoted to distinguishing the most advanced examples of each series present in the houses at Olynthos since these are the most nearly contemporary with the time of the destruction in point of time of manufacture. In the main, Attic pots in deposits have been compared with Attic pots from Olynthos, a major and necessary exception being the comparison of Corinthian skyphoi of Attic type with Attic skyphoi found at Olynthos. The writer is aware of indications for slight re-inhabitation of Olynthos after 348 in a restricted area there: see David

is necessary. The problem of the establishment of what pieces are of the time of the destruction, or in use at that time, has been approached from several directions, each providing a measure of control, with the result that a considerable degree of reliance, it is believed, can be placed on the dating of this pottery to that time. The main block of Mummian material comes from the South Stoa wells, from fillings which can plausibly be associated with the destruction, owing to the presence in them of great quantities of pieces of numerous architectural elements of the South Stoa, evidently representing an overall, extensive destruction of the building suitable to that occasion. This indication of destruction is further supplemented by broken statue bases from which the statues had been hacked, broken furnishings of various kinds, fragments of the stone well curbs, fragments of inscriptions, and some indication of burning. It was initially clear, if only on the basis of reason, that this material, if Mummian, was not likely to have been thrown in the wells until the time of the establishment of the Roman colony in 44 B.C. In many cases some Roman additions, pottery, glass, or coins, were actually present in these destruction fillings, indicating that the disposal of the fillings in the wells actually took place in the time of the Roman colony, in some cases soon after 44 B.C., in others after a lapse of some years, thus providing evidence that the destruction fillings were to be attributed to Mummius' activities in 146 B.C. rather than to some earlier, unrecorded event. The supplementary indications for date provided by the Hellenistic coins and amphora handles in the fillings pointed to the same occasion. In the initial stages of this study it seemed justifiable, then, to regard the material from these fillings as having been in use in 146 B.C. Further testing of the attribution in the course of the present study, in relation to deposits of earlier times, with repeated scrutiny as the histories of all the shapes represented in the destruction fillings were studied and written, has entirely confirmed the attribution. The pottery studied here is entirely Corinthian. It is *a priori* likely that all production of pottery ceased in Corinth at the time of the destruction.[7] The examples of shape series studied here from deposits attributed to the destruction are in the main the most advanced of their series (fragments of some earlier material are of course inevitably present), hence representing the last stage of pottery produced in Greek Corinth. The attribution of this important block of material to the time of Mummius' destruction is supplemented and

M. Robinson and J. Walter Graham, *Excavations at Olynthus*, VIII, *The Hellenic House*, Baltimore, 1938, pp. 1–13; David M. Robinson and Paul Augustus Clement, *Excavations at Olynthus*, IX, *The Chalcidic Mint and the Excavation Coins found in 1928–1934*, Baltimore, 1938, pp. 363–372; Alfred R. Bellinger, "Notes on Coins from Olynthus," in *Studies Presented to David Moore Robinson on his Seventieth Birthday*, II, Saint Louis, 1953, pp. 180–186.

[6] No chronological use has been made here of clusters of deposits with potential historical connection in the summaries below (for comment see pp. 192–195). These groupings were developed at the end of this study and are intended only for future scrutiny and consideration when chronology is more refined than it is at present. It is also to be noted that no use has been made in this study of examples of shapes produced in centers foreign to Corinth which occur in deposits elsewhere for which historical associations have been suggested. It is to be expected that pottery traditions, usages, criteria for dating, speed of shape development, decorative tastes and emphases, will vary considerably among the numerous local centers of pottery production which must have existed in Hellenistic times. Though a superficial *koine* may appear to exist in Hellenistic pottery in general, it is likely that as wide a variety of local individualities will be seen to exist in Hellenistic pottery, when more local fabrics are isolated, as, for instance, there were in the Orientalizing, Archaic and Classical periods in the Greek area. Parallelisms between comparable vessels of different centers of manufacture do not seem a reliable basis for dating except in very general terms.

[7] The percentage of likelihood that some Corinthian potters may have survived to continue Corinthian pottery traditions under the Sikyonian control of the area in the desolation period from 146 to 44 B.C. seems slight. The possibility that some of the pottery may be of Sikyonian manufacture, added to the Mummian destruction debris in the years following the destruction, has also been considered and needs to be further explored. Some material at Corinth datable in the desolation period is known. For comment on this period see Harris, *Hesperia*, X, 1941, p. 158; *Asklepieion*, pp. 82–84; Grace, *Hesperia*, XXII, 1953, p. 119 and note 7; Broneer, *S. Stoa*, p. 100; Grace, *Hesperia*, Supplement X, note 19; Kent, *The Inscriptions*, p. 20, note 10.

Local Sikyonian pottery of the Hellenistic period has not been isolated and defined. The present writer has seen some material excavated at Sikyon and has formed the very tentative opinion that, though in fabric the pottery of Sikyon may be close to Corinthian, future study will probably show that there are detectable differences in the treatment and details of shape design between the products of Corinth and Sikyon.

confirmed by the material from two other deposits, 46 and 94. The attribution of the material from Deposit 46 to Mummius' destruction was suggested by the date of the latest coin in it, of the years 148–146 B.C. Subsequent study of many shape series in the deposit pertinent to the present undertaking has shown them also to be of the most advanced stage of their series.[8] Analysis of the material from Deposit 94 at an advanced stage of the study has shown it to be, evidently, an assemblage of material which gradually accumulated during the lifetime of the Greek South Stoa from the time of its first use down to the time of the destruction. Although none of the deposits or fillings attributed to the time of the destruction is what might be called an *in situ* deposit, i.e. sealed or remaining in the position it occupied as the immediate result of the destruction (certainly one may hope that such will be distinguished in future excavations in Corinth), nonetheless the attribution of the material in this study to that event, controlled by various approaches, seems a reasonably strong one. It is to be emphasized that one can feel more confidence in the attribution of Corinthian material to Mummius' destruction than one can in the case of imported material from the destruction fillings. Though imported material in the destruction fillings may share with the Corinthian some degree of likelihood that it is of 146, with it there is always present the possibility that it may have been added to the destruction debris by Sikyonians or other occasional visitors in the desolation period of 146 to 44 B.C.

The degree of reliability of the "archaeological" dating here is somewhat difficult to estimate for one closely concerned with the initial erection of a chronological framework and the establishment of criteria for dating. It will be better assesed by those who may have reason to employ the present conclusions in the future in specific archaeological situations. There has been a firm conviction in this study that good or likely dating for pottery produced in Corinth in the Hellenistic period can only be achieved by full study of the history of the various shape series from their time of introduction, whenever that may have been, to the final stages, employing the evidence, primarily, of its homeland, so that the significant criteria for dating in each series can be ascertained as fully as possible. All pertinent full sequences available at present have, accordingly, been studied here, and all those of which we have at present only partial representation. The deposit evidence is that provided by the excavations at Corinth; some evidence from neighboring Isthmia, also in the Corinthia, has been available in addition through the kindness of Professor Broneer. The reliability of likelihood in dating depends greatly on the representation of a given shape series in respect to initial, intermediate, late, and final stages, on the representation in size series, and of course, in the number, reliability, and the degree of study which has been devoted to them, of the deposits concerned in the various stages of production of the shape. In the discussions of the many shape series in this study and in the summaries the reader has been provided insofar as is practicable with the necessary information for evaluating the reliability of the dating of vessels in which he may be interested. Indication of the stages now attested in a given series (many incomplete) is given in the headings. The catalogues of the individual series are arranged by sizes for the most part, both for assessment and for use, so that the degree of representation should be readily evident. In the headings a list of all deposits concerned is also given, in addition to specific deposit references in the catalogue. In various discussions an attempt has been made to suggest the degree of sensitivity in the dating of particular series. Much remains for the future in the way of gain in dating precision: much further study of present deposit evidence, supplementation of the present deposit evidence, filling of the gaps in representation in the various series by stage and by size. This is necessarily so, since the present study is a beginning, based on the evidence now available. Some has been well recorded and interpreted, some hastily and summarily treated, some has been recaptured only with good will, experience, or sanguine imagination. Excavation is done by excavators of varying degrees

---

[8] It is not ruled out that some of the material from this deposit not studied here may be of earlier date. Some material of very high quality, both pottery and pieces of other categories, may have been in the household for some years. Also it seems likely that some material may belong to an undetected use filling.

of experience, for various reasons and with various interests in view, not always with the student of artifacts or the establishment of chronology in mind.

The present order of presentation of the deposit summaries was devised at the conclusion of this study with the thought not only of making clear, insofar as possible in brief space, the nature of the deposit evidence available, but of making strengths, weaknesses, and gaps readily comprehensible. It has also been arranged so that evidence which will become available in the future can readily be integrated, with the hope that eventually there may exist a more tightly interwoven mesh of deposit evidence for chronology, not only of pottery but of other varieties of artifacts of the times. Toward this end the present deposits have been arranged in three major categories, each with smaller clusters of deposits interrelated in various ways, clusters of deposits which need to be considered in relationship to one another, either with regard to present dating or with respect to dating in future studies. A list of all the deposits, which will serve as an index and also as a quick means of general appraisal of the deposits, is provided here for purposes of general comprehension and discussion. In the case of deposits of long range the dates given in the list are those of the lower limit of range. In the case of deposits in which several fillings are concerned, the one given is the lower date of the particular filling of major interest here.

I. Deposits other than graves and South Stoa
   6th century B.C., *3rd quarter*
   1. Agora SCW, Well at T-U: 2
   2. Southeast Building, Well at I: 23
   Early 5th century B.C.
   3. Agora SC, Well at I-J: 24–25
   4. Pit II in new road west of Shear's house
   5th century B.C., *first half*
   5. Isthmia, the Large Circular Pit
   6. Potters' Quarter, Road Deposit
   7. Potters' Quarter, Deposit in Stelai Shrine A
   450 and 4th century B.C., *third quarter*
   8. Museum West, Well at K 23
   9. Potters' Quarter, Circular South Shrine
   Ca. 420 B.C.
   10. Agora SW, Well at E-K: 30–37 ⎫
   11. South Basilica, Well at S: 11   ⎬ Earthquake (?) deposits
   12. South Basilica, Well at K: 14 ⎭
   13. Potters' Quarter, Rectangular South Pit
   375 to 350 and 4th century B.C., *3rd quarter*
   14. St. John's, unidentified well or cistern
   15. South Basilica, Well in E. cryptoporticus at IV: 15
   16. Isthmia, Pottery Pit in Theater Cave
   17. New Museum East, Well J at O-P: 10
   4th century, third quarter (?) to 275 B.C.
   18. Potters' Quarter, deposits in Terracotta Factory ⎰ Earthquake
                                                          ⎱ deposits
   19. North Stoa, Gold Hoard
   20. Asklepieion, Votive Deposit V in Well QQ 22
   21. Baths of Aphrodite: Section C, West Well (Well I) ⎱
   22. Baths of Aphrodite: Cistern Complex in Room L   ⎰ Stratigraphical relationship

23. Temple E, Cistern II
24. Well at Kretika
25. Tile Works, Well B ⎫
26. Tile Works, Well C ⎭ Early Kiln
27. Tile Works, Well A ⎫
28. Tile Works, Large Kiln ⎭ Later Kiln
29. Anaploga Cistern Area, Manhole 7 ⎫
30. Anaploga Cistern Area, Manhole 8 ⎪
31. Anaploga Cistern Area, Manhole 10 ⎬ Simultaneous abandonment (?)
32. Anaploga Cistern Area, Manhole 11 ⎭
33. North of School, Well R
34. Baths of Aphrodite, East Well (Well II)
35. Museum West, Manhole at G:2
36. New Museum East, Well A ⎫
37. New Museum East, Cistern at I-L: 15–16 ⎬ Terracing

3rd century B.C., *second quarter*
38. Well by Excavation Dump
3rd century B.C., *third and last quarters*
39. New Museum, "Well" (cistern) 41a ⎫ Connected with
40. New Museum, "Well" (cistern) 49a ⎪ planning and
41. New Museum, Well X ⎬ construction of temenos
42. New Museum, Well Z ⎪ of Hellenistic predecessor
43. Well at NW corner of precinct of Temple E ⎭ of Temple E?
44. St. John's, Cistern at D-34
2nd century B.C., *first quarter*
45. Sanctuary of Demeter and Kore, Pit B
Destruction of Corinth in 146 B.C.
46. Southeast Building, Well at N-20
47. Anaploga, destruction filling of 1st Cleaning and Dyeing Works
Early Roman period
48. Anaploga, Well in Grave 12

II. Graves
   5th century B.C., *last quarter*
49. North Cemetery, Field of Panages Kondyles, Grave 54A
Trefoil oinochoe graves, 5th century last quarter to 4th century B.C., *last quarter*
50. North Cemetery, Field of Panages Kondyles, Grave 23A
51. North Cemetery, Grave 339
52. North Cemetery, Grave 348
Pyxis and trefoil-oinochoe-with-shoulder-stop graves, 350 to 4th century B.C., *last quarter*
53. North Cemetery, Deposit 36
54. North Cemetery, Deposit 28
55. North Cemetery, Grave 40
4th century B.C., *3rd quarter*
56. Grave outside Kenchrean Gate
Corinthian skyphos, Attic Type and unguentarium graves, 4th century, late third quarter to ca. 275 B.C.
57. Graves on road to Acrocorinth, Grave 4
58. Graves on road to Acrocorinth, Grave 9

59. Grave (9) near "Justinian's Wall"

60. North Cemetery, Grave 372

61. Grave NW of Acrocorinth

62. North Cemetery, Grave 369

63. North Cemetery, Grave 50

64. Grave VII outside city wall on road to Hexamilia

65 A. Anaploga Cistern Area, Grave 1, lower burial

65 B. Anaploga Cistern Area, Grave 1, upper burial

66. Anaploga Cistern Area, Grave 3

67. Graves on road to Acrocorinth, Grave 3B

68. Graves on road to Acrocorinth, Grave 10

69. Roman Tomb, Grave 5

Hexamilia kantharos graves, 3rd century B.C., *second quarter to early last quarter*

70. North Cemetery, Grave 269

71. Area of Roman tomb north of village, group of pots between Tomb I and Grave 11

72. Tomb VIII outside city wall on road to Hexamilia

73. Cheliotomylos, Trench D burial vault

3rd century B.C., *second half*

74. Roman tomb north of village, Grave 16

75. Anaploga, rock cutting 4

76. Irrigation Ditch NE of City, Burial DD

1st century B.C., *last quarter*

77. West Wall of City, Grave I ⎫
78. West Wall of City, Grave III ⎬ (evidence for Mummian destruction of City Wall)

III. Deposits connected with the history of the South Stoa

Planning and preparation for construction: *ca.* 375 to 350 B.C.

Construction of Stoa and terracing: *ca.* 350 or early third quarter of 4th century to *ca.* 330 B.C.

Period of use of Stoa in Greek times: *ca.* 330 to 146 B.C.

Destruction of Stoa by Mummius: 146 B.C.

79. Agora SC, Well at b-c: 18–19 ⎫
80. Agora SC, Drain at b-f: 19–20 ⎪
81. Southeast Building, Well at P-27 ⎬ Planning and preparation
82. South Stoa, Great Reservoir, filling of oval manhole ⎭

83. South Stoa, Great Reservoir, filling of eastern entrance

84. South Stoa, footing trenches, Shop and Storeroom I

85. South Stoa, footing trench of east wall of Stoa

86. South Stoa, fill around foundation of pier 31 of Ionic colonnade — Planning,

87. South Stoa, Pre-Stoa Well north of Shop IV and filling of building north of Shop IV — construction, and completion

88. Tavern of Aphrodite, South Stoa Construction Fill, South Stoa Terrace Filling, and earlier — (some deposits

89. Agora SC, V-X: 24–26, Underground Sanctuary — involved in

90. Agora SC, Pit at N-O: 21–23 — several phases)

91. Filling under cobble pavement of South Stoa Terrace

92. Agora SC, filling over stereo at V-Y: 13–20

93. South Stoa, Deposit in Shop XXXII

94. South Stoa, Shop I, Pottery Deposit
95. South Stoa, Well II
96. South Stoa, Well III
97. South Stoa, Well IV
98. South Stoa, Well V
99. South Stoa, Well VII
100. South Stoa, Well VIII
101. South Stoa, Well IX
102. South Stoa, Well X
103. South Stoa, Well XI
104. South Stoa, Well XII
105. South Stoa, Well XIII   Use.
106. South Stoa, Well XIV
107. South Stoa, Well XV   Destruction in 146 B.C.
108. South Stoa, Well XVI
109. South Stoa, Well XVIII
110. South Stoa, Well XIX
111. South Stoa, Well XX
112. South Stoa, Well XXII
113. South Stoa, Well XXVII
114. South Stoa, Well XXVIII
115. South Stoa, Well XXX
116. South Stoa, Well XXXI
117. South Stoa, Well XXXIII
118. South Stoa, from various shop wells

The division of the deposits into three categories is a natural one along the lines of the kinds of evidence the deposits provide as a whole. First, a category in part an exclusive one: deposits other than grave groups and deposits connected with the history of the South Stoa. This includes Deposits 1-48. They were found in various areas in Corinth and at Isthmia. They are mainly well and cistern groups with a few from other kinds of sources. In this major category there are various lesser clusters. 10-12 of ca. 420 B.C. form one cluster deserving of further close scrutiny and study since it has been suggested that an earthquake may have been responsible for the disposal of the material they include. If indeed an earthquake was the motivating factor it is entirely conceivable that this cluster may be extensively increased in the future and provide closely datable chronological information of much material in use at one moment. 18-37, some twenty deposits, form the very suggestively largest chronological cluster of a fairly limited period in this category. Probably no single event in the years they cover, according to present dating, from the latter years of the 4th century through the first quarter of the 3rd, is the cause of the disposal of the material in them. Several successive events seem more likely. There is indication that another earthquake may be responsible for one deposit (actually a group of deposits): 18, the Terracotta Factory of the Potters' Quarter. Whether or not other deposits in this cluster owe their disposal to this event is open to speculation and scrutiny. One thinks in this connection of the wholesale disposal of votives of the Asklepieion, represented by 20, and others not treated here. Perhaps also the abandonment of the later Tile Works, represented by 27 and 28, may have been involved. The political events of these troubled years may also be reflected in this cluster. Is the burial of the Gold Hoard of 19 to be connected with one such event? May the abandonment of the enormous cistern system, represented by 29-33, be due to another such event? Some deposits of the time seem more likely to be connected with construction rather than destruction, e.g. 36-37, which were involved in a terracing operation. Two deposits, 21-22, are connected by a stratigraphical relationship, a cistern constructed above a well in close sequence, though the nature of their fillings does not provide a particularly useful chronological sequence of material. A further cluster, 39-43, and perhaps 44, is conceivably an association of a different kind and worthy of scrutiny together for this reason, a topographical one, potentially perhaps as extensive a topographical grouping as those concerned with the history of the South Stoa. The wells and cisterns of this group all were located within the confines of a temple temenos, to a large extent still hypothetical, believed to have occupied in Hellenistic times the area later covered by the temenos of Temple E. It seems a fair possibility that all the members of this group may have been involved in operations connected with the clearing of the temenos area for construction. The present dating for the final filling of these wells and cistern in the third and last quarter of the 3rd century B.C. is based primarily on the catalogued material since at present the context material is not accessible for study. Further study of the context material when it becomes available[9] may conceivably reveal even closer contemporaneity in time of final deposit among these deposits than is now indicated. There is, of course, a further possibility that excavation within the considerable limits of the temenos will provide additional deposits also involved in the clearance of the temenos area and the construction of the temenos, thus forming an important cluster of the still extensively enigmatic 3rd century. The potentialities of the small cluster of two deposits, 46, 47, connected with the Mummian destruction, is, of course, readily apparent.

The second major category of deposits, 49-78, consists of grave groups. These afford the possibility of valuable lesser clusters of considerable importance for relative chronology and potentially important for absolute chronology also, in cases where closely datable coins are involved. A number of such clusters, the basis for each cluster being the presence in each of the grave groups of one or more examples of particular shape series, are seen in the list. One cluster, 57-69, for example, provides a closely knit sequence of grave groups which have been of considerable importance in the present study for chronology from the latter third quarter of the 4th century through the early years of the Hellenistic period. The cluster is bound together by the presence in its deposits of unguentaria or skyphoi of Attic type or both. The relative sequence these forms provide is pertinent also to the chronology of at least a dozen other shape series because of the differing components of each grave group. Some numismatic evidence present in this series may eventually yield greater precision for the cluster than is possible at present, and future additions to this important initial Hellenistic cluster should do much in the direction of chronological precision. It is conceivable that eventually, with the addition of further grave groups of the times yet to be excavated, it will be possible to form a closely interlocking mesh of such grave groups of the period, knitting together various clusters. The list makes the present paucity of single-burial grave groups of Hellenistic times in Corinth only too evident. Future filling of this important gap is much to be wished since it will contribute much to precision in dating of other kinds of deposits and, by chain reaction, to precision in dating of architectural structures and even ultimately, through linking with the deposits of the first category, to providing closer precision in the dating of those deposits which may have resulted from historical events in Hellenistic Corinth. Two of the grave groups in this cluster are, incidentally, in a stratigraphical relationship, 65 A and 65 B.

The third major category, 79-118, is composed of deposits which have to be considered in relationship to one another chronologically since in one way or another they are all concerned with the South Stoa: the planning and preparation for its construction; the actual construction and completion of the building itself; supplementary activities concerned with terracing in front of the building so as to make it accessible for use from the valley at the north (the later open area of the Roman Agora); the period of use of the Stoa in the Greek period; and, of course, the destruction of the building in 146 B.C. Deposits

---

[9] Re-organization of the inheritance of context material of many years of excavation at Corinth is currently being undertaken.

connected with one aspect of the history of the Stoa necessarily have to be considered chronologically in relation to those concerned with other aspects. A modification in date in respect to one deposit will in many instances affect the dating of others, one often controlling that of another. In the present study consideration of all these deposits in relation to one another has resulted in the opinion that the planning and preparation for the Stoa (condemnation of property existing in its area, negotiations probably in several instances with religious establishments, fund raising presumably, and the like) may have occupied the entire second quarter of the 4th century;[10] that construction of the building probably began around 350 B.C. or in the early third quarter of the 4th century;[11] that construction of it, the terracing and its paving to the north were complete, making it possible to use the building by *ca.* 330 B.C.; and that the Greek period of use of the Stoa extended from *ca.* 330 to 146 B.C. when Corinth was destroyed by Mummius. The indications provided by the deposits toward these conclusions are summarized below in connection with the individual deposits. The date of *ca.* 330 B.C. for the completion of the Stoa construction program and the beginning of its use, it should be noted, has been arrived at by a consideration of, on the one hand, the evidence of deposits associated with the planning and construction, and, on the other hand, the earliest material from the use fillings of the South Stoa shop wells, preserved to us despite probably successive cleanings of the wells, in a number of deposits. Though consideration of one kind of evidence alone might permit greater latitude in dating the completion of the Stoa program, consideration of both kinds vis-à-vis each other much reduces the possibility of latitude.[12]

With regard to the period of use of the Stoa in the Greek period and the chronological use here of material from the shop wells which served it (Deposits 95–118), the position adopted here in consideration of the various kinds of evidence is that the wells were constructed as an integral part of the building program[13] and came into use, if not actually during the construction, then at the time of completion of the entire building and terracing program. Thus they are here regarded as having been in the main in use from *ca.* 330 B.C. to the time of destruction with the one possible exception of 110, whose use seems to have been truncated earlier, and conceivably also that of 97. It seems inevitable that use over so long a period necessitated cleaning out the well accumulations at intervals, since no doubt these

[10] The lower limits of four deposits in the area eventually occupied by South Stoa terracing, 79–82, representative of several establishments, are indicative of this. They are on present dating graduated through the course of the second quarter. The establishments to which Deposits 87, 88, and 89 belonged were evidently also involved in planning and preparation, though these deposits also reflect actual Stoa construction activities.

[11] Primarily Deposits 83–93 in combination with evidence from the use fillings of various Stoa wells, especially 96, 109, 110, 111; see also below, pp. 218–223.

[12] The conclusions here with regard to the date of the Stoa are in general agreement, though with some modifications, with those reached by Professor Broneer (*S. Stoa*, pp. 94ff.) and with those reached on the date of the building on the basis of the architectural mouldings by Lucy Shoe Meritt (*ibid.*, p. 96). Different opinions have been expressed by R. Martin, *Rev. Et. Gr.*, LXIX, 1956, pp. 213–216, and by G. Roux, *L'Architecture de l'Argolide aux IVe et IIIe siècles avant J.-C.*, Paris, 1961. The latter (p. 348, footnote 6) says with reference to Professor Broneer's dating: "Je me rangerais volontiers à l'opinion de R. Martin (*R.E.G.* 69, 1956, pp. 213–216) qui propose d'abaisser la date de quelques decades." His preference as to a lower date is, however, unclear. On p. 414 the terracotta simas are dated 320–270 B.C.; on p. 421 the Ionic capitals are dated at the end of the 4th century; on p. 417 the Ionic interior columns are dated at the beginning of the 3rd century. One gets the impression of a building constructed from the top downward! One presumes that his dating is based on stylistic sequences of these various elements, the sequences being composed of examples from various cities and areas. Comparison between architectural and ceramic practice cannot of course be pressed, since different factors influencing the dating are present in each. The present writer, however, has observed that in the pottery products of different centers shapes, shape development, and decorative elements of comparable pots may differ strongly in both rate of change and in kind, and wonders if there may not be to some degree similar differences in the architectural practices of different centers. Conceivably a study of Corinthian architectural sequences might show a more rapid development than that of some other centers represented in the sequences studied by M. Roux. More advanced and developed architecture today is undoubtedly to be observed in large and wealthy cities than in the smaller and less prosperous.

[13] A structural consideration, among others, leads to this conclusion. It would seem necessary for them to have been plotted and laid out prior to the construction of the shop walls, for visibility, in order to have achieved their attested alignment with the Peirene channel which provided their water. See also Hill, *The Springs*, p. 62; for the plan, *ibid.*, pl. III, and Broneer, *S. Stoa*, plan IX.

often rose to high enough levels to cut off the flow of water through the small inlets from the Peirene channel.[14] Thus in the use accumulations of the wells probably in no case have we the full accumulation of the *ca.* 180 years of their use. Some material of the initial stages of accumulation is preserved to us in either catalogued or context material in a number of wells, notably Deposits 96, 109, 110, 111, and to some extent probably also in 95, 106, and 113. Material of the subsequent period of use is progressively more abundant, though truncated in range of period by varying degrees in the various wells and no doubt very much decimated in all through the cleanings. Evidently only Deposit 94, the circumstances of whose place of disposal perhaps did not require cleaning out and disposal elsewhere, provides a probably very complete accumulation of the period of use of the Stoa.

The general category of deposits related to the history of the South Stoa may well be increased through future excavations. A number of the shop wells remain to be excavated. In addition, further deposits pertinent to the planning and final terracing may be revealed (conceivably still sealed in place by the cobble pavement: see Deposit 91) in front of the building at the east where excavation seems not as yet to have been carried down to levels contemporary with the time of the Stoa.

[14] For the inlets see Hill, *The Springs*, p. 61, and Broneer, *S. Stoa*, pp. 59–60.

DEPOSIT SUMMARIES

I. DEPOSITS OTHER THAN FROM GRAVES AND THE SOUTH STOA

1. Agora SCW, Well at T–U: 2
Range in date: 600 to 540 B.C.

Bibliography:

Charles H. Morgan, *Hesperia*, XXII, 1953, p. 132, fig. 1: pp. 135–136; pl. 46, a, 1–3 (preliminary report).

Brann, pp. 350–374 (full publication of the deposit).

Summary:

The well was located at little less than two meters north of the stylobate of the South Stoa, in front of Shop XXVII (Morgan, *op. cit.*, p. 132, fig. 1: lower left, well cut by grave; cf. Broneer, *S. Stoa*, plan V). The filling of the well, which has a range in period from *ca.* 600 to 540 B.C., was evidently thrown in at one time (Brann, p. 350, footnote 2). It includes 126 pottery vessels of various categories. The question is raised, p. 121, footnote 8, as to whether or not **648** (C-53-134) actually belongs to the 6th century filling.

Objects published:

C-53-93: **239**   C-53-153: **235**
C-53-134: **648**

2. Southeast Building, Well at I: 23
Range in date: 6th century B.C., third quarter

Bibliography:

Oscar Broneer, *Hesperia*, XVI, 1947, pp. 237–238; pl. 55, 4–5 (preliminary report).

Weinberg, *The Southeast Building*, p. 4; plan I (brief summary).

Summary:

The well was located just west of the eastern line of inner supports of the building, between the second and third from the north (Weinberg, *The Southeast Building*, plan I; cf. *ibid.*, p. 5, fig. 1). The material from the filling of the shaft, which included 300 pottery vessels, lamps, terracottas, has been dated in the third quarter of the 6th century in the preliminary notices. Broneer, *op. cit.*, suggests that the pottery came from a shop or potters' establishment.

Objects published or noted:

C-47-748: **214**	C-47-751: **201**
C-47-749: **236**	C-47-752: p. 50[38]
C-47-750: **119**	C-47-755: **240**

3. Agora SC, Well at I–J: 24–25
Range in date: *ca.* 550 to 500–480 B.C.

Bibliography:

Charles H. Morgan II, *A.J.A.*, XLI, 1937, p. 547; p. 548, fig. 10; and pl. XIII, 2 (preliminary report).

Campbell, pp. 557–611 (full publication of deposit).

Summary:

The well was located *ca.* 7 meters north of the stylobate of the South Stoa in the area in front of Shop XXII (Morgan, *op. cit.*, pl. XIII, 2: VIth century well; cf. Broneer, *S. Stoa*, plan IV). The filling of the well, which has a range in period from *ca.* 550 to sometime between 500 and 480 B.C., was thrown in at one time. It included 222 pottery vessels of various categories, numerous lamps, some architectural tiles, loomweights, a terracotta and a stone palette.

Objects published or noted:

C-37-942: p. 107	C-37-1081: **203**
C-37-949: **202**	C-37-2048: p. 108[8]
C-37-972: **216**	C-37-2056: p. 57[44]
C-37-973: **215**	C-37-2058: p. 120[7]
C-37-984: p. 107	C-37-2059: p. 120[7]
C-37-985: p. 107	C-37-2060: p. 120[7]
C-37-1051: **204**	C-37-2062a: **693**
C-37-1066: p. 107	

4. Pit II in New Road west of Shear's House
Range in date: *ca.* 500 or early 5th century B.C.

Summary:

The pit was located in the line of the modern road running between Oakley House and Hadji Mustapha. The section of the road in which the pit was situated, excavated in 1931, evidently lay south of the atrium of the Roman building just outside the northwest corner of the precinct of Temple E (see Henry S. Robinson, *Corinth, A Brief History of the City and a Guide to the Excavations*, Athens, 1964, fig. 4). The dating of the material from the filling of the pit, 12 pottery vessels and one lamp, needs further study. At present it would seem to have been deposited about 500 B.C. or in the early years of the 5th century.

Objects published:

C-31-171: **217**   C-31-172: **218**

5. Isthmia, the Large Circular Pit
   Range in date: ca. 7th century, third quarter to ca. mid-5th century B.C.
   Bibliography:
   Oscar Broneer, *Hesperia*, XXVIII, 1959, pp. 301–303, and fig. 2; pp. 327–328, nos. 2, 8, and 11; pp. 334–336, nos. 4, 5, and 10; XXXI, 1962, pp. 1–3 and fig. 1; pp. 22–24, nos. 1–12.
   Oscar Broneer, *Isthmia*, II, pp. 135–136.

   Summary:
   An extremely large well which was, according to the preliminary reports, probably filled up at one time about mid-5th century B.C., the material in the filling evidently of considerable range in period including pottery as early as Early and Middle Corinthian. The objects from the pit are being studied by Professor D. A. Amyx who may well suggest modifications of the dates indicated here.

   Objects noted:

   IP 2303: p. 50[38]   IP 2352: p. 50[38]

6. Potters' Quarter, Road Deposit
   Range in date: from ca. 600 well into the 5th century B.C.
   Bibliography:
   Agnes N. Stillwell, *PQ* I, pp. 15, 21, and pl. 51; *PQ* II, p. 22 and pl. 60 (the deposit, terracotta figurines, lamps, and miscellaneous).

   Summary:
   "A thick layer of discarded material, mostly pottery, with many lamp fragments also, from the roadway outside the South Long Building and the North Long Building, particularly the latter. This material is datable throughout the 6th century and well into the 5th."

   Objects published:

   KP 361: **219**

7. Potters' Quarter, Deposit in Stelai Shrine A
   Range in date: 5th century B.C., first half
   Bibliography:
   Agnes N. Stillwell, *PQ* I, pp. 22–23, and pl. 51; *PQ* II, p. 22 and pl. 60 (the deposit, terracotta figurines, and a lamp).

   Summary:
   "A mass of vases, figurines, and a little other material found packed into a small walled en-

closure, and probably to be dated mainly in the first half of the 5th century."

Objects published:

KP 1312: **259**

8. Museum West, Well at K: 23
   Range in date: from ca. early 6th century perhaps into 5th century B.C., third quarter
   Bibliography:
   Saul S. Weinberg, *A.J.A.*, XLIII, 1939, pp. 596–598, figs. 7, a–b, 8, and 9 (preliminary report); *Hesperia*, XXIII, 1954, pp. 128–129, and footnotes 123, 127, 129, 131; pl. 30, m, b, d, g.

   Summary:
   The well was located in the area just north of the northeast corner of the foundations of Temple E (see *A.J.A.*, XLIII, 1939, p. 594, fig. 4, "Well"). There seems to have been no use filling in the well and it is reported to have been filled up at one time. The significant range in period represented by the objects from the filling, which included 366 pottery vessels, many lamps and terracottas, loom weights and some objects of bone and stone, is from the beginning of the 6th century to the middle of the 5th century B.C., perhaps into the third quarter.

   Objects published or noted:

C-39-7: **228**	C-39-102: **209**
C-39-22: p. 57[44]	C-39-168: p. 66[60]
C-39-86: **253**	C-39-211: **555**
C-39-99: **208**	C-39-253: **200**
C-39-100: **227**	C-39-278: **688**
C-39-101: **222**	

9. Potters' Quarter, Circular South Shrine
   Range in date: 5th century B.C., third quarter
   Bibliography:
   Agnes N. Stillwell, *PQ* I, p. 32 and pl. 51; *PQ* II, p. 23 and pl. 60.

   Summary:
   "A small walled enclosure around which a great number of vases and figurines were found, all probably belonging to the third quarter of the 5th century."

   Objects published:

   KP 367: **237**

10–12.

   These three well deposits form a chronological group with a common lower limit of ca. 420 B.C. Conceivably other deposits in Corinth will be found, on further study, to be suitable for addition to this group.
   Pease, p. 257, footnote 3: "Three wells in the southern part of the Agora (this well [i.e. 10] and S:11 [i.e. 11] and K:14 [i.e. 12] in the

South Basilica) were filled in contemporaneously, perhaps as the result of some sudden catastrophe, as one of the earthquakes familiar in Corinth. In the Basilica Wells (i.e. 11 and 12) the pottery was thrown in by kinds, as though swept in series off the shelves of a pottery shop." Miss Pease's date for 10 has been fully adopted here and has proved very satisfactory indeed in relative placement of shape series. Her date for 11 and 12 have also been adopted. No further analysis of them has, however, been attempted here. They seem very worthy of future attention and study since they will presumably supplement our present knowledge of pottery of this time.

Weinberg, *The Southeast Building*, p. 59, evidently refers to both 11 and 12 in the following: "The first well to be filled was that in the southwest corner of the cryptoporticus; the pottery in it belongs largely to the early fifth century and some of it is even earlier. A well in the southwest corner of the core, about ten meters northeast of the other one, was also filled in the fifth century and much of the debris is from the first half of that century." The date given by Weinberg for 11, "largely to the early fifth century and some of it is even earlier," is evidently due to a clerical error in the excavation records whereby the objects from 11 were assigned to a different well in the Basilica.

10. Agora SW, Well at E–K: 30–37
    Range in date: 460 to 420 B.C.
    Bibliography:
    Richard Stillwell, *A.J.A.*, XL, 1936, pp. 41–42, and fig. 20 (preliminary report).
    Pease, pp. 257–316 (full publication of deposit).
    Location:
    In "the area at the foot of the great stair or ramp that led through the central portion of the West Shops up to the precinct in front of Temple E."
    Summary:
    The entire filling of the well was thrown in at one time. The objects in the filling, including 343 catalogued pottery vessels of various categories, range in period from 460 to 420 B.C.
    Objects published or noted:

C-34-347: **220**	C-34-946: **283**
C-34-923: p. 115	C-34-947: **282**
C-34-926: **617**	C-34-948: **284**
C-34-940: p. 133	C-34-955: p. 108[8]
C-34-943: **669**	C-34-956: p. 108[8]
C-34-944: **676**	C-34-979: p. 107
C-34-945: **689**	C-34-1020: **221**

C-34-1028: **751**	C-34-1139a: **677**
C-34-1046: p. 29[14]	C-34-1194: **285**
C-34-1092: p. 66[60]	C-34-1195: **298**
C-34-1093: p. 66[60]	C-34-1196: **299**
C-34-1095: p. 29[14]	C-34-2513: **618**
C-34-1135a: **678**	C-34-2514: **619**

11. South Basilica, Well at S:11
    Range in date: 5th century to 420 B.C.
    Location:
    In the southwest corner of the cryptoporticus of the South Basilica: see Weinberg, *The Southeast Building*, p. 59 and plan V.
    Objects published or noted:

C-36-1057: **750**	C-36-1116: p. 57[44]
C-36-1074: **230**	

12. South Basilica, Well at K:14
    Range in date: 5th century to 420 B.C.
    Location:
    In the southwest corner of the core of the South Basilica: see Weinberg, *The Southeast Building*, p. 59 and plan V.
    Note:
    The paucity of objects catalogued from the well vis-à-vis the comments of Miss Pease and of the excavator in his notebook record indicate that the contents of the well have not been fully mended up.
    Objects published:
    none

13. Potters' Quarter, Rectangular South Pit
    Range in date: 5th century B.C., end of the third quarter and beginning of the last
    Bibliography:
    Agnes N. Stillwell, *PQ* I, p. 31; *PQ* II, p. 23 and pl. 60, D 11 (the deposit, terracotta figurines, lamps, and miscellaneous).
    Summary:
    "A cutting containing mostly pottery, with some mould fragments and figurines, which seem to be datable around the third quarter of the 5th century, probably at the end of that quarter and the beginning of the next."
    Objects published:

KP 715: **229**	KP 963: **246**
KP 719: **238**	KP 964: **241**
KP 930: **223**	KP 2503: **622**

14. St. John's, unidentified well
    Range in date: ca. 450 to 375 B.C.
    Bibliography:
    Possible reference in Richard Stillwell, *A.J.A.*, XL, 1936, p. 41.
    Summary:
    This is a group of vessels all of which have the same record of provenience. Their character sug-

gests that they belong to the use filling of a well. The range in period which they represent is from *ca.* 450 to 375 B.C. The information available about them indicates that the well from which they presumably derive was located in the area of St. John's (for this area see Stillwell, *op. cit.*, pl. I) and dug in April, 1935. Conceivably it is the second of the two wells referred to by Stillwell, *op. cit.*, p. 41:

> "In clearing the area at the foot of the great stair or ramp that led through the central portion of the West Shops up to the precinct in front of Temple "E", two wells were found, one excavated in the fall, the other in the spring campaign."

The first of the two wells is that published by Pease, pp. 257–316 (Deposit 10 here).

Objects published or noted:

C-35-638: p. 137	C-35-641: p. 137[22]
C-35-640: **733**	C-35-642: p. 137[22]

15. South Basilica, Well at IV–15
Range in date: 4th century B.C., first and early second quarters
Bibliography:
　　Weinberg, *The Southeast Building*, p. 59 and plan V (brief mention).
Summary:
　　The well was located in the southern part of the east aisle of the cryptoporticus. The filling of the well, which included 20 pottery vessels, a terracotta, and two loomweights, seems to be primarily of the first and early second quarters of the 4th century.
Objects published:

C-36-969: **336**	C-36-976: **211**
C-36-971: **664**	C-36-977: **232**
C-36-973: **250**	C-36-986: **681**

16. Isthmia, Pottery Pit in Theater Cave
Date: ca. 350 B.C.
Bibliography:
　　Oscar Broneer, *Hesperia*, XXXI, 1962, p. 6; pp. 24–25, nos. 13–21; pl. 2, c; pl. 3, b; and pl. 12, a–f; *Isthmia*, II, p. 41 and note 37.
Summary:
　　A group of complete vessels, including a fine-ware trefoil olpe, coarse-ware, blister-ware, and cooking-ware vessels, stacked upside down in a pithos set in one corner of the western court of the Theater Cave. They are here regarded as having been in use contemporaneously and to have been deposited about 350 B.C. on the basis of present studies of the series of vessels to which those noted below belong.
Objects noted:

IP 2230: p. 147[16]	IP 2239 A: pp. 125[12], 130
IP 2231: p. 147[16]	IP 2239 B: pp. 129, 130
IP 2232: p. 109[9]	IP 2240: p. 109[9]
IP 2234: pp. 120[7], 138[24]	IP 2241: pp. 120[7], 138[24]
IP 2235: pp. 120[7], 139[24]	IP 2243: pp. 122[9], 138[24]
IP 2236: pp. 120[7], 138[24]	

17. New Museum East, "Well J" at O–P, 10
Range in date: 4th century B.C., third quarter
Bibliography:
　　Saul S. Weinberg, *Hesperia*, XVII, 1948, pp. 239–240, no. 6, and pl. 88, 6 (publication of one object).
Summary:
　　The "well", evidently actually a fairly shallow pit (L. 1.10; W. 0.55; Depth 1.00 m.), was located *ca.* 5.00 m. west of the northwest corner of the northern group of the West Shops (see Weinberg, *op. cit.*, p. 198, fig. 1: the well is not shown, but it was partly under the eastern end of the dogleg rubble wall at this point). Weinberg, *op. cit.*, p. 239, has suggested that this pit was filled at the same time as Deposits 36 and 37, which are now seen to have been filled *ca.* 275 B.C. The two pottery vessels catalogued from the filling of the pit do not bear out this assumption since both seem to be of the third quarter of the 4th century. Comments of the excavator in his field notebook, however, indicate that the sherds from the pit have never been mended up. It has not been possible to examine them in connection with the present study.
Objects published:

　　C-40-465: **363**

18. Potters' Quarter, Deposits in the Terracotta Factory
Date:
　　In publishing the terracotta figurines, moulds, lamps, and miscellaneous objects from the Terracotta Factory, Mrs. Stillwell (*PQ* II, pp. 23–24) distinguished nine deposits, indicating that two were of the late 5th century and that some of the others were of the third quarter of the 4th century B.C., i.e. presumably of the time of the destruction of the Terracotta Factory by an earthquake (*PQ* I, pp. 37 and 47). At present (1966) Mrs. Stillwell's assignment of pots to deposits in the Terracotta Factory has not been established and, accordingly, in the present study all pots from it which are published or cited have been put under a single heading. It seems clear that (though some undoubtedly are very much earlier) all the pots from the Terracotta Factory will be anterior to one lower limit in date, the time of the earthquake because of which the factory was abandoned. Many presumably were currently in use or stored in the factory at that time. Mrs.

Stillwell, in discussing the numismatic evidence for the destruction of the building, considered two alternative dates: sometime after 338 B.C. or after 316 B.C., concluding with a preference for the earlier. In the course of this study consideration of the Terracotta Factory pottery as a whole was not feasible. In connection with the few pots from the factory which have actually been included here (with the kind permission of Mr. J. L. Benson) the earlier date has generally been accepted or has seemed reasonable. In one case, **185**, a date in the last quarter of the 4th century has seemed obligatory, providing some indication that the dating of the pottery from the factory as a whole should be reviewed. It is expected that a prospective study by Mr. Martin Price on the Corinthian bronze Pegasos/Trident coin series, of which eight were included in the numismatic evidence for the destruction, will have bearing in reconsidering the date of the material involved in it. A list which presumably includes all the specific coins considered by Mrs. Stillwell in this connection has been prepared by the present author and is on file in the Corinth Museum.

Bibliography:
PQ I, pp. 34–49, *passim; PQ* II, pp. 23–24.

Location of factory and the deposits:
PQ II, pl. 60.

Objects published:
Terracotta figurines, moulds, lamps, and miscellaneous objects:
see lists, PQ II, pp. 23–24.

Pottery:

KP 121: **234**	KP 688: **260**
KP 218: **185**	KP 701: **565**
KP 230: **271**	KP 702: **277**
KP 231: **272**	KP 834: **244**
KP 677: **569**	KP 835: **264**
KP 682: **278**	KP 837: **567**
KP 684: **265**	KP 876: **273**
KP 685: **581**	KP 2525: **256**

19. North Stoa, Gold Hoard
Date: between 325 and 315 B.C.

Bibliography:
F. J. deWaele, *A.J.A.,* XXXV, 1931, pp. 396, 405, and pp. 418–422, figs. 1 and 11, and pl. 6 (preliminary report).

Katharine M. Edwards, *Hesperia,* VI, 1937, pp. 246–247 (preliminary notice of coins).

Sidney P. Noe, *A Bibliography of Greek Coin Hoards* (2nd ed., *Numismatic Notes and Monographs,* no. 78), New York, 1937, p. 81, no. 267.

Scranton, *The Lower Agora,* p. 174, pl. 73, and plans K and M (comment on hoard in relation to North Stoa).
Davidson, *Minor Objects,* p. 256, no. 2055, pl. 109 (the gold necklace).
Margaret Thompson and G. R. Edwards, *A.J.A.,* LXXIV, 1970, pp. 343–350, joint studies of the coins and the pottery saucer.
The account of the excavation of the coins has also been consulted:
F. J. deWaele, Field Notebook 109, pp. 40, 41, 43, 44, Corinth Museum.

Summary:
This group consists of a hoard of 51 gold staters, now in the Numismatic Museum in Athens, and a pottery saucer, **183**. A gold necklace, now Athens, National Museum, 15457, is probably to be associated. The place of concealment was a cutting in bedrock, 1.20 m. long, in the form of a tube cut in half lengthwise, widening out at one point to a hemispherical hollow 0.10 m. in diameter. This lay at the northeast corner of the eleventh of the preserved internal piers (counting from the east) of the North Stoa beneath an earth filling 0.10 m. deep whose surface formed the floor of the building. Fifty of the coins lay in the hemispherical hollow, which was covered, apparently deliberately, by the saucer. The fifty-first lay a little toward the west in the cutting. The necklace was found "just beside the hoard, a little to east, and not immediately on the rock" (deWaele, Notebook). DeWaele, at the time of excavation, regarded the necklace as not having been buried, but later (*A.J.A.,* XXXV, 1931, p. 405) associated it with the coins and the saucer. In the preliminary notices the coins have been assigned in part (41) to Philip II of Macedon (359–336 B.C.), and in part (10) to Alexander the Great (336–323 B.C.). There has been general agreement in them about the date of concealment. DeWaele: "at the end of the fourth century." K. M. Edwards: "The date of hiding cannot be far from the end of the Macedonian Period." Scranton: "The proportion [of staters of Philip to those of Alexander] would indicate that the collection was made during the lifetime of Alexander, and very likely the burial occurred during the same general period." The attribution of the coins will be further discussed by Miss Thompson. In the meantime the present writer suggests that the saucer was made in the early last quarter of the 4th century and that the date of burial which it seems to indicate may lie between *ca.* 325 and 315 B.C.

Objects published:
Coins and necklace: see bibliography above.
Pottery: C-30-150: **183**

20. Asklepieion, Votive Deposit V, in Well QQ 22

Range in date: ca. 425 to 4th century B.C., last
quarter

Bibliography:

Asklepieion, pp. 113–142. *Votives:* nos. 2, 3, 9,
11–14, 17, 20–25, 28–30, 32–36, 38–41, 43–45,
47, 49, 50, 52–56, 59–62, 65–72, 77, 80–82,
84–87, 91–102, 106–108, 112, 115, 117. *Lamps:*
nos. 1–8, 10–12. *Pottery:* nos. 6–78. *Terracotta
figurines:* nos. 38, 39.

Saul S. Weinberg, *Hesperia,* XXIII, 1954, p.
126 and footnote 111; pl. 28, a.

Summary:

The well was located *ca.* 2.50 m. north of the
north wall of the Temple of Asklepios (indicated
on plan of the Early Temenos, *Asklepieion,* p. 9,
fig. 3). There was no use filling in this well
(*Asklepieion,* p. 134). The character of the objects
at various levels in the well suggests that the
filling was introduced at one time. Roebuck
(*Asklepieion,* p. 113) came to the conclusion that
this deposit and the two others (II, IV) were
made at the same time, shortly after 315 B.C.
The range of period which he suggests that the
objects represent (*Asklepieion,* p. 137) lies between
the last quarter of the 5th century and the time
of the deposit. The pottery studied here falls
within this range, from *ca.* 425 B.C. into the
third quarter of the 4th century. The filling also
included numerous lamps and terracottas.

Objects published or noted:

C-31-66: **300**	C-31-421: p. 96[92]
C-31-390: **338**	C-31-443: p. 109[9]
C-31-391: **327**	C-31-448: p. 109[9]
C-31-405: p. 29[14]	C-31-451: p. 71[66]
C-31-406: p. 34[19]	C-31-453: **339**
C-31-409: **66**	C-31-454: **340**
C-31-417: **761**	C-31-455: **337**
C-31-418: **756**	

21–22. These two deposits form a group since 22 is
stratigraphically later than 21. The mouth of 21,
a well, was covered by a wall dividing the two
chambers of 22, a cistern complex, and the floors
of the chambers.

**21. Baths of Aphrodite, Section C. Well I (West
Well)**

Range in date: use fill: late 5th century to
375 B.C.; dump fill: late 7th century to
4th century B.C., third quarter

Bibliography:

Henry S. Robinson, *Hesperia,* XXXI,
1962, p. 124.

Summary:

The well was located near the west end
of Trench II of the Baths of Aphrodite
excavations (Robinson, *op. cit.,* p. 123, fig.

8). Its use fill accumulated during the
period from the latter 5th century to *ca.* 375
B.C. It was filled up during the third quarter
of the 4th century, the material in this fill
ranging in date from the late 7th century
to the time of deposit.

Objects noted:

C-60-244: p. 145[8]	C-60-247: p. 137[21]
C-60-246: p. 137[22]	

**22. Baths of Aphrodite, Cistern Complex in
Room L**

Range in date: 4th century, second quarter
to *ca.* 300 B.C.

Bibliography:

Henry S. Robinson, *Hesperia,* XXXI,
1962, p. 124, and footnote 98.

Summary:

This cistern complex of two chambers
was located in the western part of Trench
II of the Baths of Aphrodite excavations
(Robinson, *op. cit.,* p. 123, fig. 8) above the
well, Deposit 21. It was evidently constructed
in the third quarter of the 4th century and
served as a cistern to about 300 B.C. The
filling then employed for the northern chamber, which was not fully excavated, included
pottery with a range in period from at
least the second quarter of the 4th century
to the time of deposit. The pottery from
the southern chamber, filled at the same
time, was more nearly contemporary with
the time of deposit. No objects from this
chamber have been catalogued.

Objects published or noted:

C-60-250: **343**	C-60-255: **773**
C-60-251: p. 30[14]	C-60-261: **744**
C-60-254 a, b: **556 a, b**	

23. Temple E, Cistern II

Range in date: 4th century, second quarter to *ca.*
300 B.C.

Bibliography:

Richard Stillwell, Robert L. Scranton, and
Sarah Elizabeth Freeman, *Corinth,* I, ii,
Architecture, Cambridge, Mass., 1941, p. 169;
figs. 106 and 108; pl. XVIII.

Summary:

The cistern was located at the southwest corner
of the Lower Foundation, that is, the foundation
for the Roman predecessor of Temple E (*op. cit.,*
pl. XVIII). Whether there was one or more
fillings has not been determined, and the material
from the fill has not been fully examined. The
range in period of the catalogued pottery appears
to be from the second quarter of the 4th century
to *ca.* 300 B.C. The material in the filling also in-

cluded some lamps, loom weights, a terracotta figurine, a cover tile, and four coins.
Objects published or noted:

C-32-48: p. 29[14]   C-32-50: **346**

24. Well at Kretika
Date: 4th century B.C., last quarter
Summary:

Two pieces of pottery of the last quarter of the 4th century B.C. are reported to have been "found at Kretika in a well dug by the Gylaina brothers." Kretika is understood to be the name of an area of the town of Old Corinth in the vicinity of the Tile Works.
Objects published:

CP-2169: **730**

25–28. Four deposits of the Tile Works

Four deposits come from the Tile Works, which was located just outside the city wall to the north, between the Long Walls to Lechaion. Its location is indicated by Henry S. Robinson, *Corinth, A Brief History of the City and a Guide to the Excavations*, American School of Classical Studies, Athens, 1964, plan I, at 6. These four form a chronological group. Two are connected with the earlier establishment here, and two with the Later Kiln. A brief report of the excavations appears in *Arch. Anz.*, LV, 1940, cols. 205–206.

25–26.

These two deposits from the Tile Works form a close, earlier unit, since, according to the excavator's summary, the two wells from which they came were put out of use and filled at the same time, in the "early Vth century (1st half of the century)," in connection with the destruction and abandonment of the earlier establishment in this area, and the construction of the later. The two wells were located within five meters of one another in the southwestern part of the excavated area near to the Early Kiln.

25. Tile Works, Well B, at R'–S', 2–3
Date: ca. 500 B.C.
Summary:

The well was located in the southwestern part of the excavated area, *ca.* 16 m. west of the west side of the Later Kiln. There was no use filling. Three separate fills were noted. Only three pieces of pottery, all from the topmost fill, were catalogued. The two published here are believed to be of *ca.* 500 B.C.
Objects published:

C-40-39: **225**   C-40-40: **226**

26. Tile Works, Well C, at L'–N', 6–8
Range in date: late 6th century and 5th century B.C., first half
Bibliography:

Saul S. Weinberg, *Hesperia*, XXIII, 1954, p. 130, fig. 2, c, and footnote 132 (publication of one object).
Summary:

This well was located in the southwestern part of the area excavated, *ca.* 11 to 12 m. west of the west side of the Later Kiln and *ca.* 4.50 m. northeast of 25. There was no use filling. Arthur W. Parsons, in his field summary of the well, dated the filling in the "1st ½ of the Vth century or earlier, mostly late VIth."
Objects published:
none

27–28.

These two deposits are connected as 27, a well, evidently served the Later Kiln during the later part of the period when it was in operation, and 28, the filling in the Later Kiln, was introduced after the Kiln went out of use.

27. Tile Works, Well A, at I–N, 59–64
Range in date: use fill, 4th century B.C., second to last quarters
  later fills: 1. 4th century, last quarter
  2. 5th century to early 2nd century B.C.
Summary:

This well was located *ca.* 22 m. north of the front of the Later Kiln. The excavator believed that this well was probably used as a water supply for the period in which the Later Kiln was in use. There was a use filling, from which all the pottery published here comes. The catalogued pottery from the use fill ranged in period from the second quarter into the last quarter of the 4th century. There were evidently two additional fills, the first probably of about the time when the well was abandoned as a water supply, the second (topmost) probably a supplementary fill introduced appreciably later, composed of material of a considerable range in period, from the 5th century into the early 2nd century B.C.
Objects published or noted:

C-40-56: **69**   C-40-61: **318**
C-40-57: **39**   C-40-62: p. 45[30]
C-40-59: **342**   C-40-63: **634**
C-40-60: **319**   C-40-64: p. 113[14]

28. Tile Works, Fill of Later Kiln

Range in date: two earlier fills, *ca.* 350 to 3rd century B.C., first quarter

Summary:

According to the excavator's field notes, "No fill that could be ascribed definitely to the kiln's period of use was found," and "all the pottery obtained from the kiln represented the period after it went out of use." Two fills entered the kiln simultaneously, and two others subsequently. The pottery published here is all from the two earlier fills. The catalogued and context pottery from them has a range in period from *ca.* 350 into the first quarter of the 3rd century B.C. Presumably, bearing in mind the use filling of Deposit 27 which served the kiln, the Later Kiln went out of use around 300 B.C. and the two earlier fills were washed in from the slopes above, bearing with them appreciably earlier material, in the early years of the 3rd century.

Objects published or noted:

C-40-21: **371**	C-40-29: **657**
C-40-22: **138**	C-40-32: **372**
C-40-24: **574**	C-40-34: p. 37[22]

29–32. Four deposits in Anaploga Water Tunnel System

These four deposits form a connected group since all are fillings of manholes of side branches of the Anaploga Water Tunnel System. Three of the manholes were located at intervals in one branch and one in the second. The main line of the system, not fully excavated as yet, may have drawn water from the fountain of Hadji Mustapha, at the bottom of the north slope of Acrocorinth. Its attested course runs from a point northwest of the fountain to a considerable distance further northwest, north of the village of Hagioi Anargyroi. The two branches ran on separate courses from it toward the north slope of Acrocorinth. The system has been described by Henry S. Robinson in *Hesperia*, XXXVIII, 1969 pp. 1–35. At present it is clear that the system was in use as early as the 4th century B.C.

29–31.

Date:

It seems a good possibility, though further study will be needed, that the three manholes of the western branch were put out of use at one time as part of a single operation. The original fillings which were present or introduced at the time of the abandonment of each have, on present information, the same lower limit, in the close vicinity of 300 B.C. Each manhole in the course of time received additional, supplemental fillings, since the tunnels connecting them were conducive to settling.

29. Anaploga Water Tunnel System, Manhole 7

Summary:

The original abandonment filling included four complete vessels which probably represent the last year of use of the cistern. One is here dated in the last quarter of the 4th century B.C. The three others, coarse wine amphorae, seem suitable to this date. A subsequent filling, of the early 3rd century, including quantities of small fragments of pottery from Geometric times to the 4th century B.C., evidently filtered in around them and filled the shaft to a high level. A final supplementary filling at the top, including fragments of Classical pottery, was evidently introduced in the 5th century after Christ.

Objects published:

C-63-687: **741**

30. Anaploga Water Tunnel System, Manhole 8

Summary:

The original abandonment filling included a number of complete vessels, which may represent the last year of use of the cistern, as well as sherds (infiltration from later fills?) from Geometric to Early Hellenistic times. Two subsequent fillings were probably introduced in the Hellenistic period prior to 146 B.C. The fourth filling may conceivably have been introduced during the period 146 to 44 B.C. when Corinth lay desolate. Some of the material probably is of pre-destruction times. An amphora handle has been dated by Miss Virginia Grace in the early 1st century B.C. Other pieces conceivably, but not certainly, are of the same time. The two latest fillings were evidently introduced after the foundation of the Roman colony in 44 B.C., the last perhaps in the 2nd century after Christ.

Objects published:

C-63-717: **707**	C-63-718: **629**

31. Anaploga Water Tunnel System, Manhole 10

Summary:

The original abandonment filling, I, included material of the third and last quarters of the 4th century B.C. Two subsequent fillings were necessitated during the course of the 3rd century and the first half of the 2nd century. The catalogued pottery from filling IV suggests that this filling was introduced closely prior to the destruction of Corinth in 146 B.C. The final filling entered the cistern in the early Roman period, receiving further infiltration until the 3rd or 4th century after Christ.

Objects published or noted:

Fill I : C-65-289: p. 37[22]
Fill IV: C-65-96: p. 91[87]   C-65-98: **796**
   C-65-97: pp. 89–90, 180[44]

32. Anaploga Water Tunnel System, Manhole 11

It is within possibility that this manhole, of the eastern branch of the Anaploga Cistern System, was put out of use at the same time as the three preceding, but this must await further study.

Range in date: ca. 350 to 3rd century B.C., last quarter

Summary:

The material found in this manhole has not at present (1966) been mended up. Whether there was one or more fillings has not been determined. The range in period of all the material found in the manhole and in the tunnel is from *ca.* 350 to the last quarter of the 3rd century B.C. with a strong emphasis on the earlier years of this period.

Objects published:

C-64-335: **802**   C-64-386: **472**
C-64-375: **515**

33. North of School, Well R

Range in date: 6th century to 3rd century B.C., first quarter or later

Bibliography:

Weinberg, *The Southeast Building,* p. 59 and plan V.

Summary:

The well was located beneath the footing trench of the north wall of the core of the South Basilica (Weinberg, *The Southeast Building,* plan V). Only six objects from this well have been catalogued, those recovered sufficiently complete for immediate cataloguing during excavation. From the comments of the excavator in his field notebook it is evident that the material from the well has never been mended up. The records suggest that there was no use filling. The filling above, if it was a single filling (which is not yet known), was

introduced at least as late as *ca.* 280 B.C. and perhaps still later in the 3rd century. It was evidently composed of material with a considerable range in period, possibly from as early as the 6th century. Weinberg, *The Southeast Building,* p. 59, "... of fourth century date ...," with reference to this well, is to be emended.

Objects noted:

C-34-278: p. 29[14]   C-34-300: p. 87[81]

34. Baths of Aphrodite, Well II (East Well)

Range in date: 7th century to *ca.* 275 or early second quarter of 3rd century B.C.

Bibliography:

Henry S. Robinson, *Hesperia,* XXXI, 1962, pp. 125–126, pl. 46, e; pl. 47, a, c, d.

Summary:

The well was located just to the east of the Turkish Stair of the Baths of Aphrodite (Robinson, *op. cit.,* p. 123, fig. 8, Trench II). The use filling accumulated during the period from *ca.* 330 to *ca.* 275 B.C. It was filled and put out of use, apparently in one operation, about 275 B.C. or in the early second quarter of the 3rd century, the material from this filling having a wide range in period from as early as the 7th century B.C. down to the time of deposit.

Objects published or noted:

C-60-263: p. 30[14]   C-60-285: p. 113[14]
C-60-269: p. 40[26]   C-60-287: **746**
C-60-270: **745**   C-60-288: **724**
C-60-280: **320**   C-60-289: **735**
C-60-283: **552**   C-60-290: **743**

35. Museum West, Manhole at G:2

Range in date: ca. 400 to *ca.* 275 B.C.

Bibliography:

Saul S. Weinberg, *A.J.A.,* XLIII, 1939, p. 593, fig. 5, and p. 596.

Summary:

The manhole was located in the area to the north of the northeast corner of the foundation of Temple E (see Weinberg, *op. cit.,* p. 594, fig. 4, manhole at upper left corner of trench). There may have been more than one fill. The range in period of the catalogued pottery, 55 pieces, is from *ca.* 400 to *ca.* 275 B.C.

Objects published:

C-38-560: p. 45[30]   C-38-571: **620**
C-38-563: p. 45[30]   C-38-592: **762**

36–37.
These two deposits, from a well and a cistern, form a chronological group. Both the well and the cistern are regarded as having been put out of use and filled at the same time in consequence of the terracing of the area in which they were

located. This is discussed by Saul S. Weinberg, *Hesperia*, XVII, 1948, pp. 229–240. The date of the filling of the well and cistern, and consequently the date of the terracing operation, suggested by Weinberg has now been lowered to *ca.* 275 B.C. because of re-attribution of some of the pertinent coins by Martin Price.

36. New Museum East, Well A
  Range in date: 5th century, last quarter
    to *ca.* 275 B.C.
  Bibliography:
    Weinberg, *op. cit.*, pp. 229–235, pls. 85–86, "Group E" (publication of 25 selected pieces).
  Summary:
    The well was located *ca.* 4.00 m. west of the back wall of the second from the north of the northern group of the West Shops (see Weinberg, *op. cit.*, p. 198, fig. 1, "4th century well, E"). The well was evidently in use over a long period. The identity of the objects from the use filling is, however, not known. The pottery from the well which has been studied indicates a range in period from the last quarter of the 5th century down to the time of the final filling in *ca.* 275 B.C.
  Objects published or noted:

C-40-393: p. 45[30]	C-40-433: **137**
C-40-399: **60**	C-40-434: **95**
C-40-407: **311**	C-40-435: **710**
C-40-413: **301**	C-40-437: **70**
C-40-419: p. 139[26]	C-40-439: **357**
C-40-423: **763**	C-40-440: **439**
C-40-424: **766**	C-40-444: **449**
C-40-432: **139**	

37. New Museum East, Cistern at I–L, 15–16
  Range in date: ca. 4th century, third quarter
    to *ca.* 275 B.C.
  Bibliography:
    Weinberg, *op. cit.*, pp. 229–230; 235–239, pls. 87 and 88, b–d, "Group F" (publication of 12 selected objects).
  Summary:
    The cistern was located *ca.* 6.00 m. west of the back wall of the northernmost of the northern group of the West Shops (Weinberg, *op. cit.*, p. 198, fig. 1, "Cistern F"). The entire filling was introduced in a single operation. The significant range in period of the pottery is from at least the third quarter of the 4th century (perhaps still earlier) down to the time of the filling in *ca.* 275 B.C. The attribution of some of the coins in Weinberg's list, *op. cit.*, p. 236,

has been twice changed since his publication. Among the changes, two, to Antigonos Gonatas, affect the lower limit of the range in period of the fill. The pottery is in general agreement with placement of the lower limit shortly after the beginning of his reign, in 279 B.C.
  Objects published or noted:

C-40-16: p. 2[3]	C-40-468: p. 37[22]
C-40-467: **136**	

38. Well by the Excavation Dump
  Range in date: use fill, *ca.* 350 to 3rd century B.C.,
    second quarter
    upper filling, *ca.* 350 to 250 B.C.
  Bibliography:
    Henry S. Robinson, *Hesperia*, XXXI, 1962, pp. 116–118, pl. 45, a–b (preliminary report).
  Summary:
    The well was located about 600 m. southwest of Temple E. For its position see the plan, *Hesperia*, XXXI, 1962, p. 96, fig. 1, at E. The dating of the fillings in the well provided by the present author in Robinson, *op. cit.*, p. 117, has been since modified. The range in period of the pottery in the use filling extends from *ca.* 350 into the second quarter of the 3rd century B.C. The upper limit is, however, provided by a vessel of extremely durable fabric, C-60-73, hence the time of the actual beginning of use of the well may not actually have been quite so early. The well was put out of use with a filling composed of successive but evidently almost contemporary dumpings, the range in period represented in the catalogued and context material from it being much the same as that of the use filling, from *ca.* 350 to perhaps as late as 250 B.C. Material derived from house construction in the upper filling may suggest that the well was abandoned because of destruction of some kind (perhaps no more than for peaceful new construction) of the house it served. Some of the pottery listed below comes from the use filling, some from the upper filling. **625** is probably, but not certainly, from this well.
  Objects published or noted:

C-60-58: **190**	C-60-68: **776**
C-60-60: **649**	C-60-69: **446**
C-60-61: p. 121[7]	C-60-70: **404**
C-60-62: p. 113[14]	C-60-71: **453**
C-60-63: **21**	C-60-72: p. 50[36]
C-60-64: **23**	C-60-73: p. 40[26]
C-60-67: **625**	

39–43. These five deposits seem good candidates for a group to be studied together in the future for both chronological and topographical purposes.

The wells and cisterns from which they come were filled up, according to the present chronology of Hellenistic pottery and the information (unfortunately incomplete) available, within a period of about 50 years, between the late second quarter and the early last quarter of the 3rd century B.C. Study of them as a unit and examination of their context material, not now feasible, may conceivably show that they are more nearly contemporary in filling up than is now indicated. It is possible that their filling up may have been caused by a construction program of a Hellenistic temple and temenos in the area above the Greek "Agora" to the west. The possibilities of the existence of such a temple and temenos have been discussed by Henry S. Robinson, *The Urban Development of Ancient Corinth*, American School of Classical Studies, Athens, 1965, pp. 17–21, and the area which they may have occupied, corresponding to that later occupied by Temple E and its temenos, is indicated on his plan of Corinth in *ca.* 150 B.C., p. 18, fig. 12. All five deposits were located within the line of the temenos as indicated there, at various points within *ca.* 20 m. south of its northern boundary. Four were situated in the northeast quadrant of this area, beneath the present Corinth Museum, the fifth lay just within the northwest corner of the temenos. Professor Robinson's suggestion is based in part on the unpublished work of Professor William B. Dinsmoor. It is understood that Professor Dinsmoor believed that the front line of the later West Shops, restored in a solid line in Robinson's fig. 12, was originally the east wall of the Hellenistic temenos. This wall, which would have served also as a terrace wall, is to be distinguished from the earlier terracing, of *ca.* 275 B.C., with which Deposits 36 and 37 are connected.

39. New Museum, "Well" (actually Cistern) 41a
Range in date: 4th century, second quarter to 3rd century B.C., third quarter
Summary:

The location of the cistern is best indicated by reference to a plan of the area immediately to the east of it, *Hesperia*, XVII, 1948, p. 198, fig. 1. It was approximately 22 m. west of the back wall of the West Shops and *ca.* 19 m. south of the south face of the south wall of the temenos of Temple C, probably within the section of the Corinth Museum shown on that plan. Whether there was one fill or more is not known. The catalogued pottery indicates that the significant range in period of this filling is from the second quarter of the 4th century into the third quarter of

the 3rd century B.C. Two much later coins evidently represent intrusion.
Objects published or noted:

C-31-08: **2**	C-31-22: **422**
C-31-9: p. 30[14]	C-31-23: **406**
C-31-10: p. 45[30]	C-31-24: **403**
C-31-12: **445**	C-31-25: **386**
C-31-13: **28**	C-31-26: **387**
C-31-14: **26**	C-31-27: **457**
C-31-15: **765**	C-31-29: **388**
C-31-21: **441**	

40. New Museum, "Well" (actually Cistern) 49a
Range in date: End of 4th century to 3rd century B.C., third quarter
Summary:

The location of the cistern is best indicated by reference to a plan of the area to the east of that in which it was found, *Hesperia*, XVII, 1948, p. 198, fig. 1. It was approximately 42 m. west of the back wall of the West Shops and *ca.* 20 m. south of the projected line of the south wall of the temenos of Temple C, well within the area now occupied by the Corinth Museum. Whether there was one filling or more is not known. The catalogued pottery indicates that the range in period of the filling is from at least as early as the end of the 4th century into the third quarter of the 3rd century B.C.
Objects published or noted:

C-31-33: **495**	C-31-37: **22**
C-31-34: p. 30[14]	C-31-38: **421**
C-31-35: **24**	C-31-39: **379**
C-31-36: p. 30[14]	

41. New Museum, Well X
Range in date: 7th century to third century B.C., third quarter
Bibliography:

Saul S. Weinberg, *Corinth*, VII, i, *The Geometric and Orientalizing Pottery*, Cambridge, Mass., 1943, p. 44., no. 143; pp. 49–50, nos. 174–182.

Summary:

The location of the well is best indicated by reference to the plan of the area just to the west of that in which it was found, *A.J.A.*, XLIII, 1939, p. 594, fig. 4. Its position was about six meters east of the northwest corner of the present Corinth Museum, the western side of which is seen on that plan. Whether there was one filling or more is not known. The range in period of the catalogued pottery is remarkable, as well as the degree of completeness of the pieces of various times within the range. It includes a number of pieces of the 7th century, some of the 3rd, down into the third quarter. Conceivably this represents the conflation of a 7th century use filling with one or more later fillings introduced after the abandonment of the well as a source of water. Alternatively it may represent a gradual accumulation over the centuries, or a mixture derived from a dump, such as that of a sanctuary. A closely similar extreme range in period is also seen in the adjacent Deposit 42.

Objects published:

C-31-131: **254**	C-31-151: **132**
C-31-147: **68**	C-31-152: **1**
C-31-148: **162**	

42. New Museum, Well Z

Range in date: Early 7th century to 3rd century B.C., last quarter

Bibliography:

Saul S. Weinberg, *Corinth*, VII, i, *The Geometric and Orientalizing Pottery*, Cambridge, Mass., 1943, pp. 42–44, nos. 136–142.

Summary:

The location of the well is best indicated by reference to a plan of the area to the west of that in which it was found, *A.J.A.*, XLIII, 1939, p. 594, fig. 4. It lay under the northwest corner of the present Corinth Museum, the western side of which is shown on that plan. The range in period represented by the catalogued pottery is extreme, as well as the degree of completeness of the pieces of various times within the range. There is much of the 7th century from early to third quarter, some of the 6th and 5th centuries, and a very great deal of the 4th and 3rd centuries, down into the last quarter of the 3rd century B.C. Whether there was one filling or more in the well is not known. The records indicate that some of the 7th century material was found at relatively high levels in the well, with very late material both below and above. Conceivably, then, the material was derived from a dump which had accumulated over this very long period. Of the 97 catalogued pieces of pottery some 16 were votives.

Objects published or noted:

C-31-192: **205**	C-31-195: p. 30[14]
C-31-194: p. 30[14]	C-31-196: p. 30[14]
C-31-197: p. 30[14]	C-31-236: p. 37[22]
C-31-198: p. 30[14]	C-31-237: **566**
C-31-199: p. 29[14]	C-31-238: **305**
C-31-200: **174**	C-31-246: **161**
C-31-201: **11**	C-31-247: **178**
C-31-202: **12**	C-31-248: **177**
C-31-202 bis: **8**	C-31-249: **341**
C-31-203: **13**	C-31-250: **344**
C-31-206: **380**	C-31-251: **355**
C-31-207: **382**	C-31-259: p. 30[14]
C-31-220: p. 30[14]	C-31-260: p. 30[14]
C-31-221: p. 30[14]	C-31-261: p. 30[14]
C-31-223: **163**	C-31-262: **55**
C-31-224: **173**	C-31-263: **59**
C-31-225: **553**	C-31-264: p. 34[19]
C-31-226: p. 30[14]	C-31-265: **100**
C-31-229: **331**	C-31-269: **583**
C-31-230: **313**	C-31-274: **261**
C-31-231: **358**	C-31-280: **306**
C-31-232: **63**	

43. Well at the northwest corner of the precinct of Temple E

Range in date: 4th century, second quarter, to 3rd century B.C., last quarter

Summary:

For the area in which the well was located see Henry S. Robinson, *Corinth, A Brief History of the City and a Guide to the Excavations*, American School of Classical Studies, Athens, 1964, figs. 4 and 10 (area shaded in the latter). The excavator believed that the entire filling was deposited at one time. The pottery from the filling shows a fairly even distribution over the period from the second quarter of the 4th century into the last quarter of the 3rd century B.C.

Objects published or noted:

C-53-227: **767**	C-53-247: p. 30[14]
C-53-228: p. 148[17]	C-53-250: **576**
C-53-229: **770**	C-53-255: **81**
C-53-230: **381**	C-53-256: **176**
C-53-231: **456**	C-53-257: **172**
C-53-232: **454**	C-53-258: p. 42[29]
C-53-233: **443**	C-53-259: **180**
C-53-234: **440**	C-53-260: **34**
C-53-235: **455**	C-53-261: **32**
C-53-236: **383**	C-53-263: **51**
C-53-237: **353**	C-53-264: **27**
C-53-238: **349**	C-53-267: p. 39[25]
C-53-239: p. 99[93]	C-53-268: p. 124[11]
C-53-245: **62**	C-53-269: **624**
C-53-246: p. 30[14]	

44. St. John's, Cistern at D-34

Range in date: 5th century to *ca.* 200 B.C.

Bibliography:

Richard Stillwell, *A.J.A.*, XL, 1936, pp. 43–45, figs. 22–25.

Scranton, *The Lower Agora*, p. 5.

Davidson, *Minor Objects*, nos. 285, 1024–1025, 1483.

Summary:

The cistern was located just to the west of the Temple of Poseidon (Temple J) in the area of the terrace between it and the West Shops (Scranton, *The Lower Agora*, fig. 1). Whether there was one filling or more in the cistern has not been determined and the context material has not been examined. If it was a single fill the information available suggests that it was one of considerable range, from the 5th century to perhaps 200 B.C.

Conceivably the filling of this cistern was motivated by the construction of the Hellenistic temenos discussed under Deposits 39–43, above, though its location at *ca.* 20 m. east of the presumed east wall of the temenos is perhaps a bit too distant for it to have been affected.

45. Sanctuary of Demeter and Kore, Pit B

Range in date: 5th century to 2nd century B.C., first quarter

Bibliography:

Ronald S. Stroud, *Hesperia*, XXXIV, 1965, pp. 8–11; pl. 3, a–c.

Summary:

The Sanctuary is located on the north slopes of Acrocorinth (Stroud, *op. cit.*, pl. 1, a). The location and character of the pit is indicated in Stroud, *op. cit.*, p. 3, fig. 1, and p. 9, fig. 2. The pit evidently was filled in one operation since it is reported (Stroud, *op. cit.*, p. 10) that there was no stratification and "fragments of pottery found at the top of the pit joined pieces which lay at the bottom." This fact, coupled with the character and date of the material, makes it seem likely that the filling was derived from an accumulation elsewhere in the sanctuary. The pottery from the pit has been only summarily studied in connection with the present publication. At the moment a considerable range of period seems to be represented. The earliest so far noted is of the 5th century B.C. In Stroud, *op. cit.*, p. 10 and footnote 15, the present author suggested that the lower limit was at the end of the 4th century or in the early 3rd. It now seems possible that the lower limit may be rather later, perhaps down into the first quarter of the 2nd century B.C.

Objects published or noted:

C-61-381: **146**	C-61-386: p. 129
C-61-382: **179**	C-61-424: **181**
C-61-383: **186**	C-61-425: **184**
C-61-385: **736**	

46. Southeast Building, Well at N-20

Bibliography:

Oscar Broneer, *Hesperia*, XVI, 1947, p. 238 (preliminary report).

Saul S. Weinberg, *Hesperia*, XVIII, 1949, pp. 148–149; pls. 13–14, 1–7.

Weinberg, *The Southeast Building*, pp. 4 and 12; pl. 8, 4.

Summary:

The well was located in a deep foundation trench at a point less than 1.00 m. southeast of the third from the north of the western line of inner supports of the building (Weinberg, *The Southeast Building*, plan I; cf. p. 25, fig. 4). How the well was filled is not fully determined. There may have been a small use filling whose lower limit would evidently be 146 B.C., the time of the destruction of Corinth by Mummius. A filling above, probably introduced in the very early years of the Roman city after 44 B.C., is largely composed of material of the time of the destruction, as indicated by a coin of 148–146 B.C. in it and study of many series of vessels from it. A supplemental fill related to the construction of the first Roman building on the site was apparently introduced very shortly after. The objects catalogued from the well included 70 pottery vessels of various categories.

Objects published or noted:

C-47-787: **821**	C-47-816: **106**
C-47-790: **919**	C-47-817: p. 28[11]
C-47-791: **921**	C-47-818: p. 33[17]
C-47-792: p. 160[17]	C-47-819: **89**
C-47-794: p. 160[17]	C-47-820: **76**
C-47-795: **811**	C-47-821: **31**
C-47-796: p. 172[26]	C-47-822: **558**
C-47-797 a, b: **839**	C-47-826: **656**
C-47-798: **820**	C-47-827: p. 108
C-47-802: p. 87	C-47-829: **749**
C-47-803: p. 44	C-47-830: **732**
C-47-804: p. 36[20]	C-47-831: **723**
C-47-807: p. 36[20]	C-47-835: **702**
C-47-809: p. 40[26]	C-47-836: **646**
C-47-810: p. 28[10]	C-47-851: **197**
C-47-811: **124**	C-47-852: pp. 50[37], 180[42]
C-47-812: p. 36[21]	C-47-853: **778**
C-47-813: **169**	C-47-854: **879**
C-47-814: **155**	C-47-891: **708**
C-47-815: **182**	MF 9246: p. 30[14]

47. Anaploga, Destruction fill of first cleaning and dyeing works

Date: 146 B.C.

Summary:

For the location of the establishment see Henry S. Robinson, *Hesperia*, XXXVIII, 1969, p. 2, fig. 1.

The filling is evidently to be attributed to the time of the destruction of Corinth in 146 B.C. It includes a slight amount of intrusive material of the early Roman period as well.

Objects published or noted:

C-63-487: **798**   C-63-737: **131**
C-63-490 a–c: **901**   C-63-738: p. 40²⁶

48. Anaploga, Well in Grave 12
Date: 6th century to 1st century B.C.
Summary:

The location of the well, above which a Roman grave was later placed, is indicated in Henry S. Robinson, *Hesperia*, XXXVIII, 1969, p. 2, fig. 1.

There seems not to have been a use filling. The material from the well was very fragmentary and no satisfactory division into fills was therefore possible. It seems very likely that the entire filling was introduced in the early Roman period. In it there is representation of various times from the 6th century down to that date. Such a mixture of extremely scrappy material may have resulted from levelling of the area at that time in preparation for new construction.

Objects published or noted:

C-62-247: p. 30¹⁴   C-62-249: **150**

II. GRAVES

49. North Cemetery, Field of Panages Kondyles, Grave 54 A
Date: 5th century B.C., last quarter
Summary:

This group combines eight vessel shapes: miniature mug, duck askos, squat banded lekythos, skyphos, miniature pyxis, squat aryballos, miniature trefoil oinochoe, and trefoil olpe. The squat aryballos and the trefoil olpe suggest a date in the last quarter of the 5th century B.C.

Objects published:

CP-829: **242**

50–52.

Three graves form a sequence connected by stages of the small trefoil oinochoe.

50. North Cemetery, Field of Panages Kondyles, Grave 23 A
Date: 5th century B.C., last quarter
Bibliography:

S. B. Luce, *A.J.A.*, XXXIV, 1930, p. 341, fig. 5, no. 13 (lekythos). Pease, under nos. 1–2, and 172 (references to this grave).

Summary:

This group combines five vessel shapes: Corinthian skyphos, small trefoil oinochoe, white-ground lekythos, and lekanis, and an Attic band cup. Miss Pease, in publishing a group of 460–420 B.C., regarded this grave group as "somewhat later" (*op. cit.*, under nos. 1–2). Hence a date in the last quarter of the 5th century has been adopted here.

Objects published:

CP-608: **255**

51. North Cemetery, Grave 339
Date: ca. 350 B.C.

Bibliography:

N. *Cemetery*, pp. 278–279, grave 442.
Summary:

This group combines four vessel shapes, all Corinthian: Corinthian type of skyphos, miniature cup, small trefoil oinochoe, round-mouth oinochoe.

Objects published:

T 2533: **262**

52. North Cemetery, Grave 348
Date: 4th century B.C., last quarter
Bibliography:

N. *Cemetery*, p. 285, grave 463 and pl. 26.
Summary:

This group combines two vessel shapes, both Corinthian: skyphos and small trefoil oinochoe.

Objects published:

T 2617: **258**

53–55.

These three graves form a small sequence connected by examples of the pyxis with domed, slipover lid and the small trefoil oinochoe with shoulder stop.

53. North Cemetery, Deposit 36
Date: ca. 350 B.C.
Bibliography:

N. *Cemetery*, p. 308, Deposit 36, and pl. 73.
Summary:

This group combines five vessel shapes, all Corinthian: skyphos, small black-glazed jug, small trefoil oinochoe, miniature hydria, and pyxis with domed, slipover lid.
Objects published:

T 2369: **559**   T 2371 a: **577**
T 2370: **276**   T 2371 b: **562**

54. North Cemetery, Deposit 28
   Date: ca. 350 B.C.
   Bibliography:
      N. *Cemetery,* p. 307, Deposit 28, and pl. 92.
   Summary:
      This group combines five vessel shapes. Four are Corinthian: miniature skyphos, small trefoil oinochoe with shoulder stop, small trefoil oinochoe, and lekanis. One is Attic: a squat palmette lekythos, which in form seems comparable to ones found in houses at Olynthos, thus evidently in use in 348 B.C.
   Objects published:

      T 2651: **274**

55. North Cemetery, Grave 40
   Date: 4th century B.C., last quarter
   Bibliography:
      N. *Cemetery,* pp. 291–292, grave 494, and pl. 76.
   Summary:
      This group consists only of a pyxis with domed, slipover lid and a strigil.
   Objects published:

      T 1097 a: **578**   T 1097 b: **563**

56. Grave outside Kenchrean Gate
   Date: 4th century, third quarter
   Summary:
      This group combines four vessel shapes, all Corinthian: skyphos of Corinthian type, black-glazed small jug, pyxis with slipover lid, and miniature column krater. The skyphos suggests a date in the third quarter of the 4th century B.C.
   Objects noted:

      C-60-239: p. 96[92]

57–69.
      These fourteen graves (including one double grave) form a closely knit group and sequence. They are primarily connected by examples of late stages of the Corinthian skyphos of Attic type and examples of early stages of the unguentarium, often occurring in conjunction in these graves and thus providing relative sequence. The earliest graves in this group are of the latter third quarter of the 4th century B.C. This date is partly based on the fact that unguentaria do not occur at Olynthos; hence one must look to a date later than 348 B.C. for the beginning of their importation. The earliest typologically are found in Corinth in conjunction with Corinthian skyphoi somewhat more advanced in shape than those at Olynthos, thus to be placed on estimate within the third quarter of the 4th century. Although it is by no means certain that the Corinthian skyph-

os developed at the same rate as the skyphoi of fabrics represented at Olynthos it seems probable that this estimate may be fairly near the mark since one of the grave groups, 58, included a silver coin of Corinth of 338 B.C. The lower limit suggested for this group of deposits, *ca.* 275 B.C., is perhaps a generous allowance. The latest of the graves in this group, 69, includes what must be the final stage of the Corinthian skyphos of Attic type. The placement of it at 275 B.C. may prove to be, when more is known of the chronology of the series, too late rather than too early. Some further precision in the dating of this group of deposits and in that of the unguentarium and skyphos series may be anticipated from the dating of two silver coins, one each from Graves 65 A and 66, which have not yet been studied by an expert.

57. Graves on road to Acrocorinth, Grave 4
   Date: 4th century B.C., latter third quarter
   Bibliography:
      Henry S. Robinson, *Hesperia,* XXXI, 1962, pp. 118–119, grave 5, fig. 1.
   Summary:
      Of the grave offerings in this damaged tomb there remained only the upper parts of two imported unguentaria of the earliest stage.
   Objects published:

      none

58. Graves on road to Acrocorinth, Grave 9
   Date: 4th century B.C., latter third quarter
   Bibliography:
      Henry S. Robinson, *Hesperia,* XXXI, 1962, pp. 118–120, grave 10, fig. 1 and pl. 46, b.
   Summary:
      This group combines two vessel shapes: unguentarium and Acrocorinth kantharos. A silver obol of Corinth has been dated *ca.* 338 B.C.
   Objects published:
      C-60-227: **451**

59. Grave (9) near "Justinian's Wall"
   Date: 4th century B.C., latter third quarter
   Summary:
      The group combines three vessel shapes: skyphos, Attic type, a small jug form, and unguentarium.
   Objects published:
      C-30-01: **360**

60. North Cemetery, Grave 372
   Date: 4th century B.C., third quarter
   Bibliography:
      N. *Cemetery,* pp. 292, 293, grave 496, and pls. 77, 82, 100.

Summary:
   This group combines seven vessel shapes. Six are Corinthian: miniature skyphos, small trefoil oinochoe, a small jug form, handle-ridge jug, covered, glaze-banded bowl, and semi-glazed bowl. Imported: unguentarium.
Objects published:

T 2720: **14**   T 2722: **641**

61. Grave northwest of Acrocorinth
    Date: 4th century B.C., third quarter
    Summary:
       This group combines five vessel shapes, all Corinthian: skyphos, Attic type, small trefoil oinochoe, small round-mouth pitcher, squat lekythos (?), and handle-ridge jug.
    Objects published:

    C-60-232: **362**   C-60-236: **639**

62. North Cemetery, Grave 369
    Date: 4th century B.C., latter third quarter
    Bibliography:
       N. Cemetery, p. 292, grave 495, pls. 78, 122.
    Summary:
       This group combines five vessel shapes: skyphos, feeding cup, pyxis with slipover lid, small chytra and lid, and unguentarium.
    Objects published:

    T 2698 a: **690**   T 2703 a: **582**
    T 2698 b: p. 120[7]   T 2703 b: **572**

63. North Cemetery, Grave 50
    Date: 4th century B.C., latter third quarter
    Bibliography:
       N. Cemetery, p. 291, grave 491, pls. 76, 122.
    Summary:
       This group combines five vessel shapes. Four are Corinthian: skyphos, Attic type, small trefoil oinochoe, a small jug form, and a small pyxis receptacle. Imported: two unguentaria.
    Objects published:

    T 1158: **361**   T 1164: **263**
    T 1159: **571**

64. Grave VII outside City Wall on road to Hexamilia
    Date: 4th century B.C., early fourth quarter
    Bibliography:
       Broneer, *Terracotta Lamps*, p. 137, no. 90, and pl. II (lamp).
    Summary:
       This group combines four vessel shapes. Three are Corinthian: skyphos, miniature trefoil oinochoe, miniature round-mouth jug.

Imported: unguentarium.
Objects published:

65 A. Anaploga Cistern Area, Grave 1, lower burial
    Date: No later than 4th century B.C., early fourth quarter
    Summary:
       This group consists of a small jug, a lamp, and a silver coin not yet identified. Earlier than 65 B (Anaploga Cistern Area, Grave 1, upper burial), which lay over it.
    Objects published:

65 B. Anaploga Cistern Area, Grave 1, upper burial
    Date: 4th century B.C., early fourth quarter
    Summary:
       This group combines two vessel shapes: skyphos and unguentarium, both Corinthian.
    Objects published:

    C-63-662: **585**

66. Anaploga Cistern Area, Grave 3
    Date: ca. 300 B.C.
    Summary:
       This group combines five vessel shapes: miniature trefoil oinochoe, miniature round-mouth pitcher, skyphos, Attic type, miniature flat-bottomed dish, all Corinthian, and an imported unguentarium.
    Objects published:

    C-63-658: **364**

67. Graves on road to Acrocorinth, Grave 3 B
    Date: ca. 300 B.C.
    Bibliography:
       Henry S. Robinson, *Hesperia*, XXXI, 1962, pp. 118–119, grave 4, fig. 1 and pl. 45, c–e.
    Summary:
       This group combines five vessel shapes. Three are Corinthian: skyphos, Attic type, miniature trefoil oinochoe, miniature convex pyxis. Two are imported: unguentarium and amphora employing the unguentarium form.
    Objects published:

    C-60-221: **347**

68. Graves on road to Acrocorinth, Grave 10
    Date: ca. 300 B.C.
    Bibliography:
       Henry S. Robinson, *Hesperia*, XXXI, 1962, pp. 118–120, grave 11, fig. 1 and pl. 46, c, d.

Summary:

This group combines three vessel shapes: Corinthian skyphos, Attic type, miniature round-mouth jug, imported unguentarium. A silver coin of Corinth has been dated *ca.* 400–338 B.C.

Objects published:

C-60-229: **348**

69. "Roman Tomb," Grave 5
Date: ca. 275 B.C.
Summary:

This group combines two vessel shapes: skyphos, Attic type, miniature round-mouth jug, both forms Corinthian. The skyphos is of the final stage of its series.

Objects published:

C-61-14: **365**

70–73.

These four graves form a close sequence probably of fairly short duration. They are tied together by examples of several adjacent stages of the Hexamilia kantharos. The relative placement of the entire group between the second quarter and the early last quarter of the 3rd century B.C. is indicated by an example of a blister-ware lamp and examples of advanced stages of the echinus bowl and the bowl with outturned rim. No evidence for absolute chronology is provided by these grave groups and there is none for the short series of Hexamilia kantharoi in general.

70. North Cemetery, Grave 269
Date: 3rd century B.C., third quarter
Bibliography:
 N. Cemetery, pp. 293, 294, grave 498, and pls. 78, 100, 119.
Summary:

This group combines six[15] vessel shapes: Hexamilia kantharos, miniature trefoil oinochoe, miniature round-mouth oinochoe, echinus bowl, bowl with outturned rim, and ointment-pot.

Objects published or noted:

T 2312: **516**	T 2316: **84**
T 2313: p. 30[14]	T 2317: **590**
T 2314: **589**	

71. Area of Roman Tomb north of village, group of pots between Tomb I and Grave 11
Date: 3rd century B.C., third quarter

Summary:

This group combines four vessel shapes: Hexamilia kantharos, miniature round-mouth pitcher, miniature bowl with outturned rim, and ointment-pot. They were found together, all intact, between the graves.

Objects published or noted:

C-61-36: **591**	C-61-39: p. 33[17]
C-61-37: **518**	

72. Tomb VIII outside City Wall on road to Hexamilia
Date: ca. 225 B.C.
Bibliography:
 Broneer, *Terracotta Lamps,* p. 146, no. 170, and pl. IV (lamp).
Summary:

This group combines three vessel shapes: Hexamilia kantharos, miniature round-mouth pitcher, and two-handled ointment-pot. Miss Judith Perlzweig has suggested that the blister-ware lamp cited above is probably not earlier than *ca.* 250 and probably not later than the end of the 3rd century B.C.

Objects published:

C-27-18: **519**	C-27-22: **587**
C-27-19: **588**	

73. Cheliotomylos, Trench D, burial vault
Date: 3rd century B.C., early last quarter
Summary:

This group combines four vessel shapes: Hexamilia kantharos, miniature round-mouth pitcher, miniature trefoil pitcher, and ointment-pot.

Objects published:

T 2018: **520**	T 2023: **594**

74. Roman tomb north of village, Grave 16
Date: 3rd century B.C., third quarter
Summary:

The offerings in this grave were two identical ointment-pots. A third, of slightly different shape, may possibly belong also.

Objects published:

C-61-28: **599**	C-61-29: **598**

75. Anaploga, Rock Cutting 4
Date: 3rd century B.C., third quarter
Summary:

This assembly may or may not be a grave group. If it is, it represents a disturbed burial.

---

[15] It seems likely that *N. Cemetery,* 498–3 may belong to grave 454 (Grave 269) of the third quarter of the 4th century, rather than to this grave. The shape does not seem to have survived into the 3rd century in Corinth.

It can only be said that the combination of a drinking cup (a cyma kantharos), a lamp, and a coin have precedent in other Corinthian graves. Miss Judith Perlzweig has dated the lamp as early in the second half of the 3rd century B.C. The silver coin has not yet been identified. The kantharos is placed on estimate in the third quarter of the 3rd century.
Objects published:

C-63-38: **450**

76. Irrigation ditch northeast of city, Burial DD
Range in date: ca. 250 to 200 B.C.
Summary:

This group consists of an imported coarse-ware stamnos used as a cinerary urn and an imported echinus bowl used as a lid.
Objects noted:

C-62-26: p. 105[4]   C-62-27: p. 105[6]

77. West Wall of City, Grave I
Date: 1st century B.C., last quarter
Summary:

The grave was evidently located on the north slope of the hill to the north of the modern road passing through the Phliasian Gate. Some of the bones were lying in the space formerly occupied by the City Wall, hence the grave was seen to be later than the destruction of the Wall. The combination of three Early Roman "onion" unguentaria and an imported unguentarium of Hellenistic form suggests a date in the last quarter of the 1st century B.C. This is presumably one of the graves referred to in Rhys Carpenter and Antoine Bon, *Corinth*, III, ii, *The Defenses of Acrocorinth and the Lower Town*, Cambridge, Mass., 1936, p. 75: "Roman graves containing objects of early Imperial date were excavated immediately above the bed of the wall and in its very course so that there is archaeological indication in favor of supposing that this particular stretch of wall was dismantled and destroyed by Mummius."
Objects published:

78. West Wall of City, Grave III
Date: 1st century, after 44 B.C.
Summary:

The grave was evidently located on the same slope as 77, but apparently not in the line of the City Wall. The grave furniture consisted of two imported unguentaria of different fabrics of Hellenistic form and a cooking pot, uncatalogued, containing an incineration.
Objects published:

III. DEPOSITS CONNECTED WITH THE SOUTH STOA

79. Agora SC, Well at b–c: 18–19
Range in date: ca. 425 through 4th century B.C., first quarter
Bibliography:
Charles H. Morgan II, *A.J.A.*, XLI, 1937, pp. 547–548, fig. 11, and pl. XIII, 2 ("Vth c. Well").
Summary:

The well was located north of Shop XVIII of the South Stoa, *ca.* 6.00 m. north of the projected line of the Terrace Wall of the Stoa and *ca.* 14.00 m. south of the west exedra of the Bema complex.

The well seems never to have been used. The excavator believed that the well was never finished and that digging was abandoned before water was reached. The top of the well was seen to have been cut down in the process of grading preparatory to laying the cobblestone pavement in the area north of the Terrace Wall of the Stoa. The pavement covered and sealed the mouth of the well. It was very probably filled in a single operation, though this cannot be demonstrated. Conceivably the filling occurred independently, prior to the laying of the cobblestone pavement, though further study of the material may suggest that they are more nearly contemporary. The extremely heavy concentration of pottery in the well (an average of one five-gallon tin of sherds for each 0.12 m. of depth) inclines one to suspect a direct relationship between the filling of the well and the laying of the pavement. At present the range of period of the pottery from it, some 222 catalogued pieces, seems to be from *ca.* 425 through the first quarter of the 4th century B.C.[16]
Objects published or noted:

C-37-415: **759**	C-37-434: **332**
C-37-416: **757**	C-37-435: **321**
C-37-424: **43**	C-37-451: **287**
C-37-425: **64**	C-37-454: **288**
C-37-428: **333**	C-37-466: p. 148[17]

---

[16] Morgan, *op. cit.*, p. 547, dated the material in the late 5th century. A note in the field records indicates that M. Z. Pease subsequently placed it in the first quarter of the 4th century.

C-37-467: p. 145[10]	C-37-510: **243**
C-37-468: p. 145[10]	C-37-511: p. 145
C-37-469: p. 145[10]	C-37-535: p. 121[7]
C-37-484: **210**	C-37-537: p. 137[20]
C-37-485: **231**	C-37-540: **666**
C-37-493: p. 29[14]	C-37-545: **729**

80. **Agora SC, Filling of drain at b–f: 19–20**

Range in date: 4th century B.C., first quarter into second quarter

Bibliography:

Charles H. Morgan II, *A.J.A.*, XLI, 1937, p. 547, pl. XIII, 2, and pl. XIV, 1.

Davidson, *Minor Objects*, pp. 17–18, 23, Deposit XI.

Summary:

A stretch of this drain *ca.* 14.00 m. long was found running from southeast to northwest. Its most southerly part, where it terminated or began in Manhole H of the Peirene System (Hill, *The Springs*, pl. III) at a point *ca.* 15 m. south of the southeast corner of the west exedra of the Bema complex, would have touched or passed a little beneath the line of the Terrace Wall of the South Stoa if it existed here.

The records indicate that the filling of the drain was in part sealed by the cobblestone pavement laid north of the Terrace Wall of the South Stoa or in parts where it was undisturbed for the most part except for some intrusion, including Byzantine. The excavator regarded the drain as unfinished, presumably in part because of the irregular depth of the bottom and also because "there was no trace of the action of water at the bottom nor indeed anywhere in the drain." It seems likely, though this cannot be demonstrated, that the drain was filled up in one operation. The records suggest that the drain was filled with an unusually heavy concentration of sherds and other material, which may in itself indicate that the filling was put in in direct anticipation of the laying of the cobble pavement above to serve as strong support for it. The bulk of the pottery seems to cover a relatively short range, the first quarter of the 4th century into the early second quarter. A few pieces were noted in the context pottery which may be as late as the middle of the 4th century B.C. 172 pieces of pottery have been catalogued.

Objects published or noted:

C-37-170: **335**	C-37-245: **289**
C-37-171: **334**	C-37-246: **296**
C-37-172: **367**	C-37-247: **295**
C-37-173: **368**	C-37-248: **297**
C-37-180: **44**	C-37-312: **621**
C-37-202: p. 96[92]	C-37-313: **623**
C-37-214: p. 33[17]	C-37-557: p. 137[22]

C-37-216: p. 33[17]	C-37-559: **659**
C-37-219: **41**	C-37-560: **663**
C-37-240: **293**	C-37-561: **694**
C-37-241: **292**	C-37-564: **680**
C-37-242: **290**	C-37-569: p. 137[22]
C-37-243: **291**	C-37-576: p. 137[22]
C-37-244: **294**	C-37-1083: **45**

81. **Southeast Building, Well at P-27**

Range in date: original filling, 4th century B.C., first quarter into second quarter; supplemental filling, 2nd century B.C., first half

Bibliography:

Weinberg, *The Southeast Building*, p. 4; plan I (brief mention).

Summary:

The well was located in the northwest corner of the building, about 1.00 m. northwest of the second from the north of the western line of inner supports (Weinberg, *op. cit.*, plan I; cf. p. 25, fig. 4). The material from the filling of the well seems to have been primarily of the first quarter of the 4th century, with some of the second quarter. How the well was filled up is not known, though it seems likely that the original filling or fillings were supplemented by another at least as late as the first half of the 2nd century B.C. It is conceivable that the well was put out of use because of the projected construction of the adjacent South Stoa.

Objects published or noted:

C-47-464: p. 84[80]	C-47-870: p. 129
C-47-856: **323**	C-47-872: **212**
C-47-857: **322**	C-47-873: **772**
C-47-858a: **309**	C-47-874: p. 148[17]
C-47-858b: **307**	C-47-878: **755**
C-47-859: **308**	C-47-889: **675**
C-47-866: **42**	

82–83. **Deposits in South Stoa, Great Reservoir**

Bibliography:

Charles H. Morgan II, *A.J.A.*, XLII, 1938, p. 364; XLIII, 1939, p. 255.

Broneer, *The South Stoa*, pp. 11–16, and 95, pl. 4, 3–4, pl. 24, 3, and plans VII, VIII.

Henry S. Robinson, *Hesperia*, XXXI, 1962, p. 133.

The Great Reservoir is located for the most part beneath Shops and Storerooms XXVII–XXXIII of the South Stoa, one branch, however, extending beyond them to the south, and another extending to the north into the area of the 28th Ionic column of the colonnade. The Reservoir was put out of use by the construction of the South Stoa. Although many deposits in it reflect intrusive activities of much later times, two have been noted which have relevance to establishing the date of construction of the Stoa.

82. South Stoa, Great Reservoir, filling of oval
    manhole in South Gallery
Bibliography:
    Broneer, *S. Stoa*, p. 13, and footnote 8;
        p. 95; pl. 24, 3, and plans VII, VIII.
Summary:
    The location of the manhole is seen in
Broneer, *op. cit.*, plan VII, beside S¹. The
filling at the bottom of the manhole, which
included four pottery vessels and three terracotta lamps, was regarded by the excavator
as belonging to the period of use of the cistern
and hence antedating its abandonment and the
time of construction of the South Stoa. For
the lamps, Broneer, *S. Stoa*, p. 95, has noted
that they have "the well-developed profile
common in the first half of the fourth century." Examples cited from Olynthos, where,
he notes, their type is the most common one,
support the dating. Of the pottery from the
filling a Corinthian skyphos of Attic type,
325 (Broneer, *S. Stoa*, pl. 24, 3), is at present
the most useful for dating. It is very close in
proportions to several skyphoi found in houses
at Olynthos (*Olynthus*, XIII, nos. 583, 585, 587)
and thus presumably in use in 348 B.C. It is
here dated in the second quarter of the 4th
century. The nature and contents of the upper
filling or fillings of the manhole, part of which
remains undug, are not known.
Objects published:

   C-52-1: **325**

83. South Stoa, Great Reservoir, filling of eastern
    entrance
Bibliography:
    Charles H. Morgan II, *A.J.A.*, XLII, 1938,
        p. 364.
    Broneer, *S. Stoa*, pp. 12–13, pl. 4, 3, and
        plans V, VII, and VIII.
Summary:
    The location of the entrance can be seen in
Broneer, *S. Stoa*, plans V and VII. The foundation of the 28th (from the east) Ionic column
of the inner colonnade of the South Stoa was
set down into it. Morgan, *op. cit.*, p. 364,
reports with reference to excavation here in
1937 that "A considerable amount of pottery
and other objects was found thrown in about
this foundation. Since none of these is of
later date than the beginning of the fourth
century, this material considerably strengthens

this date for the building of the Stoa..."
No pieces from this fill were catalogued and
it has unfortunately not been possible as yet
to locate and examine the context material.
The context pottery from further excavation
in this entrance in 1952 consists of Classical
coarse-ware sherds.
Objects published:

84. South Stoa, footing trenches, Shop and Store-
    room I
Summary:
    The fillings are those of footing trenches for a
part of the east wall of Shop I and for the southeast and southwest corners of Storeroom I.[17] The
most pertinent piece excavated, noted below, is a
section of an Attic echinus bowl, C-63-509, very
close in proportions to two found in houses at
Olynthos (*Olynthus*, XIII, nos. 768 and 774) and
thus probably in use in 348 B.C.
Objects noted:

   C-63-509: p. 30[14]

85. South Stoa, footing trench of east wall of Stoa
Summary:
    The part of the wall concerned is that which
lies between the front of Shop I and the outer
colonnade. The footing trench was examined on
the inner face of the wall. Much of the pottery
recovered was either indicative of later disturbance
or noncommittal.[18] The one catalogued piece,
C-52-4, a red-figure sherd, from a very low level,
was regarded by the excavator as antedating the
Stoa.
Objects noted:

   C-52-4: p. 218

86. South Stoa, fill around foundation of pier 31 of
    Ionic colonnade
Summary:
    The filling on the south and east sides of the
foundation was excavated. That on the east side
was found undisturbed. The pottery[19] includes a
Corinthian red-figure sherd, not yet dated, and
the base and rim of a skyphos of Attic type
datable about 350 B.C.
Objects noted:

   C-52-3: p. 218[19]

87. South Stoa, top filling of well north of Shop IV
    and fill of building north of Shop IV

---

[17] Context pottery: Corinth Lots 3837–3839.
[18] Corinth Lots 3835–3836.
[19] Catalogued: C-52-3. Context pottery: Corinth Lots 3832–3834.

Bibliography:
Oscar Broneer, *Hesperia*, XVI, 1947, p. 238;
XX, 1951, pp. 294–296, pl. 93, c, d.
Broneer, *S. Stoa*, pp. 7–8; p. 95 and footnotes
53–54; pl. 4, 1; pl. 24, 1; and plan I.

Summary:
The location of the well and building are seen in Broneer, *S. Stoa*, plan I. The two-room structure extends from just inside Shop IV of the Stoa northward to within *ca.* 1.00 m. of the foundation for the fourth column of the inner colonnade. The well is located in the southwest corner of the northern room.

The two fillings, from the top 0.50 m. of the well shaft and from within the confines of the two rooms, dug at different times, are here regarded as essentially and in bulk one, for the most part introduced at the time of the construction of the South Stoa. To this evidently a certain amount of supplementary filling was added at a later date, seemingly in the early 3rd century B.C. Two still later coins are apparently casually intrusive. This interpretation cannot be demonstrated since no stratification was reported, but it seems probable in the light of the implications of the physical circumstances of the filling and the indications provided by the other evidence for the dating of the construction of the Stoa.

The well long antedated the Stoa, for it was put out of use in the second quarter of the 6th century. It is evident that the filling extended originally to the top of the shaft and remained at this level during the lifetime of the building, which was erected over it at some undetermined later date. The building clearly antedates the beginning of construction of the Stoa and it is reasonable to assume that the filling was introduced within its rooms at the time of construction of the Stoa, rather than earlier, to bring the level up to that planned for the floors of the colonnade and shop. It seems likely that the settling of the original well fill occurred later, causing the building filling to collapse into the top of the well shaft and necessitating the addition of a supplementary fill containing later material above, in the immediate vicinity of the shaft.

Professor Broneer, in *S. Stoa*, p. 95, has already pointed out the pertinence of the filling in the top of the well shaft to the date of construction of the South Stoa. The present interpretation supports his view of its relevance. An Attic calyx kantharos from this fill, C-50-27 (*Hesperia*, XX, 1951, pl. 93, c) is comparable in stage of development to ones found at Olynthos (*Olynthus*, V, nos. 513, 517). An Attic skyphos, C-50-28 (*Hesperia*, XX, 1951, pl. 93, d, right), is close in form to *Olynthus*, XIII, nos. 585 and 587. A Corinthian skyphos of Attic type (*Hesperia*, XX, 1951, pl. 93, d, left) is here dated in the second quarter of the 4th century B.C.

For the filling above, within the two rooms, no objective division of the material between original and supplementary fills can be made, nor can it be demonstrated that the supplementary material came only from the area of the shaft. A slight point in favor of the isolation of the supplementary fill to the area of the shaft, however, is seen in the character of the context material from the south room (Corinth Lot 3816) which does not include material demonstrably later than about the middle of the 4th century. Two catalogued pieces from the south room can perhaps, then, be added as relevant to the date of construction of the Stoa. C-46-114, an Attic rolled-rim plate, is close in stage of development to one from a house at Olynthos (*Olynthus*, XIII, no. 865). An imported drinking(?) vessel, C-46-126, cannot now be dated closely. In the features it evidently imitates from Attic it seems suitable to the same time.

The bulk of the pottery from the filling in the rooms is of the first half of the 4th century and beginning of the third quarter. A very little is of the late 4th century and the first quarter of the 3rd century B.C.

Objects published or noted:

C-46-108: **494**	C-46-129: **696**
C-46-113: **351**	C-46-130: p. 30[14]
C-46-114: p. 37[22]	C-46-133: **665**
C-46-119: **771**	C-46-135: **679**
C-46-122: **98**	C-50-27: p. 219
C-46-126: p. 219	C-50-28: p. 219
C-46-128: **668**	C-50-29: **352**

88. Tavern of Aphrodite, South Stoa Construction Fill, South Stoa Terrace Fill, and earlier

Bibliography:
Charles H. Morgan II, *A.J.A.*, XLIII, 1939, p. 258 and fig. 4; *Hesperia*, XXII, 1953, pp. 131–140, pls. 45, 46.
Broneer, *S. Stoa*, pp. 8–10, fig. 1, pl. 3, 2, and plan V.

Summary:
The Tavern of Aphrodite was located north of Shops XXVII–XXX of the South Stoa.[20] It is attested to have extended from a point *ca.* 5.00 m. north of the Terrace Wall of the Stoa southward to the foundations of the stylobate of the outer

[20] The Tavern of Aphrodite is to be equated with Building III, re-examined in 1971. See Williams, *Hesperia*, XLI, 1972, pp. 173 f. (Ed.)

colonnade of the Stoa. No doubt at the south it extended still further into the area occupied by the Stoa.

The Tavern was originally constructed in the 6th century. It was abandoned because of the construction of the South Stoa whose outer colonnade and terrace wall were erected across it.

Considerations of terrain make it likely that the Tavern was put out of use in the early days of construction of the South Stoa. The stone for the Stoa, very conceivably derived from a large quarry extending due west from the fountain of Glauke, could seemingly be transported practically to the site of the Stoa only via a route from the northwest crossing the area occupied by the Tavern. Physical evidence that the area of the Tavern was actually on the route of transport from this direction is provided by wheel grooves, one very marked, running from northwest to southeast across the threshold of the Tavern (*Hesperia*, XXXII, 1953, p. 132, fig. 1, at E). Such grooves have also been reported in the northern pavement of the building (*op. cit.*, p. 137). It seems reasonable to suppose that construction of the Stoa proceeded from east to west. The route presumably would have been required for access through all stages of the construction of the Stoa proper and its colonnades, and thus presumably the Tavern area would have been one of the latest to receive the final fillings introduced between the foundations of the outer colonnade and the Terrace Wall and from the Terrace Wall northward in a gradual slope to the lower central part of the Agora valley.

Much later inhabitants of Corinth removed most of the final fillings and the paving of cobblestones which is presumed to have covered them in this area, and we are evidently thus deprived of practically all the evidence which once existed here for the date of completion of the construction of the Stoa and its approaches from the north. Of the cobble pavement, however, there existed at the time of excavation a small patch a bit beyond the northeast corner of the Tavern, well north of the Terrace Wall. A bronze coin of the Pegasos/Trident series found in the fill beneath it was assigned by Martin Price in 1963, with reservations because of poor condition, to his Group II of 360–345 B.C. Probably some allowance must be made for circulation of this coin, though perhaps not a great one since it had slight commercial value and the construction of the Stoa may suggest that the times were prosperous. Another coin of the same series was covered by the laying of the Terrace Wall over the Tavern, an operation which must have been one of the latest elements of the program. Mr. Price, again with reservations because of its poor condition, suggested that it may possibly be of his Period III, *ca.* 350–340 B.C.[20 bis] Some 51 coins in all were found in fillings taken to be pertinent to Stoa activities in the Tavern area. Most were in too poor condition for cleaning or identification. Of those legible, however, none is known to date later than the two above.

The present writer has prepared a list, on file in the Corinth Museum, of catalogued objects of all kinds from the excavations of Mr. Morgan in the Tavern which he in his field records indicated were found in undisturbed fillings connected with construction activities of the Stoa. With the exception of the two coins mentioned all objects come from the area between the south face of the Terrace Wall and the foundations for the outer colonnade of the Stoa. The fillings in many cases contained material suitable to construction, disintegrated adobe, probably from the walls of the Tavern, poros chips and dust presumably from the work of trimming and setting the blocks of the two foundations, and the like. This list includes much that relates to activities in the Tavern during its use down to the time of its abandonment. Some may have been dropped by the builders of the Stoa. Probably little if any (aside from the 2 coins) relates to the final fillings and paving. The pottery is all of Classical times, some of it as early as the 6th century. Many of the pieces, such as miniature vessels, are not susceptible of close dating. A number, however, are of series which provide quite sensitive criteria for dating, both Attic and Corinthian: skyphoi of the Corinthian and the Attic types, a variety of stemless kylix, the echinus bowl and calyx kantharoi. The latest of these are very close in stage of shape development to ones found in houses at Olynthos and thus presumably in use in 348 B.C. A few seem very slightly more advanced than the Olynthian examples. Placement of them in the early third quarter of the 4th century seems reasonable. The pertinent context pottery, not retained for the most part evidently, according to the excavator's notes on it, included nothing of later date. Much was appreciably earlier.

The evidence from the Tavern of Aphrodite, then, suggests that construction of the South Stoa began early in the third quarter of the 4th century B.C. The absence of pottery of later date

---

[20 bis] Cf. J. Warren, "The Trihemidrachms of Corinth," *Essays in Greek Coinage presented to Stanley Robinson*, Oxford, 1968, p. 143 and note 1.

combined with the numismatic evidence for the laying of the Terrace Wall and for filling and paving north of it suggests that, with due allowance for the circulation of the coins, the full program was probably completed within the third quarter. Additional evidence having bearing on the time of completion of the program and the beginning use of the South Stoa is provided by the earliest material from the Stoa wells (p. 197) whose construction was evidently an integrated part of the program.

Objects published or noted:

C-53-14: p. 107	C-53-59: **317**
C-53-53: p. 107	C-53-60: **304**
C-53-54: p. 106	C-53-62: **661**
C-53-57: p. 137[20]	C-53-63: **660**
C-53-58: **314**	

89. Fill of Underground Sanctuary, Agora SC, V–X: 24–26
Bibliography:
Charles H. Morgan II, *A.J.A.*, XLI, 1937, pp. 545–547, fig. 8, and pls. XIII, 1–2, XIV, 2.
Oscar Broneer, *Hesperia*, XI, 1942, pp. 142–145, fig. 2.
Broneer, *S. Stoa*, p. 8, pl. 3, 1, and plans III–IV.
Summary:
The sanctuary was located north of Shop XIX of the South Stoa. The projected line of the Stoa's Terrace Wall crosses over it. If the Terrace Wall actually existed here[21] virtually the entire structure would have been covered, either by the Wall itself or by filling behind it to the south. The bedding of a Roman pavement was preserved over most of the area occupied by the shrine.

The Sanctuary was constructed during the 6th century. A fill of ash, cinders, and lamb and pig bones, attributed to the time of use of the Sanctuary, lay over the floor. A fill above was evidently introduced at the time when the Sanctuary was put out of use, presumably because of the construction of the South Stoa. Two coins provide a *terminus post quem* for the filling, one of Aigion dated after 404 B.C., and a bronze Corinthian coin of the Pegasos/Trident series. The beginning of the latter series is placed by Martin Price in 394 B.C. This particular coin has not yet been assigned to a group in the series. Fragments of Attic calyx kantharoi, catalogued (C-63-501) and uncatalogued, little if any advanced beyond the

latest from Olynthos, suggest that the filling took place in the early third quarter of the 4th century. Many fragments throughout the filling of a fine pebble mosaic with a representation of a griffin and a horse (*A.J.A.*, XLI, 1937, p. 546, fig. 8) evidently represent the dismantling of a house, fortifying the thought that the filling resulted from activities in preparation for construction of the South Stoa. A final filling was introduced at the top evidently to serve as a bedding for the Roman pavement.
Objects noted:

C-63-501: p. 221

90. Agora SC, Filling of Pit at N–O: 21–23
Bibliography:
Charles H. Morgan II, *A.J.A.*, XLI, 1937, p. 547, pl. XIII, l, h, and 2 (cistern).
Summary:
The pit was located north of Shop XXI of the South Stoa, its southwest corner being about 2.00 m. north of the projected line of the Terrace Wall of the Stoa and a little to the northwest of the Underground Sanctuary (Deposit 89).

This pit has a number of strange features. It is trapezoidal in plan. Four internal steps provided access from above at the southwest corner. On the bottom along the east and near the northeast corner narrow trenches are reported. On the long sides, in the earth above the stereo in which the pit was cut, were ledges, broad on one side, narrow on the other. The field records and the published notice have suggested, seemingly without much conviction in the case of the former, that it was a cistern. No waterproof plaster seems to have been preserved in it, however, and it does not seem in general very suitable for this purpose.

Study and repeated testing of the material from this pit indicates that it was originally filled in the early third quarter of the 4th century B.C., probably at the same time and for the same reason (imminent construction of the South Stoa) as the Underground Sanctuary. Though it cannot be objectively demonstrated, it seems likely that the pit was covered through most of antiquity by the cobble pavement which is attested to have been laid over the fill north of the Terrace Wall of the South Stoa, preserved close by, beginning just west of the Bema and continuing eastward. The filling of the pit seems to have remained intact

---

[21] Broneer, *S. Stoa*, p. 8, assumes that it did, reporting, however, that all traces of it in the area have been removed: cf. also his p. 90, with reference to the Terrace Wall in the area north of Shops XV–XXII. It seems a bit odd, however, that no trace of the wall is preserved in the Sanctuary itself since its floor was not at a very low level. Possibly there was some deviation of the line of the Terrace Wall in this vicinity. Morgan has suggested, alternatively (*A.J.A.*, XLIII, 1939, p. 258), "The lack of a central section of wall is explained by the height of hardpan at that point, for it rises about level with the top of the wall, and needed no retention."

until Byzantine times when a kind of bothros was excavated over most of its area, the digging and use of which introduced not only an accumulation of that period but, as might be expected, a certain amount of material of Greek times appreciably later than the time of original deposit.

The use of a deposit so affected is vulnerable and certainly further testing of it is indicated. The amount of material from the fill regarded as original, which seems in the very great bulk to have been confined to the lower part of the pit, occupying *ca.* 0.50 to 0.75 m. of its depth of 1.05 m., is very considerable. In addition to a few lamps and miscellaneous finds there are 180 catalogued pieces and a very great amount of context pottery. In the vessels some 40 different shapes are represented. Generally speaking the material seems to fit well in the range adopted here, mainly in the second quarter of the 4th century and into the early third quarter. Some fourteen of the shape series have been studied here in detail and some have been studied also in lesser degree. The placement of examples of the series studied in the period suggested has, in each case, proved relatively entirely satisfactory. Many of the pieces are Attic and find close parallels in stage of development of shape with the latest from Olynthos, thus supporting the lower dating suggested. Quite apart from chronological and topographical considerations, additional fragments of the griffin mosaic (*A.J.A.*, XLI, 1937, p. 546, fig. 8), most of which was found in the filling of the Underground Sanctuary, were found in the filling of the pit, thus supporting the thought that the two deposits were made at one time.

Some aspects of the material, in addition to the unusual features of the pit's construction, suggest that there may have been a functional connection with the Underground Sanctuary. The provision of steps may suggest that it was also an underground cult room. Cinders and ashes were mixed with the earth and clay of the filling. Of the vessels from the filling some 50 are miniatures, presumably votive. This and the seemingly short range in period of the pottery in general may suggest that the pit in the end served as a final favissa for the sanctuary.

Objects published or noted:

C-37-2491: **324**	C-37-2520: **198**
C-37-2492: **312**	C-37-2521: **302**
C-37-2493: **328**	C-37-2522: **354**
C-37-2494: **315**	C-37-2523: **326**
C-37-2506: p. 124[11]	C-37-2524: **356**
C-37-2509: **667**	C-37-2525: **329**
C-37-2510: **734**	C-37-2526: **310**
C-37-2512: **697**	C-37-2527: **369**
C-37-2528: **316**	C-37-2588: **159**
C-37-2532: p. 29[14]	C-37-2589: **73**
C-37-2533: p. 29[14]	C-37-2590: **20**
C-37-2534: p. 29[14]	C-37-2597: p. 96[92]
C-37-2535: pp. 29[14], 178	C-37-2604: p. 30[14]
C-37-2536: **49**	C-37-2605: p. 30[14]
C-37-2537: **57**	C-37-2606: p. 30[14]
C-37-2538: **46**	C-37-2607: p. 30[14]
C-37-2539: **61**	C-37-2608: p. 30[14]
C-37-2540: **58**	C-37-2609: p. 30[14]
C-37-2541: **96**	C-37-2610: **65**
C-37-2542: **97**	C-37-2611: **37**
C-37-2543: p. 29[14]	C-37-2614: **145**
C-37-2544: **36**	C-37-2615: **144**
C-37-2545: p. 29[14]	C-37-2617: **157**
C-37-2546: **99**	C-37-2619: **143**
C-37-2547: p. 30[14]	C-37-2641: **602**
C-37-2582: **147**	C-37-2645: **603**
C-37-2583: **171**	C-37-2662: **303**
C-37-2584: **148**	C-37-2666: **9**
C-37-2585: **156**	C-37-2667: **3**
C-37-2586: **158**	C-63-503: **610**
C-37-2587: **142**	C-63-504: p. 106

91. Filling under cobble pavement of South Stoa Terrace

Bibliography:

Charles H. Morgan II: *A.J.A.*, XL, 1936, p. 475, and fig. 5, E; XLI, 1937, p. 543 and pl. XIII, 1; *Hesperia*, XXII, 1953, p. 140.

Scranton, *The Lower Agora*, p. 76, and note 6.

Broneer, *S. Stoa*, pp. 88–91 (the Terrace Wall).

Summary:

The construction of a terrace immediately in front of the South Stoa and a graded slope beyond the Terrace Wall was evidently a necessary part of the South Stoa construction program to provide access from the central area to the north which, in Hellenistic times, was at an appreciably lower level than that of the stylobate of the Stoa. It is reasonable to assume that the terrace was paved, as presumably was the floor of the colonnade of the Stoa, although apparently no evidence for paving here has been forthcoming. Paving of the graded slope north of the terrace is, however, attested since a paving of cobblestones set in tough clay *ca.* 0.20 m. thick was preserved at the time of excavation in various places. Some was removed in excavation in order to reach deposits or graves beneath it, but much still remains *in situ*. No doubt more will be found in place in future excavation, particularly at the east where excavation has evidently not reached the pavement level. Fill and deposits beneath it may be expected to yield further, well-sealed evidence concerning the South Stoa construction program. Specific deposits found sealed by the paving or thought to have been sealed when the paving, missing above them, was laid have been summarized separately (Deposits 79, 80, 88, 89(?), 92). The present heading is intended to cover objects from general fillings found actually sealed by the paving, either in past or future excavations. The few objects, including a coin, from a small patch of the paving due north of Shop XXVII of the Stoa, have been included here in the list of Deposit 88. Deposit 92 includes a few additional objects from a patch of filling which probably was found sealed by the paving, though we do not have a specific statement to that effect. The paving is attested, more extensively preserved, just to the east and south of the Bema and still further east for a bit south of the line of the Central Shops. The dating adopted here for the completion of the South Stoa construction program leads to the assumption that objects found in the filling beneath the pavement will antedate *ca.* 330 B.C. The objects now known to have been found under existing pavement are few, including some pieces of pottery, terracottas, and loomweights. The number may be increased by further scrutiny of the field records and by an examination of context material, which has not been located for examination as yet.

Objects published:

92. Agora SC, fill over stereo at V–Y: 13–20
Bibliography:
Charles H. Morgan II, *A.J.A.*, XLI, 1937, p. 543, pl. XIII, 1 and 2 (location).
Summary:
This patch of filling lay *ca.* 10–12 m. southwest of the southwest corner of the west exedra of the Bema complex, and *ca.* 6.00 m. north of the projected line of the Terrace Wall of the South Stoa, in the immediate vicinity of Graves A and B of the late Geometric cemetery (Morgan, *op. cit.*, pl. XIII, 2). Morgan indicates that the area of the cemetery was found covered by the cobblestone pavement laid north of the Terrace Wall of the South Stoa and though there is no specific statement that this patch of filling was sealed by

the pavement it seems a reasonable inference that it was.

Two pieces are datable in the first and second quarters of the 4th century B.C. The few others are not at present independently datable.
Objects noted:

C-37-584: p. 107

93. South Stoa, Deposit in Shop XXXII
Bibliography:
Oscar Broneer, *A.J.A.*, XXXVII, 1933, p. 556.
Davidson, *Minor Objects*, p. 17, Deposit VII.
Broneer, *S. Stoa*, pp. 11–12.
Summary:
The area beneath Shops XXXI and XXXII (Broneer, *S. Stoa*, pp. 11–12 and plan VI) was occupied prior to the construction of the Stoa by a structure of which there remain parts of the east and west walls, and a paved floor (in Shop XXXI) at −1.75 m. below Stoa toichobate level. Professor Broneer has associated with this structure three rectangular cuttings in stereo in Shop XXXII, the floor of the larger of which is −2.50 m. below Stoa toichobate level. The structure presumably went out of use at some time appreciably earlier than the time of the construction of the Stoa. A manhole leading into the Great Reservoir (Deposits 82, 83) was subsequently cut through the east wall of the structure. The time of the abandonment of the structure is thus seen to have been earlier than the time of the construction of the Stoa by the extent of the use period of the Great Reservoir at least.

The field records and to some extent the published accounts tend to suggest that the entire filling in Shop XXXII from the level of the Stoa toichobate down to bottom, which contained a very large amount of pottery, some lamps and miscellaneous finds, and over 50 coins, was a single filling at one time. No stratification was reported, and in fact joins were found between pieces at different levels.[22] It seems more likely that there were in fact several fillings. It is to be expected that some of the filling within this shop is attributable to the time of use of the early structure mentioned above and its abandonment.

---

[22] Joining fragments at different levels could readily be present in a filling dumped in successive loads from different angles and thus having various slopes. This would very likely have been the case in filling up the area within the foundations of the Stoa shop after the disruption of lower fills caused by laying the blocks of the foundations. The conclusion that the fill, of up to 2.50 m. in depth, was a single one is not reasonable nor likely since it implies that at least until far into the Hellenistic period the interior of the shop was a gaping hole with no usable floor and no accumulation of fill representing the various pre-Stoa and Stoa activities. There is, it is true, an instance of omission of fill and flooring within Shop I (Deposit 94), but there this would seem to be due to the special circumstance that much of the shop was occupied by a stairway. The depth below toichobate to bedrock in Shop I was, in any case, slight as compared with that in Shop XXXII.

It also seems likely that a further amount was introduced at the time of the construction of the manhole in Shop XXXI, and that still another filling was required when the South Stoa was constructed, to serve as a basis for the floor of the shop, which is attested to have existed here at a point 0 to –0.10 m. below toichobate level. The floor evidently was broken through in the course of the use of the shop and the material in the upper part of the filling, which included all the coins, all of which are dated after 400 B.C., was evidently gradually introduced in subsequent years, some as late as mediaeval.

The existence of the various fillings suggested cannot be objectively demonstrated. The catalogued pottery from the entire filling has a very considerable range, from at least the 6th century B.C. down to at least as late as the 3rd century B.C.

Objects published:

C-33-116: **267**   C-33-227: **500**

94. South Stoa, Shop I, Pottery Deposit

Bibliography:

Oscar Broneer, *A.J.A.*, XXXIX, 1935, pp. 54–56, figs. 1 and 3.

Broneer, *S. Stoa*, pp. 48–49, fig. 26, and pp. 68–69 (stairway); pp. 94 and 97 (deposit); pls. 7 and 27 and plan I.

Summary:

The deposit occupied the area beneath the stairway in Shop I. The filling or fillings concerned evidently extended from stereo to the level of the toichobate of the Stoa here, a depth of *ca.* 0.80 m.

The following interpretation of the deposit is not fully demonstrable, but various indications are recorded which make it a possible one.[23]

It seems likely that the deposit represents a casual and very gradual accumulation of material initiated when the Stoa began to be used and continuing all through the lifetime of the Greek Stoa. The bulk of it would seem to have gathered by the time of the destruction of the Stoa by Mummius in 146 B.C. It may possibly contain an indication of a partial destruction of the Stoa during this time and it seems quite likely that there is also indication of the destruction of the Stoa by fire at the time of Mummius. A slight amount of material may represent activities in the early days after the establishment of the Roman colony in 44 B.C.

Professor Broneer in his field records and publications has already pointed out that the deposit was made after the construction of the Stoa, not before. The footing trench of the east wall of the Stoa (Deposit 84) was not cut through the deposit here, and in fact it is indicated by the records that the inner faces of the foundation blocks of the shop remained visible and accessible after they had been laid for they show signs of wear and mutilation. This is compatible with the thought that the builders of the Stoa provided no floor proper here, leaving the area as it was on completion of the construction. There would have been no reason to provide a floor, for no traffic would have been expected here beneath the stairway. Professor Broneer has pointed out that the area was in fact restricted in access at least for part of the Stoa's time of use (Broneer, *S. Stoa*, p. 69), and probably for the most part it was accessible only to the users of Shop II. It was evidently partly shut off on the west by a crude wall, at least to some height. The area can be visualized in terms of a modern hall closet beneath stairs to the upper floor. And like a hall closet it seems to have accumulated junk. No doubt there were frequent contributions to it, predominantly broken vessels from the users of Shop II. The range of these extends from the very early days of the Stoa, from *ca.* 325 or perhaps a bit earlier, right down through, with occasional representations of the years in between, to the time of the destruction in 146 B.C. Some of the material, particularly the numerous coins, whose dates span this period and extend in some cases earlier, may have been dropped through the openings in the wooden stair, which presumably would have lacked risers, by people ascending to or leaving the upper floor. A deposit accumulating in this way, objects being thrown or dropped in from time to time from various angles and levels, could not be expected to show easily detectible stratification or consistency in date from level to level. In fact, some of the latest material was found quite close to or at bottom, a situation compatible with the thought of an accumulation of the material in various sloping strata. The records indicate that there were two layers of burning, one at –0.50 and the other at –0.20 m.,

---

[23] Alternatively, it has been suggested by Professor Broneer (bibliography above) that the area was a deliberately excavated hollow, presumably dug either for the reception of the deposit or concerned with an alteration of the Stoa which involved lowering the floors. These possibilities seem to the present writer less likely. There is little if anything in the deposit to suggest the former interpretation in any case. Votives are conspicuously absent. An additional thought that part of the material represents the cleaning out of one of the Stoa wells, e.g. Well II, during the Greek period of use is possible, but it is evident that this would not completely account for the deposit.

evidently sloping, for it was noted that the two merged at one point. The pottery deposit proper is stated to have been below a burned layer, though which of the two is not clear. The uppermost burned layer seems attributable to burning of the Stoa by Mummius. It is not excluded that both layers refer to the same event, though an earlier conflagration seems possible. Pieces of Corinthian roof tiles are reported from between the two levels of burning. Apparently above them both, in the area, other fragments of Greek tiles were found, among them one, FS 654, which provides an association with Mummius' destruction since it joined FS 512, found in the Mummian filling of Well II. The amount of material which may have been added in the early years of the Roman colony is certainly not great and it is not absolutely certain at present that any of the material is actually of this time. A curious inscribed pottery disk (for magical use?), C-34-27, is from an unknown depth in the fill. It is unique and cannot be claimed with any conviction as Hellenistic of pre-destruction times. Conceivably it is early Roman.

The deposit so interpreted provides an interesting cross-section of the life and activities in the South Stoa during its Greek period, as much if not more than any of the use fillings of the wells. Its material in character and composition is quite like that of many of the accumulations of the Greek period in the wells, a point in favor of its being an accumulation from everyday life in the Stoa.

Objects published or noted:

C-34-16: p. 50[36]	C-34-392 a, f: **424**
C-34-17: p. 30[14]	C-34-392 b: **502**
C-34-19: **116**	C-34-392 c: **503**
C-34-21: **5**	C-34-392 d: **504**
C-34-22: **30**	C-34-392 e: **505**
C-34-23: **134**	C-34-392 g: **506**
C-34-24: **82**	C-34-393: p. 33[17]
C-34-27: p. 225	C-34-394: **460**
C-34-30: **483**	C-34-395: **490**
C-34-31: **484**	C-34-396: **467**
C-34-33: **731**	C-34-397: **489**
C-34-34: **437**	C-34-471: **706**
C-34-35: **700**	C-34-2497: p. 88
C-34-37: **532**	C-34-2499: **128**
C-34-38: p. 44	C-35-128: **908**

95. South Stoa, Well II

Bibliography:

Broneer, *S. Stoa*, p. 63 and pl. 14, 5 (two kantharoi); plan I (location of well).

Summary:

In this well there were evidently two fillings, a use fill entirely below water level and a filling from below water level to the top (with a hiatus of about 4.50 m. evidently caused by pieces of tile blocking the shaft at a high level). The two fills cannot be objectively separated since no doubt pieces from the upper filling penetrated into the lower when the former was thrown in. The catalogued pottery, lamps, and miscellaneous finds all came from the lowest part of the well and are likely to belong to the use fill. The pottery ranges in date from the early last quarter of the 4th century to 146 B.C. Amphora handles, also from the same depth, are of the 3rd century and the first half of the 2nd century B.C. The coins from the entire filling of the well are of the 4th and 3rd centuries B.C. Some were from the lowest part of the well, including those evidently latest, which may of course have been minted in the 2nd century, Philip V, 220–179 B.C. The material of the final filling consisted almost entirely of architectural pieces, both stone members and roof tiles, evidently largely from the Stoa. The well is thus believed to have been in use from at least the early last quarter of the 4th century to the time of the destruction of Corinth in 146 B.C. The absence of material of later date in the well is taken to indicate that it was filled up with destruction debris in the very early years of the Roman colony, after 44 B.C. Pieces of tiles from the upper filling join others from the Mummian destruction filling in Well V.

Objects published or noted:

C-47-106: **464**	C-47-116: **79**
C-47-107: **536**	C-47-117: **122**
C-47-112: **480**	C-47-118: p. 40[26]
C-47-113: **469**	C-47-119: **400**

96. South Stoa, Well III

Bibliography:

Broneer, *S. Stoa*, plan I (location of well).

Summary:

The filling of the well from top to water level is not known. This was apparently dug in the early days of excavation at Corinth; the records of its excavation and the objects found have not been identified.

What remained to be excavated below water level in 1947 indicated two fillings, primarily a use filling at bottom with a slight amount of an upper filling containing architectural members, both stone and tile.

The pottery, catalogued and uncatalogued, to be assigned to the use fill indicates that the well was continuously in use from some time in the third quarter of the 4th century to the time of the destruction of Corinth in 146 B.C. The earliest pottery in the context material (Corinth Lot 3608–3611), including a number of pieces of skyphoi of Attic type somewhat more advanced in shape than the latest examples of the form from Olynthos, is fragmentary, suggesting that the well had been cleaned out at least once in the course of the nearly 200 years of use. There is fairly even representation among the rest from *ca.* 300 to 146 B.C. The numerous coins are primarily of the 4th and 3rd centuries with a few of dates overlapping the 3rd century and the first half of the 2nd century. A proportion of these no doubt are infiltrative from the later filling. The assignment of the meager amount of architectural material to the destruction of Mummius, presumably thrown in in the very early years of the Roman colony, seems reasonable.

Objects published or noted:

C-47-86: **409**	C-47-120: **510**
C-47-87: **416**	C-47-121: **493**
C-47-89: **605**	C-47-122: **399**
C-47-90: **606**	C-47-123: **417**
C-47-91: **607**	C-47-124: **435**
C-47-92: **393**	C-47-125: **487**
C-47-93: **398**	C-47-126: **4**
C-47-94: **433**	C-47-128: **224**
C-47-97: p. 50[38]	C-47-146: **511**
C-47-98: p. 102[99]	

97. South Stoa, Well IV

Bibliography:

Oscar Broneer, *Hesperia*, XVI, 1947, p. 242 and pl. LXII, 23 (terracotta mould).

Broneer, *S. Stoa*, plan I (location of well).

Davidson, *Minor Objects*, nos. 1478 and 1479, pl. 89 (lead shovels).

Summary:

It is thought that there were three separate fillings in this well, though they cannot be objectively demonstrated.

The amount of material which can be attributed to the period of use of the well, probably including all the pottery published here, is meager. It seems very likely that the well had been very extensively cleaned out shortly before going out of use. Of the catalogued pottery one piece is probably of *ca.* 250 B.C. Whether or not the other pieces may actually be as late as 146 B.C. is open to question since they are of series with scanty representation and their dates will need review when more is known of these series.

Above, between depths –8.80 and –3.00 m., two different kinds of earth were noted, below a red fill, above a black fill with much ash and carbon. Both contained pieces of roof tiles, some at least from the Stoa, and both contained fragments of terracotta figurines. These two are regarded as probably a single fill. The coins from –3.00 to bottom (aside from one intrusive Byzantine coin,

no doubt filtered in between the two periods of excavation) were all of the 4th and 3rd centuries with a few of dates overlapping the 3rd century and the first half of the 2nd. The presence of broken roof tiles suggests some destruction of the Stoa involving the roof. The absence of other kinds of architectural members, usually present in the fillings attributed to the Mummian destruction, is perhaps notable. Conceivably the filling in which the tiles appear is attributable to some pre-Mummian, presumably localized fire. As a parallel, there is an indication in the Mummian filling of Well XIX suggesting that the Stoa was in process of some repair and redecoration at the time of Mummius.

The filling at the top, which contained little, though including two Pergamene fragments, is thought to be a supplementary one, introduced at the time when the marble pavement of the Roman Room B (Broneer, *S. Stoa*, pp. 106–107) was laid.

Objects published:

C-34-25: **687**	C-47-148: **140**
C-47-147: **628**	C-47-149: **194**

98. South Stoa, Well V

Bibliography:

Oscar Broneer, *A.J.A.*, XXXVII, 1933, p. 564 and fig. 8 (marble gaming board).

Broneer, *S. Stoa*, pl. 15, 1 (marble gaming board) and pl. 24, 4 (two lamps: CL 3787–3788); plan I (well).

Kent, *The Inscriptions*, no. 42.

Davidson, *Minor Objects*, no. 491, pl. 47 (bronze lock of hair).

Summary:

Though it cannot be fully demonstrated it is believed that this well contained two fillings, a use fill at bottom and a final filling from a point near water level to the top.

The pottery attributed to the use filling covers the range from the last quarter of the 4th century probably to 146 B.C. The filling above, at least to –5.00 m., perhaps to –4.00 m., contained a wide variety of Stoa architectural material, both stone and tile, indicative of an extensive destruction of the Stoa. The upper filling, though evidently not characterized by destruction filling, may belong since pottery joins were noted between it and lower levels. The coins from the entire filling (aside from two Byzantine, no doubt introduced during World War II years between the two periods of excavation) are primarily of the 4th and 3rd centuries B.C. with some overlapping into the first half of the 2nd century. From the earth of the well derived from excavation of World War II debris and the ancient filling below water level came a coin of Patras,

146–32 B.C., and a Corinthian coin of the early Roman duovir series. These plus Arretine and Samian fragments mixed with the upper fill suggest that the final fillings of the well took place in the period of the early Roman colony after 44 B.C. and that the bulk of the final filling represents clean-up and disposal of material deriving from the Mummian destruction of the Stoa. The well was covered by the same marble pavement of Room B as Well IV.

Objects published or noted:

C-33-433: **914**	C-47-150: p. 33[17]
C-33-985: **695**	C-47-151: **245**
C-33-986: **712**	C-47-152: p. 50[38]
C-33-1119: p. 33[17]	C-47-153: **471**
C-33-1461: **850**	C-47-154: **486**
C-33-1462: p. 28[11]	C-47-155: **485**
C-33-1463: p. 40[26]	C-47-157: **779**
C-33-1471: pp. 28[12], 33[17]	C-47-158: **738**
C-33-1473: **501**	C-47-159: **726**
C-47-88: **473**	

99. South Stoa, Well VII

Bibliography:

Broneer, *S. Stoa*, pl. 14, 2 (well curb); plan II (well).

Kent, *The Inscriptions*, no. 28.

Davidson, *Minor Objects*, no. 1681, fig. 37 and pl. 99 (bone counter).

Summary:

In this well there was evidently a slight accumulation of the use period. The pottery assigned to it covers the range from *ca.* 250 to 146 B.C. Very likely the well had been subject to a cleaning out during its period of use which removed early accumulation. Whether there was one filling or more in the well subsequent to this cannot be objectively demonstrated. Conceivably there were two, one from –8.85 to –4.70 m. in which architectural elements are prevalent, representing clean-up of Mummian destruction debris and a second from –4.70 to top in which little or no architecture is present, perhaps a supplementary fill introduced at the time of the laying of the flooring of the Roman Agonotheteion above (Broneer, *S. Stoa*, pp. 107–111, plans II and XV). The final filling of the well, whether in one or two stages, had evidently occurred by some time in the second half of the 1st century after Christ. The few coins from the well (the entire shaft) are rather earlier, some of the 3rd century and the first half of the 2nd century, one of Patras, 146–32 B.C., and one Corinthian of the Early Roman period duovir series. An appreciable quantity of Arretine and Samian pieces and fragments of blown glass come from various levels in the upper filling and a lamp

of Broneer's Type XXII from near the top, at –1.75 m.

Objects published or noted:

C-33-1220: p. 87	C-47-226: **7**
C-47-222: **497**	C-47-227: p. 30[14]
C-47-223: **192**	

100. South Stoa, Well VIII

Bibliography:

Oscar Broneer, *A.J.A.*, XXXIX, 1935, pp. 72–73, fig. 17.

Broneer, *S. Stoa*, pp. 111–115, pls. 32, 33, plans II and XVI (Well VIII and Room D); pl. 32, 2 (marble bench support).

Summary:

The bottom of the well was not certainly reached in excavation and there is no real indication of a use filling, though a lamp and pieces of Stoa roof tiles at bottom may reflect the Greek lifetime of the Stoa and its destruction by Mummius. The filling of the entire well otherwise is probably a single one introduced within the second half of the 1st century after Christ, after Nero. The material from it is, with the exception of a few earlier pieces and coins, predominantly Roman.

Objects published:

101. South Stoa, Well IX

Bibliography:

G. R. Edwards, *Hesperia*, XVIII, 1949, pp. 151–152 and pl. 16, 14.

Broneer, *S. Stoa*, pp. 111–115, pls. 32, 33, plans II and XVI (well and Room D).

Summary:

It is not absolutely certain that bottom was reached in excavating this well. The amount of material attributable to the use of the well is neither particularly characteristic nor extensive. Much of the depth below water level was taken up by seven or eight complete coarse amphorae. The pottery with them covers a range from *ca.* 250 to 146 B.C. Evidently either a cleaning of the well had removed earlier material of the time of use or it remains to be discovered beneath the appreciable depth of water. What is regarded as a single filling from just below water level to –1.25 m. (the shaft was empty at top) is to be attributed to a clean-up of Mummian destruction debris, which included many architectural elements of the South Stoa, in the very early years of the Roman period after 44 B.C. The coins from the entire shaft, including none of Roman times, date in the 4th and 3rd centuries with some overlapping into the first half of the 2nd century B.C. A few scraps of early Roman material (Augustan barbotine and Samian) indicate the time when the clean-up took place.

Objects published:

C-48-53: **129**	C-48-61: **915**
C-48-59: **488**	C-48-245: **604**

102. South Stoa, Well X

Bibliography:

Broneer, *S. Stoa*, p. 115 and plans II and XVI (well and entrance to South Basilica).

Davidson, *Minor Objects*, nos. 1124, 1185, 1186, 1188, 1783, 2511, pls. 74, 76, 101, 122.

Summary:

It seems possible that there was a slight use filling in the well, including some material of the 3rd century B.C., though this cannot be objectively demonstrated. Probably two other fillings are also represented in this well. That from below water level to –2.70 m. is regarded as a clean-up of Mummian destruction debris introduced probably early in the Roman colony after 44 B.C. Along with tiles, including ones from the Stoa, pieces of the well curb and a statue base, was much Hellenistic pottery. A Samian fragment suggests the time of the introduction of this filling. A filling from –2.70 m. to top is regarded as supplementary, probably to compensate for settling, and was presumably introduced at the time of the construction of the entrance portico of the South Basilica above. This filling seems to be entirely of Roman material.

Objects published or noted:

C-34-82: **85**	C-34-1621: p. 91
C-34-153: pp. 91	C-34-1622: **789**
C-34-470: pp. 39[25], 40[26]	C-34-1623: pp. 30[14], 33[17]
C-34-474: p. 33[17]	C-34-1624: p. 162[21]
C-34-1602: p. 37[22]	C-34-1640: p. 30[14]
C-34-1603: **107**	C-34-1645: **777**
C-34-1604: p. 40[26]	C-34-1738: **715**
C-34-1605: p. 30[14]	C-34-1740: p. 162[21]
C-34-1607: p. 37[22]	C-34-1742: **929**
C-34-1608: **704**	C-34-2489 a, b: **686**
C-34-1609: **711**	C-47-228: **775**
C-34-1610: **713**	C-47-233: p. 50[34]
C-34-1611: **685**	C-47-234: **633**
C-34-1612: **699**	C-47-235: **6**
C-34-1613: **658**	C-47-236: **822**
C-34-1614: **714**	C-47-237: **797**
C-34-1615: **109**	C-47-238: p. 180[43]
C-34-1616: **33**	C-47-241: **832**
C-34-1617: **153**	C-47-242: **626**
C-34-1618: p. 33[17]	C-47-256: **705**
C-34-1619: **213**	C-47-901: **527**
C-34-1620: **87**	

103. South Stoa, Well XI

Bibliography:

Broneer, *S. Stoa*, p. 115, and plans II, III, XVI (location of well, and entrance portico to South Basilica).

Summary:

The bottom of the well was not reached in excavation and evidently at least 1.00 m. of the filling remains to be dug. Probably only one or two of the pieces recovered represents, then, the use filling (presumably **742** is one). It is believed that there were two subsequent fillings. One from below water level to –7.75 m. is taken to represent a clean-up of Mummian destruction debris, including architectural material from the Stoa, probably introduced early in the Roman period. The pottery noted below, with the exception of **742**, is regarded as of the time of the destruction. Fragments from the Mummian filling of Well X joined a number of these. The coins from this level are all of the Greek period, of the 4th and 3rd centuries with some overlapping into the first half of the 2nd century B.C. Some Arretine sherds reported from this level indicate the time of the introduction of this fill. The filling from *ca.* –7.75 to –5.50 m., containing little and that Roman, is regarded as supplementary, perhaps in connection with the construction of the entrance portico of the South Basilica above. Coins of Marcus Aurelius and Antoninus Pius in it indicate that it was introduced in the 2nd century after Christ. The shaft of the well was empty from –5.50 m. to top where it was sealed by the floor of the portico.

Objects published or noted:

C-47-233: p. 50[34]	C-47-241: **832**
C-47-234: **633**	C-47-245: **742**
C-47-235: **6**	C-47-246: **654**
C-47-236: **822**	C-47-247: **655**
C-47-237: **797**	C-47-248: p. 124
C-47-238: p. 180[43]	

104. South Stoa, Well XII

Bibliography:

Richard Stillwell, *A.J.A.*, XL, 1936, pp. 32–39 (Fountain House).

Broneer, *S. Stoa*, pp. 115–128, plans III and XVI (well and Fountain House).

Davidson, *Minor Objects*, no. 2886, pl. 136 (bronze wheel).

Summary:

The bottom of the well was evidently not reached in excavation. A large stone at –10.25 m., below water level, could not be removed. There is thus nothing which can certainly be attributed to the period of use of the well. That the entire filling of the well (up to –1.10 m., the top being empty) was introduced at one time cannot be objectively demonstrated, though it seems likely. This filling, which included a variety of architectural elements and part of the well curb, is regarded as representing clean-up of Mummian destruction debris in the early years of the Roman colony after 44 B.C. The coins from the entire shaft were of the 4th and 3rd centuries with overlapping into the first half of the 2nd century B.C. A coin of Corinth of the duovir series evidently represents the time of the introduction of the filling. A coin of Valentinian, from searching the earth of the well, is probably not pertinent. The well was sealed over by the cement base for the floor of the Roman Fountain House above.

Objects published or noted:

C-35-116: p. 173[28]	C-35-721: **717**
C-35-117 and	C-35-723: **684**
C-35-719: **845**	C-35-830 and C-35-651
C-35-649: **110**	and C-35-912: p. 91[87]
C-35-650: **118**	C-35-831: p. 37[22]
C-35-651 and C-35-830	C-35-832: p. 37[22]
and C-35-912: p. 91[87]	C-35-833: **718**
C-35-653: **911**	C-35-912 and C-35-830
C-35-718: p. 30[14]	and C-35-651: p. 91[87]
C-35-719 and	C-47-258: p. 162[21]
C-35-117: **845**	C-47-261: **673**
C-35-720: **716**	

105. South Stoa, Well XIII

Bibliography:
> Broneer, *S. Stoa*, pp. 115–128, plans III and XVI (well and Fountain House).
> Davidson, *Minor Objects*, nos. 289, 353, and 1729, pls. 24, 31, and 100.
> Kent, *The Inscriptions*, no. 31.

Summary:

It is not entirely certain that bottom was reached in this well in excavation. There is no material which suggests a use fill. Though it cannot be objectively demonstrated that the filling of the well (empty to –1.50 m.) was a single operation, it seems likely. It included many architectural elements and tiles and is taken to represent a clean-up of Mummian debris in the early years of the Roman colony after 44 B.C. An Arretine sherd evidently represents the time of the introduction of the filling. Only two coins were found, both of Corinth of the Pegasos/Trident series. The well was sealed by the floor of the Roman Fountain House above.

Objects published or noted:

C-33-304: p.	C-33-1001: **674**
C-33-306: **113**	C-34-2419: **662**
C-33-998: p.	

106. South Stoa, Well XIV

Bibliography:
> Oscar Broneer, *Hesperia*, XVI, 1947, p. 240 and pl. LVIII, 11.
> Broneer, *S. Stoa*, pp. 124–128, plans III, XVI, XVII (well and Room F).

Summary:

The appreciable amount of material which can be assigned to the use filling of this well, from water level to bottom, extends in date from *ca.* 330 to 146 B.C. At least the bulk of the remainder of the filling of the shaft, from water level to at least –2.25 m., is regarded as a single filling representing a clean-up of Mummian destruction debris. This included a mass of architectural material, both stone and tile. The coins from the entire shaft are of the Greek period, of the 4th and 3rd centuries, with some overlapping into the first half of the 2nd century B.C. There seems to be no admixture of early Roman material in this filling, hence it is assumed that it must have been introduced into the well very early in the time of the Roman colony, soon after 44 B.C. In the upper part of the well, a red fill with almost nothing in it is reported from –2.25 to –1.25 m. and above this some "mixed fill." These may or may not be part of the same filling as that immediately below them.

Objects published or noted:

C-47-268: **475**	C-47-294: **496**
C-47-269: **189**	C-47-295: **479**
C-47-271: **395**	C-47-296: **482**
C-47-282: p. 50[35]	C-47-297: **774**
C-47-288: **389**	C-47-298: **643**
C-47-289: **466**	C-47-299: **206**
C-47-290: **420**	C-47-300: **207**
C-47-291: **463**	C-47-301: p. 121[7]
C-47-292: **394**	C-47-302: **522**
C-47-293: **465**	C-47-303: pp. 122[9], 138[23]

107. South Stoa, Well XV

Bibliography:
> Oscar Broneer, *Hesperia*, XVI, 1947, pp. 239–242; pl. LVII, 8, lower right; pl. LXI, 19; pl. LXII, 22.
> Broneer, *S. Stoa*, pp. 126–128, plans III, XVII (well and Room F).
> G. R. Edwards, *Hesperia*, XXVI, 1957, pl. 80 (C-46-51 b).
> Kent, *The Inscriptions*, nos. 22 and 25.

Summary:

There is no indication of a use filling in this well. It seems likely, however, that there were at least two other separate fillings in the well shaft. One, from bottom to *ca.* –6.00 m., with joining fragments at various levels, represents a clean-up of Mummian destruction debris thrown in soon after the foundation of the Roman colony in 44 B.C. It includes some tiles and architectural blocks and fragments of the complete well curb. Three amphora handles in the fill are of the second quarter of the second century B.C. and two are of the earlier 2nd century. Coins from this level are of the Greek period, of the 4th and 3rd centuries with some overlapping into the first half of the 2nd century B.C. Some of the material from this filling probably has relevance to repair and redecoration of the Stoa at the time of the Mummian destruction (see under Well XIX).

The filling from –6.00 m. to top would seem to represent at least one if not more supplementary fills in the advanced Roman period. It contained a mixture of Hellenistic and Roman material extending probably into the 1st century after Christ. The single Roman coin from this fill (the only one in the well) is of the Corinthian duovir series. The mouth of the well was covered in Roman times by the marble pavement of the Roman Room F.

Objects published or noted:

C-46-15: **38**	C-46-63: p. 176[32]
C-46-26: **683**	C-46-64: **813**
C-46-28: p. 122	C-46-65: **121**
C-46-38: **653**	C-46-66: **105**
C-46-41: p. 123[10]	C-46-68: **672**
C-46-42: **83**	C-46-69 a–c: p. 160[17]
C-46-43: **102**	C-46-71: p. 30[14]
C-46-45: p. 30[14]	C-46-73: **141**
C-46-46: **91**	C-46-79: p. 122
C-46-56: **836**	C-46-80: p. 133[16]
C-46-57: **825**	C-47-35: **93**
C-46-58: **249**	C-47-36: **126**
C-46-59: **682**	C-47-37: **92**
C-46-60: **112**	C-47-43: **892**
C-46-62: p. 30[14]	

108. South Stoa, Well XVI

Bibliography:

Oscar Broneer, *Hesperia*, XVI, 1947, pl. LIX, 13 (2 kantharoi).

Broneer, *S. Stoa*, pp. 128–129, plan III (well and Kenchrean Road); pl. 24, 4, upper right (lamp).

Davidson, *Minor Objects*, nos. 1332, 1333, 2900, pls. 82 and 137.

Summary:

Though it cannot be objectively demonstrated, at the bottom there was evidently a small accumulation from the use period of the well, of the 3rd century and probably down to 146 B.C. A filling probably extending from near water level to –5.70 m. is regarded as representing a clean-up of Mummian destruction debris in the early days of the Roman colony after 44 B.C. This included

many fragments of Stoa roof tiles, some other architectural members and pieces of the well curb. The coins from the well, with the exception of two of the 4th century after Christ, which are probably intrusive via the loosely fitting cover of the mouth of the well in the Kenchrean Road, are all of the Greek period, of the 4th and 3rd centuries B.C. The well shaft was empty from –5.70 m. to top.

Objects published or noted:

C-35-115: p. 159	C-47-307: **691**
C-35-636: p. 92[89]	C-47-309: **478**
C-35-674: **720**	C-47-310: **434**
C-35-675: p. 37[23]	C-47-311: **521**
C-47-272: **413**	C-47-312: **166**
C-47-273: p. 88	C-47-313: **80**

109. South Stoa, Well XVIII

Bibliography:

Oscar Broneer, *Hesperia*, XVI, 1947, p. 240 and pl. LVIII, 10 (amphora lids).

Broneer, *S. Stoa*, pp. 129–132, plans III and XVII (well and Bouleuterion).

Summary:

There evidently was a certain amount of filling of the time of use at the bottom. A great deal of pottery including some very heavy water jars and other coarse pottery is reported. Animal bones are also reported at this level. The catalogued pieces include ones datable in the late 4th and early 3rd centuries and ones here dated in the first half of the 2nd century. A few scraps are datable in the course of the third quarter of the 4th century. They may or may not be significant for the time of the first use of the well. Others of this time were also found in the upper fill and hence these may, in this case, be infiltrative.

Whether the fill above, from near water level to top, was introduced in one or more fillings is not fully demonstrable. Evidently at least up to –6.75 m. a clean-up of Mummian destruction debris is represented, for quantities of Stoa tiles of various kinds were found at this level. Fragments of pottery vessels and tiles from this fill joined others from the Mummian fill of the adjacent Well XIX suggesting contemporaneity in disposal of the two fillings, one of the joining pieces coming from the filling of XVIII between –3.00 and –4.75 m. The coins from the entire filling of the shaft of XVIII are all of the Greek period, of the 4th and 3rd centuries with some overlapping into the first half of the 2nd century B.C. Whether one or more fillings were needed to fill the shaft, all were evidently thrown in in the Roman period. A piece of blown glass was found low in the tile fill. Other Roman pieces, including a

Samian rim fragment, are reported from close to the top of the shaft.

Objects published or noted:

C-36-499 a–e and	C-47-328: pp. 162[21], 184[52]
C-48-62: **873**	C-47-329: **897**
C-47-281 a–c: **512**	C-47-330: p. 30[14]
C-47-314: **286**	C-47-331: p. 91
C-47-322: **233**	C-47-335: p. 157[8]
C-47-323: p. 42[29]	C-47-337 a–e: **936**
C-47-325: **135**	C-47-338: **513**
C-47-326: **165**	C-47-900: p. 105[4]

110. South Stoa, Well XIX

Bibliography:

G. R. Edwards, *Hesperia*, XVIII, 1949, p. 152, pls. 16–17, 15–23.

Margaret Thompson, *Hesperia*, XX, 1951, pp. 355–367 (Ptolemaic coins).

Marie Farnsworth, "Ancient Pigments," *Journal of Chemical Education*, XXVIII, 1951, pp. 28–29.

D. A. Amyx, *Hesperia*, XXVII, 1958, p. 212 and footnote 90 (inscribed chytra).

Broneer, *S. Stoa*, pp. 129–132, plans III and XVII (well and Bouleuterion).

Kent, *The Inscriptions*, no. 501.

Summary:

Four fillings, distinguished by multiple joins of fragments, are attested in this well. At bottom there was an early use fill. The earliest pieces in it are fragments (in context pottery) of skyphoi of Attic type of the third quarter of the 4th century. Catalogued pieces of pottery range in date from *ca.* 325 to about the end of the 3rd century B.C. The coins from this filling, which are probably not intrusive from fillings above, are of the 4th and 3rd centuries. This fill was effectively sealed by a mass of pebbles, rough stones, and sherds covered with an adhesive, white, ashlike substance. Above this, appreciably above water level at the time of excavation, there was what may have been a second use filling, an accumulation at any rate, of a depth of somewhat over a meter. The pottery is primarily of the first half of the 2nd century. The coins, some of which no doubt were infiltrative from the fill above this, include one of the 4th century, a number of the 3rd and others with dates overlapping from the 3rd into the 1st half of the 2nd century B.C. A third filling, from –2.10 m. to 8.00 m., evidently represents clean-up of Mummian destruction debris of 146 B.C. Elements of four parts of the Stoa roof were repre-

sented and stone fragments of the well lining and well curb, all indicative of an extensive destruction of the building. A stone altar and the base for a large bronze statue, which had been hacked off, were also included. The coins from this filling are primarily of the 4th and 3rd centuries, with many overlapping into the first half of the 2nd century. No pottery in the filling has been identified as of the period after the establishment of the Roman colony in 44 B.C., though no doubt it was soon after this that the filling was introduced. The character and homogeneity of the filling suggests that most if not all of the material in it was actually in use or stored in the shop at the time of the destruction, and that probably it represents an assemblage of materials concerned with repairs, particularly redecoration, of the Stoa. This included quantities of pigments of a wide range of colors, along with some pots which had been used as pigment containers, and other substances whose chemical composition and use have not been fully determined. In addition there were many bronze nails and tacks and about 30 fragments of large iron spikes. The pottery from the filling is practically unique in Corinth and very largely foreign, of undetermined centers of manufacture.

Professor Broneer has already suggested (*S. Stoa*, p. 94) that various repairs and changes were made in the Stoa in the course of its Greek period, and thought of the end of the 3rd century or the beginning of the 2nd century B.C. as the time. It may reasonably be expected that there was more than one occasion for repairs in the course of the presumed *ca.* 175 or 200 years of use of the Stoa. The indications from this filling of Well XIX may be taken to suggest that one such was in progress at the time of Mummius' destruction in 146 B.C. Quite possibly it was connected with redecoration of the colored elements of the Stoa stone architecture, though much more needs to be known about the suitability of the various pigments and other substances to architectural decoration. The wide range of colors (eleven shades) may seem too great for architectural use in these times but no doubt many were mixed, as now, to obtain the tones desired. The nails and spikes could presumably have been employed for scaffolding for the work. It is to be noted that pigments were also found in some quantity in the filling attributed to the Mummian destruction in Well XV.[24]

---

[24] In *Hesperia*, XVIII, 1949, p. 152, it was suggested that the filling in Well XIX concerned represented a painter's supply shop or perhaps an artist's studio. The present thought that the assemblage of material has direct bearing on the architecture of the Stoa itself was suggested by Judith Perlzweig (Binder). Dr. Perlzweig has also suggested that the quantities (175) of peculiar, crude, foreign vessels found, probably all, in the Mummian filling of Well XV (examples:

The fourth and last filling, in the top two meters of the well, is evidently a supplementary one, perhaps as late as the 2nd or 3rd centuries after Christ.

Objects published or noted:

C-48-62 and	C-48-98: **90**
C-36-499 a–e: **873**	C-48-99: **18**
C-48-65: pp. 120[6], 121[7]	C-48-100: p. 66[58]
C-48-66: **719**	C-48-101: **168**
C-48-67: p. 105[4]	C-48-102: **154**
C-48-69: p. 105[4]	C-48-103: p. 33[17]
C-48-70: p. 105[4]	C-48-104: p. 30[14]
C-48-71: p. 105[4]	C-48-104 bis: p. 28[8]
C-48-72: p. 105[4]	C-48-105: **477**
C-48-72 bis: p. 105[4]	C-48-106: **444**
C-48-73: p. 105[4]	C-48-107: **415**
C-48-74: p. 105[4]	C-48-108: p. 102[99]
C-48-75: p. 105[4]	C-48-110: **609**
C-48-76: p. 105[4]	C-48-112: **612**
C-48-77: p. 105[4]	C-48-117: p. 172[26]
C-48-82: p. 105[4]	C-48-118: **595**
C-48-83: **88**	C-48-119: **584**
C-48-86: **824**	C-48-120: **652**
C-48-87: p. 158	C-48-121: **709**
C-48-90: **918**	C-48-122: **722**
C-48-92: **848**	C-48-123: p. 121
C-48-93: **554**	C-48-124: **650**
C-48-94: **10**	C-48-126: **647**
C-48-95: p. 37[22]	C-48-127: **281**
C-48-96: p. 37[22]	C-48-195: pp. 137[19], 138
C-48-97: **86**	

111. South Stoa, Well XX

Bibliography:

Oscar Broneer, *Hesperia*, XVI, 1947, p. 241, pl. LX, 18 (lower right: lamp); pl. LXI, 20; pl. LXIII, 24, 25.

Broneer, *S. Stoa*, p. 95, pl. 24, 2, left (skyphos) and plan IV (location of well).

Kent, *The Inscriptions*, no. 15.

Summary:

It is thought that there were three fillings in this well, though their identity is not fully demonstrable. The accumulation at the bottom of the well, taken to represent the period of use of the well in the Greek period, is unusual in that it included 21 miniature one- and two-handled cups suitable as votives, and some 60 knucklebones, many sawn or perforated (*Hesperia*, XVI, 1947, p. 241). The miniature vessels are evidently of the early days of the Stoa for their shapes probably

were not produced in Corinth beyond the end of the 4th century B.C. A skyphos of Corinthian type already cited by Professor Broneer (*S. Stoa*, pl. 24, 2, left) is also of this time. Numerous fragments in the context pottery from the lowest levels attest still earlier use of the well, beginning some time in the third quarter of the 4th century. They are primarily from skyphoi of Attic type and from calyx kantharoi, examples of both forms being but little if any advanced beyond the latest stages of the shapes found at Olynthos. The use filling is presumed to have had as a lower limit the time of the destruction of the Stoa in 146 B.C. The filling from –10.90 to top was evidently introduced in Roman times, as indicated by the presence of Roman sherds at various levels. Some difference between the fillings between –10.90 and –7.00 m. and that above prompts the suggestion of two operations. The lower of the two included numerous tile fragments representing various elements of the Stoa roof which suggest that this is clean-up of Mummian destruction debris. The coins from –7.00 and below in the well (none were found above –7.00 m.) are all of the Greek period, of the latter 4th and 3rd centuries, some overlapping into the first half of the 2nd century B.C. The pieces certainly of Roman times in this fill suggest that the filling was introduced in Augustan times or perhaps soon after.

The filling above –7.00 m., particularly above –5.00 m., seems to have included a much larger proportion of Roman pottery and tiles, as well as fragments of Broneer's Type XXII and XXVIII lamps. This is taken to be a supplementary filling introduced at an appreciably later time than the preceding.

Objects published or noted:

C-47-274: p. 158	C-47-356: **396**
C-47-275: pp. 90[84], 180[42]	C-47-357: **397**
C-47-339: **542**	C-47-360: **152**
C-47-340: **846**	C-47-362: **78**
C-47-342: p. 160[17]	C-47-386: **56**
C-47-344: p. 162[21]	C-47-390: **611**
C-47-345: p. 176[32]	C-47-391: **608**
C-47-346: p. 176[32]	C-47-399: **627**
C-47-347: p. 176[32]	C-47-400: p. 40[26]
C-47-351: **830**	C-47-401: **614**
C-47-352: p. 66[58]	C-47-402: **692**
C-47-353: **103**	C-47-403: p. 37[23]
C-47-355: p. 111[13]	C-47-410: **280**

Hesperia, XVI, 1947, pl. LXII, 22) were employed as temporary handles for heated metal rods or tools used in sealing colors on stone in the encaustic process of painting. The absence of these vessels from Well XIX and their great quantity in Well XV may be indication, if this is indeed their use, that Shop XIX was the place where the painters stored their supplies and that they were actually at work redecorating in the immediate vicinity of Shop XV in the last days of Corinth before its destruction.

C-47-415: p. 33[17]　　　C-47-417: p. 30[14]
C-47-416: p. 30[14]　　　C-47-419: pp. 90[85], 180[44]

112. South Stoa, Well XXII

Bibliography:

> G. R. Edwards, *Hesperia*, XVIII, 1949, p. 151, pl. 15, 12, 13.
> Broneer, *S. Stoa*, pp. 138–144, plans IV and XXI (well and Room H); p. 143 and pl. 46, 2 b (lamp from top filling).

Summary:

A small deposit at the bottom of the well represents the period of use of the well in the Greek period. The pieces range in date from about 300 into the first half of the 2nd century B.C. The coins from this fill are of the 4th and 3rd centuries B.C. A second filling above, from –10.30 to –3.50 m., was introduced at one time, as indicated by multiple joins at various levels, probably in the latter 1st century after Christ. It is a mixture of Hellenistic and Roman pottery, Hellenistic tiles of the Stoa and Roman tile fragments. The coins are in part of the Greek period and in part Roman, apparently not later than Augustus. Broneer Type XXII lamp fragments are taken to indicate the rather later date of the introduction of the filling. A third filling at top, distinguished by joins, is evidently a supplementary fill, primarily of tile fragments, tightly packed in great quantity, introduced in the late 2nd or early 3rd century after Christ to provide a firm basis for the marble pavement of Room H above.

Objects published or noted:

C-48-2: **644**	C-48-31: **933**
C-48-14: **843**	C-48-32: p. 28[9]
C-48-15: **193**	C-48-33: **17**
C-48-16: **114**	C-48-34: p. 137[20]
C-48-17: **120**	C-48-35: **748**
C-48-18: **117**	C-48-36: **740**
C-48-19: p. 30[14]	C-48-37: **651**
C-48-20: p. 28[8]	C-48-39: **645**
C-48-21: p. 28[11]	C-48-40: **29**
C-48-22: p. 28[13]	C-48-41: p. 50[34]
C-48-23: p. 28[8]	C-48-42: **701**
C-48-24: **108**	C-48-49: **837**
C-48-25: **125**	C-48-50: **856**
C-48-28: p. 162[21]	C-48-51: **786**
C-48-29: p. 45[31]	C-48-244 a, b: **903**
C-48-30: p. 160[17]	C-48-247: p. 119

113. South Stoa, Well XXVII

Bibliography:

> G. R. Edwards, *Hesperia*, XVIII, 1949, pp. 150–151, pl. 15, 8–11.
> Broneer, *S. Stoa*, p. 60, fig. 38 (well curb), pp. 145–151 (Roman bath); plan V (location of well).

Summary:

Two main fillings are attested in this well, distinguished by independent series of joins. A fairly abundant use filling at bottom has a range in date from the early last quarter of the 4th century to 146 B.C. A second filling from below water level to –1.30 m. is clearly a clean-up of Mummian destruction debris introduced very early in the period of the Roman colony after 44 B.C. It included many architectural pieces, tiles, column drums, column and anta capitals, wall block (?) fragments and the complete well curb. These give evidence of burning. The coins from the shaft from –1.30 m. to bottom are all of the Greek period, of the latter 4th and 3rd centuries, and some with dates overlapping into the first half of the 2nd century. One represents the period of desolation at Corinth: Thespiai 146–27 B.C. There is no Roman admixture in this filling from –1.30 downward. In probably the 3rd century after Christ a drain for the Roman Bath in this part of the Stoa was cut through part of the top of the well shaft, introducing a certain amount of material of this time between levels 0 and –1.30 m., including a coin of Julia Domna.

Objects published or noted:

C-47-430: **195**	C-47-465: **461**
C-47-440: **74**	C-47-466: **642**
C-47-443: **67**	C-47-467: **247**
C-47-444: **279**	C-47-468: **248**
C-47-449: p. 165[23]	C-47-469: **573**
C-47-450: **805**	C-47-470: **557**
C-47-451: **188**	C-47-471: **560**
C-47-452: **373**	C-47-472: **727**
C-47-453: **374**	C-47-473: **728**
C-47-454: **438**	C-47-474: **739**
C-47-455: **470**	C-47-475: **737**
C-47-457: **428**	C-47-476: pp. 137[19], 138
C-47-458: **431**	C-47-477: **616**
C-47-459: **432**	C-47-478: **670**
C-47-460: **427**	C-47-479: **698**
C-47-461: **390**	C-47-480: **196**
C-47-462: **405**	C-47-483: **25**
C-47-463: **391**	C-47-484: p. 28[8]

114. South Stoa, Well XXVIII

Bibliography:

> Broneer, *S. Stoa*, plan V (location of well).

Summary:

The contents of the well from top to –6.80 m. are not known. The filling below included much that is precedented in use fillings of the South Stoa wells and some suggestion of the presence of a Mummian destruction filling. Evidently this was, however, much disturbed, even to bottom, in Byzantine times.

Objects published:

C-47-422: **426**	C-47-430: **195**
C-47-423: **491**	C-47-431: **523**
C-47-424: **476**	C-47-433 a, b: **615**
C-47-425: **596**	C-47-435: **481**

115. South Stoa, Well XXX
Bibliography:
Oscar Broneer, *Hesperia*, XVI, 1947, pls. LVII, 9, and LIX, 14.
Broneer, *S. Stoa*, plan VI (location of well).
Davidson, *Minor Objects*, no. 836, pl. 62.
Summary:

It is believed that there were three separate fillings in this well, though their identity is not fully demonstrable.

The material from the bottom of the well, with a range from the last quarter of the 4th century B.C. to the second quarter of the 2nd century B.C., is attributed to the period of use of the well. A filling above, from near water level to –4.00 m., is regarded as representing a clean-up of Mummian destruction debris probably thrown in in the early years after the foundation of the Roman colony in 44 B.C. The coins from –4.00 m. to the bottom of the shaft, with the exception of an evidently intrusive coin of Constantius II, A.D. 355–361, are all of the Greek period, of the 4th and 3rd centuries, some with dates overlapping into the first half of the 2nd century B.C. There was apparently but slight admixture of Roman material in this filling, one piece being a section of a stamped Roman amphora (*Hesperia*, XVI, 1947, pl. LVII, 9). A final filling of the well, between –4.00 m. and top, seems to have occurred perhaps as late as the 5th or 6th century after Christ.

Objects published or noted:

C-38-676: **16**	C-47-65: **410**
C-38-678: p. 40[26]	C-47-66: **401**
C-38-679: **721**	C-47-67: **414**
C-38-681: **829**	C-47-68: **429**
C-38-683: **807**	C-47-69: **468**
C-47-45: **458**	C-47-70: **419**
C-47-46: **474**	C-47-71: **423**
C-47-48: **541**	C-47-72: **462**
C-47-49: p. 37[22]	C-47-73: **459**
C-47-50: **546**	C-47-74: **392**
C-47-54.1: p. 89	C-47-75: **378**
C-47-55: **94**	C-47-76: **430**
C-47-57: **115**	C-47-77: **376**
C-47-58: **638**	C-47-78: p. 121[7]
C-47-60: **551**	C-47-79: **636**
C-47-61: **408**	C-47-129: **613**
C-47-62: **411**	C-47-130: **631**
C-47-63: **402**	C-47-131: **632**
C-47-64: **418**	C-47-133: **640**

C-47-134: **635**	C-47-139: **637**
C-47-135: p. 30[14]	C-47-145: **492**
C-47-136: **164**	

116. South Stoa, Well XXXI
Bibliography:
Broneer, *S. Stoa*, plan VI (location of well).
Davidson, *Minor Objects*, nos. 430 and 834, pls. 39 and 62.
Summary:

The well was excavated only to –7.60 m., considerably above water level. No material, then, from the use filling has been recovered. Though it is not objectively demonstrable it seems likely that there were two fillings in the excavated portion of the shaft. That from –7.60 to –4.50 m. is regarded as representing a clean-up of Mummian destruction debris, probably in the early years of the Roman colony after 44 B.C. It included, along with Hellenistic pottery and other objects, a great many broken roof tiles, some evidently of the South Stoa. The filling above, from –4.50 m. to top, contained entirely Roman material and was presumably introduced in the 2nd or 3rd centuries after Christ. The only legible coin from the entire filling of the shaft is of the Greek period.
Objects published:

C-33-1443: **528**	C-33-1451: **111**
C-33-1450: **119**	

117. South Stoa, Well XXXIII
Bibliography:
Broneer, *S. Stoa*, plan VI.
Davidson, *Minor Objects*, no. 1343, pl. 83.
Summary:

The well was excavated only to –8.00 m., above water level. No material, then, from the use filling has been recovered. Though it cannot be objectively demonstrated it is likely that there were two fillings in the excavated portion of the shaft. One, from –8.00 to –4.60 m., is regarded as representing a clean-up of Mummian destruction debris probably early in the years after the foundation of the Roman colony in 44 B.C. It included, along with Hellenistic pottery and other objects, many fragments of roof tiles, some at least from the South Stoa, and fragments of the well curb. A few coins are of the Greek period. The filling from –4.60 to top was composed entirely of Roman material probably introduced in the 2nd century after Christ.
Objects published:

C-33-204: **851**

118. South Stoa, from various shop wells
Summary:

The pottery collected under this heading is merely an assembly of pieces evidently found in shop wells of the South Stoa. The identity of the specific wells in which they were found is not known. To some degree, the value being shaded because of lack of record, the pieces share the indications for dating provided by association with the history of the South Stoa and its wells. Two pieces, **375** and **425**, are probably among those extracted from well fillings from below via the openings from them into the Peirene Channel

(Hill, *The Springs*, p. 62). Others, of coarse and cooking ware, were recomposed of fragments discarded in excavations of 1946–1947.

Objects published:

C-33-42: **375**	C-46-91: **671**
C-33-43: **425**	C-46-92: **703**
C-46-90: **725**	

CONCORDANCE I

INVENTORY NUMBERS IN CORINTH:
PUBLICATION NUMBERS OR PAGE REFERENCES

C-27-7	p. 105[4]	C-28-89	**600**	C-30-143 a-c	**841**	C-31-117	p. 162[21]
C-27-18	**519**	C-28-90	**345**		p. 167	C-31-131	**254**
C-27-19	**588**	C-28-113	**882**	C-30-144	pp. 156,	C-31-147	**68**
C-27-22	**587**	C-28-125	**880**		157[8]	C-31-148	**162**
C-27-24	p. 29[14]	C-28-130	p. 183[49]	C-30-145	**895**	C-31-151	**132**
C-28-37	**809**	C-29-99	**534**		p. 167	C-31-152	**1**
	p. 166		p. 22	C-30-148	**783**	C-31-171	**217**
C-28-46	**834**	C-29-115	p. 172[26]	C-30-149	pp. 180[42,44]	C-31-172	**218**
	p. 167	C-29-116	**885**	C-30-150	**183**	C-31-192	**205**
C-28-51	**800**	C-29-146	**860**		p. 203	C-31-194	p. 30[14]
	pp.166,167	C-29-149	p. 99[93]	C-31-08	**2**	C-31-195	p. 30[14]
C-28-52 and		C-29-202	p. 157[9]	C-31-9	p. 30[14]	C-31-196	p. 30[14]
C-28-57	**833**	C-30-01	**360**	C-31-10	p. 45[30]	C-31-197	p. 30[14]
	pp.166,167	C-30-36	**844**	C-31-12	**445**	C-31-198	p. 30[14]
C-28-53	**781**		p. 167	C-31-13	**28**	C-31-199	p. 29[14]
C-28-54	**127**	C-30-37	**808**	C-31-14	**26**	C-31-200	**174**
	pp.22-23,		p. 166	C-31-15	**765**	C-31-201	**11**
	91	C-30-38	**814**	C-31-21	**441**	C-31-202	**12**
C-28-55	**857**		pp.165,166		pp. 20-21	C-31-202 bis	**8**
C-28-57 and		C-30-39	**812**;	C-31-22	**422**	C-31-203	**13**
C-28-52	**833**		*v.* **875**	C-31-23	**406**	C-31-206	**380**
	pp.166,167		pp. 166,	C-31-24	**403**	C-31-207	**382**
C-28-58	**858**		174[29]	C-31-25	**386**	C-31-220	p. 30[14]
C-28-59	**823**	C-30-40	**815**		p. 20	C-31-221	p. 30[14]
	pp.166,167		pp.165–167	C-31-26	**387**	C-31-223	**163**
C-28-60	**871**	C-30-58	p. 91		p. 20	C-31-224	**173**
C-28-65	p. 87	C-30-73	**442**;	C-31-27	**457**	C-31-225	**553**
C-28-66	**910**	C-30-100	p. 37[22]	C-31-29	**388**	C-31-226	p. 30[14]
C-28-67 a, b	**530**;	C-30-103 bis	p. 87[81]		p. 20	C-31-229	**331**
	v. **531**	C-30-116	**35**	C-31-33	**495**	C-31-230	**313**
	pp. 39,	C-30-129	p. 176[32]		p. 83	C-31-231	**358**
	180[44]	C-30-130	**874**	C-31-34	p. 30[14]	C-31-232	**63**
C-28-68	**544**	C-30-131	**926**	C-31-35	**24**	C-31-236	p. 37[22]
C-28-69	**531**	C-30-133	**803**	C-31-36	p. 30[14]	C-31-237	**566**
	pp. 39,		p. 166	C-31-37	**22**	C-31-238	**305**
	180[44]	C-30-134 a-c	**537**	C-31-38	**421**	C-31-246	**161**
C-28-70	p. 2[3]		p. 22	C-31-39	**379**	C-31-247	**178**
C-28-71	**859**	C-30-135 a	**539**	C-31-66	**300**	C-31-248	**177**
C-28-72	p. 162[21]		pp. 22-23		p. 60	C-31-249	**341**
C-28-74	**855**	C-30-135 b	**540**	C-31-102	**889**		p. 62[53]
C-28-74 a	**828**		pp. 22-23	C-31-104	**877**;	C-31-250	**344**
	p. 166	C-30-137	p. 162[21]		*v.* **878**		p. 62[53]
C-28-82	p. 33[17]	C-30-138	p. 183[49]	C-31-107	**893**	C-31-251	**355**
C-28-85	**266**	C-30-141	p. 162	C-31-111	**54**		p. 62[53]
C-28-86	**601**			C-31-113	**890**	C-31-259	p. 30[14]

C-31-260	p. 30[14]	C-33-304	p. 45[31]	C-34-21	5	C-34-940	p. 133
C-31-261	p. 30[14]	C-33-306	113	C-34-22	30	C-34-943	669
C-31-262	55	C-33-316	447	C-34-23	134	C-34-944	676
C-31-263	59		p. 65	C-34-24	82	C-34-945	689
C-31-264	p. 34[19]	C-33-318	499	C-34-25	687	C-34-946	283
C-31-265	100		p. 65	C-34-27	p. 225	C-34-947	282
	p. 35	C-33-390	19	C-34-29	104	C-34-948	284
C-31-269	583	C-33-391	160	C-34-30	483	C-34-955	p. 108[8]
C-31-274	261	C-33-394	p. 72		p. 65	C-34-956	p. 108[8]
C-31-280	306	C-33-395	50	C-34-31	484	C-34-979	p. 107
C-31-390	338	C-33-416	570	C-34-33	731	C-34-1020	221
C-31-391	327	C-33-424	187	C-34-34	437	C-34-1028	751
C-31-405	p. 29[14]		pp. 24, 25		p. 65	C-34-1046	p. 29[14]
C-31-406	p. 34[19]	C-33-426	543	C-34-35	700	C-34-1092	p. 66[60]
C-31-409	66	C-33-433	914	C-34-37	532	C-34-1093	p. 66[60]
C-31-417	761		p. 154		pp. 18, 22	C-34-1095	p. 29[14]
C-31-418	756	C-33-985	695	C-34-38	p. 44	C-34-1135 a	678
C-31-421	p. 96[92]	C-33-986	712	C-34-44	p. 50[34]	C-34-1139 a	677
C-31-443	p. 109[9]	C-33-998	p. 36[20]	C-34-82	85	C-34-1194	285
C-31-448	p. 109[9]	C-33-1001	674	C-34-135	p. 91	C-34-1195	298
C-31-451	pp. 64, 65	C-33-1003	p. 176[32]	C-34-166	894		p. 60
	71[66]	C-33-1008	810	C-34-213	p. 176[32]	C-34-1196	299
C-31-453	339		pp. 154[3],	C-34-227	p. 47		p. 60
C-31-454	340		165-167	C-34-259	524	C-34-1602	p. 37[22]
C-31-455	337	C-33-1053	920	C-34-278	p. 29[14]	C-34-1603	107
C-31-478	826	C-33-1119	p. 33[17]	C-34-300	p. 87[81]	C-34-1604	p. 40[26]
	pp. 166, 167	C-33-1220	p. 87	C-34-304	904	C-34-1605	p. 30[14]
C-31-479	931	C-33-1375	p. 176[32]		p. 154	C-34-1607	p. 37[22]
C-31-480	827	C-33-1377	861	C-34-307	547	C-34-1608	704
	p. 166	C-33-1378	867	C-34-347	220	C-34-1609	711
C-31-481	785	C-33-1383	p. 176[32]	C-34-356	p. 172[26]	C-34-1610	713
C-31-482	937	C-33-1443	528	C-34-392 a, f	424	C-34-1611	685
C-31-483	917		pp. 39, 90		p. 65	C-34-1612	699
C-32-38	752	C-33-1450	119	C-34-392 b	502	C-34-1613	658
C-32-48	p. 29[14]	C-33-1451	111		p. 64		p. 122[9]
C-32-50	346		p. 42	C-34-392 c	503	C-34-1614	714
C-32-56	48	C-33-1461	850		p. 65	C-34-1615	109
C-32-214	330		pp. 154,	C-34-392 d	504		p. 42
C-32-231	p. 172[25]		158, 159		p. 65	C-34-1616	33
C-32-280	849	C-33-1462	p. 28[11]	C-34-392 e	505	C-34-1617	153
	p. 167	C-33-1463	p. 40[26]		p. 65	C-34-1618	p. 33[17]
C-32-281	838	C-33-1463	906	C-34-392 g	506	C-34-1619	213
	pp. 154, 167	C-33-1464	p. 176[32]		p. 65	C-34-1620	87
C-32-290	p. 148[18]	C-33-1466	p. 2[3]	C-34-393	p. 33[17]	C-34-1621	pp. 91, 91[87]
C-33-42	375	C-33-1466 A	p. 2[3]	C-34-394	460	C-34-1622	789
C-33-43	425	C-33-1467	793	C-34-395	490	C-34-1623	pp. 30[14],
C-33-102	930	C-33-1468	792	C-34-396	467		33[17]
C-33-106	71		p. 154		p. 65	C-34-1624	p. 162[21]
C-33-116	267	C-33-1470	878	C-34-397	489	C-34-1640	p. 30[14]
C-33-123	p. 50[36]	C-33-1471	pp. 28[12],		pp. 20, 24,	C-34-1645	777
C-33-185	883		33[17]		65		p. 145
C-33-204	851	C-33-1472	p. 183[49]	C-34-470	pp. 39[25],	C-34-1738	715
	p. 159	C-33-1473	501		40[26]	C-34-1740	p. 162[21]
C-33-205	498		p. 64	C-34-471	706	C-34-1742	929
	p. 65	C-34-16	p. 50[36]	C-34-474	p. 33[17]	C-34-1856	p. 37[22]
C-33-227	500	C-34-17	p. 30[14]	C-34-923	p. 115	C-34-2007	934
	p. 65	C-34-19	116	C-34-926	617		

Number	Reference	Number	Reference
C-37-2322	p. 172[26]	C-37-2610	65
C-37-2345	p. 45[30]	C-37-2611	37
C-37-2346	77	C-37-2614	145
C-37-2390	pp. 140[26,27]	C-37-2615	144
C-37-2399	924	C-37-2617	157
C-37-2422	p. 44	C-37-2619	143
C-37-2423	788	C-37-2641	602
C-37-2424	p. 161[19]		pp. 99[94], 100
C-37-2491	324		
C-37-2492	312	C-37-2645	603
C-37-2493	328		pp. 99[94], 100
C-37-2494	315		
C-37-2506	p. 124[11]	C-37-2662	303
C-37-2509	667	C-37-2666	9
C-37-2510	734	C-37-2667	3
C-37-2512	697	C-37-2668	550
C-37-2520	198		pp. 22, 39
C-37-2521	302	C-37-2681	886
C-37-2522	354	C-37-2693	p. 161[19]
C-37-2523	326	C-37-2695	526
C-37-2524	356		v. 912
C-37-2525	329		p. 171
C-37-2526	310	C-37-2698	898
C-37-2527	369	C-37-2700	p. 161[19]
C-37-2528	316	C-37-2701	909
C-37-2532	p. 29[14]		p. 154
C-37-2533	p. 29[14]	C-37-2702	p. 176[32]
C-37-2534	p. 29[14]	C-37-2703	p. 180[42]
C-37-2535	p. 29[14]	C-37-2704	790
C-37-2536	49	C-37-2705	869
C-37-2537	57	C-37-2709	900
C-37-2538	46	C-37-2712	922
C-37-2539	61	C-37-2714	p. 176[32]
C-37-2540	58	C-37-2715	899
C-37-2541	96	C-37-2716	864
C-37-2542	97	C-37-2717	p. 157[8]
C-37-2543	p. 29[14]	C-37-2718	p. 176[32]
C-37-2544	36	C-37-2719	p. 160[17]
C-37-2545	p. 29[14]	C-37-2720	p. 183[50]
C-37-2546	99	C-37-2724	865
C-37-2547	p. 30[14]	C-37-2725	935
C-37-2582	147	C-37-2731	866
C-37-2583	171	C-37-2732	p. 176[32]
C-37-2584	148	C-37-2734	870
C-37-2585	156	C-37-2735	pp. 176[32], 178
C-37-2586	158	C-37-2737	818
C-37-2587	142		p. 166
C-37-2588	159	C-37-2738	852
C-37-2589	73		p. 159[13]
C-37-2590	20	C-37-2739	905
C-37-2597	p. 96[92]	C-37-2740	927
C-37-2604	p. 30[14]	C-37-2742	p. 176[32]
C-37-2605	p. 30[14]	C-37-43	p. 161[19]
C-37-2606	p. 30[14]	C-38-560	p. 45[30]
C-37-2607	p. 30[14]	C-38-563	p. 45[30]
C-37-2608	p. 30[14]	C-38-571	620
C-37-2609	p. 30[14]		

Number	Reference	Number	Reference
C-38-592	762	C-40-32	372
C-38-628	768		p. 71
C-38-629	764	C-40-34	p. 37[22]
C-38-634	448	C-40-39	225
	v. 389	C-40-40	226
	pp. 65	C-40-56	69
C-38-637	p. 173[28]	C-40-57	39
C-38-640	507	C-40-59	342
	p. 65	C-40-60	319
C-38-644	508	C-40-61	318
	p. 65	C-40-62	p. 45[30]
C-38-645	509	C-40-63	634
	p. 65	C-40-64	p. 113[14]
C-38-649	533	C-40-393	p. 45[30]
	p. 22	C-40-399	60
C-38-660	p. 173[28]	C-40-407	311
C-38-676	16	C-40-413	301
C-38-678	p. 40[26]	C-40-419	p. 139[26]
C-38-679	721	C-40-423	763
C-38-681	829	C-40-424	766
	pp. 154[3], 164, 167	C-40-432	139
		C-40-433	137
C-38-683	807	C-40-434	95
	pp. 154[3], 166, 167	C-40-435	710
		C-40-437	70
C-38-691	p. 176[32]	C-40-439	357
C-38-692	p. 176[32]	C-40-440	439
C-38-698	831	C-40-444	449
	pp. 166, 167	C-40-465	363
C-38-699	p. 183[49]	C-40-467	136
C-38-704	p. 176[32]	C-40-468	p. 37[22]
C-38-705	840	C-40-469	377
	pp. 154, 164, 168	C-46-10	801
C-39-7	228		pp. 165, 166
C-39-22	p. 57[44]	C-46-15	38
C-39-86	253	C-46-26	683
C-39-99	208	C-46-28	p. 122
C-39-100	227	C-46-38	653
C-39-101	222	C-46-41	p. 123[10]
C-39-102	209	C-46-42	83
C-39-168	p. 66[60]	C-46-43	102
C-39-211	555		p. 37
C-39-253	200	C-46-45	p. 30[14]
C-39-278	688	C-46-46	91
C-39-351 a,b	875	C-46-56	836
	p. 166		p. 167
C-39-352	876	C-46-57	825
C-39-390	p. 39[25]		pp. 165, 167
C-39-438	pp. 176[32], 178	C-46-58	249
		C-46-59	682
C-40-16	p. 2[3]	C-46-60	112
C-40-21	371	C-46-62	p. 30[14]
C-40-22	138	C-46-63	p. 176[32]
C-40-24	574	C-46-64	813
C-40-29	657		pp. 154, 166
		C-46-65	121
		C-46-66	105

C-47-356	396 p. 21	C-47-466	642	C-47-817	p. 28[11]	C-48-28	p. 162[21]
C-47-357	397 p. 21	C-47-467	247	C-47-818	p. 33[17]	C-48-29	p. 45[31]
C-47-360	152	C-47-468	248	C-47-819	89	C-48-30	p. 160[17]
C-47-362	78	C-47-469	573; v. 560	C-47-820	76	C-48-31	933 p. 154[3]
C-47-386	56	C-47-470	557	C-47-821	31	C-48-32	p. 28[9]
C-47-390	611 p. 104[2]	C-47-471	560	C-47-822	558	C-48-33	17
C-47-391	608	C-47-472	727	C-47-826	656 p. 123	C-48-34	p. 137[20]
C-47-399	627	C-47-473	728	C-47-827	p. 108	C-48-35	748 p. 139
C-47-400	p. 40[26]	C-47-474	739	C-47-829	749 p. 58	C-48-36	740
C-47-401	614	C-47-475	737	C-47-830	732	C-48-37	651
C-47-402	692	C-47-476	pp. 137[19], 138	C-47-831	723	C-48-39	645
C-47-403	p. 37[23]	C-47-477	616 p. 134	C-47-835	702	C-48-40	29
C-47-410	280	C-47-478	670	C-47-836	646 p. 132	C-48-41	p. 50[34]
C-47-415	p. 33[17]	C-47-479	698	C-47-851	197	C-48-42	701
C-47-416	p. 30[14]	C-47-480	196	C-47-852	pp. 50[37], 180[42]	C-48-49	837 p. 167
C-47-417	p. 30[14]	C-47-483	25	C-47-853 a, b	778 p. 145	C-48-50	856
C-47-419	pp. 90[85], 180[44]	C-47-484	p. 28[8]	C-47-854	879	C-48-51	786 v. 886 pp. 173, 174
C-47-422	426	C-47-748	214	C-47-856	323	C-48-53	129 p. 91
C-47-423	491 p. 65	C-47-749	236	C-47-857	322	C-48-59	488
C-47-424	476 p. 65	C-47-750	199	C-47-858 a	309	C-48-61	915 p. 154
C-47-425	596 p. 100	C-47-751	201	C-47-858 b	307	C-48-62 and C-36-499 a-e	873 v. 874 pp. 166, 168, 171
C-47-430	195	C-47-752	p. 50[38]	C-47-859	308		
C-47-431	523	C-47-755	240	C-47-866	42		
C-47-433 a, b	615	C-47-787	821 pp. 154[3], 164, 166	C-47-870	p. 129	C-48-65	pp. 120[6], 121[7]
C-47-435	481	C-47-790	919 p. 154	C-47-872	212	C-48-66	719
C-47-440	74	C-47-791	921 v. 922 p. 154	C-47-873	772	C-48-67	p. 105[4]
C-47-443	67			C-47-874	p. 148[17]	C-48-69	p. 105[4]
C-47-444	279 p. 54[42]	C-47-792	p. 160[17]	C-47-878	755	C-48-70	p. 105[4]
C-47-449	p. 165[23]	C-47-794	p. 160[17]	C-47-889	675	C-48-71	p. 105[4]
C-47-450	805 pp. 154, 164, 166	C-47-795	811 pp. 154[3], 165-167	C-47-891	708	C-48-72	p. 105[4]
				C-47-893	816 pp. 154[3], 166	C-48-72 bis	p. 105[4]
C-47-451	188; v. 189 pp. 20, 134	C-47-796	pp. 166, 172[26]	C-47-894	436	C-48-73	p. 105[4]
C-47-452	373	C-47-797 a, b	839 p. 167	C-47-900	p. 105[4]	C-48-74	p. 105[4]
C-47-453	374	C-47-798	820 pp. 166, 167	C-47-901	527 pp. 39, 87	C-48-75	p. 105[4]
C-47-454	438 p. 64	C-47-802	p. 87	C-48-2	644	C-48-76	p. 105[4]
C-47-455	470	C-47-803	p. 44	C-48-14	843 pp. 154, 163, 167	C-48-77	p. 105[4]
C-47-457	428	C-47-804	p. 36[20]	C-48-15	193	C-48-82	p. 105[4]
C-47-458	431	C-47-807	p. 36[20]	C-48-16	114	C-48-83	88
C-47-459	432	C-47-809	p. 40[26]	C-48-17	120	C-48-86	824 pp. 165, 166
C-47-460	427	C-47-810	p. 28[10]	C-48-18	117	C-48-87	p. 158
C-47-461	390	C-47-811	124	C-48-19	p. 30[14]	C-48-90	918
C-47-462	405	C-47-812	p. 36[21]	C-48-20	p. 28[8]	C-48-92	848 p. 167
C-47-463	391	C-47-813	169	C-48-21	p. 28[11]	C-48-93	554 p. 94
C-47-464	p. 84[80]	C-47-814	155	C-48-22	p. 28[13]	C-48-94	10
C-47-465	461	C-47-815	182	C-48-23	p. 28[8]		
		C-47-816	106	C-48-24	108		
				C-48-25	125		

C-64-335	**802**	CP-350	**568**	T 2722	**641**	T 603	p. 54[42]
	pp.154,164	CP-370	**252**	CP-2253 a	**575**	T 655	p. 99[93]
	166, 167	CP-371	**251**		v. 561	T 1060	p. 54[42]
C-64-375	**515**	CP-398	**149**	CP-2253 b	**561**	T 1067	p. 54[42]
C-64-386	**472**	CP-399	**151**		v. 575	T 1097 a	**578**
C-65-15	p. 126	CP-400	**167**	KP 121	**234**	T 1097 b	**563**
C-65-96	p. 91[87]	CP-463	**758**	KP 213	**384**	T 1158	**361**
C-65-97	pp. 89-90,	CP-464	**753**	KP 218	**185**		p. 66[59]
	180[44]	CP-465	**754**		p. 203	T 1159	**571**
C-65-98	**796**	CP-466	p. 148[17]	KP 230	**271**	T 1164	**263**
	pp. 154[3],	CP-471	p. 50[34]	KP 231	**272**	T 1440	p. 54[42]
	165–167	CP-515	**123**	KP 361	**219**	T 1550	p. 53
C-65-169	**275**	CP-518	**938**	KP 367	**237**	T 2018	**520**
C-65-289	p. 37[22]	CP-519	p.180[42,44]	KP 677	**569**		p. 62[53]
C-65-323	p. 126	CP-520	**842**	KP 682	**278**	T 2023	**594**
C-65-372	**939**		pp. 154[3],	KP 684	**265**	T 2250	p. 105
	p. 156[6]		167	KP 685	**581**	T 2312	**516**
C-65-377	**944**	CP-521	p. 176[32]	KP 688	**260**		p. 87
	pp. 22, 23,	CP-522	p. 162[21]	KP 701	**565**	T 2313	p. 30[14]
	39, 88[83]	CP-526	p. 161[19]	KP 702	**277**	T 2314	**589**
C-65-379	pp. 65,83[79]	CP-608	**255**	KP 711	p. 54[42]	T 2316	**84**
C-65-391	p. 56[43]	CP-829	**242**	KP 715	**229**	T 2317	**590**
C-65-394	p. 120[5]	CP-889	p. 173[28]	KP 719	**238**	T 2346	pp. 99[93],
C-66-3	**940**	CP-908	**888**	KP 834	**244**		100[95], 101[98]
	p. 159[14]	CP-909	**784**	KP 835	**264**	T 2369	**559**
C-66-4	**942**	CP-953	**804**	KP 837	**567**	T 2370	**276**
	pp. 163[22]		p. 166	KP 876	**273**		
C-66-96,	pp. 64, 65	CP-971	p. 40[26]	KP 930	**223**	T 2371 a	**577**
	75[75]	CP-991	p. 173[28]	KP 963	**246**		v. 562
C-66-104	p. 2[3]	CP-1572	**819**	KP 964	**241**	T 2371 b	**562**
C-66-143	p. 2[3]		p. 166	KP 1312	**259**		v. 577
C-66-151	**943**	CP-1607	p. 162[21]	KP 2503	**622**	T 2413	**257**
	pp.23,90[86]	CP-1923	p. 173[28]	KP 2525	**256**	T 2533	**262**
C-66-153	p. 2[3]	CP-1926	p. 162[21]	KP 2702	p. 76[77]	T 2560	p. 54[42]
C-66-155	p. 2[3]	CP-1928	p. 162[21]	MF 1040	p. 172[26]	T 2582	**269**
C-66-158	p. 38[24]	CP-1929	**817**	MF 1041	p. 172[26]	T 2617	**258**
C-66-159	p. 2[3]		pp.166,167	MF 9179	**525**	T 2651	**274**
C-66-165 a, b	p. 47[32]	CP-1930	**923**		p. 171	T 2666	**268**
C-66-225	**941**	CP-1931	**835**	MF 9246	p. 30[14]	T 2698 a	**690**
	p. 160[18]		p. 167	MP 76	**385**	T 2698 b	p. 120[7]
C-67-56	p. 159[14]	CP-1932	p. 176[32]		p. 62[53]	T 2703 a	**582**
C-67-112 a, b	p. 84[80]	CP-1933	**916**	MP 124	p. 72		v. 572
C-3217	v. 300	CP-2169	**730**	MP 143	**270**	T 2703 b	**572**
CP-20	**760**	CP-2245	**517**	MP 208 a	**579**		v. 582
CP-21	**769**		p. 87		v. 564	T 2720	**14**
CP-198	**191**	CP-2250	**592**	MP 208 b	**564**		
	pp.47,48	CP-2251	**593**	T 602	p. 54[42]		

CONCORDANCE II

PUBLICATION REFERENCES: PUBLICATION NUMBERS OR PAGE REFERENCES

A.J.A., XXXIX, 1935

p. 71, fig. 14	**532**
fig. 16	p. 50[34]
72, fig. 15, a	**437**
fig. 15, b	**489**
fig. 15, c	**483**
fig. 15, d	**467**
fig. 15, e	**490**

Carl W. Blegen, Hazel Palmer, Rodney S. Young, *Corinth*, XIII, *The North Cemetery*, Princeton, 1964 (= *N. Cemetery*)

442–5	**262**
463–2	**258**
491–5	**361**
491–6	**263**
494–2	**563**
494–2	**578**
495–5	**572**
495–5	**582**
495–6	**690**
496–12	**641**
496–14	**14**
498–4	**516**
498–7	p. 30[14]
498–9	**589**
498–10	**590**
D 28–b	**274**
D 36–c	**276**
D 36–e	**562**
D 36–e	**577**
D 36–f	**559**
X–176	**257**
X–179	**269**
X–181	**268**

Oscar Broneer, *Corinth*, I, iv, *The South Stoa and its Roman Successors*, Princeton, 1954 (= Broneer, *S. Stoa*)

p. 29, fig. 7, and pl. 7, 3	p. 50[34]
63, fig. 41	**489**
pl. 14, 5, left	**464**
5, right	**400**
24, 1, left	**352**
3, upper right	**325**

Hesperia, III, 1934, pp. 311–480 (= Thompson)

B 33	p.60[51]

Hesperia, VI, 1937, pp. 257–316 (= Pease)

no. 124	**221**
138	**751**
151	**283**
152	**282**
153	**284**
190	**617**
191	**618**
192	**619**
208	**676**
209	**689**
222	p. 66[60]
223	p. 66[60]

Hesperia, VII, 1938, pp. 557–611 (= Campbell)

no. 63	**202**
64	**216**
65	**215**
67	**204**
68	**203**
150	p. 57[44]
163	**693**

Hesperia, XVI, 1947

pl. LVIII, 11	**189**
LIX, 13, left	p. 88
14, left	**408**
14, right	**458**
15, left	**464**
15, right	**400**

Hesperia, XVII, 1948

pl. LXXXV, E 3	**311**
E 4	**357**
E 5	**439**
E 11	**766**

Hesperia, XVIII, 1949

pl. 13, 1, center	p. 87
1, right	pp. 50[37], 180[42]
3	p. 36[20]
14, 4	pp. 166, 172[26]
15, 8–9	p. 165[23]
10	**438**
11	**188**
16, 14	**129**
16, left	p. 105[4]
17	p. 105[4]
17, 19	p. 105[4]
23	**647**

Hesperia, XXV, 1956, pp. 350–374 (= Brann)

no. 56	**239**
58	**235**
69	**648**

Hesperia, XXXI, 1962

pl. 11, c	p. 50[38]
12, b	p. 122[9]
e	pp. 125[12], 129[14]
f	p. 147[16]
45, b, center	**190**
46, b, right	**451**

Hesperia, XXXIV, 1965

pl. 3, b	**736**

Carl Roebuck, *Corinth*, XIV, *The Asklepieion and Lerna*, Princeton, 1951 (= *Asklepieion*)

pl. 46, 71	**339**
47, 72	**340**
73	**337**
48, 6	**338**
7	**327**
22	p. 34[19]
49, 33	**761**
34	**356**
50, 60	**700**

INDEX I

GRAFFITI, DIPINTI, AND MOULDED IRSCRIPTIONS

COMPLETE OR RESTORED

Ἀλυ[πίας: ΑΛΥ. **510** (C-47-120). *Ca.* 325–275 B.C. Graffito.

Ἀντέρωτος: ΑΝΤΕΡѠΤΟC. **438** (C-47-454). 4th century, early fourth quarter, B.C. Graffito.

Ἀσφαλείας: ΑCΦΑΛΕΙΑC. **475** (C-47-268). *Ca.* 300 B.C. Graffito.

Ἀσφα]λεί[ας: ΛΕΙ. **501** (C-33-1473). *Ca.* 325–275 B.C. Graffito.

Ἀσφα]λε[ίας: ΛΕ. **502** (C-34-392 b). *Ca.* 325–275 B.C. Graffito.

Διονύσου: ΔΙΟΝΥCΟΥ. **409** (C-47-86). 3rd century, third quarter, B.C. Graffito.

Διονύσου: ΔΙΟΝΥCΟΥ. **464** (C-47-106). 3rd century, third quarter, B.C. Graffito.

[Διὸς Σ]ω[τῆ]ρος: Ω[ ]ΡΟΣ. **424** (C-34-392 a, f). *Ca.* 300 B.C. Graffito.

Διὸς [Σωτῆρος]: ΔΙΟC. **447** (C-33-316). *Ca.* 330 B.C. Graffito.

Διὸς Σωτῆρος: ΔΙΟCCѠΤΗΡΟC. **458** (C-47-45). 4th century, advanced last quarter, B.C. Graffito.

Διὸς Σ]ωτῆρος: ѠΤΗΡΟC. **474** (C-47-46). *Ca.* 325 B.C. Graffito.

Διὸς Σω]τῆρ[ος: ΤΗΡ. **498** (C-33-205). *Ca.* 325–275 B.C. Graffito.

Διὸ]ς Σωτῆρ[ος: CCѠΤΗΡ. **499** (C-33-318). *Ca.* 325–275 B.C. Graffito.

Διὸς Σω]τῆρ[ος: ΤΗΡ. **503** (C-34-392 c). *Ca.* 325–275 B.C. Graffito.

Δι]ὸς [Σ]ωτῆρ[ος: ΟC[ ]ѠΤΗΡ. **514** (C-50-25). *Ca.* 325–275 B.C. Graffito.

Εἰ]ράνας: ΡΑΝΑC. **437** (C-34-34). 4th century, early fourth quarter, B.C. Graffito.

Ἔρωτος: ΕΡѠΤΟC. **480** (C-47-112). *Ca.* 250 B.C. Graffito.

Εὐ]νοίας:]ΝΟΙΑC. **500** (C-33-227). *Ca.* 325–275 B.C. Graffito.

Ἡδ[ο]νῆς: ΗΔ[ ]ΝΗC. **476** (C-47-424). *Ca.* 300 B.C. Graffito.

Ἡ[δον]ῆς: Η[ ]ΗC. **493** (C-47-121). *Ca.* 300 B.C. Graffito.

Ἡ]δυλ[ογίας: ΔΥΛ. P. 75, note 75 (C-66-96). Graffito.

Ἡδύοινος: ΗΔΥΟΙΝΟΣ. **454** (C-53-232). *Ca.* 300 B.C. Graffito.

Ἡδύ[οινος: ΗΔΥ. **512** (C-47-281 a–c). *Ca.* 325–275 B.C. Graffito.

Ο]ἰνῶπ[ος: ΙΝѠΠ. **407** (C-50-1). 3rd century, second quarter, B.C. Graffito.

Παυσικρηπά[λου: ΠΑΥCΙΚΡΗΠΑ. **416** (C-47-87). 3rd century, third quarter, B.C. Graffito.

Πιωνε[ ]υς: ΠΙѠΝΕ[ ]ΥC. **492** (C-47-145). *Ca.* 300 B.C. Graffito.

[Ποδα]λ[ίρι]ος: Λ[ ]ΟC. **389** (C-47-288). *Ca.* 330 B.C. Graffito. Cf. C-31-451. Pp. 65, 71, note 66. Dipinto.

Σώζων: CѠΖѠΝ. **491** (C-47-423). *Ca.* 300 B.C. Graffito.

Ὑ]γείας: ΓΕΙΑC. **448** (C-38-634). 4th century, fourth quarter, B.C. Graffito.

Ὑγιείας: ΥΓΙΕΙΑC. **400** (C-47-119). 4th century, early fourth quarter, B.C. Graffito.

Ὑ]γι[είας: Γι. **505** (C-34-392 e). *Ca.* 325–275 B.C. Graffito.

Φιλίας: ΦΙΛΙΑC. **483** (C-34-30). 4th century, advanced last quarter, B.C. Graffito.

Ὦ παρ' ἐλπίδας φανεῖς: ѠΠΑΡΕΛΠΙΔΑCΦΑΝΕΙC. **489** (C-34-397). 4th century, last quarter, B.C. Graffito.

FRAGMENTARY

Α[: Α. **913** (C-36-2350). *Ca.* 160–146 B.C. Moulded.

]α[: Α. **506** (C-34-392 g). *Ca.* 325–275 B.C. Graffito.

]α[or Α[: Α. **915** (C-48-61). *Ca.* 160–146 B.C. Moulded.

]ας: ΑΣ. **452** (C-50-24). *Ca.* 325 B.C. Dipinto.

]ας: ΑC. **507** (C-38-640). *Ca.* 325–275 B.C. Graffito.

Ατ[or]ατ[: ΑΤ. **909** (C-37-2701). *Ca.* 160–146 B.C. Moulded.

Ατ[or]ατ[: ΑΤ. **912** (C-37-2256). *Ca.* 160–146 B.C. Moulded.

]ατω[ ]ου: ΑΤѠ[ ]ΟΥ. **911** (C-35-653). *Ca.* 160–146 B.C. Moulded.

ΔΙ or δι: ΔΙ. **316** (C-37-2528). 4th century, second quarter, B.C. Graffito.

]ιας: ΙΑC. **467** (C-34-396). *Ca.* 325 B.C. Graffito.

]ιας: ΙΑC. **509** (C-38-645). *Ca.* 325–275 B.C. Graffito.

]νερεις: ΝΕΡΕΙC. **508** (C-38-644). *Ca.* 325–275 B.C. Graffito.

]οδι[: ΟΔΙ. **838** (C-32-281). 3rd century, last quarter, to 146 B.C. Moulded.

Ομ[: ΟΜ. P. 83, note 79 (C-65-379). Graffito.

Πι[: ΠΙ. **511** (C-47-146). *Ca.* 325–275 B.C. Graffito.

πρ[: ΠΡ. **904** (C-34-304). *Ca.* 150–146 B.C. Moulded.

]ρ[: P. **914** (C-33-433). *Ca.* 160–146 B.C. Moulded.

Σ: Σ. **337** (C-31-455). 4th century, first quarter, B.C. Graffito.

TE : TE. **340** (C-31-454). 4th century, second quarter, B.C. Graffito.

THΛ : THΛ. **339** (C-31-453). 4th century, second quarter, B.C. Graffito.

]υη[: YH. **504** (C-34-392 d). *Ca.* 325–275 B.C. Graffito.

]χου: XOY. P. 176, note 32 (C-33-1464). *Ca.* 150–146 B.C. Moulded.

INDEX II

GENERAL INDEX

Unless otherwise indicated, shapes are Corinthian wheelmade fine ware. Principal entries are *italicized*, catalogue numbers are in **bold type**. References to specific catalogue entries are given only where they supplement the text.

ALEXANDRIA: basketball askos in, 103; mould for brazier lug found at, 119[3]

Amphora, Attic Classical: no equivalent in Corinthian Hellenistic, 19, 44

based (coarse ware): 206, 227; I, *111*; II, *112*; III, *112*

neck: blister ware, reason for production, 145; normal clay, influenced by blister ware, 145

unguentarium form: 214

West Slope: Attic, 11, 19[3], 44; Corinthian, 11, 18, 24, 25, *44*; gray ware, 44; unknown fabric, 44

Amphora handles, stamped: as evidence for dating deposits, 127[13], 189, 190, 206, 225, 230, 234

Amphoriskos. *See* Ointment-pot

Anaploga deposits: Cistern Area, graves, 194, *214*, water tunnel system, 193, *206–207*; cleaning and dyeing works, 193, *211–212*; rock cutting 4, 194, *215*; well in Grave 12, 193, *212*

Apollo, epithet of, 65. *See also* Graffito inscriptions; Motifs on Figured Bowls

Apollo, Peribolos of: findspot of graffito inscription, 65

Appliqué: head on askos, 103; lug in form of bearded head, on imported brazier, 119; mask, on askos, 103, on brazier, 119, 120, on bowl, 171, 172[25]; medallion on conical bowl, 26, 90–92, 171; "thorns" on wheelmade Megarian bowl, 88. *See also* Decoration, applied clay; Rim, moulded; Supports

Ariston. *See* Signatures

Aryballos (blister ware): decoration rather than shape as dating criterion, 8, 146; fabric, fragile, 145; intended for oil, 144; linear, 147, 148; squat, *146–148*, 149, chief blister-ware shape, 144; imitated in normal fabric, 145, produced in Athens until *ca.* 200 B.C., 147[15]

Asklepieion: deposit, 192, 195, *204*; mortars from, 109; no ointment-pots found in, 100

Askos, basketball: 18, *102–103*, 180[44]

Askos, duck (blister ware): 145, *148–149*, 212; incised decoration on, 146

Athena: head, as appliqué medallion, **549**, as appliqué support, 171, 174. *See also* Motifs on Figured Bowls

Attic pottery: Corinthian derivations from, 7, 10, 19, 30, 33, 38, 71, 88–89, 101, 145, 152, 154, 156, 161, 162, 177; Corinthian imitations of, 6–7, 19, 37, 44, 46, 66, 72, 145, 157, 159–160; decoration imitated in Corinthian, stamping and rouletting, 19, glazed wheel-run bands, 20, West Slope, 24; foreign imitations of, 6–7, 72, 152, 156, 157, 159, 160, 161; shapes not found in Corinthian, 11, 18–19. *See also* Amphora, West Slope; Bowl, conical, echinus, hemispherical, pine-cone, wheelmade Megarian, with outturned rim; Brazier; Cup, calyx; Decanter II, III; Dish, bevelled rim; Funnel; Kantharos, articulated, calyx, cyma, metallic foot, one-piece, thorn; Krater, bolster, column, hemispherical; Kyathos, loop handle; Lid I; Mastos; Mortar; Moulded relief ware; Myke; Oinochoe, trefoil, shape 9; Plate, fish plate (Attic type), flat-rim, rolled-rim, with offset rim; Pyxis, domed slipover lid; Skyphos of Attic type; Unguentarium; Water pitcher, small (coarse ware)

BAKING DISH (COOKING WARE): *133–134*

Baking pan (cooking ware): *133*

Basin: Attic, comparable to coarse-ware krater, 108[8]; milk, "mortar" as, 110

Baths of Aphrodite: deposits, 192, *204, 207*

Beater-and-anvil technique. *See* Cooking ware

Benson, J. L.: 145[11]

Blister ware: at Isthmia, 202; dating criterion, color as, 7, 10, decoration as, 8, 146, 147, fabric as, 7, 10, 145, 147–148, 149, handle form as, 148, method of manufacture as, 7, 146; decoration, relief, 145, 146, lunate impressions, 146, "thumb print", 145, 146, vertical ribbing and incision, 146; fabric, 10, 145–146, 147, not used for Classical lamps, 146; imitations in normal clay, 145, 148; intended for oil, 144–145; manufactured in other centers, 144; shapes native to Corinth, 10, handmade until Hellenistic period, 146. *See also* Aryballos; Askos, duck; Cup; Filter vase

Bols: à bossettes et à imbrications, 151, 155; *à décor (uniquement) végétal et floral*, 151, 155, 156; *à*

double dipped, 4, 66, 115; fugitive, 18, 30, 38, 64, 99, 103, 155, 163; matt black, 183; red, intentional (?) on bowl, 27, **72**, on interior of coarseware vessels, 104, 108, 114, 114[16, 18]. *See also Bols à glaçure*; Slip

Glaze-banded vessels: 10, 20, 27, 28, 29, 49, 58, 59, 60, 60[51], 61, 214

Glaze lines: 117, 122[9], 125, 129, 131, 137[21], 138–139, 141. *See also* Decoration, stroke burnishing

Glazing: full, 4, 27, 35–36, 49, 63; partial (semiglazed), 4, 10, 27, 35–36, 49, 63, 93, 107, Corinthian tradition, 27; trends in, 4, 36; unglazed fine ware, 10, 47, 48, 49, 51, 55, 56, 62, 72, 74, 94, 100, 101, 121[7]; wheel, 4, 72. *See also* Glaze-banded vessels

Gold vessels: as mould prototypes, 156[7]. *See also* Decoration, gilding

Grace, V. R.: 127[13], 189, 206

Graffito inscriptions: 9, *64–66*, 75[75], 78, 82, 83, 84; none on skyphoi, 66. *See also* Calligraphy; Dipinto inscriptions; Index I

Grammatika ekpomata. See Graffito inscriptions

Grave: groups, 2, 4, 67, 67[63], 86, 94–95, 101[98], 193–194, 196, 212–216; offerings, 2, 53, 55, 100, 130, 144, 147[14]; pyre groups, Attic, 57, 67[62]

Gray ware: 30[14], 33[17], 36, 37[22, 23], 40[26], 44, 50[37], 66[58], 90[85], 91, 172[25], 176[32], 177, 180[42, 44], 183[50]

HALIEIS: Corinthian calyx krater found at, 45[30]

Hand grip: bolster, on mortar, 109, 110; piecrust, on mortar, 111

Handles: criterion for dating, 68, 147–148; double loop, on aryballos and cup, 148, 150, cf. lamps, 150, on kantharos, 76, 78, 82; double strap, on decanters, 57, 59, 60, 143; for metal rods, 232[24]; frying pan, 131, wooden (?), 125, 132; grooved, 59, 76, 78, 112, 132, 150; kylix, on bowl kantharos, 2[3], on kantharos, 71, 73, 74; loop and pinch, on kyathoi, 47–49; on bowls with appliqué supports, 172[25], 174; on trefoil olpai, development of, 51; pierced for suspension, 47, 48, **188**, **189**; plastic, on askos, 103; recurved, on drinking bowls, 62, 93, 94; ribbed, on decanters, 58, 59, 61; spirally ridged, 132; thumb rest, bolster, 74, 137[19], Herakles knot, 74, 76, 78, 82, rotelle, 138, **497**, spur, 87, strap, 74, 76, 78, 83; triple ring, on askos, 103; twisted rope, 138; without handle plate, on kraters, 107[7]. *See also* Amphora handles; Hand grip; *and shape names* (main entry)

Handmade vessels: blister ware, 8, 146, 147, 148, 150. *See also* Shapes, handmade

Head: appliqué medallion, 92

Hexamilia. *See* Kantharos; Mug

Holmos: 110[12]

Homeric bowls. *See* Bowls, Homeric

Household ware: 2, 18, 45, 49, 68, 104, 113, 117, 141, 155, 191[8]. *See also* Drinking vessels; Wine, shapes for

Hydria: Attic Classical, no equivalent in Corinthian Hellenistic, 19; Corinthian, 212. *See also* Kalpis; Pitcher, hydria

ICONOGRAPHY ON FIGURED BOWLS: 163–168

Indented bottom: 118, 135, 137–138, 139, 140, 141, 142, 143

Inkwell: Attic, 181; Corinthian, 18, *102*

Isthmia: Corinthian pottery found at, 54[42], 59[49], 75[76], 88, 113[15], 120[7], 191, 195; Large Circular Pit (Deposit 5), 50[38], 192, *200*; Pottery Pit, Theater Cave (Deposit 16), 109[9], 120[7], 125[12], 129, 138[24], 147[16], 192, *202*

JAR. *See* Ointment-pot

Jug (blister ware): 144–145, 146, 147[14], intended for oil, 144; shapes imitated in normal fabric, 145
(coarse ware): handle-ridge, 10, 49–50, *113–115*, 214; semi-glazed (red), 10, 104; shape history, 10
(fine ware): 213, 214; black-glazed, 212, 213; round-mouth, 214, 215

Juglet: 56; imported forms, 50; production period unknown, 49; shape history, 10, 19[4]; unglazed, 10

KALOS NAMES: 9

Kalpis (blister ware): 144[3]

Kantharoi: dating of, 6; graffito inscriptions on, 9; in foreign fabrics, 72; similar shape elements among, 6; vertical ribbing on, as dating criterion, 8, thorn decoration, 87; West Slope Earlier Phase decoration, 24

Kantharos, Acrocorinth: *82–83*, 213; capacity, 62[53]; graffito inscriptions on, 64, 82; relation to cyma kantharos, 77[78], 82; shape history, 19[6], 63; West Slope and other decoration on, 20, 82

articulated: Attic, 83, 84; Corinthian, 68, *83–86*, graffito inscriptions on, 64, 83, shape history, 19[6] 63, 152; West Slope decoration on, 21, 84

bowl, kylix handles: not discussed, 2[3]

calyx: Attic, 19[3], 219, 221, applied rim, 73[71], metallic foot, 74, spur-handled, 72[67]; Corinthian, 61, 62, 63, 220, 232, kylix handles, 71–72, *73–74*, dipinto inscription on, 64, 71[66], gilded, 62, metallic foot, 71–72, *74*, moulded rim, 72, *73–74*, only decorated Classical shape, 19, pedestal foot, *73–74*, shape history, 19[2], 63, 72, 73, West Slope and other decoration on, 21, 63

cyma: 68, *76–82*, 152, 216; graffito inscriptions on, 64, 78; related to Acrocorinth kantharos, 82; shape history, 19[6], 63; useful for dating, 64; West Slope and other decoration on, 20, 21

Hexamilia: *86–87*, 152, 215; capacity, 62[53]; dipped, 63; fabric, 62; shape history, 19[6], 63. *See also* Mug, Hexamilia

metal. *See* Metal vessels

one-piece: Attic, 75; Corinthian, *74–76*, capacity, 62[53], graffito inscription on, 64, 75[75], shape

Slip: 58, 107, 109, 111, 149, 150

South Basilica: deposits, 192, *201, 202*

Southeast Building: deposits, 192, 193, 194, *199, 211, 217*

South Stoa: date of construction, vi, 197; deposits connected with history of, 77, 191, 194–195, 196–198, *216–235*; findspot of graffito inscriptions, 64; religious use of, 100; wells, v, 76, 83, 100, 140, 190, 195, 197–198, *225–235*

Stamnos: Attic Classical, no equivalent in Corinthian Hellenistic, 19, 105; imported and early Roman examples, 105[4], 176[32], 216

Stamped inscriptions: on ointment-pots, 99

Stamps: for relief-ware moulds, Figured Bowls, 153, 155, 163, Foliage Bowls, 153, 157, 158, 159, **940, 941**, Linear Bowls, 153[2], 175[30]. *See also* Amphora handles

Stew pot (cooking ware): Attic, 123; Corinthian, *122–124*, with glaze lines, 138[24]; imported, with indented bottom, 138[23]

Stopper: 114

String marks: 47, 48, 53, 55, 100, 101, **942**

Supports, appliqué: 62, 165, 174, **786**; Athena head, on Figured Bowls, 171, 174; masks, on Figured Bowls, 171–173; shells, on wheelmade hemispherical bowls, 88, 171; significance for dating, 165, 171

Suspension holes. *See* Handles, pierced for suspension

Tarentum: silver kantharos from, 74

Tavern of Aphrodite: deposit, 194, *219–221*

Temple E, peribolos: deposits, 193, 196, *200, 204, 209, 210*; findspot of graffito inscription, 65

Thompson, H. A.: 1, 151

Thompson, M.: 189

Tile Works: deposits, 193, 195, *205–206*

Trends: in care of execution, 4, 8, 24; toward ease and speed of production, 4, 9, 88–89, 153; toward loss of articulation, 4; toward vestigiality of components of forms, 4. *See also* Decoration; Glazing; Motif, degeneration of; Shape development

Unguentarium: Attic, blister ware, 145; Corinthian, 4, 18, *98–99*, associated with skyphoi in graves, 67, 196, 213–215, fabric, 98–99, replaced blister ware, 145, shape history, 19[5], 67; early Roman, "onion", 216; imported, 216

Votive pottery: 210, 222, 224[23], 232; not miniature in Hellenistic Corinth, 2

Water pitcher (coarse ware): Attic, 113; Corinthian, 56, *112–113*, shape history, 10

(fine ware): Attic, 50, 56, in pyre groups, 56–57; Corinthian, *56–57*, 112, shape history, 19[5], 49, unglazed, 10

West Slope decoration: Attic, 24; Corinthian, 2[3], 8, 11, *20–26*, 36, 39, 45, 46, 73, 75, 76, 78, 82, 83, 84, 89–91, **187, 943, 944**, date, 20, 24, figured representations, 11, influenced by Moulded relief ware, 8, 26, 89, 91, lip zone, **527, 532, 536, 537, 539–541, 544–546**, shapes attested for Earlier and Later Phases, 24, three-dimensionality, 11, 25–26; other centers, 26. *See also* Decoration, incision; Medallion, floral; Moulds; Workshops

Wheel marks: 55, 72, 93, 109[10], 121, 123, 124, 125, 131, 134, 139, 140, 143, 148, 149

Wine: shapes for, 18, 45, 47, 49, 50, 61, 62, 63, 114, 143, West Slope decoration on, 20; fine-ware wine jugs, small, undecorated, 49. *See also* Fabric; Graffito inscriptions; Resin

Workshops: distinctions not discussed, 6; identification of Corinthian West Slope style artists, 8

PLATES

1:2

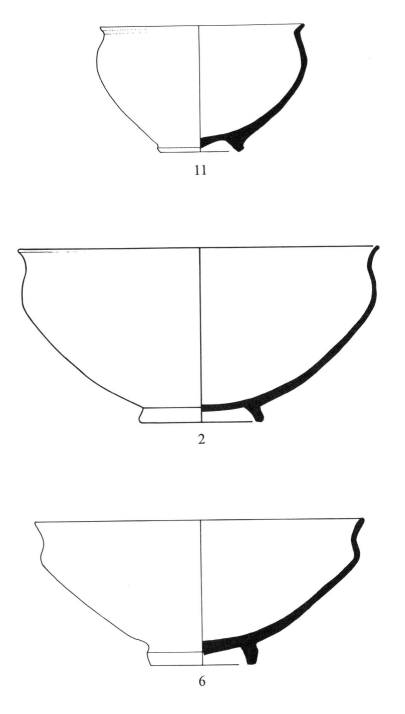

11

2

6

Semi-glazed bowl

1:2

PLATE 2

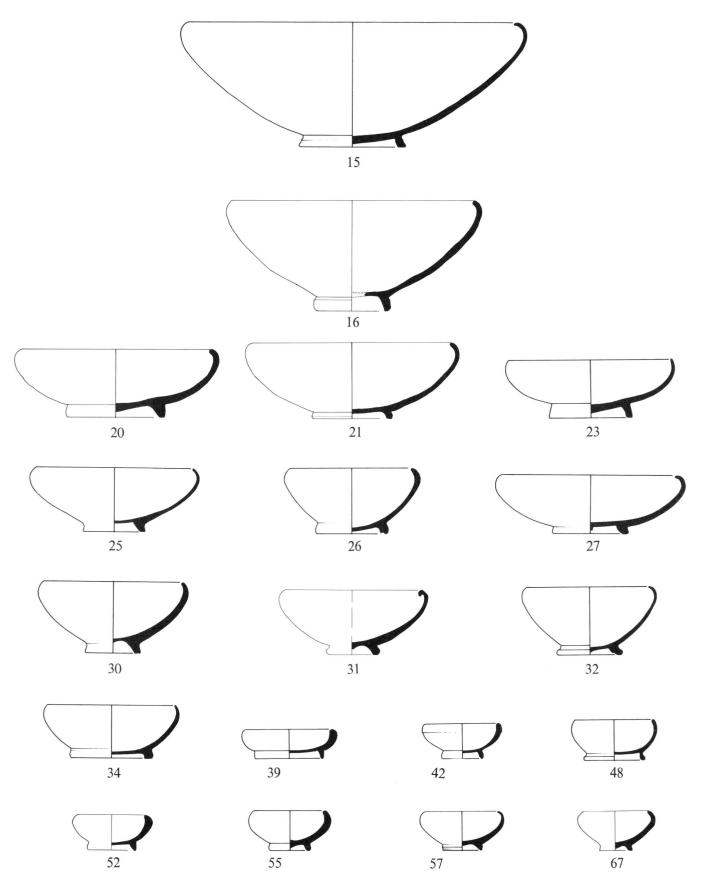

15

16

20

21

23

25

26

27

30

31

32

34

39

42

48

52

55

57

67

Echinus bowl

1:3

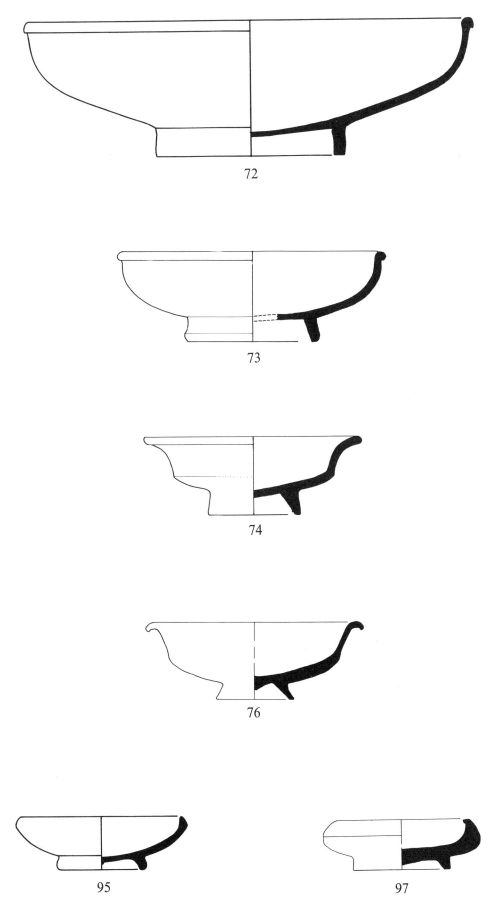

72

73

74

76

95 97

Bowl, outturned rim
Dish, bevelled rim

1:2

PLATE 4

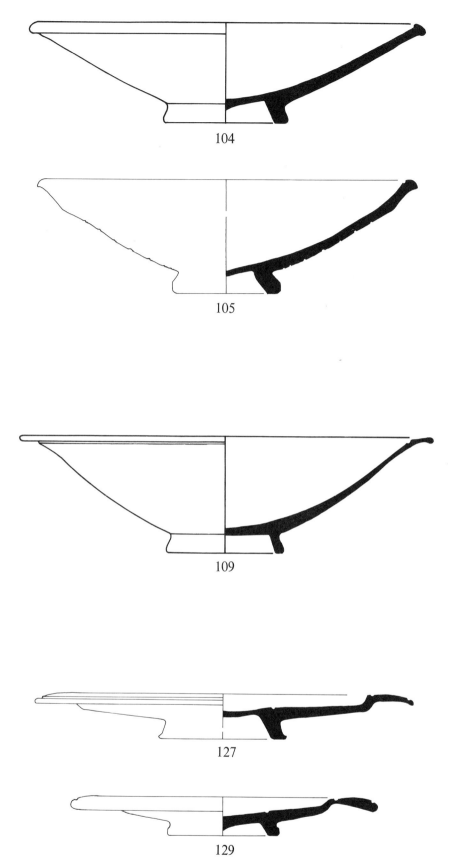

104

105

109

127

129

Plate: Rolled-rim; Flat-rim;
offset rim

1:2

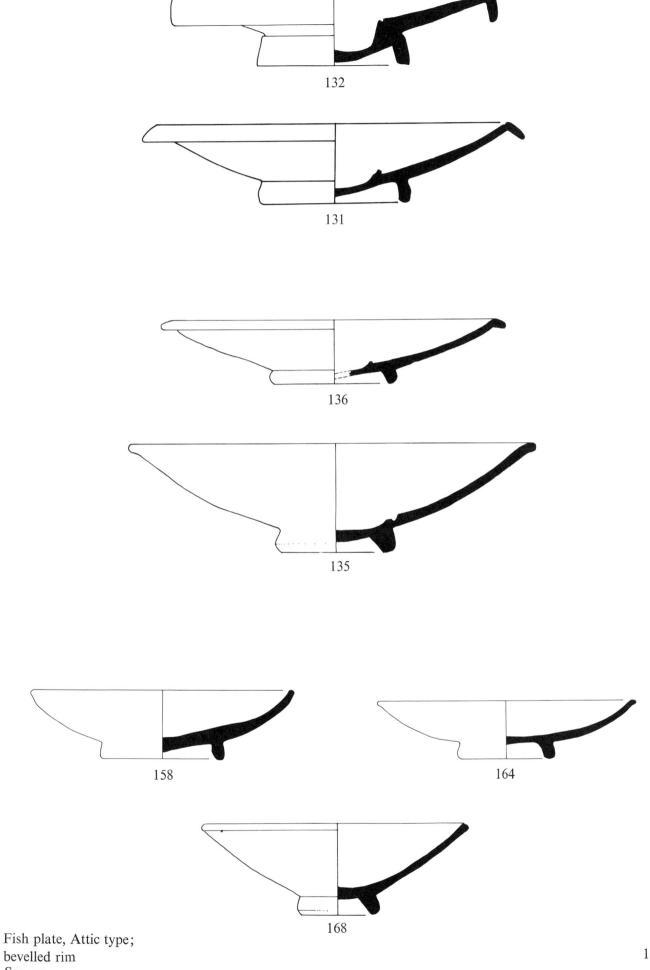

132

131

136

135

158

164

168

Fish plate, Attic type;
bevelled rim
Saucer

1:2

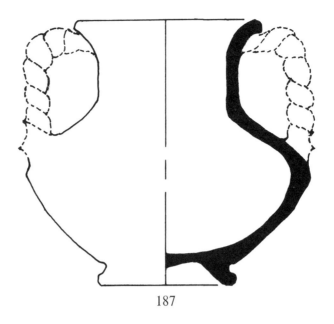

187

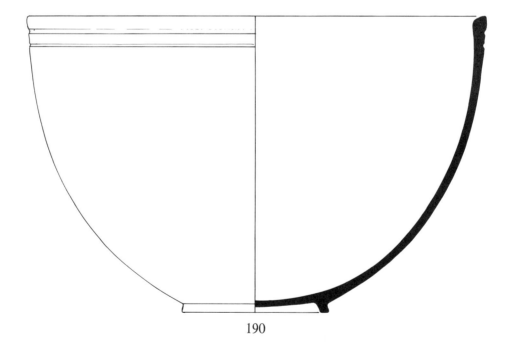

190

West Slope amphora
Hemispherical krater

1:1
1:2

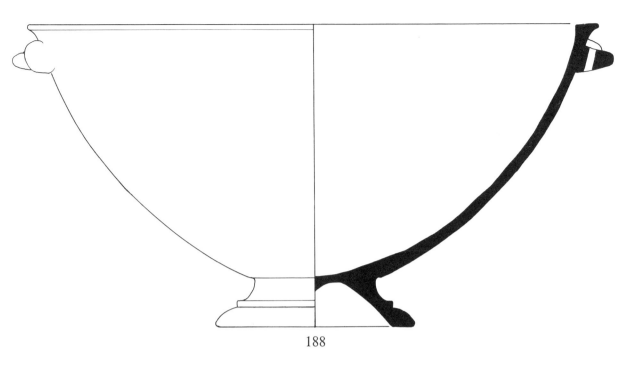

188

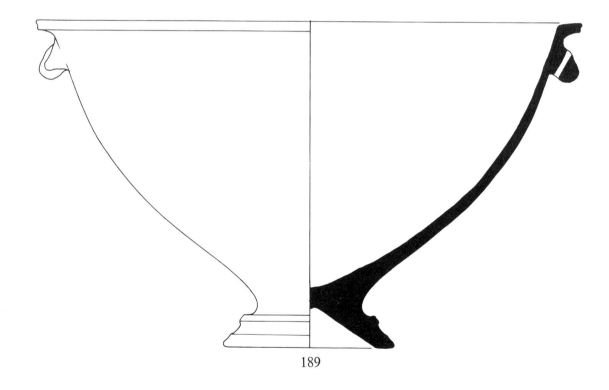

189

Bolster krater

1:2

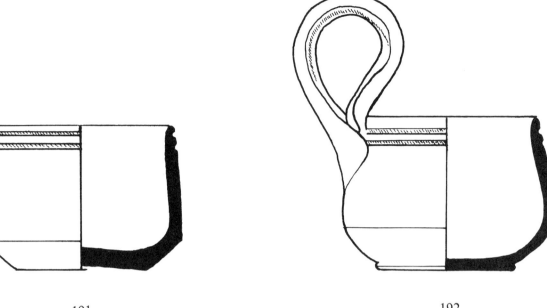

191

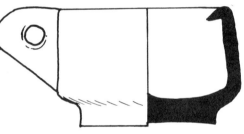

192

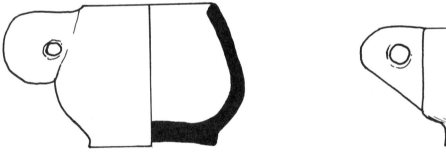

194

195

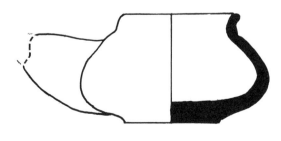

197

Kyathoi

1:1

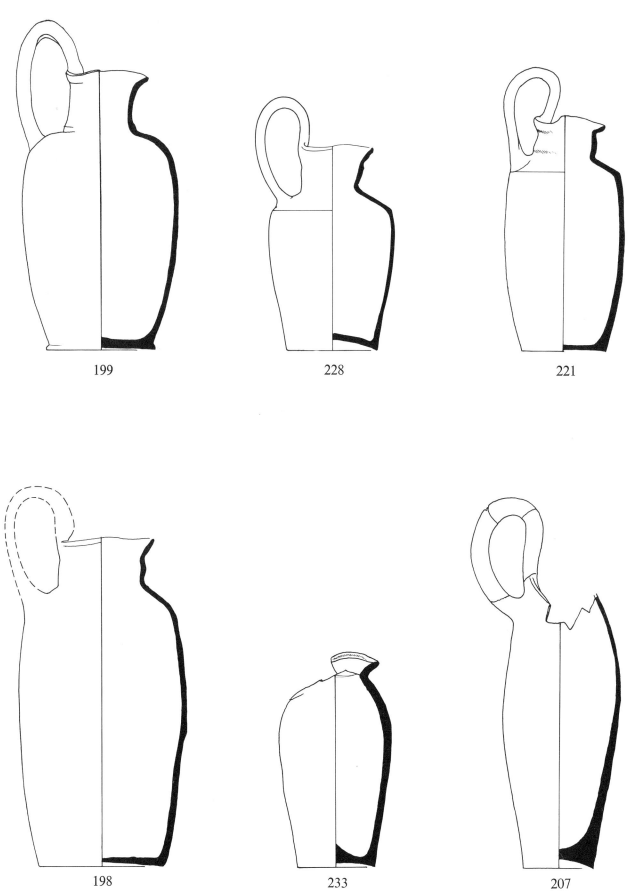

199

228

221

198

233

207

Trefoil olpe

1:2

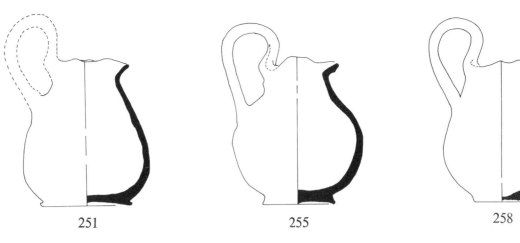

251   255   258

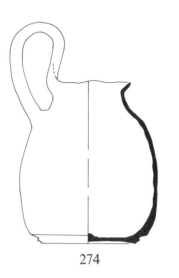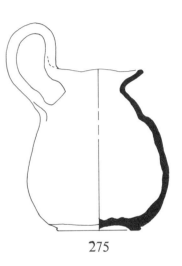

273   274   275

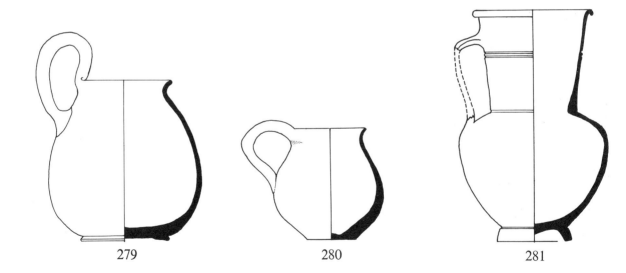

279   280   281

Trefoil oinochoai   1:2
Juglet
Water pitcher

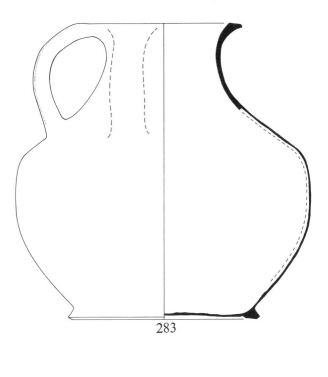

283

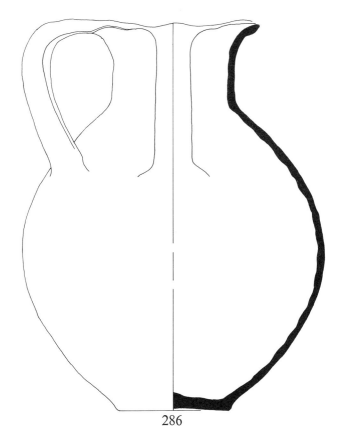

286

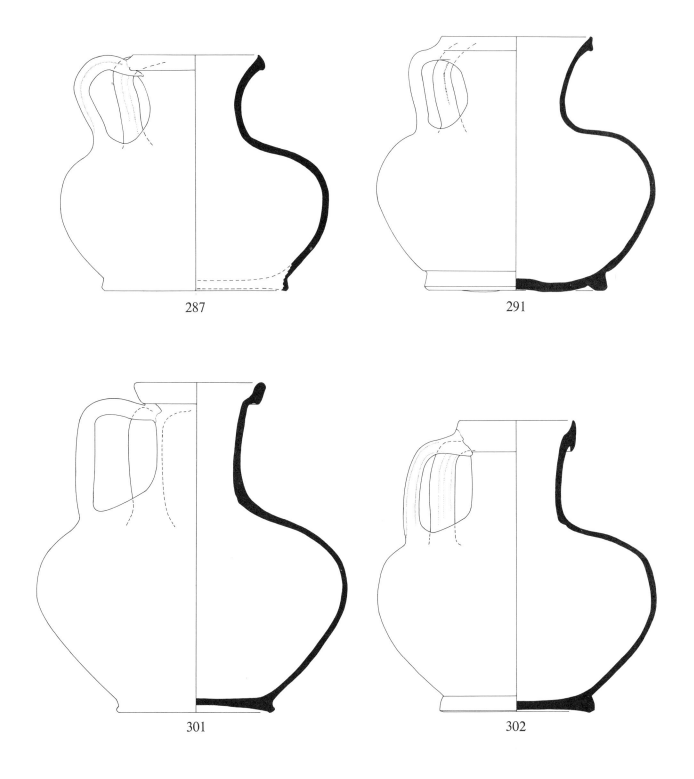

287

291

301

302

Decanters II, III

Slightly less than   1:2

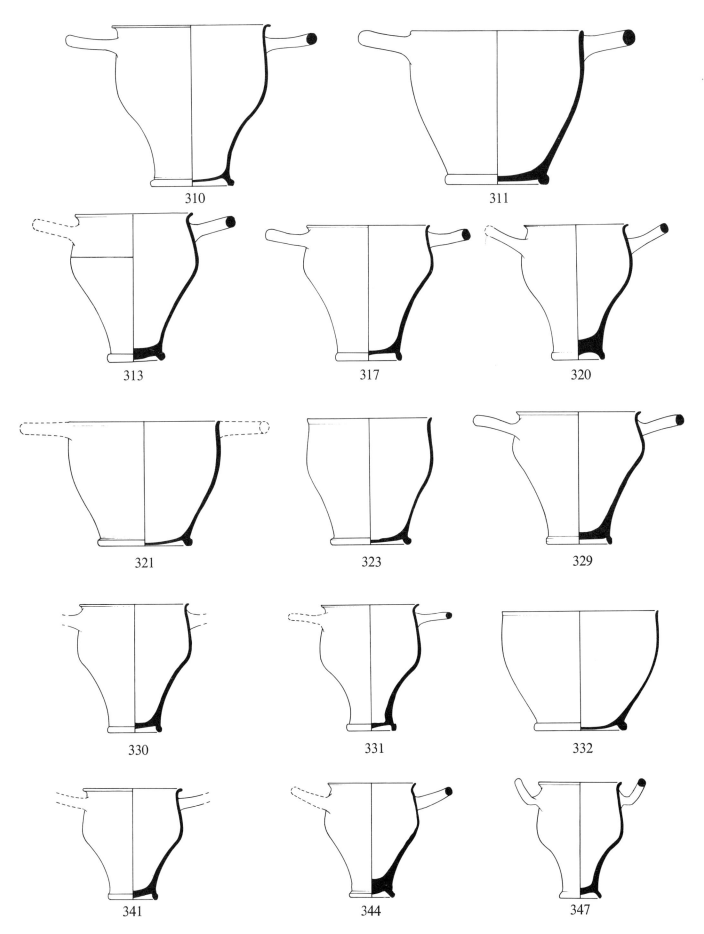

310

311

313

317

320

321

323

329

330

331

332

341

344

347

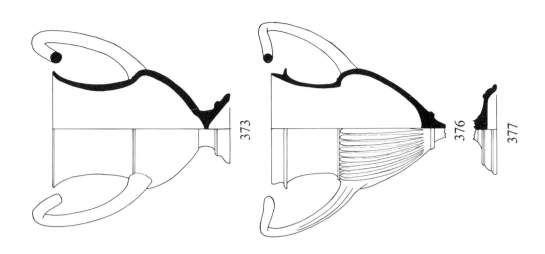

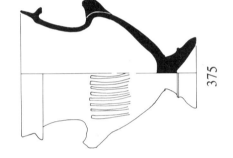

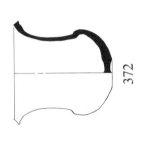

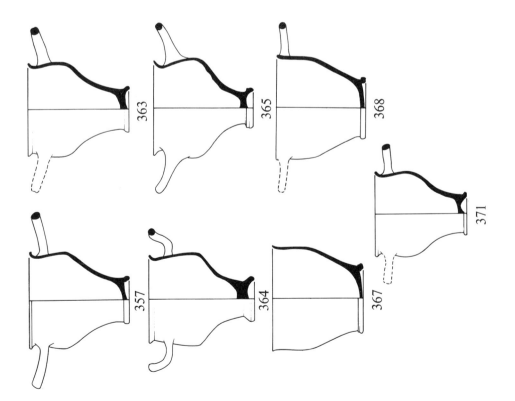

Skyphos, Attic type
Calyx cup
Calyx kantharoi

Skyphos 1:3

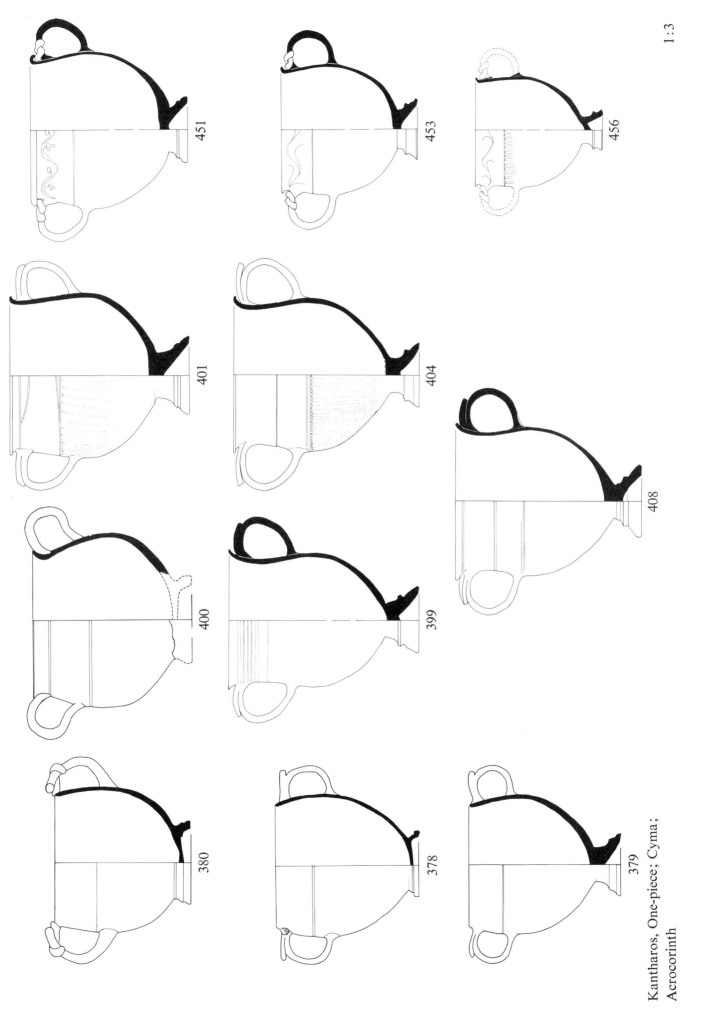

Kantharos, One-piece; Cyma; Acrocorinth

1:3

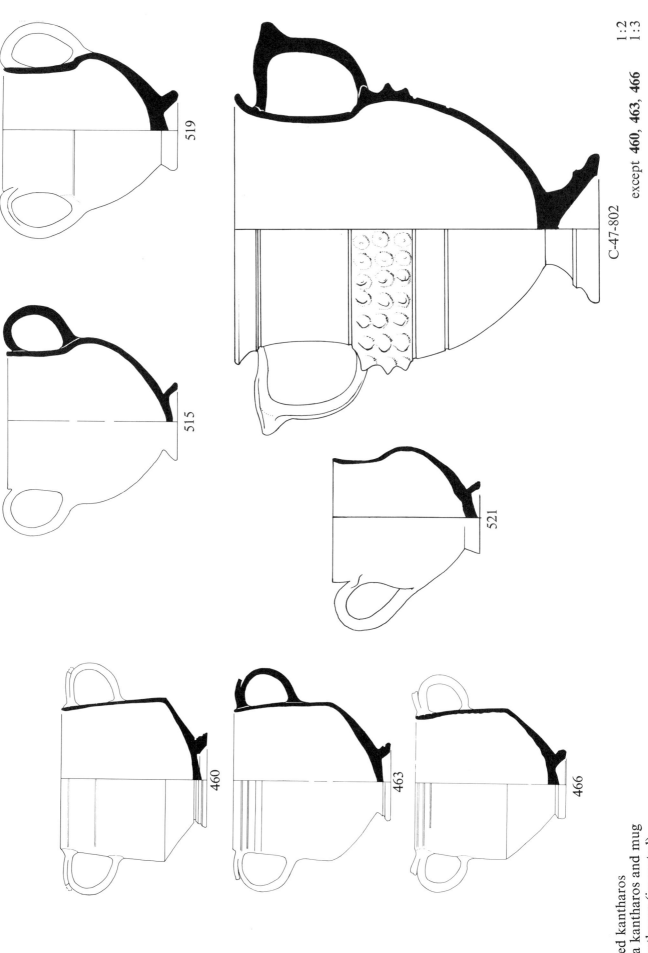

519

515

C-47-802

521

460

463

466

Articulated kantharos   1:2
Hexamilia kantharos and mug   1:3
Thorn kantharos (imported)

except **460**, **463**, **466**

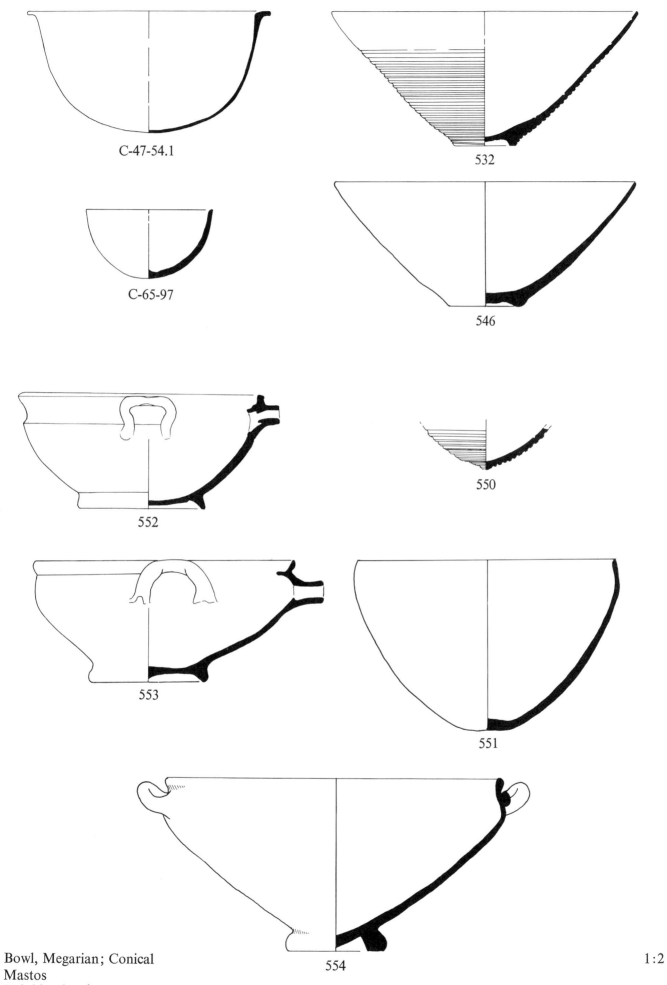

C-47-54.1

532

C-65-97

546

552

550

553

551

554

Bowl, Megarian; Conical
Mastos
Drinking bowls

1:2

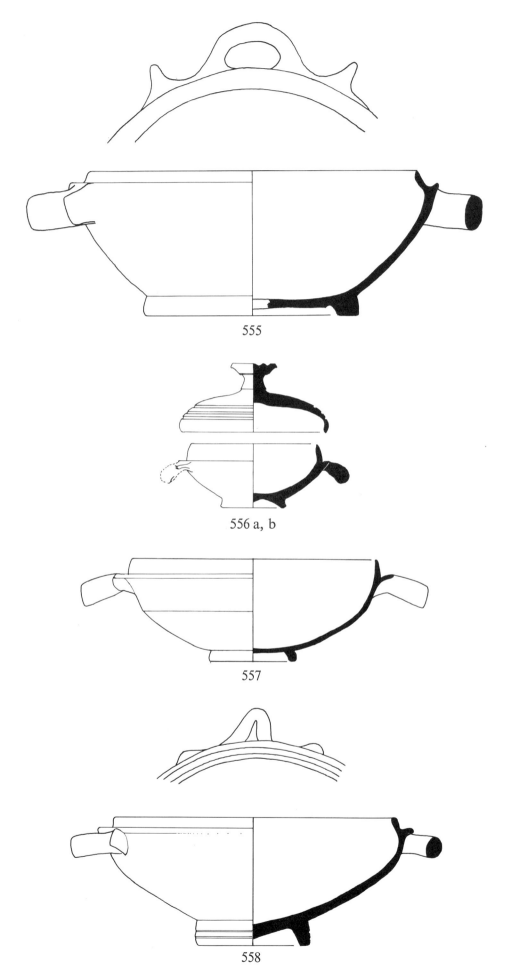

555

556 a, b

557

558

Lekanis

1:2

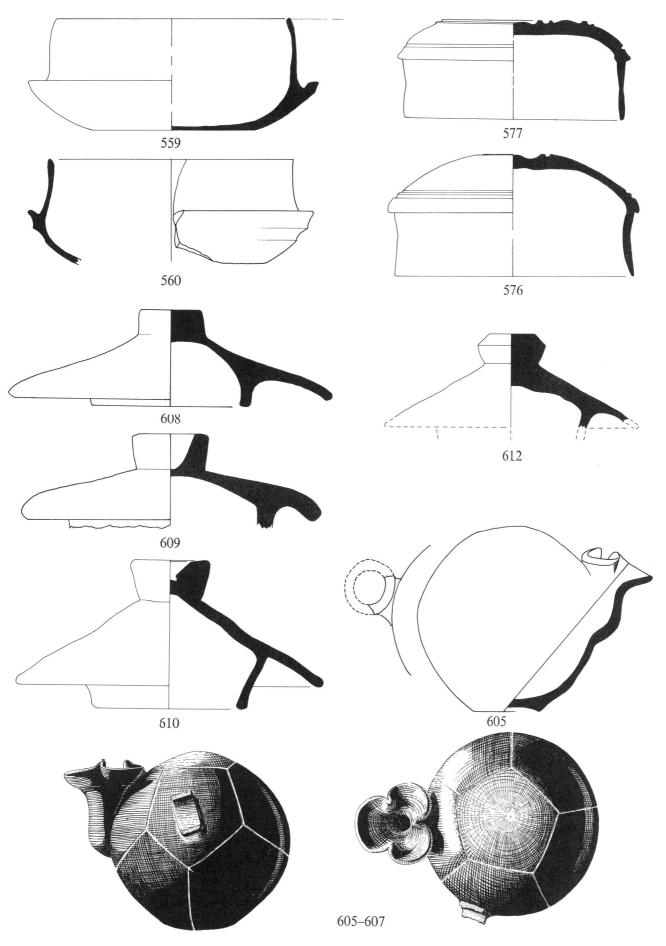

559

577

560

576

608

612

609

610

605

605–607

Pyxis, receptacles and lids
Stamnos lid
Basketball askos

1 : 2

PLATE 20

587

596

591

602

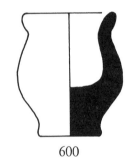

600

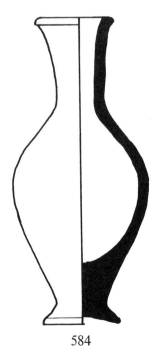

584

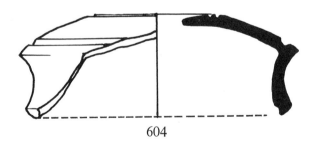

604

Unguentarium
Ointment-pots
Inkwell

1:1

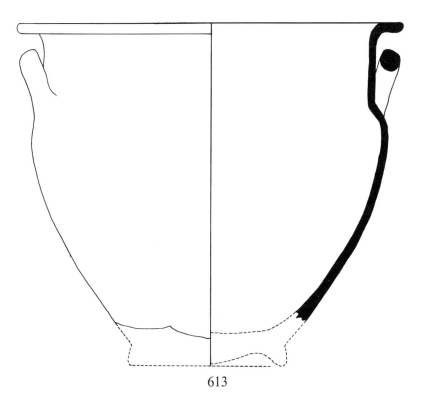

613

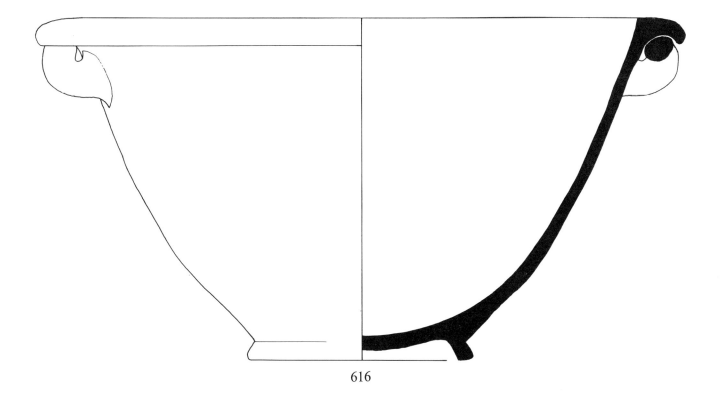

616

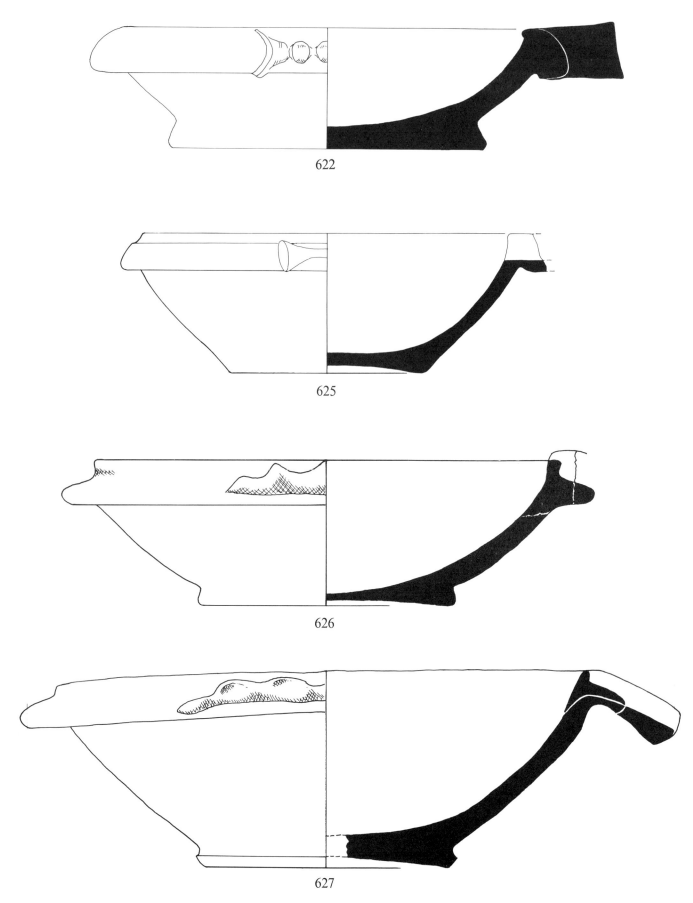

622

625

626

627

Mortar I, II

1:2

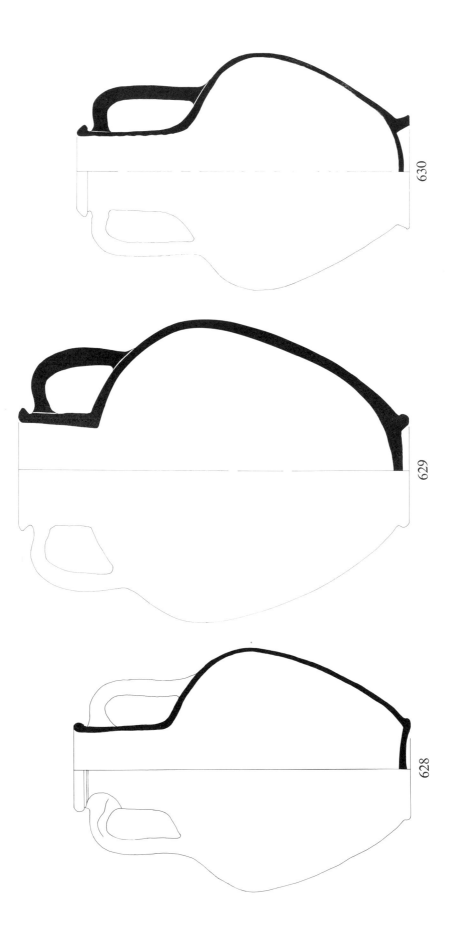

630

629

628

Based amphoras I–III

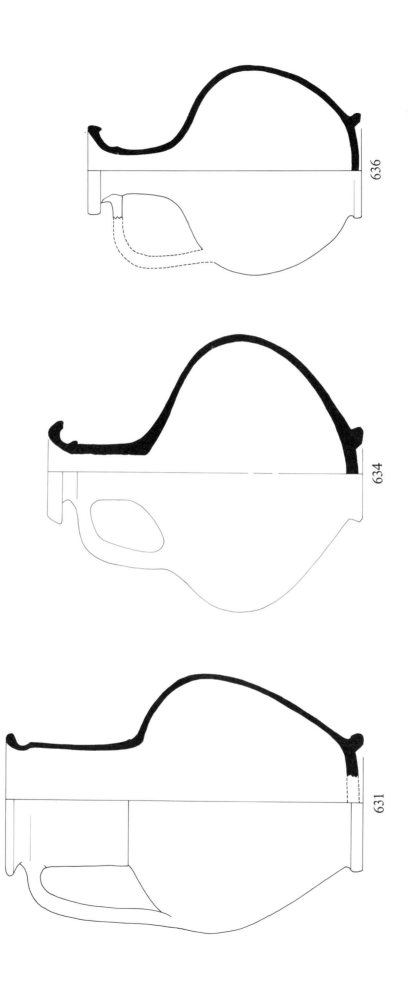

636

634

631

Water pitcher
Handle-ridge jug 1:3

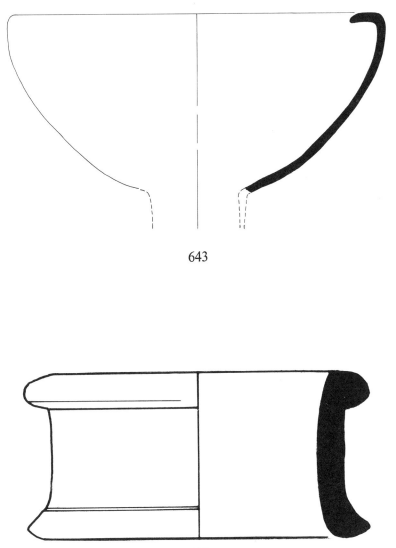

643

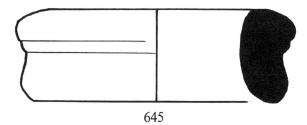

644

645

Funnel

Ring stand

1:1

except funnel   1:2

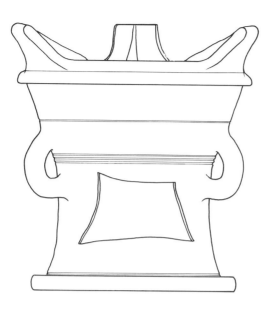

646

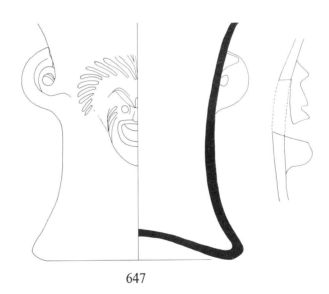

647

Brazier

1:4

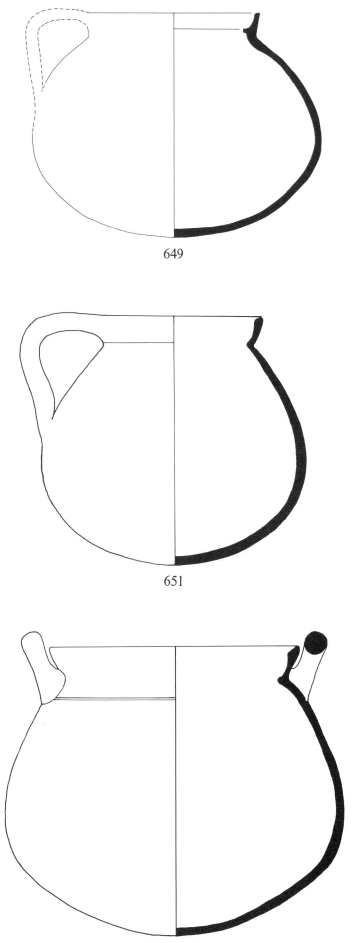

649

651

656

Chytra
Stew pot

1:2

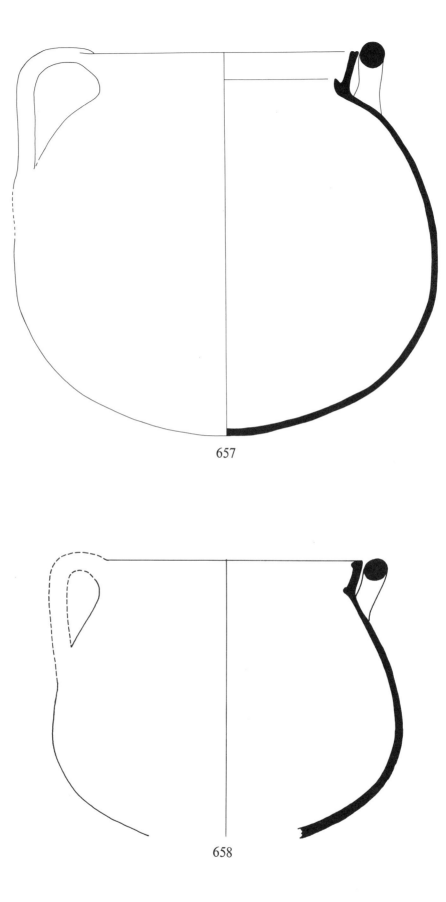

657

658

Stew pot, one vertical, one
tilted horizontal handle

1:2

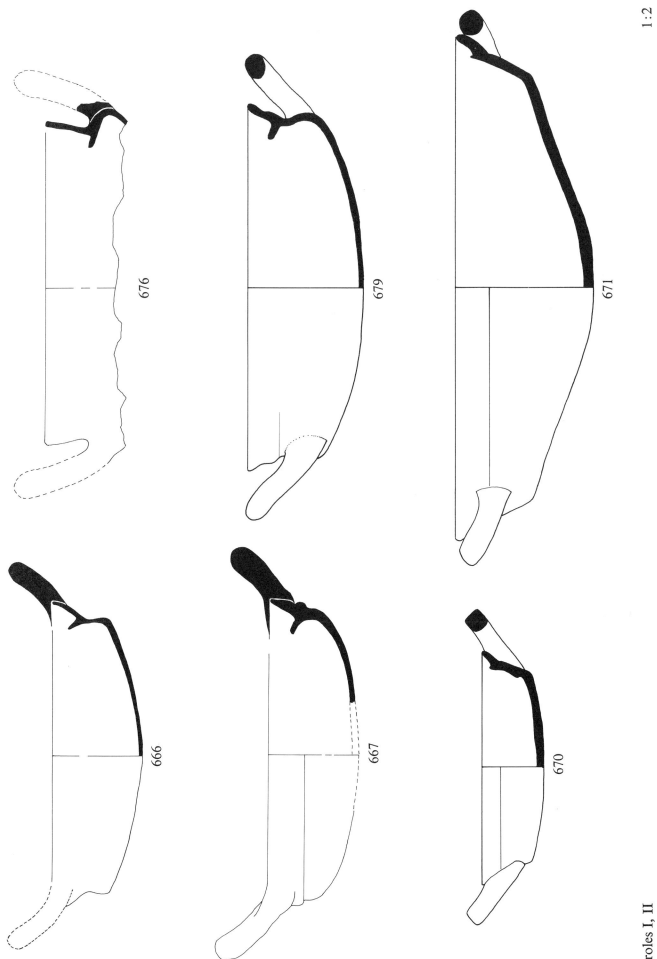

676

679

671

666

667

670

Casseroles I, II

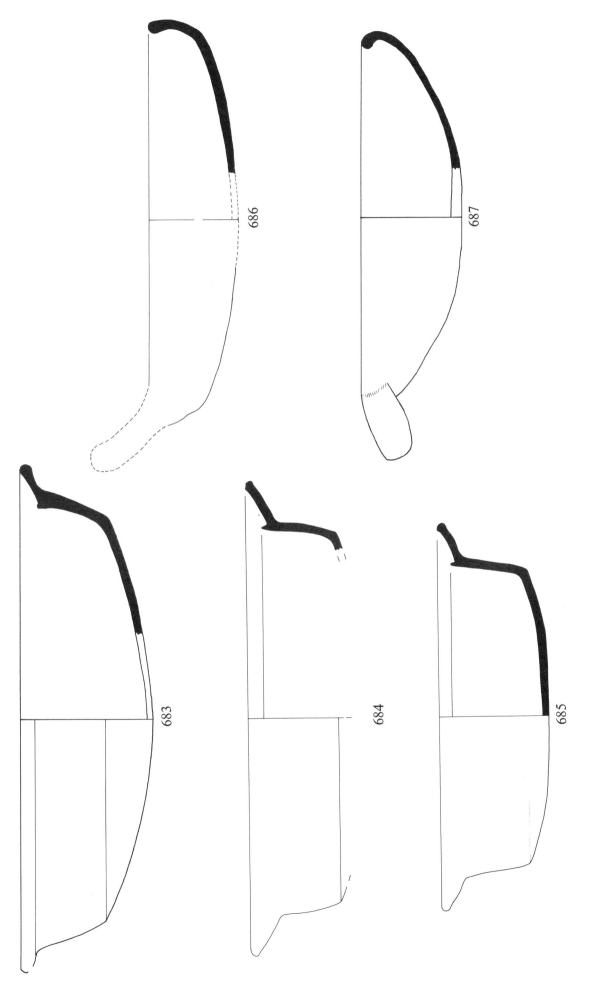

683

684

685

686

687

Casserole without handles
Saucepan

Casserole 1:2

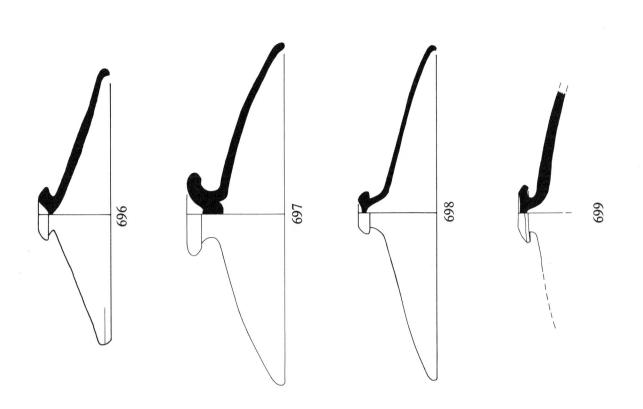

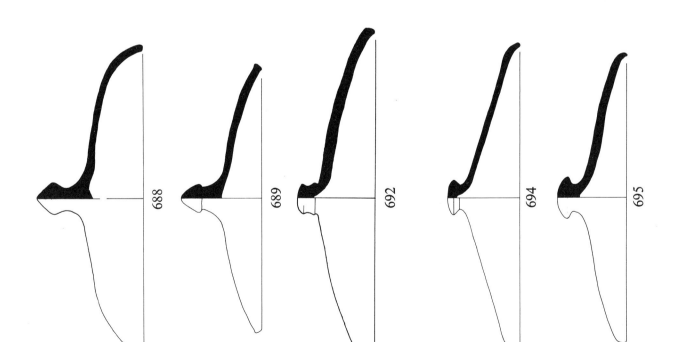

Lids I–III   1:2

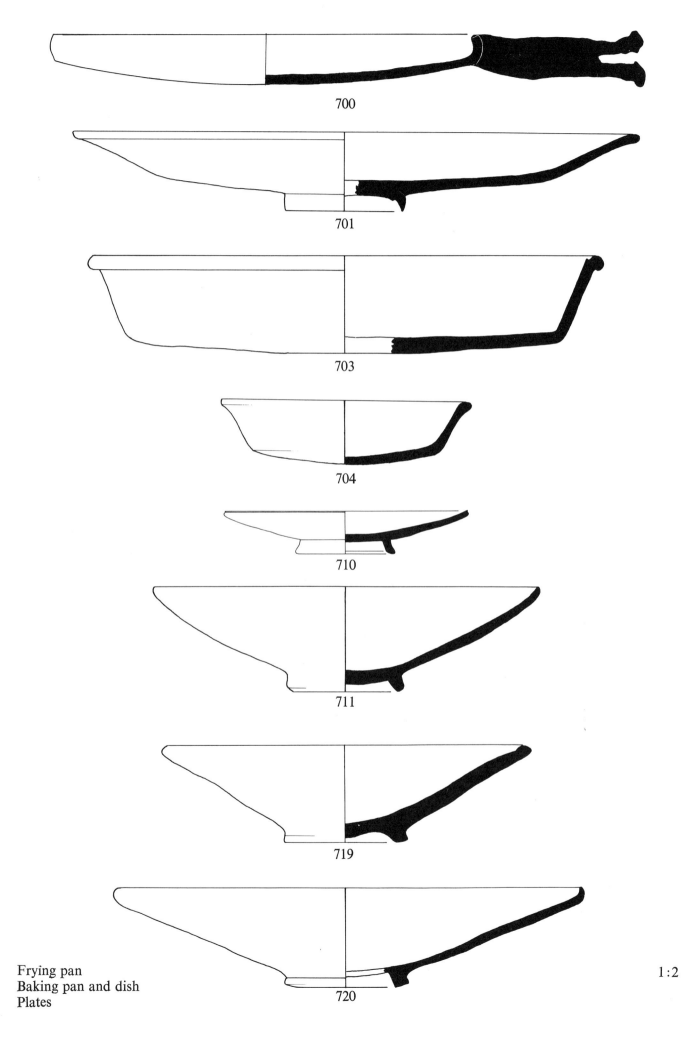

700

701

703

704

710

711

719

Frying pan
Baking pan and dish
Plates

720

1:2

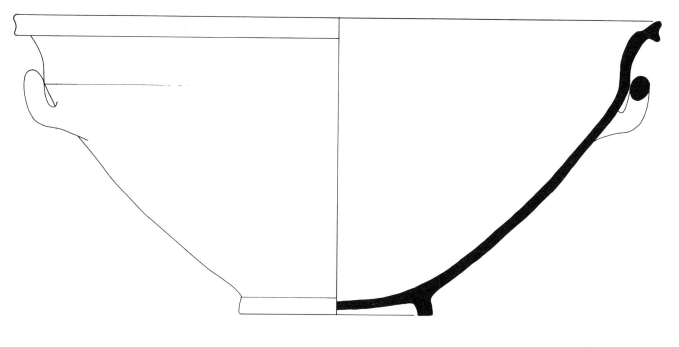

705

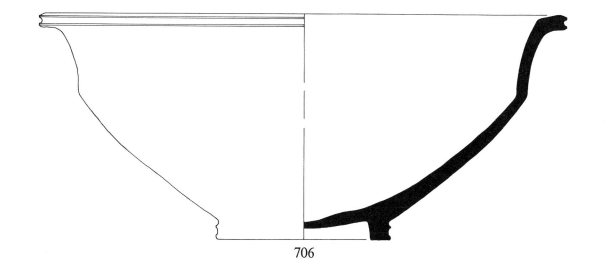

706

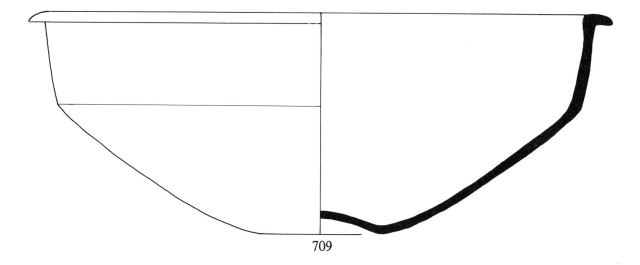

709

Krater

Bowl

1:2

705 slightly less than 1:2

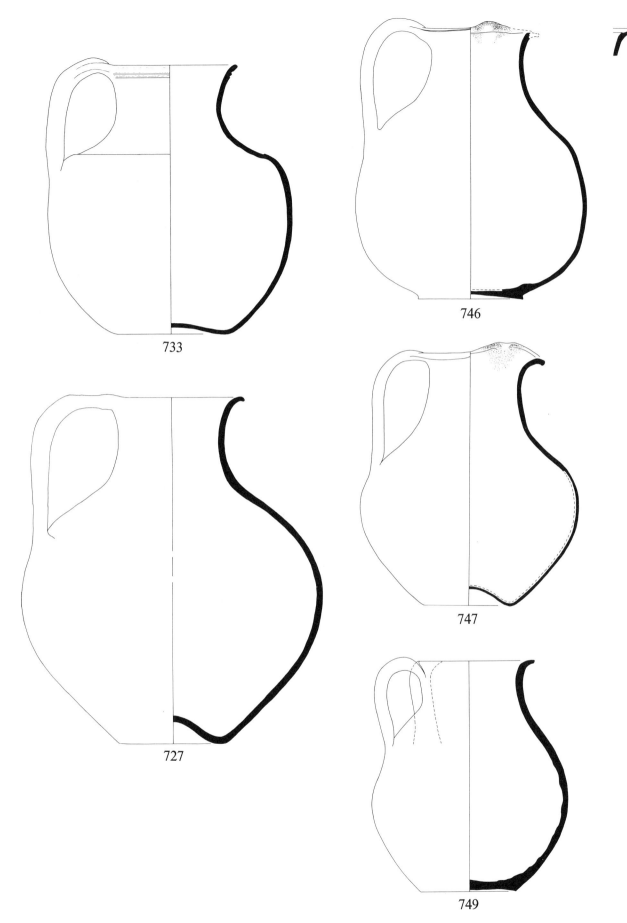

733

746

727

747

749

Pitcher, Round-mouth; Trefoil
Decanter.

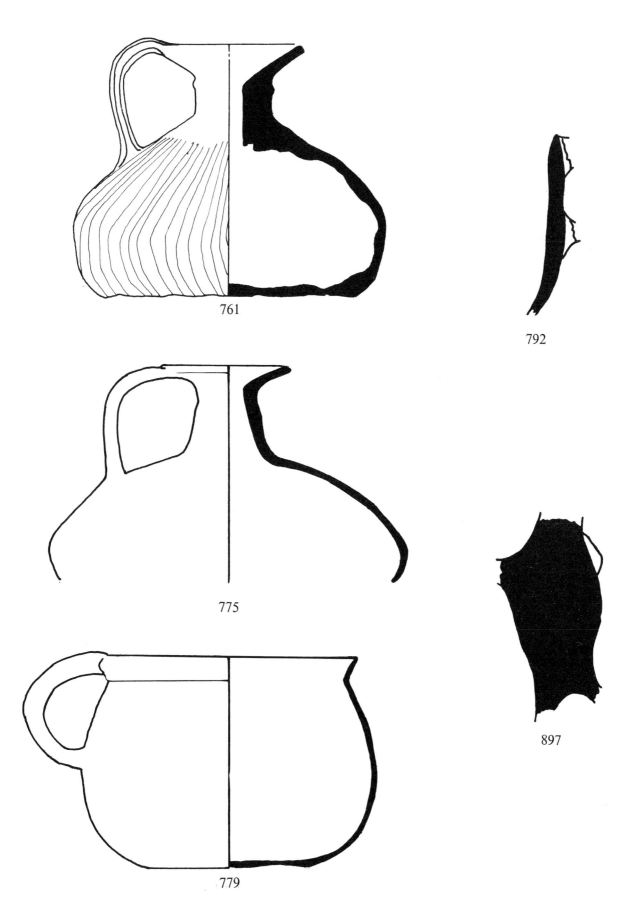

761

792

775

897

779

Aryballos
Cup
Moulded relief-ware fragments

1:1

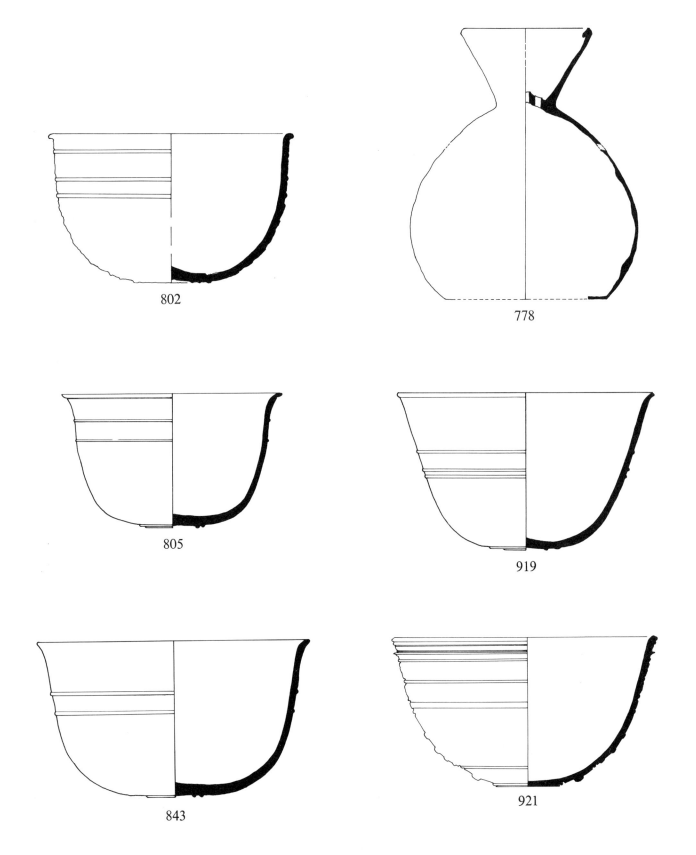

802

778

805

919

843

921

Filter vase
Moulded relief-ware bowl

1:2

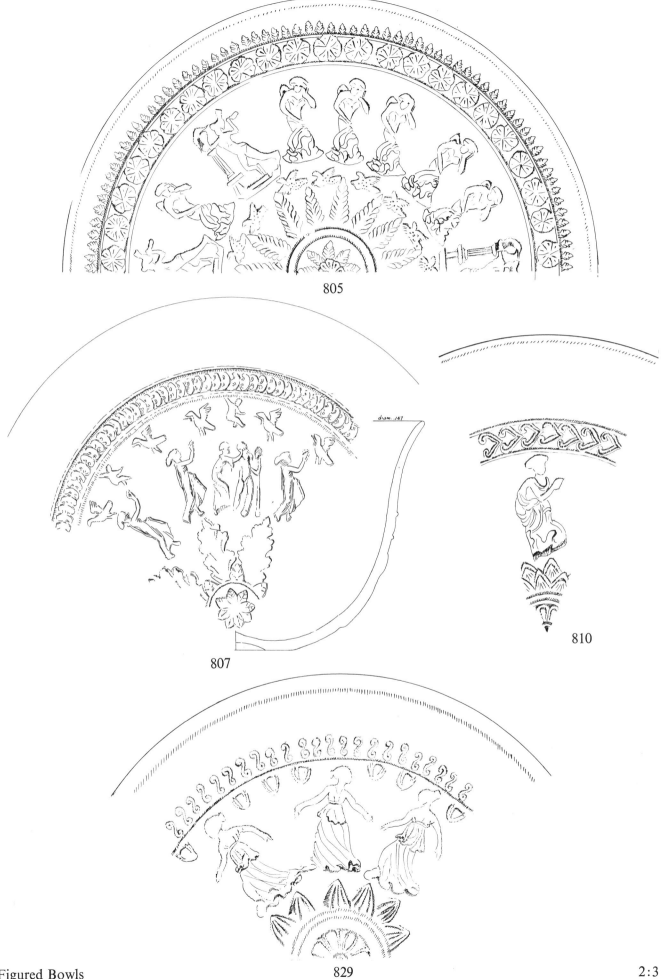

805

807

810

829

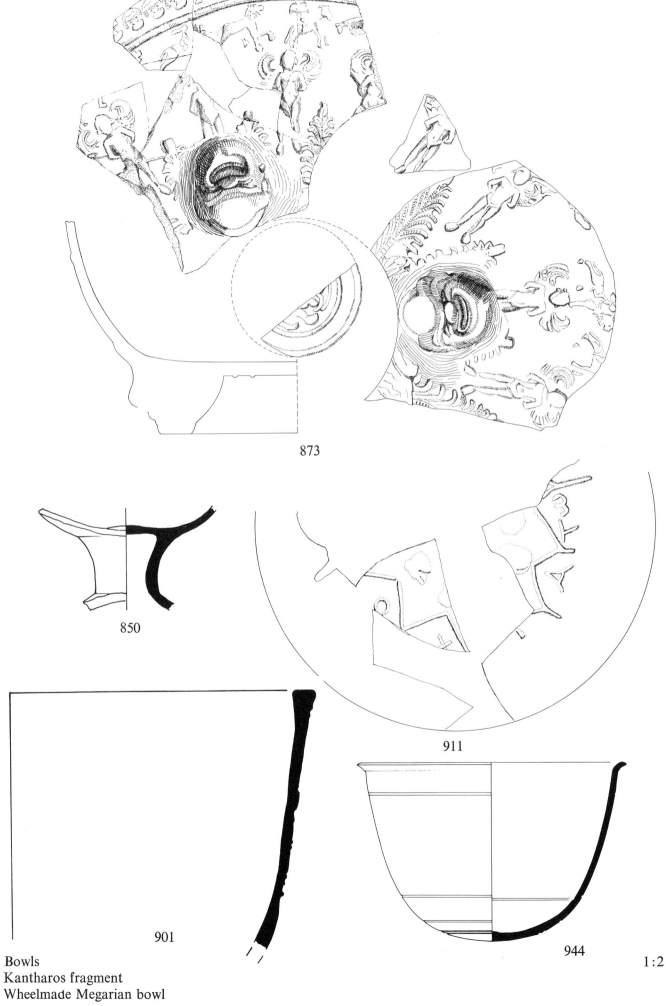

873

850

901

911

944

1:2

Bowls
Kantharos fragment
Wheelmade Megarian bowl

442

189

489

513

412

190

494

464

188

418

408

428

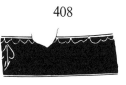

480

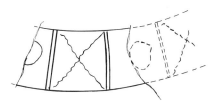

396, 397

441

1:2

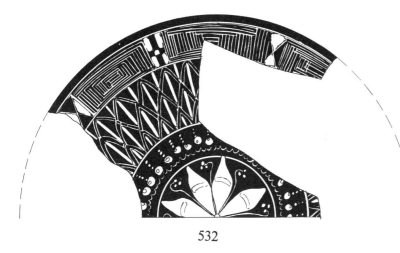

532

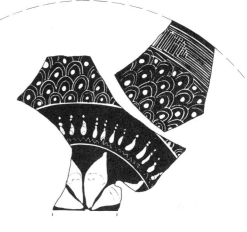

537

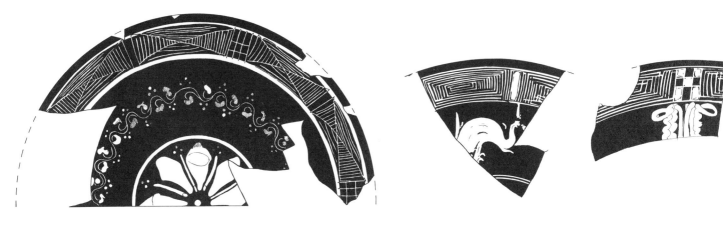

536

539   540

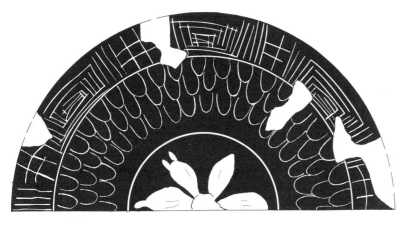

546

541

1:2

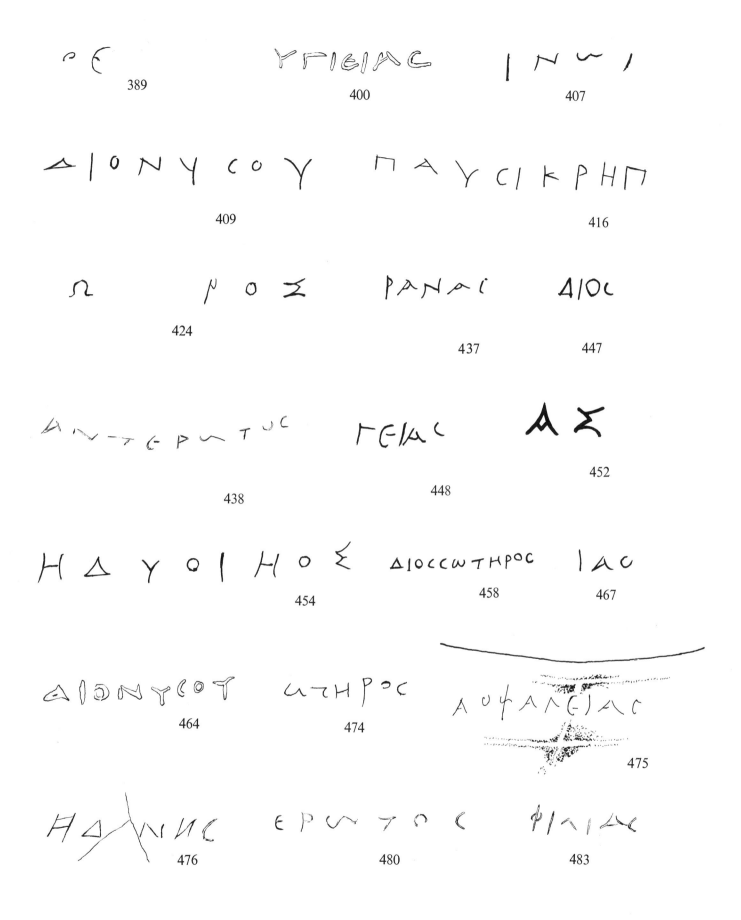

᷁Ε
389

ΥΓΙΕΙΑΣ
400

Ι Ν ω /
407

ΔΙΟΝΥΣΟΥ
409

ΠΑΥΣΙΚΡΗΠ
416

Ω
424

ΡΟΣ

ΡΑΝΑΣ
437

ΔΙΟΣ
447

ΑΝ-ΤΕΡωΤΟΣ
438

ΓΕΙΑΣ
448

ΑΣ
452

Η Δ Υ Ο Ι Η Ο Σ
454

ΔΙΟΣΣωΤΗΡΟΣ
458

ΙΑΣ
467

ΔΙΟΝΥΣΟΥ
464

ωΤΗΡΟΣ
474

ΑΨΑΛΕΙΑΣ
475

ΗΔ ΝΗΣ
476

ΕΡωΤΟΣ
480

ΦΙΛΙΑΣ
483

1:1

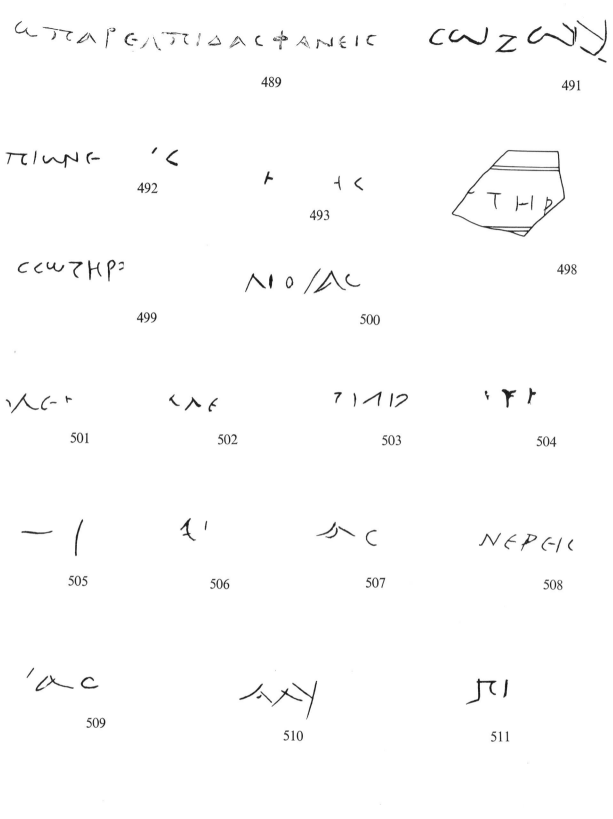

489

491

492

493

498

499

500

501

502

503

504

505

506

507

508

509

510

511

512

514

1:1

2

6

11

15

16

20

21

23

Semi-glazed bowl
Echinus bowl

2:5

26

27

30

31

32

34

39

42

48

52

55

57

67

73

74

76

95

97

Echinus bowl
Bowl, outturned rim
Small dish, bevelled rim

2:5

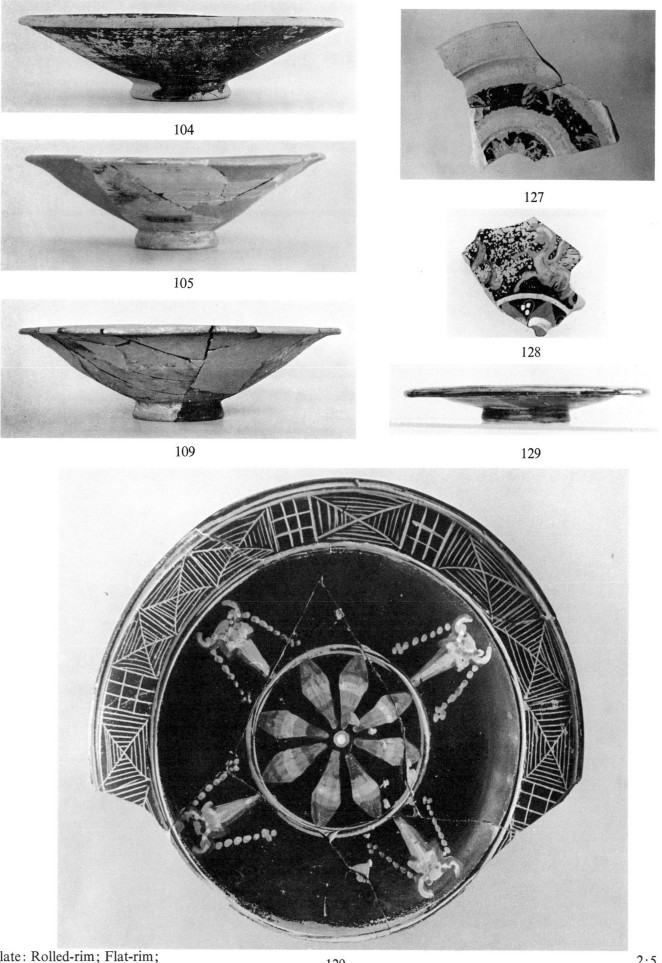

104

105

109

127

128

129

Plate: Rolled-rim; Flat-rim;
offset rim

129

2:5
except **128** 3:5, **129** interior 4:5

132

131

136

135

158   164

168

Fish plate, Attic type;   2:5
bevelled rim
Saucer

187

188

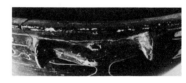

188

189

189

189

190

West Slope amphora   2:5
Bolster krater   except bottom, **189, 190**   1:5
Hemispherical krater

192

193

194   195   197

198   199   207   221   228   233

251   255   258

273   274   275   279

Kyathoi
Trefoil olpe
Trefoil oinochoai

2:5
except olpai   1:5

280

281

283

286

287

291

301

302

Juglet
Water pitcher
Decanters I–III

1:5
except top   2:5

PLATE 50

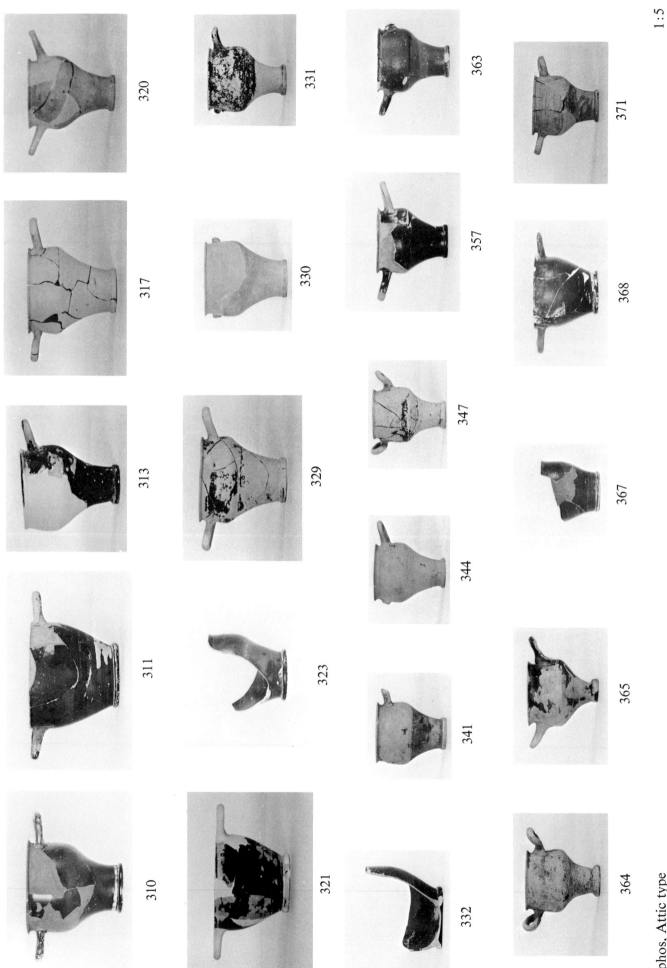

Skyphos, Attic type

Skyphos 1:5

PLATE 51

311

317

347

372

316

336

373

376

374

375

377

Skyphos, Attic type, details
Calyx cup
Calyx kantharoi

1:5
except **376**, **377** 2:5,
details approx. 1:2

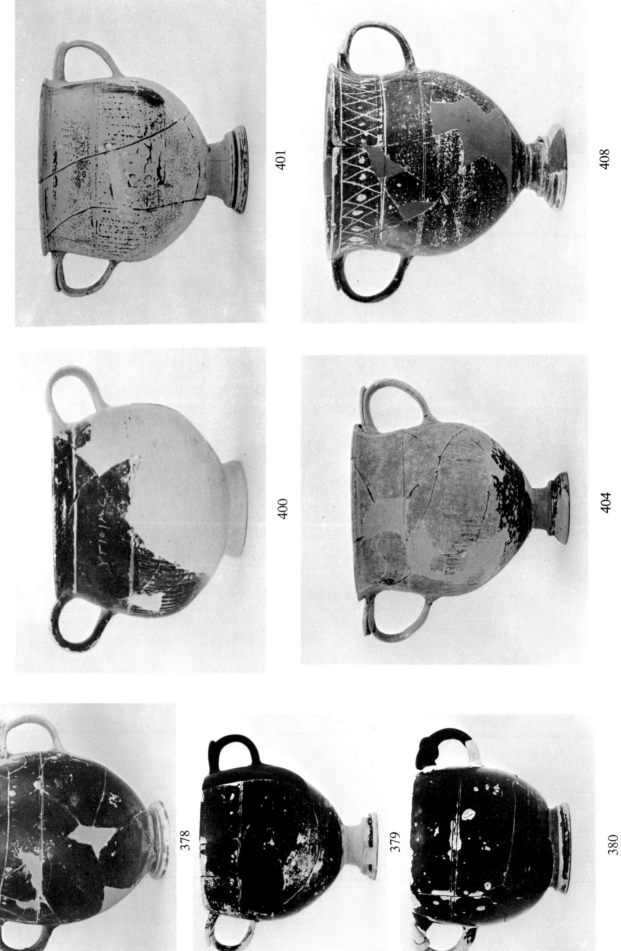

401

408

400

404

378

379

380

2:5

Kantharos: One-piece; Cyma

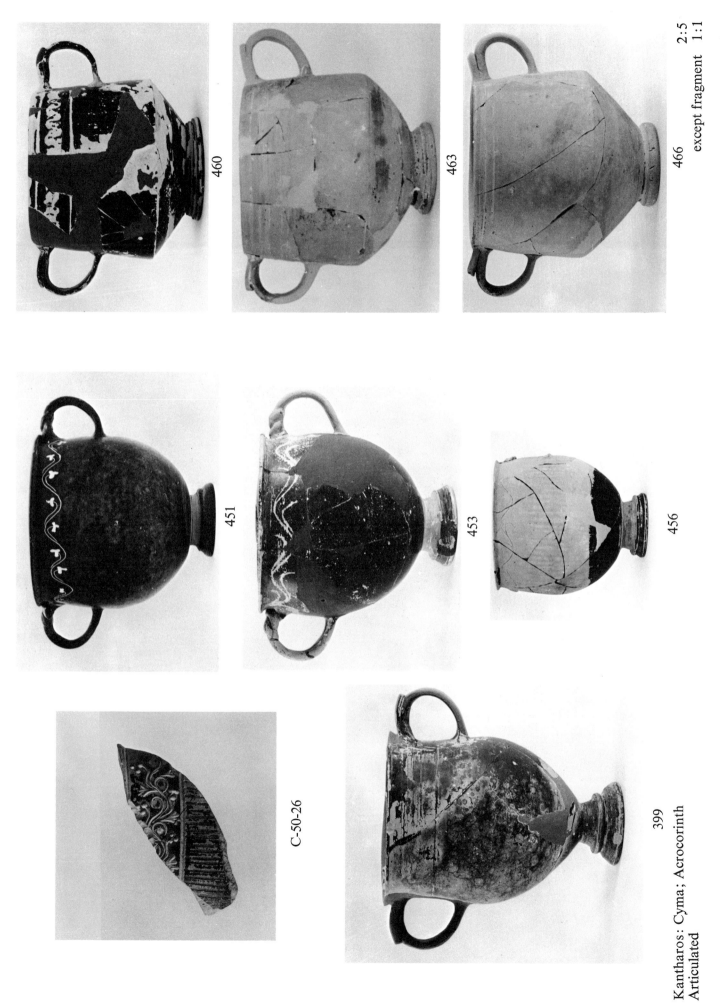

460

463

466

2:5
except fragment 1:1

451

453

456

C-50-26

399

Kantharos: Cyma; Acrocorinth
Articulated

515

519

521

524

526

527

exterior

528

interior

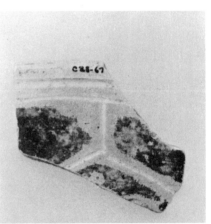

530

exterior

529

interior

Hexamilia kantharos and mug
Details: thorn kantharos,
hemispherical and Megarian bowls

2:5
except details **527–530** 1:1

534

538

532

535

540

539

532

534

541

542

543

547

549

Conical bowl

2:5
except fragments   3:5

exterior

550

interior

551

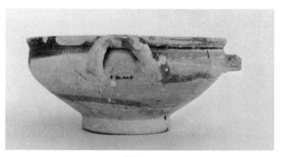

552

554

553

554

555

556

556 b

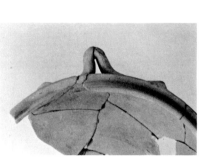

558

555

557

558

559

560

562   564+579   576

Lekanis
Pyxis, receptacles and lids

above   1:5, below   2:5

handles about   2:5

PLATE 58

584

585

586

587

591

596

600

602

605

604

Unguentarium
Ointment-pots
Inkwell
Basketball askos

1:2
except ointment-pots   1:1

608

609

610

612

613

616

622

625

626

627

Stamnos lids I–IV
Kraters
Mortars I, II

1:5

628

629

630

631

633

643

634

636

644

645

Based amphoras I–III
Water pitcher
Handle-ridge jug
Funnel; Ring stand

1:5
except mortars   2:5

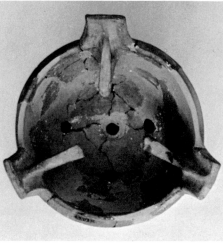

front   top   back
                              646

front   side   back
                              647

649   656

657

651   658

Brazier   1:5
Chytrai I, II
Stew pots

667

671

670

679

683

684

687

685

688

689

692

694

695

696

699

701

697

700

703

698

704

705

706

709

710

711

719

720

727

733

746

747

749

Vessels not intended for use with heat

1:5

750   751   754   756

768   774   775

778 a

776, top

778 b

776   777   779

Squat aryballos
Duck askos   2:5
Filter vase   except askos, top view 3:5,
Cup   fragment 777 1:1

780

781

782

783

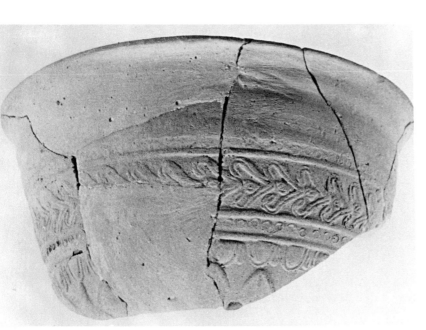

789

786

787

791

792

Leaf-and-tendril bowl
Imbricate bowl

1:1
except **789** less than 1:1

793

794

795

Ivy bowl
Foliage Bowl, unclassified

1:1

801

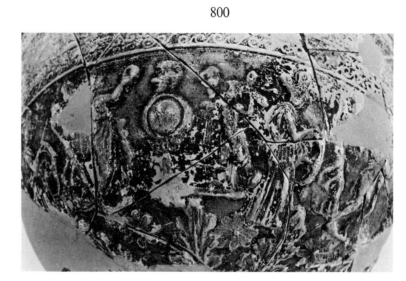

800

797

802

805

807

803

808

812

814

Figured Bowls   1:1

810

810

810

817

821

825

827

831

838

Figured Bowls

829

1:1

823

836

Figured Bowls

841

1:1

842

842

Figured Bowls 3:5

842

843

Figured Bowls

842 3:5
843 4:5

840

844

845

Figured Bowls

1:1

846

848

849

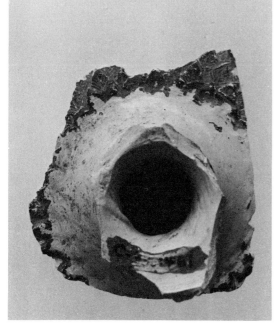

850

850

Figured Bowls
Figured kantharos (?)

1:1

873

873

873

874

879

875

Figured Bowls
Relief supports

1:1
except **873** 3:5

889

897

897

893

898

902

904

Relief supports
Long-petal bowl

906

1:1

908

909

910

Net-pattern bowl

1:1

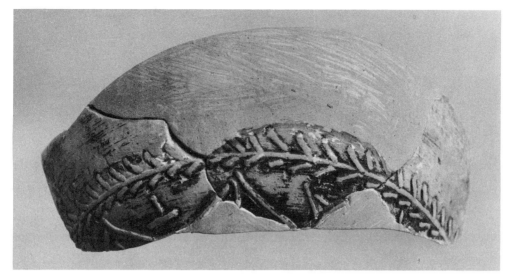

912

913

914

915

920

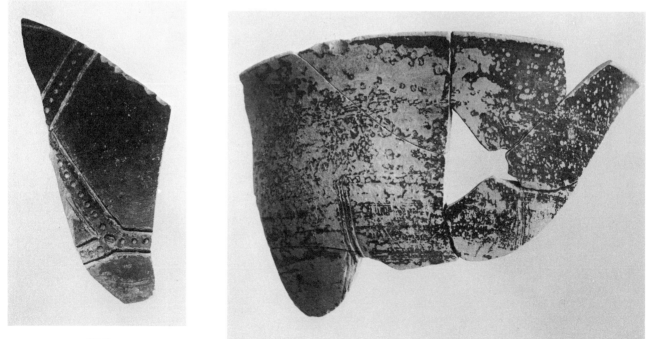

917

918

Net-pattern bowl

1:1

919

921

Net-pattern bowl   2:3
Concentric-semicircle bowl

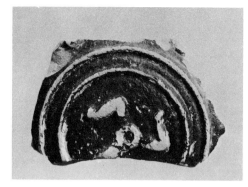

928

929

931

933

Concentric-semicircle bowl
Linear-leaf bowl

1:1

936

938

Linear-leaf bowl   1:1

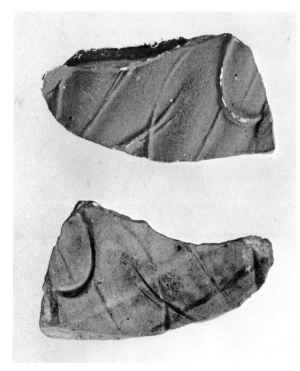

940

941

939

942

Megarian bowl
Moulds and impressions

943

944

Conical bowl
Wheelmade Megarian bowl

1:1

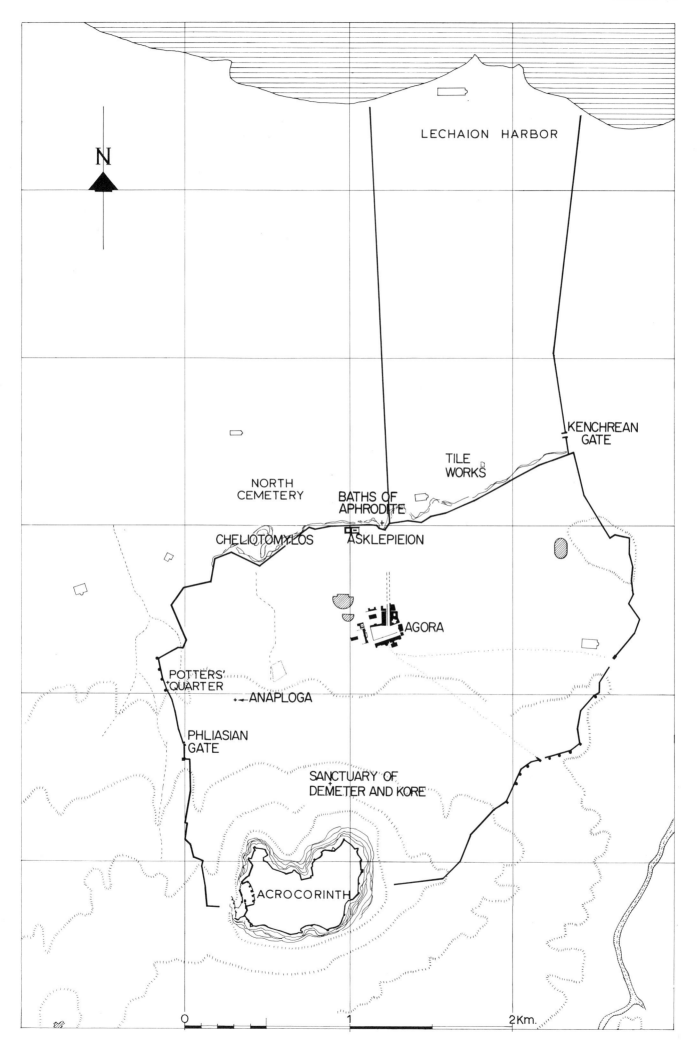

N

LECHAION HARBOR

KENCHREAN GATE

TILE WORKS

NORTH CEMETERY

BATHS OF APHRODITE

CHELIOTOMYLOS

ASKLEPIEION

AGORA

POTTERS' QUARTER

ANAPLOGA

PHLIASIAN GATE

SANCTUARY OF DEMETER AND KORE

ACROCORINTH

0   1   2 Km.

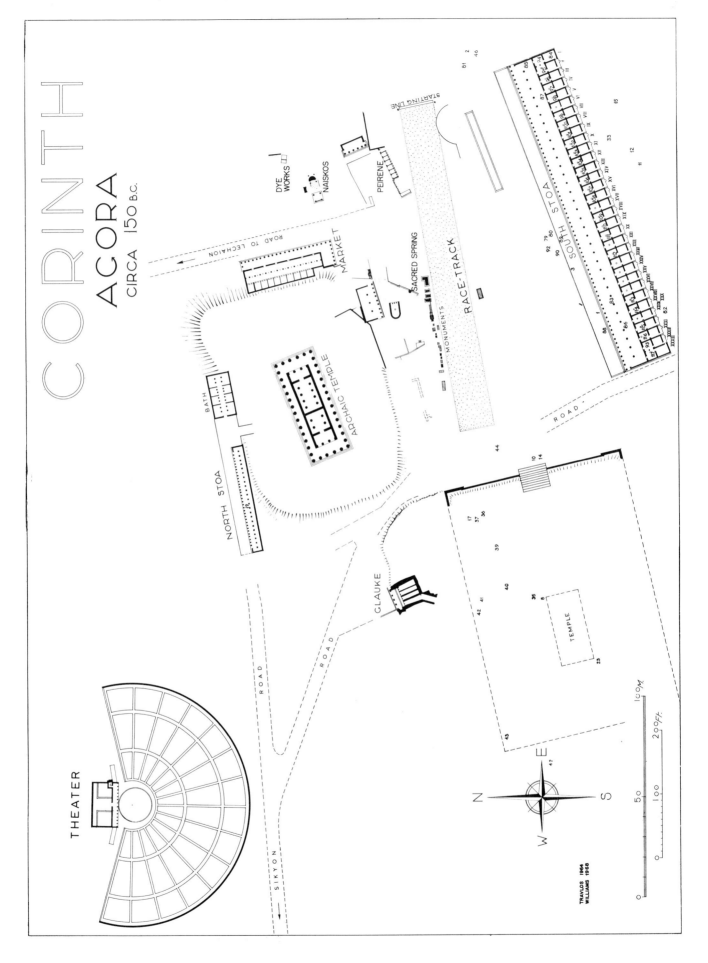